Global Corruption Report: Sport

Sport is a global phenomenon engaging billions of people and generating annual revenues of more than US$145 billion. Problems in the governance of sports organisations, the fixing of matches and the staging of major sporting events have spurred action on many fronts. Attempts to stop corruption in sport, however, are still at an early stage.

The *Global Corruption Report* (GCR) on sport is the most comprehensive analysis of sports corruption to date. It consists of more than 60 contributions from leading experts in the fields of corruption and sport, from sports organisations, governments, multilateral institutions, sponsors, athletes, supporters, academia and the wider anti-corruption movement.

This GCR provides essential analysis for understanding the corruption risks in sport, focusing on sports governance, the business of sport, the planning of major events and match-fixing. It highlights the significant work that has already been done and presents new approaches to strengthening integrity in sport. In addition to measuring transparency and accountability, the GCR gives priority to participation, from sponsors to athletes to supporters – an essential to restoring trust in sport.

Transparency International (TI) is the global civil society organisation leading the fight against corruption. Through more than 100 chapters worldwide and an international secretariat in Berlin, TI raises awareness of the damaging effects of corruption and works with partners in government, business and civil society to develop and implement effective measures to tackle it.

"Transparency International have for years undertaken valuable, authoritative work on governance issues of vital importance in sport, and the concerns they have raised have been repeatedly vindicated. The research and insights in this book provide another major contribution to the recognition that sports must be true to the love people have for them."

–David Conn, The Guardian

"At last a truly comprehensive, critical and impassioned look at the whole range of governance and corruption issues that have engulfed global sport. For those that want to know what has been going on, why, and how to do something about it, this book will be their first point of call."

–David Goldblatt, award-winning author of The Game of Our Lives: The Meaning and Making of English Football

Global Corruption Report: Sport

TRANSPARENCY INTERNATIONAL

LONDON AND NEW YORK

First published 2016
by Routledge
2 Park Square, Milton Park, Abingdon, Oxon OX14 4RN

and by Routledge
711 Third Avenue, New York, NY 10017

Routledge is an imprint of the Taylor & Francis Group, an informa business

© 2016 Transparency International

Editor: Gareth Sweeney, Associate Editor: Kelly McCarthy

The right of Transparency International to be identified as the author of the
editorial material, and of the authors for their individual chapters, has been
asserted in accordance with sections 77 and 78 of the Copyright, Designs
and Patents Act 1988.

British Library Cataloguing-in-Publication Data
A catalogue record for this book is available from the British Library

Library of Congress Cataloging-in-Publication Data
A catalog record for this book has been requested

ISBN: 978-1-138-90589-4 (hbk)
ISBN: 978-1-138-90592-4 (pbk)
ISBN: 978-1-315-69570-9 (ebk)

Typeset in Helvetica
by Keystroke, Station Road, Codsall, Wolverhampton

MIX
Paper from
responsible sources
FSC® C013604
www.fsc.org

Printed and bound by CPI Group (UK) Ltd, Croydon, CR0 4YY

Contents

Illustrations

Figures

Preface

Cobus de Swardt, Managing Director,
Transparency International

Sport gives people hope. It provides joy to billions of people across the world, from the favelas of Rio de Janeiro to the boroughs of London. As fans we have a love affair with our favourite game. When our teams win we are ecstatic; when they lose we are devastated. When results – of games, of contests to host events or of elections to run sports bodies – are determined not by fair competition but by corruption, however, we feel betrayed. Cleaning up sport is therefore essential, not only for the good of the game but for the good of society as a whole.

For more than 20 years Transparency International (TI) has led the fight against corruption, through more than 100 independent national chapters around the world, which take action to stop corruption and promote transparency, accountability and integrity at all levels and across all sectors of society.

The *Global Corruption Report* (GCR) is a strong foundation to support this fight. This 11th edition, for the first time complemented online through our new Corruption in Sport Initiative, provides an authoritative look at the state of corruption in a given sector through contributions from over 50 leading experts in the field. These are complemented by case studies from TI national chapters that show how TI is tackling the problem at the national and local levels. The aim is to provide clear recommendations for change.

Sport touches the lives of billions. No one wants to think that his or her favourite pastime is tainted. This became unavoidable for football fans in May 2015, however, with the indictment by the United States of nine current and former FIFA officials on charges of racketeering and money-laundering, confirming the worst suspicions of many. These crises at the heart of sport illustrate well-known issues: a culture of impunity at the top of sporting organisations that gives free rein to bribery and obscures financial black holes. Implementing necessary and long-lasting reforms will prove far more difficult.

Needless to say, corruption in sport is not limited to football, and the importance of fighting corruption is not limited to the effect on sport only. Sport is a symbol of fair play around the world, and often provides a release from daily hardships for many, whether it is taking part in or supporting a local team. If trust in sport is lost and people can no longer believe what they are seeing on the field of play or hearing from those in charge, then public trust in *any* institution may be irreparably undermined.

The issues addressed in the GCR can draw from the experience of TI and the anti-corruption movement in other sectors. There are so many people who want to have a say in sports – from the citizens in cities where big events are held to the parents of kids in grass-roots clubs – and it is imperative that this wider sports family is heard. It is for this reason that the current GCR focuses on participation as key to strengthening sport integrity.

We at Transparency International recognise that the fight against corruption in sport is not new, and we are indebted to those individuals who, long before it was on our agenda, dug deep at great personal risk to uncover the truth. Our goal is for the new GCR and the

Corruption in Sport Initiative to help to bring these voices together in one place. We also hope to continue to provide an open space for new analysis and recommendations.

Everyone has a stake is keeping sports clean. Our chapters around the world will continue to demand clean sports, but the voices of athletes, supporters, governments, sponsors, journalists and, primarily, those within sports organisations need to combine to send a strong message that integrity matters, for the good of the game and the good of the global fight against corruption.

Now is the time.

Foreword

Raí Souza Vieira de Olivera, founder of the Gol de Letra Foundation and captain of the Brazilian 1994 World Cup winning team

What would become of humanity if the act of simply playing the game to enjoy yourself did not exist? If playfulness did not exist? If competition did not exist? We would probably be identical, dispassionate beings, losing much of the grace, humour and beauty that we have been given.

Sport is nothing more than natural fun and healthy play packaged in rules to create just conditions among participants and contain the excesses that any impassioned activity or competition awakens. From this is born the expression 'the spirit of sport'. Health, fun, justice, passion – these are basic values for any child, any human being, any society: values transformed into rules, rights and laws.

For the development of sport, it was necessary to create organisations – associations, federations and confederations – to impose and administer these collective values. Hierarchies of power began to develop without guarantees of a democratic, participatory and transparent system. Sport is a large source of inspiration, but it is run with an absurd autonomy, without effective checks.

Sporting administrative bodies have evolved to take ownership of an enormous and notorious public interest, involving soul and passion. They even win freely the right to represent countries and nations. These organisations operate almost as independent states, however, without effective counterbalances and with vast possibilities to manoeuvre to remain in power. They claim legitimacy for their promotion, but demand complete autonomy in self-management, and even in self-punishment.

Corruption is for sport as doping is for competition, and for the health of the athlete. This framework has provided many reasons, motivations, contradictions and counter-intuitions, which build and today form one of the most enabling environments for acts of corruption to take place and proliferate, allowing the corrupt and greedy to gain an interest in sport, and impunity to take hold.

To rethink this, let us return to the basics: health, fun, justice and passion!

If we really want sport to be the basis for a better society, to be one of the pillars for human and social development, we need to rethink the rules of sports governance and their criteria of representation and accountability – and build something new, transparent and committed.

For this we need (in the same way that we created and systematically perfected sports themselves) to evolve in terms of governance, building a system in which fair play always prevails. We need to create a clean and healthy structure and new rules that guarantee complete transparency and democratic participation.

Transparency International's work on sport integrity – including the report before you – provides a good framework for reform. The responsibility now lies with the participants of sport, from the grass-roots to elite professionals, fans, sponsors, governments and, most of all, sport organisations themselves, to demand the changes that are clearly needed, for the good of sport and the good of humanity.

Acknowledgements

This *Global Corruption Report* on sport is a partnership and collaboration between Transparency International (TI) and its authors, whose expertise has provided us with the highest quality of content. We are very honoured to have worked with everyone involved and hope that these relationships may continue long beyond this report.

We are especially grateful for the guidance of a group of distinguished experts who kindly served on our Expert Advisory Panel and who were actively engaged throughout: Jens Andersen, Wolfgang Baumann, Pâquerette Girard Zappelli, Tony Higgins, Jacques Marnewicke, Richard Pound and Ben Shave.

We are also, as always, hugely indebted to the expert peer reviewers who devoted their energies to improve the content: Paul Anderson, Mark Baber, Robert Barrington, Amita Baviskar, Trish Bradbury, Gonzalo Bravo, Benjamin Bendrich, Scarlett Cornelissen, Pete Dawson, Juan de Dios Crespo, Peter Donnelly, Jocelyn East, Iain Edmondson, Esther Enkin, Neil Fergus, Leonardo Fernandes, Gyongyi Szabó Foldesi, John Foster, John Fourie, Jason Genovese, David Greenspan, Oleg Golubchikov, Sean Hamil, Barry Houlihan, Dionne Koller, Helen Lenskyj, Mike McNamee, Felix Majani, Jean-Paul Marthoz, Maira Martini, Luiz Martins de Melo, Laura Misener, Matthew Mitten, Severin Moritzer, Martin Müller, Bridget Niland, Walter Palmer, Katarina Pijetlovic, Denis Primakov, Stephen Pritchard, Dino Ruta, Chris Smith, Harry Arne Solberg, Ulrike Spitz, Joe Stead, John Sugden, Eleni Theodoraki, Ilija Trojanovic, George Turner, Pedro Velasquez, Geoff Walters, John Wilson and Serhat Yilmaz.

As the work of TI continues to expand, we are indebted to our national chapters, whose country case studies illustrate the approaches of the anti-corruption movement in tackling corruption in sport. In particular, we would like to extend our thanks to Sylvia Schenk and Ulrike Spitz for their valuable proposals during the initial scoping of our work. We are also thankful to colleagues at the Transparency International Secretariat who lent their perspectives and expertise. We are indebted to Deborah Unger, who is a real champion of our Secretariat work in sport and a pleasure to work alongside. We would also like to thank Marie Terracol for essential coordination work, Matthew Jenkins for initial mapping research, Eric Fichtl for online design and creation of the TI Corruption in Sport Initiative, Nicky Rehbock for online support, Thomas Coombes and Chris Sanders for communication, Kerstin Deinert and Michael Sidwell for print design, Rachel Beddow for libel coordination, and Bruno Brandao and Solange Falcetta for helping to arrange a number of outstanding contributors. As ever, the *Global Corruption Report* has been guided by Robin Hodess, and now also with the generous oversight of Casey Kelso. Finally, and especially, the team would like to thank our former associate editors Samira Lindner, for her enthusiasm, sharp intellect and unwavering commitment to the fight against corruption, and Kelly McCarthy, for her Herculean resolve and keen editorial eye in seeing the *Report* past the final post.

Further afield, copy-editor Mike Richardson once again excelled and kept us in check, and we are forever indebted. We were also delighted to work once more with Agur Paesüld, whose graphics continue to give life to dry text. And, to those for whom the details are never lost, we would like to thank our industrious fact-checkers: Oisín Bourke, Krista Brown,

Adam DeJulio, Natacha Draghi, Tyler Klink, Michelle McAlarnen, Holly Nazar, Sylvia Plaza and Philippa Williams.

We are very happy to continue our collaboration with Routledge, and in particular we extend our thanks to Helen Bell and Edward Gibbons for their continued support.

Finally, the *Global Corruption Report* team would like to acknowledge Liverpool FC, Kilkenny City AFC (defunct), Ipswich Town FC and the Republic of Ireland national football team for inspiring a love of sport and the desire to fight for its integrity.

Executive summary

Gareth Sweeney, Transparency International[1]

Sport is a global phenomenon engaging billions of people and generating annual revenues of more than US$145 billion.[2] While corruption in sport is not new,[3] the recent pervasiveness of poor governance and corruption scandals threatens to undermine all the joy that sport brings and the good that it can do. For Transparency International (TI), the pace of building integrity in sport has been too slow, and now it must be rapidly accelerated.

The indictments on 27 May 2015 of nine current and former Fédération Internationale de Football Association (FIFA) officials on charges of racketeering and money-laundering[4] changed the landscape overnight. Suddenly a system of 'rampant, systemic and deep-rooted corruption' was brought starkly into global focus. The re-election two days later of the FIFA president who had presided over this culture of impunity, and who was therefore either complicit or oblivious (and, either way, had failed in his duties), exposed to the watching world just how much football exists in a parallel universe of unaccountability. It is easy to understand why public trust in FIFA is at an all-time low, and is set to go even lower if promises for reform turn out to be business-as-usual.[5]

The context

Yet corruption in sport is not limited to football. Cricket, cycling, badminton, ice hockey, handball, athletics and other sports, including US collegiate sports, suffer similar credibility gaps. The reasons related to each are broadly similar.

Sport is a public interest, played and viewed by billions, whose tax dollars often fund the hosting of major sporting events. Sport is also organised on the historic principle of autonomy,[6] however, and sports organisations – whether international organisations, regional confederations or national associations – are subsequently afforded 'non-profit' or 'non-governmental organisation' status in most jurisdictions. This allows them to operate without any effective external oversight (or interference, depending on perspective). The statutes of most sports associations therefore require that reforms are initiated and approved by the same individuals who will be most directly affected by them. It stands to reason, then, that the murkiest sports will be the most resistant to self-incrimination and change.

Even the corporate structures of sport are largely archaic. The administration of sport is often overseen by ex-athletes with little prior experience in management, operating through very linear hierarchical organisational models. While these models may have worked in the past, many international sports organisations (ISOs), regional confederations and national sports organisations (NSOs) have simply not kept pace with the huge commercial growth of the sector, and have even chosen not to adapt in order to protect certain self-interests, including high salaries, bonuses and virtually limitless tenures.

Finally, this insular environment is facilitated by the countries that host these organisations, such as Switzerland and the United Arab Emirates, which traditionally afford favourable legal status and generous tax breaks in order to attract and keep ISOs resident.[7] Changes to tighten legal accountability are under way,[8] but these are usually tempered with caution since ISOs may simply relocate if the screws are tightened.

The solutions

When Sepp Blatter vowed to step down as FIFA president on 2 June, he declared: 'While I have a mandate from the membership of FIFA, I do not feel that I have a mandate from the entire world of football – the fans, the players, the clubs, the people who live, breathe and love football . . .' This short statement struck at the heart of the problem. Sports organisations, from ISOs to local community clubs, have a responsibility for their sport, and should be accountable to all those affected by their sport, from displaced communities to migrant construction workers, from grass-roots fans to World Cup winners.

The current outcry against corruption at FIFA shows that, once roused, the wider sporting community can become as interested in what goes on off the field of play as on it. Tackling the roots of corruption must come primarily from within the sports community, though, starting with an acknowledgement of the problem. There must be a sincere and verifiable commitment to realise sport's principles on inclusiveness and fair play, 'to comply with the highest standards in terms of transparency, democracy and accountability'.[9]

At the same time, internal reform must be open to external perspectives, including inputs from athletes and supporters, governments, sponsors and civil society. The 'sports family' needs to welcome those with know-how in anti-corruption activities, good governance, human rights, labour rights and development outside the world of sport as allies in the greater interest of sport. The *Global Corruption Report: Sport* therefore places particular focus on participation as a fundamental element of good governance in sport, and dedicates a full chapter to the voices of key participants and their respective roles.

The *Global Corruption Report: Sport* provides a comprehensive overview of the root causes of corruption across sport, presenting key participants' perspectives side by side, as well as the work of TI national chapters on the ground. It focuses on current challenges in sports governance as the gateway through which all other forms of corruption in sport take hold, including, for example, the regulation of club ownership and the transfer markets (here the *Report* focuses on football). The *Report* gives special attention to the bidding, awarding and planning of major sporting events as a particularly vulnerable area for widespread corruption, as evidenced from the 1998 International Olympic Committee (IOC) Salt Lake City scandal[10] to ongoing investigations. It then looks at global developments around the criminalisation and prevention of match-fixing, and what needs to be done. Space is also provided for a chapter on the unique corruption risks inherent in the structure of US collegiate sports, and its compromising influence on academic integrity. There are contradictory opinions within the *Report*, and much still to tackle, but the wealth of information illustrates how vibrant the field of sport and corruption has become in the past decade.

Drawing from this expert analysis of structural issues presented in the *Global Corruption Report: Sport*, Transparency International identifies the following key recommendations to restore public trust in sport.

Governance

Some reform recommendations in sport can be put in place very quickly, while others will require a more incremental consultative approach. A step-by-step reform process, suitable to the size and capacity of respective sports organisations, should incorporate many of the good governance principles that guide other sectors.

- Heads of ISOs should, as a rule, be elected by an open vote of members. National members/associations of ISOs should be accountable for their positions to their national constituencies.
- Executive decision-makers should be elected rather than appointed.
- There should be a clear separation between the administrative and commercial operations of all ISOs/NSOs.
- Decision-making bodies should contain at least one independent executive member.
- The gender balance of decision-making bodies should at least reflect the gender balance of participation in the respective sport as a whole.
- All ISO heads and decision-making body members should be bound by fixed terms, with mandatory gaps in service before being eligible for re-election.
- Integrity checks should be required for all senior ISO committee and secretariat staff, to be organised centrally and with independent external oversight. Due diligence criteria should include potential commercial conflicts of interest, as well as any ongoing investigations related to improper conduct. Integrity checks should be periodically reviewed.
- ISOs should put in place internal governance committees, presided over by an independent non-executive or lead director on governance issues, to provide ongoing external oversight of sport organisational decisions. Any review committees should have the mandate to review past as well as present activities.
- Sports organisations should establish independent ethics commissions/ethics advisers, with effective oversight and disciplinary authority related to codes of conduct and ethics guidelines.
- Specialised units should be created within ISOs to regularly monitor member associations and provide support in terms of governance and accountability.
- Structural reforms put in place in ISOs (elections, terms limits, integrity checks, codes of conduct, ethics and compliance structures and authority, financial transparency) should also be required to be applied uniformly to the structures of regional sports organisations as applicable as a prerequisite to membership of ISOs.
- The IOC, in consultation with all relevant stakeholders, should give serious consideration to the creation of an independent global anti-corruption agency for sport.

Transparency

- Sports organisations should establish cultures of transparency so that good work is not just done but is seen to be done. Access to information policies should be integrated and promoted.
- The publication of ISO finances – expenditures, revenues and disbursements – should be disaggregated and go far beyond minimum legal requirements in host countries so as to meet public expectations.
- Sports organisations should adhere to strict disclosure requirements, including financial reporting, and adequately communicate their activities to their internal stakeholders and the general public through accessible open data platforms.
- International and national sports organisations should publish the pay scales, as well as the salaries and costs, of senior executives/members of the executive committee, remuneration for board members, etc.
- The disbursement of funding to national member associations should be contingent on the receipt of annual financial accounts and activity reports, to be made available to the public via their national websites, and searchable on the websites of ISOs.

- ISOs should adopt the use of governance benchmarking tools such as the BIBGIS or the Sports Governance Observer to measure progress over time,[11] and should periodically publish the results and lessons learnt, to be included as a section in their annual reports.

Participation

The primary responsibility for reform lies with sports organisations, from ISOs to the grassroots bodies. This needs to be matched by sustained engagement with intergovernmental organisations, governments, athletes, sponsors, supporters and civil society.

- Any reform process to address systemic governance issues in sport should formally provide for inputs by relevant stakeholders, including athletes, supporters, governments, sponsors and human rights, labour and anti-corruption organisations. ISOs should commit themselves to honouring the recommendations of any reform process or providing formal responses for recommendations that are rejected.
- NSOs should support increased transparency and accountability, whether in speaking out for institutional reform or publicly supporting reformist platforms around elections.
- Sponsors should demand that whoever they sponsor should live up to the same anti-corruption and human rights standards that they are expected to adhere to in their own operations and in their own supply chains. As individual sponsors may fear a 'first-mover disadvantage', major sponsors should align to apply collective pressure for change. Sponsors should therefore consider the creation of a Sports Integrity Group that sets out their shared commitment to integrity in sport and allows major sponsors to advance a common position for integrity in sport.
- Sponsors should conduct due diligence on any organisation they sponsor – just as they do for their other business partners. They should also review their relationships with intermediaries and sports marketing companies to ensure that the companies meet their standards of integrity.
- Sponsors should ensure that their employees who work with ISOs, sports marketing companies and other intermediaries are properly trained on their code and integrity standards.
- Professional sport is nothing without supporters. Supporters' groups can play an even larger role than they do now, by mobilising a collective voice for key structural reforms in ISOs and NSOs and demanding a seat at the table.
- National and local governments should ensure adequate legislation to address match-fixing and organised crime in grassroots sports. In the case of US collegiate sports in particular, such legislation should protect the well-being of student athletes ahead of commercial interests. Governments should also provide whistleblower protection for those reporting malfeasance in sport, and effectively enforce access-to-information laws so as to facilitate and ensure the effective monitoring of the planning and hosting of sports events.
- Intergovernmental organisations should continue to facilitate the coordination and sharing of lessons learnt among national governments, and should develop indicators, benchmarks and self-assessment tools to help national governments identify policy gaps, needs, solutions and progress in promoting integrity in sport.

Major events

There are multiple entry points for corruption related to major sporting events. These include the selection process for bids and the related canvassing, the courting of international delegates and the use of high-priced consultants for global bidding. There are also corruption risks during the awarding process and related bribery risks. Finally, the planning and hosting of events and the attendant large-scale procurement and construction risks put local organising committees under intense pressure to provide the required infrastructure and logistics on time. ISOs, as event owners, must ensure that the process is one of integrity, from the pre-bidding phase to the closing ceremony and far beyond.

- ISOs should require a national consultation process at the pre-bidding stage. A summary of national consultation outcomes should be publicly available, and must then be presented as part of the bid criteria.
- ISOs should establish clear, obligatory anti-corruption, labour rights, human rights and environmental and social sustainability criteria as objective admissibility safeguards for the first round of bidding. They should then be assessed by internal and external joint committees at this first round.
- Official bid documents must be publicly available and bidders must include a commitment to publish detailed policies and plans for all of the above.[12]
- Official bids should be required to provide a breakdown of anticipated expenditure by sport- and non-sport-related development, as well as by the cost carrier.
- ISOs should establish an internal compliance process from the opening of the bidding phase, covering ISO member and bid countries alike, to include, at a minimum, clear policies and reporting on ethics, conflicts of interest, a register of lobbyists, gift and travel registry and whistleblower protection. This should be publicly accessible through the continued rollouts of content on open data platforms.
- Major sporting events should, as a rule, be awarded through an open vote by ISO members.
- ISOs must formally recognise through the amendments of statutes that they bear a responsibility to protect human rights, labour rights, anti-corruption activities and sustainable development.
- Host contracts must include an agreement that a serious failure to uphold fundamental anti-corruption, human rights and labour standards, and the host country's own bid commitments, can result in loss of the major event.
- ISOs should require host countries to detail all major procurement processes, contracts and expenditures related to the bidding, planning and hosting of major events through an open data platform.
- ISOs should develop a clear set of assessment indicators, in consultation with external experts, to measure performance related to the above over time. External independent experts should also be part of the review process.
- ISOs should revisit tax arrangements for major sporting events and share surpluses so that host countries are not expected to host events at a net loss while ISOs extract the vast majority of revenues.
- Independent impact assessments should be carried out following events, covering all dimensions, namely the thematic (economic, social, environmental and political), the scale (local to global), the temporal (bid phase to legacy stage) and the actors (event owners, event producers, event consumers), addressing both positive and negative impacts. These can be earmark-funded by ISOs from event revenues.
- To ensure that promises on event legacies are kept, measurable legacy criteria must be a mandatory element of bids. These should include strengthening documentation of the factual evidence on the results of hosting such events, which should be made public and

maintained. Any failure to meet legacy criteria can then be weighed against admissibility for hosting future sporting events, and should be acknowledged across ISOs as required elements of subsequent bidding criteria.

Match-fixing

The manipulation of competitions is now fully acknowledged as a real threat to the integrity of sport. Any sport is vulnerable to manipulation by organised crime or for sporting reasons, such as promotion or relegation.

- States should ratify the Council of Europe's Convention on the Manipulation of Sport Competitions. It commits states to investigate and sanction all match-fixing, to have cross-border cooperation on cases and to ensure prevention, including the provision of comprehensive and continuous education on the issue.
- Sport organisations should establish whistleblower systems that are independent, confidential and secure, and follow Transparency International's international whistleblower guidelines.
- Governments should cooperate with NSOs to establish national focal points for sport integrity, including national ombudspersons for sport.
- ISOs should prohibit professional athletes from gambling on their own sport.
- National gambling regulations should oblige betting operators to report information on suspicious betting activity to the authorities or the relevant national platform and provide concrete guidelines as to what constitutes 'suspicious' activity.
- All people involved – athletes, coaches, referees, officials, parents – should know how to detect match-fixing before any manipulation takes place, through mandatory preventative training courses provided by national associations. Athletes and other concerned individuals must be fully informed about the rules and the consequences for violations.

Notes

1 Gareth Sweeney is chief editor of the *Global Corruption Report* at Transparency International.
2 PricewaterhouseCoopers, *Changing the Game: Outlook for the Global Sports Market to 2015* (London: PricewaterhouseCoopers LLP, 2011), *www.pwc.com/gx/en/hospitality-leisure/changing-the-game-outlook-for-the-global-sports-market-to-2015.jhtml*.
3 The 1998 Salt Lake City scandal, for example, resulted in major reforms within the International Olympic Committee, while the work of investigative journalists continued to expose corruption in governance and match-fixing across sport.
4 United States District Court, Eastern District of New York, Indictment 15 CR 0252 (RJD) (RML), 20 May 2015, *www.justice.gov/opa/file/450211/download*.
5 According to a Transparency International/Football Addicts poll of 35,000 fans in 30 countries on 26 May 2015, 17 per cent of fans responded that they had no confidence in FIFA. See *www.transparency.org/news/pressrelease/4_in_5_football_fans_say_blatter_should_not_stand_for_fifa_president_poll_o*.
6 See Jean-Loup Chappelet, Chapter 1.3 'Autonomy and governance: necessary bedfellows in the fight against corruption in sport', in this report.
7 Michaël Mrkonjic, 'The Swiss regulatory framework and international sports organisations', in Jens Alm (ed.), *Action for Good Governance in International Sports Organisations: Final Report* (Copenhagen: Danish Institute for Sports Studies, 2013), *www.playthegame.org/fileadmin/documents/Good_governance_reports/AGGIS-report_-_12The_Swiss_regulatory_*

framework__p_128-132_.pdf; BBC (UK), 'Cricket chiefs move base to Dubai', 7 March 2005, *http://news.bbc.co.uk/sport2/hi/cricket/4326601.stm*.

8   See Lucien W. Valloni and Eric P. Neuenschwander, Chapter 6.4 'The role of Switzerland as host: moves to hold sports organisations more accountable, and wider implications', in this report.

9   Jacques Rogge (president of the IOC from 2001 to 2013), 'Good sport governance', speech given at 'The Rules of the Game: First International Governance in Sport Conference', Brussels, 26 February 2001.

10 Bill Mallon, 'The Olympic bribery scandal', *Journal of Olympic History*, vol. 8 (2000).

11 See Arnout Geeraert, 'Indicators and benchmarking tools for sports governance', in this report.

12 The United Nations Office on Drugs and Crime (UNODC) 'Strategy for safeguarding against corruption in major public events' offers a useful reference framework in relation to corruption. See UNODC, *The United Nations Convention against Corruption: A Strategy for Safeguarding against Corruption in Major Public Events* (Vienna: UNODC, 2013), *www.unodc.org/documents/corruption/Publications/2013/13-84527_Ebook.pdf*.

PART 1

Governance of sport:
the global view

1.1
Sport as a force for good

Bob Munro[1]

Sport has the power to change the world. It has the power to inspire. It has the power to unite people in a way that little else does. It speaks to youth in a language they understand. Sport can create hope where once there was only despair.

Nelson Mandela, Laureus World Sports Awards, Monaco, 2000

Since the eighth century BC, when the first Olympic Truce allowed athletes to travel safely to the Olympic Games, sport has been largely regarded as an inspirational force for good.[2] Sport has helped transcend often divisive geographic, political and cultural differences by bringing people and nations together to celebrate athletic achievements. Surprisingly, concerted efforts to expand sport as a force for good accelerated only in the last two decades. More surprisingly, the youth in Nairobi's Mathare Valley, one of Africa's largest and poorest slums, were pioneers in using sport for community development and peace. Although the initial examples in this chapter are from that project, today many different sports are now used as a force for good in tackling a remarkably wide range of serious health, social and environmental challenges – and even conflicts – around the world.

Learning life lessons and skills through sport

For me and many other boys growing up in the Canadian town of St. Catharines in the 1950s, school was what we did in between Saturdays. With our fathers as voluntary organisers and coaches, on Saturdays we put on our team uniforms and proudly bicycled through town to play with or against our friends in summer baseball and winter ice hockey leagues. On those eagerly awaited Saturdays, we won or lost the bragging rights for the next week.

Through sport, we learnt vital lessons and social skills, which helped us then and later in life. We learnt that achievement is our reward for self-discipline and constant training, for getting fit and staying healthy and, most importantly, for extra effort and teamwork. We learnt to cope with losing as well as winning, gaining new insights into our weaknesses from our losses and earning new self-confidence from our victories. We also learnt to respect the rules, the referees, our coaches, our team-mates and even our opponents. Our leagues were also a miniature United Nations (UN) in which multiculturalism thrived as many players were young refugees from faraway places such as Estonia, Hungary, Latvia, Slovakia and Ukraine. Once we put on our team uniforms, though, they ceased being foreigners and soon became our team-mates and friends.[3]

Without those many kind-hearted volunteers and the early life lessons and social skills I learnt while playing in their youth leagues, my character would have had much sharper edges and my life been far less user-friendly. As they made sport such a force for good in my life, I owed them a debt of gratitude that I wanted to repay some day.

Combining sport with community service

Three decades later the Mathare Youth Sports Association (MYSA) became my payback. In August 1987 in the huge Mathare slums near the UN headquarters in Nairobi, I stopped at a little dirt field to watch some barefooted kids excitedly playing with their homemade *juala* football.[4] Their joy triggered a flashback to my own youth and this thought: why shouldn't these kids also get a chance to play and learn useful life lessons in leagues with real footballs, coaches and referees?

A few days later I met with some young leaders in the slums to start organising a few youth leagues. I set only one non-negotiable condition: 'If you do something, I'll do something, but if you do nothing, I'll do nothing.' They agreed and the first MYSA leagues kicked off two weeks later with over 500 youth in 27 boys' football teams and six girls' netball teams.

The Mathare youth leaders and members adopted the same approach, which soon transformed MYSA from just a few youth leagues into a self-help community development project using sport as a starting point. For example, the huge piles of uncollected garbage were major causes of disease and deaths in the slums, so environmental clean-ups became an integral part of all MYSA leagues. While teams get three points for a victory, MYSA teams also earn six points for each completed clean-up project. Then, and still today, MYSA likely has the only sports leagues in the world where the standings include the points for games won or tied *plus* points for garbage clean-ups.

MYSA's community service activities expanded in response to many different needs and risks in the slums. In 1994, when Adrian, a shy and popular teenager on the Undugu[5] street kids team, suddenly grew thin and died of an unusual and unfamiliar disease, MYSA started an HIV/AIDS awareness and prevention programme which is still in existence today. Training in AIDS prevention as well as child rights and protection against sexual abuse are embedded in all staff, coaching and other courses in the MYSA Sports and Leadership Training Academy.

By the mid-1990s MYSA's pioneering sport-for-development activities attracted a few brave partners,[6] enabling MYSA to add innovative new programmes such as training youth in music, photography, dance and drama which focused on serious health and other risks in the slums; providing leadership awards to help the best young volunteers stay in school; feeding and freeing jailed kids; expanding activities for kids with disabilities; stopping child labour; and creating slum libraries and study halls for members and local school classes.[7] Today in the Mathare slums, over 30,000 boys and girls[8] participate annually in the MYSA self-help youth sports and community service programmes. In addition to helping themselves, the Mathare youth also help over 10,000 youth in similar projects in and outside Kenya, which receive technical and training support from MYSA.[9]

Linking sport for development with peace

The MYSA youth also became peacemakers outside and later in the Mathare slums. In 1999 inter-ethnic violence escalated among the over 70,000 refugees in the Kakuma Refugee Camp in north-west Kenya. As two-thirds of the refugees were youth, the UNHCR asked MYSA to start a similar self-help youth sport-for-development project in the camp. Within six months the inter-ethnic tensions and violence had dropped dramatically. Many youth were from South Sudan and, after the 2005 peace agreement, they returned to Rumbek, the then administrative capital, where former child soldiers also demobilised. MYSA therefore helped start another project there, which continues today.

Sadly, in late 2006 inter-ethnic violence also flared up in the Mathare slums, with hundreds of innocent women and kids fleeing and camping on a field near a MYSA office. As the government and nearby UN agencies initially ignored their desperate situation, the Mathare youth took the funds intended for MYSA's 20th anniversary celebrations and instead used the money to rent tents and buy blankets, clothing, food and medicine for the displaced families. MYSA also organised peace-themed sports activities for the kids and, with later donations from MYSA friends in Norway and UN-Habitat, bought new uniforms and textbooks so the children could go back to school.[10]

During the devastating post-election violence in early 2008 the MYSA youth also organised special Football4Peace tournaments and activities throughout the slums.[11] Even the top clubs in the Kenyan Premier League (KPL), then chaired by Mathare United FC, got directly involved in helping mend the post-election rifts after the government and the Kenya Football Federation (KFF) had both declared that they lacked funds for the national team to join the 2010 Fédération Internationale de Football Association (FIFA) World Cup qualifying rounds. To help heal their divided country, the 16 KPL clubs urgently met in early May 2008 and agreed to fund the national team themselves.[12] Over the next six months national pride and unity rose, and Kenyans packed the stadium to cheer their national team as it climbed an astonishing 52 places in the FIFA world rankings.[13] Even FIFA acknowledged that it was likely the first time in world football history that a national team had been funded entirely by the clubs.

Expanding sport-for-development initiatives worldwide

National governments and other international organisations had largely ignored sport as a serious development activity until the early 1990s, when MYSA's new approach to sport for development started attracting attention in the Kenyan[14] and international media,[15] and even an academic journal.[16] The new approach and potential of sport for development gradually gained international recognition. For example, the 1991 Commonwealth Heads of Government meeting first recognised the unique role of sport in helping reduce poverty and promote development. In 1993 the UN General Assembly adopted Resolution 48/11 on 'Building a Peaceful and Better World through Sport'. Key milestones early in the new millennium included the appointment in 2001 of a new UN Special Adviser on Sport for Development and Peace and the creation in 2002 of the UN Inter-Agency Task Force on Sport for Development and Peace, which produced a trailblazing report on how sport can contribute to achieving many of the Millennium Development Goals.[17]

New international non-governmental organisations and networks also emerged for supporting and linking sport-for-development projects around the world. The process started in 2000 with the new Laureus World Sports Academy and Laureus Sport for Good Foundation, which adopted MYSA as its first flagship project.[18] Committed to 'using the power of sport as a tool for social change', today Laureus has national foundations in eight countries on four continents, and, with additional support from Comic Relief, now assists over 150 sport-for-development projects in 35 countries.[19]

In 2004 the streetfootballworld network was inaugurated 'to change the world through football' by creating new partnerships for sharing knowledge and experience among the fast-growing number of football-for-development-and-peace projects around the world. Headquartered in Berlin, today streetfootballworld has regional offices in Brazil, South Africa and the United States, and helps link over 100 organisations and projects in 66 countries.[20]

Other major global initiatives include Peace and Sport, founded in 2007 for 'building sustainable peace through sport', which focuses mainly on long-term peace-building programmes for reintegrating vulnerable children; peace-promotion programmes linked to major sports events; and emergency aid for humanitarian disasters through sports.[21]

A summary simply cannot do justice to the thousands of innovative sport-for-development projects not cited above that have also started, and achieved often remarkable results, during the last 15 years. Examples include the use of football by Spirit of Soccer to reduce deaths from landmines among children in Cambodia, Iraq, Jordan, Laos and Moldova;[22] the use of basketball combined with peace-building and leadership training by PeacePlayers International for youth in divided communities in Cyprus, Israel and the West Bank, Northern Ireland and South Africa;[23] the use of various youth sports to reduce AIDS infections and teach life skills in the Kicking AIDS Out network of 22 organisations on four continents;[24] and the use of boxing and martial arts combined with education by the delightfully named Fight for Peace, initially in Rio de Janeiro but now with a network of projects helping over 250,000 street and slum kids in over 25 countries on four continents.[25]

The local and global sport-for-development-and-peace projects and organisations are now so numerous and so successful that they even have their own highly competitive annual awards such as the Laureus Sport for Good Award, the Beyond Sport Summit Awards and the Peace and Sports Awards.[26]

Creating new role models and leaders

Since the first Olympic Games, in 776 BC, sport has created many heroes – but too few role models. While MYSA teams won many tournaments from local to global levels,[27] MYSA's greatest achievement by far has been the creation of new heroes *and* role models. With its motto of 'Giving youth a sporting chance on *and* off the field', MYSA provides youth with a chance to test and develop their social and leadership skills so they can better help themselves and others. MYSA also applies an 11-point Fairplay Code, subtitled 'For those who want to be winners on *and* off the field'. Today the over 125,000 MYSA alumni include doctors, lawyers, marketing executives, bank managers, IT experts, teachers and many other high achievers, who have helped themselves and their families escape poverty.

A major reason for MYSA's success is the fact that it is owned and run by the youth themselves. The more than 200 elected youth leaders, coaches and volunteers are on average only 16 years old, and half of the elected leaders are girls.[28] Although politicians like saying that the youth of today are the leaders of tomorrow, in the Mathare slums the youth have been the leaders of today for nearly three decades. More than ten former MYSA leaders have also been elected to municipal and county councils in the last two national elections.[29] It would not be surprising if a MYSA graduate even became the president of Kenya someday, and he or she then included sport for poverty reduction and peace among his or her top priorities.

Using sport to tackle corruption

Tackling corruption in sport can reinforce anti-corruption efforts in other sectors. For example, in early 2003 the newly elected Kenyan government inherited several complex mega-scandals that would inevitably involve lengthy investigations. So, as an initial signal of its sincerity, the government also targeted the notoriously mismanaged KFF.[30] In February 2003, the government disbanded the national U17 team for fielding over-age players, withdrew from the African youth tournament and launched investigations on corruption in the KFF.[31] To the surprise of many sceptical Kenyans, in June 2003 several top KFF officials were arraigned in court on corruption charges.[32]

Sport can also show the way forward in tackling corruption through stakeholder-led reforms.[33] For example, in 2003 the KFF rejected over 50 reform proposals submitted by its own clubs. Most top clubs then left the KFF and set up their own league and company – the Kenyan Premier League Limited (KPL) – plus a Transparency Cup with the theme 'Kicking Corruption Out of Sport'. In mid-2004 FIFA persuaded the top clubs to rejoin the KFF but also supported continued club management of the KPL.[34] As a result, today the KPL is one of the most corruption-free, highly competitive and professionally managed leagues in Africa.[35]

Protecting sport as a force for good

In parallel with the rapid growth of so many and different sport-for-good initiatives, over the last two decades some global sports bodies such as FIFA and the International Olympic Committee (IOC) have also emerged as major geopolitical actors in the international community. Their leaders are often better known than many heads of state and their decisions on sports rules, disputes and the hosting of major sports events now have significant political, social and economic ramifications within and among countries.

Their income has also grown dramatically. For example, FIFA's income of US$2.1 billion in 2014[36] was equivalent to more than 75 per cent of the 2014 UN programme budget[37] and larger than the gross national income of over 25 countries.[38] FIFA also generated a 'surplus' of US$2.6 billion from the 2014 World Cup,[39] which would place it among the top 100 most profitable Fortune 500 companies.[40]

Despite their prominence on the world stage, global sports bodies remain largely a law unto themselves. While UN member states must respect many different *international* treaties, laws and judicial bodies, global sports bodies are bound only by their own internal statutes, the Court of Arbitration for Sport (CAS) and the *national* laws and courts of the countries where they are headquartered.[41] Moreover, unlike the over 30 UN organisations headquartered in over 17 countries under standardised agreements with the host countries, there are no standardised host-country agreements on the rights *and* responsibilities of global and regional sports bodies. Sadly, that autonomy has been abused, as shown by the results of the new *Sport Governance Observer* study which reveals that international sports bodies often lack proper procedures and tools against corruption, undemocratic procedures and other critical poor governance traits.[42]

The huge rise in revenues and lack of external as well as internal accountability pose a serious threat to sport as a force for good. In too many international sports bodies and their national associations, once elected the officials often handle the organisation as if it is their private property, treat the athletes and teams as if they are the enemy, marginalise them in decision-making bodies and then ignore or change the rules to perpetuate themselves in power.[43] As a result, while match-fixing still poses a serious threat, corruption in sport is more prevalent and destructive off the field than on it. For future reforms, a key challenge is to ensure that the teams, coaches and athletes who make the sport on the field have a much greater role in making decisions about their sport off the field.

Sport has a rare and universal power to transcend the many political, cultural, social and economic differences within and among countries on our still-divided planet. For example, for the first time in its 44-year history, the Norway Cup this year will feature a unique 'Colourful Friendship' team with half the players from Norway and half from the Mathare slums in Nairobi.[44] For decades environmentalists have urged the UN and other international agencies and governments to 'think globally and act locally'. In sport, however, what is needed is for more international sports bodies to act globally, more like the way thousands of sport-for-development-and-peace organisations are already acting locally.

Today, thousands of local and global projects and organisations involve millions of young athletes carrying out sport-for-development-and-peace activities. Using many different sports, they tackle a wide range of health, social, environmental and other problems. Their achievements – and the dreams of millions of young athletes hoping to use their athletic talents to help themselves and their families escape poverty – will be overshadowed and compromised, however, unless the corruption in sport issues highlighted later in this report are also tackled.

Corrupt sports officials are not just stealing money. They are also stealing the future of our youth, the future of our athletes and the future of our sports. This is why no one should stand on the sidelines or remain seated in the stands during the continuing struggle for corruption-free sport and for sport as a force for good.

Notes

1   Bob Munro is the Managing Director of XXCEL Africa Ltd. Since 1985 he has lived and worked in Africa as a senior policy adviser on sustainable development for African governments and the United Nations. He is also the founder/chairman of the Mathare Youth Sports Association (1987), the founder/chairman of Mathare United FC (1994) and a founding director of the Kenyan Premier League Ltd (2003).
2   See Olympic Movement, 'Olympic Truce', *www.olympic.org/content/the-ioc/commissions/public-affairs-and-social-development-through-sport/olympic-truce*.
3   Multiculturalism also prevails in many 'national' teams today, especially in Europe. For example, the 2010 FIFA World Cup team from Germany had players with roots in nine different countries on three continents: Brazil, Bosnia-Herzegovina, Ghana, Nigeria, Poland, Spain, Tunisia and Turkey, as well as Germany.
4   The *juala* balls are made by the children using waste plastic bags tied with old string. In 2010 a made-in-Mathare *juala* ball sold at a charity auction in Dubai for US$205,000; it is probably the world's most expensive football. The purchaser then donated it to the IOC, and it is now on display in the Olympic Museum in Lausanne, Switzerland.
5   Father Arnold Grol, the Undugu Society founder, dedicated his life to helping streetkids, and first took me to the Mathare slums during one of my many UN missions to Kenya in the early 1980s.
6   The Mathare Youth Sports Association's first major partners were the Norwegian Ministry of Environment, Norad and the Strømme Foundation. A few years later the new Laureus Sport for Good Foundation and then Comic Relief also became key partners. During the last two decades over 30 bilateral and international organisations and companies partnered with MYSA, as well as several Kenyan agencies and companies such as K.D. Wire.
7   For more information, see *www.mysakenya.org* and *www.facebook.com/MathareYouth SportsAssociation*.
8   In 2015 MYSA has 26,420 players in 1,811 teams, including 6,000 girls in 398 teams, playing in over 120 leagues in 16 MYSA zones. In addition, more than 5,000 youths participate in the MYSA community service programmes.
9   MYSA leaders and trainers have provided technical advice and assistance to projects in Botswana, India, Mozambique, Senegal, South Africa, South Sudan, Tanzania, Uganda, Vietnam and Zambia.
10 See Bob Munro, 'Sport for peace and reconciliation: young peacemakers in the Kakuma Refugee Camp and Mathare slums in Kenya', paper presented at the 6th Play the Game World Communication Conference on Sport and Society, Coventry, UK, 11 June 2009, *www.playthegame.org/uploads/media/Bob_Munro-Sport_for_peace_and_reconciliation.pdf*.
11 To help reduce pre-election tensions, the MYSA Football4Peace tournaments had special rules. For example, all the teams had to include at least five girls and only the girls were allowed to score.

12 I chaired this meeting, which became one of my proudest moments in sport. After only ten minutes all the top clubs unanimously agreed to use their limited funds to pay for the Kenyan national team.

13 In May 2008, when KPL started funding and helping the national team, Kenya was 120th in the FIFA world rankings. By the end of 2008, Kenya was ranked 68th in the world. On that 2008 national team, which achieved the best results in Kenyan football history, over half the players and both the head coach and team manager were from MYSA and Mathare United FC.

14 See, for example, *Standard* (Kenya), 'Youth clean up Mathare', 23 April 1989; Inter Press Service, 'Football sets development rolling in slums', 29 November 1989.

15 See, for example, *New York Times* (US), 'In Nairobi slums, soccer gives poor youths hope', 14 October 1991, *www.nytimes.com/1991/10/14/world/nairobi-journal-in-nairobi-slums-soccer-gives-poor-youths-hope.html*; *Christian Science Monitor* (US), 'Soccer playing youths clean up: Nairobi program combines sports and community service', 31 August 1992; *Reader's Digest* (US), 'Miracle in the Mathare slums', April 1994.

16 Bob Munro, 'Children and the environment: a new approach to youth activities and environmental cleanup in Kenya', *Journal of Environment and Urbanization*, vol. 4 (1992).

17 See United Nations, *Sport for Development and Peace: Towards Achieving the Millennium Development Goals* (New York: UN, 2003).

18 In 2004 MYSA also won the Laureus Sport for Good Award at the World Sports Academy Awards in Lisbon.

19 The eight Laureus national foundations are in Argentina, Germany, Italy, the Netherlands, South Africa, Spain, Switzerland and the United States. For more information on Laureus, see *www.laureus.com/home*.

20 For more information on streetfootballworld, see *www.streetfootballworld.org*.

21 For more information on Peace and Sport, see *www.peace-sport.org*.

22 For more information on Spirit of Soccer, see *www.spiritofsoccer.org*.

23 For more information on PeacePlayers International, see *www.peaceplayersintl.org*.

24 For more information on the Kicking AIDS Out network and projects, see *www.kickingaidsout.net*.

25 For more information on Fight for Peace, see *www.fightforpeace.net*. To fully understand and also stay updated on the special and still growing power of sport as a force for good worldwide, go to the international platform on sport and development (*www.sportanddev.org*), built and hosted since 2003 by the Swiss Academy for Development. It includes a comprehensive history and links to many good local and global sport and development projects, as well as a series of excellent project case studies on key issues such as sport and disability, disaster response, education, gender, health and peace building. Moreover, for those tempted to start a project in their own community or country, it also includes a detailed toolkit with practical advice on implementation, along with references to other helpful and reliable manuals.

26 In addition to the annual Laureus Sport for Good Awards, at the Beyond Sport Summit annual awards are given in a wide range of categories, including sport for education, for environment, for health, for social inclusion, for conflict resolution and for overall leadership in sport, and include organisations in 145 countries from 37 different sports. See *www.beyondsport.org*. The Peace and Sport Awards have eight distinct categories – see *www.peace-sport.org/en/forum/awards/presentation/les-categories.html*.

27 For example, MYSA is second to a club from Brazil for the most gold medals won at the world's oldest and largest international youth tournament, the Norway Cup. MYSA teams also won the first two FIFA Football for Hope tournaments, held during the 2006 and 2010 World Cups.

28 Mathare Youth Sports Association internal governance statistics – see *www.mysakenya.org/resources.html*. In 2009 FIFA acknowledged that the youngest elected football official in

the world was probably the 11-year-old MYSA girl Charity Muthoni, the elected chairman in Kayole, one of MYSA's largest zones with over 2,000 players. See FIFA.com, 'Charity elected as youngest MYSA chairman', 4 November 2009, *www.fifa.com/sustainability/news/y=2009/m=11/news=charity-elected-youngest-mysa-chairman-1128176.html*.

29   In the 2007 national elections, 25-year-old Joel Achola, a leader in the MYSA 'Jailed Kids' project, became the youngest elected councillor in Kenya. See *Sunday Nation* (Kenya), 'Age has nothing to do with it', 27 January 2008.

30   See, for example, *The People* (Kenya), 'KFF lands in serious trouble as government disbands U17 team', 15 February 2003; *Daily Nation* (Kenya), 'Prosecute soccer crooks', editorial, 17 February 2003.

31   Ibid. This may be another Kenyan first in world sport, as friends in FIFA could not recall any government ever voluntarily withdrawing its national team from an international tournament because of age cheating.

32   See *Kenya Times*, 'KFF officials appear in court to face corruption charges', 7 June 2004.

33   See Bob Munro, 'From grassroots to gold medals: are stakeholder-led reforms and ownership a way forward for African football?', paper presented at the 1st African Football Executive Summit, Accra, Ghana, 27 May 2011.

34   This may be the first time FIFA ever supported clubs over their national association member. Had it not been for FIFA, and especially its then deputy general secretary, Jérôme Champagne, the KPL would not have survived the attacks by an unholy alliance of corrupt football officials and politicians.

35   *Guardian* (UK), 'Kenya leads the way in ending blight of corruption in African football', 11 July 2010, *www.theguardian.com/football/2010/jul/11/kenyan-premier-league*.

36   For access to all of FIFA's Financial Reports, see *www.fifa.com/about-fifa/official-documents/governance/index.html#financialReports*. See *FIFA: Financial Report 2014* (Zurich: FIFA, 2015), p. 142.

37   The 2014 UN programme budget was US$2.7 billion; United Nations, *Proposed Programme Budget for the Biennium 2014–15: Foreword and Introduction* (New York: UN, 2013).

38   See World Bank, *World Development Report 2014: Risk and Opportunity – Managing Risk for Development* (Washington, DC: World Bank, 2013), pp. 296–298.

39   See FIFA (2015), p. 36.

40   See 2015 List of Fortune 500 Companies: *http://fortune.com/fortune500*.

41   Many global sports bodies are headquartered in Switzerland, including seven of the ten largest for football (FIFA, UEFA), volleyball (FIVB), basketball (FIBA), hockey (FIH), handball (IHF) and the Olympics (IOC). Those for cricket (ICC), rugby (IRB) and athletics (IAAF) are headquartered in Dubai, Ireland and Monaco, respectively.

42   Developed by Play the Game/Danish Institute for Sports Studies and the University of Leuven in cooperation with other partners, the Sports Governance Observer is a new benchmarking tool for assessing how well sports organisations perform on the basis on 38 key governance indicators. See Play the Game (Denmark), 'Most sports federations fail to meet basic principles of good governance', 10 July 2015, *www.playthegame.org/news/news-articles/2015/0056_most-sports-federations-fail-to-meet-basic-principles-of-good-governance* and Arnout Geeraert, Chapter 1.8 'Indicators and benchmarking tools for sports governance', in this report.

43   For example, in 2012 the Congress of the Confederation of African Football (CAF) blatantly changed the rules so that only elected members of the CAF Executive Committee could run for the CAF presidency. At a subsequent congress, the 70-year age limit for members of the CAF Executive Committee was also lifted, primarily so that the ageing incumbent, already in power for 27 years, could run yet again in the next CAF elections. See Inside World Football (UK), 'African rule changes ensure there will be no change', 15 April 2015, *www.inside worldfootball.com/osasu-obayiuwana/16821-osasu-obayiuwana-african-rule-changes-ensure-there-will-be-none.*

44 With over 30,000 boys and girls playing on over 1,500 football teams from 50 countries during the last week of July every year, the Norway Cup is one of the world's best examples of the truly 'beautiful game' and 'Colourful Friendship' through sport. Before the 2015 Norway Cup, the under-16 Norwegian and Mathare players on their combined Colourful Friendship team spent a week training together at the MYSA Football for Hope Centre in Nairobi and another week living and training together in Norway. The Colourful Friendship team's sponsors and partners include the Norwegian Football Coaches Association (NFT), Norwegian SANA Foundation, Norwegian Football Federation (NFF), Norway Cup and MYSA's Friends in Norway (MViN).

1.2

Fair play

Ideals and realities

Richard H. McLaren[1]

Introduction

Pierre de Coubertin, often heralded as the father of modern Olympism, viewed the concept of fair play as vital to the Olympic spirit.[2] Coubertin was responsible for the initiative that established the International Olympic Committee (IOC), whose Olympic Charter holds that 'the practice of sport is a human right', and describes the Olympic spirit as one of 'friendship, solidarity and fair play'.[3] Fair play is more than a philosophical ideal that athletes subscribe to; it is a mode of social organisation that demands dedication. It requires adherence to written rules, respect for unwritten rules and respect for fellow players, referees, opponents and fans. Fair play requires valuing friendly rivalries, team spirit, fair competition, equality, integrity, solidarity, tolerance, care, excellence and joy for sport. The ideals of fair play begin at the grass roots and extend through to Olympic and professional athletes. More importantly, in the modern world, sport stands apart from other, scripted, forms of entertainment that have predetermined outcomes.

Fair play is integral to the continued success of sport, and yet is everywhere under attack. Acts of corruption undermine the ideal of fair play by taking control of and manipulating the variables that define sport and the Olympic ideal in order to benefit specific individuals or groups. In doing so, sport is deprived of its most fundamental feature: the uncertainty of outcome.

Corrupt governance and match-fixing damage public perceptions of the integrity of sport as an arena for competition, from grassroots competitions to international mega-events. This is alarming, particularly because international sporting institutions increasingly face allegations of corruption. The Fédération Internationale de Football Association (FIFA) and the International Association of Athletics Federations (IAAF) have been embroiled in controversy because of alleged kickbacks to selection committees during bidding processes and bribery in governance elections.[4] The May 2015 arrest of nine FIFA officials and five affiliated corporate executives for 'racketeering, wire fraud and money laundering conspiracies'[5] demonstrated the capacity and willingness of the US government to fight corruption on an international scale. Subsequently, Australia, Colombia, Costa Rica and Switzerland each launched independent investigations targeting alleged bribery, money-laundering and bidding process irregularities. Qatar's successful bid to host the 2022 men's football World Cup has been met with sustained criticism and allegations of bribery. Moreover, the human rights abuses of migrant workers who labour on stadium and facility construction under the 'kafala' system in Qatar have created international pressure on the country to abolish the system, but to date the government has not done so.[6] Although corporate sponsors have expressed concern about these conditions, so far no 2022 World Cup sponsors have withdrawn financial support as a result of the bribery allegations or working conditions. As participants, these companies have the capacity to effect change.

In North America, the National Collegiate Athletic Association (NCAA) faces a continuing backlash over its corporate sponsorship practices, which yield hundreds of millions of dollars per year in profit by exploiting athletes who, in return, receive little more than the dim and fragile hope of a professional career following their collegiate experience.[7] These collegiate experiences may compromise education in favour of training elite 'amateur' athletes who produce success and profit for teams and schools.

Media coverage[8] of poor governance or athletes transgressing the ideals of fair play gives the public a cause for concern as to the validity of competition, fair play and enforcement. Proving that officials accepted kickbacks, athletes used banned substances or matches were fixed can have a dramatic effect on the public's opinion of sport. Such findings call into question every aspect of the sporting relationship, from the highest levels of governing organisations all the way to individual athletes.

The discovery and prosecution of corrupt practices create the same perception problem, leaving the public to wonder how long such practices went undetected and what historic moments in sport may have been compromised by corruption on and off the field. Corrupt practices are therefore parasitic, because they undermine and destroy the ideals of fair play, which are integral to the continued success and growth of sport. The endemic corruption across sporting bodies undermines the ideals of fair play, and yet international sport remains a multi-billion-dollar industry.

Ideals

International sporting organisations (ISOs) make it their objective to promote fair play and meaningful competition for all participants involved in their respective sports. Promoting fair play involves clear statements on ethical values,[9] the development of anti-doping programmes[10] and the promotion of participation in sport. As this *Global Corruption Report* shows, however, the realities are often very different from the ideals.[11]

Enforcement is often controversial and litigious, even where it is limited in scope. The World Anti-Doping Agency (WADA) is one of the best-known proactive institutions, but its mandate is limited to combating doping in sport; WADA does not address corruption in other forms. WADA's director-general, David Howman, has suggested that it is time to create a sport integrity agency to address corruption beyond WADA's current scope, including gambling, match-fixing and bribery.[12] These acts of corruption engage the interests and stakes of all parties: athletes; fans; coaches; sport organisations; stakeholders; corporate sponsors; and, when public actors are involved, national governments. The FBI's FIFA investigation marks a turn in enforcement methods: charges were laid under the United States' 'RICO' statute,[13] a law typically used to prosecute organised crime.

The spectre of corruption haunts notions of fair play in sport and undermines the ideals of modern Olympism. A sport integrity agency, similar in structure to WADA, could enlist and leverage the combined efforts of government and sport organisations in order to proactively target corruption. Existing institutions, such as WADA and the newly developed Voluntary Anti-Doping Association (VADA),[14] offer frameworks for a broader regulatory and administrative solution that places positive obligations on those involved in corrupt practices. While aspects of a broader solution to stamp out corruption in sport exist, more needs to be done to reach the ideal espoused by ISOs and the Olympic movement.

Realities: moving forward

Promoting and achieving fair play in sport by eradicating corruption requires the engagement of all stakeholders and the introduction of authoritative enforcement mechanisms. Battling corruption in sport requires more than statements espousing Olympic ideals. The discovery and prosecution of corruption attracts public scrutiny and undermines the credibility of not just the sport, but its governing organisation as well. If ISOs are viewed as ineffective at purging corruption from their respective sports, fair play will continue to operate as an illusory ideal instead of a reality.

Notes

1   Richard McLaren is the CEO of McLaren Global Sport Solutions Inc., an organisation dedicated to the development of best practices in governance and integrity in sport, and Professor of Law at Western University, London, Canada.
2   Pierre de Coubertin, *Olympism: Selected Writings* (Lausanne: IOC, 2000), p. 588.
3   International Olympic Committee, *Olympic Charter: In Force as from 8 December 2014* (Lausanne: IOC, 2014), p. 11, *www.olympic.org/Documents/olympic_charter_en.pdf*.
4   *The Globe and Mail* (Canada), 'Three FIFA board members under investigation in World Cup bid corruption probe', 27 November 2014, *www.theglobeandmail.com/sports/ soccer/three-fifa-board-members-under-investigation-in-world-cup-bid-corruption- probe/article21820656*. See also *Guardian* (UK), 'Questions for IAAF president's son over $5m request to Doha amid 2017 bid', 10 December 2014, *www.theguardian.com/ sport/2014/dec/10/questions-for-iaaf-presidents-son-over-5m-request-to-doha-amid- 2017-bid*.
5   US Department of Justice, 'Nine FIFA officials and five corporate executives indicted for racketeering conspiracy and corruption', 27 May 2015, *www.justice.gov/opa/pr/ nine-fifa-officials-and-five-corporate-executives-indicted-racketeering-conspiracy-and*.
6   *Al Jazeera America*, 'Amnesty: Qatar lagging on labor reforms', 21 May 2015, *http://america. aljazeera.com/articles/2015/5/21/amnesty-qatar-lagging-on-labor-reforms.html*.
7   *New York Times* (US), 'Day of reckoning for NCAA', 6 June 2014, *www.nytimes.com/2014/ 06/07/opinion/nocera-day-of-reckoning-for-ncaa.html?_r=0*.
8   See, for example, a discussion on the various scandals plaguing FIFA during Sepp Blatter's 17-year presidency: *New York Times* (US), 'FIFA scandals while Sepp Blatter has been president', 22 May 2015, *www.nytimes.com/aponline/2015/05/22/sports/soccer/ap-soc- fifa-election-scandals.html*. On television, John Oliver's two FIFA specials on *Last Week Tonight*, a late-night US comedy show, have together received over 15 million views online. The high-profile public arrests of FIFA officials created international news coverage, from small newspapers to international newspapers of record. With respect to the NCAA, the alleged educational institutions' use of athletics and athletes for profit has also become part of the public discourse; see *The Atlantic* (US), 'Why hasn't Congress investigated corruption in the NCAA?', 9 April 2014, *www.theatlantic.com/entertainment/archive/2014/04/ why-hasnt-congress-investigated-corruption-in-the-ncaa/360391*.
9   See, for example, the preamble of FIFA's Code of Ethics: Fédération Internationale de Football Association, *FIFA Code of Ethics: 2012 Edition* (Zurich: FIFA, 2012), *www.fifa.com/ mm/document/affederation/administration/50/02/82/codeofethics2012e.pdf*.
10 See, for example, the programme changes introduced by Brian Cookson after he had been elected president of the Union Cycliste Internationale (UCI) in 2013, including, but not limited to, partnerships with anti-doping ISOs, internal and external legal counsel, policy

boards directed at doping prevention and rigid use of the Athlete Biological Passport: Union Cycliste Internationale, 'UCI anti-doping programme', *www.uci.ch/clean-sport/anti-doping*.

11   See, for example, International Weightlifting Federation, 'Mission', *www.iwf.net/focus-on-iwf/ about*.

12   David Howman, 'Supporting the integrity of sport and combating corruption', *Marquette Sports Law Review*, vol. 23 (2013), p. 247.

13   Racketeer Influenced and Corrupt Organization, part of the Organized Crime Control Act of 1970: USC tit. 18 §§1961–1968 (1970).

14   See the VADA website: *http://vada-testing.org*.

1.3

Autonomy and governance

Necessary bedfellows in the fight against corruption in sport

Jean-Loup Chappelet[1]

Autonomy is a combination of the Greek words *auto* and *nomos*, meaning 'those who make their own law'. It is a long-established concept in the moral sciences that was developed, most notably, by the eighteenth-century German philosopher Immanuel Kant and later taken up by English-speaking thinkers under the expressions 'self-rule' and 'self-governance'. It was also a presiding principle in colonies obtaining self-rule and then independence from European countries during the nineteenth and twentieth centuries. The management and political sciences gave a new dimension to the concept with the emergence of the ideas of so-called new public management (NPM) and the granting of autonomy to entire sectors of public administration in the 1990s.[2] Throughout almost the entire twentieth century traditional associative sports organisations (clubs and federations) enjoyed a large degree of autonomy in governing sport.[3] Some European countries (such as France and Italy) even gave them monopolistic public service missions in sport. As explained below, for sport's governing bodies, autonomy is seen as fundamental both to sport and to their organisations.

Governance, a seventeenth-century French word designating the territory controlled by a governor,[4] became an important concept in the management and political sciences in the 1990s. The concept has now been defined and analysed in so many ways it would be impossible to summarise them all here.[5] The term has now become part of the common lexicon, thanks to the adoption by intergovernmental organisations such as the World Bank[6] and the European Union[7] of the expression 'good governance' – a concept that applies just as much to public and not-for-profit organisations as it does to companies. Governance is an important issue for sport and for the organisations that co-produce sport (clubs, federations, governing bodies, etc.), which increasingly have to work in conjunction with public bodies, non-governmental organisations (NGOs), other non-profit organisations and commercial companies, most notably sports equipment companies, sponsors and the media.[8]

In these early decades of the twenty-first century, the concepts of 'autonomy' and 'governance' have become major issues in international, national and – sometimes – local debates over sport. They have largely replaced the issue of the 'specific nature of sport', which was finally recognised in Europe in 2009 by article 165 of the Lisbon Treaty on the Functioning of the European Union after the Declaration of Nice (2000), as mentioned below. Autonomy and governance are of concern to non-profit sports organisations just as much as they are to public authorities (local or regional sports departments, ministries) and intergovernmental (European Union, Council of Europe, United Nations, etc.) and non-governmental (International Olympic Committee [IOC], international sport federations, Transparency International, etc.) organisations. This chapter reviews the history of these two concepts in the field of international sport and shows how they are closely linked to the development of policies to combat corruption in sport and improve the management of sports organisations. A number of conclusions are drawn in order to orient discussions about how sport – now a very important sector of society – should be managed and regulated, especially in terms of meeting certain criteria relating to the environment, society and governance.

Autonomy

The Olympic Charter, a sort of constitution for the elite Olympic sports organisations (also known as the 'Olympic Movement'), first made reference to autonomy in 1949.[9] At this time, state interference in sport was starting to make itself felt, especially in the countries of the Soviet bloc, which were beginning to join the Olympic Movement (the USSR first took part in the Olympic Games in 1952, in Helsinki). For members of the IOC, making recognition of a country contingent on the autonomy of its national Olympic committee (NOC) and, thus, authorising its participation in the Olympics was a way of resisting these government pressures.

The concept was not new, however, and had imbued the Olympic Movement from its beginnings at the turn of the twentieth century. In 1909 Pierre de Coubertin, the then IOC president, declared: 'The goodwill of all the members of any autonomous sport grouping begins to disintegrate as soon as the huge, blurred face of that dangerous creature known as the state makes an appearance.'[10] In a controversial speech following the Palestinian terrorist attack during the Munich Olympics in 1972 ('the Games must go on'), Avery Brundage, one of Coubertin's successors, reiterated this idea in his statement: 'The games of the 20th Olympiad [in Munich 1972] have been subjected to two savage attacks. We lost the Rhodesian battle against naked political blackmail.' (This was a reference to the threat of boycotts by African governments, which led the IOC to withdraw its invitation to Rhodesia – now Zimbabwe – to take part in the 1972 Olympics just before the Games were held.)

The concept of autonomy was reiterated in the 1992 European Sport Charter (based on the principles of the 1975 Sport for All Charter), adopted by the Council of Europe: 'Voluntary sports organisations have the right to establish autonomous decision-making processes within the law. Both governments and sports organisations shall recognise the need for a mutual respect of their decisions' (article 3.3). EU heads of state and heads of government confirmed this principle in the Nice Declaration of 2000 without using the word 'autonomy': 'The task of sporting organisations is to organise and promote their particular sport, in line with their objectives, with due regard for national and Community (i.e. European) legislation and on the basis of a democratic and transparent method of operation. They enjoy independence and the right to organise themselves.'

These statements by intergovernmental organisations came at a time when the 1995 Bosman ruling by the European Court of Justice declared illegal the football players transfer sporting rules in the European Union and forced the Fédération Internationale de Football Association (FIFA) to change its transfer rules for footballers. The sports movement saw this ruling as interference in sporting affairs and led it to call upon governments to recognise the 'specific nature of sport'. (This status, which it was thought would exempt sport from European law, was finally accorded under the 1999 Treaty on the Functioning of the European Union; it had few real consequences, however, because of the imprecision of the concept, and it certainly did not exempt sport from European law.) In 2004 the IOC's revised Olympic Charter reaffirmed: 'The NOCs must preserve their autonomy and resist all pressures of any kind, including but not limited to political, legal, religious or economic pressures, which may prevent them from complying with the Olympic Charter' (article 28.6).

Although the 2006 Meca–Medina case led to a ruling by the European Court of Justice in favour of the sports organisations involved against two Romanian swimmers who contested their doping sanctions, the court declared: 'If the sporting activity in question falls within the scope of the [European] Treaty, the conditions for engaging in it are then subject to all the obligations which result from the various provisions of the Treaty.' In other words, all sporting rules (including, in this case, doping rules) were potentially subject to the laws governing the European Union. The ruling did not include anything new compared with the Nice Declaration, but the IOC reacted by calling a seminar, held in Lausanne, on the autonomy of sports organisations.

A 2007 EU White Paper on sport confirmed the sports movement's fears and prompted the IOC to organise a second seminar on the autonomy of the Olympic Movement that same year. The resolution adopted by this seminar underlined the fact that good governance in sports organisations is 'the fundamental basis to secure the Autonomy of Olympic and Sports organisations and to ensure that this Autonomy is respected by our stakeholders' (point 6 of the resolution). The IOC's deliberations concluded in February 2008 with the introduction of the 'basic universal principles for good governance of the Olympic and sports movement', or 'BUPs',[11] organised into seven chapters. BUP 7 is called 'Harmonious relations with governments while preserving autonomy'.

Thomas Bach, who became the IOC president in 2013, presented the BUPs in his speech to the 2009 Olympic Congress. Entitled 'Unity in diversity', this speech was a plea for autonomy and good governance in sport. Following their adoption by the Congress (point 41 of the Final Document of the Congress) and subsequent incorporation into the IOC's Code of Ethics, the BUPs became obligatory for the Olympic Movement: 'The Basic Universal Principles of Good Governance of the Olympic and Sports Movement, in particular transparency, responsibility and accountability, must be respected by all Olympic Movement constituents' (point C1 of the IOC Code of Ethics). The Congress's Final Document states: 'The Olympic Movement is founded on the concept of the autonomy and good governance of sport, which recognises and respects our individuality and achieves unity through diversity' (point 3.27).

This doctrine was subsequently refined in the revised version of the Olympic Charter, published in 2011: 'Recognising that sport occurs within the framework of society, sports organisations within the Olympic Movement shall have the rights and obligations of autonomy, which include freely establishing and controlling the rules of sport, determining the structure and governance of their organisations, enjoying the right of elections free from any outside influence and the responsibility for ensuring that principles of good governance be applied' (Fundamental Principle 5 of the Olympic Charter). This principle uses the author's[12] definition of autonomy but does not really explain why sports organisations should enjoy autonomy as a right.

Several organisations within the Olympic Movement, including two essential components of the movement – international federations (IFs) and national Olympic committees – used the autonomy recognised by the Olympic Charter to adopt their own codes of ethics. This was the case for FIFA in 2004 (revised in 2013) and the Swiss Olympic Association in 2012.

At the turn of the twenty-first century, sports organisations in numerous countries, including Afghanistan, Gambia, Ghana, India, Kuwait, Nigeria, Pakistan, Panama and Poland, denounced cases of state intervention in sport. These complaints led the IOC to temporarily suspend the NOCs of Afghanistan, Kuwait and India, preventing them taking part with their flag in the Sydney 2000, London 2012 and Sochi 2014 Winter Olympics, respectively. As early as the 1970s the IOC had protested, unsuccessfully, against a law (the Amateur Sport Act) passed by the US Congress creating the United States Olympic Committee (USOC) and giving it property rights over the Olympic rings in the United States. Historically, however, it can be seen that the countries excluded from the Olympics or other world events have all been relatively minor in terms of either their size or sporting results.

It goes without saying that, within a constitutional state, there are limits to autonomy, and complete autonomy is not possible. Different authors have referred to this situation as 'conditional autonomy',[13] 'negotiated autonomy'[14] or 'pragmatic autonomy'.[15] The IOC president evoked the idea of 'responsible autonomy'[16] in front of the General Assembly of the United Nations in New York in 2013, and it is now the IOC doctrine:

> *Regardless of where in the world we practise sport, the rules are the same. They are recognised worldwide. They are based on a common 'global ethic' of fair play, tolerance and friendship. But to apply this 'universal law' worldwide and spread our values globally, sport has to enjoy responsible autonomy. Politics must respect this sporting autonomy. For only then can sport organisations implement these universal values amidst all the differing laws, customs and traditions. Responsible autonomy does not mean that sport should operate in a law-free environment. It does mean that we respect national laws which are not targeted against sport and its organisations alone, sometimes for chiefly political reasons.*

In the Western tradition, the freedom of peaceful association – proclaimed in the Universal Declaration of Human Rights (article 20.1) – allows people to create sports organisations, adopt the rules they wish and apply these rules to all members of the organisation, as long as they do not disturb public order or contravene the laws of the country in which the organisation is based. Such associations (clubs, federations) formed the basis of the modern sports movement, which began in Europe in the nineteenth century. Hence, a boxing organisation based in Switzerland can decide how its president is elected, as long as it respects articles 60–79 of the Swiss Civil Code (laws governing associations), and stipulate any rule of boxing, as long as it does not impose fights, for example, 'to the death' (which would be against public order). On the other hand, some organisations' rules for sports events may conflict with national or international laws, such as laws on nationality or laws regulating the European single market (as demonstrated in the Bosman ruling). Conflicts can also arise if national governments pass laws contradicting existing sporting rules. This occurred in India in 2011, when, against the wishes of the Indian Olympic Association, the government of India tried to limit the age and length of tenure of the leaders of the country's sports federations. Commercial partners (sponsors and the media) may also exert pressure to change sporting rules. The abolition of protective helmets in amateur boxing, in order to give spectators a better view of the boxers' faces, is just one example among many (tie breaks in tennis, disqualification after two false starts in athletics, etc.).

Sports autonomy becomes difficult to justify outside the Western world, and, even here, some authors feel it is no more than a myth. According to some researchers,[17] this is the case in Denmark. In the United Kingdom, where government intervention in sport is not common, the government has set up public bodies (such as UK Sport) known as QUANGOs (quasi-autonomous non-governmental organisations) to support UK sports organisations and elite sport. In China, government bodies and sports organisations are known as GONGOs (governmental non-governmental organisations) in order to underline the closeness of their ties with the government and their lack of autonomy from the state ('gong' is the Chinese word for 'public'). For example, China's Olympic Committee is run by more or less the same people who run the country's sports ministry. In several countries around the world, the national Olympic committee's president is also the president of the country or its sports minister.

Nowadays it is difficult to host a major sports event, or organise the fight against doping, violence in sport or match-fixing, without close cooperation with states. In fact, sports organisations welcome this type of cooperation, as long as their autonomy is respected (see BUP 7). The most common justification for the autonomy of sports organisations is that sport has to remain outside politics. The least that can be said is that this ideal – just like amateurism, finally abandoned by the Olympic Movement in the 1980s – has been impossible to achieve and runs counter to the rationale behind the revival of the Olympics.[18] Keeping sport free from political interference and scrutiny has been the traditional way for sport organisations to ensure they can justify autonomy. A better justification today would be that the twenty-first-century state cannot do everything; therefore, from a liberal point of view, governments should delegate what they can to other bodies, including self-financed private organisations, such as sports organisations, as long as the state retains control over legislation and the regulation of the sector in question.

Thomas Bach recognised these necessary limits to autonomy in his 'Unity in diversity' speech to the 2009 Olympic Congress and reiterated his faith in the concept in the manifesto he drew up for his successful bid to become IOC president in 2013. He even saw it as one of the main challenges facing the Olympic Movement and the IOC in the coming years:

> *Sport must be politically neutral, but sport cannot be apolitical. This is why the Olympic Movement needs responsible autonomy and partnership with politics at the same time. This can be achieved by a dialogue in mutual respect between the Olympic Movement and government authorities at all levels, including the United Nations, intergovernmental organisations and national governments. We should more clearly define the concept of responsible autonomy and better communicate its advantages for both politics and sports to all parties. [. . .] Because of the way the Olympic Movement is structured, an attack on the autonomy of one of its members represents an attack on the autonomy of the whole Olympic Movement. A lack of autonomy of a national federation, for instance, always leads to a lack of autonomy for the relevant NOC and IF. Therefore, going beyond our preventive measures, we should optimise and harmonise our sanction system even more. Each IF and each continental association of NOCs and IFs should appoint an expert at the highest executive level to be called upon whenever a problem of autonomy arises. The sanctions imposed by the IOC should be respected and applied by as many IFs as possible, since such a united approach is the most efficient.[19]*

After his election, Bach appointed Irishman Patrick Hickey, also a representative of the NOCs, to the IOC's Executive Commission, as the IOC member responsible for autonomy.

Governance

The term 'governance' first took hold in the language of international sport in 1998, during what would become known as the 'Salt Lake City scandal'.[20] The IOC was forced to investigate around 30 of its members, accused of receiving favours (such as luxury travel and holidays, study grants or jobs, free goods or services) from Salt Lake City's 2002 Winter

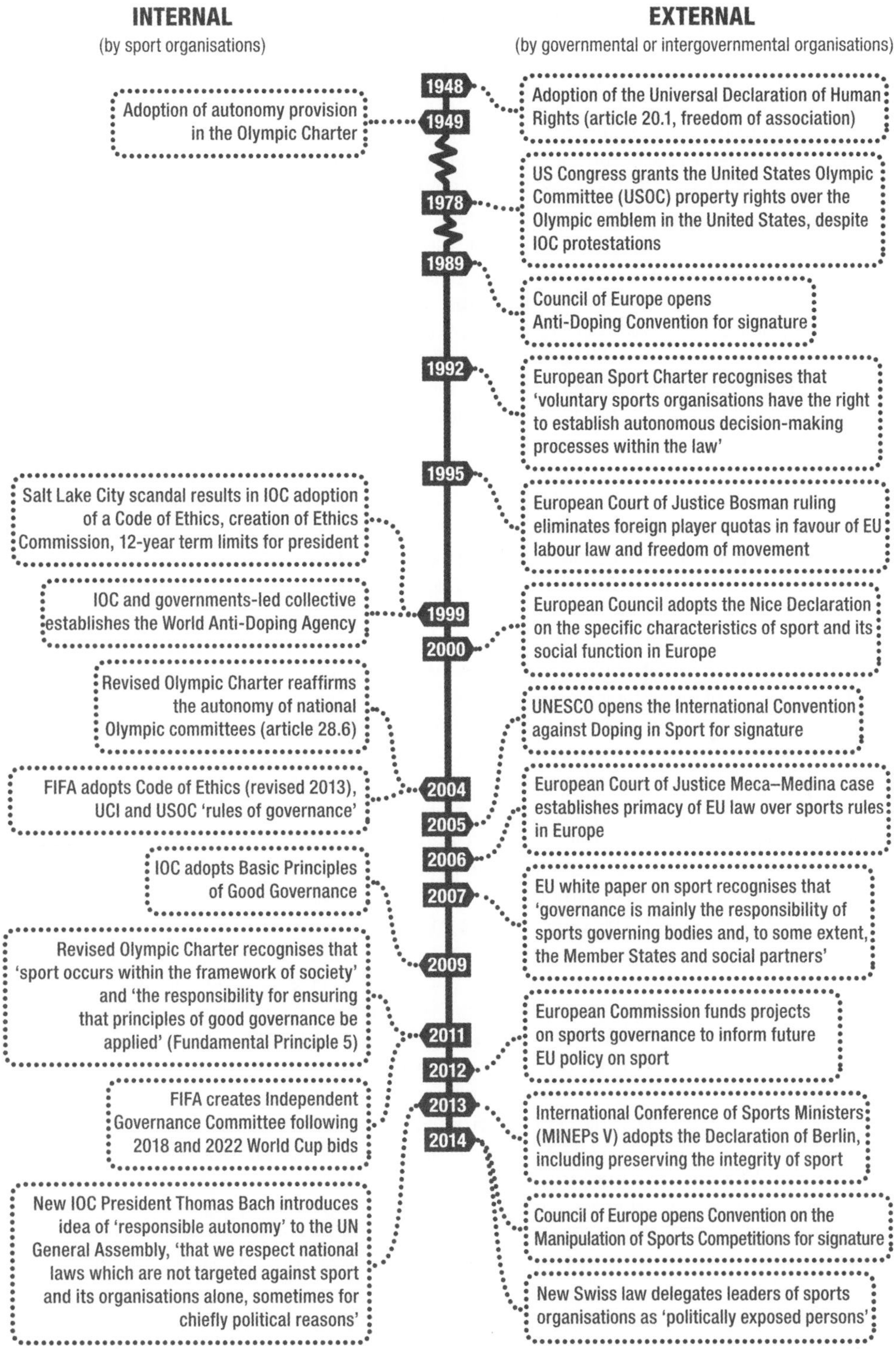

INTERNAL
(by sport organisations)

EXTERNAL
(by governmental or intergovernmental organisations)

1948
1949
Adoption of autonomy provision in the Olympic Charter

Adoption of the Universal Declaration of Human Rights (article 20.1, freedom of association)

1978
US Congress grants the United States Olympic Committee (USOC) property rights over the Olympic emblem in the United States, despite IOC protestations

1989
Council of Europe opens Anti-Doping Convention for signature

1992
European Sport Charter recognises that 'voluntary sports organisations have the right to establish autonomous decision-making processes within the law'

1995
Salt Lake City scandal results in IOC adoption of a Code of Ethics, creation of Ethics Commission, 12-year term limits for president

European Court of Justice Bosman ruling eliminates foreign player quotas in favour of EU labour law and freedom of movement

1999
2000
IOC and governments-led collective establishes the World Anti-Doping Agency

European Council adopts the Nice Declaration on the specific characteristics of sport and its social function in Europe

Revised Olympic Charter reaffirms the autonomy of national Olympic committees (article 28.6)

UNESCO opens the International Convention against Doping in Sport for signature

2004
2005
FIFA adopts Code of Ethics (revised 2013), UCI and USOC 'rules of governance'

European Court of Justice Meca–Medina case establishes primacy of EU law over sports rules in Europe

2006
2007
IOC adopts Basic Principles of Good Governance

EU white paper on sport recognises that 'governance is mainly the responsibility of sports governing bodies and, to some extent, the Member States and social partners'

2009
Revised Olympic Charter recognises that 'sport occurs within the framework of society' and 'the responsibility for ensuring that principles of good governance be applied' (Fundamental Principle 5)

2011
2012
European Commission funds projects on sports governance to inform future EU policy on sport

2013
2014
FIFA creates Independent Governance Committee following 2018 and 2022 World Cup bids

International Conference of Sports Ministers (MINEPs V) adopts the Declaration of Berlin, including preserving the integrity of sport

New IOC President Thomas Bach introduces idea of 'responsible autonomy' to the UN General Assembly, 'that we respect national laws which are not targeted against sport and its organisations alone, sometimes for chiefly political reasons'

Council of Europe opens Convention on the Manipulation of Sports Competitions for signature

New Swiss law delegates leaders of sports organisations as 'politically exposed persons'

Figure 1.1 Key decisions in the evolution of 'sports autonomy'

Olympics bid committee. In 1995 the IOC's members had awarded the Games to the city in Utah (United States), which it duly hosted in 2002 under a new president (the former organising committee president had resigned but was acquitted of all charges in 2003). It was also revealed that similar behaviours had been part of earlier bidding processes.[21]

By the end of the IOC-led inquiry, four members of the IOC had resigned or had died, six members had been expelled and ten members had been reprimanded. This scandal shook the IOC so deeply that, in 1999, it introduced substantial reforms to its governance by setting up an ethics commission, drawing up a code of ethics to sanction unacceptable behaviours and limiting terms of office, most notably for the IOC president (a maximum of 12 years). It also had to accept new members representing its main stakeholders: athletes, NOCs and IFs. These reforms allowed the IOC to escape from the media and sponsor spotlight, and enjoy the success of the 2000 Summer Games in Sydney. At first the term 'governance' was used mostly by the media and the IOC's sponsors, but it was quickly picked up by governments, which, in 1999 and in conjunction with the Olympic Movement, founded the World Anti-Doping Agency (WADA) in order to jointly fight a phenomenon that sports organisations had proved unable to control and govern alone.

In February 2001 the European Olympic Committees (EOC, the umbrella organisation for Europe's 49 IOC-recognised NOCs), in partnership with the International Automobile Federation, which provided the finance, held a conference in Brussels called 'The rules of the game: first international governance in sport conference'. Jacques Rogge, who would be elected president of the IOC a few months later, used this conference to expound on one of his campaign themes: 'Since sport is based on ethics and competition on fair play, the governance of sport must comply with the highest standards in terms of transparency, democracy and accountability.'[22] These ideas were greatly influenced by Sunder Katwala, a British researcher of Indian and Irish descent.[23]

The word 'governance' appeared in the Olympic Charter for the first time in 2004, in article 19.3.2: '[The IOC Executive Board] approves all internal governance regulations relating to its organisation.' More significantly, in 2011 governance was included in the IOC's first mission: 'To encourage and support the promotion of ethics and good governance in sport as well as education of youth through sport and to dedicate its efforts to ensuring that, in sport, the spirit of fair play prevails and violence is banned' (article 2.1). Also in 2011, the fifth fundamental principle of the Olympic Charter closely linked the concepts of governance and autonomy (see above). This principle was implemented, at least partly, in 2012, when the IOC used some of the above-mentioned BUPs to evaluate the 28 IFs that wanted to remain on the programme for the Summer Olympics and the seven IFs that were applying to join the programme.[24] The result of this evaluation was the provisional exclusion of wrestling, because its IF had no women on its decision-making bodies and no athletes' commission, and failed to follow unspecified precepts of 'good' governance.

'Rules of good governance' were introduced by the Union Cycliste Internationale in 2004, closely followed by other sports organisations, including the Dutch NOC (called NOC*NSF) and the United States Olympic Committee in 2005, the Commonwealth Games Federation in 2006 and the European Team Sports Association in 2008.[25] Governmental or intergovernmental organisations such as UK Sport (in 2004), the European Union (in 2000 and 2007) and the Council of Europe (in 2004 and 2005) did likewise. Since the early 2000s innumerable definitions of governance have been put forward; the author and Michaël Mrkonjic have identified more than 35 sets of 'good governance' principles in sport alone, most of which have been written in the conditional tense.[26] On the other hand, there are very few examples of tools for measuring sports organisation governance. Exceptions include, for instance, UK Sport's 11 'Governance Requirements', the Australian Sports Commission's 20 'Mandatory Sports Governance Principles'[27] and the 63 'Basic

Indicators for Better Governance in International Sport' (BIBGIS).[28] The IOC systematically refers to the more than 100 indicators that can be deducted from the BUPs, even though they have proved difficult to apply.[29] Despite the introduction of all these principles, a 2009 report by Transparency International[30] condemned a continuing lack of transparency and accountability – two key precepts of sports organisation governance.

At the end of 2010, during and after the selection of the host countries for the 2018 (Russia) and 2022 (Qatar) football World Cups, FIFA was shaken by a similar crisis to the one that had rocked the IOC ten years earlier. Several members of FIFA's executive committee were expelled, suspended or forced to resign. Transparency International sent FIFA a report called *Safe Hands: Building Integrity and Transparency at FIFA*,[31] which listed several concrete measures that could be taken. FIFA responded to this crisis by creating, in 2011, an Independent Governance Committee (IGC) and nominating Mark Pieth, a Swiss expert, as its president. Pieth's analysis of the organisation, called *Governing FIFA*,[32] was followed by several IGC reports recommending possible actions football's governing body could take. These reports resulted in the 2012 and 2013 FIFA congresses approving a series of measures to improve the organisation's governance. In Bach's bid for the IOC presidency, he said he wished to copy one of these measures: the creation of two branches for investigation and adjudication within the Ethics Commission to further its independence.[33]

From 2012 to 2013 the European Commission financed several projects in the field of sports governance in order to prepare Europe's sports policy for the period from 2014 to 2017, which has been introduced following the adoption of article 165 of the Treaty on the Functioning of the European Union (Lisbon Treaty). Projects included 'Action for Good Governance in International Sport'[34] and 'Good Governance in Grassroots Sport'.[35]

These different approaches to sports governance raise two important issues. The first is the need to harmonise the fundamental requirements of sports organisation governance: what is essential and what is just 'nice to have'? The second issue – the urgent need for indicators that can be used to measure a sports organisation's level of governance, as is done for other public or private organisations, and even for states (see the World Bank's Worldwide Governance Indicators) – arises from the first. These indicators must probably include analogous measurement tools to those included in the BIBGIS.[36]

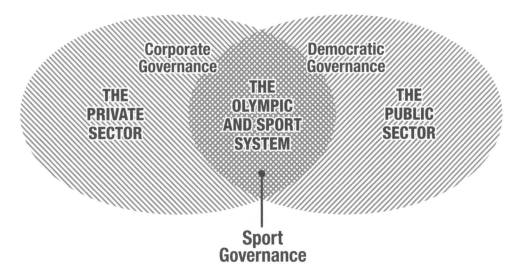

Figure 1.2 The need for governance

From this point of view, it would be judicious to talk about 'better governance' rather than 'good governance'. In fact, sports organisations have a lot of catching up to do in this respect, as was demonstrated by the IOC/Salt Lake City scandals in 1998/1999 and the FIFA scandals in 2010–2013 and 2015. The governance of these two governing bodies is better today, but it is not perfect. Moreover, who can legitimately say that an organisation's governance is 'good'? The legal statutes of associations, especially sports associations, mean that reforms have to be approved by a general meeting of the association in question – that is, by the very people who will be most affected by them. Moreover, there are many agent–principal problems. As Daniel Mason, Lucie Thibault and Laura Misener write: 'The same individuals are involved in both the management and control of decision making.'[37] This is why governance reforms are so slow and so difficult to implement. One way of getting round this difficulty is to approve reforms for implementation at a later date (sparing agents and/or postponing difficulties).

Of course, autonomy and governance are not the only issues facing sports organisations. The IOC and FIFA have been criticised over the 2014 Sochi Winter Olympics and the 2014 World Cup in Brazil with respect to their mega-events' sustainability, in the wider sense of the term. But the IOC and FIFA cannot be held responsible for all the problems facing Russia or Brazil (although they could have refused to allow these countries to host these mega-events). Nor can the local organising committees for these mega-events be held responsible, however autonomous they are and however well they are governed. Good governance is an essential element in combating corruption in sport, but this fight also involves other issues, as discussed below.

Autonomy, governance and corruption in sport

The large amounts of money that began flowing into sports organisations in the 1970s and 1980s led to the development of corruption in (formerly known as amateur) elite sport. Autonomy can also hide corruption. Corruption/cheating in sport can take several forms, including – in a broad definition – doping, match-fixing, money-laundering, the fraudulent attribution of sponsoring, broadcasting or construction contracts, kickbacks, election-rigging, illegal transfers and the manipulation of event-bidding processes, etc. There are two main categories of sports corruption: on-the-field (of play) corruption by athletes, referees and athletes' entourages, etc.; and off-the-field corruption by sports organisation decision-makers, which often occurs in offices, away from competition venues.

Off-the-field corruption is mostly a question of governance. In Switzerland, where numerous international sports organisations are based, this form of private corruption can be fought under article 102.2 of the Criminal Code, as the Swiss and German branches of Transparency International have pointed out to Swiss sports organisations.[38] Under article 102.2, an association – like any other organisation – can be punished for corruption by its members if it has not taken all reasonable and necessary measures to prevent corruption. Fines, which can be up to 5 million CHF (some US$5.3 million), are determined according to the seriousness of the offence, the measures taken by the organisation to prevent corruption, the damage caused and the organisation's ability to pay. Unfortunately, Swiss judges can prosecute such organisations only if a complaint is filed by either the corrupter or the corrupted, which rarely happens. Following a recommendation by the Council of Europe's Group of States against Corruption (known as GRECO), in 2015 Switzerland's parliament approved an amendment to the Criminal Code that allows such offences to be prosecuted by a state prosecutor without a complaint being filed (for all kinds of organisations).

To prevent corruption in 'major public events' (including sporting events), one can refer to the strategy published in 2013 by the United Nations Office on Drugs and Crime following the adoption by most countries of the United Nations Convention against Corruption.[39] It contains more than 200 recommendations pertaining to major public events, organised in 11 dimensions. The International Organization for Standardization (ISO) has also recently decided to create a new standard against corruption (ISO/PC 278) that can be applied to all organisations.

In contrast, on-the-field corruption can take a wide variety of forms and can affect even very well-governed organisations and their athletes. The fight against this form of private corruption has resulted in international treaties, such as the United Nations Educational, Scientific and Cultural Organization's International Convention against Doping in Sport, adopted in 2005, and the Council of Europe's Convention on the Manipulation of Sports Competitions, signed in 2014. In addition, the attribution and organisation of sports events, large and small, give rise to numerous possibilities for corruption via the votes, contracts and constructions they involve. In theory, all the decisions linked to these events can be taken autonomously by the organisations that own them or that organise them locally. In practice, public opinion expects these decisions to take into account factors other than just governance (and economic considerations), especially environmental and social factors. Sport organisations must take these factors into consideration at the organisation and bidding stages (before their decision to award their event).

Companies and other types of organisation are increasingly being called upon to focus on the triple bottom line – that is, the balance between economic, social and environmental criteria (for sports organisations, at least since the publication of a United Nations Environment Programme report in 2001).[40] In 1994 the IOC made the environment the third dimension of Olympism (with education and culture) and started promoting sustainability in sport (article 2.13 of the Olympic Charter). The social dimension must not be forgotten either, because sports organisations are first and foremost social organisations whose goal is to promote participation in (their) sport in order to 'place sport at the service of humanity', as the Olympic Charter proclaims. From this point of view, the corporate social responsibility programmes launched by numerous sports organisations may appear as 'greenwashing' – that is, unsuitable or inappropriate – as they are based on criteria that are removed from these original social goals.[41]

The IOC felt this keenly when it began promoting the long-term legacy of the Olympic Games as a major reason for hosting them (article 2.14 of the Olympic Charter). In 2003 it began requiring organising committees of the Olympic Games (OCOGs) to carry out Olympic Games Global Impact (OGGI, then OGI) studies.[42] Then, in conjunction with the OCOGs for Vancouver 2010 and London 2012, the Union of European Football Associations (UEFA) and Transparency International, it turned towards a sports event 'sector supplement' of the Global Reporting Initiative (GRI), proposed by the same-name NGO, which promotes the use of sustainability reporting. This work led to the creation of the ISO 20121 standard for sports events.[43] In 2014 the IOC included in clause L of the host-city contract governing its relations with future organising committees sections relating to non-discrimination, the environment, health, safety and labour laws. In 2015, the Sport and Rights Alliance (SRA) was formed to ensure protection of human rights and implementation of anti-corruption measures in the lead-up to and during Olympic Games by well-known NGOs, including Amnesty International, FIFPro (World Football Players' Union), Football Supporters Europe, Human Rights Watch, the International Trade Union Confederation, Supporters Direct Europe, Terre des Hommes and Transparency International Germany.

Events can also take as their inspiration the well-known environmental, social and governance (ESG) performance indicators, which were devised as a way of judging the quality of an investment. In fact, organisers and event owners could view sports events as investments in the communities (local, regional, national) that host them. The United Nations' 'principles for responsible investment' (UNPRI) acknowledge the importance of ESG factors. These principles cover environmental issues (climate change, hazardous waste, nuclear energy, etc.), social issues (diversity, workplace safety, human rights, consumer protection, sin stocks, animal welfare, housing eviction, etc.) and governance (management structure and accountability, employee relations, executive compensation, transparency, etc.), all of which concern, closely or distantly, the attribution or organisation of sports events and corruption. As a result, human rights and environmental protection issues in countries hosting major events could take precedence over questions of organising committee governance.

Although sports organisations cannot be held responsible for all the social and environmental problems affecting a country, they are responsible for attributing and organising their events in ways that avoid these problems or reduce them as far as possible, as highlighted by the experiences of four European NOCs that, in 2013, saw the public reject their bids to host the Olympic Games.[44] Evaluating compliance with these responsibilities is necessary in order to re-establish confidence in the Olympic and sports movements, whose images have become tarnished in recent decades.[45]

Conclusion

Although autonomy is one of the foundation stones on which the sports movement was built, it was not until the years after the Second World War that the IOC formally stated its attachment to this principle. Sport's vision of itself as a universal ideal goes hand in hand with sports organisations' long-standing claim that sport is apolitical. This attachment was reaffirmed quite recently in the face of the European Union's and other governments' desires to more closely regulate sport, a sector that has become an extremely important element in the social fabric of states.

Despite reiterating the importance of autonomy, sports organisations have realised that they have political influence and must be seen by governments and other partners (sponsors, broadcasters and the media) to deserve this autonomy from the state. Thus, in the early decades of the twenty-first century, they have begun introducing a form of sports governance inspired by corporate governance and democratic governance.[46] The IOC now considers 'good sports governance' a principle of the Olympic and sports movements that is intrinsically linked to the principle of autonomy.

The Sochi Winter Olympics and the football World Cup in Brazil, both held in 2014, seem to have pushed questions of autonomy and governance to the background, to be replaced by problems of corruption, environment or human rights in the host countries. Such problems are a real trap for sports organisations, which generally attribute their flagship events many years in advance, and to general indifference. Consequently, future bid evaluations need to be more political than technical. Similarly, the problem of match-fixing has put sports corruption (by on-the-field actors such as athletes and referees) under the spotlight.[47] This issue is the subject of a 2014 Council of Europe international convention, but it remains to be stemmed through joint actions by sports organisations, governments and, if necessary, other stakeholders, such as betting operators. Similarly, a new balance between political, economic, social and sporting forces needs to be found to fight overall corruption in sport.

Notes

1   Jean-Loup Chappelet is a Professor of Public Management at the Swiss Graduate School of Public Administration (IDHEAP), University of Lausanne, Switzerland.

2   See, for example, Christopher Hood, 'A public management for all seasons?', *Public Administration*, vol. 69 (1991).

3   Jean-Loup Chappelet, *Autonomy of Sport* (Strasbourg: Council of Europe Publishing, 2010).

4   See Bernard Quemada (ed.), *Trésor de la langue française: dictionnaire de la langue du XIXe et du XXe siècle (1789–1960)* (Paris: Centre national de la recherche scientifique, 1971).

5   Following on from, for example, Jan Kooiman (ed.), *Modern Governance: New Government–Society Interactions* (London: Sage, 1993); Adrian Leftwich, 'Governance, the state and the politics of development', *Development and Change*, vol. 25 (1994); and Roderick A.W. Rhodes, 'The new governance: governing without government', *Political Studies*, vol. 44 (1996).

6   Jonathan Isham, Daniel Kaufmann and Lant Pritchett, *Governance and Returns on Investment: An Empirical Investigation*, Policy Research Working Paper no. 1550 (Washington, DC: World Bank, 1995).

7   European Union, *European Governance: A White Paper* (Brussels: European Union Commission, 2001).

8   Jean-Loup Chappelet, 'The global governance of sport: an overview', in Ian Henry and Ling-Mei Ko (eds), *Routledge Handbook of Sport Policy* (London: Routledge, 2013).

9   Chappelet (2010), p. 89.

10 Pierre de Coubertin, *Une campagne de vingt-et-un ans (1887–1908)* (Paris: Éducation physique, 1909), p. 152.

11 Chappelet (2013).

12 Chappelet (2010), p. 49.

13 Stephen Weatherill, 'On overlapping legal orders: what is the "purely sporting" rule?', in Barbara Bogusz, Adam Cygan and Erika Szyszczak (eds), *The Regulation of Sport in the European Union* (London: Edward Elgar, 2007).

14 Chappelet (2010).

15 Arnout Geeraert, Michaël Mrkonjic and Jean-Loup Chappelet, 'A rationalist perspective on the autonomy of international sport governing bodies: towards a pragmatic autonomy in the steering of sports', *International Journal of Sport Policy and Politics* (2014), *www.tandfonline.com/eprint/k7VVVmEvIwFBYF8FWh36/full*.

16 Thomas Bach, 'Unity in diversity: candidature for the presidency of the International Olympic Committee' (8 July 2013), *www.olympic.org/Documents/IOC_President/Manifesto_Thomas_Bach-eng.pdf*.

17 Lone Thing and Laila Ottesen, 'The autonomy of sports: negotiating boundaries between sports governance and government policy in the Danish welfare state', *International Journal of Sport Policy*, vol. 2 (2010), p. 233.

18 Jean-Loup Chappelet, 'A long lasting marriage arranged by Coubertin', in Dikaia Chatziefstathiou and Norbert Müller (eds), *Olympism, Olympic Education and Learning Legacies* (London: Cambridge Scholars Publishing, 2013).

19 Thomas Bach, 'Statement on the occasion of the adoption of the resolution "Building a Peaceful and Better World through Sport and the Olympic Ideal"' (6 November 2013), *www.olympic.org/Documents/IOC_President/2013-11-6_Speech_IOC_President_Bach-Olympic_Truce_adoption_Speech_4_November.pdf*.

20 Stephen Wenn, Robert Barney and Scott Martyn, *Tarnished Rings: The International Olympic Committee and the Salt Lake City Bid Scandal* (Syracuse, NY: Syracuse University Press, 2011).

21 Ibid.

22 Jacques Rogge, 'Good sport governance', speech given at 'The rules of the game: first international governance in sport conference', Brussels, 26 February 2001.

23 Sunder Katwala, *Democratising Global Sport* (London: Foreign Policy Centre, 2000).

24 International Olympic Committee, *Evaluation Criteria for Sports and Disciplines – 2012* (Lausanne: IOC, 2012).

25 Jean-Loup Chappelet and Michaël Mrkonjic, *The Basic Indicators for Better Governance in International Sport*, Working Paper no. 1/2013 (Lausanne: Swiss Graduate School of Public Administration, 2013).

26 Ibid.
27 Australian Sports Commission, *Mandatory Sports Governance Principles* (Canberra: Australian Sports Commission, 2013).
28 Chappelet and Mrkonjic (2013).
29 Emilie Romon, 'La gouvernance des organisations sportives: une application des principes universels de base de bonne gouvernance du Mouvement Olympique et sportif du CIO', unpublished master PMP thesis, Swiss Graduate School of Public Administration, 2011.
30 Transparency International, *Corruption and Sport: Building Integrity and Preventing Abuses*, Working Paper no. 03/2009 (Berlin: TI, 2009).
31 Transparency International, *Safe Hands: Building Integrity and Transparency at FIFA* (Berlin: TI, 2011).
32 Mark Pieth, *Governing FIFA: Concept Paper and Report* (Basel: Basel University, 2011).
33 Bach (2013, 'Unity in Diversity'), p. 8.
34 Jens Alm (ed.), *Action for Good Governance in International Sports Organisations: Final Report* (Copenhagen: Danish Institute for Sports Studies, 2013).
35 International Sport and Culture Association, *Guidelines for Good Governance in Grassroots Sport* (Copenhagen: ISCA, 2013).
36 Chappelet and Mrkonjic (2013).
37 Daniel Mason, Lucie Thibault and Laura Misener, 'An agency theory perspective on corruption in sport: the case of the International Olympic Committee', *Journal of Sport Management*, vol. 20 (2006).
38 Swiss Olympic Asociation, *Transparence dans le sport structuré: Guide pratique à l'intention des fédérations* (Bern: Swiss Olympic Association, 2010).
39 United Nations Office on Drugs and Crime, *The United Nations Convention against Corruption: A Strategy for Safeguarding against Corruption in Major Public Events* (Vienna: UNODC, 2013).
40 David Chernushenko, Anne van der Kamp and David Stubbs, *Sustainable Sport Management: Running an Environmentally, Socially and Economically Responsible Organization* (New York: UNEP, 2001).
41 Juan Paramio Salcines, Kathy Babiak and Geoff Walters (eds), *Routledge Handbook of Sport and Corporate Social Responsibility* (London: Routledge, 2013).
42 Christophe Dubi, Pierre-Alain Hug and Pascal van Griethuysen, 'Olympic Games management: from the candidature to the final evaluation, an integrated management approach', in Miguel de Moragas, Christopher Kennett and Nuria Puig (eds), *The Legacy of the Olympic Games 1984–2000* (Lausanne: IOC, 2003).
43 Fiona Pelham, 'Sustainable event management: the journey to ISO 20121', in Jill Savery and Keith Gilbert (eds), *Sustainability and Sport* (Champaign, IL: Common Ground, 2011).
44 Austrian Olympic Committee, German Olympic Sports Confederation, Swedish Olympic Committee and Swiss Olympic Association, *The Bid Experience: Evaluation of the Winter Games Bids 2010–2018 and Recommendations for the IOC's Olympic Agenda 2020* (Frankfurt: Proprojekt, 2014), p. 13.
45 John Milton-Smith, 'Ethics, the Olympics and the search for global values', *Journal of Business Ethics*, vol. 35 (2002).
46 Chappelet (2013).
47 Jean-Loup Chappelet, 'The fight against match-fixing: the Olympic approach', in Jean-Patrick Villeneuve and Martial Pasquier (eds), *International Sports Betting: Integrity, Deviance, Governance and Policy* (London: Routledge, 2015).

1.4

Obstacles to accountability in international sports governance

Roger Pielke Jr[1]

Introduction

It was like a scene out of a Jason Bourne movie. At 6:00 a.m. on 27 May 2015, plain-clothed Swiss police entered the posh Baur au Lac Hotel in Zurich, Switzerland, looking to arrest members of an alleged international criminal syndicate.[2] The surprise raid at the early hour meant that seven suspects were taken into custody without incident, although one was able to escape the hotel without being caught, because he saw the arrests being made as he had his breakfast.[3] The suspects were quickly ushered out of the hotel behind white sheets to save them the embarrassment of the arrests.

The identities of the suspects were not kept quiet for long, thanks to Twitter and a hard-working press corps. They included top officials from the Fédération Internationale de Football Association (FIFA), the Swiss-based international organisation which oversees football competitions around the world, and several of its business partners. The police action was the result of an unprecedented coordinated effort between the US and Swiss governments. It also marked the onset of a global crisis for FIFA. Less than a week later its president announced his intention to step down within a year and call a new election to choose FIFA's next leader. The crisis did not stop there, as the US government promised more arrests and more details emerged of alleged bribes and corruption involving governments, businesses and FIFA itself. FIFA, it turns out, is not unique.

To understand why international sport organisations are so often the subject of allegations and findings of corruption, it is necessary to understand the unique standing of these bodies in their broader national and international settings. Through the contingencies of history and a desire by sports leaders to govern themselves autonomously, international sports organisations have developed in such a way that they have less well-developed mechanisms of governance than many governments, businesses and civil society organisations. The rapidly increasing financial interests in sport and associated with sport create a fertile setting for corrupt practices to take hold. When they do, the often insular bodies have shown little ability to adopt or enforce the standards of good governance that are increasingly expected around the world.

This chapter describes why improved governance is needed and why it is so hard to achieve. First, it recounts a number of recent and ongoing scandals among sports governance bodies. Second, it discusses the growing economic stakes associated with international sport. Third, it provides an overview of the unique history and status of international sports organisations, which helps to explain the challenge of securing accountability to norms common in other settings.

Recent and ongoing scandals

Actual and alleged corruption has been a long-standing issue for many international sports bodies. Some scandals are well known. For instance, in the 1990s the International Olympic Committee (IOC) was embroiled in a scandal over the Salt Lake City Winter Olympic games, involving alleged bribes for votes.[4] This scandal was particularly notable because of the IOC's leadership role across international sport. The episode led to the IOC instituting reforms to encourage greater transparency and accountability, such as the creation of an Ethics Commission and the introduction of conflict of interest guidelines.[5]

More recently, FIFA has faced a barrage of allegations over its process for selecting the venues of the 2018 and 2022 World Cups, won by Russia and Qatar, respectively. The accusations range from the sordid – cash in brown paper envelopes[6] – to the incredible – alleged gifts of paintings from the archives of Russia's State Hermitage Museum in St. Petersburg[7] – and everything in between. The US Department of Justice claims that arrests in May 2015 in Switzerland are just the start of a longer-term criminal investigation.

These episodes involve the largest and most visible sports organisations; allegations of corrupt practices can be found among less well-known bodies as well, however, including the following.

- The International Weightlifting Federation (IWF), located in Budapest, Hungary, has been accused of financial mismanagement, with millions of dollars provided by the IOC unaccounted for.[8]
- The international volleyball federation, the FIVB, located in Switzerland, has faced accusations of illegitimate political actions to keep a leadership regime in power,[9] as well as accusations of financial mismanagement of funding.[10]
- The international cycling union, the UCI, also located in Switzerland, in association with the doping scandal involving Lance Armstrong and his team-mates, has faced accusations of bribery and financial conflicts of interest.[11]
- The International Association of Athletics Federations stands accused of covering up institutionalised doping by Russian athletes and of other corrupt practices.[12]
- CONCACAF, one of the regional football federations within FIFA, discovered alleged bribery and tax evasion within its leadership in a 2013 integrity investigation.[13] CONCACAF sits at the centre of the ongoing US Department of Justice investigation.

Corruption, defined as 'the abuse of entrusted power for private gain',[14] is a global problem, and a risk wherever power and politics are practised (which is to say, everywhere). Some organisations are better than others, however, at discouraging corrupt practices and rooting them out when they do occur. For instance, there is a well-developed body of experience on the role of conflict-of-interest guidelines and disclosures.[15] Avoiding such best practices can be tempting, however, because of the large and growing stakes involved in international sport. Securing the implementation of best practices requires effective leadership but also a more general commitment to good governance.

Sport and money: big, and getting bigger

Sport is increasingly big business and, crucially, associated with big business, thus providing opportunity and motivation for corrupt practices. For instance, the IOC reported total revenues of about US$5 billion for the three-year period ending with the London 2012 games.[16] To place this number into context, it is comparable to the collective total revenues of the top 15 European football clubs over their 2013–2014 season.[17] Following the 2010 World Cup, FIFA boasted financial reserves of more than US$1.3 billion,[18] with an additional US$2 billion in revenue from the 2014 World Cup.[19]

In the broader context of business, however, international sports organisations do not turn over particularly large amounts of money. For instance, Tesco, the British supermarket chain, had revenues of about US$100 billion in 2013[20] and Royal Dutch Shell, an oil company, had revenues of about US$450 billion.[21] Stefan Szymanski has shown that, as part of the overall economy, sport and sport-related economic activity constitute a fairly small element.[22] Even so, the turnover of billions of dollars within the largest sporting organisations represents a significant increase from past years and provides considerable opportunity and incentive for corrupt behaviours. The growth in the financial stakes associated with sport shows no sign of slowing down.[23]

Although the revenues associated with international sport organisations are not comparable to the biggest businesses in the global economy, sport can be considered big business nonetheless. In particular, mega-events such as the Olympic Games and the FIFA World Cup result in the mobilisation of tens of billions of dollars in state-sponsored infrastructure expenses. For example, the 2014 Winter Olympic Games in Sochi, Russia, reportedly cost more than US$50 billion.[24] The cost of the 2022 World Cup in Qatar, by some estimates, will top US$200 billion.[25] These enormous expenditures attract a wide range of interests, not only in the projects associated with the games but also in the decision-making leading to the selection of host venues. Sports organisations make decisions with billion-dollar implications, and with corresponding winners and losers.

The peculiar history and organisation of sports bodies

Even though international sport and its broader financial context have grown in size and significance, the organisations that govern the games are typically not businesses but, rather, a special class of non-profit associations. The fact that sports organisations sit in such an odd place in the panoply of international organisations will come as a surprise to many; they are not governmental, not intergovernmental, not corporations and not international bodies like the United Nations or World Health Organization. It is, arguably, this special, non-profit status that is at the heart of challenges to hold such bodies accountable to the same rules and norms that govern other international bodies. There are many examples of businesses, international organisations and civil society organisations that have seen governance shortfalls exposed and then improved. A recent list of examples might begin with the international banking sector, the International Monetary Fund (IMF) and Greenpeace.[26]

Professor Mark Pieth of the Basel Institute of Governance, and from 2011 to 2013 chair of FIFA's internal governance reform effort, has written that, despite its non-profit status, FIFA is 'a potent corporate entity. This calls for a sequence of particular governance measures developed in the corporate world.'[27] This view holds for other sports organisations as well. Because of their unique governance structures, however, such bodies are not easily held accountable to standards of good governance. For instance, companies and other organisations typically have formal accountability to stakeholders (shareholders, for example, in the case of public companies) and are often overseen by independent directors. International sports bodies have more diffuse and complex stakeholder relationships, and very few have any external directors (the World Anti-Doping Agency offers an exception).

To understand international sports requires understanding the peculiar history and organisation of the institutions that oversee international sports.[28] The most significant governance body is the International Olympic Committee, created in 1894. The IOC oversees what it calls the 'Olympic Movement', defined as 'the concerted, organised, universal and permanent action, carried out under the supreme authority of the IOC, of all individuals and entities who are inspired by the values of Olympism'.[29] By 'Olympism', the IOC is referring to its guiding philosophy, which is 'based on the joy found in effort, the educational value of good example and respect for universal fundamental ethical principles'.[30] In 2015 more than 50 different sports are part of the Olympic Movement, as elements of the Olympic Summer and Winter Games.[31]

The IOC coordinates the activities of national Olympic bodies and collaborates with international sports federations, such as FIFA, the FIVB and the IWF, among many others. The international federations have many other responsibilities, which go far beyond their collaboration with the IOC. For instance, FIFA oversees the quadrennial World Cup, and also oversees and coordinates the national football associations, which, in turn, oversee (with varying degrees of influence) the most popular professional leagues in the world, including the English Premier League and the German Bundesliga.[32] There are also, of course, many significant sports leagues, such as the National Football League in the United States, that sit apart from the Olympic Movement, and thus follow different sorts of governance models.

About 60 international sports organisations are headquartered in Switzerland, including the IOC and FIFA.[33] The IOC may seem like an international body, and it does have a close relationship with the United Nations, including special recognition by the UN and the sharing of programmes with the UN.[34] Despite appearances, however, the IOC is not itself a part of the UN or any other multilateral institution. It is actually a non-profit organisation incorporated under the provisions of Swiss law, which – along with several other global sports bodies – receives special treatment under Swiss law, including tax and property privileges.[35]

For the IOC and other sports organisations, these arrangements with the Swiss government date to more than a century ago, when the Swiss were recruiting international governmental and non-governmental organisations to their country. The historical interest of the Swiss in hosting international organisations is not particular to sport, with almost 300 such bodies headquartered in the small country.[36]

Unique governance practices stymie accountability

In a 2013 research paper I asked why it is that FIFA, the subject of frequent allegations of corruption and poor governance practices, has been so difficult to hold accountable.[37] The answer that I have reached is more broadly applicable, relating to international sports organisations that share similar characteristics.

Specifically, I drew on research on international organisations that identified seven different mechanisms of accountability. These are:

1. *hierarchical accountability*: the power that superiors have over subordinates within an organisation;
2. *supervisory accountability*: relationships between organisations;
3. *fiscal accountability*: mechanisms of control over funding;

4. *legal accountability*: the requirement that international bodies and their employees must abide by the laws of relevant jurisdictions in which those laws are applicable;
5. *market accountability*: influence that is exercised by investors or consumers through market mechanisms;
6. *peer accountability*: the evaluation of organisations by their peer institutions; and
7. *public reputational accountability*: the reputation of an organisation.

Because most international sports bodies are incorporated as associations – that is, voluntary membership organisations – and are legally characterised as non-profits, in general they are not subject to national or international laws or norms that govern business practices.

The difference in governance practices between public corporations, multilateral institutions and sports organisations is striking. For example, if one wants to know the compensation of Ban Ki-Moon (about US$240,000), the secretary general of the United Nations, one can find that information online.[38] The same transparency goes for the president of the United States (US$400,000 in 2014)[39] and the CEO of Nestlé (US$10.6 million in 2013),[40] one of the largest Swiss companies. If one wishes to know the salary of Sepp Blatter, the president of FIFA, however, that information is simply not available, and has in fact been refused to be released by FIFA.[41] FIFA can keep this information secret because none of the mechanisms of accountability have much influence on FIFA, and thus it can do as it wishes with very little in the way of consequences.

Leadership compensation disclosure is just one of many areas in which private, non-profit sports organisations differ from governmental, corporate or other non-governmental multi-lateral organisations. Good governance, of course, goes well beyond transparency. In 2011 Pieth was commissioned by FIFA to draft a paper on how the organisation might improve its governance practices. Transparency International published a report on FIFA governance the same year.[42] Among the recommendations of these reports is a focus on the following areas of governance:[43]

● executive term limits;
● the establishment of a compensation committee with external membership;
● salary disclosure;
● non-executive directors on the executive committee;
● the adoption of best-practice anti-corruption protocols;
● the adoption of best-practice conflict-of-interest guidelines;
● greater financial disclosure at all levels of FIFA and its member organisations;
● greater transparency in anti-corruption investigations and proper due process; and
● greater adoption of democratic procedures in various FIFA election processes.

Such recommendations are not unique to FIFA or football. For instance, a 2012 review of the International Cricket Council (ICC) led by Lord Woolf concludes: 'The reputation of the ICC and international cricket as a whole is at risk if the right standard of Boardroom behaviour is not seen to be in place.'[44] Transparency International agreed, concluding that 'today's sports governing bodies have to start operating as big businesses, using best business practices'.[45] In fact, there exists considerable commonality in recommendations being made for sporting bodies in general. The recent investigation into doping in international cycling, for instance, has made similar recommendations for governance reform.[46]

Several scholars have looked more comprehensively at governance across international sports bodies, finding many to fall well short of best practices. For instance, Jean-Loup

Chappelet and Michaël Mrkonjic survey the academic, evidence-based literature to identify 63 indicators of good governance across seven families of indicators in order to develop a governance scorecard for international sports bodies.[47] They apply their scorecard to the IOC and FIFA, finding notable improvement by the IOC from 1998 to 2012, but with FIFA still falling short. In another recent analysis, Arnout Geeraert, Jens Alm and Michael Groll apply criteria of good governance to 35 Olympic sport governing bodies, concluding that 'recent high-profile corruption scandals have been institutionally induced'.[48] There is a general consensus among observers of international sport that governance practices could be much improved across many sports organisations.

Pieth argues that sports organisations ought to follow the practices widely used by corporations and international bodies alike, such as oversight by independent directors: 'They are close to international organisations, but they are also businesses. There is a certain logic in applying the standards of both worlds.'[49] In general, however, adopting such standards has proved difficult in practice, as sports organisations have been held to different standards to other organisations, and because of these different standards it is typically easier (though often still challenging) to identify and address corruption in corporate and other international settings than it is in sports organisations. The expectations of governance may be changing, however.

A good example of the challenges facing international sports organisations is provided by the Confederation of North, Central American and Caribbean Association Football (CONCACAF), which is one of six regional confederations under FIFA. In 2013 CONCACAF released the report of an internal integrity committee, empanelled to look at the practices of former management. The report uncovers a wide range of corrupt practices, including allegations of fraud, financial mismanagement and violations of CONCACAF's ethics code and fiduciary responsibilities.[50] The officials implicated in the report are no longer associated with CONCACAF, but have not otherwise been sanctioned (though certain investigations continue), and the organisation has begun to implement some changes to its governance practices.[51]

For those sports organisations that are located in Switzerland, there are additional challenges. These bodies are subject to the provisions of Swiss law, and the Swiss government has historically been lax in its oversight of these organisations. For example, as recently as 2006 certain kinds of bribery in the private sector were not illegal under Swiss law.[52] The Swiss government has taken steps to tighten its oversight of sport bodies. In December 2014 it passed a law that would classify the leaders of sports organisations as 'politically exposed persons', thus allowing investigators to examine their financial holdings and transactions.[53] The legislation is part of a broader set of reforms known as 'Lex FIFA' (after the football body), which will be further considered in 2015.[54]

In addition, other countries, notably the United States, have extended the reach of their anti-corruption investigations beyond their own borders. At present the US FBI is reportedly investigating FIFA, and the United Kingdom's Serious Fraud Office has been asked to open its own investigation.[55] The FBI has reportedly secured the cooperation of a US citizen implicated by the CONCACAF integrity report mentioned above.[56] To date, however, fiscal and legal accountability has been scarce.

In terms of market accountability, all international sports organisations have corporate sponsors, and some have very large television contracts. Sponsors have shown little interest in holding these bodies accountable when allegations of corruption have surfaced, however. Occasionally a sponsor will issue a statement of concern,[57] but, so long as sport proves popular and makes money, sponsors tend to show little interest in much else.

Similarly, with respect to public reputation accountability, sport is continuing to grow in popularity, and there is scant evidence to suggest that its popularity is threatened by alleged or actual corrupt practices among governance bodies. Some argue that the corruption of sport, such as via doping or match-fixing, has proved to be a greater threat to the integrity of sport than shortfalls in governance.[58]

Conclusion

This chapter has argued that international sports bodies are particularly fertile settings for corruption to take root in and, accordingly, difficult to reform. Sports organisations have come to resemble corporations and other international institutions, but their governance practices, not only to address issues of corruption, but beyond, have not kept pace. Although sports bodies play the role of international organisations, they are with very few exceptions neither governmental nor business operations, which helps to explain why their governance practices have developed in a unique fashion.

As sport has gained in popularity, so too has the amount of money involved in the various games and in building associated infrastructure, especially for events such as the Olympic Games and football World Cup. The vast amount of money flowing through these bodies, coupled with the financially significant decisions they make, often at the highest levels of politics and in the absence of best practices in place for governance, creates settings amenable to corrupt practices.

Recent decades have seen greater attention being devoted to achieving best practices of governance on the part of states, businesses and non-profits, but sport organisations have lagged behind. They will continue to face pressures to improve their governance. Athletes, sponsors, supporters, governments and other parties all have interests in participating in this process. To date, however, progress has been slow. If sport organisations prove incapable of introducing effective reform, they may find change being forced upon them. So far, at least, change has proved difficult.

Notes

1   Roger Pielke Jr is professor and director of the Center for Science and Technology Policy Research at the University of Colorado.
2   *New York Times* (US), 'In a five-star setting, FIFA officials are arrested, the Swiss way,' 27 May 2015, *www.nytimes.com/2015/05/28/sports/soccer/in-a-five-star-setting-fifa-officials-are-arrested-the-swiss-way.html.*
3   *Bloomberg* (US), 'The man who got away ate breakfast as police raided FIFA hotel', 3 June 2015, *www.bloomberg.com/news/articles/2015-06-03/the-man-who-got-away-ate-breakfast-as-police-raided-fifa-hotel*
4   Roger Pielke Jr, 'How can FIFA be held accountable?', *Sport Management Review*, vol. 16 (2013).
5   Ibid.
6   See *Guardian* (UK), 'Official "was offered $40,000" after Mohamed bin Hammam presentation', 30 May 2011, *www.theguardian.com/football/2011/may/30/mohamed-bin-hammam-fifa.*
7   *Les Échos* (France), 'Russie: Platini dément toute corruption', 30 November 2014, *www.lesechos.fr/sport/football/sports-699346-russie-platini-dans-une-affaire-de-corruption-1069682.php#*
8   Play the Game (Denmark), 'IWF president under suspicion of financial mismanagement', 14 May 2013, *www.playthegame.org/news/news-articles/2013/iwf-president-under-suspicion-of-financial-mismanagement.*
9   Play the Game (Denmark), 'FIVB accused of violating statutes to oust former presidential candidate', 29 October 2014, *www.playthegame.org/news/news-articles/2014/fivb-accused-of-violating-statutes-to-oust-former-presidential-candidate.*

10   See Around the Rings (US), 'FIVB exec not worried about legal claims', 23 March 2005, *http://aroundtherings.com/site/A__26134/Title__FIVB-Exec-Not-Worried-About-Legal-Claims/292/Article*; and, for background, see Play the Game (Denmark), 'FIVB stops practice that has enriched former president Acosta', 21 April 2009, *www.playthegame.org/news/news-articles/2009/fivb-stops-practice-that-has-enriched-former-president-acosta*.

11   Reed Albergotti and Vanessa O'Connell, *Wheelmen: Lance Armstrong, the Tour de France, and the Greatest Sports Conspiracy Ever* (London: Headline, 2013).

12   *Guardian* (UK), 'Crisis at IAAF that threatens to bring athletics to its knees', 13 December 2014, *www.theguardian.com/sport/blog/2014/dec/13/iaaf-crisis-drugs-allegations-athletics?CMP=share_btn_tw*.

13   See Confederation of North, Central American and Caribbean Association Football, *Integrity Committee Report of Investigation* (Miami: CONCACAF, 2013), *www.guardian.co.tt/sites/default/files/story/FinalReport.pdf*.

14   See Transparency International: *www.transparency.org/whatwedo*.

15   For instance, I helped to produce this review on conflicts of interest in science advisory processes: *http://bipartisanpolicy.org/library/science-policy-project-final-report*.

16   See International Olympic Committee, 'Factsheet: IOC financial summary: update – July 2014' (Lausanne: IOC, 2014), *www.olympic.org/Documents/Reference_documents_Factsheets/IOC_Financial_Summary.pdf*.

17   Deloitte, 'Football money league' (London: Deloitte, 2015), *www2.deloitte.com/uk/en/pages/sports-business-group/articles/deloitte-football-money-league.html*.

18   Fédération Internationale de Football Association, 'Income' (Zurich: FIFA, 2011), *www.fifa.com/aboutfifa/finances/income.html*.

19   See Fédération Internationale de Football Association, *FIFA: Financial Report 2014* (Zurich: FIFA, 2015), *www.fifa.com/mm/document/affederation/administration/02/56/80/39/fr2014weben_neutral.pdf*.

20   Tesco, 'Five-year record' (Dundee: Tesco, 2015), *www.tescoplc.com/index.asp?pageid=30*.

21   See Royal Dutch Shell, 'Royal Dutch Shell plc fourth quarter and full year 2013 unaudited results' (The Hague: Royal Dutch Shell, 2014), p. 11, *http://s00.static-shell.com/content/dam/shell-new/local/corporate/corporate/downloads/quarterly-results/2013/q4/q4-2013-qra.pdf*; and 'Royal Dutch Shell plc fourth quarter and full year 2013 results announcement' (The Hague: Royal Dutch Shell, 2014), *www.shell.com/global/aboutshell/investor/news-and-library/2014/fourth-quarter-2013-results-announcement.html*.

22   Wladimir Andreff and Stefan Szymanski (eds), *Handbook on the Economics of Sport* (Cheltenham: Edward Elgar, 2006).

23   PricewaterhouseCoopers, *Changing the Game: Outlook for the Global Sports Market to 2015* (London: PricewaterhouseCoopers LLP, 2011), *www.pwc.com/gx/en/hospitality-leisure/changing-the-game-outlook-for-the-global-sports-market-to-2015.jhtml*.

24   Deutsche Welle (Germany), 'Sochi the most extravagant Winter Olympics ever', 6 February 2014, *www.dw.de/sochi-the-most-extravagant-winter-olympics-ever/a-17411857*.

25   Al Arabiya (Saudi Arabia), 'Record World Cup costs put Qatar in losing game', 16 July 2014, *http://english.alarabiya.net/en/business/economy/2014/07/16/Record-World-Cup-costs-put-Qatar-in-losing-game.html*.

26   International Monetary Fund, 'IMF board approves far-reaching governance reforms', 5 November 2010, *www.imf.org/external/pubs/ft/survey/so/2010/NEW110510B.htm*; *New York Times* (US), 'After the scandal, more of the same at the IMF', 15 June 2011, *http://wcfia.harvard.edu/publications/after-scandal-more-same-imf*; *Financial Times* (UK), 'Greenpeace, Amnesty and Oxfam agree code of conduct', 2 June 2006; *Spiegel Online* (Germany), 'Financial scandal: organizational change has led to chaos in Greenpeace', 23 June 2014, *www.spiegel.de/international/business/greenpeace-financial-scandal-how-the-organization-lost-millions-a-976868.html*.

27   Mark Pieth, *Governing FIFA: Concept Paper and Report* (Basel: Basel University, 2011), *www.fifa.com/mm/document/affederation/footballgovernance/01/54/99/69/fifagutachten-en.pdf*.

28 For an overview, see Jean-Loup Chappelet and Brenda Kübler-Mabbott, *The International Olympic Committee and the Olympic System: The Governance of World Sport* (Abingdon: Routledge, 2008).
29 International Olympic Committee, 'The Olympic Movement', *www.olympic.org/content/the-ioc/governance/introductionold*.
30 International Olympic Committee, 'Olympism in action', *www.olympic.org/olympism-in-action*.
31 International Olympic Committee, 'Sports', *www.olympic.org/sports*.
32 Web.archive.org, 'The Premier League and other football bodies', *http://web.archive.org/web/20060716102915/www.premierleague.com/fapl.rac?command=setSelectedId&nextPage=enSimpleStories&id=2851&type=com.fapl.website.stories.SimpleStories&categoryCode=Who+We+Are&breadcrumb=about_breadcrumb*.
33 Reuters (UK), 'Swiss to increase oversight of FIFA, other sports bodies', 5 December 2014, *www.reuters.com/article/2014/12/05/us-soccer-fifa-switzerland-idUSKCN0JJ1II20141205*.
34 Olympic.org (France), 'IOC and UN Secretariat agree historic deal to work together to use sport to build a better world', 28 April 2014, *www.olympic.org/news/ioc-and-un-secretariat-agree-historic-deal/230542*.
35 See Chappelet and Kübler-Mabbott (2008), pp. 106–127 (chapter 6: 'Governments and the Olympic System').
36 Federal Department of Foreign Affairs (Switzerland), 'International organizations in Switzerland', *www.eda.admin.ch/eda/en/fdfa/foreign-policy/international-organizations/international-organizations-switzerland.html*. For historical background, see Michael Gunter, 'Switzerland and the United Nations', *International Organization*, vol. 30 (1976).
37 Pielke (2013).
38 Public Broadcasting Service (US), 'Kofi Annan: center of the storm', *www.pbs.org/wnet/un/life/job.html*; Fox News (US), 'After calls by Ban Ki-Moon for austerity measures, UN staffers get pay hike', 23 August 2011, *www.foxnews.com/world/2011/08/23/after-calls-by-ban-ki-moon-for-austerity-measures-un-staffers-get-pay-hike*; United Nations, 'Salaries and post adjustment', *www.un.org/Depts/OHRM/salaries_allowances/salary.htm*.
39 US Senate, 'Salaries of federal officials: a fact sheet', *www.senate.gov/reference/resources/pdf/98-53.pdf*.
40 *Financial Times* (UK), 'Nestlé cuts chief executive Paul Bulcke's pay amid Swiss scrutiny', 11 March 2014, *www.ft.com/intl/cms/s/0/6ae9ca98-a93c-11e3-b87c-00144feab7de.html*.
41 The Least Thing, 'Further thoughts on Sepp Blatter's FIFA salary', 17 June 2013, *http://leastthing.blogspot.com/2013/06/further-thoughts-on-sepp-blatters-fifa.html*.
42 See Transparency International, *Safe Hands: Building Integrity and Transparency at FIFA* (Berlin: TI, 2011), *www.transparency.org/whatwedo/pub/safe_hands_building_integrity_and_transparency_at_fifa*.
43 Roger Pielke Jr, 'An evaluation of the FIFA governance reform process of 2011–2013', in Stephen Frawley and Daryl Adair (eds), *Managing the Football World Cup* (Basingstoke: Palgrave Macmillan, 2014).
44 Lord Woolf, *An Independent Governance Review of the International Cricket Council* (London: PricewaterhouseCoopers LLP, 2012), *http://static.espncricinfo.com/db/DOWNLOAD/0000/0093/woolfe_report.pdf*.
45 Transparency International, 'Defining the boundaries: a blue print for enhancing cricket administration', 31 January 2012, *http://blog.transparency.org/2012/01/31/defining-the-boundaries-a-blue-print-for-enhancing-cricket-administration*.
46 Cycling Independent Reform Commission, *Report to the President of the Union Cycliste Internationale* (Aigle, Switzerland: UCI, 2015), *https://docs.google.com/viewerng/viewer?url=www.cyclisme-dopage.com/actualite/2015-03-08-circ-report.pdf*.
47 Jean-Loup Chappelet and Michaël Mrkonjic, *Basic Indicators for Better Governance in International Sport (BIBGIS): An Assessment Tool for International Sport Governing Bodies*, IDHEAP Working Paper no. 1/2013 (Lausanne: Swiss Graduate School of Public

Administration, 2013), *www.idheap.ch/idheap.nsf/view/D6156F1EF87ACB07C1257B39005 38D87/$File/IDHEAP%20Working%20Paper%201-2013.pdf*.

48   Arnout Geeraert, Jens Alm and Michael Groll, 'Good governance in international sport organisations: an analysis of the 35 Olympic sport governing bodies', *International Journal of Sport Policy and Politics*, vol. 6 (2014).

49   Pieth (2011).

50   The Least Thing, 'The CONCACAF integrity report', 21 April 2013, *http://leastthing. blogspot.com/2013/04/the-concacaf-integrity-report.html*. See CONCACAF (2013).

51   For example, Chuck Blazer, a former top CONCACAF official from the United States, is reportedly working with the FBI: *New York Daily News* (US), 'Soccer rat! The inside story of how Chuck Blazer, ex-US soccer executive and FIFA bigwig, became a confidential informant for the FBI', 1 November 2014, *www.nydailynews.com/sports/soccer/soccer-rat-ex-u-s-soccer-exec-chuck-blazer-fbi-informant-article-1.1995761*. On changes to its governance practices, see CONCACAF, 'CONCACAF focuses on reform during congress', 10 June 2014, *www.concacaf.com/article/ordinary-congress-finalized*.

52   See State Secretariat for Economic Affairs (Switzerland), 'Swiss criminal law on corruption', *www.seco.admin.ch/themen/00645/00657/00659/01395/index.html?lang=en*.

53   Inside World Football (Switzerland), 'FIFA on alert as Swiss tighten laws to keep a closer eye on sports bodies', 15 December 2014, *www.insideworldfootball.com/fifa/16033-fifa-on-alert-as-swiss-tighten-laws-to-keep-a-closer-eye-on-sports-bodies*.

54   BBC (UK), 'FIFA and Olympic leaders face new financial checks', 12 December 2014, *www.bbc.com/news/business-30451609*.

55   *Guardian* (UK), 'Serious Fraud Office considers criminal investigation into World Cup bids', 26 November 2014, *www.theguardian.com/football/2014/nov/26/serious-fraud-office-criminal-world-cup-bids*.

56   *New York Daily News* (1 December 2014).

57   See, for example, Reuters (UK), 'FIFA's Blatter juggles sponsor pressure, voters', 31 May 2011, *www.reuters.com/article/2011/05/31/us-soccer-fifa-idUSTRE74S16320110531*.

58   For instance, on match-fixing, see LawInSport (UK), 'Match fixing: the biggest threat to sport in the 21st century?', part 1, 5 June 2011, *www.lawinsport.com/articles/anti-corruption/item/match-fixing-the-biggest-threat-to-sport-in-the-21st-century-part-1*; and, on doping, see European Gaming and Betting Association (Belgium), 'Doping remains greatest threat to sports integrity', 10 November 2011, *www.egba.eu/doping-remains-greatest-threat-to-sports-integrity*.

1.5

Political interference, power struggles, corruption and greed

The undermining of football governance in Asia

James M. Dorsey[1]

Football, arguably Asia's most popular sport, has been marred across the continent by multiple scandals, ranging from Asia-based criminal organisations fixing matches globally,[2] to corruption in regional and national governance, to a lack of transparency and accountability that facilitates undemocratic management[3] and even boosts support for autocratic regimes.[4] The root of the lack of good governance within the Asian Football Confederation (AFC), the continent's football governing body, as well as the Olympic Council of Asia, is corruption, enabled by the dominance over sport that is exercised by executive committee members with close political ties to often undemocratic or hybrid regimes that see football as a tool to strengthen their grip on power and project themselves internationally in a positive light.[5]

The extent of the problem is illustrated by a string of scandals, questionable actions and incidents of political manipulation in the last four years, some of which were also related to the lack of proper governance in the administration of global football by the Fédération Internationale de Football Association (FIFA). These have included the following:

- The 2011 banning for life from involvement in professional football of then AFC president and FIFA vice president Mohammed Bin Hammam, a Qatari national.[6]
- The burial by Sheikh Salman Bin Ebrahim Al Khalifa, the current AFC president and FIFA vice president, of an independent audit of AFC finances carried out by PricewaterhouseCooper (PwC) that warned of possible tax evasion, money-laundering, sanctions-busting and a series of illicit payments to national, regional and global football executives and questioned the integrity of a US$1 billion master rights agreement to commercialise AFC assets, including broadcast rights, with a Singapore-based company.[7]

- The failure to act decisively on allegations that a senior AFC official had sought to tamper with or destroy documents related to corruption investigations.[8]
- The election of an AFC president who has been tainted by allegations of involvement in the detention and torture of scores of athletes and sports officials in his native Bahrain.[9]
- The manipulation of AFC election procedures for FIFA Executive Committee seats to ensure that specific candidates were successful on preferential terms.[10]
- The failure to distance the AFC from endorsements of Iranian restrictions on women attending public sporting events by one of its senior officials.[11]
- Allegations of vote-buying in Sheikh Salman's election to the AFC presidency in 2013 that remain uninvestigated.[12]

Governance in the AFC: worsening rather than improving?

The AFC, despite its lofty statements and a pledge to establish an ethics committee,[13] has shown no intention of institutionalising principles of good governance or fair play. If anything, its president, Sheikh Salman – a member of the Bahraini ruling family who as head of the Bahrain Football Association failed to stand up for members of the national football team who were reportedly arrested and tortured after joining a march to protest against the government and has been tainted by allegations of involvement in their detention[14] – has used his first two years in office to centralise power, favour his closest associates, marginalise reformers and turn his back on any attempt to clean up the organisation.[15]

Sheikh Salman's burial of the audit and failure to act on its recommendations has meant a lack of good governance within the AFC on multiple levels. In a taped and written statement recorded by a FIFA security officer in July 2012 that became public in April 2015, the AFC's finance director, Bryan Kuan Wee Hoong, asserted that AFC general secretary Dato' Alex Soosay had asked him to 'tamper [with] or hide any documents' related to the general secretary that could figure in the PwC audit.[16] The AFC said in a statement four days after the allegations became public that it was assessing the veracity of the allegations, yet it only collected a copy of the tape over two weeks later.[17] Soosay was finally suspended in May 2015.[18] The audit was commissioned by the AFC, allegedly in a bid to create a legal basis to oust Bin Hammam from his AFC presidency and FIFA vice presidency.[19]

The PwC report had earlier identified Soosay and Kuan as two of three AFC officials who had authorised questionable payments under Bin Hammam for which the Asian group could be held legally liable:

> Our transaction review revealed that items sampled were, in most cases, authorised by the General Secretary or Deputy General Secretary and the Director of Finance. As signatories these parties hold accountability for the authorisation of these transactions. We also note the Internal Audit and Finance Committees were aware of this practice.[20]

Implications for governance in national associations: the case of Nepal

The lack of governance and accountability at the regional level extends to the national level as well. Take, for example, the case of Nepal, where Ganesh Thapa was suspended by FIFA as a member of the AFC executive committee and as head of the All Nepal Football Association (ANFA) pending an investigation into corruption charges, but still controls the group, according to ANFA board members.[21] Similarly the AFC appointed as match commissioner Thapa's son, Gaurav, who was not suspended but was named in the PwC audit as a recipient of questionable payments from Bin Hammam.[22]

Two ANFA vice presidents sent a letter to the FIFA general secretary, the AFC general secretary and a member of the Ethics Committee of FIFA's investigatory chamber regarding Thapa's violation of ANFA's statutes by continuing to operate during his suspension, and his failure to share critical information on ANFA, including audits, with executive members.[23] FIFA and the AFC have yet to respond to the letter.[24]

The overlap of politics and governance in Asian football

The AFC's problems are rooted in the fact that, like FIFA, it is an inherently political grouping, despite its insistence on the fiction of a separation of sports and politics. As football czars, Bin Hammam and Salman emerged as two of the most senior governors of the world's most popular sport on the world's largest and most populous continent at a time when Asia's fortunes were rising. The composition of the AFC's Executive Committee under both men bears witness to the group's political nature, as do the boards of many of the national associations that constitute its membership.

Nowhere is this more prevalent than among the AFC's 13 Middle Eastern members, which account for 28 per cent of the confederation's 46 member associations. Six of the AFC Executive Committee's 21 members in the period from 2011 to 2015 hailed from the Middle East: Salman, a member of Bahrain's minority Sunni Muslim ruling family; Prince Ali Bin Al Hussein, a half-brother of Jordan's King Abdullah, who was a reformer and thorn in Salman's side; the United Arab Emirates' Yousuf Yaqoob Yousuf Al Serkal, who maintains close ties to his country's ruling elite; Sayyid Khalid Hamad Al Busaidi, a member of Oman's ruling family; Hafez Al Medlej, a member of the board of Saudi Arabia's tightly controlled football association who made his career in the kingdom's state-run media; and Palestine's Susan Shalabi Molano. That number has risen to seven in the Executive Committee elected in April 2015, which includes Sheikh Salman and Shalabi Molano as well as Mohammed Khalfan Al Romaithi, deputy commander-in-chief of the Abu Dhabi police force, and representatives of Kuwait, Lebanon and Saudi Arabia, and the head of the Islamic Republic of Iran Football Federation (IRIFF). Other members of the committee include Prince Abdullah Ibni Sultan Ahmad Shah, the crown prince of Pahang, Malaysia's third largest state; Makhdoom Syed Faisal Saleh Hayat, who served as a minister in various Pakistani governments and is a member of the Pakistan People's Party; and North Korea's Han Un-gyong.

Conclusion

Reform of the governance of the continent's football associations will require a paradigm shift. Tinkering with reforms of the AFC's current government structure is unlikely to tackle the group's fundamental, long-standing problems that are embedded in its corporate culture. To achieve this paradigm shift, the AFC will have to ensure that management is expanded at the club, national and regional levels so that it includes all stakeholders, including players and fans. The AFC, like other regional and international sports associations, will have to develop principles enshrined either in a charter or a code of conduct that governs the relationship between sports and politics, addressing proportional representation. These will have to provide the safeguards against football governance being politically manipulated or driven, as well as proper oversight of the relationship to guarantee the sport's independence as well as its transparent and accountable management. To ensure sound rules and regulations for international tournaments, the AFC should consider the criteria for the awarding of mega-events from the International Olympic Committee's Agenda 2020. This reform should incorporate international human labour and gender rights and standards; increase public engagement in the national and host city decision-making processes; and enhance the transparency of the infrastructural requirements for hosts, and the terms of the agreement between the sports association and the host.

Notes

1   James M. Dorsey is a senior fellow at the S. Rajaratnam School of International Studies at Singapore's Nanyang Technological University, co-director of the Institute of Fan Culture of the University of Würzburg, Germany, and the author of the blog 'The turbulent world of Middle East soccer' and a forthcoming book with the same title.
2   Zaihan Mohamed Yusof, *Foul! The Inside Story of Singapore Match Fixers* (Singapore: Straits Times Press, 2014).
3   The Turbulent World of Middle East Soccer, 'AFC suspends General Secretary as it keeps damning audit buried', 13 May 2015, *http://mideastsoccer.blogspot.sg/2015/05/afc-suspends-general-secretary-as-it.html*.
4   James M. Dorsey, 'Asian football: a cesspool of government interference, struggles for power, corruption, and greed', *International Journal of History of Sport*, vol. 32 (2015).
5   Ibid.
6   Heidi Blake and Jonathan Calvert, *The Ugly Game: The Qatari Plot to Buy the World Cup* (London: Simon & Schuster, 2015); The Turbulent World of Middle East Soccer, 'Qatar's Bin Hamman banned for life, faces humiliation', 27 July 2011, *http://mideastsoccer.blogspot. com/2011/07/qatars-bin-hammam-banned-for-life-faces.html*.
7   Blake and Calvert (2015); The Turbulent World of Middle East Soccer (27 July 2011).
8   The Turbulent World of Middle East Soccer, 'Alleged AFC cover-up effort highlights Asian football's lack of proper governance', 25 April 2015, *http://mideastsoccer.blogspot. sg/2015/04/alleged-afc-cover-up-effort-highlights.html*; The Turbulent World of Middle East Soccer, '*Malay Mail*: explosive "tamper or hide" AFC probe video surfaces/Soosay: where's this coming from, why now?', 25 April 2015, *http://mideastsoccer.blogspot.co.uk/2015/04/ malay-mail-explosive-tamper-or-hide-afc.html*.
9   Confidential evidence submitted to the English High Court of Justice, Queen's Bench Division, Divisional Court, in the case of *FF* vs *Director of Public Prosecutions*, October 2014; YouTube, 'Shaik Nasser Bin Hamad Al-Khalifa talking on Bahrain TV', 16 August 2011, *www.youtube. com/watch?v=mAXjGidl_JU*; The Turbulent World of Middle East Soccer, 'Torture investigation of Bahraini prince puts IOC and AFC on the spot', 7 October 2014, *http://mideastsoccer. blogspot.sg/2014/10/torture-investigation-of-bahraini.html*; Bahrain News Agency, 'منتسبي الحركة الرياضية بعض' 'الشيخ ناصر يصدر قرارا بتشكيل لجنة تحقيق رسمية في التجاوزات التي صدرت من', 11 April 2014, *www.bna.bh/portal/news/452380?date¼*.
10 WorldSoccer.com, 'Sheikh Ahmad plots path that may lead to presidency of FIFA', 16 April 2015, *www.worldsoccer.com/columnists/keir-radnedge/sheikh-ahmad-plots-path-that-may-lead-to-presidency-of-fifa-360888*.
11 Sportsflash.com, 'Iran: AFC "broad-minded" on Iranian women ban', 23 January 2015, *www.sportsflash.com.au/NewsArticle.aspx?spname=SOC&articleid=52371*.
12 The Turbulent World of Middle East Soccer, 'AFC election marred by interference allegations and candidates' track records', 26 April 2015, *http://mideastsoccer.blogspot.sg/2013/04/ afc-election-marred-by-interference.html*.
13 The Turbulent World of Middle East Soccer, 'New AFC president sets about reform as battle for change looms', 5 May 2015, *http://mideastsoccer.blogspot.sg/2013/05/new-afc-president-sets-about-reform-as.html*.
14 *The Times of Northwest Indiana* (US), 'Bahrain soccer stars pay price for protesting', 27 August 2011, *http://www.nwitimes.com/sports/soccer/professional/bahrain-soccer-stars-pay-price-for-protesting/article_e800a879-dc13-5969-b5aa-38a9bb093a9d.html*;

The National (UAE), 'From heroes to pariahs: Bahrain athletes pay a steep price', 31 August 2011, *www.thenational.ae/sport/other-sport/from-heroes-to-pariahs-bahrain-athletes-pay-a-steep-price*; Bahrain Youth Society for Human Rights, 'List of sport players, referee and clubs targeted because of their involvement in the protests', 24 April 2011, *http://byshr.org/wp-content/List-of-sport-players-Referees-and-Clubs-targeted-Because-of-their-involvement-in-the-protests-BYSHR.doc*.

15 The Turbulent World of Middle East Soccer, 'AFC's Salman re-elected amid renewed corruption and governance questions', 2 May 2015, *http://mideastsoccer.blogspot.sg/2015/05/afcs-salman-re-elected-amid-renewed.html*.

16 The Turbulent World of Middle East Soccer, 'Haresh says: when (AFC) silence is not golden', 29 April 2015, *http://mideastsoccer.blogspot.co.uk/2015_04_01_archive.html*; The Turbulent World of Middle East Soccer, 25 April 2015 ('*Malay Mail*'); The Turbulent World of Middle East Soccer, 25 April 2015 ('Alleged AFC cover-up').

17 The Turbulent World of Middle East Soccer, 29 April 2015.

18 Asian Football Confederation. 'AFC general secretary suspended', 13 May 2015, *www.the-afc.com/media-releases/afc-general-secretary-suspended*.

19 The Turbulent World of Middle East Soccer, 'FIFA focuses on Bin Hammam's management of the AFC after dropping bribery charges', 14 December 2012, *http://mideastsoccer.blogspot.de/2012/12/fifa-focuses-on-bin-hammams-management.html*.

20 The Turbulent World of Middle East Soccer, 29 April 2015; The Turbulent World of Middle East Soccer, 25 April 2015 ('Alleged AFC cover-up').

21 The Turbulent World of Middle East Soccer, 2 May 2015 ('AFC's Salman re-elected').

22 The Turbulent World of Middle East Soccer, 29 April 2015; The Turbulent World of Middle East Soccer, 25 April 2015 ('Alleged AFC cover-up').

23 Reuters (UK), 'Exclusive Nepal FA chiefs ask FIFA to investigate own president', 18 October 2014, *http://uk.reuters.com/article/2014/10/18/uk-soccer-nepal-idUKKCN0I70AD20141018*.

24 Interview by the author with ANFA vice president Karma Tsering Sherpa, 16 May 2015.

1.6
Corruption in African sport
A summary

Chris Tsuma[1]

2015 was the golden jubilee of the All-Africa Games, the continent's equivalent of the Olympics, but there has not been much else to celebrate 50 years after the holding of the first Games, in Brazzaville in 1965. Sporting excellence on the field of play continues to elude Africa, despite the continent's immense natural athletic talent.

Africa remains stunted by a combination of talent drain (mainly to Europe), a lack of government investment and policy guidelines, corruption and gross mismanagement. International sporting life just seems to pass Africa by. The 2010 football World Cup finals came to South Africa only because of a deliberate continental rotation policy by the Fédération Internationale de Football Association (FIFA).[2] No African city has come anywhere near mounting a serious bid for the Olympics, or even the Commonwealth Games: Abuja, the Nigerian capital, failed with a poor attempt for the 2014 event – won by Glasgow – its bid found wanting in the key areas of transportation, information and communication technology, accommodation, the proposed games village and sports venues and finance.[3] Africa has produced close to 200 (13 per cent) of the medals on offer in the ten most recent World Athletics Championships, nearly five times the total tally of Asia, which hosted its fourth championship in Beijing in 2015, after Osaka (2007), Tokyo (1991) and Daegu (2011).[4] Meanwhile, the World Athletics Championships have still not come to Africa.

The African Union (AU, then the Organisation of African Unity) originally conceived of an All-Africa Games managed by the now defunct Supreme Council for Sports in Africa (SCSA), composed mostly of political appointees with little or no experience in managing sport. The AU resisted proposals to turn the management of the Games over to the Association of National Olympic Committees of Africa (ANOCA) despite promises in 2011,[5] transferring administration to the AU Sports Commission in July 2013.[6] Since 1987 the Games have continued to provide a case study of poor organisation and management, failing to capture the imagination of Africans or the world, resulting in diminished competitiveness and commercial value, and largely shunned by the continent's top athletes.

Governance

According to a 2009 International Olympic Committee (IOC) report, football, basketball, volleyball, athletics (track and field), swimming and boxing are the most popular sports among Africans.[7] Each of these sports is managed by national associations, often a grouping of affiliates within national borders. These national associations are in turn affiliated to regional bodies, such as ANOCA or the Confédération Africaine de Football (CAF), through which they gain admittance to international organisations. These administrative structures also serve as participation/competition levels from the smallest village tournament to the world championships.

The classic cases of abuse of office and clinging to power are still widespread within sports organisations in Africa. Reflecting its universal popularity, football is always prone to forces of corruption. The first area of abuse and malpractice in football is the election of administrators. In what passes for sports elections, vote-buying, manipulation and other corrupt practices are rampant. In 2014 FIFA cancelled the re-election of Cuthbert Dube as the president of the Zimbabwe Football Association (ZIFA), citing irregularities that included claims of vote-buying and manipulation.[8]

Within CAF, president Issa Hayatou is into his 28th year in charge, following his unopposed re-election in Marrakech, Morocco, in 2013.[9] A rule change barring non-executive members of CAF from running prevented Ivorian Jacques Anouma from standing against the Cameroonian, whose stay at the top of CAF beyond 2017 is clearly likely after the removal of another rule setting an age limit of 70 years for members of its executive committee.[10]

At the national level, by way of example, in the election of officials to the Kenyan Football Federation (KFF) the sports media covering the poll would hear claims that top candidates for the position of chairman/president denied their rivals access to delegates (often a bare majority would be sufficient to win) by paying for the delegates' transport, and providing room and board in hotels watched by the candidates' henchmen right until they went to vote.[11] There was never any actionable proof, but during the 2004 KFF elections, which came about after another of the many FIFA interventions in Kenyan football administration, the then sports minister, Najib Balala, sought to put an end to this practice by ordering the deployment of anti-corruption police to guard against any form of bribery and manipulation of delegates.[12]

Football suffers under these elected officials because they have an eye on other things – such as politics, or simply the amassing of wealth. As a result, there is a chronic lack of professionalism in the management of the game. At the national level the approach to matches, even big internationals, is shockingly casual. Money meant for looking after the team – players' allowances and bonuses – is pocketed by the administrators in the football associations. Even national team selection is not free of corruption. In conversations with players while on the football beat for the *Daily Nation* in Nairobi, this writer heard how one local coach of the national team would demand a cut from the allowances and bonuses of certain players, especially the peripheral ones, or he would drop them. The well-documented strikes by African national teams, most notoriously Cameroon,[13] Nigeria just before the 2013 Confederations Cup,[14] and Togo (at the 2006 FIFA World Cup),[15] and the famous airlift of cash in bonuses to the Ghanaian players in Brazil during the 2014 World Cup,[16] are a reflection of the shocking cases of corruption the Africa game suffers. While players risk public ridicule, many say that if they don't resort to such measures the administrators will pocket their money.

In Kenya, a 2015 report by the Ethics and Anti-Corruption Commission (EACC), which led to the suspension of several government ministers, implicated the Football Kenya Federation (FKF) president, Sam Nyamweya, in the alleged embezzlement of federation funds.[17] In 2013 claims had emerged that Nyamweya and his executive committee could not account for more than US$410,146 received between November 2011 and December 2012.[18] In addition, a FIFA report during the January 2015 crisis, which delayed the new Kenya Premier League (KPL) season kick-off, questioned the promotion of Shabana FC, a team closely associated with Nyamweya, to the KPL. Indeed, the contentious expansion of the KPL from 16 to 18 teams by the FKF seemed to have been designed to accommodate Shabana, whose promotion was just as controversial, with the curious awarding of points off the field of play.[19]

In Zambia, Kalusha Bwalya is one of the continent's best football talents, a former winner of the African Player of the Year award, and captain of the national team that perished in a plane crash off the coast of Gabon in 1993 (he was the only player not on board). He is now the president of the Football Association of Zambia (FAZ), and is being investigated by the country's anti-corruption authorities over US$80,000 he said was received during the 2011 FIFA Congress in Qatar in the name of the FAZ, but that was paid into his personal account.[20]

Financial misappropriation is not limited to football, however. Apart from having the country's biggest doping scandal happen on their watch,[21] the Athletics Kenya (AK) president, Isaiah Kiplagat, and his deputy, David Okeyo, are also being investigated by Kenyan police over a US$200,000 grant that was deposited in the AK account in Nairobi but could not be accounted for.[22] Kiplagat stepped down as AK president on 1 May 2015, after 23 years in charge, not in relation to allegations and ongoing investigations but, ostensibly, to focus on his campaign for the International Association of Athletics Federations (IAAF) vice presidency.[23]

Match-fixing

Match-fixing has emerged as a huge threat to sport in Africa. The story of the cricket scores emerging from the lower tiers of Nigerian domestic competition indicated to the world how low the African game was sinking at the hands of those bent on manipulating results.[24] The continent's football is replete with tales of match-fixing. In 2014 a South African referee, Clifford Malgas, was jailed for two years for corruption and two years for perjury for his role in trying to manipulate the outcome of lower league promotion play-off games in 2011.[25] A former South Africa assistant coach, Phil Setshedi, got a three-year term for his part in the scam. He was caught in a sting operation as he tried to bribe an undercover policeman posing as another referee.[26]

There is also an external angle to match-fixing in Africa, involving criminal betting syndicates, especially from Asia. In 2013 reports surfaced of a convicted match-fixer, Wilson Raj Perumal, using referees to manipulate exhibition matches before the 2010 FIFA World Cup in South Africa.[27] One such referee, Ibrahim Chaibou, is under investigation by FIFA for his role in what is seen as manipulation of the results in two friendly matches played by South Africa against Guatemala and Colombia in May 2010. South Africa beat Guatemala 5–0, with three suspicious penalties being awarded by Chaibou, all for handball.[28]

In 2012 ZIFA banned its CEO, Henrietta Rushwaya, and 15 players, a coach and two journalists for life for their role in the fixing of matches involving Zimbabwe during a tour of Asia between 2007 and 2009.[29] After this ban, reports emerged that the country's top domestic championship was riddled with match-fixing. In 2011 ZIFA imported referees from Zambia and South Africa for the country's top knockout competition, the Mbada Diamonds Cup, amid claims of bribery and match-fixing among local referees.[30]

Human trafficking and African sport

Poverty is common in Africa, so sport affords a way out. This, combined with the abundance of talent and the globalisation of international sport, means that many top sports competitions and clubs around the world look to Africa to provide cheap talent. Getting a professional sports contract is the ultimate dream of many young Africans, and this leaves them vulnerable to unscrupulous scouting agents, who dump them in Europe and other parts of the world when they cannot secure their dream contract.

Charities such as the Paris-based Culture Foot Solidaire (CFS) campaign against the trafficking of young players.[31] CFS estimates that, each year, some 700 boys are smuggled into Europe from Cameroon alone by rogue agents.[32] A 2013 CNN report states that, according to CFS's founder, Jean-Claude Mbvoumin, the charity was at one time monitoring more than 1,000 boys in France, many of them taken from football academies in Africa.

The global push for popularity by the US National Basketball Association (NBA) is now seen as another avenue of abuse by human traffickers.[33] While social responsibility programmes such as the NBA's Basketball without Borders bring young basketball players around the world together for specialised coaching and to encourage positive change in the fields of education and health,[34] the story of Nigerian player Chukwuemeka Ene is evidence that rogue agents are involved in the recruitment of basketball players. Ene was brought to the United States along with two other players by a basketball scout, who promised him a college education and a shot at a professional game, but subsequently abandoned him.[35]

Defections of African athletes

A 2003 *Economist* report referred to the defection of African athletes to rich countries as the 'brawn drain from Africa'.[36] Kenya has borne the brunt of these defections of track stars, with a 2013 report by the *Daily Nation* in Nairobi reporting that there had been 40 known defections of young Kenyans to the Gulf, mainly Qatar and Bahrain. Following in the footsteps of Wilson Kipketer, who ran for Denmark in the 1990s, Saif Saeed Shaheen, previously known as Stephen Cherono, became the most high-profile Kenyan to defect to the Gulf, winning gold for Qatar at the World Athletics Championships in Paris in 2003.

After Shaheen's success, Qatar and Bahrain went full-throttle in recruiting Kenyan runners.[37] The IAAF's rules allow any athlete who has not run for one country at senior level to turn out for another country of his or her choice. Local agents swarmed Rift Valley training camps and the Kenyan athletics belt of Iten, Nandi and Marakwet, targeting young runners for recruitment to become nationals of the two countries, leading, for example, to the Bahraini team of ten runners at the 2015 World Junior Championships including three Kenyan-born teenage girls.[38] Ordinarily, decisions to change citizenship are personal, but in the case of Kenyan runners it has involved monetary incentives for the runners and their parents.[39] The targeted runners are teenagers. AK officials might not have been complicit in the scheme, but they are guilty of not having tight in-house rules to prevent the poaching of young Kenyan talent by other countries.

Doping

Kenya, once an epitome of clean running, is in the grip of an unprecedented doping scandal, with 19 positive tests and bans in the last two years alone.[40] The latest, involving Rita Jeptoo, a triple winner of the Boston and Chicago marathons, for the blood-boosting agent EPO, is the most prominent so far.[41] Matthew Kisorio, the other elite runner to be banned, claimed that doping is widespread among Kenyan runners and that doping doctors have set up shop in Kenya's athletics belt for their business.[42]

Jeptoo and Kisorio have not been the only high-profile African track stars to be banned for doping offences. Amantle Montsho, the former World and Commonwealth Games 400-m champion, and South Africa's top sprinter, Simon Magakwe, were both banned in early 2015 for doping.[43] To combat this menace, Kenyan athletes, under the Professional Athletes Association of Kenya (PAAK), are running a campaign called Run Clean to educate each other, and especially young runners, about the dangers of doping.[44]

The big event: the gravy train for joy riders

Major events are a main avenue of abuse and corruption in sport in Africa. The selection of national teams for the Olympics, the All-Africa Games, the Commonwealth Games and the World Athletics Championships is determined by meeting individually set qualifying marks. There are times, however, when the respective federations have the discretion to pick an athlete or player through a wildcard system. This is prone to abuse, as it can be used to favour or victimise athletes, or even to smuggle people. In 2003 a Kenyan volleyball player who thought she had been unfairly dropped from the All-Africa Games team publicly sought the intervention of the sports minister.[45]

Delegations of African teams to these big events are always bloated, with officials of federations, and even government functionaries, further abusing such occasions by taking mistresses, friends and relatives along for the ride, all at the expense of the taxpayer.[46] In the case of Nigeria it was decided not to send a government delegation to the 2012 London Olympics, as reports said an anti-corruption investigation had been launched after government officials ran up a huge bill at the 2010 World Cup in South Africa.[47]

It is clear that the belated appreciation by Africa's policy-makers of sport's economic and social value means that the continent's sport industry is much more vulnerable to corruption. Formulating policies on sport, even for countries with a rich sporting history such as Kenya, is only now occurring 50 years after independence. Corruption and governance issues in African sport are also criminal offences, and need to be understood as such. National federations need to work more closely with the police and other government agencies to protect the integrity of sport.

Fighting corruption and poor governance in sport can be helped by better and more insightful reporting. Sports journalism is viewed as the classical representation of the 'dumbing down' of news, with more emphasis on the entertainment and celebrity element for light reading.[48] This means that the weightier matters of corruption, doping, mismanagement and other vices in sport are often put on the back-burner. There is a need for the mainstreaming of these issues in the media in order to help raise the media profile of sports corruption.

Bearing in mind the viciousness and criminal nature of those involved in match-fixing and human trafficking, those journalists who write on these issues are to be applauded for revealing the little that they can. It is important that they are provided with the skills, equipment and incentives to be able to continue reporting on corruption in sport, thus raising people's awareness of the problem.

Notes

1   Chris Tsuma is a journalist, independent consultant and author for the Africa Center for Open Governance (AfriCOG), based in Nairobi.
2   FIFA.com, 'Rotation ends in 2018', 29 October 2007, *www.fifa.com/worldcup/news/y=2007/m=10/news=rotation-ends-2018-625122.html*.
3   Commonwealth Games Federation, *The Report of the CGF Evaluation Commission for the 2014 Commonwealth Games* (London: Commonwealth Games Federation, 2007), *www.thecgf.com/media/games/2014/2014_Evaluation_Report.pdf*.
4   International Association of Athletics Federations, 'Medal table: 147th IAAF World Championships', *www.iaaf.org/competitions/iaaf-world-championships/14th-iaaf-world-championships-4873/medaltable*.
5   *Vanguard* (Nigeria), 'All Africa Games: Popoola hails SCSA dissolution', 27 October 2011, *www.vanguardngr.com/2011/10/all-africa-games-popoola-hails-scsa-dissolution*.

6　Allsports.com (Ghana), 'It's the same old, sorry story for All African Games', 21 July 2014, *http://allsports.com.gh/other_sports/lost-hope-its-the-same-old-sorry-story-for-all-african-games-id2999997.html*.

7　International Olympic Committee, *Report on the 26 Core Sports for the XXXI Olympiad* (Lausanne: IOC, 2009), *www.olympic.org/results?q=report_on_the_26_core_sports_for_the_xxxi_olympiad*.

8　Insidethegames.biz (UK), 'FIFA annuls Zimbabwe Football Association elections amid vote buying claims', 1 April 2014, *www.insidethegames.biz/articles/1019244/fifa-annuls-zimbabwe-football-association-elections-amid-vote-buying-claims*.

9　BBC (UK), 'Issa Hayatou is re-elected unopposed as CAF president', 10 March 2013, *www.bbc.co.uk/sport/0/football/21733665*.

10　*Vanguard* (Nigeria), 'CAF elections: Nigeria loses, Hayatou returns', 11 March 2013, *www.vanguardngr.com/2013/03/caf-elections-nigeria-loses-hayatou-returns*; Africa Review.com (Kenya), 'CAF rule changes will ensure no change in football governance', 18 April 2015, *www.africareview.com/Sports/Much-to-worry-about-Caf-rule-changes/-/979186/2690198/-/view/analysis/-/1589t6iz/-/index.htm*.

11　AllAfrica.com, 'Kenya: branch delegates told to vote wisely', 16 December 2004, *http://allafrica.com/stories/200412150865.html*.

12　AllAfrica.com, 'Kenya: police to monitor bribery of delegates', 14 February 2004, *http://allafrica.com/stories/200402160360.html*.

13　*Guardian* (UK), 'World Cup 2014: Cameroon squad refuse to fly to Brazil in pay dispute', 8 June 2014, *www.theguardian.com/football/2014/jun/08/cameroon-squad-refuse-travel-brazil*.

14　BBC (UK), 'Confederations Cup 2013: Nigeria settle bonus dispute', 14 June 2013, *www.bbc.co.uk/sport/0/football/22895513*.

15　*Independent* (UK), 'Fifa threat ends Togo players' strike', 19 June 2006, *www.independent.co.uk/sport/football/international/fifa-threat-ends-togo-players-strike-404619.html*; *New York Times* (US), 'African teams head home, cash in hand', 30 June 2014, *www.nytimes.com/2014/07/01/sports/worldcup/world-cup-2014-african-soccer-overshadowed-by-protests.html*.

16　Canadian Broadcasting Corporation, 'Ghana flies in cash for World Cup players', 25 June 2014, *www.cbc.ca/sports/soccer/brazil2014/ghana-flies-in-cash-for-world-cup-players-1.2687321*.

17　AllAfrica.com, 'Kenya: Nyyamweya named in EACC dossier', 31 March 2015, *http://allafrica.com/stories/201503311431.html*.

18　StandardMedia.co (Kenya), 'Football Kenya Federation challenges official to present evidence on alleged financial scam', 10 August 2013, *www.standardmedia.co.ke/article/2000090559/football-kenya-federation-challenges-official-to-present-evidence-on-alleged-financial-scam*.

19　StandardMedia.co (Kenya), 'FKF defies FIFA man: Niema accused of acting ultra vires, FKF still wants 18 clubs', 28 January 2015, *http://webmail.standardmedia.co.ke/sports/article/2000149522/fkf-defies-fifa-man-niema-accused-of-acting-ultra-vires-fkf-still-wants-18-clubs*.

20　Zambian Eye, 'Qatar 2022 World Cup: Kalusha mentioned in bribery scandal', 2 June 2014, *http://zambianeye.com/archives/20965*; AllAfrica.com, 'Zambia: ACC still investigating Kalusha's US$80,000 Qatar bribe' 13 April 2015, *http://allafrica.com/stories/201504140836.html*.

21　*Forbes* (US), 'Kenyan marathoners: the next great doping scandal?', 17 November 2014, *www.forbes.com/sites/marcedelman/2014/11/17/kenyan-marathoners-the-next-great-doping-scandal*.

22　StandardMedia.co (Kenya), 'AK in deeper hole: officials fail to explain connection between federation and marketing company', 14 December 2014, *www.standardmedia.co.ke/sports/article/2000144710/ak-in-deeper-hole-officials-fail-to-explain-connection-between-federation-and-marketing-company*.

23   Radio Citizen (Kenya), 'Athletics Kenya president Isaiah Kiplagat steps aside', 13 April 2015, *www.radiocitizen.co.ke/index.php/news/item/28259-athletics-kenya-president-isaiah-kiplagat-steps-aside/28259-athletics-kenya-president-isaiah-kiplagat-steps-aside.*

24   BBC (UK), 'Nigerian players banned for life in match-fixing scandal', 22 July 2013, *www.bbc.co.uk/sport/0/football/23412227.*

25   ESPN (US), 'South African referee convicted of corruption, jailed for four years', 15 November 2014, *www.espnfc.com/league-name/story/2147693/headline.*

26   *The Sowetan* (South Africa), 'Phil Setshedi sentenced to 8 years for match fixing', 13 February 2013, *www.sowetanlive.co.za/sport/2013/02/13/phil-setshedi-sentenced-to-8-years-for-match-fixing.*

27   *Independent* (UK), 'Matches were fixed before 2010 World Cup, says Fifa', 15 December 2012, *www.independent.co.uk/sport/football/news-and-comment/matches-were-fixed-before-2010-world-cup-says-fifa-8420032.html.*

28   *New York Times* (US), 'Fixed soccer matches cast shadow over World Cup', 31 May 2014, *www.nytimes.com/2014/06/01/sports/soccer/fixed-matches-cast-shadow-over-world-cup.html.*

29   *Guardian* (UK), 'Zimbabwe suspends 80 players as part of "Asiagate" match-fixing probe', 1 February 2012, *www.theguardian.com/world/2012/feb/01/zimbabwe-footballers-suspended-asiagate-match-fixing.*

30   *NewsDay* (Zimbabwe), 'Match-fixing allegations in Premier Soccer League', 2 November 2012, *www.newsday.co.zw/2012/11/02/match-fixing-allegations-in-premier-soccer-league.*

31   See the charity's website: *www.footsolidaire.org.*

32   CNN (US), 'Human traffic: Africa's lost boys', 28 March 2013, *http://edition.cnn.com/2013/03/28/sport/football/football-trafficking.*

33   *Harper's* (US), 'American hustle: how elite youth basketball exploits African athletes', April 2015, *http://harpers.org/archive/2015/04/american-hustle.*

34   See *www.nba.com/bwb/mission.html.*

35   *Bloomberg* (US), 'African victims of basketball's global push', 19 March 2015, *www.bloombergview.com/articles/2015-03-19/african-victims-of-basketball-s-global-push.*

36   *The Economist* (UK), 'The brawn drain from Africa: Qatar's poaching of African champions', 28 August 2003, *www.economist.com/node/2026223.*

37   *Daily Nation* (Kenya), '40 defections later, Kenyan athletes still find grass greener on the other side', 17 August 2013, *http://mobile.nation.co.ke/Sports/Why+the+defections/-/1951244/1957996/-/format/xhtml/-/hpgsnf/-/index.html.*

38   Qatarsucks.com, 'Kenyan athletes are exploited like "slaves" and Qatar is leading the way!', 3 May 2008, *www.qatarsucks.com/Qatar_Buys_Kenyan_Athletes.*

39   Mwakilishi.com (Kenya), 'How scent of oil cash lures Kenyan children to Gulf state of Bahrain', 23 July 2014, *www.mwakilishi.com/content/articles/2014/07/23/how-scent-of-oil-cash-lures-kenyan-children-to-gulf-state-of-bahrain.htm.*

40   *Irish Times*, 'Dark cloud of doping hanging over Kenyan athletics', 12 November 2014, *www.irishtimes.com/sport/other-sports/dark-cloud-of-doping-hanging-over-kenyan-athletics-1.1996620.*

41   Yahoo! Sports, 'Marathon champ Rita Jeptoo receives two-year ban for positive drug test', 30 January 2015, *http://sports.yahoo.com/blogs/the-turnstile/marathon-champ-rita-jeptoo-receives-two-year-ban-for-positive-drug-test-141220783.html.*

42   *Guardian* (UK), 'Kenya's Matthews Kisorio doped because he "wasn't the only one"', 30 October 2013, *www.theguardian.com/sport/2013/oct/30/kenya-athletics-doping-matthews-kisorio.*

43   BBC (UK), 'Amantle Montsho given two-year ban for doping at Commonwealths', 18 March 2015, *www.bbc.com/sport/0/athletics/31953218*; *The Times* (South Africa), 'Simon Magakwe banned for two years', 15 April 2015, *www.timeslive.co.za/sport/other/2015/04/15/simon-magakwe-banned-for-two-years.*

44   AllAfrica.com, 'Kenya: athletes launch anti-doping campaign dubbed "Run Clean"', 6 April 2015, *http://allafrica.com/stories/201504060642.html.*

45 AllAfrica.com, 'Kenya: Ayuma's plea draws quick Balala move', 25 September 2003, *http://allafrica.com/stories/200309250147.html*.

46 AllAfrica.com, 'Kenya: no chance for joy-riders in Melbourne', 9 February 2006, *http://allafrica.com/stories/200602080915.html*.

47 BBC (UK), 'Olympics 2012: Nigeria bans government delegation', 5 July 2012, *www.bbc.co.uk/news/world-africa-18720212*.

48 See Ian Hargreaves, *Journalism: Truth or Dare* (Oxford: Oxford University Press, 2003). Hargreaves is a former editor of the *Financial Times* and *The Independent*, and has written widely on journalism.

1.7

Impunity and corruption in South American football governance

Juca Kfouri[1]

The intangibility of its assets means that sport, and not just football, is one of the sectors of the entertainment industry most prone to money-laundering.

How much is Lionel Messi worth: €200 million? Gareth Bale of Wales was worth €100 million to Real Madrid. Is Messi worth two Bales? 'No,' some would say; 'he's worth three!' It will never be known how much he is worth, however, and what the true amount paid would be should he be transferred, as was also the case with the nebulous transaction that brought Neymar da Silva Santos Júnior of Brazil to Barcelona.

The trajectory of Havelange, FIFA and CONMEBOL

Following the election of João Havelange as president of the Fédération Internationale de Football Association (FIFA) in 1974, with the help of the Dassler family of Adidas, the entity was transformed into a large multinational that resembles the Cosa Nostra more than it does the Red Cross.[2]

The repercussions throughout Brazil and South America were immediate. Havelange had presided over the Brazilian Sports Confederation for 18 years, from 1956 to 1974. He capitalised on the fame of Pelé to collect votes in Africa and defeat Stanley Rous of England, who had presided over FIFA since 1961.[3]

Taking advantage of this 'global village',[4] Havelange aimed to make football big business, and profitable, especially for those who surrounded and supported him. This included even his son-in-law, Ricardo Teixeira, then married to his only daughter. In 1989 Havelange successfully lobbied for him to become president of the Brazilian Football Confederation (CBF).[5]

The South American Football Confederation (CONMEBOL) was similarly transformed into a fiefdom of patronage from which shadowy and folkloric figures emerged, such as the late Julio Grondona, who presided for decades over the Argentine Football Association. Grondona wore a ring with the inscription 'Todo pasa' (in English, 'Anything goes' or 'In time, it will all be fine'), reflecting his method for managing the scandals and crises that surrounded him.[6]

In the same circle was the Paraguayan Nicolás Leoz, president of CONMEBOL from 1986 to 2013, who is alleged to have offered his vote in support of the UK bid to host the 2018 World Cup on the condition that the queen would grant him a knighthood.[7] With full confidence of impunity – indeed, the CONMEBOL headquarters in Paraguay had 'embassy' status – the heads of the national associations and the confederation operated to a large extent as if they were part of an immense and untouchable gang.

Less concerned with football and more preoccupied with its luxurious benefits, these leaders had their operators to make sure that the ball was bouncing on the field and that the sponsors were attended to. Furthermore, although they are referred to as sports marketers, in reality many such companies throughout South America have been a screen for all sorts of fraud.[8] Sports marketing companies in South America often serve as intermediaries for large contracts and distribute payments, from sponsors or broadcasters to football association executives, in a manner that guarantees, in the small world of these fortunate ones, that everybody gets along. Sports marketing executives from Kléfer and Traffic (both of Brazil) and Torneos Y Competencias (Argentina) are reportedly under investigation, linked to business deals with national and international football officials.[9] It is a vicious cycle that has the virtue of keeping everyone – including the marketers, sponsors, broadcasters and football executives – satisfied.

Impunity in South American football governance

It is in South America where, thanks to this prevailing sense of impunity, less caution is taken with such fraudulent behaviour, to the point that it is discussed with a smile on one's face, as a sign of expertise. This brazenness is what led to the downfall of the former president of the CBF, José Maria Marin, who is now in prison in Zurich awaiting his likely extradition to the United States, charged in May 2015 with racketeering conspiracy, money-laundering conspiracy and wire fraud conspiracy.[10]

An octogenarian, a servant of the former Brazilian dictatorship and a millionaire thanks to a lifetime of scandal,[11] Marin was caught in a conversation taped by a convicted defendant working for the FBI, José Hawilla, the owner and founder of Traffic Group, the sports marketing company that controlled the television rights for the 2014 World Cup in Brazil as well as the Copa Libertadores, the Copa America and the Copa do Brasil.[12] Hawilla admitted that he had paid bribes to association heads across the continent in the course of his work.[13]

Teixeira, Marin's predecessor as president of the CBF, had resigned from his position in 2012, amid various corruption allegations, and moved to Florida.[14] To Marin's dismay, Teixeira continued to receive commissions from CBF contracts.[15] Marin had indicated to Hawilla that Teixeira no longer deserved such privileges, and said that they should instead be transferred to him and his successor as CBF president, Marco Polo Del Nero,[16] speculated to be the unidentified 'co-conspirator 12' in the FBI indictment of May 2015.[17]

The problem with the CBF, like other national associations in the region, and like CONMEBOL and like FIFA, is structural. There is a need to change the rules, rather than individuals, in order to reform the governance of football in South America. Otherwise, any individual aiming to rise up the ranks will have to play the game that is dictated by vested interests in which the end always justifies the means.

There is an urgent need to break away from the undemocratic methods for reaching the top, be it term limits or, more importantly, giving voice to the athletes. It is the athletes who are the main actors in sports, yet they are mere spectators of what happens in their governing bodies, and victims of their decisions.

It became clear that the 'emperor had no clothes', and sponsors began to depart. Yet other sponsors have nonetheless stepped in, confident that the magic of football will mesmerise all and that the fans won't see Adidas as a sponsor of FIFA but instead of the

World Cup, or, in the case of Brazil, that they won't see Nike as a sponsor of the CBF but, rather, the Brazilian national team.

Movements for change

Occasionally fans mobilise, form movements and denounce what goes on behind the scenes. In the case of Brazil, the 1980s saw the Corinthian Democracy, an ideological movement for the sound management of clubs led by the famous Brazilian footballer Socrates. Today the Bom Senso FC movement represents over 1,000 players who stand for fair financial play and the democratisation of access to power.

The Brazilian government has also taken steps, namely by proposals for new legislation on the governance of clubs in the quest to modernise Brazilian football. There have been difficulties in passing these ideas through the National Congress, however, which is heavily influenced by the 'bancada da bola', or the 'ball bench' – a group of congressmen and senators who are close to and guided by the CBF.[18]

Brazil and the rest of South America are still far from seeing football as an opportunity for all, fans in particular, to enjoy and benefit from. To the contrary, they still operate under the logic that the accumulation of capital comes first. It is difficult to predict the future of football in South America and to imagine a structure free of corruption, given how engrained these practices are and the amount of money involved. It is hoped that CONMEBOL and the national associations will look to other regions and countries, to learn from their mistakes as well as their best practices.

Notes

1 Juca Kfouri is a columnist for *Folha de São Paulo* and Universo Online (UOL), and a leading sports writer in Brazil.
2 ESPN (US), 'Havelange to Blatter: the dynasty based on corruption', 28 February 2002, *www.espnfc.com/global/news/2002/0228/20020228featjenningsmain.html*.
3 David Yallop, *How They Stole the Game* (London: Poetic Publishing, 1999).
4 The 'global village' is a term coined by Marshall McLuhan to describe the increasingly small world as a result of growing networks of communication.
5 *Guardian* (UK), 'Fifa corruption intrigue deepens as Brazil's Ricardo Teixeira resigns', 12 March 2012, *www.theguardian.com/football/2012/mar/12/fifa-ricardo-teixeira-resigns*; World Soccer, 'Ricardo Teixeira: how 25 years of absolute power came to an end', 26 January 2014, *www.worldsoccer.com/columnists/keir-radnedge/ricardo-teixeira-how-25-years-of-absolute-power-came-to-an-end-344414*.
6 *Clarín* (Argentina), 'El Señor del anillo', 30 July 2014, *www.clarin.com/deportes/Muerte_de_Julio_Grondona-murio_Julio_Grondona_0_1184281997.html*.
7 *Guardian* (UK), 'Former MP claims Nicolás Leoz made earlier request for British honour', 11 May 2011, *www.theguardian.com/football/2011/may/11/mp-nicolas-leoz-honour*.
8 United States District Court, Eastern District of New York, Indictment CR 14-609 (RJD), 12 December 2014, *www.justice.gov/opa/file/450216/download*.
9 *Wall Street Journal* (US), 'Brazil, Argentina probe soccer industry', 28 May 2015, *www.wsj.com/articles/brazil-kicks-off-soccer-graft-probe-1432845022*; *The Washington Post* (US), 'Here's who the FBI arrested in connection to its FIFA investigation', 27 May 2015, *www.washingtonpost.com/blogs/early-lead/wp/2015/05/27/heres-who-the-fbi-arrested-in-connection-to-its-fifa-investigation*.
10 *Washington Post* (US), 'After FIFA arrests, Brazilians ask: why didn't we do this?', 29 May 2015, *www.washingtonpost.com/blogs/worldviews/wp/2015/05/29/after-fifa-arrests-brazilians-ask-why-didnt-we-do-this*.

11   *The Blizzard* (UK), 'A troubled history: José Maria Marin', June 2014, *www.theblizzard.co.uk/ articles/a-troubled-history-jose-maria-marin*; *New York Times* (US), 'A region's soccer strongmen are facing a hard fall', 27 May 2015, *www.nytimes.com/2015/05/28/world/ americas/a-regions-strongmen-are-facing-a-hard-fall.html*.

12   *Folha de Sao Paulo* (Brazil), 'Réu confesso, Hawilla colabora com o FBI desde o final de 2013', 4 June 2015, *www1.folha.uol.com.br/esporte/2015/06/1637703-reu-confesso-hawilla-colabora-com-o-fbi-desde-o-final-de-2013.shtml*; *Guardian* (UK), 'Brazil starts congressional inquiry into corruption after Fifa arrests', 29 May 2015, *www.theguardian. com/football/2015/may/29/brazil-corruption-fifa-arrests-romario*.

13   Ibid.

14   BBC (UK), 'Brazil football boss Ricardo Teixeira resigns', 12 March 2012, *www.bbc.co.uk/ news/world-latin-america-17345455*; *Folha de Sao Paulo* (Brazil), 'A year after leaving the presidency of the CBF, Ricardo Teixeira enjoys luxury homes and cars in Florida', 27 February 2013, *www1.folha.uol.com.br/internacional/en/sports/2013/02/1237583-a-year-after-leaving-the-presidency-of-the-cbf-ricardo-teixeira-enjoys-luxury-homes-and-cars-in-florida.shtml*.

15   *Folha de Sao Paulo* (Brazil), 4 June 2015.

16   Ibid.

17   Reuters (UK), 'Brazil soccer head to review suspicious deals, rules out resignation', 29 May 2015, *http://in.reuters.com/article/2015/05/29/ soccer-fifa-brazil-idINKBN0OE1ZQ20150529*.

18   UOL (Brazil), '10 fatos sobre a bancada da bola no Congresso Nacional', 15 June 2015, *http://esporte.uol.com.br/futebol/ultimas-noticias/2015/06/15/10-fatos-sobre-a-bancada-da-bola-no-congresso-nacional.htm*.

1.8

Indicators and benchmarking tools for sports governance

Arnout Geeraert[1]

Introduction

Notwithstanding recent internal and external efforts, the impression is that there is still inertia hampering the establishment of better governance in the sports world.[2] To a large extent, this can be explained by the lack of a generally accepted, homogeneous set of core principles and benchmarking tools for good governance in international sport organisations (ISOs). Arguments that underline the importance of indicators and benchmarking tools for sports governance are threefold. First, ISOs need to be informed as to how they can organise their affairs in a sustainable and effective manner. Existing codes usually include principles that are extremely broadly defined and, therefore, rather impractical.[3]

Second, there is a need to put external pressure on ISOs in order to push for change towards better governance. Whereas empirical evidence suggests that international sport organisations lack good governance, internal accountability deficits render change from within an unrealistic scenario.[4] Benchmarking has the potential to inflict the reputational costs associated with naming and shaming, which has been known to change the behaviour of powerful international actors.[5]

Third, benchmarking instruments are needed in order to evaluate governance reform processes. In certain cases, governance scandals have led to governance reforms.[6] Most recently, for instance, the governance reform process in the Fédération Internationale de Football Association (FIFA) resulted in some major organisational changes. The problem is, however, that several important reform proposals were not implemented, on account of a lack of internal support.[7] In the absence of independent benchmarking systems, it is difficult to fully appreciate the adequacy (or lack thereof) of the process.

This chapter highlights the challenges in developing benchmarking tools, as well as the limits and opportunities of existing tools. In addition, it aims to identify the way forward.

The challenges in developing benchmarking tools for sports governance

Good governance principles must always take account of the specificity of the relevant organisation. Consequently, there are important differences in existing codes across international boundaries, both at a commercial and non-profit level. In their capacity as regulators/promoters of their sports, ISOs comprise organisational structures that are found within state, market and civil society entities. Because of the *sui generis* structures of these organisations, existing codes from other sectors cannot simply be applied to them. They can serve as important sources for inspiration, however, so long as attention is paid to preserving sufficiently high standards in relevant areas.

Benchmarking tools for sports governance thus need to take into account the specificity of ISOs. At the same time, they have to be sufficiently generic in order to be applicable to the many different structures that can be discerned within these organisations, which only adds to the complexity of the issue. This implies that benchmarking tools can never capture all the nuances that exist within the governance structures of each organisation. Taking account of these considerations, it is possible to identify core elements for good governance in ISOs around which concrete indicators can be constructed.

Core elements for good sports governance

The core elements for good sports governance that emerge from the literature on good governance in both the public and private area are transparency, democracy, checks and balances, social responsibility, and equity and diversity.

Transparency

Transparency in general can be defined as 'the availability of information about an organisation or actor allowing external actors to monitor the internal workings or performance of that organisation'.[8] It is commonly assumed that increased transparency will lead to decreased misuse of power, financial mismanagement and corruption.[9] It may also lead to stronger democracy, since it allows for better debate.

In order to be transparent, ISOs should adhere to strict disclosure requirements, including financial reporting, and adequately communicate their activities to their internal stakeholders and the general public. More specifically, they should produce regular narrative accounts that seek to justify decisions, actions and results and engage in a constructive dialogue with those who are publicly contesting these. Not every form of transparency benefits stakeholder empowerment and trust, though. The risk of misinformation, information overload and unjust blaming underlines the importance of publishing clear, objective and timely information.[10]

Democracy

Participation in policy processes by those who are affected by the policy is a cornerstone of democracy.[11] Democratic principles and procedures in the decision-making of ISOs ensure that those who govern can be held accountable by their primary stakeholders. The main way in which member federations can hold their respective ISOs accountable is through their statutory powers. Most notably, these relate to the election of the people who govern the organisation – i.e. the members of the executive body of the organisation – but they also relate to the selection process of the ISO's major event.

Member federations are not the only primary stakeholders of ISOs, though. Among those affected by ISOs' policies and decisions are clubs, referees, coaches and, most importantly, athletes. According to Barrie Houlihan, sports policy is 'rarely [carried out] in consultation with athletes, and almost never in partnership with athletes'.[12] Specific attention should therefore be paid to involving stakeholders, notably athletes, in decision-making processes. It is widely accepted that this leads to more long-term effectiveness and to sustainable solutions for policy issues, on the one hand, and a reduced likelihood of corruption and concentration of power, on the other.[13]

Checks and balances

Mutual control procedures are paramount, to prevent the concentration of power and ensure that decision-making is robust, independent and free from improper influence. They also ensure that no manager or board member or department has absolute control over decisions, and clearly define the assigned duties.[14] Checks and balances should apply to all (senior) officials and staff working in the different departments of an ISO. To achieve this, the organisation should at the very least have an internal audit and ethics committee, financial controls, an ethics code and conflict-of-interest rules in place.

Social responsibility

ISOs carry a responsibility to society at large. Given the socio-cultural value of sport, sports federations have the potential to make a positive contribution to social cohesion, cultural understanding and global dialogue. They are expected to 'give something back' to society, as sports activities often rely on public funds. It is important to determine clear standards in order to prevent such efforts from serving merely as 'window dressing'.

An ISO's social responsibility should encourage it to invest in the global development of grassroots activities, mitigate the negative externalities of international organised sports, including environmental degradation, improve the circumstances of marginalised and/or fractured communities and adopt legacy requirements for the hosting of its major event.

Equity and diversity

Diversity is needed in ISOs in order to ensure that everybody's best interests are being looked after. For instance, whereas sports governance is still male-dominated, studies indicate that female inclusion on boards leads to improved governance and reduces the influence of the 'old boys' network'.[15] At the same time, it is important that equity is also promoted at lower levels, since grassroots sports often form the foundation from which the leading sports officials of the future emerge.

Existing benchmarking tools

In recent years important progress has been made in the literature on good governance in sport.[16] This has been translated not just into checklists for good governance in international sport organisations but also into concrete benchmarking tools. Especially noteworthy is the work by Jean-Loup Chappelet and Michaël Mrkonjic,[17] the 'Action for Good Governance in International Sport' (AGGIS) organisations group[18] and the 'Sport For Good Governance' (s4gg) project.[19]

Although all three of these tools use a Likert-type scale for measuring good governance, they are distinct in that they use different indicators and different measuring systems (self-evaluation, expert assessment and pre-defined scoring). The s4gg project devised an easy-to-use self-evaluation tool that is mainly targeted at sports federations operating at the national level. The tool consists of a set of indicators that are sufficiently broad to be applied to ISOs as well. The main advantage of the s4gg tool is that it is supported by the sports federation community. Self-evaluation precludes naming and shaming, however, and influences the reliability of outcomes.

Chappelet and Mrkonjic have suggested the 'Basic Indicators for Better Governance in International Sport' (BIBGIS), which are organised along seven dimensions: organisational transparency, reporting transparency, stakeholders' representation, democratic process, control mechanisms, sport integrity and solidarity. Their measuring system is based on expert assessment, and thus requires (independent) experts to give a score for each indicator.

The AGGIS group have devised the 'Sports Governance Observer', a benchmarking tool consisting of four dimensions, namely transparency and public communication, democratic process, checks and balances and solidarity. Each of the (roughly) ten indicators per dimension is quantified by means of a predetermined scoring system.

Conclusion: the way forward

The benchmarking of good governance in ISOs is necessary in order to induce better governance in (international) sport. The different benchmarking tools that are emerging fill a void that to some extent impeded improvements in sports governance. These tools can coexist and complement each other, in the sense that they serve distinct goals and each have specific benefits.

It is important that they are tested and improved on a continuous basis, however.[20] Special attention should be paid to concerns regarding their validity (the degree to which a tool succeeds in describing or quantifying what it is designed to measure) and reliability (the degree to which a tool generates the same results under the same conditions). Including stakeholders, notably ISOs, more in this process than thus far has been the case would facilitate exchanges of knowledge and increase the likelihood that the sports world will pay attention to the principles of good governance that are being promoted. This, of course, underlines the need for ISOs to 'take the leap' and adopt one or more of these benchmarking tools.

Box 1.1 The Sports Governance Observer

Play the Game

The concept of good governance in sport has climbed to the top of the global political agenda in the course of the past few years. Good governance is increasingly regarded as an essential quality if sports organisations are to become efficient partners in solving a number of complex international challenges: the fight against match-fixing, doping and other forms of corruption in sport; the demand for more sustainable international events; the social and gender imbalances in sport; and the decreasing level of physical activity across the globe.

Politicians worldwide increasingly expect the international sports movement to engage with these challenges. This was expressed, for instance, in the 2013 Berlin Declaration, which was approved by governments from more than 125 countries at the Fifth International Conference of Ministers and Senior Officials Responsible for Physical Education and Sport (MINEPS V). In addition, the European Union and the Council of Europe regard sports governance as a key issue in their range of activities, and the International Olympic Committee (IOC) intends to reinvigorate its efforts in the field.

In order to inspire international sport to raise its governance standards to a higher level, Play the Game and the Danish Institute for Sports Studies (Idan) have introduced the Sports Governance Observer, a benchmarking tool developed in cooperation with six European universities that is based on the best scientific theory and yet easily applicable in the day-to-day work of the various national and international sports federations. The Sports Governance Observer has been further elaborated with a robust scoring system, and in 2014 and 2015 the 35 international federations that support the IOC by governing each sport at a global level were analysed on the basis of the instrument.

The aim of the Sports Governance Observer is to enable an in-depth analysis of good governance in international sports federations, firmly rooted in state-of-the art governance and management theory and building on the best international practices. A thorough knowledge of the state of affairs in this regard can lead to better-informed and more effective policy choices for these federations, and ultimately to a better relationship between sport and society in general.

Notes

1   Arnout Geeraert is a research fellow at the Leuven International and European Studies (LINES) Institute, Catholic University of Leuven, and also works for the Danish Institute for Sports Studies.
2   Arnout Geeraert, Jens Alm and Michael Groll, 'Good governance in international sport organisations: an analysis of the 35 Olympic sport governing bodies', *International Journal of Sport Policy and Politics*, vol. 6 (2014).
3   International Olympic Committee, *Basic Universal Principles of Good Governance of the Olympic and Sports Movement* (Lausanne: IOC, 2008); EU Expert Group 'Good governance', 'Deliverable 2: principles of good governance in sport', *http://ec.europa.eu/ sport/library/policy_documents/xg-gg-201307-dlvrbl2-sept2013.pdf*.
4   Geeraert *et al.* (2014); Mark Bovens, 'Analysing and assessing accountability: a conceptual framework', *European Law Journal*, vol. 13 (2007).
5   Thomas Risse, Stephen Ropp and Kathryn Sikkink (eds), *The Power of Human Rights: International Norms and Domestic Change* (Cambridge: Cambridge University Press, 1999).
6   Mark Pieth (ed.), *Reforming FIFA* (Zurich: Dike Verlag, 2014); Jean-Loup Chappelet and Brenda Kübler-Mabbott, *The International Olympic Committee and the Olympic System: The Governance of World Sport* (Abingdon: Routledge, 2008).
7   Pieth (2014).
8   Stephan Grimmelikhuijsen, 'Transparency and trust: an experimental study of online disclosure and trust in government', PhD thesis (Utrecht: Utrecht University, 2012), p. 55.
9   Christopher Hood, 'What happens when transparency meets blame-avoidance?', *Public Management Review,* vol. 9 (2007), p. 207.
10   Frank van Eekeren, 'Transparency', in Jens Alm (ed.), *Action for Good Governance in International Sport Organisations: Final Report* (Copenhagen: Danish Institute for Sports Studies, 2013).
11   Sherry Arnstein, 'A ladder of citizen participation', *Journal of the American Institute of Planners*, vol. 35 (1969).
12   Barrie Houlihan, 'Civil rights, doping control and the World Anti-Doping Code', *Sport in Society*, vol. 7 (2004), pp. 421–422.
13   Oran Young, *International Governance: Protecting the Environment in a Stateless Society* (Ithaca, NY: Cornell University Press, 1994); Bovens (2007).
14   Peter Aucoin and Ralph Heintzman, 'The dialectics of accountability for performance in public management reform', *International Review of Administrative Sciences*, vol. 66 (2000).
15   David Brown, Debra Brown and Vanessa Anastasopoulos, *Not Just the Right Thing . . . But the 'Bright' Thing* (Ottawa: The Conference Board of Canada, 2002).
16   Jean-Loup Chappelet and Michaël Mrkonjic, 'Existing governance principles in sport: a review of published literature', in Alm (2013).

17 Jean-Loup Chappelet and Michaël Mrkonjic, *Basic Indicators for Better Governance in International Sport (BIBGIS): An Assessment Tool for International Sport Governing Bodies*, IDHEAP Working Paper no. 1/2013 (Lausanne: Swiss Graduate School of Public Administration, 2013).

18 See Arnout Geeraert, 'AGGIS: action for good governance in international sports organisations', *http://ec.europa.eu/sport/library/documents/eusf2013-1-2-wkshp2-5b-danish-institute.pdf*.

19 See *www.s4gg.eu*.

20 Play the Game, an international initiative under the auspices of the Danish Institute for Sports Studies, is currently in the process of reviewing the 35 Olympic sports federations on the basis of the Sports Governance Observer benchmarking tool. Results are expected in the first half of 2015.

1.9

Examples of evolving good governance practices in sport

Michael Pedersen[1]

Although a holistic framework can offer a useful basis for considering all relevant aspects of sport governance, national and international sport governing bodies are very different in terms of size, resources and management challenges – and therefore also in terms of which specific solutions add the most value to them. This chapter highlights three succinct examples of evolving good governance practices across several sports and countries.

Netball New Zealand and its model for professionalising the boardroom

As early as 1999, way ahead of most other sport governing bodies throughout the world, Netball New Zealand went through a comprehensive governance modernisation. A particularly noteworthy outcome was the organisation's decision to build the foundation for good and effective decision-making by creating a skills-based, eight-person-strong board with no or few conflicts of interest and financial compensation to board members.

In accordance with the governance standards[2] that were put in place, the eight-person board of Netball New Zealand consists of three elected members, four appointed members and the chief executive of the sport governing body. The three elected members are chosen by the membership of Netball New Zealand, for a three-year term, including the president. There is no automatic board representation for specific geographical membership groups. The elected president mainly has a representational role, as it is the role of the chairman to lead the board.

The four appointed members of the board are recruited by a so-called Appointment Panel, also for a three-year term. The panel is composed of three people nominated by the board, including a member of the Institute of Directors in New Zealand. There is a process in place for receiving and considering applications from candidates. Any person can apply. There are no specific requirements either of affiliation with netball or of independence from the sport.

The commencement of the terms in office for board members is staggered, so as to ensure a rotation of board members over a three-year period. The board appoints one of its members as chairman. All board members, except for the chief executive, can serve on the board for a maximum of nine years.

At the beginning of every board meeting the members are asked to declare any potential conflicts of interest related to the agenda items of the meeting – personal as well as institutional ones. Furthermore, beyond the reimbursement of relevant and appropriate travel expenses, board members are given a yearly honorarium payment in appreciation of their work. In 2012 board members received US$8,500 each, while the chairman received US$21,000.[3]

The Badminton World Federation and its model for democratising sport

Unlike most other sport governing bodies, nationally as well as internationally, the Badminton World Federation (BWF) does not have a democratic governance system along the lines of 'one member association, one vote' at its general assembly. Rather, member associations are allocated a minimum of one and a maximum of five votes on the basis of criteria that favour those that prove able to contribute the most to the further development of badminton.

The allocation of votes to member associations is made for one four-year period at a time, based on a four-year retrospective assessment period. Accordingly, under the precondition that a member association is in good standing, the number of votes it has at the general assembly is allocated in line with the criteria shown in Table 1.1a.[4]

One vote	A member of the Badminton World Federation.
One additional vote	More than 10,000 registered players in each of the four years of the assessment period.
One additional vote	Participation in seven out of 12 international events during the assessment period: the Sudirman Cup (two events), individual Continental Championships (a maximum of two events), World Championships (three events), the Olympic Games (one event) and the World Junior Team Championships (four events).
One additional vote	Having one player or more in the top 40 world ranking in any of the five disciplines as per the world ranking list for qualifying for the most recently held Olympic Games.
One additional vote	Hosting at least one of these events in three out of the four years of the assessment period: the Super Series, Grand Prix or International Challenge.

Table 1.1a Vote weighting in the Badminton World Federation

Rights and responsibilities go hand in hand for member associations in the Badminton World Federation. The actual size of a member association's membership fee is determined according to a scale of units, which is a function of the number of votes allocated to the association. The scale of units is as shown in Table 1.1b.

The BWF covers travel expenses for all its member associations to send one representative to attend the general assembly. Voting by proxy is not allowed; only member associations directly represented at the general assembly are in a position to cast votes.

Total number of votes at the general assembly	Total units to be applied when calculating the size of the actual membership fee
One vote	1
Two votes	4
Three votes	9
Four votes	26
Five votes	31

Table 1.1b Vote weighting in the Badminton World Federation

The South African Rugby Union and its model for annual reporting

Although annual reports are critical means of maintaining and increasing trust with key stakeholders, internally as well as externally, many sport governing bodies have yet to create and publish such reports. The annual reports of the South African Rugby Union (SARU) are particularly noteworthy, in as much as they are integrated: not only do they provide the consolidated financial statement, they also provide a range of governance measures, strategies, activities and results achieved throughout the year.

A substantial part of SARU's 2013 annual report[5] consists of governance measures relating to the political management of the sport governing body. Notably, details are given regarding the composition of the Executive Council and committees (including individual actual attendance at meetings), the terms of reference for committees and a list of independent members of committees (in areas such as audit and risk and human resources and remuneration). Another significant piece of information is the figure for the total compensation of Executive Council members (approximately US$1.1 million).

As for governance measures related to the operational management of the South African Rugby Union, one of the more striking accounts is of the organisation's HIV/AIDS policy, aimed at promoting a non-discriminatory work environment for employees with HIV/AIDS. Other notable details are the figure for the total expenses of the CEO's office (some US$870,000) and the total numbers of male and female employees (143 women, 433 men).

Finally, the auditing of the consolidated financial statement is noteworthy in at least two ways. First, it is carried out in accordance with International Standards on Auditing. This reflects SARU's commitment to comply with the Companies Act 2008 and the so-called 'King Code of Governance Principles' in South Africa, despite not being incorporated and, therefore, not being legally required to do so. Second, SARU appoints both internal and external auditors; for the 2013 annual report, KPMG was the internal auditor, while PwC was the external auditor.

Notes

1   Michael Pedersen is the founder of M INC. and the former Head of the World Economic Forum's 'Partnering against Corruption Initiative'.
2   Constitution of Netball New Zealand Inc.
3   Netball New Zealand, *Annual Report 2012* (Auckland: Netball New Zealand, 2012).
4   Badminton World Federation constitution.
5   South African Rugby Union, *Annual Report 2013* (Cape Town: SARU, 2013).

1.10

For the good of the game?

Governance on the outskirts
of international football

Steve Menary[1]

In those small football associations at the bottom of Fédération Internationale de Football Association (FIFA) rankings, participation in the finals of a major tournament is usually accepted as impossible. These associations often have a handful of players, at best, with any experience of playing professionally, and the imperative is on grassroots development. This is the key challenge with governance at small national associations, which are often charged with developing the game in areas no larger than a small town in most larger countries. With such a small pool of players, the national teams are usually unsuccessful and go largely ignored, yet their executives, as inexperienced off the pitch in international football as their players are on it, can rise to the well-remunerated upper echelons of FIFA while at times completely oblivious to the standards of governance needed at the national level.

When Tahiti qualified for the 2013 Confederations Cup in Brazil by winning the 2012 Oceania Football Confederation (OFC) Nations Cup,[2] the outgunned team was predictably sneered at by parts of the mainstream media, many of which previously had cause to mention the French overseas collective and football in the same article only in the context of corruption.[3] This illustrates the dichotomy at the heart of media coverage of football in smaller nations and territories. It is all too easy for the lack of international media exposure to work to the disadvantage of those attempting to improve the quality of the governance in the minor associations on the periphery of international football.

Although FIFA has 209 members, media priorities, usually generated by consumer demand, dictate that coverage focuses on those countries and teams with the most support.[4] As Roger Pielke Jr has identified in another chapter, through the desire for autonomous development, national sports bodies often have 'less well developed mechanisms of governance than many governments, businesses and civil society organisations'.[5]

FIFA and the non-interference rule

Local journalists attempting to uncover issues of poor governance and corruption can face vilification or isolation in small countries, where the size of the population is more akin to that of a minor city in a larger country. Attempts to draw the attention of local politicians to concerns about the governance of national football can be stifled by conflicts of interest and FIFA's insistence on independence from political interference for national football associations.

Such violations of independence led to 5 per cent of the member associations being suspended between 2005 and 2010.[6] This insistence can discourage positive intervention on occasions when politicians witness genuine poor governance or suspect corruption.[7] In places where everyone knows everyone else, sporting autonomy can supersede the rule of national law, and instances of poor governance or corruption can go unchecked for years.

Take, for example, French Caledonia, where Jacques Zimako was elected as vice president of the Fédération Calédonienne de Football (FCF) in July 2011, only to fall out, for reasons unclear, with president Edward Bowen, who then suspended Zimako.[8] A civic tribunal ruled that the suspension was illegal, but this ruling was ignored.[9] FIFA then appointed Bowen to its Disciplinary Committee at the 2013 annual congress, even though the FCF president had failed to disclose that he was facing criminal charges in Nouméa, the French Caledonian capital, for violence against local civil servants.[10] Bowen was subsequently convicted, but the OFC president, David Chung, wrote to Bowen offering his support to the disgraced FCF president, who was jailed in December 2013.[11] According to the FCF's statutes, Zimako should have taken over as president at this point, but he continues to be ignored, and Bowen was only belatedly removed from his FIFA position last year, after Zimako supporters had written directly to Michael Garcia, when he was still on FIFA's Ethics Committee.[12]

The leap from small football associations to lucrative international positions

Bowen is hardly the first local football official to have established a domestic position of power through intimidation and then win promotion to a well-paid executive-level position at a regional or international body.[13] Moreover, making the transition can be difficult; and the sudden leap in income can also have a detrimental impact on the behaviour and expectations of newly enriched sporting officials. Whereas in richer economies, notably in western Europe, there is less of a discrepancy between the pay for national football association members and that of other high-level civic or business positions,[14] the gulf between average national salaries and those of regional or international football associations can be enormous, particularly when officials secure a paid position at FIFA, where the average annual salary is £128,000 (some US$194,000).[15]

In 2010 the then Guyana Football Federation (GFF) president, Colin Klass, insisted on flying first-class to the United Kingdom to watch his national team, at a cost of US$10,576.[16] Ultimately, Klass decided against making this trip for unknown reasons, but the incident illustrates the types of demands made by former domestic officials from poorer economies when they obtain the elite, five-star lifestyle of the international football executive. Ignoring or becoming enmeshed in poor governance is often the next step. If FIFA intervenes, this often happens only after a long period of poor governance that must surely have been known at some level in the world body but went ignored. FIFA later, in September 2011, suspended Klass for 26 months from all football activities,[17] but elections to vote in a new president were not held until April 2013.[18] His replacement, Christopher Mathias, proved so unpopular that some elements of Guyanese football wanted Klass back, and there was no intervention taken by FIFA until Mathias had excluded virtually all overseas players from the national team and had libelled a football agent on live television.[19]

Poor governance and the failure of FIFA to press for change

Only after numerous instances of poor governance had been exposed on a wider level in the international media did FIFA belatedly take action and appoint a normalisation committee to run the game in Guyana.[20] This is the last resort for FIFA, and all too often such action is taken only when domestic governance has completely broken down – to the detriment of all levels of the game. The disappearance of nearly US$1 million worth of FIFA funds from a GOAL development project[21] in Antigua and Barbuda was repeatedly exposed at the local level for a decade, with journalist Ian 'Magic' Hughes even losing his job over the issue in 2005.[22] It was not until March 2014 that FIFA finally suspended the annual US$250,000 Financial Assistance Programme (FAP) payment; it also imposed a fine of Swiss Fr. 30,000 (some US$31,500) on the Antigua and Barbuda Football Association, after it had been accused on a wider international level of trying to mortgage the site for the GOAL project even though it had been purchased using FIFA funds.[23]

Too often officials are allowed to disregard basic standards of governance and accountability because of the freedom they are given through a combination of ennui among the international media, local conflicts of interest and the inability of politicians – in times of real need – to intervene. In the British Overseas Territory of Anguilla, Raymond Guishard, the president of the national association, the Anguilla Football Association (AFA), was suspended by FIFA from all football activity for 45 days for his part in the 2011 Port of Spain bribery scandal that also led to the banning of Colin Klass.[24] Guishard did not explain this suspension to the AFA, in part due to the inopportune timing of his suspension during an ongoing dispute between the AFA and three disenfranchised clubs over both youth development and overseas players.[25] It was reported that, in February 2012, the disenfranchised clubs had not had access to information on the 2011 or even 2010 AFA financial accounts.[26] Damien Hughes, from Antigua, was the acting general secretary of the Caribbean Football Union (CFU) at the time, during which the CFU took no action.[27] Between 2000 and 2010 the AFA received US$3.5 million from FIFA in FAP and GOAL funds, yet managed to play just 17 internationals.[28] Only in 2015 did Anguilla finally play its first ever full international match on the island, even though in 2010 FIFA president Sepp Blatter had inaugurated a US$653,976 football centre, which was funded mainly by a US$400,000 GOAL grant and another US$200,000 grant from the world body's FAP.[29]

Implications of poor governance and challenges for grassroots football development

Further down the FIFA rankings, there is often a disconnect between international and grassroots football. Some FIFA members only play senior male internationals in World Cup qualifying, which can mean there is a four-year gap between matches.[30] If children do not have a national team to which they aspire, they can easily give up on the game entirely. A lack of opportunities after primary school was another main concern of the disenfranchised AFA clubs.[31] Anguilla is among the world's least active national teams, but the most inert in the first decade of the new millennium was that of São Tomé e Príncipe, which played just seven matches.[32] After losing to Libya in 2003, its Federação Santomense de Futebol (FSF) subsequently cancelled four national club championships and merged another.[33] São Tomé e Príncipe disappeared from the FIFA rankings, and only after FSF president Manuel Dende had left in 2010, after 12 years in charge, did the country's football association then stage another international.[34] In the decade prior to Dende's departure the FSF received US$3.9 million from FIFA, and the end result was no development from club through to international football.[35] With senior national teams not playing and clubs in turn complaining about a lack of youth development from the national association, this suggests an obvious lack of priorities and therefore poor governance despite the large financial incentives from FIFA.

The lack of senior international participation is not always due to poor governance, and for some of the more remote national associations, particularly in areas such as Oceania, the cost of playing internationals can be prohibitive. Sara Barema, the CEO of Football Federation Samoa (FFS), described senior international matches as a 'waste of resources in terms of air fares and preparation costs'.[36] The FFS is now focused on grassroots development and junior participation, but this only came after the FFS had been suspended by FIFA in 2008 for playing too few internationals to meet FIFA requirements and running up huge debts, and a normalisation committee was sent to run the game there.[37]

In some smaller, poorer countries, FAP funds can be a significant tool in both helping compensate for the lack of government investment in grassroots sport and also for generating much-needed employment opportunities, which then empower both the association and the president – but not always for the good of the game. Local calls for accountability following alleged misuses of funds or poor governance are hard to sustain without government backing, as FIFA prohibits such government involvement, but the example of Belize shows this can be achieved. In April 2011, the central American country's sports minister, John Salvidar, asked Bertie Chimilio, the president of the Football Federation of Belize (FFB), to answer questions about 'numerous irregularities, misconduct and improprieties', and the country's clubs threatened to form their own association if no answers were forthcoming.[38] The result of this standoff was that the FFB agreed to rewrite its statutes and hold open elections, which resulted in Chimilio departing office in 2013.[39] The FFB was left broke and no action was taken against Chimilio, but a positive change that improved governance was achieved not because of but in spite of FIFA.[40]

Conclusions

FIFA has frequently been found wanting when trying to police governance at smaller associations.

FIFA insists that 'members which do not participate in at least two of all FIFA competitions over a period of four consecutive years shall be suspended from voting at the Congress until they have fulfilled their obligations in this respect',[41] but there is no financial penalty for inaction or lack of development. The only conditions for stopping development money are if 'funds may not have been used in accordance with the approved application in every respect'.[42]

Much of Blatter's support has traditionally come from associations that are grateful for this financial support from FIFA, however, and often they are equally indebted to the international media for its lack of interest in their governance. A solution has been offered by FIFA presidential candidate Jérôme Champagne, whose manifesto included proposals for a Division of National Associations to monitor all member associations daily and to provide support and improve governance.[43]

Even if Champagne's admirable initiative is not enacted, another, simpler, solution could be found. The FAP began in 1999, and FIFA distributes US$250,000 a year to all member associations, sometimes more in World Cup years.[44] In return, FIFA should demand that all 209 members be paid only when detailed annual financial accounts and the results of executive votes and personnel changes are made available to the public via its website. While FIFA does publish financial accounts, the results of votes and personnel changes could be expanded upon as an example for the world body's members. This would provide valuable information that could be used by clubs, politicians and the media – or a coalition of all three – to monitor governance and would, surely, be for the good of the game everywhere.

Box 1.2 FIFA and the non-interference rule

Mark Baber[45]

The Statutes of the Fédération Internationale de Football Association (FIFA) state that all member associations have an obligation to 'manage their affairs independently and ensure that their own affairs are not influenced by any third parties'.[46] FIFA's director of member associations and development, Thierry Regenass, has described political interference in the following terms: 'FIFA has the mandate to control association football worldwide, in all its aspects. This mandate is delegated to the national association, to control association football at the national level . . . The associations have the obligation to do it on their own, in an autonomous way without outside interference, from the government or any other parties. In general, political interference is when a government tries to take direct control.'[47]

In practice, however, recent cases have demonstrated a different dynamic. Although protecting football officials from unreasonable government behaviour is uncontroversial, FIFA's so-called 'non-interference rule' appears to be being used as a pretext to defend national federations from legitimate demands for transparency in the spending of public resources (government money is often essential to the running of football) and from the desire of individuals to see fairness in elections and an end to corruption in the running of football administration. Political figures aiming to hold national football federations or their officials accountable often feel that they have their hands tied; no one wants to risk FIFA's suspension of the national football federation, and therefore risk significant support from their football-loving constituencies. This threat often keeps governments from responding to the most blatant examples of corruption in national football administration.

In Nigeria, FIFA has aggressively invoked the non-interference rule and the threat of suspension, intervening a number of times in an ongoing factional crisis within the national association, the Nigeria Football Federation (NFF).[48] FIFA's interventions are presumed to have been in order to protect one group within the NFF from government interference as well as from attempts by rival factions and individuals to enforce their own civil rights through local civil courts. Most recently, in October 2014, the Nigerian Federal Court annulled the results of a disputed NFF election that had been carried out in defiance of a court order.[49] Soon afterwards, FIFA secretary general Jérôme Valcke wrote to one of the two men claiming to be the head of the NFF, insisting that the Federation would be suspended if the case were not withdrawn from the civil courts.[50]

Although in Nigeria FIFA's actions have, ostensibly, been to prevent football matters being dragged through the courts, in Kenya the organisation has stood aside while the Football Kenya Federation (FKF) instituted civil court proceedings, in early 2015, in an attempt to have the leadership of the widely praised Kenyan Premier League, who were seen as an obstacle to the Federation's commercial ambitions (and, it has been alleged, to the ambitions of the president of the FKF to favour a club from his home area), imprisoned for contempt of court as part of a court action brought by the Federation to close down the country's top league.[51]

Questions need to be asked as to why the non-interference rule has not been effectively and consistently applied to prevent political interference from all countries, including some of the more powerful ones (such as the alleged role of the French and German governments in influencing

World Cup bids).[52] Questions also need to be asked about why the rule has not been used to prevent the involvement of football in government campaigns. For example, FIFA remained silent when the government of Bahrain, including Sheikh Salman bin Ebrahim Al-Khalifa, then candidate for the AFC presidency and FIFA Executive Committee, cracked down on peaceful demonstrators, including football administrators and referees.[53] In a meeting of the Bahrain Football Association (BFA), Sheikh Salman bin Ebrahim Al-Khalifa insisted the BFA remove individuals proven to have participated in the peaceful protests.[54] The rule also continues to be used as a tool of legitimacy for authoritarian regimes in which there is no separation between political power and football administration, such as Qatar.[55]

Notes

1   Steve Menary is a freelance journalist who contributes to *World Soccer* magazine and the World Football show on BBC World Service on football in smaller members of FIFA. He is also an author and visiting lecturer at the University of Winchester and Southampton Solent University.

2   This was the result of a grassroots development programme started in 2010 by the same coach, Eddy Etaeta. Before winning the OFC Nations Cup, Tahiti had reached the finals of the 2009 U20 World Cup and the final of the 2011 OFC U17 Championship. *World Soccer* (UK), 'Brazil awaits', November 2012.

3   After Tahiti's showing in the Confederations Cup, BBC football commentator Robbie Savage said that 'poor' teams like Tahiti 'devalue tournaments'. In 2010 Tahitian FIFA Executive Committee member Raymond Temarii was suspended for his involvement in the votes-for-sale scandal: Fédération Internationale de Football Association, 'Statement of the Chairman of the Adjudicatory Chamber of the FIFA Ethics Committee', 13 November 2014, *www.fifa. com/mm/document/affederation/footballgovernance/02/47/41/75/statementchairman adjcheckert_neutral.pdf.*

4   Fédération Internationale de Football Association, 'Associations', *www.fifa.com/ associations/index.html.*

5   See Roger Pielke Jr, Chapter 1.4 'Obstacles to accountability in international sports governance', in this report.

6   *When Saturday Comes* (UK), 'Carrot on a stick', February 2010.

7   For further reading on the arguments for and against the autonomy of national football associations, see Jean-Loup Chappelet, Chapter 1.3, 'Autonomy and governance: necessary bedfellows in the fight against corruption in sport', in this report.

8   *World Soccer* (UK), 'FIFA steps in at troubled federation', November 2014.

9   Ibid.

10 Ibid.

11 A copy of Chung's letter is in the author's possession.

12 Letter from Le COLLECTIF pour la Défense des Intérêts et du Développement Technique du Football, 15 April 2013, in the author's possession.

13 Letter from Le COLLECTIF pour la Défense des Intérêts et du Développement Technique du Football, 12 June 2014, to FIFA president Sepp Blatter, in the author's possession. In this letter, the Collective claim to 'not go a week without aggression'.

14 The average Union of European Football Associations salary is £97,000 (US$147,000): *Guardian* (UK), 'Said and done', 11 April 2015, *www.theguardian.com/football/2015/apr/11/ said-and-done-sepp-blatter-issa-hayatou.*

15 Ibid.; Sporting Intelligence (US), 'FIFA paid $88.6m in salaries in 2014: we can guesstimate Blatter's take at $6m+', 20 March 2015, *www.sportingintelligence.*

com/2015/03/20/fifa-paid-88-6m-in-salaries-in-2014-we-can-guesstimate-blatters-take-at-11m-200301.

16 Details of the travel reservation are available to the author.

17 In September 2011 Klass was banned by FIFA from all football activity for 26 months: Fédération Internationale de Football Association, 'Ethics Committee bans Guyana FA president Colin Klass for 26 months', 23 September 2011, www.fifa.com/aboutfifa/organisation/news/newsid=1515457.

18 News Source (Guyana), 'Klass resurfaces after FIFA ban', 1 January 2014, http://news sourcegy.com/sports/klass-resurfaces-after-fifa-ban/.

19 World Soccer (UK), 'In Guyana, overseas players are not wanted', October 2014.

20 Guyana Chronicle (Guyana), 'FIFA names GFF normalisation committee', 28 October 2014.

21 The GOAL project is an initiative by FIFA to assist countries around the world to construct their own football facilities for the development and continued progress of football activities. In Antigua, FIFA granted applications for three GOAL projects on the same site for a total of US$1.3 million, but only a minor amount of work has been undertaken to build walls around the site. An estimated US$1 million remains missing/unspent. Play the Game (Denmark), 'Something rotten in the football state of Antigua', 9 November 2005, www.playthegame.org/news/news-articles/2005/something-rotten-in-the-football-state-of-Antigua. See also Fédération Internationale de Football Association, 'Antigua and Barbuda GOAL programme', www.fifa.com/development/facts-and-figures/association=atg/index.html; and Play the Game (Denmark), 'Antigua's field of gold', in Play the Game Magazine 2006, p. 2, www.playthegame.org/upload/magazine%202005/realtransparency.pdf.

22 Play the Game (2006).

23 World Soccer (UK), 'Where did the money go?', April 2014.

24 Reuters (UK), 'Soccer: FIFA bans six more Caribbean officials', 18 November 2011, http://uk.reuters.com/article/2011/11/18/soccer-fifa-bans-idUKL3E7MI2K120111118.

25 Letter from Roaring Lions, Strikers and KICKS United to the author, 15 March 2012.

26 World Soccer (UK), 'Caribbean Union hit by fresh controversy', May 2012.

27 Ibid.

28 The Blizzard (UK) 'What's a vote worth? How FIFA's attempt to devolve power could be a bribers' charter', December 2011.

29 World Soccer (May 2012), with details on Anguilla's FIFA grants available here: www.fifa.com/development/facts-and-figures/association=aia/index.html.

30 The Bahamas and Tonga did not play a senior international between the 2014 and 2018 World Cup qualifiers, while Papua New Guinea dropped off the FIFA rankings altogether after not playing a match between July 2007 and August 2011.

31 Ibid.

32 The Blizzard (December 2011).

33 Ibid.

34 Ibid.

35 Ibid.

36 Author interview with Sara Barema, 13 May 2013.

37 When Saturday Comes (February 2010).

38 Irish Times, 'Northern Ireland is the most successful country ever in World Cup finals', 12 June 2014, www.irishtimes.com/sport/soccer/northern-ireland-is-the-most-successful-country-ever-in-world-cup-finals-1.1828661.

39 Ibid..

40 News 5 (Belize), 'No witch hunt for former F.F.B. President, Dr. Bertie Chimilio', 27 March 2012, http://edition.channel5belize.com/archives/68549.

41 Fédération Internationale de Football Association, FIFA Statutes: Regulations Governing the Application of the Statutes – Standing Orders of the Congress (Zurich: FIFA, 2008), article 14.4, p. 12.

42 Fédération Internationale de Football Association, General Regulations for FIFA Development Programmes (Zurich: FIFA, 2013), www.fifa.com/mm/document/footballdevelopment/

generic/02/22/32/94/12_11_2013_generalregulationsforfifadevelopmentprogrammes_
neutral.pdf.

43 Jérôme Champagne, 'My agenda for the twenty first century FIFA', letter no. 6, annex 1,
20 October 2014, *www.jeromechampagne2015.com/documents/document_fusionne_en.pdf.*

44 Fédération Internationale de Football Association, *Regulations: FIFA Financial Assistance
Programme (FAP)* (Zurich: FIFA, 2013), *www.fifa.com/mm/document/footballdevelopment/
fap/50/16/69/12_11_2013_fapregulations_neutral.pdf,* and *FIFA Circular no. 1463, http://
resources.fifa.com/mm/document/affederation/administration/02/49/61/02/circularno.1463-
fifafinancialassistanceprogramme2015%28fap%29andbonusrelatingtothe2011-2014financial
resultsregulationsandadministrativeguidelinesfor2015_neutral.pdf.*

45 Mark Baber is a Director of 11v11 and a contributor to Inside World Football.

46 Fédération Internationale de Football Association, *FIFA Statutes* (Zurich: FIFA, 2015), p. 13,
article 13(1)(i), *www.fifa.com/mm/Document/AFFederation/Generic/02/58/14/48/2015FIFAS
tatutesEN_Neutral.pdf.*

47 Fédération Internationale de Football Association, 'Regenass: we have strong principles',
19 October 2011, *www.fifa.com/about-fifa/news/y=2011/m=10/news=regenass-have-
strong-principles-1528544.html.*

48 Inside World Football, 'FIFA orders Nigeria to withdraw court case or face seven-month
ban', 29 October 2014, *www.insideworldfootball.com/world-football/africa/15742-
fifa-orders-nigeria-to-withdraw-court-case-or-face-seven-month-ban.*

49 Ibid.

50 Ibid.

51 Inside World Football, 'FIFA "monitoring situation" as court decides fate of Kenyan football',
6 March 2015, *www.insideworldfootball.com/world-football/africa/16561-fifa-monitoring-
situation-as-court-decides-fate-of-kenyan-football.*

52 Reuters (UK), 'French, German presidents tried to influence World Cup votes: Blatter in
paper', 5 July 2015, *www.reuters.com/article/2015/07/05/us-soccer-fifa-blatter-
idUSKCN0PF0JF20150705.*

53 Football Rights, 'Bahrain human rights group asks FIFA to withdraw Salman from AFC
elections', 26 April 2013, *http://footballrights.org/2013/04/26/bahrain-human-rights-
group-asks-fifa-to-withdraw-salman-from-afc-elections.*

54 Ibid.

55 Soccer Politics (US), 'Qatari foundations', 26 August 2013, *https://sites.duke.edu/wcwp/
2013/08/26/qatari-foundations.*

1.11

Image-laundering by countries through sports

Naomi Westland[1]

Fifty years ago this summer, from the sidelines at Wembley, the so-called 'Russian linesman' flagged for England's controversial third World Cup final goal against West Germany, helping to drive Bobby Moore's team to a 4–2 victory and, to date, England's only World Cup win.[2]

The linesman's name was Tofiq Bahramov, and he wasn't actually from Russia but Azerbaijan, and – until recently – that country's only real sporting claim to fame.[3] That all changed in the summer of 2015, however, when Baku hosted the first ever European Games, an event devised by the European Olympic Committees (EOC) as a continent-wide sporting extravaganza to rival the Asian and Pan-American Games, with some 6,000 athletes from 50 countries taking part in 20 sports.

Those already having heard of the event are unlikely to have done so for the sport. It's far more likely to have been for things that Azerbaijan's government would have much preferred the public did not know, such as the systematic dismantling of civil society in the run-up to the Games, which saw journalists, lawyers, opposition politicians and youth activists intimidated, harassed, arrested and locked up on trumped-up charges.[4] There are at least 20 people designated as prisoners of conscience by Amnesty International in Azerbaijan, jailed simply for criticising or challenging the government, and there could be up to 100 political prisoners.[5]

Azerbaijan, as described below, is one of various examples of image-laundering by countries or heads of state through sports, in order to attract positive attention both from the global community and at home, and often to divert concerns over serious allegations of corruption and human rights. Such strategies are made worse when leaders or administrations, for private or undue interests, garner this attention through sport by the use of massive amounts of public funds that could otherwise be used for far better purposes in the interest of their citizens.

Image-laundering and human rights concerns in Azerbaijan

Azerbaijan wanted to use the European Games, and the international media attention it hoped they would bring, to convince the world that it is a modern, dynamic, progressive country. This image-laundering exercise turned into a disaster, however, when the world cottoned on to the human rights abuses going on behind the glitz and glamour of the event. The government then did itself no favours by banning Amnesty International from entering the country to launch a new report on the crackdown the day before the opening ceremony.[6] Then, as if it did not realise that this had attracted enough of the wrong kind of attention, it blocked journalists from *The Guardian*, Radio France International and Germany's ARD channel from covering the event.[7]

The European Games are not the only sporting pie into which Azerbaijan has stuck its fingers. Baku will host Formula 1 in 2016, as well as three group stage games and one quarter-final in the European Football Championships in 2020.[8] The country has bid twice for the Olympics.[9]

To avoid a repeat of the PR catastrophe of the European Games when these other events come to town, the Azerbaijani government will need to make some urgent improvements to the country's human rights record. It could start by freeing all those who have been wrongly jailed, such as Intigam Aliyev, a prominent human rights lawyer who was sentenced to a seven-and-a-half-year jail term in April 2015 on trumped-up charges of tax evasion, illegal business dealings and abuse of power, after he had successfully taken a number of cases against the Azerbaijani government to the European Court of Human Rights.[10]

Another example is Rasul Jafarov, the head of a non-governmental organisation (NGO) called the Human Rights Club, sentenced to six and a half years on similar charges, also in April 2015. He had organised the Sing for Democracy campaign when the Eurovision Song Contest was held in Baku in 2012, and had been planning to launch a Sport for Rights campaign around the European Games.[11]

Then there is Khadija Ismayilova, an award-winning journalist for Radio Free Europe/Radio Liberty, who had been investigating claims of corruption at the highest levels of government when she was arrested in December 2014.[12] She was accused of 'inciting a colleague to suicide' and other false charges.[13] The colleague later said that he had been forced to file the complaint and that his suicide attempt was nothing to do with her.[14] Ismayilova has been harassed by the authorities over many years, and if she is found guilty of the charges currently against her she could be sentenced to 12 years in prison.[15]

Olympic Games are supposed to embrace the concepts of peace, respect and mutual understanding.[16] It is hard to see how these ideals could ever have been honoured in a country with an already repressive regime that escalated its human rights crackdown in the run-up to an Olympic event. Despite this, few in the Olympic Movement spoke out. Amnesty International heard nothing from the International Olympic Committee (IOC), nothing from the EOC and nothing from the vast majority of national Olympic committees that had sent teams to compete. Only the German and Swedish Olympic Committees raised their concerns publicly.[17]

Image-laundering is not limited to mega-events, but applies more broadly in sports as well, as reflected on the shirts of Atlético Madrid players, which for the last three seasons had 'Azerbaijan, Land of Fire', emblazoned across the front (the slogan changed to 'Baku 2015' as the Games approached), and on the club's website, which features promotional materials on tourism and business opportunities in the country.[18]

Azerbaijan, however, is not the only country with a poor human rights record guilty of using sport – and in particular mega-events – for political gain. A pattern is starting to emerge of these being awarded to countries with money to burn and images to burnish, either as a way of attracting outside investment or consolidating power at home.

Further concerns of image-laundering and human rights: Brazil, Russia and Qatar

In the run-up to the 2014 men's football World Cup in Brazil, a powerful campaign got under way, highlighting the lack of government investment in public transport, schools and hospitals against the spending on the World Cup. The police response to the street protests was brutal, however. Policemen fired rubber bullets and tear gas and beat protesters with hand-held batons.[19] There have also been forced evictions of whole communities to make way for infrastructure for the World Cup and the 2016 Summer Olympics in Rio de Janeiro.[20] This means that thousands have been turfed out of their homes, often violently, and not offered adequate alternative accommodation.[21] If they are offered anything at all, it tends to be miles away from their schools, work, family and friends.[22]

Meanwhile, the Winter Olympics in Sochi in 2014 exposed Russia's appalling record on lesbian, gay, bisexual and transgender (LGBT) rights, environmental protection and freedom of expression. These issues will again come to the fore, no doubt, when the country hosts the 2018 World Cup. In 2015, in a move that Amnesty International described as the latest in an unprecedented crackdown on NGOs, the Russian government introduced a new law banning foreign organisations deemed to be undermining 'state security', 'national defence' or 'constitutional order'.[23] It will also punish Russian activists and civil society groups for maintaining ties with 'undesirable' organisations.[24]

In the Middle East, Qatar is building for the 2022 World Cup. Those doing the actual building – migrant workers, mostly from India and Nepal – are being subjected to horrendous working conditions, however, including having their wages withheld and being prevented from leaving the country without permission from their employer.[25] A recent Amnesty International analysis of progress made on improving migrant workers' rights since the Qatari government promised a number of reforms in 2014 showed not only that the government's pledges had offered too little in the first place, but that it had delivered even less.[26] To complete the picture there is the choice the IOC faces in July 2015, when it announces the winning bid for the 2022 Winter Olympics. At the time of writing, Lviv in Ukraine, Krakow in Poland and Stockholm in Sweden had dropped out of the race, leaving only Almaty, Kazakhstan, and Beijing, China, in the running, both of which have unenviable human rights records.[27]

The need for reform: actions from international sports governing bodies

For too long, sports governing bodies have buried their heads in the sand regarding their responsibility to ensure that their events do not lead to, or exacerbate, human rights abuses. Improvements to bidding criteria are key to turning around this sorry state of affairs, but they must be more than a tick-box exercise. This means that human rights need to be central to the whole process of hosting an event, from initial bids to delivery to evaluation and legacy, and awarding bodies need to make a solid assessment of whether a country or city can and will comply with any promises made on paper.

In December 2014 the IOC approved Agenda 2020, which provides new standards for Olympic events, including clauses on labour rights and respect for LGBT rights, as well as a requirement for host cities to use existing sports infrastructure in order to keep costs down.[28] If they are implemented effectively, these reforms could go some way to prevent governments from using sports mega-events as a vehicle for laundering their images for undue interests. The almost complete silence of the Olympic movement over the European Games perhaps indicates that the spirit of Agenda 2020 is far from being wholly embraced, however. The key test of the IOC's commitment to change will be the 2024 Summer Olympics, from when Agenda 2020 applies, with applications to bid having closed in September 2015.

FIFA, for its part, has promised revised bidding criteria for the hosting of World Cups, but has yet to provide detail on what they will contain. What is clear, though, is that human rights need to be at the heart of all stages of the hosting process, and, when abuses happen, those responsible for upholding these values and ensuring that promises are kept must hold host governments to account. If they don't, major sports events will continue to leave large-scale despair in their wake.

Box 1.3 France, Qatar and the purchase of Paris Saint-Germain

Kelly McCarthy[29]

Image-laundering is a clear example of the undue influence of politics in sport. The circumstances that saw the overlap of the Qatari purchase of Paris Saint-Germain (PSG) football club and the French support for the Qatar 2022 World Cup bid raise similar concerns for undue political influence in sport.

In November 2010, one month before the Executive Committee of the Fédération Internationale de Football Association (FIFA) voted on the host countries for the 2018 and 2022 World Cups, then president of France and PSG supporter Nicolas Sarkozy reportedly hosted a lunch in the Élysée Palace attended by Tamim bin Hamad al-Thani, the crown prince of Qatar, Sebastien Bazin, the European representative of PSG's then 95 per cent majority owners Colony Capital[30] and the president of the Union of European Football Associations (UEFA), Michel Platini, who was also one of 22 FIFA Executive Committee members empowered with a vote for the 2018 and 2022 World Cup bids.[31]

Sarkozy is reported to have encouraged the purchase of the club by Qatar Sports Investments (QSI), a state-owned entity of the Qatari government, which was then in the process of bidding to host the 2022 event.[32] Also reportedly part of the three-pronged deal, in addition to the PSG purchase and the World Cup vote, was the opportunity for the Qatari state-owned Al Jazeera network to buy a stake in the broadcast rights of France's Ligue 1.[33] Platini was allegedly encouraged by the president to vote for the Qatari bid.[34] Indeed, referring to the then French and German presidents, FIFA president Sepp Blatter stated in July 2015 that 'Messrs Sarkozy and Wulff tried to influence their vote-makers . . . That is the reason why we now have a World Cup in Qatar.'[35]

Platini did ultimately cast his vote for the successful Qatar 2022 World Cup bid.[36] Six months later, in May 2011, QSI purchased 70 per cent of PSG.[37] The details of the sale were not made public, but the amount is understood to have been between €30 million (US$43 million) and €40 million (US$58 million).[38] Three weeks after QSI's purchase of the club, Al Jazeera bought the rights to broadcast France Ligue 1, Ligue 2, Coupe de la Ligue and Trophée des Champions matches internationally, for €192 million (US$274 million) a year from 2012 to 2016, thus gaining an interest in promoting French football as widely as possible.[39] Al Jazeera also purchased the rights to broadcast a portion of Ligue 1 matches within France, for €90 million (US$129 million) a year, also from 2012 to 2016, which came at a time when it was thought that Ligue 1 TV revenues were on the verge of declining.[40] The chairman of QSI is also the president of PSG as well as the general manager of Al Jazeera Sport.[41] Platini has maintained that his vote for the Qatari World Cup bid was not linked to any political pressure.[42] Soon afterwards, in early 2012, Platini's son became the chief executive at Burrda, a QSI subsidiary,[43] and in January 2015 he became a legal adviser for QSI's European operations.[44]

QSI ultimately purchased the remaining 30 per cent of PSG in March 2012, for an amount understood to have been about €30 million (US$43 million).[45] QSI has spent £300 million (US$470 million) on player transfers since its 2011 purchase of the club, thus helping propel the team to the top of the Ligue 1 standings.[46] Since the takeover, PSG has gone from a fourth place finish in Ligue 1 in the 2010–2011 season to winning its third consecutive league title in May 2015.

Notes

1   Naomi Westland is media manager at Amnesty International UK, covering issues of sport and human rights, Europe, Latin America, lesbian, gay, bisexual and transgender issues and refugees.
2   Amnesty International (UK), 'Azerbaijan, "the Russian linesman" and other dodgy sporting decisions', 20 March 2015, *www.amnesty.org.uk/blogs/global-voices/azerbaijan-russian-linesman-european-games-baku-sports-human-rights.*
3   Ibid.
4   Amnesty International (UK), 'Azerbaijan: European Games legacy tainted by repressive crackdown', press release, 26 June 2015, *www.amnesty.org/en/press-releases/2015/06/azerbaijan-european-games-legacy-tainted-by-repressive-crackdown-1.*
5   Radio Free Europe/Radio Liberty (Czech Republic), 'US official, BBG slam raid on RFE/RL's Baku bureau', 27 December 2014, *www.rferl.org/content/azerbaijan-rferl-baku-bureau-raided/26763449.html.*
6   *Daily Express* (UK), 'Human rights activists banned from European Games in Azerbaijan', 10 June 2015, *www.express.co.uk/news/world/583533/Amnesty-Platform-banned-European-Games-in-Azerbaijan.*
7   Amnesty International (26 June 2015).
8   Union of European Football Associations, 'UEFA EURO 2020 hosts: London to hold final', 19 September 2014, *www.uefa.com/uefaeuro-2020/news/newsid=1844904.html.*
9   *USA Today*, 'Azerbaijan says 2024 Olympic bid possible', 23 June 2015, *www.usatoday.com/story/sports/olympics/2015/06/23/azerbaijan-says-2024-olympic-bid-possible/29160343.*
10   Amnesty International (UK), 'European Games: Amnesty urges Lord Coe to speak out against human rights abuses in Azerbaijan ahead of opening ceremony', press release, 2 June 2015, *www.amnesty.org.uk/press-releases/european-games-amnesty-urges-lord-coe-speak-out-against-human-rights-abuses.*
11   *Independent* (UK), 'Singing in Azerbaijan: but not for democracy', 12 May 2012, *www.independent.co.uk/news/world/europe/singing-in-azerbaijan--but-not-for-democracy-7737804.html*; Amnesty International (2 June 2015).
12   Amnesty International (2 June 2015).
13   PEN (US), 'Khadija Ismayilova, Azerbaijan', *www.pen.org/defending-writers/khadija-ismayilova.*
14   Organized Crime and Corruption Reporting Project, 'About Khadija Ismayilova', *www.occrp.org/freekhadijaismayilova/khadija-ismayilova.php.*
15   Ibid.
16   International Olympic Committee, *Olympic Charter: In Force as from 8 December 2014* (Lausanne: IOC, 2014), *www.olympic.org/Documents/olympic_charter_en.pdf.*
17   Amnesty International (26 June 2015).
18   Atlético de Madrid, 'Azerbaijan: land of fire', *http://en.clubatleticodemadrid.com/atm/azerbaijan-3.*
19   BBC (UK), 'Brazil World Cup: clashes at Sao Paulo and Rio protests', 13 June 2014, *www.bbc.co.uk/news/world-latin-america-27811657.*
20   International Business Times (US), 'Forced evictions in Brazil shadow Olympic, World Cup preparations', 14 August 2012, *www.ibtimes.com/forced-evictions-brazil-shadow-olympic-world-cup-preparations-746530.*
21   National Public Radio (US), 'As Brazil gears up for Olympics, some poor families get moved out', 27 February 2014, *www.npr.org/sections/parallels/2014/02/27/276514012/as-brazil-gears-up-for-olympics-some-poor-families-get-moved-out*; *Guardian* (UK), 'Forced evictions in Rio favela for 2016 Olympics trigger violent clashes', 3 June 2015, *www.theguardian.com/world/2015/jun/03/forced-evictions-vila-autodromo-rio-olympics-protests.*
22   National Public Radio (27 February 2014); *Guardian* (3 June 2015).
23   *Independent* (UK), 'Putin signs new law to ban "undesirable" organisations from Russia', 24 May 2015, *www.independent.co.uk/news/world/europe/putin-signs-new-law-to-ban-*

undesirable-organisations-from-russia-10273199.html; Amnesty International (UK), 'Russia: law on "undesirable organizations" will further tighten the noose on dissent', 20 January 2015, *www.amnesty.org/en/latest/news/2015/01/russia-law-undesirable-organizations-will-further-tighten-noose-dissent.*

24   *Independent* (24 May 2015); Amnesty International (20 January 2015).

25   Amnesty International (UK), 'Qatar: the grim reality behind the World Cup 2022', 10 November 2014, *www.amnesty.org.uk/qatar-grim-reality-behind-world-cup-2022#.VXm7cEv5LjQ.*

26   Amnesty International (UK), 'Mounting risk of World Cup built on abuse as Qatar fails to deliver on reforms', 21 May 2015, *www.amnesty.org/en/latest/news/2015/05/mounting-risk-of-world-cup-built-on-abuse-as-qatar-fails-to-deliver-reforms.*

27   Fox News (US), 'China, Kazakhstan roll out bids for 2022 Winter Olympics', 8 June 2015, *http://latino.foxnews.com/latino/sports/2015/06/08/china-kazakhstan-roll-out-bids-for-2022-winter-olympics*; Amnesty International (UK), 'China: Amnesty International Report 2014/15', *www.amnesty.org/en/countries/asia-and-the-pacific/china*; Amnesty International (UK), 'Kazakhstan: Amnesty International Report 2014/15', *www.amnesty.org/en/countries/europe-and-central-asia/kazakhstan.*

28   International Olympic Committee, *Olympic Agenda 2020: 20+20 Recommendations* (Lausanne: IOC, 2014), *www.olympic.org/Documents/Olympic_Agenda_2020/Olympic_Agenda_2020-20-20_Recommendations-ENG.pdf.*

29   Kelly McCarthy is associate editor of the *Global Corruption Report: Sport.*

30   Unprofessional Foul, 'PSG is for sale. Sort of', 29 December 2010, *http://unprofessionalfoul.com/2010/12/29/psg-is-for-sale-sort-of.*

31   *Guardian* (UK), 'Qatar cash is stirring French football revolution at Paris St-Germain', 22 November 2011, *www.theguardian.com/football/blog/2011/nov/22/qatar-psg-french-football-al-jazeera*; Goal, 'UEFA inquiry into sponsorship deals highlights problematic fight against corruption', 6 February 2013, *www.goal.com/en-sg/news/3883/features/2013/02/06/3730377/uefa-inquiry-into-sponsorship-deals-highlights-problematic-fight.*

32   *Daily Mirror* (UK), 'Qatar hero? Why Michel Platini might not be the man to save FIFA', 29 May 2015, *www.mirror.co.uk/sport/football/news/qatar-hero-michel-platini-might-5783843.*

33   Goal (6 February 2013).

34   *Guardian* (22 November 2011).

35   Reuters (UK), 'French, German presidents tried to influence World Cup votes: Blatter in paper', 5 July 2015, *www.reuters.com/article/2015/07/05/us-soccer-fifa-blatter-idUSKCN0PF0JF20150705.*

36   *Daily Mirror* (29 May 2015).

37   Ibid.

38   SportsPro, 'QSI completes PSG buyout', 7 March 2012, *www.sportspromedia.com/news/qsi_completes_psg_buyout.*

39   SportsPro, 'Al Jazeera Sports wins Ligue 1 distribution rights', 31 May 2011, *www.sportspromedia.com/news/al_jazeera_sports_wins_ligue_1_international_distribution_rights.*

40   ESPN (US), 'Al Jazeera make move into Ligue 1', 23 June 2011, *www.espnfc.com/story/930049/al-jazeera-make-tv-move-into-french-football.*

41   Ibid.

42   *Daily Telegraph* (UK), 'Qatar World Cup 2022: France embroiled in corruption scandal', 2 June 2014, *www.telegraph.co.uk/sport/football/world-cup/10871065/Qatar-World-Cup-2022-France-embroiled-in-corruption-scandal.html.*

43   *Guardian* (UK), 'Michel Platini: "All the decisions I make are for the good of football"', 24 May 2013, *www.theguardian.com/football/2013/may/24/michel-platini-uefa-football.*

44   *Daily Telegraph* (2 June 2014).

45   SportsPro (7 March 2012).

46   *Sport 360°* (UAE), 'Inside story: PSG have transformed under QSI's huge investment', 25 May 2015, *http://sport360.com/article/european/37199/inside-story-psg-have-transformed-under-qsi%E2%80%99s-huge-investment.*

1.12

Opening the door to corruption in Hungary's sport financing

Miklós Ligeti and Gyula Mucsi[1]

As a member of the European Union, Hungary has a democratic system with institutions that were originally established to respect the separation of powers and legal checks and balances. Even though institutionalised corruption and moderate respect for the rights of the political opposition have made democracy vulnerable, a political consensus existed that legislative, executive and judicial powers need to be separated and that the government needs to be controlled by independent institutions.

The government of the Fidesz party,[2] based on an overwhelming majority in parliament resulting from successive landslide victories in national elections, has broken this consensus and 're-engineered' the public arena to its own liking. Essentially, Fidesz has constructed a de facto 'upper house' of government by appointing to public institutions its own loyalists, with often questionable professional careers but with a clear political bias. The government's determination to follow this path has in some cases run contrary to European standards.[3]

A number of examples indicate the government's intention to grant privileges to certain economic actors by legal means, such as the nationalisation and subsequent redistribution of tobacco kiosk concessions, or the same process in the financial sector, with savings cooperatives first being nationalised by law and then reprivatised to an entrepreneur close to the government. In these cases the regulations were tailor-made, hurting market incumbents and favouring new players with close links to the government.[4]

By 2014, when the last session of the previous parliament ended, the edifice of democratic checks and balances in Hungary had been disrupted, its institutional capacity to build equilibrium in public life weakened. In the view of Transparency International Hungary (TI-H), the steps taken by the government have increased corruption risks and have steered the country in the direction of a managed democracy with an Eastern type of state capitalism, and the imminent danger that political influence over independent institutions, the media, business and civil society may be exercised.

Non-governmental organisations (NGOs) that have been critical of the government in the past have come under increased scrutiny from the Government Control Office, primarily Ökotárs, a foundation responsible for coordinating the distribution of European Economic Area (EEA) Grants and Norway Grants.[5] The nature and legitimacy of these audits have been contested both by members of Hungarian civil society and by their Norwegian partners.[6] TI-H maintains that the government's audit stands on shaky legal ground.[7]

The government's overwhelming power coupled with an unprecedentedly high level of centralisation has resulted in a situation of 'state capture', whereby powerful oligarchs either outwit the government or are in symbiosis with influential public decision-makers, allowing them to extract public money from the system through intentionally designed and profession-ally managed channels. This has been followed by the rise of rent-seeking tendencies and cronyism, which distort the functioning of the market economy.

Specific forms of corrupt practices in sports

Hungary's government is proud of the country's outstanding sports traditions. The drive to make Hungarian sports teams, especially football clubs, excel at the European and international levels is widely regarded as sufficiently legitimate grounds for pouring immense sums of public money into the development of sports infrastructure and manufacturing a system of opaque company donations for the promotion of sports clubs and young athletes.

TI-H's judgement is that there are two specific forms of investment into sport that unaccountably absorb taxpayers' money and open the door to corruption in sport financing. One of these is the financial support going to sports clubs through company donations; the other is the public construction of sports facilities, primarily soccer stadiums. Both types fit into the country's current situation of widespread state capture.

Company donations to sports clubs and federations

To attract financial supporters in order to boost Hungarian sporting life, the government introduced a new tax benefit scheme in 2011. Based on the idea that 75 per cent of Hungary's active sports community comes from five branches of sport – football, basketball, handball, ice hockey and water polo, referred to in the law as 'spectator team sports' – the government devised a new system to significantly increase the amount of donations to sport clubs and federations of these five branches. Since 2011, HUF 204 billion (€656 million) have been donated this way.

Under the tax benefit scheme, all corporations subject to corporate income tax in Hungary may give a donation – of up to 80 per cent of their corporate tax – to one of these five branches of sport to gain two types of tax benefits. Companies may reduce their pre-tax profit by the amount of their donations. Moreover, they may also deduct donations from their corporate income tax calculations; donations thus increase companies' overall profit.[8] This does not entitle donor companies to expect a quid pro quo from the supported sports clubs, however, making this donation different from regular sport sponsorship.

This new system of donations has serious transparency implications and raises genuine corruption risks.

- *Lack of transparency of the donations*. Tax-deductible company donations are treated as pure corporate donations, whereas in reality they are more like a form of government subsidy offered by repurposing corporate tax. The opinion that these subsidies are not private donations is supported by the European Commission, which assessed the tax-benefit scheme. According to the Commission "state resources are clearly involved in the scheme since the Hungarian central budget suffers a loss of fiscal revenue as a result of the scheme." Unfortunately since the Hungarian Government views the subventions as private donations, the granting process lacks the transparency necessary to ensure the elimination of corruption risks.[9]

As these company donations do not qualify as public money, they are exempt from requests for public interest information. A recent change in legislation,[10] adopted at breakneck speed during the 2014 Christmas period, lifted this interpretation to the regulatory level, with a realistic prospect of further curtailing the accessibility of information relating to the use of public funds, thus decreasing the transparency of the donation processes. In practice, this means that the recipients of tax-deductible company donations – that is, sports clubs and sports federations – are considered civil society groups in the eyes of the law and are not to be troubled with freedom of information tools. This means that the identity of the donors can remain a secret, thus concealing collusion and all kinds of corrupt practices.

- *Biased selection of eligible sports clubs*. Suspicions of corruption in the selection of sports clubs eligible for donations are twofold. On the one hand, when the government and parliament defined the five 'spectator team sports', they virtually excluded other branches of sports from tax-deductible donations. Even though 75 per cent of Hungary's active sports community participates in spectator team[11] sports, it could be that the government's financial considerations, unknown to the public, lie behind this decision. This claim is further supported by the marked increase in the erection and reconstruction of stadiums in recent years.

  On the other hand, the sports clubs of the five selected spectator team sports have to apply for authorisation from their respective sports federations in order to be eligible for tax-deductible company donations. Sports clubs' applications can be refused if the applicant's programme to be approved is not in line with the long-term strategic goals of the federation,[12] which gives considerable leeway to federations, and raises concerns as to whether inappropriate considerations might be being taken into account. The impartiality of the selection process may be in jeopardy if the decision to approve or dismiss a programme can be based on subjective reasons. There is a clear risk of corruption when sports federations decide which applicants are eligible for donations if this very evaluation process lacks any publicly available regulation and transparency. There is some hope for a measure of transparency, since the Hungarian authorities agreed to submit yearly reports to the European Commission on the activities and outcomes under the tax refund scheme.[13] This, however, does not provide the necessary oversight.

- *Favouritism in the appointment of sports federation leaders*. Sports federations in the spectator team sports have a crucial role in the distribution of company donations, which may correlate to their leadership's political ties. The Hungarian Football Federation (Magyar Labdarúgó Szövetség: MLSZ), the largest recipient of company donations, is chaired by Sándor Csányi, the CEO of OTP-Bank, the country's biggest commercial bank and one of Hungary's richest people; he is also a well-known ally of the prime minister, Viktor Orbán. The Hungarian Basketball Federation is headed by Ferenc Szalay, the Fidesz mayor of Szolnok, a medium-sized Hungarian city. Miklós Német, who until recently presided over the Hungarian Ice Hockey Federation, is also the CEO of Közgép, a construction company that has received a very high level of public contracts and that belongs to the interest group of Lajos Simicska, who was perhaps the most influential friend of Orbán.[14]

- *Disproportionate distribution of donations*. Orbán is an ardent football fan, and in his personal dedication to promoting Hungarian football he has founded in Felcsút, his home town, the Felcsút Foundation for the Promotion of Young Athletes, which is the operator of the Felcsút football team and the recipient of the biggest chunk of tax-deductible corporate donations. Each year over 1100 football clubs receive HUF 74.5 billion

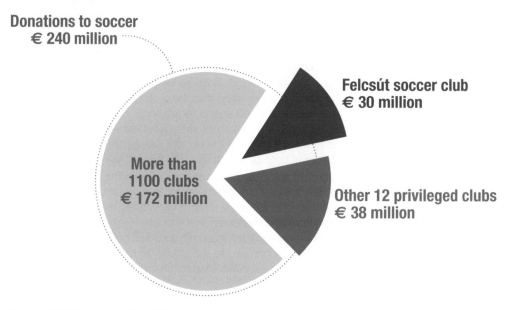

Figure 1.3 Privileged soccer clubs, 2011–14

Source: Hungarian Football Federation, *http://www.mlsz.hu/fejlesztesek*; Freedom of information requests submitted by Transparency International Hungary

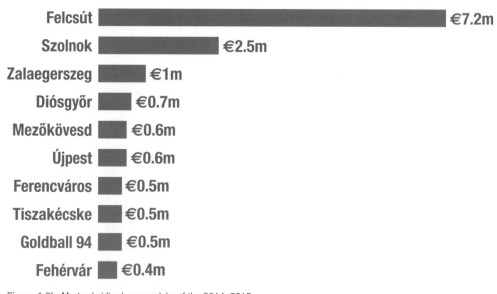

Figure 1.3b Most subsidized soccer clubs of the 2014–2015 season

Source: Hungarian Football Federation, *http://www.mlsz.hu/fejlesztesek*; Freedom of information requests submitted by Transparency International Hungary

(€240 million) in donations over a span of four years. Almost one-third went to 13 clubs (€68 million). Felcsút absorbed over 12 per cent of all donations (€30 million). This imbalance suggests that subjective considerations may override rational aspects in the grant-making process.[15]

- *Backdoor deals and opaque lobbying*. Corporate donations to the Felcsút football team and various other privileged clubs are widely accepted in the country as a form of bribing companies' way into lucrative businesses and winning public contracts. TI-H's recent study on the Hungarian lobbying landscape[16] has uncovered that participants in sports events – especially in football games, and corporate donors to football clubs through the MLSZ – play a prominent role in lobbying in Hungary. These kinds of sports donations are perceived as a distorted form of lobbying, whereby grants are donated to the preferred sports clubs of influential people and decision-makers in an attempt to curry favour with them.

All in all, the new system of sports subsidisation suggests that the government is ready to employ parliament's regulatory power to achieve political leaders' personal goals.

According to publicly available data, clubs of spectator team sports received tax-deductible company donations totalling HUF 204 billion (€656 million) since the start of the tax-benefit scheme in the span of four years.[17] It is worth noting that football clubs and the MLSZ absorbed some 90 per cent of all tax-deductible company donations, whereas the four remaining branches of spectator team sports and their respective federations received a much smaller amount of funding.[18] Although football is the most popular sport in Hungary out of the aforementioned five, the ratios still seem disproportionate.

Sports clubs in sports other than the five specified spectator sports receive normative grants from the government that are less exposed to corruption. This is the case with teams and federations in 16 other branches of sport, which are to receive a substantial amount of direct government support.[19] Organisations active in these branches of sport altogether will receive HUF 135 billion (some €430 million) by the end of 2020.[20]

It remains to be seen whether such robust investments will result in improved performance on the part of Hungary's sports teams, as there are as yet no real positive signs, except for a modest increase in the number of licensed athletes in these sports.[21]

Sports facility construction

As opposed to the system of corporate donations, which mainly channels private and corporate incomes to designated sports clubs, investments into sport infrastructure are funded directly from public resources. It should come as no surprise that the majority of the funds go to improving and building football stadiums. According to publicly accessible data on sports investments, the following major sports grounds have been erected or recently rebuilt, or are planned to be built in the near future:

- a stadium at Debrecen – HUF 12.3 billion (€39 million) of public resources;[22]
- a stadium for Ferencvárosi TC soccer club – HUF 13.5 billion (€43 million), government-funded;[23]
- a stadium at Hódmezővásárhely – HUF 1 billion (€3.2 million), out of which HUF 702 million (€2.2 million) is tax-deductible corporate donations and HUF 301 million (€963,000) is the local government contribution;[24]
- a stadium at Diósgyőr – HUF 4.5 billion (€14.4million), public resources;[25]
- a stadium at Szombathely – HUF 9.2 billion (€29.4 million), public resources;[26]
- a stadium at Székesfehérvár – HUF 9 billion (€28.8 million), public resources;[27]
- the National Olympic Centre (Nemzeti Olimpiai Központ) – HUF 128 billion (€410 million), public resources disbursed over a period of four years;[28] and

- a stadium at Felcsút – HUF 3.8 billion (€12.2 million), 70 per cent of which comes from corporate donations, the remaining 30 per cent being the owner's contribution.[29]

Despite these considerable investments, however, the numbers of spectators are dwindling in these brand new, state-of-the-art stadiums.[30] The average number of football enthusiasts attending the matches in person is showing a downward trend.[31] It is also worth noting that attendance at the most popular event, the National Championship league, has also taken a big hit, with the number of fans falling by 4,897 this season so far compared with the previous season and a decrease of 624 in average spectators per match.[32]

The goal of these grandiose constructions is questionable as well, in light of these modest numbers. The stadiums have been built to accommodate much larger crowds than the current ones; for example, the stadium of the Felcsút team Puskás Akadémia, called Pancho Arena, can hold up to 3,500 spectators, while the average match attendance in the 2013/2014 season was around 1,400. The stadium of the Debreceni Vasas Sport Club, based in Debrecen, can potentially welcome 20,000 visitors, but attendance is nowhere near that number, with a match average of 3,400, and some 7,500 spectators for the most popular match.[33]

The reopening ceremony of the Ferencvárosi TC football club's stadium was a public event at which the world-famous UK team Chelsea played against the local team; numerous Hungarian dignities visited the game and some of the air force's jet fighters flew past during the inauguration ceremony.[34] The Ministry of Defence, when requested to reveal the cost of the fly-past, answered at first that the flight was no more than a regular and pre-scheduled pilot-training exercise – a surprising reaction in light of Budapest's restricted airspace. Later the ministry announced that it had classified all relevant information until 2044.[35]

As stadium construction is funded from public resources, entrepreneurs are selected through public procurement – one of the most corrupt areas in Hungary.[36] Therefore, bias can easily develop in the selection process, putting public spending at risk of misappropriation. For example the small town of Kisvárda received HUF 800 million (€2.57 million) to build a state-of-the-art soccer stadium, plus HUF 120 million (€386,000) in government donations after the town's MP Miklós Seszták was appointed Minister of National Development. The town has only 16,000 people and was only recently promoted to the second league for the first time. Mezőkövesd, home of Deputy Minister of National Economy András Tállai, received HUF 800 million (€2.57 million) to build a new stadium, although the team only played one season in the first league.[37] Another example is the stadium in Felcsút,[38] which was built mainly on land owned by the Prime Minister's wife, adjoining his family house. A large proportion of the construction work for the Felcsút stadium has been allocated to companies that belong to the interest group of this municipality's mayor and CEO of the Felcsút Foundation for the Promotion of Young Athletes, Lőrinc Mészáros, who is undisputedly one of Orbán's closest allies. Though almost bankrupt in 2007,[39] he is now Hungary's 86th richest person, with a wealth of approximately HUF 8.4 billion (almost €27 million).[40] He claimed publicly in an interview that he owed his breathtaking enrichment to God, good luck and his friendship with the premier.[41]

Notes

1   Miklós Ligeti is legal director, Transparency International Hungary. Gyula Mucsi is project manager, Transparency International Hungary.
2   Fidesz is a right-wing party that belongs to the EU-wide European People's Party. Fidesz has been using nationalist conservative rhetoric with an anti-EU tone since 2010.

3 *Guardian* (UK), 'Hungary's election offers some disturbing lessons for Europe', 9 April 2014, *www.theguardian.com/commentisfree/2014/apr/09/hungary-election-europe-prime-minister-viktor-orban.*

4 The two cases referred to here have provoked immense media interest. See Politics.hu, 'Transparency International points to corruption in government takeover of tobacco business', 13 April 2013, *www.politics.hu/20130429/transparency-international-points-to-corruption-in-government-takeover-of-tobacco-business*; Politics.hu, 'Court orders release of tobacco retail tender documents', 12 May 2014, *www.politics.hu/20140512/court-orders-release-of-tobacco-retail-tender-documents*; Global Voices Online (Netherlands), 'Hungary: government limits FOIA transparency law', 8 May 2013, *http://advocacy.globalvoicesonline.org/2013/05/08/hungary-government-limits-foia-transparency-law.*

5 Hungary Today, 'Police raids Eea/Norway Grants foundation Ökotárs', 9 September 2014, *http://hungarytoday.hu/cikk/police-raids-eeanorway-grants-foundation-okotars-114*; The Budapest Beacon (Hungary), 'Hungarian NGOs react to Ökotárs raid with bewilderment and fear', 12 September 2014, *http://budapestbeacon.com/featured-articles/hungarian-ngos-react-to-okotars-raid-with-bewilderment-and-fear*; Politics.hu, 'Tax authority suspends tax numbers of Ökotárs', 23 September 2014, *www.politics.hu/20140923/tax-authority-suspends-tax-numbers-of-okotars.*

6 *Diplomacy and Trade* (Hungary), 'Police raid Norway Grants distributor in Budapest', 8 September 2014, *www.dteurope.com/politics/hungary/police-raid-norway-grants-distributor-in-budapest.html*; Politics.hu, 'Norway objects strongly to raid on NGO offices', 10 September 2014, *www.politics.hu/20140910/norway-objects-strongly-to-raid-on-ngo-offices.*

7 Transparency International Hungary, 'TI turns to the ombudsman regarding recent government audit', 30 June 2014, *www.transparency.hu/TI_turns_to_the_Ombudsman_regarding_recent_government_audit?bind_info=index&bind_id=0.*

8 Amendments introduced in 2015 expect donor companies to pay a mandatory fee called a 'supplementary sport sponsorship', which amounts to 12.5 per cent of the donation given from the donor company's pre-tax profit. The goal of this was to encourage traditional sport sponsorships while keeping the new tax scheme appealing to companies.

9 European Commission C(2011)7287, p. 14, point (65).

10 Transparency International Hungary publicly criticised this law: see *http://korrupcio.blog.hu/2014/12/16/gratulalunk_a_kormanynak.*

11 European Commission, 'Supporting the Hungarian sport sector via tax benefit scheme' (Brussels: European Commission, 2011), p. 7, *http://ec.europa.eu/competition/state_aid/cases/240466/240466_1271180_52_3.pdf.*

12 For the requirements of the application, see MLSZ-hu, 'A TAO: Pályátatásról', *www.mlsz.hu/blog/2013/10/14/fejlesztes-tao-palyaztatas*; Sporttámogatás.hu, 'Főoldal', *www.sporttamogatas.hu/fooldal.* For the requirements for each individual sport, see Sporttámogatás.hu, 'Fontos Tudnivalók', *www.sporttamogatas.hu/fontos-tudnivalok.*

13 European Commission (2011), p. 13, para. 57.

14 International Ice Hockey Federation, 'New president for Hungary', 2 July 2010, *www.iihf.com/home-of-hockey/news/news-singleview/?tx_ttnews%5Btt_news%5D=4798&cHash=6e26f00c878d95e2c9880ee16695c74a*; Hungarian Spectrum, 'A different kind of media war: Lajos Simicska versus Viktor Orbán', 6 February 2015, *http://hungarianspectrum.org/2015/02/06/a-different-kind-of-media-war-lajos-simicska-versus-viktor-orban*; The Budapest Beacon (Hungary), 'Meet Lajos Simicska: Fidesz's enigmatic oligarch', 10 February 2015, *http://budapestbeacon.com/politics/meet-lajos-simicska-fideszs-enigmatic-oligarch.*

15 TI-H Freedom of Information requests.

16 The study is titled *Lifting the Lid on Lobbying: Lobbying in an Uncertain Business and Regulatory Environment* (Budapest: Transparency International Hungary, 2014), *www.transparency.hu/uploads/docs/lobbi2014_web_eng.pdf.*

17 TI-H Freedom of Information requests from the five spectator team sports federations and the state bodies involved (Prime Minister's Office, Ministry of Human Capacities and Ministry for National Economy).

18 During the 2011/2012 season the Hungarian Basketball Federation received HUF 700 million (some €2.2 million) in donations, the Hungarian Handball Federation HUF 500 million (€1.6 million), the Hungarian Ice Hockey Federation HUF 400 million (€1.3 million) and the Hungarian Water Polo Federation HUF 200 million (just over €0.6 million): *www.nupi.hu/tao/ jegyzek*; *http://atlatszo.hu/2012/10/02/tao-penzek-megint-a-focistak-jarnak-jol.*

19 The branches of sport referred to here are table tennis, athletics, wrestling, rowing, judo, kayaking/canoeing, cycling, skating, boxing, the pentathlon, volleyball, shooting sports, tennis, gymnastics, swimming and fencing.

20 !!444!! (Hungary), 'Megfelelő emberek érkeztek az elnöki székbe, jöhet a százmilliárd a sportszövetségekhez' ['Now that the right people are in the presidential seats, it's time for the hundred billion forints for the federations'], 19 January 2015, *http://444.hu/2015/01/19/ megfelelo-emberek-varjak-a-tizmilliardokat-a-sportszovetsegek-elen.*

21 Adó Online (Hungary), 'Siker a látványcsapatsport-támogatás' ['Spectator sports funding is a success'], 20 November 2012, *http://ado.hu/rovatok/ado/siker-a-latvanycsapatsport- tamogatas.*

22 Daily News Hungary, 'Hungarian stadium building program marches on', 10 March 2014, *http://dailynewshungary.com/hungarian-stadium-building-program-marches-on.*

23 Ibid.

24 Delmagyar.hu, '2014-re megújulhat a vásárhelyi stadion', 3 September 2011, *www. delmagyar.hu/hodmezovasarhely_hirek/2014-re_megujulhat_a_vasarhelyi_stadion/2238222.*

25 Atlatzo.hu, 'Jövőre sem enyhül a stadionépítési láz – közel százmilliárd forint sportlétesítményekre', 25 October 2013, *http://atlatszo.hu/2013/10/25/jovore-sem- enyhul-a-stadionepitesi-laz-kozel-szazmilliard-forint-sportletesitmenyekre.*

26 Daily News Hungary (10 March 2014).

27 Ibid.

28 Ibid.

29 Origo (Hungary), 'Ne a stadionnal foglalkozzanak, hanem a saját dolgukkal!', 18 August 2013, *www.origo.hu/itthon/20130718-felcsutiak-a-stadionepitesrol.html*; FourFourTwo.hu, 'Kérdések és válaszok az épülő felcsúti stadionról', 2 August 2013, *www.fourfourtwo.hu/ hirek/magyarorszag/nb-i/kerdesek-es-valaszok-az-epulo-felcsuti-stadionrol.*

30 Hungarian Spectrum, 'No good players, no spectators but more and more stadiums', 6 December 2013, *http://hungarianspectrum.org/2013/12/06/no-good-players-no- spectators-but-more-and-more-stadiums.*

31 These are not exact numbers but an estimate based on the tickets sold in each season.

32 *Nemzeti Sport* (Hungary), 'Hiába az új stadionok, az FTC-nél és az NB I-ben is csökkent a nézőszám', 8 December 2014, *www.nemzetisport.hu/labdarugo_nb_i/nezoszam-2381393.*

33 Paraméter (Slovakia), 'Kinek építi az Orbán-kormány a több tízezres stadionokat?', 28 November 2013, *www.parameter.sk/rovat/kulfold/2013/11/28/kinek-epiti-az-orban- kormany-tobb-tizezres-stadionokat-az-atlagos-nezoszam.*

34 *Budapest Business Journal* (Hungary), 'Socialists: Gripens used for goverment propaganda', 14 August 2014, *www.bbj.hu/politics/socialists-gripens-used-for-goverment- propaganda_83732.*

35 Origo (Hungary), 'Gripen-parade: classified until 2044', 4 September 2014, *www.origo.hu/ itthon/20140903-harminc-evig-titokban-marad-a-gripenek-legi-paradeja.html.*

36 PricewaterhouseCoopers EU Services, *Identifying and Reducing Corruption in Public Procurement in the EU: Development of a Methodology to Estimate the Direct Costs of Corruption and Other Elements for an EU-Evaluation Mechanism in the Area of Anti- Corruption* (Brussels: PwC EU Services, 2013), *http://ec.europa.eu/anti_fraud/documents/ anti-fraud-policy/research-and-studies/identifying_reducing_corruption_in_public_ procurement_en.pdf.*

37 Kisvárda: *Hungarian Journal*, 2014, vol. 136, page 39, *http://www.kozlonyok.hu/nkonline/ MKPDF/hiteles/MK14136.pdf*; Mezőkövesd: Government Decree 1438/2013 (VII. 11), *http://www.kozlonyok.hu/nkonline/MKPDF/hiteles/MK13119.pdf.*

38 *New York Times* (US), 'A village stadium is a symbol of power for Hungary's premier', 3 April 2014, *www.nytimes.com/2014/04/04/business/international/the-village-stadium-a-symbol-of-power-for-hungarys-premier.html?_r=0.*

39 The Budapest Beacon (Hungary), 'Shepherd to challenge pipe-fitter billionaire Lorinc Meszaros for Felcsut mayor's seat', 7 July 2014, *http://budapestbeacon.com/politics/shepherd-to-challenge-pipe-fitter-billionaire-lorinc-meszaros-for-felcsut-mayors-seat.*

40 *Heti Világgazdaság* [*World Economy Weekly*] (Hungary), 'Még mindig Csányi a leggazdagabb magyar, Simicska a 10, Mészáros Lőrinc a 86' ['Csányi is still the most richest Hungarian, Simicska is 10th, Lőrincz Mészáros is 86th'], 14 May 2015, *http://hvg.hu/vallalat_vezeto/20150514_Meg_mindig_Csanyi_a_leggazdagabb_magyar.*

41 Index.hu (Hungary), 'A Jóisten is szerepet játszott Mészáros Lőrinc meggazdagodásában' ['Even God had a hand in the enrichment of Lőrinc Mészáros'], 24 April 2014, *http://index.hu/belfold/2014/04/24/a_joisten_is_szerepet_jatszott_meszaros_lorinc_meggazdagodasaban.*

1.13

Challenges and approaches to ensuring good governance in grassroots sport

Mogens Kirkeby[1]

> *'Grassroots sport' covers all sport disciplines practiced by non-professionals and organized on a national level through national sport. . . .'[N]on-professionals]' are individuals who neither spend the bulk of their time practicing sport, nor who take the bulk of their revenue from the practice of sport.*
> *(Definition of 'grassroots sport' in recent European Union study)[2]*

Why grassroots sport matters

Governance is a topic that is high on the agendas of all sectors – public, private and non-profit. It is equally important for the grassroots sport sector to be part of this drive, as a prerequisite for organisational legitimacy, autonomy and – ultimately – survival. If grassroots sport is not governed in an appropriate and legitimate way, it will lose not only its good reputation but also the significant financial support from its members and from public authorities that it currently receives.

Clearly, the governing structure of grassroots sport differs radically in different countries and regions. In a number of countries grassroots sport is primarily an activity within the school system, but in most countries the basic governing structure for the sector comprises local associations, often connected nationally or regionally. In all cases, the good governance of these associations has implications not only for participants but for the economy as a whole, and for the health sector in particular.

For most people, it is quite obvious why good governance is a relevant issue for performance-oriented elite sport and highly commercialised sports entertainment. Often, however, it is not as well understood why good governance of grassroots sport is also of importance, and increasingly so. This is probably based on two key myths about sport. The first is that the sport system is a pyramid, with grassroots sport at the bottom and elite sport/sports entertainment at the top, and with each tier strongly interconnected. This is still a prevalent view, particularly among organisations with an interest in painting a picture of themselves as covering and representing the whole 'sport family'.[3] Grassroots sport, in its original meaning, is a popular phenomenon, and not something that lies at the bottom of a 'pyramid'; this model fails to reflect today's very diverse and pluralistic sport sectors, which encompass non-governmental, governmental and, not least, corporate actors as operating, governing and delivering bodies. Other recently developed models, such as the so-called 'church' model of sport,[4] depicted in Figure 1.4, present a more accurate picture of today's sport sectors, and show that the interdependence between mass grassroots sport participation and the comparatively small elite level no longer applies.

The second myth is that elite sport creates the most economic activity and impact. A study carried out across the European Union in 2011 and 2012 illustrates the significant economic impact of the sport sectors; together, they constitute a major industry, generating more than 2 per cent of EU gross domestic product.[5] The report also shows that the vast majority of this

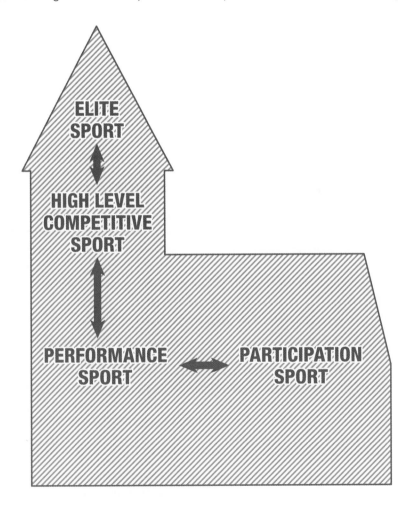

Figure 1.4 The church model of sport.

Adapted from: Jeroen Scheerder and Steven Vos, 'Belgium: Flanders', in Kirstin Hallmann and Karen Petry (eds), *Comparative Sport Development: Systems, Participation and Public Policy* (New York: Springer Science, 2013).

impact is created not by the relatively few sports stars' astronomical salaries, sales of media rights and merchandise, but by citizens' individual spending in mass-participation sport.[6]

Why governance matters in grassroots sport

There are at least four reasons why good governance of the grassroots sport sector is of huge and growing importance. First, grassroots sport has by far the highest level of popular participation and direct involvement. Citizens participate in grassroots sport or recreational physical exercise in various settings and in massive numbers. Second, the grassroots sport sector comprises the largest number of governing bodies, primarily local associations or sports clubs, and the environment in which they govern has become more complicated and diverse. Third, as detailed above, the grassroots sport sector generates the greatest economic impact in the overall sport sector, with its most significant financial contributions coming from individual citizens and, to some extent, public authorities. Finally, the grassroots sport sector is the arena in which most people exercise their 'right to participate in sport',[7] and in which the 'right to freedom and peaceful assembly and to freedom of association with others' are practised.[8]

The EU-supported 'Good Governance in Grassroots Sport' (GGGS) project of the International Sport and Culture Association (ISCA) shows how good governance can be introduced into the grassroots sport sector and how steps towards setting up good governance structures can be encouraged regardless of varying management structures, differences in staffing capacity, etc.

Box 1.4 The 'Good Governance in Grassroots Sport' project

'Good Governance in Grassroots Sport' is a transnational project led by ISCA in partnership with five universities and knowledge centres, ten national grassroots sport organisations, four international sport organisations and three municipalities.[9]

The project has developed guidelines and an online self-assessment tool for governing bodies in grassroots sport based on the principles of democracy, transparency, accountability and the inclusion of stakeholders.[10] While it is hoped that other stakeholders might benefit from them as well, the principles and guidelines are meant primarily for organisations that (1) are non-governmental, not-for-profit and democratic, based on a membership structure; (2) organise sport and physical activities on a regular basis for purposes other than high-level performance; (3) operate on a basis of voluntary board leadership in cooperation with salaried staff and further volunteers (coaches, helpers, etc.); and (4) may be national-level (umbrella) organisations or regional-/local-level organisations/clubs.

The self-assessment tool had over 12,000 page views and 4,600 users worldwide from its launch in August 2013 to mid-October 2014. A further 190 users completed the self-assessment tool in preparation for the ISCA General Assembly, which was held in late October 2014.

The project has been supported financially by the EU 'Preparatory Actions' in the field of sport.

The GGGS project recognised that grassroots sport's governing bodies comprise a variety of stakeholders, from small local clubs to national and regional organisations, with a mix of elected voluntary leaders and contracted employed staff. Many of the local, regional and national bodies are governed by board members elected at general assemblies. They are often volunteers who offer their time and enthusiasm to the governing of the entity. Most of the people who provide grassroots sport and exercise activities, including trainers, instructors and coaches, also work as volunteers. This volunteerism does not lessen the responsibility given to the individual, but the conditions of employment and potential penalties, such as sanctions for not fulfilling tasks, are different from those for employees operating on a formal work contract.

Naturally, the cultural, economic and political contexts in which these grassroots sport volunteers operate are also diverse. The number of citizens whom their organisations reach, the scope of their activities and their economic turnover all vary considerably. What their organisations have in common, though, is that they are the delivery bodies located closest to and involving the most citizens in physical activity on a daily basis.

Key findings and lessons learnt

'If it ain't broke, don't fix it'

When leaders of grassroots sport bodies are approached about good governance, often their first reaction is to say: 'We are working as volunteers for a good cause; we are doing nothing wrong.' For the most part, these leaders are creating and delivering positive services and activities for the benefit of people other than themselves, with no or very little material compensation, and the vast majority intend only to govern their organisations in a proper and appropriate way. GGGS's aim in facilitating good governance in grassroots sport is therefore not to try to fix something that is not broken but, rather, to help grassroots sport leaders reflect on governance procedures and to assist them in keeping their systems intact. In other words, GGGS aims to create awareness and tools for handling potential governing issues.

How can this rationale be presented to leaders of the grassroots sport sector? First, it needs to be communicated that good governance is not about uncovering governance problems in individual grassroots sport entities, but about preventing future governance problems in the increasingly complex sporting landscape. Second, practical examples can demonstrate that, despite the conviction in many organisations that they do not have any governing problems, the reality is that the leaders of any sport club or governing body can face situations and dilemmas every day that potentially involve risks, conflicts of interest and maybe even undue advantages (see Box 1.5).

Box 1.5 Examples of risks to grassroots good governance

Conflicts of interest

- The board of a non-profit sports club has to decide on the awarding of a contract. The husband of the vice president of the club is employed by one of the bidding companies.
- The manager of a sport federation is going to employ a new coach. One of the people who applies for the job is the manager's niece.

Undue advantages

- Two months after the conclusion of a sponsorship contract between a non-profit sports club and a company, the sponsor's manager presents high-quality sporting equipment to the president of the sports club.
- A sport equipment manufacturer invites the president of a sports club and his wife to sit in the VIP box of the local premier league football club. Some months later the president and his colleagues on the board decide on a large order of sporting equipment.

Finally, it needs to be acknowledged that no single model will fit all circumstances, and therefore the GGGS project principles and guidelines are flexible and can be adapted to each organisation's capacity and context.

Good governance: from the elite to everyday reality

One of ISCA's overall concerns was the reception the GGGS would get: how great would the interest and uptake be among the target organisations and leaders in the sector? When introducing a topic such as good governance, it is necessary to provide practical, simple tools and processes based on the everyday practical aspects of running clubs and organisations, which can initiate awareness, reflections and first steps towards practical solutions. In the event, the subject was well received by grassroots sport leaders at various levels, indicating that they have an organisational and personal interest in learning and using tools that can help them perform better and validate their decisions.

In general, the grassroots sport sector is doing reasonably well in terms of governance, but in an increasingly complex political and societal reality there is always room for improvement to allow for more open and transparent communication and decisions. This drive for self-improvement is in itself the essence of good governance in grassroots sport.

Notes

1 Mogens Kirkeby is president of the International Sport and Culture Association (ISCA). The chapter has been co-authored by Rachel Payne, fundraising and communications officer at ISCA, and Saska Benedicic Tomat, head of projects.
2 European Commission, *Study on the Funding of Grassroots Sports in the EU: Final Report*, vol. I (Brussels: European Commission, 2011), *http://ec.europa.eu/internal_market/top_layer/docs/FinalReportVol1_en.pdf*.
3 For example, from the European Commission: 'In Europe, the governance of sport is traditionally organised along a pyramid structure. . . . At the bottom of the pyramid one finds the sport clubs. One level above are the national federations, usually one per discipline. They cover both high-level (elite) and grassroots sport. Each national federation plays a leading role in implementing regulations and organizing championships. . . . At the top of the pyramid one finds the International sport federations and/or Continental federations.' Opinion of the Committee of the Regions on 'The European Model of Sport', 27 June 2011, *http://ec.europa.eu/internal_market/top_layer/docs/FinalReportVol1_en.pdf*.
4 Jeroen Scheerder, Hanne Vandermeerschen, Charlotte Van Tuyckom, Remco Hoekman, Koen Breedveld and Steven Vos, *Understanding the Game: Sport Participation in Europe: Facts, Reflections and Recommendations* (Leuven: Research Unit of Social Kinesiology and Sport Management, Catholic University of Leuven, 2011), *http://faber.kuleuven.be/spm/download.php?f=SPM10.pdf*.

5   SportsEconAustria, *Study on the Contribution of Sport to Economic Growth and Employment in the EU: Final Report* (Vienna: SportsEconAustria, 2012), *http://ec. europa.eu/sport/library/studies/study-contribution-spors-economic-growth-final-rpt.pdf.*

6   Sport England, 'Economic value of sport in England' (London: Sport England, 2013), *www.sportengland.org/media/177230/economic-value-of-sport.pdf.*

7   Council of Europe, 'European Sport for All Charter', article 1, *www.coe.int/t/dg4/sport/ resources/texts/spchart2_en.asp.*

8   Office of the United Nations High Commissioner for Human Rights, 'International Covenant on Civil and Political Rights', articles 21 and 22, *www.ohchr.org/EN/ProfessionalInterest/ Pages/CCPR.aspx.*

9   International Sport and Culture Association, *Good Governance in Grassroots Sport: What Does Good Governance Mean to Grassroots Sport?* (Copenhagen: ISCA, 2014), *www.isca-web.org/files/GGGS_WEB/Files/GGGS_Final_Report.pdf.*

10 Ibid., chap. 4.2.

1.14

The Code of Ethics for sport in the Municipality of Milan

A grassroots approach against organised crime and corruption in sports

Paolo Bertaccini Bonoli and Caterina Gozzoli[1]

The problem

The city of Milan and the Lombardy region are traditional areas of industry and professional services, providing approximately 25 per cent of Italy's GDP, and are historically characterised by a respect for the rule of law. However, the last decade has witnessed a gradual increase in organised crime,[2] with judicial investigations repeatedly uncovering the presence of the Mafia in building, waste cycle management, trade, major infrastructure projects and retail commerce. Greater attention was drawn in early 2014 in connection with the organisation of Expo 2015 in Milan, when serious cases of corruption surfaced.[3]

Nonetheless, it still surprised many in Milan that organised crime extended to the world of grassroots sport. In March 2011 the Ripamonti sports facility in via Iseo was impounded as part of the Milanese anti-Mafia operation 'Redux-Caposaldo'. The operation found that the facility was being managed by the Flachi clan, 'which exercises all the powers typical of dominus: deciding on staff, resolving disputes, managing services and raking in the profits. And the City, as the owner of the centre, was unaware that it was funding the Flachi group by supporting its economic initiatives.'[4] As a result of the seizure, the facility was closed by the prefetto (the central state authority) and the licence was revoked by the municipality. A further arson attack on 8 October 2011 seriously damaged the building, and was clearly committed for purposes of intimidation.[5]

Actions taken

The city of Milan and the Lombardy region have undertaken various measures to tackle corruption and organised crime, including an Anti-Mafia Committee, which reports directly to the mayor of Milan, a Municipality Council Anti-Mafia Commission and a 'Head of Corruption

Prevention and Transparency' in Lombardy.[6] The city of Milan also undertook its first whistleblowing procedure in October 2014.[7]

Specific to sport, it was in the shadow of the Ripamonti case and wider issues at the apex of Italian sport[8] that public opinion first became sensitised to the risks of organised crime and illegality in sport, even at the grassroots level. Against this background, the City of Milan initiated a policy to prevent and combat criminal infiltration of public sports facilities, thus integrating sport into its anti-Mafia agenda. This was led by the Commissione Consigliare Antimafia (Anti-Mafia Advice Committee) through its chairman, David Gentili, in coordination with the Assessorato allo Sport (Department of Sport) and the Commissione Consigliare Sport (Sports Advice Committee).

The chosen instrument was a Code of Ethics in sport, to be adopted by the management licensees of the city's municipal facilities (110 facilities managed by private sport clubs or companies as a result of public bidding procedures) and the public company Milanosport (which manages 24 municipal sports facilities).

In order to construct the Code and develop a plan for its implementation, the city of Milan signed a memorandum of understanding with Avviso Pubblico[9] and Transparency International Italia[10] on a voluntary basis to work alongside technical experts and representatives of public administration, starting with a preliminary collection of information and views on the issue.

It became clear from the outset that what was needed was not an approach limited to countering infiltration by organised crime, but an 'overall' approach to the contemporary issue of ethics in sport. The final proposed version of the Code set out 12 areas to reach the two key interrelated goals of combating organised crime and fostering integrity in sports practices.

Box 1.6 Elements of the Code of Ethics for grassroots sport in the city of Milan[11]

1. The principle of the supremacy of the 'rule of law' in social dynamics and in sport.
2. Self-regulation in the management of sports clubs.
3. Protection from the misuse of sport and from the effects of illegal, criminal and Mafia interests.
4. Effective participation on the part of members in the activity and decisions of sports associations/clubs, promoting awareness and individual and collective responsibility.
5. Strengthening the interchange between the sports clubs/associations and the local community.
6. Principles of fairness, honesty and loyalty in competitive and non-competitive sport and in social relationships; sports associations/clubs to select their leaders on the basis of these principles.
7. Developing sport to respect nature and promote environmental sustainability.
8. Strengthening the content and perception of sport as a clean and proper environment in which there are no concealed or unverifiable interests.
9. Generating awareness that lawlessness and minor non-compliance within sports associations/clubs increases the risks of criminal infiltration.
10. Promoting full transparency in order to make reporting and selection criteria for activities accessible and verifiable.

11. Recognising sport as important in the proper development and expression of the personality of the child and the adult, thereby also assigning to sport an educational and cultural function in the improvement of society and quality of life for individuals and communities.

12. Recognising that the principles promoted by sports associations/clubs also apply to all people involved in the organisation and promotion of sports activities, including the local authority and public administration.

The Code was conceived in recognition of the fact that sport plays a positive role in the growth of the individual, so the Code itself is a tool for protecting, strengthening and making more visible and explicit the ethical component of sport. A strategic choice was also taken to consider the 'cultural and behavioural context'. The trend in recent years has been a watering down of the sporting spirit: excessive competition; the use of sport for financial ends; personal grandstanding; foul and abusive language; insufficient technical skills in sports performance; and family interference in the work of instructors. In addition, inefficient models of sports organisation in Italy have encouraged minor misdemeanours, contributing to a sharp reduction in public and private grants. The Code therefore addresses the use of language by participants, information-sharing with families, the link between training capacities and learning goals, risk management and procedures to be adopted in controversial situations.

The process for the adoption and implementation of the Code is particularly innovative, as it is both inclusive – open to all clubs in the area – and participatory, inviting inputs from the same clubs to shape the initial draft. An initial tutoring phase involving six pilot clubs will lead to a final compulsory adoption by all clubs on the basis of a shared, tried and tested text. The Code can then be used by any legal entity active in the field of sports, from joint-stock companies to non-profit grassroots associations. Unlike other codes, the Code also empowers decision-makers to evaluate situations critically with a range of options, avoiding the risk of the Code merely being adopted in form but not in substance, with the paradoxical consequence of lowering self-responsibility. Instead, clubs are compelled to look at themselves critically and take decisions tailored to their own circumstances.

Preliminary lessons learned and next steps

By the end of 2014 the Code and the implementation plan were being shared with the 110 licensees for possible improvements, with six sport clubs already in the process of formally adopting it. In 2015 a dedicated website to the Code was launched to support networking among licensees, the public authorities and citizens. From February to May 2015 an appointed commission evaluated the effectiveness of the application of the Code by the pilot clubs so that additional clubs and the public administration itself can address gaps and begin to tailor policies.

Among many emerging aspects, four key lessons can be drawn. The first is the importance of having reliable data. The absence of systematic preliminary information on grassroots sports' connections to illegality, beyond the single case of the Ripamonti sport centre, proved a challenge in terms of persuading potential stakeholders to take part. To remove this obstacle, three steps have been taken: a training/information programme is currently under elaboration; two stakeholder focus group meetings will take place; and fundraising for dedicated research on a local scale is under way.

The second lesson is the importance of public–private partnerships, whereby the public institution plays a start-up and accompanying role, and civil society and private actors lead the programme. The involvement of NGOs such as Transparency International and Avviso Pubblico, and their good reputation, made it possible for the municipality to roll out the initiative in a credible and consistent way. Equally, active cooperation with local sport clubs is decisive, not least in avoiding possible future fall-outs.

A third element is the importance of training sessions to support decision-makers in clubs on implementation: most do not have the skills base to oversee ethics initiatives. Once the issues of 'corruption' and 'crime infiltration' have been understood, the lack of tools becomes immediately tangible to operators themselves. The organisation of tailored training sessions will require additional time and resources.

Finally, the development of the Code of Ethics for sport of the Milan municipality has shown that mobilising the grassroots sports movement as a force for the promotion of ethical behaviour requires considerable effort by clubs, and it is therefore important to ensure that a ready set of services can be delivered to them, for free or with reduced fees, so that this effort/investment is feasible and of benefit. This will require resources, such as a permanent assistance desk for critical situations, a shared mechanism to cooperate with potential sponsoring companies interested in corporate social responsibility projects, and shared public opportunities to foster the importance of ethics towards managers, trainers, family and all participants in grassroots sport.

Notes

1   Paolo Bertaccini Bonoli works for Transparency International Italia and Caterina Gozzoli is the director of the Alta Scuola di Psicologia Agostino Gemelli (ASAG) at the Catholic University of Milan. This chapter is the result of personal experience in formulating the Code of Ethics and its implementation programme, providing coordination expertise and being directly involved in the process, and representing Transparency International Italia and the Catholic University of Milan.

2   The consciousness-raising as a result of the presence of the Mafia in Milan has been quite shocking for a city that saw itself as immune to organised crime. See CaféBabel (UK), 'Milan is the true capital of the 'Ndrangheta', 9 April 2010, *www.cafebabel.co.uk/society/article/milan-is-the-true-capital-of-the-ndrangheta.html*. See also DissentMagazine.org (US), 'The anti-Mafia movement in Milan', 2 April 2014, *www.dissentmagazine.org/online_articles/the-anti-mafia-movement-in-milan*. Nando dalla Chiesa, son of the Carabinieri general Carlo Alberto Dalla Chiesa, who was murdered by the Mafia in Palermo in 1981, has been one of the leaders of civil society movements against organised crime since the early 1980s, and was appointed by the mayor of Milan in 2011 as chair of the Milan Anti-Mafia Committee. See also *Gazzetta del Mezzogiorno* (Italy), 'Suspected 'Ndrangheta mobsters arrested in Lombardy', 18 December 2014, *www.lagazzettadelmezzogiorno.it/english/suspected-ndrangheta-mobsters-arrested-in-lombardy-no678971*.

3   Many corruption cases have emerged in recent months; see *Il Fatto Quotidiano* (Italy), 'Antonio Acerbo, commissario Expo indagato per corruzione su "Vie d'acqua"', 17 September 2014, *www.ilfattoquotidiano.it/2014/09/17/expo-il-commissario-delegato-acerbo-indagato-per-corruzione-e-turbativa-dasta/1123624*; and ItalyChronicles.com, 'Corruption scandal hits Milan Expo 2015 preparations', 8 May 2014, *http://italychronicles.com/corruption-scandal-hits-milan-expo-2015-preparations*. The concern about illegal practices was nonetheless significantly present from the very beginning of the organisation, leading to the adoption of a specific 'Protocol of Legality': Expo2015.org (Italy), 'Protocol of Legality', *www.expo2015.org/en/transparency/legal-notes/protocol-of-legality*; this has proved to be largely ineffective, however: ExpoLeaks.it (Italy), 'Mafia and unclear bids, "Controls on Expo 2015 are not enough" says Antimafia Committee', 8 August 2014,

www.expoleaks.it/mafia-and-unclear-bids-controls-on-expo-2015-are-not-enough-says-antimafia-committee.

4   On 13 March 2011, order by Milan public prosecutor Giuseppe Gennari. See the text of the order in the Italian Parliament Acts: *www.camera.it/_dati/leg16/lavori/stenografici/sed533/pdfbt13.pdf.*

5   *Corriere della Sera*, 'Pisapia: avvertimento della 'ndrangheta l'incendio di via Iseo', 10 October 2011, *http://milano.corriere.it/milano/notizie/cronaca/11_ottobre_10/incendio-iseo-ndrangheta-1901773343877.shtml*; *Il Giorno*, 'Rogo al centro sportive ex feudo della malavita', 8 October 2011, *www.ilgiorno.it/milano/cronaca/2011/10/08/596841-incendio_centro_sportivo_feudo_della_malavita.shtml.* See also MilanoX.eu (Italy), 'Un anno fa la 'Ndrangheta bruciava il palazzetto di via Iseo', 8 October 2012, *www.milanox.eu/un-anno-fa-la-ndrangheta-bruciava-il-palazzetto-di-via-iseo.*

6   The region of Lombardy introduced this position in May 2013: *www.regione.lombardia.it/cs/Satellite?c=Redazionale_P&childpagename=Regione%2FDetail&cid=1213619980676&pack edargs=NoSlotForSitePlan%3Dtrue%26menu-to-render%3D1213582351799&pagename=RGNWrapper.*

7   The implementation process has been under way since the council finally gave approval on 10 October 2014: *Il Fatto Quotidiano* (Italy), 'Corruzione, Comune di Milano adotta il "whistleblowing": che Expo ha rifiutato', 11 October 2014, *www.ilfattoquotidiano.it/2014/10/11/corruzione-comune-di-milano-adotta-il-whistleblowing-che-expo-ha-rifiutato/1150186.*

8   This includes the 2011 match-fixing scandal in football: see Wikipedia, '2011–12 Italian football scandal', *http://en.wikipedia.org/wiki/2011%E2%80%9312_Italian_football_scandal*; and the 'Schwazer case' of doping before the Olympic Games in London 2012: ESPN (US), 'Alex Schwazer caught doping', 6 August 2012, *http://espn.go.com/olympics/summer/2012/trackandfield/story/_/id/8239963/2012-london-olympics-2008-olympic-race-walker-champion-alex-schwazer-caught-doping.* See also the recent important interview with Italian public prosecutor Guido Rispoli: *La Gazzetta dello Sport* (Italy), 'Caso Schwazer, parla il procuratore Rispoli: "Ecco le nuove armi contro il doping"', 23 September 2014, *www.gazzetta.it/Atletica/23-09-2014/caso-schwazer-parla-procuratore-rispoli-ecco-nuove-armi-contro-doping-90535055331.shtml*; and, on fan-based violence, see CNN (US), 'Violence mars Italian Cup final in Rome as fan remains critical in hospital', 7 May 2014, *http://edition.cnn.com/2014/05/03/sport/football-italy-napoli-violence-ultras*; and ANSA (Italy), 'Soccer: "Genny the Scumbag" arrested over Cup trouble – update', 22 September 2014, *www.ansa.it/english/news/2014/09/22/soccer-genny-the-scumbag-arrested-over-cup-trouble-update_8114ef27-b072-44b0-861a-cd3ef8b9ee0e.html.* The reference essay on racism in Italian football is that by Mauro Valeri, *Che razza di tifo: Dieci anni di razzismo nel calcio italiano* (Rome: Donzelli, 2010).

9   Avviso Pubblico is a primary Italian association that was founded in 1996 and associates local public institutions (municipalities, provinces and regions); see *www.avvisopubblico.it/home/associazione/chi-siamo/about-us.* In 2012 the 'Charta of Pisa' for transparency and fairness in public administration was launched, now updated in the 'Charta of Avviso Pubblico'; see *www.avvisopubblico.it/home/progetti/progetti-in-corso/carta-di-avviso-pubblico.*

10 Transparency International Italia is, in turn, collaborating with the masters programme in sport at the Catholic University of Milan in the field of psychosocial intervention through sport, within the advanced institute ASAG, directed by Caterina Gozzoli (*http://asag.unicatt.it*); see *http://asag.unicatt.it/asag-sport-e-intervento-psicosociale-ix-edizione-presentazione.*

11 Summary of the key principles of the code of ethics. The full code will be made available online at *www.codiceeticosportmilano.net.*

PART 2

Money, markets and private interests in football

2.1

Offside

FIFA, marketing companies and undue influence in football

Jamil Chade[1]

'You have created a monster.' According to Sepp Blatter, this warning was imparted to him by João Havelange, the president of the Fédération Internationale de Football Association (FIFA) from 1974 to 1998.[2] The Brazilian was not talking about corruption, bribes or commissions, but was instead referring to the fact that multinational companies and TV networks had been invited to the game, transforming sports forever and taking it to every corner of the Earth. As there was no oversight, though, an unholy alliance had also been created that would enable a small group of officials and businessmen to control football and to kidnap the emotions of millions of fans around the world.

The evolution of FIFA

When Havelange took power in the mid-1970s, FIFA was a small entity located in the outskirts of Zurich. It had 12 employees and, according to Blatter's own account, was financially in serious difficulties. Three aspects would cause a revolution, however. The first one was political. Havelange saw the decolonisation process in Africa and Asia as an opportunity to enlarge his organisation.[3] After all, the newly independent countries across Africa and parts of Asia would need not only a flag and a seat at the United Nations, but a national football team as well. FIFA supplied financial help, uniforms and even footballs to these countries; in exchange, Havelange made allies around the world.

The second aspect of this revolution was the decision to bring in sponsors. Adidas was one of the first to sponsor, with a fundamental part of the game: the ball itself. In exchange for huge investments poured into FIFA, Adidas could claim it owned the official ball of the World Cup, as if other balls would not be appropriate for the game. A number of multinational companies would follow suit, and, today, the tour of the football World Cup trophy is actually a Coca-Cola event. A fan can hardly take a picture with the most desired cup in history without the brand of the American company being visible on the back.

It was a third element, however, that would create the conditions for football to become the richest and most popular sport on Earth: the increasing popularity of television and the initial stages of live broadcasting. In exchange for the exclusive rights to show the game, networks would pay millions of dollars to FIFA, which, in theory, the organisation would reinvest in football.

Political expansion, sponsors and the growth of television around the world would transform FIFA from a small organisation on a hilltop in Zurich into a global superpower. Today its financial reserves accumulated in Switzerland amount to some US$1.5 billion, a tenfold increase in less than a decade.[4] The last World Cup, in Brazil, generated a record revenue of US$5.7 billion for FIFA,[5] more than twice as much as the event in Germany in 2006.[6]

Where did this all lead to, though? What mechanisms were there to control what was happening and the money that football was generating? This lack of control was precisely the Achilles heel of the newly globalised structure. As football grew, the 'world government' of the sport was maintained as it had been in the 1970s, with a handful of people making all the decisions, with no transparency or need to justify contracts, but unprecedented profits to be made. What the US Department of Justice indictments of 14 FIFA officials and businessmen on 27 May 2015 showed is the result of 40 years of a structure without control.

Bribery among marketing companies, TV networks and multinationals

The indictments revealed how media and marketing companies paid commissions to those in power at FIFA, and other sports organisations, to acquire, maintain or extend lucrative contracts for the broadcasting of matches. The marketing companies would then sell on these rights across the world, in return for a large profit.

The investigations also pointed out that the structure of power and the flow of payments are not always direct. A system of intermediaries had been established, many of them to channel bribes and other illegal payments from companies to football officials. Officially, the intermediaries are presented as 'marketing companies'. According to the Department of Justice, however, they are mere facades to justify payments and corruption.[7] In slightly over 20 years they are alleged to have moved over US$150 million in bribes around the world,[8] often using offshore centres, such as the Cayman Islands.[9]

Bribery for lucrative broadcasting contracts is alleged to have included TV rights for a number of tournaments, such as the rights to broadcast the Copa América from 2015 to 2023, purchased by Datisa, a joint venture of marketing companies from Argentina. According to the May 2015 US Department of Justice indictment, the bribes in this case alone reached US$110 million for a handful of sports officials, with José Maria Marin, the former president of the Brazilian Football Confederation (Confederação Brasileira de Futebol: CBF), Eugenio Figueredo, the former head of the South American Football Confederation (CONMEBOL), and the presidents of each of the national associations in South America soliciting or intended to receive bribes.[10]

The investigation also demonstrates how businesses were ready to pay bribes in exchange for exclusive deals. The case of the major US sportswear brand and its deals with the CBF, as disclosed in the US FIFA indictments, is one of the most significant. According to the investigations, extra payments of US$40 million were deposited into Swiss bank accounts in order to ensure the deal would be maintained.[11]

Having a gold mine under their control, FIFA officials would fight long and hard to retain power and, with it, the capacity to enrich themselves by 'selling' football. Elections at FIFA and the regional confederations became not only a matter of sports, but decisive moments in establishing which groups would control these channels of payments.

Absence of accountability

There was no surprise when a proposal asking FIFA officials to establish a limit on the mandates for themselves was unapproved, and it was equally unsurprising when a proposed age limit for the presidency and members of the Executive Committee was vetoed. There was no surprise even when, in 2010, the organisation decided that it would name the venue not only for the 2018 World Cup then, but also the 2022 one. An entire generation of decisions was locked in, as well as the profits for each of the actors involved.

In addition, the legal framework did not encourage investigators to look into such decisions. FIFA had until very recently a status in Switzerland that made investigations into it almost impossible. Around the world, however, it played a very simple game: any threats of investigations by national authorities would mean that the possibility of that country hosting a big event would be almost erased. In other words: blackmail. Marketing companies, investors, TV networks and multinational companies all played the game at FIFA, and, in a way, corrupted a system that welcomed and, in fact, asked for compensations and commissions.

'The indictment alleges corruption that is rampant, systemic, and deep-rooted both abroad and here in the United States', said the attorney general, Loretta Lynch, in a press release published on 27 May 2015.[12] 'It spans at least two generations of soccer officials who, as alleged, have abused their positions of trust to acquire millions of dollars in bribes and kickbacks. And it has profoundly harmed a multitude of victims, from the youth leagues and developing countries that should benefit from the revenue generated by the commercial rights these organizations hold, to the fans at home and throughout the world whose support for the game makes those rights valuable.'[13]

Private undue influence: the case of Brazil

The undue influence of marketing companies can also be seen in national federations, with the case of Brazil providing a stark example. The CBF signed a secret contract with Saudi Arabian investors – ISE, part of the DAG Group – giving the latter the full right to organise, explore and benefit from over 100 games of the Brazilian national side until 2022.[14] According to the contract between the CBF and the DAG Group, 'CBF gives to ISE the exclusive rights to organize, host, commercialize and produce the games to be held around the world, including in Brazil.'[15]

Accordingly, the investors, in search of immediate financial results, had the right to obligate the coach to select a team that would be most attractive in terms of marketing. The contract states that 'any changes in the list [of players] will be communicated to ISE in written form and confirmed by mutual consensus. In this case, the CBF will do its utmost to substitute the player for a new one with the same level, regarding marketing value, technique and reputation.'[16]

This has significant consequences for the game, as it limits the ability of a manager to prepare the next generation of stars and a competitive team for the future. Instead, he or she will always have to play with the best and most popular athletes of that moment in time, leaving no space for investing in younger players.

Conclusion

What the FBI investigation shows, and the secret contracts reveal, is that football was kidnapped by business groups and the personal interests of a few for far too long. Breaking this structure will require law enforcement intervention, though this may not be enough in itself. As long as there are no clear rules inside and outside FIFA, no transparency in contracts for sponsors, TV rights and commercial partners, the room for undue influence from business interests will remain a threat to the sport.

Until there is reform, establishing clear guidelines for those who are elected to key positions at FIFA, the entity will continue to operate as a private, non-transparent company. Until there are limits to the mandates of officials as presidents of local federations and international organisations, FIFA will be no more than an instrument of 'football oligarchs', who will profit by exploiting and manipulating the emotions of millions of fans around the world.

Notes

1   Jamil Chade is the European correspondent for the Brazilian newspaper *O Estadão*.
2   *Financial Times* (UK), 'Sepp Blatter warns FIFA sponsors not to rebel', 29 May 2015, *www.ft.com/intl/cms/s/0/47c4986c-062a-11e5-89c1-00144feabdc0.html#axzz3f8YimKLQ*.
3   Fédération Internationale de Football Association, 'History of FIFA: a new era', *www.fifa.com/about-fifa/who-we-are/history/new-era.html*.
4   Fédération Internationale de Football Association, *FIFA: Financial Report 2014* (Zurich: FIFA, 2015), *www.fifa.com/mm/document/affederation/administration/02/56/80/39/fr2014weben_neutral.pdf*.
5   Ibid.
6   Fédération Internationale de Football Association, *FIFA: Financial Report 2006* (Zurich: FIFA, 2007), *www.fifa.com/mm/document/affederation/administration/51/52/65/2006_fifa_ar_en_1766.pdf*.
7   United States District Court, Eastern District of New York, Indictment 15 CR 0252 (RJD) (RML), 20 May 2015, *www.justice.gov/opa/file/450211/download*.
8   US Department of Justice, 'Nine FIFA officials and five corporate executives indicted for racketeering conspiracy and corruption', 27 May 2015, *www.justice.gov/opa/pr/nine-fifa-officials-and-five-corporate-executives-indicted-racketeering-conspiracy-and*.
9   United States District Court, Eastern District of New York (20 May 2015).
10 Ibid.
11 Ibid.
12 US Department of Justice (27 May 2015).
13 Ibid.
14 *O Estadão* (Brazil), 'Documentos mostram como a CBF "vendeu" a seleção Brasileira', 16 May 2015, *http://esportes.estadao.com.br/noticias/futebol,documentos-mostram-como-a-cbf-vendeu-a-selecao-brasileira,1688813*.
15 Article 3.1 of the CBF and DAG Group contract, dated 27 December 2011: see *O Estadão* (16 May 2015).
16 Article 9.3 of the CBF and DAG Group contract: see *O Estadão* (16 May 2015).

2.2

Measuring the United Kingdom's 'offshore game'

George Turner[1]

For many years the Tax Justice Network (TJN) has set out to research the effects of the offshore financial industry on the world's economic activity. The TJN's view is that the secrecy and tax avoidance services offered by what are commonly termed 'tax havens' are damaging to the global economy. Secret financial flows create opportunities for money-laundering, undermine democracy, weaken the nation state and distort economic activity.

One particular strand of the TJN's work has been to quantify the size of the offshore industry. In 2005 TJN published its first report, *The Price of Offshore*,[2] which estimated that some US$11.5 trillion was held offshore by high-net-worth individuals.

In 2012 the TJN revisited[3] that study and found that between US$21 and US$32 billion was held offshore. This was a conservative estimate, as it did not take into account real estate, yachts and other high-value luxuries. To put the figure into some perspective, the entire world produces around US$74 billion in goods and services every year.

Offshore in sport

Offshore financial flows are pervasive, and are found in every part of economic life. In the United Kingdom, for instance, even tax inspectors offshored their own office space.[4] Sport is no different. For years high-earning sports stars have based themselves in tax havens such as Monaco or Switzerland. Despite proudly displaying their national flag when competing, they seem reluctant to share their wealth with their nation.

In the British professional football leagues, a total of 34 clubs are now owned by offshore companies[5] – no fewer than 25 per cent of the country's professional football clubs. The TJN decided to try to quantify the amount of offshore finance in professional football, and ranked UK clubs in a league table that looked at both the amount of finance flowing into clubs from offshore and the secrecy of the jurisdiction from which that finance came. Our study found that, in total, around £3 billion (about US$4.8 billion) in finance is held by companies based offshore,[6] the vast majority in secrecy jurisdictions and tax havens such as the Cayman Islands and the British Virgin Islands.[7]

It is important to be clear about what the TJN sets out to do. The project is not about looking at foreign ownership or foreign people; the sole concern is with loans and shares held by companies based in offshore financial centres. Almost always these companies were found to be shell companies that had no other purpose than to control the club. The ultimate owners of these companies could be anywhere, including the United Kingdom.

A tale of two cities

Take, for example, Bolton Wanderers FC. The club, currently in the bottom half of England's second tier, has a history going back to 1874, when Bolton was a booming industrial town. It was one of the 12 founding members of the Football League in 1888. Today the club is controlled by Eddie Davies OBE, a local boy who found riches in the thermostat industry. His children still live in Bolton, although Davies lives in the Isle of Man.

Davies does not actually own the club directly, however. Instead, ownership and finance is routed through a series of tax havens. Burnden Leisure PLC, the UK holding company, is owned by the Fildraw Trust in Bermuda. Most of the money comes in the form of loans from a company called Moonshift Investments Ltd, which is rumoured to be in the British Virgin Islands.[8] The TJN could find no public record of the company registration. Although Davies has a beneficial interest in Moonshift,[9] the TJN could not establish whether or not he actually owns or controls that company. This is something that should be of concern to fans, as the club is entirely dependent on these offshore loans.

On the other hand, take Southampton FC, which is owned by Swiss industrial heiress Katharina Liebherr. Liebherr owns the shares in her own name, and not through some offshore finance company, as can be seen by the annual return of St Mary's Football Group Limited.[10] It is an interesting quirk of the offshore game that a woman from a notorious tax haven, Switzerland, owns shares in a UK football club in her own name but, for whatever reason, the owner of Bolton Wanderers, who actually comes from Bolton, owns the club through a trust registered thousands of miles away in a Caribbean tax haven. One might well ask what possible reason there could be for such an arrangement.

Only the Bolton case represents a risk in terms of financial secrecy, as somebody owning shares in a UK company in his or her own name is as transparent a set-up as the TJN could ask for.

What value in measuring the offshore game?

Although, of course, anyone could set up an anonymous offshore company in the British Virgin Islands just for the fun of it, and simply owning an offshore company does not mean in itself that anything illegal is going on, the TJN's experience is that these companies have a considerably higher risk of engaging in tax avoidance, money-laundering and other illicit financial activity.

In sport there have been several high-profile cases. For example, in 2009 Birmingham City FC was bought by Carson Yeung Ka Sing, a self-styled hairdresser turned businessman. Yeung said that he had accumulated his vast wealth from some clever property investments and stock market plays he had made using the profits from cutting the hair of the rich and famous and playing baccarat in Macau.[11] The company that he used to complete the transaction, Grandtop International Holdings, was incorporated in the Cayman Islands, and later changed its name to Birmingham International Holdings.

The Hong Kong police were sceptical, however, and started investigating the source of his funds. In 2014 Yeung was given a six-year prison sentence for money laundering.[12] It was found that he was dealing in criminal proceeds on behalf of third parties. It is more than possible that the money that was used to pay for Birmingham City also came from these sources.

Harmless financial fun?

When club directors get involved with dubious or, as some might say, 'exotic' financial transactions it is not a victimless crime. Every week millions of people go to support their club as a means of escaping from the grind of daily life. They pour their heart, soul and dreams into their club. As the experience of Scottish club Rangers FC demonstrates, however, the use of offshore structures can also place the entire existence of the club at risk.

The Glasgow-based club was advised that it could make significant savings on income tax payments if it set up Jersey trusts on behalf of its players.[13] The author of the scheme was tax adviser Paul Baxendale-Walker (who would later leave the tax profession to star in adult films).[14] In order for the scheme to work, financial secrecy was key. The trusts had to be independent of the club, and they did not report payments made to players to the football league. Rangers' management signed a number of private agreements, however, guaranteeing that the trusts would make payments to the players. This allowed the club to pay the players more, as they would not have to make tax payments.

Was this a good thing for the fans, who would see their club attract better players and more success? No. HM Revenue and Customs (HMRC) found out about the side letters and challenged Baxendale-Walker's tax structure, concluding that the Jersey trusts were simply another way of paying a salary to the players, and therefore should be taxed as such. HMRC landed the club with a large tax bill for back taxes – a tax bill that, because of the club's precarious finances, it could not pay. The club was put into administration and eventually liquidated. The tax case still rolls on, and so far the company has won every stage, but HMRC continues to appeal to higher courts.[15] A new company was set up to continue the Rangers tradition, but it had to enter at the bottom of the Scottish professional football league.

A risky business

Sport is big business. According to Deloitte, the 20 highest-earning clubs in the world earned, between them, over €6 billion (approximately US$6.7 billion) in 2013/2014.[16] The global betting industry, including the unregulated Asian markets, is said to be worth over US$1 trillion.[17] With these vast financial flows surrounding the game, there are huge opportunities for a wide range of illicit financial transactions, from tax avoidance to bribery and corruption.

Whatever the reason a club or an owner may use an offshore structure, it is undoubtedly the case that, on a structural level, running large amounts of money through lightly regulated, secretive financial centres and tax havens increases the risk that things may go wrong. The TJN's report on the 'offshore game' provides just one indicator of the level of risk in sports finance: the amount of offshore finance in club ownership. The disconcerting finding was that, in the United Kingdom at least, the practice is widespread.

The well-documented problems with the offshore economy pose a real risk to the financial health of clubs. In the interests of the game and the fans, isn't it now time for football and sporting authorities to take the issue of financial secrecy seriously?

Notes

1   George Turner is a writer and researcher for the Tax Justice Network, which is based in Chesham, United Kingdom.
2   Tax Justice Network, *The Price of Offshore*, briefing paper (Chesham, UK: TJN, 2005), *www.taxjustice.net/cms/upload/pdf/Price_of_Offshore.pdf*.
3   Tax Justice Network, *The Price of Offshore Revisited* (Chesham, UK: TJN, 2012), *www.taxjustice.net/cms/upload/pdf/Price_of_Offshore_Revisited_120722.pdf*.

4   Accountancy Age (UK), 'MPs slam HMRC "business acumen" over offshore company deal', 14 April 2010, *www.accountancyage.com/aa/news/1808456/mps-slam-hmrc-business-acumen-offshore-company-deal.*

5   See The Offshore Game (UK), 'The offshore league', *www.theoffshoregame.net/the-offshore-league.*

6   The Offshore Game (UK), '£3bn in the UK's offshore football league', 14 April 2015, *www.theoffshoregame.net/3bn-in-the-uks-offshore-football-league.*

7   Tax Justice Network, *The Offshore Game* (Chesham, UK: TJN, 2015), *www.theoffshore game.net/wp-content/uploads/2015/04/Final-Offshore-Game-Report.pdf.*

8   Ibid., p. 25: 'Online forums state that Moonshift is registered in the British Virgin Islands, but the Offshore game team could not find any official record confirming this.'

9   *Daily Telegraph* (UK), 'Bolton Wanderers must avoid Premier League relegation to tackle £110m debt', 13 January 2012, *www.telegraph.co.uk/sport/football/teams/bolton-wanderers/9014275/Bolton-Wanderers-must-avoid-Premier-League-relegation-to-tackle-110m-debt.html.*

10 See Company Check (UK), 'St Mary's Football Group Limited', *http://companycheck.co.uk/company/06951765/ST-MARYS-FOOTBALL-GROUP-LIMITED/group-structure# shareholders.*

11 *Financial Times* (UK), 'Carson Yeung, club owner who reeled from rags to riches to rags', 7 March 2014*, www.ft.com/cms/s/0/0654a212-a5ed-11e3-9818-00144feab7de.html# axzz3YuisjEIW.*

12 See the Legal Reference System website of the Hong Kong government: *http://legalref. judiciary.gov.hk/lrs/common/search/search_result.jsp?isadvsearch=0&txtSearch=dccc860% 2F2011&vm=GO%21&txtselectopt=4&stem=1&selDatabase=JU&selDatabase= RS&sel Database=RV&selDatabase=PD&selall=1&order=1&SHC=&page=1.*

13 *The Scotsman* (UK), 'The unravelling of Rangers', 16 April 2011, *www.scotsman.com/sport/the-unravelling-of-rangers-1-1587442.*

14 See Wikipedia: *http://en.wikipedia.org/wiki/Paul_Baxendale-Walker.*

15 BBC (UK), 'HMRC granted leave to appeal Rangers tax case decision', 27 August 2014, *www.bbc.com/news/uk-scotland-scotland-business-28957732.*

16 Deloitte (UK), 'Deloitte Football Money League 2015', January 2015, *www2.deloitte.com/uk/en/pages/sports-business-group/articles/deloitte-football-money-league.html.*

17 *Daily Telegraph* (UK), 'Football's authorities fighting $1trillion crime wave powered by illegal betting markets in Asia', 4 February 2013, *www.telegraph.co.uk/sport/football/international/9848868/Footballs-authorities-fighting-1trillion-crime-wave-powered-by-illegal-betting-markets-in-Asia.html.*

2.3

Unfit, improper ownership in UK football clubs

Arjun Medhi[1]

Introduction

Money-laundering and the improper ownership of football clubs are considered among the main threats to the integrity of sport.[2] Money-laundering is a process whereby criminals disguise their illicitly gained wealth so it appears as though it came from a legitimate source, and in football it can involve multifaceted aspects.[3] It is achieved through a variety of means, notably manipulating club accounts by inflating income from ticket sales, buying empty spectator seats, inventing a fake revenue stream and engaging in the development of property near stadiums. The international market for transferring players can also be a vehicle for money-laundering, as the overvaluation of a player is similar to the money-laundering protocol of inflating invoices for goods and services.[4] Another vehicle for money-laundering is the use of tax havens and the ability to use front companies and shadow directors as football club owners. Such fraud and corruption in football are frequently reported in the media, and they involve and affect the wider community, jeopardising the game and its brand value.

Football clubs, especially when they are in debt, can be attractive targets for criminals seeking to launder their dishonest income. Wealth and power are often not spread in football clubs, unlike large businesses in other sectors, leaving clubs vulnerable to the actions of one or two individuals. Football in the United Kingdom also lacks effective regulation, making it easier for criminals to outflank the systems of the football business. As a result of these factors, vulnerable clubs are more likely to accept (perhaps unwittingly) criminally laundered money.[5] Furthermore, when it is impossible to identify their actual owners or their source of wealth, UK clubs are clearly at risk of being vehicles for money-laundering. This raises the question as to why the country's football sector (its authorities and, to some extent, its fans) allows unidentified rich investors to own clubs.

Countering money-laundering and the illegal financing of clubs

There are various strategies available to counter money-laundering and the illegal financing of football clubs. These include establishing codes of conducts, introducing whistleblowing policies, setting up ethics committees, imposing sanctions, instituting training courses to raise awareness of fraud and corruption and ensuring accounts and records are audited. A key strategy the UK football authorities use to protect football from fraud and corruption, however, is the fit and proper person test. There are three such tests for potential club owners and directors, each operated by the Premier League (known as the owners' and directors' test), the Football League and the Football Association (FA), for their respective leagues. These tests aim to:

● prevent anyone who holds a criminal record from owning or directing a football club;
● protect football clubs from people who do not have the long-term business interests of the club at heart; and
● prevent anyone who lacks integrity from becoming an owner or director of a club.

A potential owner or director who undergoes these tests will be disqualified if he or she is found to have:

● an unspent criminal conviction of fraud or dishonesty, in the United Kingdom or overseas;
● been declared bankrupt;
● been declared unlawful to act as a director of a UK-registered company;
● been a director of a football club that was declared insolvent more than twice;
● been banned from a sport ruling committee, accredited association or other regulator;
● breached FA rules on betting; or
● been, or still is, on the register of sex offenders.[6]

Questions have been raised about the validity of these tests, however. Given the substantial amount of unreported fraud in the country, clubs can appoint fraudsters unwittingly.[7] The testing needs to check for spent convictions, expanding beyond the United Kingdom. If an individual has been disqualified from being a company director, he or she may still be able to purchase a club, given that it is possible to purchase a club through a company where it is sometimes impossible to identify its owner. The tests should also check owners or directors against any international data-sharing schemes and international media reports.

Most of these issues would be addressed if one were to open up a financial business in the United Kingdom. For example, one of the previous owners of Portsmouth FC, Vladimir Antonov, was considered a fit and proper person by the Football League even though the UK financial regulator would not allow Antonov's business to trade in the country (Antonov's business failed to provide the necessary information required by the UK financial regulator).[8] There is insufficient information to know why the Football League allowed Antonov to own a UK football club when he was not allowed even to trade his financial services business in the country. Generally, leagues do not disclose information pertaining to fit and proper person tests in the public domain, and release information only when someone fails the test.[9]

Three people, so far, are known to have failed the test: (1) Dennis Coleman was twice declared insolvent and was not allowed to be the director of Rotherham United;[10] (2) Stephen Vaughan, the previous owner of Chester City FC, failed the test and was forced by the Football Association to reduce his shareholdings because of involvement in a £500,000 (US$840,000) VAT fraud;[11] and (3) Louis Tomlinson, a member of the successful pop music group One Direction, failed along with a co-investor to pass the test and become a co-owner of Doncaster Rovers.[12]

Several owners and directors who are alleged to have committed fraud and corruption have passed the test without explanation, however. Thaksin Shinawatra, a business tycoon and former prime minister of Thailand, passed the Premier League's fit and proper person test to own Manchester City FC in 2007. Shinawatra had been ousted as prime minister in a military coup the previous year, following allegations of corruption and human rights violations, and he was later charged with corruption and his assets of some £800 million (around US$1.2 billion) stored in Thai banks were frozen.[13] Despite this, and being criticised by Human Rights Watch, Amnesty International and Transparency International,[14] the Manchester City board of directors and the Premier League allowed Shinawatra to become the owner of a football club. It is believed that Shinawatra passed the test because he had not been criminally convicted; moreover, Richard Scudamore, the Premier League chief executive, proclaimed that the League was unable to prevent an individual who faced criminal charges from an unelected military government from owning a club.[15] Shinawatra was eventually sentenced for corruption by a democratically elected government in Thailand, and there is a warrant for his arrest.[16] Although he had promised long-term investment in Manchester City, in 2008 he sold the club to Abu Dhabi United Group, making a profit of some £20 million (around US$30 million) in just over a year.[17] The fit and proper person test should consider disqualification of an individual from owning or directing a football club if he or she is subject to a fraud or corruption investigation or prosecution anywhere in the world.

Another possible mechanism for countering money-laundering of football clubs is the Financial Fair Play rule, introduced in 2013 by the Union of European Football Associations (UEFA). The rule is a directive to football clubs to operate their business so as to break even. This rule therefore restricts spending at football clubs, which should make it less easy, and therefore less attractive, to launder money through football. It is not clear, however, whether this is being properly enforced, as money-laundering involves disguising financial flows. To bypass Financial Fair Play regulations and to encourage dishonest investment, creative accounting techniques are required, such as inflating assets (for example, players, stadiums and properties) and hiding liabilities.

Recommendations for reform

Although information on the application of the fit and proper person test is not in the public domain, it is uncertain whether these tests are broad enough to protect football clubs. There is no evidence that they verify the source of a prospective owner's wealth, which is one of the most important financial checks for countering money-laundering.

The United Kingdom has strong money-laundering regulations, and, as a result, organised criminals are deterred from laundering their wealth through the country's banking sector.[18] Accordingly, some features of the financial sector's regime should be extended to football. The UK banking sector focuses on prevention, and an effective prevention strategy can be underpinned by enhanced vetting. This could be incorporated into the fit and proper person tests. Enhanced vetting involves a combination of objective and subjective checks, which would also help to prevent fraudsters and corrupt individuals from entering the market and to detect money-laundering at an early stage. Therefore, the fit and proper person and the owners' and directors' tests should be expanded.

As with anti-money-laundering and enhanced vetting procedures, the tests must incorporate:

● substantiated identity checking of owners, directors and other key senior staff;
● establishing the owner's source of wealth, through the use of forensic accountants;
● for foreign investors, conducting checks against politically exposed person (PEP) databases (PEPs are individuals, including their associates/family, who are entrusted with a prominent public function by a country other than the United Kingdom, the European Union or another international body);[19]

- conducting checks with information-sharing schemes, nationally and internationally, with other football authorities and with law enforcement authorities;
- considering checks with information-sharing schemes about individuals currently being investigated for fraud or corruption;
- considering internet searches, bearing in mind that the results would need to be verified;
- conducting ethics and honesty checks (involving, for example, Amnesty International and Transparency International); and
- carrying out a face-to-face meeting with the potential owner.

Given the lack of transparency in the football sector, the risk of corruption at UK football clubs is high. Although an enhanced vetting strategy might deter money-launderers, further research into the vetting strategies adopted in other sports sectors and other business sectors is critical. Every effort needs to be made to try to ensure that only fit and proper persons own and run football clubs in the United Kingdom.

Notes

1 Arjun Medhi is Technical and Development Manager at the UK's Chartered Institute for Public Finance and Accountancy.
2 Oxford Research, *Examination of Threats to the Integrity of Sports* (Frederiksberg, Denmark: Oxford Research, 2010), p. 15, *www.eusportsplatform.eu/Files/Filer/examination%20of%20 threats%20to%20sports%20integrity.pdf*.
3 Financial Action Task Force (France), 'What is money laundering?', *www.fatf-gafi.org/pages/ faq/moneylaundering*.
4 Transparency International, 'Sport', *www.transparency.org/topic/detail/sport*; Graham Johnson, *Football and Gangsters: How Organised Crime Controls the Beautiful Game* (Edinburgh: Mainstream, 2006), p. 199; Financial Action Task Force, *Money Laundering through the Football Sector* (Paris: FATF, 2009), pp. 15, 20, 21, *www.fatf-gafi.org/media/ fatf/documents/reports/ML%20through%20the%20Football%20Sector.pdf*.
5 Financial Action Task Force (2009); Johnson (2006); John Beech, 'Written evidence submitted by Dr John Beech, head of sport and tourism, Applied Research Centre for Sustainable Regeneration, Coventry University (FG69)', in House of Commons Culture, Media and Sport Committee, *Football Governance: Written Evidence – at 28 March 2011* (London: The Stationery Office, 2011), *www.publications.parliament.uk/pa/cm201011/ cmselect/cmcumeds/writev/792/792we.pdf*.
6 Sean Hamil and Geoff Walters, 'Financial performance in English professional football: "An inconvenient truth"', *Soccer and Society*, vol. 11 (2010), p. 355; Rachel Baird, Andrew Hogg, Nick Mathiason and Alex Cobham, *Blowing the Whistle: Time's Up for Financial Secrecy* (London: Christian Aid, 2010), p. 10; All Party Parliamentary Football Group, *English Football and Its Governance* (London: Thales, 2009), p. 2, *www.levelplayingfield.org.uk/ sites/default/files/contentfiles/apfg_report_on_english_football_its_governance_april_20091. pdf*; Supporters Direct, *Developing Football Regulation to Encourage Supporter Community Ownership in Football* (London: Supporters Direct, 2011), p. 25, *www.supporters-direct.org/ wp-content/uploads/2012/07/Developing-Football-Regulation-to-Encourage-Supporter- Community-Ownership-in-Football-Briefing-2.pdf*; Geoff Walters and Sean Hamil, 'Ownership and governance', in Simon Chadwick and Sean Hamil (eds), *Managing Football: An International Perspective* (Oxford: Butterworth-Heinemann, 2010), p. 27.
7 City of London Police, 'Tightening the net', *www.cityoflondon.police.uk/advice-and-support/ fraud-and-economic-crime/nfib/nfib-news/Pages/Tightening-the-net.aspx*.
8 *Baltic Times* (Latvia), 'Snoras barred from the UK', 11 February 2009, *www.baltictimes.com/ news/articles/22305*.

9   Baird *et al.* (2010), p. 14.

10 Ibid.

11 Ibid.; *Guardian* (UK), 'Chester City chief becomes first owner to fail fit and proper person test', 18 November 2009, *www.theguardian.com/football/2009/nov/18/chester-city-fit-proper-person-test.*

12 *Guardian* (UK), 'One Direction's Louis Tomlinson "misled" as Doncaster takeover bid fails', 18 July 2014, *www.theguardian.com/football/2014/jul/18/one-direction-louis-tomlinson-misled-doncaster-takeover-john-ryan.*

13 Walters and Hamil (2010); Football Supporters' Federation, 'Written evidence submitted by the Football Supporters' Federation (FG37)', in House of Commons Culture, Media and Sport Committee (2011).

14 BBC (UK), 'A fit and proper Premiership?', 31 July 2007, *http://news.bbc.co.uk/sport2/hi/football/teams/m/man_city/6918718.stm*; *Guardian* (UK), 'City blinded by money in race to bind Thais', 23 May 2007, *www.theguardian.com/sport/blog/2007/may/23/cityblindedbymoneyinrace.*

15 Walters and Hamil (2010).

16 Ibid.

17 Ibid., pp. 27–28, citing *The Daily Telegraph* (UK), 'Soap opera involving Thaksin Shinawatra and Manchester City damaging our game', 12 August 2008, *www.telegraph.co.uk/sport/football/teams/manchester-city/2542658/Soap-opera-involving-Thaksin-Shinawatra-and-Manchester-City-damaging-our-game-Football.html*; Football Supporters' Federation (2011).

18 Jackie Johnson and Desmond Lim, 'Money laundering: has the Financial Action Task Force made a difference?', *Journal of Financial Crime*, vol. 10 (2002).

19 Financial Services Authority, *Bank's Management of High Money-Laundering Risk Situations: How Banks Deal with High-Risk Customers (Including Politically Exposed Persons), Correspondent Banking Relationships and Wire Transfers* (London: FSA, 2011), p. 16, *www.fca.org.uk/static/documents/fsa-aml-final-report.pdf.*

2.4

Agents and beyond

Corruption risks in the football transfer market and the need for reform

Raffaele Poli[1]

Agents are at the heart of the transfer and labour market of football players. Among many responsibilities, agents represent both clubs and players within the context of contract or transfer negotiations, they deal with players' image rights and they carry out scouting tasks on behalf of clubs.

The main corruption issues with regard to agents in football are related to the misuse of the transfer system by the different actors involved, both within and outside club structures, as a source of personal financial benefit. The key mechanism is the payment of commission fees to agents upon the transfer of a player, which are then kicked back to the different stakeholders, in particular originating club officials and owners, with whom the agents collaborate.

Given the considerable amount of profits to be made, sports directors, scouts, coaches, club shareholders and agents often have a financial interest in transferring more players and for more money, even if doing so is detrimental to the financial health of the club. The prevalence of vested interests in the football transfer market provides a stark picture of the poor financial situation of many clubs around the world.

Data from the Transfer Matching System (TMS) of the Fédération Internationale de Football Association (FIFA) shows that expenditure for international transfers reached new highs during the two last calendar years: US$3.98 billion in 2013 and US$4.06 billion in 2014. Meanwhile, commission fees paid to intermediaries acting on behalf of clubs alone went up from US$218 million in 2013 (5.5 per cent of total transfer expenditure) to US$236 million in 2014 (5.8 per cent of total transfer expenditure).[2]

Beyond commission fees for representing clubs, dominant agents also earn considerable amounts of money by representing players. According to a report prepared by the Centre international d'étude du sport (CIES),[3] the yearly turnover of football intermediaries is above €400 million (around US$450 million) in Europe alone. Moreover, powerful intermediaries with the best connections are increasingly benefiting from transfer revenues, whether through personal entitlement to shares of deals or as advisers to investment funds and companies active in the third-party ownership business.[4]

Market concentration

As in other industries, the representation market in football is a business based on relationships, with trust playing a crucial role. This raises crucial issues with regard to opaque arrangements between business partners, corruption, unfair competition and market concentration based on privileged relations.

According to the CIES report,[5] in June 2011 694 individual agents – whether licensed or not[6] – or companies represented the 1,945 players employed by the clubs of the five major European leagues[7] for whom the authors were able to collect the relevant information. This represents nearly three-quarters of all footballers in the 'Big Five' leagues. As illustrated in Figure 2.1, the study also indicates that 50 per cent of the players were clients of 83 individual agents or agencies, and one-quarter of footballers were represented by only 24 of them. This clearly shows the high level of concentration in the representation market of top league footballers.

From the perspective of market concentration, it is useful to recall that in June 2011 there were more than 2,400 licensed agents domiciled in the countries hosting the 'Big Five' European leagues. This figure is much greater if we also include people acting as intermediaries without the possession of a licence delivered by a national association, as well as lawyers and players' relatives.

The CIES report also highlights the existence of strong entry barriers to intermediaries aspiring to work in the representation market for top league players. According to a survey of licensed agents in the 'Big Five' leagues carried out for the report, the existence of established agents dominating the market is considered to be an important hurdle for newcomers.[8]

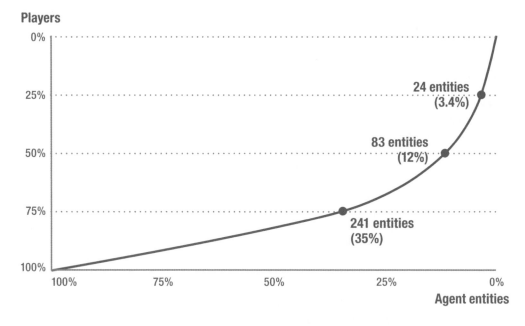

Figure 2.1 Percentage of individual agents or agencies (entities) with clients in the 'Big Five' leagues according to the percentage of players represented (2010–2011 season).

Source: CIES Football Observatory, *Football Agents in the Biggest Five European Football Markets: An Empirical Research Report* (Neuchâtel: Centre international d'étude du sport, 2012), p. 17.

The European Commission (EC) attempted to increase competition by facilitating agents' ability to obtain licences through national associations, which was put into practice by FIFA with the entry into force of a regulation on agents in 2001.[9] This has fallen short of achieving the EC's and FIFA's desired impact[10] of a more accessible representation business, however. FIFA's recent efforts to no longer require licences for agents will hardly change the situation. While more people will be able to be recognised as legitimate intermediaries, those who hold the closest relationships with club officials will maintain their hold on the market.

In addition, the direct involvement of the most influential agents in deals entitling them or other parties to shares of transfer revenues or as advisers of investment funds or companies active in this business aggravates 'cartelisation' concerns, and leads to an institutionalisation of the conflict of interest as the modus operandi in the transfer market. In fact, there are investment funds and companies that collaborate on a regular basis with a small group of intermediaries who maintain strong ties with clubs and their shareholders. These dominant networks are exercising increasing control over footballers and clubs.[11] This increases the risks of insider trading, collusion and kickbacks, and gives dominant actors and networks even more leverage over outsiders. As in all economic sectors, this oligopolistic position is indeed advantageous; specifically in football, it drives up transfer costs for players, generates ever greater profits and consolidates control of the market.

Transfer system reform

The corruption risks related to the role of football agents should be tackled from a holistic perspective. Notably, the role played by team officials and shareholders within the context of poor corporate governance at club level should be taken into account. To be effective, any action with regard to agents should take into consideration the vested interests between the multiple actors involved in the transfer market of football players.

Comprehensive reform is needed to move away from the speculative view of the transfer market, which has gained ground during the last 20 years. The key objective should be to make the transfer system better suited to fulfil the purpose for which it was first implemented and has since been adapted: for contractual stability, the promotion of training and development and fair income distribution. An efficient measure to accomplish this would be to entitle each team that a player passes through to compensation for all transfers involving the payments of fees that later take place over the course of that player's career. This could be done on a pro rata basis, according to the number of official matches played at the club. In the current situation, the contribution to clubs that developed players is limited to 5 per cent of any transfer fee.

As an example, take footballer A, who begins as a professional in club X, playing 75 matches there before being transferred to club Y. After 25 games with club Y, the player transfers to club Z. In the event of a 'fee-paying' transfer to club Z, club X is entitled to 75 per cent of the transfer fee, regardless of club Y already having paid a fee to sign the player from club X. In this scenario, obligations for increased transparency – including open negotiations, expert valuation, compulsory disclosure, sporting and financial sanctions for non-compliance – will be very important as a means of preventing the possibility of club Y hiding from club X the real deal arranged with club Z. This would allow football governing bodies to ensure that transfer incomes are evenly distributed throughout the whole chain of teams that have contributed to players' development.

With regard to contractual stability, this reform would ensure that clubs receive compensation even if the player leaves at the end of his or her contract. This could also enable teams to more easily afford hanging onto their best players for longer periods, and salary inflation might also be better kept in check.[12] This reform could also have a promising impact on development and training, making investments in clubs or youth academies more interesting from a financial standpoint. Importantly, training clubs would receive substantial money in the event of a second, third or subsequent fee-paying transfer, which are generally the most profitable. This should incentivise current or new club shareholders to invest in the training of players instead of disproportionately speculating on specific talents from a short-term profit maximisation perspective, with no real contribution to the smooth development of football, as it is often the case currently.

The reform would also be beneficial from an income distribution perspective. Although the wealthiest clubs, in their quest for success, will probably continue to spend huge amounts of money to sign players, their investments would be split more evenly throughout the whole chain of clubs that have developed them.

The increased guidance and control resulting from the proposed reform would help to address the corruption risks related to agents in the transfer market. Although it would not resolve all the concerns arising from the prevalence of vested interests in the transfer market, it would help return the system towards the critical principles underlying its creation and existence: contract stability, the reward of training and fair income distribution.

Notes

1 Raffaele Poli is the co-founder and head of the Football Observatory of the Centre international d'étude du sport, University of Neuchâtel, Switzerland.

2 Fédération Internationale de Football Association, 'International transfers break $4bn mark: FIFA TMS Annual Report', media release, 28 January 2015, *www.fifa.com/governance/ news/y=2015/m=1/news=international-transfers-break-4bn-mark-fifa-tms-annual-report-2512285.html*.

3 Raffaele Poli and Giambattista Rossi, *Football Agents in the Biggest Five European Football Markets: An Empirical Research Report* (Neuchâtel: Centre international d'étude du sport, 2012), *www.football-observatory.com/IMG/pdf/report_agents_2012-2.pdf*.

4 In this regard, see Asser International Sports Law blog, 'Blog symposium: third-party entitlement to shares of transfer fees – problems and solutions', 15 April 2015, *www.asser. nl/SportsLaw/Blog/post/blog-symposium-third-party-entitlement-to-shares-of-transfer-fees-problems-and-solutions-by-dr-raffaele-poli-head-of-cies-football-observatory*.

5 Poli and Rossi (2012).

6 In 1994 FIFA introduced a requirement for individuals to obtain a licence in order to officially operate as agents. This required no tests, but the payment of CHF 100,000 (approximately US$70,000). In a 2001 reform to open the market, tests, conducted by the national associations under FIFA guidance, were required to obtain a licence. Lawyers and players' relatives could also operate as agents. Non-licensed agents continued to be present in the market. Various additional regulations exist in each country. In April 2015 FIFA abolished its guidance on and control of the licensing system. Each national association is now responsible for the development of its own regulatory framework regarding agents, following FIFA's minimum requirements.

7 The so-called 'Big Five' leagues include the English Premier League, the Spanish Liga, the German Bundesliga, the Italian Serie A and the French Ligue 1.

8 Poli and Rossi (2012).

9 See endnote 6.

10 Stanislas Frenkiel, *Une histoire des agents sportifs en France: Les imprésarios du football (1979–2014)* (Neuchâtel: Centre international d'étude du sport, 2014).

11 For further information on the role of investment funds and third-party ownership, see the following two chapters.

12 As many clubs transfer players to avoid their leaving for free, or, alternatively, they are obliged to pay them significantly increased salaries to persuade them to extend their contracts, the reform would help limit salary inflation.

2.5

Third-party ownership of football players

Human beings or traded assets?

Jonas Baer-Hoffmann[1]

> *Today, it's shameful to see some players with one of their arms belonging to one person, a leg belonging to a funds pension located who knows where, and a third person owning his foot. It is shameful; we're dealing with a type of slavery that belongs to the past.*[2]
>
> UEFA president Michel Platini

The grip of third-party owners of economic rights in the transfers of footballers between clubs worldwide has grown stronger in recent years, increasing economic and legal risks and inviting corrupt behaviour and conflicts of interest. The three letters 'TPO' have come to symbolise the commercial exploitation of sporting talent and the ever-growing trend of profit maximisation in the transfer market for football players. Third-party ownership is considered a risk so significant to players, clubs and football's integrity that a global ban was imposed by the Fédération Internationale de Football Association (FIFA), which is now subject to legal challenge in the courts and at the European Commission (EC). This legal battle is a stand-off between those who seek reform and those benefiting from a non-transparent transfer market that is worth billions and is open to corruption.

Background

TPO is operated in different models around the world, but in the European markets arises in the following rough scenario.

- A football club needs money, usually for the 'acquisition' of new employees (players), or sometimes for other projects in a drive to boost competitiveness.
- A third party – an agent, investment fund or other entity – provides the club with the required money.
- In return, this third party does not receive a typical commercial value (such as a sponsorship) or a guarantee on the club's infrastructure, but 'acquires' the partial or complete rights to the fee the club will receive in the future for transferring the employee to a new club.[3]

The interest of the third-party investor is obvious: maximising his or her return on investment via the transfer of the player to another club during the duration of his or her contract at the maximum transfer fee, in the shortest possible timeframe. The risks of collusion and sharing in undue financial kickbacks between agents, club managers and investors are high. The football player, who at least in Europe is usually not party to these agreements and is often not even aware of such agreements,[4] thereby becomes the asset in an investment agreement, while his or her rights as a citizen and worker are at risk.

The emergence of TPO has led to an intense political struggle[5] – and, more recently, a legal battle[6] – about the impact, causes and prohibition of TPO. Proponents of TPO view it as a regular investment policy, benefiting clubs' competitiveness in a market of growing financial disparity; these are mainly TPO investment funds (such as Doyen Sports Group), agents and certain clubs deeply invested in TPO funding models.[7] The fight to remove TPO is based on concerns about infringements of human rights and labour rights, general threats to the integrity of competitions and negative medium- and long-term economic consequences, which have been characterised as setting clubs in a vicious cycle of debt and speculation.[8] The trade unions representing professional football players are natural opponents of TPO, and find support from FIFA and the Union of European Football Associations (UEFA).

Labour relations in professional football

Comprehending TPO requires an understanding of the very specific nature of the football labour and transfer market system. In professional sport, the workforce of a club or franchise is the most valuable asset of the employer, not only because of the labour the workforce provides but also because of its image and intellectual property rights, which are of immense importance to safeguard the main revenue streams – broadcasting, sponsorship and merchandise, as well as gate receipts.[9] On the other hand, having the freedom to offer their services on the labour market is the key for athletes to maximise their salary income in what is often a short-lived and precarious career.

Consequently, the history of collective labour relations in professional sport has been marked by a struggle for freedom of movement and free agency on the part of the players, against restrictive rules – such as retain and transfer systems, the reserve clause, salary caps, etc. – that help to exert control over this workforce, and its pay, for clubs' owners and management.[10] Prior to the 1995 'Bosman ruling' of the European Court of Justice, a player, even after the end of his or her employment relationship, depended on an agreement and compensation payment between the former and future employers in order to have his or her player licence transferred, and thereby being cleared to play. The Court recognised this as an infringement of freedom of movement, permitting players to move to another club at the end of a contract without a transfer fee being paid to the previous club.[11]

A subsequent investigation by the European Commission into specific labour market regulations of football culminated in an informal agreement via an exchange of letters between Mario Monti, the competition commissioner, and FIFA president Sepp Blatter in 2001.[12] This agreement settled a long dispute between the Commission and football's international federations, and, while its legal status remains questionable, it established the basis on which the current transfer system operates:

● A system of training compensation aligned with the movement of young players to reward their training by the home club, as well as a solidarity mechanism to the same effect.
● The creation of two limited periods per year (transfer windows) during which transfers of players are exclusively allowed.

- Minimum and maximum duration of contracts of, respectively, one and five years.
- A protected period during which the unilateral breach of an employment contract is subject to a sporting sanction, which in the case of the player equals a ban on participating in matches.
- Breaches of contracts to be exclusively possible at the end of a season.
- A system of financial compensation for unilateral contractual breaches by clubs or players.
- The creation of an arbitration system in which members are chosen equally by clubs and players with an independent chairman, including an appeals body; such arbitration is voluntary and does not prevent recourse to national courts.[13]

From the perspective of the players' unions around the world, the implementation and application of this agreement has failed football on various levels, and it continues to impose an imbalance of power between the vast majority of players and their clubs while limiting the application of general workers' protections.[14] It has also facilitated and sustained widespread abusive practices, such as delayed or withheld salary payments and players becoming trapped with clubs that are acting in bad faith, and has encouraged business models such as TPO.

As a result, despite the Bosman ruling and the EC intervention, football continues to operate as a market in which players and their labour are traded assets.

The relevance of TPO

This particular set of market mechanisms, paired with the accelerating commercial expansion of football (2014's US$4.1 billion in transfer compensations was the highest to date),[15] has opened the floodgates and attracted third parties seeking to exploit this opaque and at times seemingly irrational industry. It is not surprising that such a market is subject to criminal activities such as money-laundering and trafficking, as recognised by the Financial Action Task Force (FATF) in a 2009 report on the football industry.[16] Long before TPO was a topic of public debate the FATF concluded that

> money laundering . . . through the football sector is revealed to be deeper and more complex than previously understood . . . [with] a variety of money flows and/or financial transactions . . . related to the ownership of football clubs or players, the transfer market, betting activities, image rights and sponsorship or advertising arrangements. Other cases show that the football sector is also used as a vehicle for perpetrating various other criminal activities such as trafficking in human beings, corruption, drugs trafficking (doping) and tax offences.[17]

The underlying philosophy and mentality in much of professional sport is one of short-term success – the next match is in a few days, relegation or promotion are only weeks away – and, in the absence of sustainable revenue-sharing structures, poor performances and rankings can throw a club into a cycle of declining revenue and non-competitiveness. While the highest payroll does not guarantee a title, competitiveness in professional football is known to have a close correlation with expenditure on wages.[18]

The threshold to compete for the best players is based not only on the capacity to pay wages over the course of a contract, but also on the ability to pay a large up-front transfer fee. Clubs can therefore turn to high-risk budget management strategies and speculative investment models, such as TPO, in attempts to accelerate their sporting performance by 'doping' their financial capacity.

Although reliable data on TPO agreements are hard to come by, two recent studies commissioned by FIFA and the European Clubs Association, an association of some 200 leading professional football clubs across Europe,[19] projected that the market share of players under TPO in all European leagues is between 3.7 per cent and 5.7 per cent, and the value of third-party investments is between 10 per cent and 50 per cent of players' market value.[20] This amounts to an estimated US$359.52 million per season in transfer compensation. Of the total amount of transfer compensation appropriated by third parties, 97.3 per cent concerns European or South American releasing clubs.[21]

Effects of TPO

Investment by a third party with a purely commercial interest in the maximised transfer of an individual player has the potential to undermine players' fundamental freedoms to move freely, choose their employer or even decide to enter a new career path. By contrast, TPO supporters invoke the argument that investors could never blatantly interfere with employment decisions, as, without the agreement of the current employer and the player, no contract can be terminated and no transfer agreement made. While this statement may hold true on paper, one of the most relevant objections concerns the amount of freedom that the player and the current club have in giving or withholding their consent.

There exists a public misconception about the negotiating power of players vis-à-vis their current and possible future employers. The vast majority of non-'superstar' professional players from the 'secondary market' offer their services to a limited number of clubs, so the number of buyers (clubs) is small but the number of sellers (players) is large.[22] Large parts of the football industry are also prone to labour contract abuse and discriminative practices, including the late payment or non-payment of salaries, harassment, violence and discrimination in the workplace.[23] A player's career is short and precarious. Strong competition between players means that market value has to be continuously established, and any period of non-performance may limit football players' future employment opportunities. Thus these players can be very vulnerable to management's power, and their consent can be forced.

Likewise, employing clubs can lose their decision-making freedom via TPO agreements. Analysis of the few accessible TPO agreements shows the dominant position of third-party owners, assigning them direct or indirect powers regarding employment decisions at the club,[24] including fines or extended ownership rights if a club extends a player's employment contract or fails to transfer a player by a certain date or for a certain value.

The risks of corruption are further increased with the commonly understood involvement of some player agents, who are deeply engaged in TPO. Conflicts of interests are inevitable if an agent who represents a player or a club in labour negotiations is at the same time financially invested in the value of such agreements. The best personal choice of the player may very well not be the most profitable for the agent. It therefore seems clear that third-party investors can and do possess power over labour-related decisions, and thereby limit players' freedom of movement and undermine existing contracts.

TPO also affects the economic sustainability of football. Although TPO investments could add further resources, these amounts plus interest are later withdrawn, while the clubs remain reliant on the continued supply of such external funds to maintain their business models and their sporting competitiveness. TPO also has the potential to affect the sporting integrity of football. Controlling the rights of a network of players could provide third-party owners with the ability to directly impact game performance. Such power has repeatedly been cited by the

Fédération Internationale des Associations de Footballeurs Professionels (FIFPro) and UEFA as a credible threat in terms of match-fixing.[25]

Finally, recent revelations about corruption scandals in and around FIFA have led to the indictment, and guilty plea, of José Hawilla,[26] the owner and founder of Traffic Group (a multinational sports marketing conglomerate), who is reported to have detailed to US authorities his central role in a bribery scheme of more than US$100 million in the acquisition of commercial rights related to major sporting competitions.[27] While no connection has been established to these activities, it is worth noting that Traffic Group has been one of the leading TPO investors in the South American market.[28]

The regulatory response

In September 2014 FIFA's Executive Committee decided to impose a stringent prohibition of TPO, and in December that year adopted an amendment to the FIFA Regulations on the Status and Transfer of Players along the following principles:[29]

- TPO, under a more stringent definition then previously, was to be banned as of 1 May 2015;
- existing TPO agreements signed before 2015 would remain in force until their ordinary contractual expiry;
- between January and April 2015 new TPO agreements could be signed with a maximum duration of one year after the interdiction; and
- all existing TPO agreements were to be uploaded and disclosed by the clubs participating in the FIFA Transfer Matching System.

Within weeks of this decision FIFA Circular 1464 (which encompassed this ban), as well as existing domestic TPO bans,[30] were the subject of legal challenges based on EU competition law and EU internal market grounds by the football leagues in Spain and Portugal, where the practice has been quite widespread, and by Doyen Sports, one of the more prominent TPO providers, in front of the European Commission's Directorate General for Competition and in domestic courts in France and Belgium.[31] In parallel, convinced of the inherent illegality of TPO agreements on the grounds of human rights, workers' rights, competition law and EU internal market freedoms, a 'counter'-complaint was jointly filed with the European Commission in an unprecedented move by FIFPro and UEFA.[32] At the time of writing it remains to be seen which side will obtain the upper hand.

Those opposing the ban on third-party ownership present two central arguments. The first is that TPO should be regulated rather than banned, in order to allow a continued yet regulated supply of funding to clubs. It is very likely, however, that a formal acceptance of regulated TPO would spread the practice, which is dominant only in certain regions at present, to other markets, and therefore possibly lead to an overall growth in what FIFPro and UEFA view as, in its very essence, an infringement of the fundamental rights of players. Moreover, football in various other areas, such as agents and general labour relations, has shown a marked inability to manage such regulations effectively.

The second defence of TPO is as a means to counter a growing financial and sporting disparity between clubs. This speaks to an important problem of the growing financial pre-eminence of a small group of elite clubs in Europe, for which TPO seems an unsuitable and ineffective intervention. Other responses that do not target the labour market, impact the fundamental freedoms of players or carry such significant risks of corruption, but that allow a greater range of clubs, players and fans to share in the undeniable prosperity of the football industry, should be identified.

Conclusion

While the legal arguments about third-party ownership are being exchanged in the courts and in front of the European institutions, the media and the court of public opinion, it needs to be realised that TPO, significant as it is in its own right, is a symptom and a symbol of a larger malaise. Poor governance standards and an industry in which labour is a commodity of trade have created the breeding ground for many of football's most severe problems. In addition to exorbitant agent fees, the non-payment of salaries, match-fixing, money-laundering and the trafficking of minors, TPO corrupts labour relations in football for the gain of private third entities, establishes conflicts of interest and may further other financial crimes.

Ultimately, a meaningful reform of the culture and governance of football must put individual rights and freedoms over commercial and power-driven self-interests, achieve financial transparency and establish strong checks and balances and resilience against corruption.

Notes

1   Jonas Baer-Hoffmann is the director policy of FIFPro Division Europe.
2   Reuters, 'Platini delighted soccer's "modern-day slavery" is ending', 16 March 2015, *http://in.reuters.com/article/2015/03/16/soccer-platini-tpo-idINKBN0MC1B220150316.*
3   This is the general model in the European market; a slightly different principle applies in the South American market, which is explained in the next chapter of this report.
4   *Daily Mail* (UK), 'Manchester City defender Eliaquim Mangala reveals he was clueless to investment firm ownership during Porto spell', 31 August 2014, *www.dailymail.co.uk/sport/ football/article-2739023/Manchester-City-s-Eliaquim-Mangala-reveals-clueless-split-ownership.html.*
5   Reuters, 'Platini makes plea to FIFA to ban third party owners', 27 March 2014, *www.reuters.com/article/2014/03/27/us-soccer-uefa-congress-platini-idUSBREA2Q 0AX20140327.*
6   Union of European Football Associations, 'UEFA and FIFPro launch complaint against third-party ownership', 1 April 2015, *www.uefa.org/stakeholders/players-unions/news/ newsid=2230203.html*; ESPN (US), 'Doyen Sports to challenge FIFA ban on third-party ownership in court: report', 18 March 2015, *www.espnfc.com/story/2354720/ doyen-sports-challenges-fifa-transfer-third-party-ownership-ban-french-court-report.*
7   Leaders in Sport (UK), 'Daniel Lorenz, FC Porto: third-party ownership: a major source of revenue', 17 February 2015, *www.leadersinsport.com/insight/business/226/daniel-lorenz-fc-porto.*
8   Centre international d'étude du sport and Centre de droit et d'économie du sport, *Research on Third Party Ownership of Players' Economic Rights* (Neuchâtel: Centre international d'étude du sport, 2014).
9   Union of European Football Associations, *Licensed to Thrill: Benchmarking Report on the Clubs Qualified and Licensed to Compete in the UEFA Competition Season 2013/14* (Nyon, Switzerland: UEFA, 2013), p. 35, *www.uefa.org/MultimediaFiles/Download/Tech/uefaorg/ General/01/99/91/07/1999107_DOWNLOAD.pdf.*
10 Beyond the Box Score (US), 'Marvin Miller and how free agency came to baseball, part 1', 24 November 2008, *www.beyondtheboxscore.com/2008/11/24/668999/marvin-miller-and-the-how.*

11   *Wall Street Journal* (US), 'Bosman still struggling with ruling that rewards soccer's free agents', 2 July 2014, *www.wsj.com/articles/the-jean-marc-bosman-ruling-benefited-soccers-free-agents-but-the-man-himself-is-still-struggling-1404327335*.

12   European Commission, 'Commission closes investigations into FIFA regulations on international football transfers', press release, 5 June 2002, *http://europa.eu/rapid/press-release_IP-02-824_en.htm*.

13   Fédération Internationale de Football Association, *Regulations on the Status and Transfer of Players* (Zurich: FIFA, 2007), *www.fifa.com/mm/document/affederation/administration/regulations_on_the_status_and_transfer_of_players_en_33410.pdf*.

14   Fédération Internationale des Associations Footballeurs Professionnels, 'FIFPro announces legal challenge to transfer system', press release, 17 December 2013, *www.fifpro.org/en/news/fifpro-announces-legal-challenge-to-transfer-system*.

15   FIFA Transfer Matching System, *Global Transfer Market Report 2015* (Zurich: FIFA TMS, 2015), *www.fifatms.com/Global/Testimonials/Gtm/Preview-GTM15.pdf*.

16   Financial Action Task Force, *Money Laundering through the Football Sector* (Paris: FATF, 2009), *www.fatf-gafi.org/media/fatf/documents/reports/ML%20through%20the%20Football%20Sector.pdf*.

17   Ibid., p. 4.

18   Stefan Szymanski, *Money and Football: A Soccernomics Guide* (New York: Nation Books, 2015).

19   European Clubs Association, 'About ECA', *www.ecaeurope.com/about-eca*.

20   KPMG Asesores, *Project TPO* (Madrid: KPMG Asesores, 2013), *www.ecaeurope.com/Research/External%20Studies%20and%20Reports/KPMG%20TPO%20Report.pdf*.

21   Centre international d'étude du sport/Centre de droit et d'économie du sport (2014).

22   KEA European Affairs and Centre de droit et d'économie du sport, *The Economic and Legal Aspects of Transfers of Players* (Brussels: KEA European Affairs, 2013), *http://ec.europa.eu/sport/library/documents/cons-study-transfers-final-rpt.pdf*.

23   Fédération Internationale des Associations Footballeurs Professionnels, *FIFPro Black Book Eastern Europe: The Problems Professional Footballers Encounter* (Hoofddorp, Netherlands: FIFPro, 2012), *www.lefigaro.fr/assets/pdf/fifpro.pdf*.

24   KPMG Asesores (2013), p. 15.

25   Soccerex (UK), 'Third-party ownership has "no place" in football: Infantino', 20 March 2013, *www.soccerex.com/news/2013/03/third-party-ownership-has-%E2%80%9Cno-place%E2%80%9D-football-%E2%80%93-infantino*.

26   US Department of Justice, 'Nine FIFA officials and five corporate executives indicted for racketeering conspiracy and corruption', 27 May 2015, *www.justice.gov/opa/pr/nine-fifa-officials-and-five-corporate-executives-indicted-racketeering-conspiracy-and*.

27   Bloomberg (US), 'FIFA scandal unearths Brazilian power broker atop soccer fortune', 2 June 2015, *www.bloomberg.com/news/articles/2015-06-02/fifa-scandal-unearths-brazilian-power-broker-atop-soccer-fortune*.

28   Bloomberg (US), 'Soccer hedge fund betting on players gets global FIFA ban', 26 September 2014, *www.bloomberg.com/news/articles/2014-09-26/soccer-hedge-fund-betting-on-players-gets-global-fifa-ban*.

29   Fédération Internationale de Football Association, 'Regulations on the status and transfer of players: third-party ownership of players' economic rights ("TPO")', Circular no. 1464, 22 December 2014, *www.fifa.com/mm/document/affederation/administration/02/49/57/42/tpocircular1464_en_neutral.pdf*.

30   Domestic bans in Europe are currently in place in England, France and Poland.

31   Bloomberg (US), 'Hedge fund challenges European soccer-transfer market ban', 18 March 2015, *www.bloomberg.com/news/articles/2015-03-18/hedge-fund-challenges-european-soccer-transfer-market-exclusion*.

32   ESPN (US), 'UEFA, FIFPro join forces for ban against third-party ownership', 1 April 2015, *www.espnfc.com/uefa-champions-league/story/2376057/uefa-and-fifpro-join-forces-for-ban-against-third-party-ownership*.

2.6

Origins, practice and regulation of third-party ownership in South America

Alexandra Gómez Bruinewoud and Gonzalo Bossart[1]

Starting in the mid-1990s, two events – completely isolated and independent from each other – combined to give birth to what is now called third-party ownership (TPO). In South America, enormous flows of direct foreign investment, hungry for unexploited natural resources, led to substantial and sustained economic growth in the region, and consequently for new and more sophisticated business opportunities.[2] Football stood apart from this economic success story, however: several clubs were facing bankruptcy, and most were struggling to survive. Banks, sponsors and television were turning their back on the activity. Meanwhile, in Europe, the freedom of movement of individuals and workers was having a major impact on the football transfer market, since European players were no longer considered as foreigners by clubs within the European Union. This catapulted the demand for and 'prices' of players worldwide,[3] and the trend was quickly read by entrepreneurial South American businessmen as a good business opportunity: on the one hand, South American clubs were begging for new funds, and their players remained as their sole 'assets'; on the other hand, European clubs, with plenty of cash in their pockets, were thirsty for the well-known talented South American players.[4]

TPO is understood as

> the Agreement between a Club and a Third Party, such as investment funds, companies, sports agencies, agents and/or private investors, in accordance to which, a Third Party, whether or not in relation with an actual payment in favour of a club, acquires an economic participation or a future credit related to the eventual transfer of a certain football player.[5]

TPO has become a powerful and easy way for South American clubs to obtain new funds, which in turn allow them to finance their youth teams, to reinforce their squads with new players and even to cover their basic economic obligations that often cannot be afforded with the standard forms of income (broadcasting rights, sponsorship, merchandising and ticketing, among others).[6]

In practice, two types of investors partake in TPO. The first are legal persons, such as companies or investment funds, which use TPO as a way to invest alongside other investors, to benefit from the inherent advantages of working as part of a group. This takes place mainly in Argentina and Brazil, where the TPO 'culture' is more widespread.[7] The second are natural persons, such as players' agents, though an important role is also played by the so-called 'clubes puente' ('bridge clubs'), which are used to 'regularise' the ownership of an investor over the economic rights of a footballer, in order to circumvent bans on TPO, as well as to avoid taxes.[8]

The regulation of TPO in South America varies from country to country. Some football associations, such as those of Chile,[9] Colombia[10] and Uruguay,[11] have a strict ban, according to national law (Colombia and Uruguay) and the federation's internal regulations (Chile). Brazil bans the influence but not the practice – that is, a third party cannot be punished for acquiring the economic rights of a player, as long as the investor is not granted the right to decide on the player's transfer – in line with article 18 bis of the *Regulations on the Status and Transfers of Players* of the Fédération Internationale de Football Association (FIFA).[12] In Paraguay and Peru, there is no regulation of TPO.

Impact and implications of TPO on clubs and players in South America

Although the direct impact of third-party ownership on players in South America is a foremost concern, the impact on the clubs affects the players as well, and, as such, both are considered below.

TPO in South America is carried out mainly through players' agents. The phenomenon can be described as follows:

> *The Clubs, because of the need to survive, resort to agents and offer them the rights on the players who are still in formative divisions (juveniles). The Agents, taking advantage of the extreme necessity of the teams, acquire the rights on the players at very low prices in comparison to the final price in the international market.*[13]

The other form of TPO is when clubs want to acquire players whom they cannot afford, and rely on TPO to pay for their transfer fee.

From this financial perspective, the flourishing of TPO has provided clubs in need with a certain cash flow, which might seem positive, given the clubs' debts and financial obligations. In the long term, however, it has proved to be financially unhealthy,[14] since clubs enter into a never-ending cycle of debt: they borrow money to acquire a player and then receive a much lower proportion of the ultimate transfer fee, which is insufficient to replace the player; and, additionally, they owe 'favours' to the investors. Therefore, after all the years of training and educating a player, when the moment of the transfer arrives, the amount they receive is minimal. Solidarity contributions[15] – an important source of income for South American clubs – are also reduced as a result of TPO, as they are calculated after the transfer amount owned by the third party involved has been deducted.[16]

Moreover, South American clubs often acquire players they could normally not afford, using mechanisms of TPO. This ends up with clubs being unable to pay the promised salaries to the players, creating contract instability, and frustrating players, which can ultimately affect their performance. Contract stability for players is also affected since investors continuously incentivise trade, regardless of the contract terms,[17] because it is when the player is transferred that the investors receive their percentage. As an example, this is what Sporting Lisbon claims happened during Marcos Rojo's transfer to Manchester United in the summer transfer window of 2014.[18]

Most young players in South America are subject to TPO, with the level reaching almost 90 per cent in Brazil.[19] This affects the career development of the players,[20] who are seen merely as assets and are transferred at the first opportunity that seems profitable, without considering their age and experience. Inevitably, this raises social and sporting concerns. Players are often pressured by third-party owners to agree to transfer to the club that would be most profitable for the investor.[21] Generally speaking, players from South America are not as well educated as their European counterparts and come from more vulnerable environments, which makes them easier to persuade and control.

The independence of the player, the player's freedom of movement and the integrity of the game are all at stake. There is also a risk of conflicts of interest, as third parties might own various players at different clubs, which could damage the integrity of competitions.

The cases of Uruguay and Chile

Uruguay

The situation in Uruguay, historically a large exporter of high-quality footballers,[22] is quite peculiar. There are 31 clubs in the first and second professional divisions,[23] most of them located in the capital city of Montevideo, which has 1.5 million inhabitants. The disproportionate number of clubs to potential supporters makes most clubs economically vulnerable. This has opened the door to TPO, which has expanded hugely in recent decades. The occurrence of TPO is common knowledge but difficult to prove, since, as it is prohibited, it is not registered, so there are no formal figures.

In Uruguay, TPO is most commonly performed by agents who simultaneously act as intermediaries and investors, since they acquire a percentage in the future transfer of the player. As a result, there is usually a close relationship between the player and the investor, since in these cases the investor is the player's agent. This gives the agent an even stronger influence on the player's decision.

Uruguay passed a law prohibiting TPO in 1980,[24] though it has never been properly enforced. The president of the Asociación Uruguaya de Fútbol (AUF) has stated that the organisation enforces the law by prohibiting the registry of any contracts involving TPO. On the other hand, he acknowledges that it would appear that it does exist in practice.[25]

Chile

Unlike their counterparts in Uruguay, Chilean clubs enjoy a relative healthy economic situation. Broadcasting rights[26] and clubs' revised legal structures[27] have substantially increased their income, allowing them to support much of their costs. Even so, rising operating costs, in particular transfer fees and salaries,[28] impact most clubs' budgets, forcing many of them to seek 'non-conventional' funding. This is how, in spite of the prohibition set by the Football Federation of Chile, agents finance the formation of young footballers, in exchange for a percentage of the price paid in their future transfer. To a lesser extent, clubes puente have been used, albeit as a way to reduce tax obligations.[29]

Impact of the new FIFA prohibition of TPO

In South America there is a popular saying, 'Hecha la ley, hecha la trampa', which means that, when a law is created, a way to circumvent it is created as well. There is much truth in the saying, so, in practice, and regrettably, clubs will probably find ways to circumvent the new rule.

If this turns out not to be the case, however, and the rule is effectively enforced by the football associations, it will have a major impact on South American football. TPO is so widespread, and clubs' financial and competitive dependence on TPO is so deep-rooted, that it becomes difficult to see how it can disappear in the short term. It is an issue not just of finance and competition but of culture as well. If the prohibition is put into effect, in the short term it could actually bankrupt some clubs, taking into account that there are clubs that really have very little in the way of fans and economic support, and carry on only as a result of TPO. They are always late paying their players' salaries, and do not so much 'thrive' as 'survive'.

In any event, the termination of TPO will be positive for South American football, allowing clubs finally to be able to receive the whole amount of the transfer fees, and to decide, together with players, when and to which club a transfer is appropriate. The great talent of South American players will not disappear with the prohibition and, in fact, the ban will probably lead to stronger clubs that can keep their players longer by enhancing their contractual stability and giving them better development prospects. As the best-performing clubs are those with stable teams,[30] an effective TPO ban could improve the quality of the national and regional championships in South America, as well as the labour conditions of the players.

Notes

1   Alexandra Gómez Bruinewoud is a legal counsel at FIFPro and Gonzalo Bossart is a partner at Alessandri, Bossart, Pacheo and Cia law firm.
2   United Nations Economic Commission for Latin America and the Caribbean, 'Síntesis y Conclusiones', *www.cepal.org/publicaciones/xml/2/4262/sintesis.htm.*
3   Stephan Zivec, 'Freedom of movement for workers: impact on transfers of EU football players – the Bosman case', 2013, *www.academia.edu/4221444/Freedom_of_Movement_ for_Workers_-_Bosman_Case.*
4   Ariel Reck, 'Third party player ownership: current trends in South America and Europe', *EPFL Sports Law Bulletin*, vol. 10 (2012).
5   KPMG Asesores, *Project TPO* (Madrid: KPMG Asesores, 2013), *www.ecaeurope.com/ Research/External%20Studies%20and%20Reports/KPMG%20TPO%20Report.pdf.*
6   IUSport.com, '¿Qué tipo de operaciones realizan los fondos de inversión en el fútbol?', 3 August 2014, *http://iusport.com/not/2629/-que-tipo-de-operaciones-realizan-los- fondos-de-inversion-en-el-futbol.*
7   Eduardo Carlezzo, 'Investments in economic rights of football players: a Brazilian and international overview', *EPFL Sports Law Bulletin*, vol. 10 (2012); IUSport.com, 'FIFA versus fondos de inversión: ¿la estocada final?', 20 February 2015, *http://iusport.com/not/5273/ fifa-versus-fondos-de-inversion-la-estocada-final.*
8   Fédération Internationale de Football Association, 'Clubes argentinos y uruguayo sancionados por "traspasos puente"', media release, 5 March 2014, *http://es.m.fifa.com/ aboutfifa/news/newsid=2292728.html.*
9   Reglamento Asociación Nacional de Fútbol Profesional (Chile), article 152C.
10   Ley 181 de 1995 (Colombia), article 32.
11   Ley 14.996 (Uruguay), article 2.
12   Ley 9.615 ('Ley Pelé'), article 27B.
13   Sala de Redaccíon [Newsroom] (Uruguay), 'El bajo precio de la necesidad', 28 November 2011, *http://sdr.liccom.edu.uy/2011/11/28/el-bajo-precio-de-la-necesidad.*
14   Centre de droit et d'économie du sport (CDES), *Research on Third-Party Ownership of Players' Economic Rights (Part II)* (Limoges: CDES, 2014), p. 79.
15   Fédération Internationale de Football Association, *Regulations on the Status and Transfer of Players* (Zurich: FIFA, 2014), annex 5, article 1: 'If a professional moves during the course of

a contract, 5% of any compensation . . . shall be deducted from the total amount of this compensation and distributed by the new club as a solidarity contribution to the clubs . . . between the season of his 12th and 23rd birthdays.'

16   CDES (2014), p. 72.
17   Ibid., p. 71.
18   BBC (UK), 'Manchester United: Sporting reveal Marcos Rojo sale "pressure"', 3 October 2014, *www.bbc.com/sport/0/football/29474696.*
19   KPMG Asesores (2013), p. 33.
20   CDES (2014), p. 81.
21   Interview with professional players (names withheld) with author, 29 April 2015.
22   *El Observador* (Uruguay), 'Uruguay, el mayor exportador de futbolistas', 14 July 2011, *www.elobservador.com.uy/uruguay-el-mayor-exportador-de-futbolistas-n205478.*
23   *www.auf.org.uy/Portal/TOURNAMENT_URUGUAYAN/2.*
24   See footnote 9.
25   Interview with Wilmar Valdez with author, 5 May 2015.
26   Centro de Investigación Periodística (Chile), 'CDF: Cómo se reparte el "botín" más preciado del fútbol', 12 November 2012, *http://ciperchile.cl/2012/11/12/cdf-como-se-reparte-el-"botin"-mas-preciado-del-futbol.*
27   Bolsa de Santiago (Chile), 'Oportunidades de Financiamiento en Bolsa', *www.bolsadesantiago.com/Biblioteca%20de%20Archivos/Emisores/Oportunidades%20de%20financiamiento.pdf.*
28   24 Horas (Chile), 'Estos son los sueldos de los jugadores del fútbol chileno', 29 December 2014, *www.24horas.cl/deportes/futbol-nacional/estos-son-los-sueldos-de-los-jugadores-del-futbol-chileno-1540279.*
29   Marca (Argentina), 'La AFA suspende a dos jugadores a petición del Fisco', 22 August 2012, *www.marca.com/2012/08/22/futbol/futbol_internacional/argentina/1345657070.html.*
30   CDES (2014).

PART 3

Events in the spotlight

3.1

The multiple roles of mega-events

Mega-promises, mini-outcomes?

Martin Müller[1]

There was once a time when a sports event was just that: an occasion at which athletes met to see who could run faster, jump higher, throw the javelin further. Today, sport remains the anchor of the Olympic Games, the football World Cup and other mega-events – but it has become a sideshow in many other senses. Of about 360,000 accredited personnel at the London Olympic Games in 2012, fewer than 3 per cent were athletes.[2] Although the number of athletes at the Summer Olympic Games has hovered at around 10,000 for the past 20 years, the number of media representatives has almost doubled, while that of security personnel has trebled.[3] Neither does expenditure for venues and sports-related infrastructure continue to be the most expensive item in the budget. Investment in transport infrastructure or the upgrading of neighbourhoods eclipses money spent on sports, sometimes by several times.[4] Barcelona, for example, allocated 83 per cent of its budget for the 1992 Summer Olympics to urban improvement, not to sport.[5]

    Large sports events come in different shapes and sizes. They can be classified into three tiers: major events, mega-events and – for the largest of them – giga-events. Size is measured with four indicators: the number of visitors, the value of broadcasting rights, the total cost and the capital investment (see Tables 3.1 and 3.2; Figure 3.1). The Summer Olympic Games and

Size	Visitor attractiveness Number of tickets sold	Mediated reach Value of broadcast rights	Cost Total cost	Transformation Capital investment
XXL (3 points)	> 3 million	> USD 2 billion	> USD 10 billion	> USD 10 billion
XL (2 points)	> 1 million	> USD 1 billion	> USD 5 billion	> USD 5 billion
L (1 point)	> 0.5 million	> USD 0.1 billion	> USD 1 billion	> USD 1 billion

Giga-event: 11–12 points total
Mega-event: 7–10 points total
Major event: 1–6 points total

Table 3.1 Scoring matrix for event classes according to size

Event	Location	Visitor attractiveness Number of tickets sold	Mediated reach Value of broadcast rights	Cost Total cost	Transformation Capital investment	Total	Class
Olympic Games	London 2012	3	3	3	2	11	Giga
Euro	Ukraine/Poland 2012	2	2	3	3	10	Mega
Football World Cup	South Africa 2010	3	3	2	2	10	Mega
Expo	Shanghai 2010	3	0	3	3	9	Mega
Asian Games	Guangzhou 2010	2	0	3	3	8	Mega
Olympic Winter Games	Vancouver 2010	2	2	2	1	7	Mega
Commonwealth Games	Delhi 2010	2	0	2	2	6	Major
Universiade	Kazan 2013	1	0	2	2	5	Major
Rugby World Cup	New Zealand 2011	2	2e	0	0	4	Major
Pan American Games	Guadalajara 2011	1	0	0	0	1	Major
Super Bowl	New Orleans 2013	0	1	0	0	1	Major

Table 3.2 Size classification of elected events

Source: Martin Müller, 'What makes an event a mega-event? Definitions and sizes', *Leisure Studies* (2015), http://dx.doi.org/10.1080/02614367.2014.993333.
Note: e = estimate

the football World Cup are almost always the largest sports events according to these indicators, followed by the European Football Championship, the Winter Olympic Games and regional games such as the Asian Games or the Commonwealth Games. [6]

No matter the size, almost all large sports events are meant to play multiple roles beyond their primary one as sports happenings. Promoters often regard them as panacea for all kinds of social, political and economic ills. By hosting them, cities seek to reinvigorate languishing neighbourhoods; regions want to build infrastructure and boost economic growth; countries are keen to signal diplomatic stature and attract tourists; political parties strive to excite their electorate; and companies hope to fill their order books. But the grand ambitions are often not matched by the outcomes.

Economic stimulus

The expected economic impact forms an essential part of justifying bids for large sports events. The unanimous message of studies before events is that they stand to generate jobs, additional tax income and economic growth for the host region; this is a claim that almost never materialises, however. For the 1994 football World Cup in the United States,

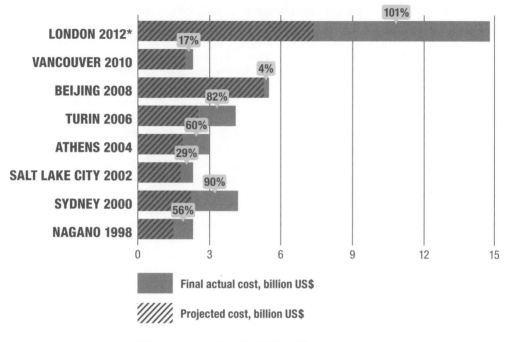

Figure 3.1 Sports-related cost overruns, 1998–2012 Olympics.

Source: Bent, Flyvbjerg and Allison Stewart, *Olympic Proportions: Cost and Cost Overrun at the Olympics 1960–2012*, working paper (Oxford: Saïd Business School, University of Oxford, 2012).

for example, studies commissioned by event promoters predicted a net economic gain of US$4 billion for the host cities. An independent examination after the event revealed that the net economic impact was, in fact, negative, and placed it in the region of US$5.5 to US$9.3 billion.[7]

One problem with predicting economic impact is that *ex ante* studies operate with overly optimistic assumptions to arrive at the desired results and sell the event to the public.[8] After all, public approval is crucial, as both a requirement for bidding and for potential referenda.[9] Once the event is over, few care to follow up on the initial estimates. The 'lowballing' of costs is particularly widespread. The Olympic Games, for example, have an average cost overrun of 79 per cent – much more than any other type of large project (see Figure 3.1).[10]

Such underestimation of costs skews cost–benefit calculations before the event. Even when the economic tally of large events may be positive, however, events may not constitute the best use for public money, since other investment opportunities may create higher returns. This is a question that studies of economic impact do not examine but that would have to form part of a balanced assessment of costs and benefits. Arguably, it is more beneficial for society if tax revenue is returned to taxpayers.

Image booster

Where economic growth is a tangible benefit, image improvements are the most frequently cited intangible benefits accruing from large events. Brands such as the Olympic Games or the football World Cup enjoy unrivalled recognition and positive associations. Thus, 93 per cent of the population recognise the Olympic rings and 73 per cent think that hosting the Olympics leaves the host city with many benefits.[11] Cities and countries hosting large sports events seek to benefit from linking themselves with these brands – a phenomenon also known as co-branding – and from the public attention that events generate, placing them in the global limelight. Who in Western countries would have known about Sochi before the 2014 Winter Games, or about the rich cultural heritage of Lviv, Ukraine, before the 2012 European Football Championship?

This putative intangible benefit is much coveted in the global attention economy. But, while some studies show that hosting a large event can create positive associations and an increase in name recognition,[12] others find that negative perceptions prevail if a country's dirty laundry is exposed to the world.[13] Thus, China and Russia saw coverage of human rights abuses and corruption during the run-up to their hosting the 2008 Summer and 2014 Winter Olympic Games, respectively.[14] Finally, large events are short-lived and follow in close succession, so the long-term image benefits remain uncertain and effects may often be short-lived.[15] Once the event is over, attention declines as the spotlight moves on to the next host, and positive associations tend to decrease, as it often becomes clear that expectations were too overdrawn in comparison with the actual benefits.[16] It is also unclear whether a better image and higher awareness translate into tangible benefits such as higher growth.

Tourist attraction

Cities and countries speculate that the global attention that large sports events generate will attract visitors, not just for the event itself, but also in the long run. Experts point to the 'Barcelona model', whereby the 1992 Summer Olympics were part of a larger package of urban renewal that turned the city into a top tourist destination.[17]

On average, large events do indeed boost tourism to host countries. One study finds an increase of 8 per cent in the year of the event.[18] This boost occurs only for the largest events, however, and only during the off-season, when event visitors do not crowd out other tourists. In destinations such as London, that already run close to full capacity, large events tend to displace other tourists rather than add significant additional demand. In the majority of cases, there is also an increased tourist inflow before the event, though not afterwards. This suggests that an event itself is not enough to radically alter the tourism growth path of a city or country.

Infrastructural catalyst

The large numbers of visitors, journalists, officials and athletes who descend on event hosts place high demands on the urban infrastructure. Among the key requirements are high-capacity airports and public transport systems, high-bandwidth information and communication technology infrastructure, a reliable energy supply and hotel accommodation in different service classes. When this infrastructure does not exist, it needs to be built. This is why some claim that large events can become catalysts for a city, 'accelerat[ing] its infrastructural development by up to 10 years'.[19] Often cities can use events as levers to extract funding from the central government and the taxpayer. This was the major reason the then mayor of London, Ken Livingstone, was interested in the 2012 Summer Olympics: 'I didn't bid for the Olympics because I wanted three weeks of sport. I bid for the Olympics because it's the only way to get the billions of pounds out of the Government to develop the East End.'[20]

Events and their immutable deadlines create a sense of urgency and political consensus among often warring political parties, thus speeding up the delivery of infrastructure. What is built is not necessarily what a city needs, however, or what city leaders promised.[21] Events often hijack urban planning, imposing event-specific requirements that do not tally with master plans, thus altering rather than merely accelerating infrastructural development – a phenomenon known as 'event takeover'.[22] When deadlines are looming and funding is running out, it is more likely that the stadium will be finished than the new bus line.

Conclusion

Large sports events are increasingly about things other than sport. The plethora of promises and expectations that a wide variety of actors – athletes, sponsors, citizens, businesses and governing bodies such as the International Olympic Committee and Fédération Internationale de Football Association – associate with events has invariably led to disappointment. If there is one constant in the hosting of large events, it can be reduced to the formula 'Overpromise, underdeliver'. As costs continue to grow, promises of what large events can achieve are becoming even grander. Despite 'boosterist' claims to the contrary, Olympics, World Cups and so on are inferior as strategies of urban and economic development. In this sense, sports events remain primarily what they have always been: great spectacles.

Notes

1   Martin Müller is a Swiss National Science Foundation professor in the Department of Geography at the University of Zurich.
2   Jean-Loup Chappelet, 'Managing the size of the Olympic Games', *Sport in Society*, vol. 17 (2014).
3   Ibid.
4   Hanwen Liao and Adrian Pitts, 'A brief historical review of Olympic urbanization', *International Journal of the History of Sport,* vol. 23 (2006).
5   John Gold and Margaret Gold, 'Olympic cities: regeneration, city rebranding and changing urban agendas', *Geography Compass*, vol. 2 (2008).
6   Martin Müller, 'What makes an event a mega-event? Definitions and sizes', *Leisure Studies* (2015), http://dx.doi.org/10.1080/02614367.2014.993333.
7   Robert Baade and Victor Matheson, 'The quest for the cup: assessing the economic impact of the World Cup', *Regional Studies*, vol. 38 (2004).
8   Andrew Zimbalist, *Circus Maximus: The Economic Gamble behind Hosting the Olympics and the World Cup* (Washington, DC: Brookings Institution Press, 2015); Brian Mills and Mark Rosentraub, 'Hosting mega-events: a guide to the evaluation of development effects in integrated metropolitan regions', *Tourism Management*, vol. 34 (2013).
9   International Olympic Committee, *2020 Candidature Acceptance Procedure: Games of the XXXII Olympiad* (Lausanne: IOC, 2011), pp. 97–98.
10 Bent Flyvbjerg and Allison Stewart, *Olympic Proportions: Cost and Cost Overrun at the Olympics 1960–2012*, working paper (Oxford: Saïd Business School, University of Oxford, 2012).
11 KantarSport, *IOC Research: Sochi 2014* (Chambourcy: Kantar Media, 2014), *www.olympic. org/Documents/Games_Sochi_2014/Research-directive-Kantar.pdf.*
12 Brent Ritchie and Brian Smith, 'The impact of a mega-event on host region awareness: a longitudinal study', *Journal of Travel Research*, vol. 30 (1991); Hyun-Jeong Kim, Dogan Gursoy and Soo-Bum Lee, 'The impact of the 2002 World Cup on South Korea: comparisons of pre- and post-games', *Tourism Management*, vol. 27 (2006).
13 Louise Heslop, John Nadeau, Norm O'Reilly and Anahit Armenakyan, 'Mega-event and country co-branding: image shifts, transfers and reputational impacts', *Corporate Reputation Review*, vol. 16 (2013).

14 Amnesty International, *Legacy of the Beijing Olympics: China's Choice* (London: Amnesty International, 2007); Jane Buchanan, *Race to the Bottom: Exploitation of Migrant Workers Ahead of Russia's 2014 Winter Olympic Games in Sochi* (New York: Human Rights Watch, 2013).

15 Ritchie and Smith (1991), p. 8.

16 Kim, Gursoy and Lee (2006).

17 Francisco-Javier Monclús, 'The Barcelona model: and an original formula? From "reconstruction" to strategic urban projects (1979–2004)', *Planning Perspectives*, vol. 18 (2003).

18 Johan Fourie and María Santana-Gallego, 'The impact of mega-sport events on tourist arrivals', *Tourism Management*, vol. 32 (2011).

19 Holger Preuss, 'Calculating the regional economic impact of the Olympic Games', *European Sport Management Quarterly*, vol. 4 (2004), p. 234.

20 *Daily Telegraph* (UK), 'Mayor tricked Govt. into 2012 Olympics bid', 25 April 2008, *www.telegraph.co.uk/sport/olympics/2298374/Mayor-tricked-Govt.-into-2012-Olympics-bid.html*.

21 Eva Kassens-Noor, *Planning Olympic Legacies: Transport Dreams and Urban Realities* (London: Routledge, 2012).

22 Martin Müller, 'The mega-event syndrome: why so many things go wrong in mega-event planning – and what to do about it', *Journal of the American Planning Association*, vol. 81 (2015).

3.2
Who bids for events and why?

Scarlett Cornelissen[1]

An important feature of major sport events today is that they have become so commercially focused, driven by business corporations from the worlds of global media, marketing, sports apparel and event organising, that their staging clusters vast volumes of transnational capital. The Summer Olympic Games and the football World Cup are the archetypal mega-events in this regard, because of their size and levels of participation and the revenues they generate. Although smaller in scale, second-order events such as the Commonwealth Games or the rugby or cricket World Cups have also become highly commoditised.[2] The commercial nature of major events partly explains their appeal to many aspiring hosts from across the globe – be they national governments or urban authorities – for which hosting such an event offers a chance to lure capital and tourists, and which seek to leverage the much-lauded branding opportunities that such an event can afford.

The motives underpinning bids

There are also other motivations for staging a major event. These include the search for global prestige and prominence; the attempt to project a particular image of the host in the international arena; and the use of an event to give force to certain diplomatic or domestic objectives.[3] It has been convincingly argued, for instance, that one of the key goals behind the People's Republic of China's bid for the 2008 Summer Olympics was to mark the country's ascendance as one of the new world powers.[4] Four decades earlier a similar objective underpinned Japan's hosting of the 1964 Summer Olympics,[5] and the Japanese government linked the staging of the games to the large-scale transformation of the capital city and an ambitious plan to double national income over the next ten years – a feat Japan went on to accomplish.[6] In a comparable way, South Africa's hosting of the 2010 Fédération Internationale de Football Association (FIFA) World Cup was the culmination of a lengthy period of experimenting with major and lesser events in the post-apartheid era in order to help meet largely unaccomplished domestic goals of socio-economic transformation, national unification and greater international visibility,[7] while much the same can be said for Brazil's recent FIFA World Cup and prospective staging of the 2016 Summer Olympics.[8]

Sometimes the political motivations outweigh the economic rationale. This seems to be the case for many aspiring hosts from the global South or the world's emerging economies, where foreign policy objectives are often placed ahead of goals like urban or national economic revitalisation that typically underpin bids from industrialised states.[9] This helps to explain why aspiring hosts are willing to spend vast amounts of money on extensive, protracted and – more often than not – unsuccessful bid campaigns as they compete for the right to stage an event. And it is not uncommon for bidding contests to be highly antagonistic or to become mired in controversy as bidders use a variety of strategies to try to outwit their opponents. Mostly these take benign forms, such as the mounting of public relations campaigns to cast an aspiring host in a more favourable light vis-à-vis other contenders.

Sometimes, however, bid contests centre on discrediting opponents' capabilities or become an arena of bickering, personalised attacks and graft.[10] Indeed, bidding wars have become part of the theatre of major events, and reveal as much about the changing nature of sport and event politics as they do about the states and cities that bid for events. It was common discourse among the football elite in South Africa, for instance, that the country was bundled out during the last stages of the contest for the 2006 FIFA World Cup as a result of backroom deals.[11] Further, the bid for the 2010 World Cup saw at times acrimonious exchanges between the South African and English bid committees about South Africa's crime situation and the country's capacity to host the event.[12]

How bids come about

Recent investigations into Russia's and Qatar's successful bids for the 2018 and 2022 FIFA World Cups, respectively, underline just how much is at stake for aspiring hosts and the extent to which bidding processes can be manipulated for strategic purposes. The organisational practices of the sport federation that holds proprietorship of the event, along with prior institutional experiences in dealing with public scrutiny or scandals, are, arguably, important factors shaping how sport federations steer bidding contests and the culture within which such contests take place. In this sense, the International Olympic Committee (IOC) experienced organisational shock much earlier than FIFA, being subject to a lot of criticism and scrutiny concerning established practices of graft surrounding bidding contests. This was the case particularly with the scandals and allegations of corruption in the lead-up to the 2002 Salt Lake City Winter Games, since when the IOC has attempted to make bid processes more transparent and to ensure stricter compliance with bidding guidelines.[13]

Most of what the public sees of bid campaigns results from extended processes of networking, strategising and alliance formation among what could often be disparate interest groups in a given domestic context, including the likes of sport associations, business groupings, political office bearers and city managers. As a rule, bids to stage a particular event can be submitted to the international sport federation in whose name the event is staged only by the national member, such as the national Olympic committee in the case of the Olympic Games, or the national football, cricket or rugby organisations in the cases of the FIFA, cricket and rugby World Cups.

By the time a bid is presented to an international sport federation it has gone through several processes of domestic consensus-building, as well as political layers. While it may be typical that campaigns to host Olympic Games are initiated by alliances between city governments and local businesses seeking to draw profit for the city (or sometimes themselves[14]), eventually their campaign would have to appeal to a wider group of political actors in order to muster national support (Figure 3.2).

To mount a campaign for a multi-city tournament such as the FIFA World Cup, numerous coalitions would have to be clustered around the national football organisation, and an array of urban authorities, local and transnational firms, and sometimes political parties and other constituencies would have to be persuaded of the potential merits of the event. In the case of

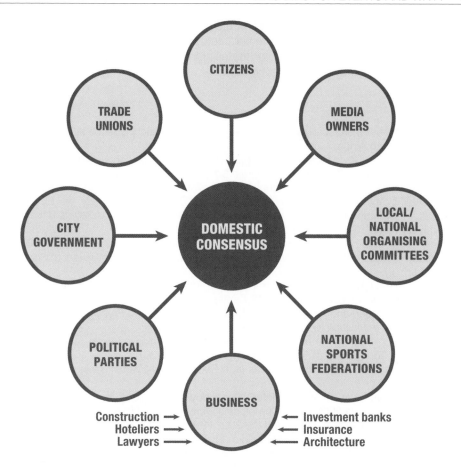

Figure 3.2 Domestic inputs to major event bids

South Africa's bids for the 2006 and 2010 finals, for instance, the national football association had to procure the support of the governing party, the country's largest trade unions and, in the later phases of the bid, the members of the Confédération Africaine de Football. Typically, therefore, bidding campaigns involve a range of stakeholders and usually unfold over several phases. It is not uncommon for the character and central messages of the bid to morph as key champions change or have to be secured.

Concluding remarks

Cities and states launch campaigns to host major sport events for a variety of reasons, and the way in which they prioritise certain objectives relative to others, be they economic or political in nature, suggests something about prevailing socio-political dynamics in the domestic settings. In all instances, the content of bid campaigns represents the outcome of extended processes of consensus-building among varied urban or national actors. However, history suggests that it is usually the interests of the most powerful corporate or political players that determine the shape, flavour and eventual impacts of events, and that most bid campaigns reflect what has been termed 'strategic misrepresentation' and 'a deep-rooted culture of deception' concerning the potential costs and benefits of staging an event.[15] Bids usually project a positive future vision for the aspirant host, but they are seldom called to reckoning when these lofty goals are not realised.

Notes

1 Scarlett Cornelissen is a professor in the Department of Political Science at Stellenbosch University, South Africa.
2 See, for instance, David Black, 'Dreaming big: the pursuit of "second order" games as a strategic response to globalization', *Sport in Society*, vol. 11 (2008).
3 David Black and Janis van der Westhuizen, 'The allure of global games for the "semi-peripheral" polities and spaces: a research agenda', *Third World Quarterly*, vol. 25 (2004).
4 Xu Xin, 'Modernizing China in the Olympic spotlight: China's national identity and the 2008 Beijing Olympiad', *Sociological Review*, vol. 54 (2006).
5 William Kelly, 'Asia pride, China fear, Tokyo anxiety: Japan looks back at Beijing 2008 and forward to London 2012 and Tokyo 2016', *International Journal of the History of Sport*, vol. 27 (2010).
6 *Japan Times*, 'Olympic construction transformed Tokyo', 10 October 2014; *Taipei Times*, 'Japan says "banzai" over Olympics', 18 September 2013.
7 Scarlett Cornelissen and Albert Grundlingh (eds), *Sport Past and Present in South Africa: (Trans)forming the Nation* (London: Routledge, 2012).
8 Christopher Gaffney, 'Mega-events and socio-spatial dynamics in Rio de Janeiro, 1919–2016', *Journal of Latin American Geography*, vol. 9 (2010).
9 Jonathan Grix (ed.), *Leveraging Legacies from Sports Mega-Events* (Basingstoke: Palgrave, 2014).
10 John Sugden and Alan Tomlinson, 'International power struggles in the governance of world soccer: the 2002 and 2006 World Cup bidding wars', in John Horne and Wolfram Manzenreiter (eds), *Japan, Korea and the 2002 World Cup* (London: Routlege, 2002).
11 *Sunday Times* (UK), 'How a humiliated old man sold SA's World Cup hopes down the river', 9 July 2000; Peter Alegi, '"Feel the pull in your soul": local agency and global trends in South Africa's 2006 World Cup bid', *Soccer and Society*, vol. 2 (2001).
12 Marcel Korthes and Manfred Rolfes, 'Unsicheres Südafrika, Unsicheres WM 2010? Überlegungen und Erkentnisse zur Medialen Berichterstattungen im Vorfeld der Fuβballweltmeisterschaft', in Christoph Haferburgh and Malte Steinbrink (eds), *Mega-Event und Stadtentwicklung im globalen Süden: Die Fuβballweltmeisterschaft 2010 und ihre Impulse für Südafrika* (Frankfurt: Brandes & Apsel, 2010).
13 Kristine Toohey and Anthony James Veal, *The Olympic Games: A Social Science Perspective*, 2nd edn (Wallingford, UK: CABI Publishing, 2007).
14 Helen Lenskyj, *Olympic Industry Resistance: Challenging Olympic Power and Propaganda* (Albany, NY: SUNY Press, 2008).
15 Bent Flyvbjerg, 'Case study', in Norman K. Denzin and Yvonne S. Lincoln (eds), *The Sage Handbook of Qualitative Research* (Thousand Oaks, CA: Sage, 2011); Bent Flyvberg, 'Policy and planning for large-scale infrastructure projects: problems, causes, cures', *Environment and Planning B: Planning and Design*, vol. 34 (2007).

3.3

The problem with sporting mega-event impact assessment

Eleni Theodoraki[1]

Introduction

Authors of reports of positive impacts from sporting mega-events attribute to them such qualities as acting as economic growth stimuli, urban regeneration catalysts, social change inspirers, destination brand developers, and so on. On the other hand, authors of reports of negative impacts describe sporting mega-events as leading to civil rights abuses, atmospheric pollution, rampant nationalism, exploitation by corrupt multinationals and bribery of officials. To look into the reason for such differences of opinion we can turn to Hippocrates, who studied medicine and understood the challenges for practising it that were created by the circumstances faced by physicians and medical professionals.

> *Life is short, and science long; the time fleeting; experience perilous, and decision difficult. The physician must not only be prepared to do what is right himself, but also to make the patient, the attendants, and externals cooperate.*
>
> *(Hippocrates, writing in 460 BC)*[2]

Like Hippocrates trying to find ways to cure patients and realising the importance of all stakeholders involved, those trying to measure mega-event impacts, or evaluate related studies, sooner or later realise the omnipresent effects of the wider context within which they find themselves, which affects what impacts are being investigated, where, when and how.

To date, assessment of the impact of sporting mega-events has been incomplete and/or biased, and not conducive to obtaining a clear view of the evidence. As one study confirms,

> *[T]he persistent under-performance of mega-projects occurs despite trends [albeit in few countries] in administrative reform seeking to impose market discipline on public projects (and in most instances mega-projects are at least part-financed by public subsidies or loans due to the vast financial commitment involved), and to scrutinise public policies and spending according to the standards of cost–benefit analysis (CBA), cost-effectiveness and value for money.*[3]

Attempts to justify expenditure by creating a positive legacy also affect the funding and research design of studies to capture impacts and legacy. In the case of the Athens 2004 Summer Olympic Games, impact assessment efforts were reported to have been affected by clientelism (giving contracts for services in return for electoral support) in academic circles and by the national election results.[4]

Box 3.1 Mega-event impact assessment: Athens Olympics 2004

In 2001 Pascal van Griethuysen and Pierre-Alain Hug developed a 150-indicator impact evaluation programme named Olympic Games Global Impact (OGGI) for the International Olympic Committee (IOC). The Athens 2004 Olympic Games organisers were to be the first to employ its methodology to assess the Games' impact, and the information collected was intended to also form part of the final official report of the organisers to the IOC. The local organising committee, ATHENS 2004, accepted initial responsibility for collecting and delivering data, and the work started in earnest in 2003, approximately one year before the Olympic Games, undertaken by a dedicated manager and research teams in Greek universities. Following the general election in March 2004 and the change of govern-ment, however, it was reported[5] that the composition of the original research teams that had started preliminary work on OGGI had been changed, to reflect the changed political interests in power, and this meant a delay in any progress with the OGGI programme. When the Games were over ATHENS 2004 quietly withdrew from its original plans to capture the Games' impacts through OGGI, and dropped the project, with the committee's senior managers suggesting that there was in fact no contractual responsibility to incorporate the programme in the report to the IOC.

The above example highlights the fact that, despite the existence of a quite comprehensive framework through which to capture impacts, the Athens OGGI programme failed to deliver because of political intervention: the composition of the research teams changed when there was a change of government following the early 2004 general election, and the new political leaders sought to reward their supporters in academic circles. It was also undermined by a lack of commitment on the part of ATHENS 2004 senior management, and a consequent failure to engage fully.[6]

Source: Pascal van Griethuysen and Pierre-Alain Hug, *Projet OGGI: Olympic Games Global Impact: Cadre d'analyse pour l'identification de l'impact global des Jeux Olympiques* (Lausanne: International Academy of Sports Science and Technology, 2001).

Image-making imperatives, contractual obligations to the event owners and nationalist agendas also influenced communication about the impact of the event to various audiences, through different means and at various stages in its life cycle. Importantly, the rhetoric varied depending on the circumstances.

A seminal systematic review on socio-economic impacts on major multi-sport events from 1978 to 2008 also confirmed this: 'No attempts have been made to bring together the large amount of research on the impact of major multi-sport events on host populations.'[7] In light of this, it is important to investigate the root cause for the weak state of, and lack of rigour in, sporting mega-event impact assessment.

Definition of problem and conceptual insights

The problem with such impact assessment has its roots in (1) the positive emotive predispo-sition of the public towards sporting mega-events, which renders them biased; and (2) the national, international and transnational mega-event governance structures and systems, which are founded on monopolistic or oligopolistic contracts. This can be illustrated with reference to relevant literature.

- 'Mega sport events achieve [the] "shared presence" . . . of significant proportions of the world's population through the medium of television [and] are powerful transmitters of messages.'[8]
- 'Mega sport events are loved by the public, who overall have strong affinity to the respective brands (event, owners, organising committees, sponsors).'[9]
- 'Mega sport events are owned by monopolistic transnational organisations.'[10]
- 'Mega sport events are gigantic, commercialized, and rely heavily on volunteer, corporate and state support.'[11] They also present unique opportunities for the development of discourses on the presence and origins of risk (leading to risk colonisation), which is described as the spread of the logic and formal managerial practice of risk management.[12]
- 'Mega sport events are presented by those in political and economic power as panacea to ills.'[13]
- 'Mega sport events present an unmovable deadline which can spearhead development and bypass due process (environmental, anti-money laundering, etc.).'[14]

Importantly, the governance of sporting mega-events presents an ironic relationship between the power and the risk-taking of the stakeholders involved, namely event owners (such as the IOC, the Fédération Internationale de Football Association, and so on), event producers (organising committees, partners, sponsors) and event hosts/consumers. As Figure 3.3 illustrates, the greater the power held by event owners, the lower the risk taken with regard to the impact outlook/result that lies with event hosts (to include local affected communities) as well as event consumers worldwide. Mega-events such as the Olympic Games are overwhelmingly funded by the public purse,[15] and yet the losers are not just host city/nation's

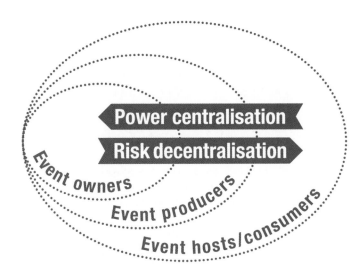

Figure 3.3 Event stakeholder power–risk irony

taxpayers but a range of other groups that one would normally expect to benefit from public spending. They include relocated communities of residents and businesses; human rights activists (if negative images and voices that can harm the Olympic brand and the host city's image are suppressed); environmental and social sustainability movements; and non-Olympic sports and other good causes, such as those sections of the arts and culture in general that suffer from the prioritisation of Olympics-related projects.[16]

The complexity of assessing the impacts of sporting mega-events is linked to the various thematic areas of conceptualising impacts (such as economic, political, social, cultural and environmental), the various geographies where impact is felt (locally, regionally, nationally and globally) and the time periods when impact is created, power exercised and risks taken (the bid phase, the build-up, the event time itself and the post-event and legacy phase). Furthermore, I believe that we cannot evaluate impact studies if we do not know the opportunity cost (what else we could have done instead) or counterfactual (what would have happened anyway) and have conducted a full CBA.

It is not possible under current circumstances to generalise findings either, as, apart from the notable exception of the Vancouver Winter Olympic Games, for which 150 indicators were used,[17] we do not have comprehensive impact studies. In contrast, the British Department of Culture, Media and Sport (DCMS) chose to focus primarily on specific positive effects of the London 2012 Olympic Games rather than set out to capture impact as the academic literature defines it, including negative as well as positive effects.[18]

Box 3.2 Mega-event impact assessment: London Olympics 2012

The DCMS report set out to 'undertake a comprehensive and robust "meta-evaluation" of the additionality, outputs, results, impacts and associated benefits of the investment in the 2012 Games'.[19] None of the 79 research questions used to guide the meta-analysis of primary and secondary research[20] were explicitly seeking to capture negative impacts of the London Games, however. Some negative impacts are mentioned in the report (such as on transport congestion, population divisions on the basis of affluence, increased population movement in and out of the area where the Games were held, the diversion of passing trade because of changes in transport, tenancy terminations and increased numbers of squatters), but the meta-evaluation did not set out to investigate negative impact along the political, social, cultural and environmental thematic areas. As a result, negative impacts are captured only when a positive impact that was anticipated, and phrased accordingly in the respective question, did not materialise. Had the study posed direct questions as to what the negative impacts had been, as reported in various studies, the meta-analysis would have reported many more impacts that are negative.

Gerry McCartney *et al.* conclude: 'Until decision makers include robust, long term evaluations as part of their design and implementation of events, it is unclear how the costs of major multi-sport events can be justified in terms of benefits to the host population.'[21] They add: 'How the impacts of events are evaluated needs to improve to allow decision makers pitching for future events to make informed judgments on the basis of known effects and known areas of uncertainty.'[22] Andrew Zimbalist, writing for the International Monetary Fund, concurs: 'The economic and noneconomic value of hosting a major event like the Olympic Games is complex and likely to vary from one situation to another. Simple conclusions are impossible to draw.'[23]

An additional complexity in assessing impact stems from the preoccupation of event owners with events' legacies and the growing demand on bidders to predefine them as part of their respective bid preparations. Both the event owners and the event franchisees (local organising committees) then engage in discussions in the public eye on event legacy, which, according to John MacAloon, 'generate a perception of common and laudable purpose' when in fact there is a strong hidden relationship between Olympic legacy manager and Olympic brand managers.[24]

Attributing effects to sporting mega-events and establishing causality is fraught with challenges. In the case of the Vancouver 2010 Winter Olympic Games, the team of academics at the University of British Columbia in charge of impact assessment used the control city of Alberta. This allowed them to account for changes to indicators that may be simply explained by looking at government policies or that may have been created by development trends (hence the need to capture baseline data on impact indicators). Their research approach, protocols, tools and careful claims of causality present the most thorough and watertight attempt at measuring sporting mega-event impact seen to date.

Having summarily defined the problem with sport mega-event impact assessment, I now turn to the conceptual literature for illumination and reflection. The concepts of effectiveness (the achievement of intended goals), efficiency (the achievement of goals in the most economical way) and equifinality (achieving the same goals via different means) have resonance with impact assessment[25] and focus at the organisational level. Sustainability is another key concept in the discussion of event impacts.[26] It links to that of effectiveness and the idea that multiple stakeholder viewpoints need to be considered when the company is not strictly for-profit only and when effects on the physical environment and social fabric are at stake. In this way, sustainability presents a conceptual lens that embraces the whole ecosystem and considers power balances and effects within it.

A more recent addition to the vocabulary of mega-event impacts is the Aristotelian[27] virtue of phronesis – 'a true and reasoned state of capacity to act with regard to the things that are good or bad for man'. Bent Flyvbjerg, Todd Landman and Sanford Schram define phronesis as the 'intellectual virtue of reason capable of action',[28] and Flyvbjerg has used phronetic social science repeatedly,[29] asking pertinent questions of mega-projects, including sporting mega-events, such as: where are we going, who gains and who loses, how, and is this development desirable? Phronetic social science can illuminate the debate on how negative and positive sport mega-event impacts balance. Figure 3.4 illustrates the concepts of effectiveness, sustainability and phronesis and their respective level of focus, from the micro-organisational to the ecosystem meso level, to the macro moral/ethical/virtue level.

Unfortunately, effectiveness offers a one-sided view, as delivering an event does not mean that the impacts promised to accompany it actually materialise. Effectiveness in the wider event and impacts sense can be somewhat elusive to ascertain, on account of the multiple themes through which we can capture it, the multiple stakeholders and their various perceptions, the many time phases during which impacts occur and the various geographies where impacts are felt. Sustainability is equally problematic when used to assess mega-events. As the Commission for a Sustainable London 2012 confirms:

> [We] have always maintained that, taken in isolation, delivering an Olympic and Paralympic Games is an inherently un-sustainable thing to do. We therefore cannot call the programme truly sustainable unless the inspirational power of the Games can be used to make a tangible, far-reaching difference.[30]

Undertaking to support the continuation of sporting mega-events in the hope that their inspirational power can counterbalance their inherently unsustainable nature seems to run

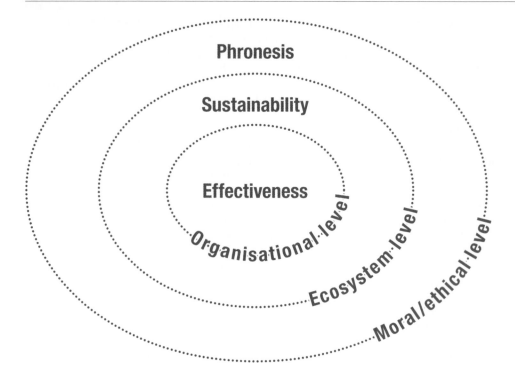

Figure 3.4 Concepts and levels of focus

contrary to any notion of phronesis and applying reason to actions. Increasingly, of late, cities have withdrawn their bids for staging such events, and in other cities currently preparing to host them loud and clear dissenting voices are heard.[31]

Regardless of the still unanswered rhetorical question of whether sporting mega-events are 'desirable' for the collective long-term development of the world's population, the challenge of impact assessment will remain as long as these events are staged, and the next section proposes an analytical framework for the endeavour of measuring them.

Epilogue and proposed framework

Evidently, unbiased mega-event impact assessment is currently unattainable because the stakes (in terms of political and capital power) are so high while the rigour of the methodology applied has, to date, been weak. Notwithstanding the fact that the challenges of event impact assessment is an under-researched area and the fact that signs of strength in the approach are becoming apparent, as, for example, in Mike Weed *et al.*'s meta-evaluation of findings,[32] the task is truly mammoth. Accusations of relativity in terms of findings and an inability to extrapolate or generalise also rightly arise from the diversity of contexts within which mega-events take place. Comparable, holistic overviews of thorough multidimensional and longitudinal studies are needed. The current focus of investigations on impacts to the event host (communities, city, country) also diverts attention away from what impacts are accrued for the event owners and producers in the form of allied companies, such as their sponsors and trusted global partners. A 360-degree approach to sporting mega-event

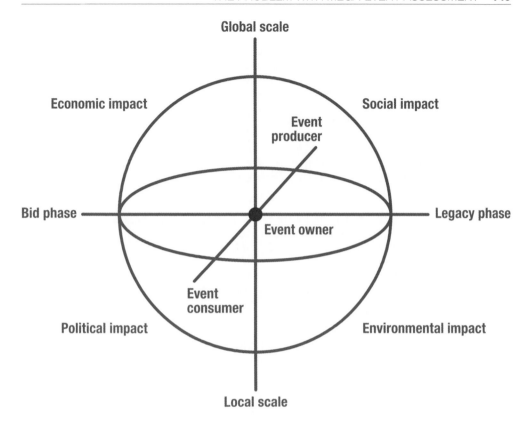

Figure 3.5 Sporting mega-event impact sphere

impact assessment would encompass impacts to them, too. Figure 3.5 attempts to do this, and to provide a framework for future assessment. It seeks to encapsulate the various dimensions of impacts, namely the thematic one (economic, social, environmental and political), the applicable scale (local to global), the temporal dimension (bid phase to legacy stage) and the actors involved (event owner, event producer, event consumer). Sporting mega-event impact assessment needs to explore both the negative and the positive effects on all the above dimensions if it is going to be adequate to capture who creates what effects, where and when, and, in so doing, affects whom.

Although, at a practical level, fully applying the impact assessment framework shown in Figure 3.5 would be politically challenging and costly in terms of the resources needed, conceptually it offers researchers an overview that would allow them to position their variables and units of analysis in the overall sphere of impact and appreciate what is still missing from their particular viewpoints.

To return to the medical analogy and Hippocrates' aphorism, I would contend that understanding the dynamics of the context of sporting mega-event impact assessment is key to understanding the root causes of the above conflicting indicators of what actually happens to the host city/nation. Having grasped the fundamental causation of a condition and studied its associated symptomatic impacts, anti-corruption agents, sports organisations and other stakeholder bodies would be able to diagnose what a host city/nation faced and what the sporting mega-event actually entailed, and could then advise corrective actions.

Notes

1   Dr Eleni Theodoraki is reader in festival and event management in the School of Marketing, Tourism and Languages at Edinburgh Napier University.

2   Elias Marks, *The Aphorisms of Hippocrates* (New York: Collins & Co., 1817).

3   Will Jennings, 'Governing the games: high politics, risk and mega-events', *Political Studies Review*, vol. 11 (2013), p. 4.

4   Eleni Theodoraki, 'Organisational communication on the impacts of the Athens 2004 Olympic Games', *Journal of Policy Research in Tourism, Leisure and Events*, vol. 1 (2009); Eleni Theodoraki, 'Expressions of national identity through impact assessments of the Athens 2004 Olympic Games', in Philip Dine and Seán Crosson (eds), *Sport, Representation and Evolving Identities in Europe* (Berne: Peter Lang, 2010).

5   Ibid.

6   Ibid.

7   Gerry McCartney, Sian Thomas, Hilary Thomson, John Scott, Val Hamilton, Phil Hanlon, David Morrison and Lyndal Bond, 'The health and socioeconomic impacts of major multi-sport events: systematic review (1978–2008)', *BMJ*, vol. 340 (2010), c.2369, p. 7, *www.bmj.com/content/bmj/340/bmj.c2369.full.pdf*.

8   Maurice Roche, 'Olympic and sport mega-events as media-events: reflections on the globalisation paradigm', in Kevin Wamsley, Bob Barney and Scott Martyn (eds), *The Global Nexus Engaged: Past, Present, Future Interdisciplinary Olympic Studies* (London, ON: International Centre for Olympic Studies, University of Western Ontario, 2002), p. 6, *http://library.la84.org/SportsLibrary/ISOR/ISOR2002a.pdf*.

9   Benoit Séguin, André Richelieu and Norm O'Reilly, 'Leveraging the Olympic brand through the reconciliation of corporate consumers' brand perceptions', *International Journal of Sport Management and Marketing*, vol. 3 (2008).

10 Eleni Theodoraki, *Olympic Event Organisation* (Oxford: Butterworth-Heinemann, 2007).

11 Jean-Loup Chappelet and Brenda Kübler-Mabbott, *The International Olympic Committee and the Olympic System: The Governance of World Sport* (Abingdon: Routledge, 2008).

12 See Will Jennings, *Mega-Events and Risk Colonisation: Risk Management and the Olympics*, Discussion Paper no. 71 (London: Centre for Analysis of Risk and Regulation, London School of Economics and Political Science, 2012), for an explanation of how mega-events are linked to broader societal and institutional hazards and threats, but at the same time induce their own unique set of organisational pathologies and biases.

13 Bent Flyvbjerg, Nils Bruzelius and Werner Rothengatter, *Megaprojects and Risk: An Anatomy of Ambition* (Cambridge: Cambridge University Press, 2003).

14 Robert Baumann and Victor Matheson, 'Assessing the infrastructure impact of mega-events in emerging economies', in Gregory Ingram and Karin Brandt (eds), *Infrastructure and Land Policies* (Cambridge, MA: Lincoln Institute of Land Policy, 2013).

15 See Reuters (UK), 'Factbox: how the Olympic Games are funded', 8 March 2012, *http://uk.reuters.com/article/2012/03/08/uk-olympics-funding-idUKBRE8270TY20120308*, for the breakdown of funding for the London 2012 Olympic Games; and Dennis Coates and Brad Humphreys, 'Do economists reach a conclusion on subsidies for sports franchises, stadiums, and mega-events?', *Econ Journal Watch*, vol. 5 (2008), for discussion on mega-event subsidies.

16 Eleni Theodoraki, 'The modern Olympic Games: governance and ownership of risk', *Royal United Services Institute Monitor*, vol. 8 (2009), *www.bl.uk/sportandsociety/exploresocsci/sportsoc/mega/governanceownership.pdf*.

17 Robert VanWynsberghe, 'The Olympic Games Impact (OGI) study for the 2010 Winter Olympic Games: strategies for evaluating sport mega-events' contribution to sustainability', *International Journal of Sport Policy and Politics*, vol. 7 (2015).

18 Department for Culture, Media and Sport, *Post-Games Evaluation: Meta-Evaluation of the Impacts and Legacy of the London 2012 Olympic Games and Paralympic Games: Summary Report* (London: DCMS, 2013), *www.gov.uk/government/uploads/system/uploads/attachment_data/file/224143/Report_5_Research_Questions_FINAL.pdf*.

19 Ibid., p. 4.
20 Ibid., pp. 251–255.
21 McCartney *et al.* (2010), p. 1.
22 Ibid., p. 7.
23 Andrew Zimbalist, 'Is it worth it?', *Finance and Development*, vol. 47 (2010), p. 11, *www.imf. org/external/pubs/ft/fandd/2010/03/pdf/zimbalist.pdf.*
24 John MacAloon, '"Legacy" as managerial/magical discourse in contemporary Olympic affairs', *International Journal of the History of Sport,* vol. 25 (2008), p. 2060.
25 See Trevor Slack and Milena Parent, *Understanding Sport Organizations: The Application of Organization Theory* (Champaign, IL: Human Kinetics, 2006), for a review of the literature and how it relates to the context of sport organisations; Wendy Frisby, 'Measuring the organizational effectiveness of national sport governing bodies', *Canadian Journal of Applied Sport Sciences*, vol. 11 (1986), for her use of the goals and systems models of effectiveness; and Eleni Theodoraki and Ian Henry, 'Perzeptionen der organisatorischen Effektivitat in nationalen Sportorganisationen Großbritanniens', in Günther Lüschen and Alfred Rütten (eds), *Sportpolitik: Sozialwissenschaftliche Analysen* (Stuttgart: Naglschmid, 1996), for the plurality of concepts and perceptions of effectiveness.
26 Sustainable development is defined as 'development that meets the needs of the present without compromising the ability of future generations to meet their own needs. It contains within it two key concepts: the concept of "needs", in particular the essential needs of the world's poor, to which overriding priority should be given; and the idea of limitations imposed by the state of technology and social organization on the environment's ability to meet present and future needs.' United Nations, *Report of the World Commission on Environment and Development: Our Common Future* (New York: UN, 1987).
27 Aristotle, *The Nicomachean Ethics* (Oxford: Oxford University Press, 2009), VI.5.
28 Bent Flyvbjerg, Todd Landman and Sanford Schram, 'Important next steps in phronetic social science', in Bent Flyvbjerg, Todd Landman and Sanford Schram (eds), *Real Social Science: Applied Phronesis* (Cambridge: Cambridge University Press, 2012), p. 287.
29 Flyvbjerg, Bruzelius and Rothengatter (2003); Bent Flyvbjerg, 'Design by deception: the politics of megaproject approval', *Harvard Design Magazine*, vol. 22 (2005); Bent Flyvbjerg, 'Truth and lies about megaprojects', inaugural speech for professorship and chair at Faculty of Technology, Policy and Management of Delft University of Technology, 26 September 2007, *http://flyvbjerg.plan.aau.dk/Publications2007/InauguralTUD21PRINT72dpi.pdf.*
30 Commission for a Sustainable London 2012, *Game Changing? Annual Review 2010* (London: Commission for a Sustainable London 2012, 2011), p. 6, *www.cslondon.org/ wp-content/uploads/downloads/2011/04/CSL-Annual-Review-20102.pdf.* The author served as core commissioner on the Commission for a Sustainable London 2012.
31 The Conversation (UK), 'There would be no shame in Brazil ditching the Olympics', 8 May 2014, *https://theconversation.com/there-would-be-no-shame-in-brazil-ditching-the-olympics-26204.*
32 Mike Weed, Suzanne Dowse, Mat Brown, Abby Foad and Ian Wellard, *London Legacy Supra-Evaluation: Final Report* (Canterbury: Centre for Sport, Physical Education and Activity Research, Canterbury Christ Church University, 2013), *www.london.gov.uk/sites/ default/files/SPEAR@CCCU%20-%20London%20Legacy%20Supra-Evaluation%20Final%20 Report%20RE-DRAFT%20V.pdf.*

3.4

Corruption and the bidding process for the Olympics and World Cup

Andrew Zimbalist[1]

The process

Every four years the International Olympic Committee (IOC) and the Fédération Internationale de Football Association (FIFA) run an international bidding competition that ends in the awarding of the Olympics or the football World Cup to a host city or country roughly seven years before the event is held. In the case of the Olympics, the international competition is often preceded by a national competition among cities in many of the potential host countries. For instance, in February 2013 the United States Olympic Committee (USOC) sent out an invitation to 50 US cities asking if they would be interested in hosting the 2024 Summer Games. In July 2014 the USOC named four cities (Washington, Boston, San Francisco and Los Angeles) as its finalists (even though Boston had never made a formal decision to be a candidate). The USOC anointed Boston as the official US candidate in January 2015.[2]

The US candidate now enters into a competition with multiple 'applicant' cities from around the world. Applicant cities pay the IOC US$150,000 for the privilege of being considered in the contest.[3] In 2016 the IOC will narrow the list down to three to five 'candidate' cities; candidate cities pay the IOC an additional US$500,000, in theory to cover the costs of the IOC's consideration of their application.[4] The IOC will pick the 'winner' in 2017. FIFA follows a similar process and timeline, with the exception that it is countries, not cities, that host the month-long final World Cup competition. In both cases, though, there is a fundamental, underlying economic reality: there is one seller (the IOC or FIFA), there is a monopoly and there are multiple bidders (and more potential bidders) from around the world. In the case of the Olympics, as indicated above, the process involving the monopoly seller with multiple bidders happens in two stages, first at the country level and then at the international level, raising the expense for the participants in the bidding game.

Well beyond these payments to the IOC or FIFA are the costs entailed in putting together a plan, hiring consultants, producing glossy brochures and videos, purchasing insurance, exploring financing options with investment bankers and public bodies, hosting IOC or FIFA executives, travelling to IOC or FIFA meetings, and so on. Chicago spent around US$100 million in its failed bid to host the 2012 Summer Olympics.[5] Other cities and countries have reported similar sums, or more: Tokyo supposedly spent US$150 million in its failed bid to host the 2016 Summer Games.[6]

In November 2014, as part of an effort to enlist more applicants, the IOC released a set of proposed reforms to make it less expensive for cities to bid. Other than some hortatory language, the only concrete change is that the IOC would pay for some of the travel expenses for applicants to attend meetings. In sum, the savings here will be a few hundred thousand dollars per applicant – a small token relative to the tens of millions of dollars typically expended in a bid.

The Netherlands has been considering a bid to host the 2028 Summer Games. According to a study by RTLnews, the largest commercial broadcaster in the country, as of 2012 the Dutch had already spent US$105 million in direct costs to study the feasibility of hosting, draw up preliminary plans, mobilise the relevant parties and organise events 'to entice IOC members to vote for us'.[7] At the time of writing (late August 2014) the Netherlands has not made a formal decision on whether to bid for the 2028 Games.

The voters at the IOC and at FIFA have appreciable power to sway the choice of a host. Examples from Nagano to Salt Lake City to Qatar abound of vote processes that have been tainted by payoffs.

What follows is a stylised model of the bidding process. The model presents three possible situations or cases under different assumptions, going from the least realistic (case 1) to the most realistic (case 3).

Case 1

● Perfect information and no principal–agent problem
● Outcome: expected net gains are bid away

In this case, it is assumed that the IOC or FIFA each has complete information about the bidders and that each of the bidders has complete information about its own bid and those of its competitors. It is further assumed that there is no principal–agent problem; this means that the body representing the city or country (the local organising committee) fairly represents the interests of the entire resident population: the local organising committee is the agent of the entire resident population (the principal). With the assumption of perfect information, each bidder will know what its potential gain is from hosting and will continue to bid until just before its gain is fully eroded. (In theory, if each bidder also knows the gains of other bidders, it will stop bidding at just above the gain to the second highest bidder, leaving a small potential gain.) Note that if the overall return to hosting approaches zero, and if there are feel-good benefits from hosting, this implies that there will be a negative financial result – that is, the host will have to pay to achieve any feel-good effects, bringing the overall net return to zero.[8] This case is the most favourable for the bidding cities or countries. It is also the least realistic of the three cases.

Case 2

● There is imperfect information and no principal–agent problem
● Outcome: winner's curse and net loss

The sole difference between this case and the prior one is that the assumption of perfect information is dropped, making case 2 a better approximation of reality. In this case, each bidder does not know what its potential benefits and costs are when it participates in the bidding competition. The winning bid in such a case usually goes to the most exuberant bidder, which not only outbids all the other bidders but also generally bids higher than the possible gain (the winner's curse). The result is a net financial loss and a net overall loss, even though the organising committee (agent) in this case is still assumed to fairly represent the interests of the local population (the principal).

Case 3

● There is imperfect information and a principal–agent problem
● Outcome: outlandish overbid

This case takes a step closer to reality by dropping one more assumption and acknowledging the existence of a principal–agent problem – in this case that the organising committee (agent) is controlled by the private interests that stand to gain the most from hosting, and that these interests are not coincident with those of the population. There is still imperfect information, which facilitates extravagant bids from each of the prospective hosts. The expected outcome is substantial financial and overall losses, which will only be exacerbated by cost overruns once construction begins.

A corrupted process

There are two manifest opportunities for corruption in this process. First, there is the exploitation by FIFA and the IOC of the bidding cities. The monopoly market power of the two organisations enables them to extract enormous rents out of the bidding process. In order to win the bid, cities and countries have to yield to the extravagance and gigantism of FIFA and IOC expectations. The costs of the bidders and the eventual 'winner' explode, as do FIFA and IOC revenues.[9] The costs are paid overwhelmingly by the taxpayers. The revenues from the event in substantial measure are not shared with the host city or country, but are retained by FIFA and the IOC for sport development and to defray high executive salaries – and, in the case of FIFA, plethoric operating expenses and ballooning reserve funds.[10]

Sepp Blatter, the FIFA president, earns a salary in excess of US$1 million on top of what seems like an unlimited expense account. Other FIFA executives earn compensation packages well into six-figure sums.[11] Blatter had been giving the 25 members of the FIFA Executive Committee annual bonuses ranging from US$75,000 to US$200,000 a year on top of their salary of US$100,000 for very part-time work. For appearances' sake, the practice of annual bonuses was ended in 2014, but FIFA's Sub-Committee on Compensation (an appointed body of Executive Committee members)[12] made up for this by secretly voting to double their pay to US$200,000, according to documents uncovered by the London *Sunday Times*. *The Sunday Times* also reported that Executive Committee members receive a US$700 per diem while doing FIFA work, travel via business class and stay in five-star hotels.[13] FIFA and its six regional confederations host myriad meetings in exotic locations each year, paying for the best hotels, restaurants, entertainment and transportation for the participants.

At the end of the four-year cycle that came with the conclusion of the 2010 South African World Cup, FIFA took in a surplus of US$631 million, which raised FIFA's accumulated reserve fund to US$1.3 billion. The anticipated surplus from the 2014 World Cup in Brazil is larger still, and the reserve fund surpassed US$1.5 billion at the end of 2014.

While the members of the IOC, including its president, Thomas Bach, are unpaid, Bach receives luxury housing in Lausanne and a lavish expense account. The IOC and its

The average profits of the 'Big Five' construction companies in South Africa rose from ZAR158 million (US$25 million) in 2004 to ZAR1.67 billion (US$200 million) the year before the World Cup.

Figure 3.6 South Africa 2010

Adapted from: Eddie Cottle (ed.), *South Africa's World Cup: A Legacy for Whom?* (Durban: University of KwaZulu–Natal Press, 2011).

various committees hold frequent meetings around the globe, stay in five-star hotels and enjoy improvident spending budgets. At the end of 2012 the IOC reportedly had a reserve fund of US$558 million.[14]

The second opportunity for corruption arises from the capture of the host city by economic interests. In either democratic or authoritarian countries, the tendency is for event planning to hew closely to the interests of the local business elite.[15] Construction companies, their unions (if there are any), insurance companies, architectural firms, media companies, investment bankers (who float the bonds), lawyers and perhaps some hotel or restaurant interests may get behind the Olympic or World Cup project. They stand to gain substantially from the massive public funding. Typically, these interests hijack the local organising committee, hire out an obliging consulting firm to perform an ersatz economic impact study, understate the costs, overstate the revenues and go on to procure political consent.[16] According to one study, in the build-up to hosting the 2010 World Cup the average profits of the 'Big Five' construction companies in South Africa rose from ZAR158 million (some US$25 million) in 2004 to ZAR1.67 billion (some US$200 million) in 2009 – a 10.5-fold increase in rand terms![17]

Thus, while the taxpayers of the city or country stand to lose from the bidding process and from hosting the event, the private interests that coalesce to push the hosting project stand to gain handsomely. Here, as elsewhere, the political process is corrupted.

Notes

1   Andrew Zimbalist is the Robert A. Woods professor of economics, Smith College, Northampton, Massachusetts. This chapter is adapted from his book *Circus Maximus: The Economic Gamble Behind Hosting the Olympics and the World Cup* (Washington, DC: Brookings Institution Press, 2015).

2   'Boston wins USOC bid to host 2024 Olympic Games', WCVB-TV, 8 January 2015, *www.wcvb.com/sports/boston-wins-usoc-bid-to-host-2024-olympic-games/30599954.*

3   See, for example, International Olympic Committee, 'IOC 2022 candidature acceptance procedure', *www.olympic.org/Documents/Host_city_elections/2022-Candidature-Acceptance-Procedure-FINAL-with-cover.pdf*, p. 25.

4   Ibid.

5   CNN (US), 'Chicago loses Olympic bid to Rio', 2 October 2009, *http://money.cnn.com/2009/10/02/news/economy/chicago_olympics_rejection/.*

6   *Asahi Shimbun* (Japan), 'Mizuno says Tokyo 2020 bid budget will be slashed', 3 December 2011, *http://ajw.asahi.com/article/behind_news/sports/AJ201112030021.*

7   Michel de Nooij, 'Mega sport events: a probabilistic social cost–benefit analysis of bidding for the games', *Journal of Sports Economics*, vol. 15 (2014), p. 412. The indirect costs are estimated at an additional US$142 million.

8   Note that cities and countries do not bid with US dollar figures. Rather, they bid with fancy facilities and appealing infrastructure and amenities. Since these have a price, their bids can be translated into US dollar figures.

9   See Bent Flyvbjerg and Allison Stewart, *Olympic Proportions: Cost and Cost Overrun at the Olympics 1960–2012,* working paper (Oxford: Saïd Business School, University of Oxford, 2012).

10 Merco Press, 'FIFA with record revenue and cash reserves, after 2014 World Cup', 23 March 2015, *http://en.mercopress.com/2015/03/23/fifa-with-record-revenue-and-cash-reserves-after-2014-world-cup.*

11 See The Least Thing, 'Further thoughts on Sepp Blatter's FIFA salary', 17 June 2013, *http://leastthing.blogspot.com/2013/06/further-thoughts-on-sepp-blatters-fifa.html.*

12 According to Domenico Scala, a member of the three-man Compensation Sub-Committee, the pay levels chosen are meant to emulate the compensation paid to executives in similarly sized companies in the private sector: *www.fifa.com/aboutfifa/organisation/footballgovernance/news/newsid=2384045/index.html.*

13 *Sunday Times* (UK), 'Fifa's chiefs pocket secret 100% pay rise', 22 June 2014.

14 *Chicago Tribune* (US), 'Pay IOC president? Yes, but . . .', 26 April 2013.

15 See Zimbalist (2015).

16 Ibid.

17 Eddie Cottle (ed.), *South Africa's World Cup: A Legacy for Whom?* (Durban: University of KwaZulu–Natal Press, 2011).

3.5

Compromise or compromised?

The bidding process for the award of the Olympic Games and the FIFA World Cup

Stefan Szymanski[1]

Introduction

History will judge the period between 1998 (when the scandal broke over bribes paid to secure votes for Salt Lake City as host of the 2002 Winter Olympic Games) and 2015 (when Sepp Blatter, president of the Fédération Internationale de Football Association (FIFA) for 17 years, resigned six days after the US Justice Department had issued indictments concerning corrupt activities by 14 senior figures in FIFA and marketing company executives) as the era when the governance of international sport came to the brink of collapse. Between the 1960s and the 1990s the administrators behind the world's two most popular sporting events, the Olympic Games (summer and winter) and the FIFA World Cup, found themselves in control of events capable of generating billions of dollars in broadcast and sponsorship revenues, while incurring negligible costs. They found themselves to be dispensers of largesse on a massive scale. The evidence suggests that many administrators within these organisations have failed in their duties and succumbed to corruption.[2] Since 1998, the International Olympic Committee (IOC) has been attempting to reform itself.[3] Under Blatter's leadership, the efforts of FIFA were, at best, half-hearted. Following his resignation, there is optimism in some quarters that a similar process can be undertaken within FIFA.

The actual process of awarding the flagship events (the Olympic Games and the football World Cup) represents only one dimension of the corruption that has been identified within the IOC and FIFA, which is itself only a subset of the instances of corruption that can be found in sports.[4] For example, most of the charges in the US Justice Department indictments of FIFA in May 2015 related not to the World Cup itself but to the sale of broadcast and marketing rights to lesser tournaments in North and South America. Nonetheless, the IOC has acknowledged corrupt practices in the process of bidding for the right to host the Olympic Games, notably in the case of Salt Lake City. At the time of writing it seems likely that corruption will be acknowledged by FIFA in relation to several World Cups, and irregularities have already been acknowledged in relation to the bidding process for the 2018 and 2022 events.[5] Investigative journalists such as Andrew Jennings, who assisted the US Justice Department ahead of the FIFA indictments, have gone much further in alleging bribery and corruption in the bidding process.[6]

Competition for the right to host these highly popular sporting events is often intense, and the decisions are often surrounded by controversy. The fundamental problem is that these are self-regulating organisations, and the scale of the events has grown much more rapidly than their capacity to manage them. The value of the broadcast rights for the Rome Olympics in 1960 was less than US$3 million (US$23 million at current values).[7] The combined value of the broadcast rights for the 2010 Vancouver Winter Games and the 2012 London Summer Games was US$3,850 million,[8] a near 170-fold increase in real terms in the space of just 14 Olympiads. Sponsorship revenues have also increased dramatically. Both the FIFA World Cup and the Summer Olympic Games generate in the region of US$6 billion in terms of broadcast, sponsorship, ticketing and merchandising.[9] A large fraction of those responsible for the governance of the IOC and FIFA are either current or former athletes, however. This is not necessarily the best preparation for business decision-making, even if these organisations now maintain large professional staffs.

The decision as to where to award both the Summer and Winter Olympic Games is made by the members of the IOC, of which there are currently 100. Twelve are appointed as current athletes, 11 are members ex officio as heads of large international sports federations. Thirty-seven members have competed in an Olympic Games themselves. The decision to award the football World Cup was, until 2013, a decision of the Executive Committee, who are appointed by confederations and associations, except the president, who is elected by the 209-member FIFA Congress. Following the alleged bribery surrounding the award of the 2022 World Cup to Qatar, future decisions, starting with the 2026 event, will be made by a vote of the full 209-member Congress.

Background

In the early years these organisations relied essentially on the goodwill of cities and governments around the world to host the events. Although some governments recognised the propaganda value of hosting (notably the Nazi government in Germany and the Berlin Olympic Games in 1936, and Mussolini's Fascist government and the 1934 football World Cup in Italy), competition was often restrained, given the limited taxpayer support either requested or offered. The 1948 Olympic Games were hosted in London because no one else was interested, and until the advent of global broadcasting these events remained relatively low-key.

From the 1960s onwards the bargaining power shifted in favour of the IOC and FIFA, and bidding intensified as the global reach provided by TV significantly enhanced the attractiveness of these events. This in turn created the incentive to pay bribes to secure victory in the bidding contest, thus necessitating the adoption of rules prohibiting such practices. Historically, both FIFA and the IOC had operated as gentleman's clubs, and, according to the received ideology, gentlemen cannot be corrupted.[10] There were other aspects of the gentleman's club mentality that caused problems. Most of the members came from Europe, and there was a strong tendency to engage in horse-trading. For example, in 1966 the hosts for the 1974, 1978 and 1982 World Cups were allocated simultaneously. At the time West Germany and Spain were both interested, and so they did a deal: Spain refrained from bidding for 1974 and West Germany withdrew its bid for 1982.[11] To insiders, this no doubt seemed a natural trade-off; to outsiders, it looked like a fix.

The 1960s and 1970s saw a huge expansion of membership of these two organisations following the end of colonialism and the expansion of the number of sovereign nations.

They brought different perspectives. While IOC founder Pierre de Coubertin and his followers had espoused an ideal of sport independent of politics and the state, many new nations saw sport and the state as intimately linked, and, indeed, in their own contexts saw the state as a major pillar in the support of sports organisations. By the 1960s the threat of boycotts from African nations if South Africa and Rhodesia were allowed to participate became evident. Throughout the 1970s and 1980s the survival of the Olympics, in particular, as a global event was challenged by the politics of national and international sport. In seeking to maintain the unity of their global organisations, the IOC and FIFA had to adapt to different cultural expectations.

Over time, the bidding process has evolved significantly. While the fiction remains that cities bid to host the Olympics and national football associations bid to host the World Cup, the reality is that both require significant government support, political and financial alike. Thus a bid usually emerges through a process of domestic lobbying for government support, leading to a formal submission of interest. A process of review lasting up to two years then culminates in a vote at the relevant congress of the IOC or FIFA.

Potential for corruption

Since the awarding of these events depends on bidding, it is not surprising that, as hosting has become more attractive, the role of inducements has grown. One problem for FIFA and the IOC has been to establish the difference between legitimate and illegitimate inducements. It can also be that attitudes to inducements can vary by culture and time. It is a matter of history, for example, that access to senior office (such as in the military or the civil service) in the nations of north-western Europe had to be bought well into the nineteenth century, and such practices were often exported to colonial administrations. By the twentieth century, though, such practices came be seen as corrupt and discredited; not everyone has followed the path of the western European nations, however, nor have they drawn the same conclusions. These differences can be seen in metrics such as those developed by Transparency International, which regularly identify European and North American nations as perceived to be among the least corrupt, and developing nations at the bottom of the list.[12]

The key moment in the development of FIFA was the 1974 electoral defeat of then president Stanley Rous, an Englishman with a barely concealed colonial mentality,[13] by João Havelange, a Brazilian, who promised to ensure that some of the riches generated by World Cup broadcast rights – mainly in Europe – would be recycled to African and Asian countries in exchange for their votes. This subsequent recycling of profits has been beneficial in terms of developing the sport in these countries. Sepp Blatter was Havelange's chosen successor, and he made it his business that a World Cup should be played for the first time in Africa. As a result, the Havelange and Blatter regimes are not universally perceived to be as unambiguously damaging as they are in Europe. This helps to explain why Sepp Blatter has managed to hold office since 1998, despite the near-universal European perception that he is corrupt.[14]

The IOC is a more European organisation than FIFA (47 per cent of IOC members are from Europe). It acted more decisively in the face of corruption allegations in relation to the awarding of major events. The scandal surrounding the award of the 2002 Winter Olympic Games to Salt Lake City caused an internal crisis. It emerged that relatives of several IOC members had received educational scholarships worth tens of thousands of dollars. Various other forms of bribery were identified, including direct payments. As a result, six IOC members were expelled in 1999, four from Africa and two from South America. The IOC took steps to limit contact between members and the bidding committees, in particular prohibiting visits by members to potential hosts – a process that gave rise to extensive opportunities for corruption.[15] Since 1999 allegations of corruption surrounding the award of the Olympics have not disappeared altogether, but the reform process has been advanced by some as a model of internal reform.[16]

One contributory factor to this change may also be the growing role of the technical assessment. Historically, the IOC has looked for guarantees and a clear plan for host cities, but in recent decades the detail required of bidders has grown considerably. Although the vote of the IOC members is still decisive, the technical assessment of the bid documents and the bid cities has become far more important. This reflects the fact that the contract between the host city and the IOC has also grown in size. For example, the technical manuals provided by the IOC for the London Olympics ran to about 4,000 pages.[17] Agreement to host the games also requires the host nation to change its laws, mainly in order to assure the IOC that its intellectual property (the Olympic rings, etc.) is fully protected. In 2014 the city of Oslo in Norway announced that it was withdrawing its bid for the 2022 Winter Olympics, largely because of the scale of demands imposed by the IOC (such as providing mobile phones to every IOC member, and seasonal fruit and cakes to be supplied in every member's hotel room).[18]

The corruption allegations surrounding the award of the 2022 World Cup to Qatar have been the most damaging to FIFA, largely because of the obvious difficulty of playing the tournament in a country where temperatures in the summer hover around 40° C.[19] In 2014 FIFA decided that the event should be played in the Northern Hemisphere's winter months, interrupting the regular league football calendar in many countries, creating further discontent. Additional concerns surround claims that hundreds of migrant workers are dying on stadium and infrastructure construction sites in Qatar,[20] and the potential problems for lesbian, gay, bisexual and transgender players, officials and fans, who risk being arrested because of their sexual identity.

In 2012 FIFA appointed Michael Garcia, a distinguished US lawyer, to investigate allegations of corruption surrounding the bid processes for the 2018 and 2022 World Cups. The report was delivered in 2014 but not published. A summary of the report, written by the chair of FIFA's Ethics Adjudicatory Chamber, German judge Hans-Joachim Eckert, was published and then immediately repudiated by Garcia, on the grounds that it did not accurately reflect the substance of his original report.[21]

In the Salt Lake City case the question of withdrawing the Games was never seriously considered by the IOC (even though the payment of bribes by the bidding committee was acknowledged), and FIFA had previously maintained that the award to Qatar would not be nullified.[22] Given the problems facing a tournament held in Qatar, however, the pressure to take the unprecedented step of nullifying the original decision has become a real possibility.[23] Given that Qatar is the first nation from the Middle East to be awarded a World Cup, and the potential for the Qataris to use their immense wealth to lobby within FIFA, there must also be a real risk of a geographical split developing within the organisation.

Conclusion

The awarding of the right to host sporting mega-events is inherently prone to corruption risks. Events involving contracts worth billions of dollars are distributed by between maybe 100 and 200 individuals, on grounds that are ultimately subjective. Those involved may have agendas that are often quite complex, and sometimes it is difficult to separate organisational objectives (such as the promotion of football) from personal objectives. The accusation of political and social bias is ever-present on all sides. Moreover, these are private organisations, not government agencies that can be forced by politicians to adopt particular rules (even if, in some cases, there is extensive overlap). Indeed, many would argue that there are large risks involved with allowing too much government interference in the running of international sports federations.

There is no doubt that greater transparency in terms of bidding processes and decision-making can help to suppress some corrupt elements, but it is unlikely that the accusation of corruption, and perhaps the reality, can ever be completely removed. The greatest challenge, for FIFA in particular at the present time, is to find a consensus on the meaning of corrupt activities and agree an agenda that enables the organisation to minimise the risks of illicit payments while preserving the commitment to transfer resources to the developing nations – a commitment that has, at least in part, helped to make it such a powerful and cohesive organisation.

Notes

1   Stefan Szymanski is Stephen J. Galetti collegiate professor of sport management at the University of Michigan School of Kinesiology and co-director of the Michigan Center for Sport Management.
2   On scandals in the IOC, see particularly the evidence relating to the award of the Winter Olympic Games of 2002 to Salt Lake City, discussed by Thomas Hamilton, 'The long hard fall from Mount Olympus: the 2002 Salt Lake City Olympic Games bribery scandal', *Marquette Sports Law Review*, vol. 21 (2010), *http://scholarship.law.marquette.edu/ sportslaw/vol21/iss1/7*. On scandals relating to the award of the FIFA World Cup, see Kate Youd, 'The winter's tale of corruption: the 2022 FIFA World Cup in Qatar, the impending shift to winter, and potential legal actions against FIFA', *Northwestern Journal of International Law and Business*, vol. 35 (2014), *http://scholarlycommons.law.northwestern.edu/njilb/ vol35/iss1/5*.
3   For the strategic roadmap of IOC planning and reform, see International Olympic Committee, 'Olympic Agenda 2020', *www.olympic.org/olympic-agenda-2020*.
4   For a survey of recent corruption in sport, see, for example, Wolfgang Maennig, 'Corruption in international sports and sport management: forms, tendencies, extent and countermeasures', *European Sport Management Quarterly*, vol. 5 (2005).
5   See Fédération Internationale de Football Association, 'Statement of the chairman of the Adjudicatory Chamber of the FIFA Ethics Committee on the Report on the Inquiry into the 2018/2022 FIFA World Cup Bidding Process prepared by the Investigatory Chamber of the FIFA Ethics Committee', 13 November 2014, *http://resources.fifa.com/mm/document/ affederation/footballgovernance/02/47/41/75/statementchairmanadjcheckert_neutral.pdf*.
6   See, for example, Andrew Jennings, *Foul! The Secret World of FIFA: Bribes, Vote Rigging and Ticket Scandals* (London: HarperCollins, 2006).
7   Holger Preuss, *The Economics of Staging the Olympics: A Comparison of the Games 1972–2008* (Cheltenham: Edward Elgar, 2004).
8   International Olympic Committee, *Olympic Marketing Fact File: 2013 Edition* (Lausanne: IOC, 2013), *www.olympic.org/Documents/IOC_Marketing/OLYMPIC_MARKETING_FACT_ FILE_2013.pdf*.
9   For Vancouver and London combined, the IOC (2013) states that total revenues were US$8 billion. For the World Cup, see Fédération Internationale de Football Association, *FIFA: Financial Report 2014* (Zurich: FIFA, 2015), *www.fifa.com/mm/document/affederation/ administration/02/56/80/39/fr2014weben_neutral.pdf*.
10 This view seems to have been especially attractive to Pierre de Coubertin, founder of the IOC, who was particularly attracted to the ideal of the English gentleman: 'The English sport ideology presupposed a certain attitude among the participants: the amateur spirit of the sport aficionado expressed most clearly in the enlightened and benevolent sportsman and

gentleman. Coubertin wanted to introduce into modern sport "the spirit of gay candour, the spirit of sincere disinterestedness which will revitalise . . . and make collective muscular exercise a true school of moral perfection".' Sigmund Loland, 'Pierre de Coubertin's ideology of Olympism from the perspective of the history of ideas', in Robert Knight Barney and Klaus Meier (eds), *Critical Reflections on Olympic Ideology* (London, ON: Centre for Olympic Studies, 1994).

11 See, for example, David Goldblatt, *The Ball Is Round: A Global History of Soccer* (London: Penguin Books, 2008).

12 The 2014 Transparency International Corruption Perceptions Index ranked perceptions of corruption in 177 countries. It put Botswana as the least corrupt African nation by some margin; 15 European nations ranked higher than this. The average ranking of European nations was 45th, the average for Asian nations was 100th and the average for African nations was 116th.

13 See, for example, the account by Goldblatt (2008), chap. 13.

14 Blatter is particularly respected in Africa, since he is credited with the award of the 2010 World Cup to Africa. Significant legitimate payments were made to developing nations, which may have partly formed the basis of his support. Given the lack of transparency of FIFA accounting, it has been hard to distinguish cronyism (meaning legitimate payments aimed at maintaining his supporter base) from outright corruption (illicit payments). See this piece of information from a poll of football fans across the world carried out in May 2015 by Transparency International: '4 in 5 football fans say Blatter should not stand for FIFA president: poll of 35,000 in 30 countries', 26 May 2015, *www.transparency.org/news/pressrelease/4_in_5_football_fans_say_blatter_should_not_stand_for_fifa_president_poll_o*; and Transparency International, 'Following FIFA World Cup corruption scandals, should Sepp Blatter be standing again for president of FIFA? Percentage who voted "no"', *www.transparency.org/files/content/pressrelease/2015_FIFAElectionInfographic_900.jpg*.

15 See, for example, Hamilton (2010).

16 On a positive note, see Roger Pielke, Jr, 'How can FIFA be held accountable?', *Sport Management Review*, vol. 16 (2013); and, on a more critical note, see Hamilton (2010).

17 Putting the requirements on paper does not rule out corruption, but it does help to focus on the relevant issues.

18 Inside the Games, '"Pompous" IOC demands "led to withdrawal of Oslo 2022 Olympic bid"', 3 October 2014, *www.insidethegames.biz/articles/1023008/pompous-ioc-demands-led-to-withdrawal-of-oslo-2022-olympic-bid*.

19 Youd (2014).

20 See, for example, *Guardian* (UK), 'Qatar World Cup 2022: 70 Nepalese workers die on building sites', 1 October 2013, *www.theguardian.com/world/2013/oct/01/qatar-world-cup-2022-nepalese-die-building-sites*.

21 See Maennig (2005).

22 See, for example, Fédération Internationale de Football Association, 'FIFA responds to independent Ethics Committee statement', media release, 13 November 2014, *www.fifa.com/governance/news/y=2014/m=11/news=fifa-responds-to-independent-ethics-committee-statement-2474201.html*.

23 *Guardian* (UK), 'Russia and Qatar may lose World Cups if evidence of bribery is found', 7 June 2015, *www.theguardian.com/football/2015/jun/07/russia-qatar-lose-world-cups-if-bribery-found-fifa*.

3.6

The planning and hosting of sports mega-events

Sources, forms and the prevention of corruption

John Horne[1]

Introduction

Writing as the revelations about alleged corruption at the Fédération Internationale de Football Association (FIFA) and the dramatic resignation speech of the organisation's president, Sepp Blatter, are still being digested,[2] it is all too easy to consider corruption as yet another form of bread and circuses entertainment provided by sport. Individuals – the 'bad guys' and the 'good guys' – are being identified, and in some cases mocked and vilified for alleged abuses of entrusted power for their own private gain (such as Blatter, Jack Warner and Chuck Blazer of, or once of, FIFA),[3] or praised and celebrated for doggedly tracking them down (such as English investigative reporter Andrew Jennings).[4] Individuals are easier to identify than complex systems, however. This can allow the structure that enables corruption to remain intact. The structure of the system is the 'elephant in the room'; just as the 'criminogenic environment of the financial system'[5] was responsible for the economic crash of 2007–2008, it is necessary to consider the crisis of international sport as part of a systemic crisis. This chapter sketches some of the ways in which corruption risks enter into the planning and hosting of sports mega-events. It recognises that the sources, forms and consequences of corruption are 'embedded within political and economic systems. Its precise role and effects will depend on the configurations and dynamics of such systems.'[6]

The concept of regional corruption binaries creates the potential for accusations of overstepping territorial jurisdiction,[7] as has happened with respect to the role of the FBI and the US attorney general in the 2015 crisis at FIFA, which served as the basis for concerns that the action taken was politically motivated against Russia (host of the 2018 World Cup) and Qatar (host of the 2022 World Cup).[8] This also raises an important question, though: how else are international sports organisations (ISOs) such as FIFA or the International Olympic Committee (IOC) to be regulated?

Corruption and sport

Why should corruption matter in sport? Because sport matters: sport in its mega-event form is used to political effect by hosts and ISOs alike; elite sport has become a transnational multi-billion-dollar industry; and it engages with the everyday lives of billions of people across the globe. In sports mega-events, this relates to activities such as vote-rigging and the use of undue influence in elections or the selection of hosts, embezzlement and fraud, and bribery. In other words, it involves non-competition decisions made by sports officials, associations and governing bodies.

Corruption in sport is as old as the ancient Olympic Games.[9] Those guilty of corruption related to the games had to erect columns of shame (*zane*) at their own expense, or that of their city, at the entrance to the Olympic stadium to atone for their actions. In contemporary sport, Wolfgang Maennig suggests that it is no greater nor 'more widespread in sport than corruption in other areas of human endeavour'.[10] The number of reported cases of management corruption in sport has been increasing, however.[11] To examine this we need to consider the context, types and circumstances in which corruption can occur in sports mega-events.

Sports mega-events

Since the 1980s rent-seeking behaviour – 'seeking control of assets and resources that can be used to extract rent from users' – has become the economic imperative.[12] This has had implications for elite sport, and in particular its flagship mega-events: the Olympic Games and the men's football World Cup. At the same time as there has been massive growth in the involvement of commercial interests in sport – creating a 'global media sports cultural complex'[13] in which the role of corporate media and sponsors especially has got bigger and bigger – regulatory systems and demands for greater transparency and accountability in governance have also emerged. In these circumstances, suspicions about the practices of self-regulating bodies claiming relative autonomy from local jurisdictions, such as international sports associations, have grown.

As the IOC and FIFA, among other sports organising bodies, have become business-oriented international non-government organisations, journalists, sociologists and other social scientists have sought to investigate shortcomings in their operations.[14] At the same time, several features of the sports mega-events that these bodies oversee have become attractive and have been used by states for a variety of non-sporting ends, such as economic and social development, nation-building and -signalling (by branding the nation) and to assist in economic and political liberalisation. As Barry Houlihan notes, the 'willingness of governments to humble themselves before the IOC and FIFA through lavish hospitality and the strategic deployment of presidents, prime ministers, royalty and supermodels is a reflection of the value that governments place on international sport'.[15]

Since the 1970s there has been concern about 'gigantism' and 'white elephants' in the Olympics – the growth in scale of the events, on the one hand, and the potential to build facilities and stadiums that will be more costly to use and maintain than they are worth, on the other. Economists and other social scientists have assessed sports mega-events in terms of their costs and benefits.[16] Bent Flyvbjerg suggests that an 'iron law of mega-projects', including sports mega-events, is that they will be 'over budget, over time, over and over again'.[17] Whether this is a constant or not, it is certainly the case that most sports mega-events since the 1970s have attracted political controversy.

There are a number of 'known unknowns' with respect to sports mega-events that have remained part of the political debate about these events.[18] These include:

- the emphasis on consumption-based development, as opposed to social redistribution, with respect to the goals of hosting sports mega-events;
- urban regeneration that often leads to the 'gentrification' of specific areas being regenerated;
- the displacement (and subsequent 'replacement') of poor and less powerful communities of people;
- the use of (often quite extensive) public sector funds to enhance private corporate sector gain;[19]
- the local host sites and spaces benefiting global flows of capital, trade and finance;
- the spatial concentration of the impact of the event;
- the impact on employment of hosting sports mega-events – and the duration of the impact;
- the impact on tourism flows is never near what is predicted by proponents of sports mega-events, mainly because 'non-sport' tourists usually defer their visit to the location of events and thus effectively are 'displaced' by 'sport-event tourists';[20]
- the way in which proponents have to resort to the manufacturing of the consent of local and national publics to get them on their side about staging the event;[21] and
- the growth of opposition event coalitions as a result of some or all of these developments.[22]

Symbolic politics – the politics of promotional culture via public diplomacy, 'soft power' and/or propaganda – are thus fundamental features of the contemporary risks of sports mega-events. Whether competing with other cities or nations to host an event, winning the right to do so or actually hosting an event, the potential for symbolic power plays, or pitfalls, is real. All such exercises in promotional politics – nation-branding, city-branding, image alteration – run the danger of heightening reputational risk to the bidders (and eventual hosts) involved. For example, according to the 2014 GfK survey of national image, hosting the 2014 World Cup, rather than boosting Brazil's reputation in the world, saw the country lose ground in the rankings, while World Cup winners Germany knocked the United States off the top spot after five years.[23]

Types and circumstances of potential corruption in sports mega-events

In a relatively simplistic formula, Robert Klitgaard suggests that 'corruption = monopoly + discretion – accountability'.[24] Where and when can corruption in sports mega-events occur? Maennig suggests that in circumstances when a sport (or sports event) enjoys high levels of popularity and attractiveness that make it capable of generating large cash flows, economic rents 'result from the fact that . . . the relevant international sports bodies have a unilateral monopoly over the awarding of sporting title honours'.[25]

In the case of sports mega-events, several factors increase the scope for corruption. The large number of disparate organisations involved in staging a sports mega-event includes the ISOs, the international federations (IFs), national organising committees (NOCs in the case of the Olympic Games), local organising committees (LOCs), bid teams and associated political and commercial entities. The membership of these organisations may vary considerably in terms of their recruitment and appointment practices and collective experience, including in the case of LOCs working within a largely inflexible timetable for the completion of projects. The intense international interest in mega-events adds considerably to the scrutiny that their organisers will face, yet this can also create the conditions where anxiety over the pressure to deliver leads to corrupt practices. Corruption in relation to the management of sports mega-events, real or suspected, can thus take a number of forms: for example, acquiring certain positions in sports associations; influencing the allocation of broadcasting or other media rights; fixing the allocation of construction contracts or subcontracts for building stadiums or facilities; or subcontracting to, for example, small- to medium-sized enterprises to undertake work in preparation for the event.[26]

One constant potential source of corruption is, of course, the governance (internal procedures) of international sports associations and related sports bodies involved in sports mega-events, as the crisis at FIFA in 2015 demonstrates. The announcement in December 2014 that the IOC would adopt 'Agenda 2020', a package of recommendations designed to change policy on a variety of issues, including ethics and good governance, promises to create a new benchmark, at least in the IOC.[27] However, sceptics might still ask if Agenda 2020 is as much a bid to restore public confidence in hosting the Olympics – at least in democratic states – as an effort to bring about fundamental reforms.

Conclusion: cultures of corruption in the management of sports mega-events

It may be possible to identify ways in which the risk of corruption could be managed better in sports mega-events. Greater democracy, transparency, solidarity and checks and balances within ISOs, NOCs and IFs would all improve governance. Five suggestions in particular have been put forward to manage corruption in sport and in general.[28]

1. Provide and publicise clear codes of conduct to measure behaviour and misbehaviour by those involved – ISOs, IFs, OCs and other agencies.
2. Ensure the fair distribution of any financial surpluses accrued by the staging of sports mega-events – whether by host cities, organising committees or sports governing organisations.
3. Have a high degree of transparency – including detailed documentation of decision-making processes, the monitoring of executive and administrative bodies by an internal auditing department to monitor staff and reducing the degrees of discretion and freedom of information legislation applicable to sport.
4. Create financial and other incentives to offset the temptations for corruption by insiders.
5. Install systematic internal auditing and control measures in sports bodies, which should bear direct responsibility for any crimes committed by subordinates.

Efforts to manage corruption risks require the establishment of certain defined procedures and protocols. These then become the new 'rules of the mega-event hosting game' that, as in other sports, can in turn be tested, tweaked and, frequently, bent to enable competing potential hosts to gain an advantage. Putting new rules into practice is difficult, however, since changing the culture of an organisation – the tacit, unwritten, unofficial ways of doing things – requires changing the rituals, routines and daily practices of the organisation. When corruption is proved there is a need to focus on anti-corruption measures and cronyism in the re-engineering of the organisation.[29]

It is possible that Michael Garcia, the former US prosecutor who investigated allegations of wrongdoing with regard to the 2018 and 2022 World Cup hosting decisions, was correct when he said as he resigned from FIFA that '[n]o independent governance committee, investigator, or arbitration panel can change the culture of an organization'.[30] This may be especially the case for organisations with the distinctive governance characteristics of ISOs that create the potential for corruption[31] mixed with an enduring belief in the 'great sport myth' – an almost 'unshakeable belief about the inherent purity and goodness of sport'.[32] One way forward may be to demand that 'sports governing bodies have to start operating as big businesses, using best business practices',[33] possibly using Play the Game sports governance indicators and other means of managing corruption risks. It needs to be remembered, though, that operating in an organisational 'culture of ethical failure'[34] is a systemic problem, not one of individual agents. Will the FIFA crisis in 2015 change everything? Probably not, but it will change some things.

Notes

1   John Horne is professor of sport and sociology at the University of Central Lancashire, based in Preston, United Kingdom.
2   See CNN (US), 'Sepp Blatter: resignation speech in full', 2 June 2015, *http://edition.cnn. com/2015/06/02/football/sepp-blatter-resigns-fifa-speech*; and BBC (UK), 'FIFA corruption crisis: key questions answered', 17 June 2015, *www.bbc.com/news/world-europe-32897066.*
3   BBC (17 June 2015).
4   *Washington Post* (US), 'How a curmudgeonly old reporter exposed the FIFA scandal that toppled Sepp Blatter', 3 June 2015, *www.washingtonpost.com/news/morning-mix/wp/2015/06/03/how-a-curmudgeonly-old-reporter-exposed-the-fifa-scandal-that-toppled-sepp-blatter.*
5   Andrew Sayer, *Why We Can't Afford the Rich* (Bristol: Policy Press, 2014), p. 273.
6   Robert Williams, 'Editorial: the new politics of corruption', *Third World Quarterly*, vol. 20 (1999), p. 488.
7   Corruption remains a slippery concept, and discussion of it tends to create binaries: the Western and Eastern blocs, developed and developing societies, democratic and authoritarian regimes, regulated and self-regulated organisations and associations. The power to define corruption may be said to lie with the dominant party, with Africa, South America and Asia often considered to be the continents and subcontinents particularly affected by corruption.
8   BBC (UK), 'Fifa scandal: is the long arm of US law now overreaching?', 4 June 2015, *www.bbc.co.uk/news/world-us-canada-33011847.*
9   Wolfgang Maennig, 'Corruption in international sports and sport management: forms, tendencies, extent and countermeasures', *European Sport Management Quarterly*, vol. 5 (2005).
10   Ibid.
11   Ibid.
12   Sayer (2014), p. 53.
13   David Rowe, *Global Media Sport: Flows, Forms and Futures* (London: Bloomsbury Academic, 2011), p. 34.
14   Vyv Simson and Andrew Jennings, *The Lords of the Rings: Power, Money and Drugs in the Modern Olympics* (London: Simon & Schuster, 1992); Andrew Jennings, *Foul! The Secret World of FIFA: Bribes, Vote Rigging and Ticket Scandals* (London: HarperCollins, 2006); John Sugden and Alan Tomlinson, *Badfellas: FIFA Family at War* (Edinburgh: Mainstream Publishing, 2003); John Sugden and Alan Tomlinson, *FIFA and the Contest for World Football: Who Rules the Peoples' Game?* (Cambridge: Polity, 1998); Alan Tomlinson, *FIFA (Fédération Internationale de Football Association): The Men, the Myths and the Money* (London: Routledge, 2014).
15   Barrie Houlihan, 'Political involvement in sport, physical education and recreation', in Anthony Laker (ed.), *The Sociology of Sport and Physical Education: An Introductory Reader* (London: Routledge, 2002), p. 194.

16   Holger Preuss, *The Economics of Staging the Olympics: A Comparison of the Games 1972–2008* (Cheltenham: Edward Elgar, 2004); David Whitson and John Horne, 'Underestimated costs and overestimated benefits? Comparing the outcomes of sports mega-events in Canada and Japan', in John Horne and Wolfram Manzenreiter (eds), *Sports Mega-Events: Social Scientific Analyses of a Global Phenomenon* (Oxford: Blackwell, 2006).

17   Bent Flyvbjerg, 'What you should know about megaprojects and why: an overview', *Project Management Journal*, vol. 45 (2014).

18   John Horne, 'The four knowns of sports mega-events', *Leisure Studies*, vol. 26 (2007), pp. 81–96.

19   Ibid.

20   Ibid.

21   Ibid.

22   Many of these issues are discussed further in the contributions to Richard Gruneau and John Horne (eds), *Mega-Events and Globalization: Capital and Spectacle in a Changing World Order* (London: Routledge, 2015).

23   GfK (Germany), 'Germany knocks USA off best nation top spot after 5 years', 12 November 2014, *www.gfk.com/news-and-events/press-room/press-releases/pages/germany-knocks-usa-off-best-nation-top-spot.aspx*; EBC (Brazil), 'Copa do Mundo não melhorou imagem do país no exterior, aponta índice britânico', 17 November 2014, *www.ebc.com.br/noticias/internacional/2014/11/copa-do-mundo-nao-melhorou-imagem-do-pais-no-exterior-aponta-indice.*

24   Robert Klitgaard, *Controlling Corruption* (Berkeley, CA: University of California Press, 1988).

25   Maennig (2005), p. 208.

26   On some of these issues with respect to the Asian Football Confederation (AFC), see James M. Dorsey, 'Reforming soccer governance: tackling political corruption alongside financial wrongdoing', 6 June 2015, *http://mideastsoccer.blogspot.sg/2015/06/reforming-soccer-governance-tackling.html.*

27   International Olympic Committee, 'Olympic Agenda 2020: 20+20 Recommendations', December 2014, *www.olympic.org/Documents/Olympic_Agenda_2020/Olympic_Agenda_2020-20-20_Recommendations-ENG.pdf.*

28   Derived and adapted from Maennig (2005) and Vito Tanzi, 'Corruption around the world: causes, consequences, scope, and cures', *IMF Staff Papers*, vol. 45 (1998).

29   The Conversation (UK), 'With Blatter gone, the hard work of changing FIFA culture starts now', 3 June 2015, *https://theconversation.com/with-blatter-gone-the-hard-work-of-changing-fifa-culture-starts-now-42776.*

30   Cited by The Conversation (UK), 'Sepp Blatter's FIFA exit opens door for prosecutors, reformers', 2 June 2015, *https://theconversation.com/sepp-blatters-fifa-exit-opens-door-for-prosecutors-reformers-42729.*

31   See Roger Pielke Jr, Chapter 1.4 'Obstacles to accountability in international sports governance', in this report.

32   Jay Coakley, 'Assessing the sociology of sport: on cultural sensibilities and the great sport myth', *International Review for the Sociology of Sport*, vol. 50 (2015).

33   Transparency International, 'Defining the boundaries: a blue print for enhancing cricket administration', 31 January 2012, *http://blog.transparency.org/2012/01/31/defining-the-boundaries-a-blue-print-for-enhancing-cricket-administration.*

34   Naomi Klein, *This Changes Everything* (London: Allen Lane, 2014), p. 334.

3.7

Preventing corruption in the planning of major sporting events

Open issues

Wolfgang Maennig[1]

Corruption in the planning of major events may start as early as during the bidding process, as demonstrated in the Salt Lake City 2002 Winter Olympic bid.[2] Likewise, corruption may not end with the opening of the event, as demonstrated in the gold medal decision in the 2002 Olympics figure skating competition in favour of the Russian skating duo.[3] The activities between these phases also provide many opportunities for corruption. Corruption affects almost all stages of the value creation chain, and in all groups of 'stakeholders', including nominations for positions, the allocation of TV or marketing rights and the commissioning of construction works for sports arenas and other venues.[4]

Truly world-leading ambitions for international sporting institutions

With the Olympic Games and the men's football World Cup, the International Olympic Committee (IOC) and the Fédération Internationale de Football Association (FIFA) control two of the most fascinating global sporting events, which attract the desire to host them in all parts of the world. These institutions have high ambitions (and positions) in promoting sports and making profits, which should be mirrored by equal ambitions to serve humankind more generally. In a sense, the IOC and FIFA are in a unique position to change the world for the better, and are potentially more influential than any other international institution, including even the United Nations and NATO, because of the prohibitively high 'costs' arising from those institutions exercising their power (alienation of sections of the global community in the event of diplomatic pressure being applied, human casualties and infrastructural destruction in the extreme case of military force being used). FIFA and the IOC could conceivably use their positions to enforce standard requirements for good governance, labour regulations and the protection of minority rights, by declaring them as a precondition for being eligible to bid or organise their events. Many nations with deficiencies in these areas might change their practices, just to be able to bid.

Any counter-argument that the IOC and FIFA do not have a general political mandate would be invalidated if these organisations made it clear that they were simply applying internationally agreed standards, developed by institutions such as the International Labour Organization (ILO), World Trade Organization, and so on, as they indeed should. Another potential counter-argument may be that such standards are biased towards current 'Western values', which even Western nations themselves did not live up to a few decades ago, and that such prescriptions imply ambitions towards a Western hegemony, including, for example, religious arrogance and/or a protectionist attempt to hinder competition from emerging regions. For this reason, if the IOC and FIFA were to reform their bidding requirements, they should do so such that they possess an inclusive character, in line with internationally accepted standards, such as those of the UN and ILO. The time is ripe for these organisations to be more ambitious, lead by example and make a genuine impact.

Referenda and participation as formal prerequisites

A general critique is that the bidding for and organising of major sporting events are 'elitist actions' that serve the interests of few (e.g. athletes, real-estate owners, construction firms, politicians), harm the lives of many (e.g. by the displacement of underprivileged people) and do not serve the majority of the population. These critiques are often linked with accusations of corrupt behaviour, for example against political officials who are accused of being misled by influential individuals and making decisions against the 'real will' of the majority. Such critiques regularly hinder the efficient planning and organising of these events.[5] Furthermore, such critiques undermine the positive image of sports organisations. The violent protests in Brazil in 2013 were a clear signal that successful sporting mega-events need to have the support of a broad majority of the population and need to be planned and managed in an accountable manner.

As a far-reaching mechanism to counter allegations of elitism and corruption, the IOC, FIFA and other sporting institutions could require *ex ante* referenda or similar processes as a precondition for bidding. This could be accompanied by an extension of the time period generally allowed for the process – from the commencement of bidding up to the opening ceremony – by an additional two years at least. The longer period of pre-bidding preparation would fit well with the ambitions of event organisers to use the Games as a tool for urban regeneration – something that is hardly feasible in multi-layered societies with well-ordered checks and balances within the present preparation period.

A requirement to hold pre-bidding referenda implies the risk of fewer cities/nations coming forward to bid in the first place. On the positive side, though, the quality of the bids would improve. Interested cities and nations would need to invest more resources into developing bidding concepts that convince their own populations (and, consequently, the decision-making bodies in the sports organisations).

Host selection: choosing a pool of future hosts

The time period between the selection and hosting of the Olympic Games or the World Cup appears to be too short for many cities and countries, if the events are interpreted as a tool for urban regeneration. It is sometimes argued that the time pressure is itself a major source of corruption and cost escalation, because decision-makers lack alternatives for completing the projects on schedule. As a response, the IOC and FIFA could change their selection modus. Instead of selecting one city seven years ahead of the Olympic Games, or one country six years in advance of the World Cup,[6] the institutions could select a pool of some three to four future hosts. The final selection of the host would take place some four years ahead of the event, based on the current status of the preparation. After each final determination of the next host, a new future host would be added to the pool. Such a mechanism would have the advantage that the host could make use of different speeds of preparation, without hindering investments, as there would be the certainty of being the host at some stage in the near future.

Looking beyond public finance for sporting mega-events

Private financing for major sporting events has been proposed as an alternative approach, in order to avoid the need to draw upon and further stress public finances.[7] When considering corruption as an intentional choice, this would make sense as well: the risk of corruption generally increases if sufficiently large bribes can be financed.

The significant increase in budgets for World Cups and Olympic Games over recent decades, which – including urban infrastructure – now easily reach double-digit billion-dollar levels,[8] provide a potential additional impulse for corruption. With private financing and no public funds, there would be much less investment for sport facilities and other infrastructure, severely limiting the scope for corruption. With effective regulations, CEOs will have far fewer incentives for allowing corruption to happen on their watches. The Los Angeles 1984 and Atlanta 1996 Summer Olympic Games were organised with minimal or no public finance, and their examples should be scrutinised by other bidding nations.[9] This method would bring the Games much closer to their roots, as a sporting event rather than an occasion for urban regeneration.

If removing public finances from the funding of major sporting events appears too far-reaching a move, at least public broadcasters should not be allowed to bid for World Cup and Olympic broadcasting rights (at least when there are private bidders willing to provide free broadcasting of the event). As such, a decrease in the TV (and marketing revenues) of major sporting events can be expected. Inevitably, this would not be a policy actively promoted by international sports organisations. With a worldwide consensus on the part of public authorities to exclude public sector institutions from bidding for TV and marketing rights, however, the available funds – and thus the risk of corruption – should be reduced.[10]

Human resources: selection, rotation, limitation, payment and accountability

The decision-making should be participatory, especially in the selection of the leadership for the bidding and organising teams. Up to now, in almost all cases, the selection process has been limited to a small circle of decision-makers in a non-transparent process. In too many instances the selection process has led to the enthroning of politically connected individuals who 'represent a greater degree of risk of corruption'.[11] Furthermore, there are various cases of bids and organisation processes for major sporting events when the leading individuals had to be removed because of inadequate performance. A selection that includes a public participation process may well increase the quality (and acceptance) of the leadership team. Such a selection process may well conclude with the decision not to install a single 'head' but, rather, a team of peers with different abilities, specialisations and backgrounds – a well-established everyday principle in almost all team sports.

It might be useful to consider making higher payments to officials working for sports organisations, especially in FIFA and the IOC, notwithstanding the above reasoning for reducing the budgets of sporting events by excluding public finance. This may imply a need to change the human resource concept for officials in such institutions, to a system whereby officials should be paid a salary that is higher than the standard market wage for equivalent activities ('efficiency wages').[12] In combination, a deferred compensation model[13] should be constructed; in other words, a large part of the officials' income would have to be paid into funds, be they pension or otherwise, which would be paid out only at the end of a corruption-free tenure. A sufficiently high perceived risk of losing this future income would decrease the corruptibility of sporting officials.

Finally, some other measures could be considered. For example, other sporting institutions should weigh up the benefits of adopting the term limits and job rotation policies of the IOC, which would tend to mitigate corruption risks by preventing too high a level of trust developing between potential providers and recipients of bribes. It might also be instructive, in the context of public finances for the sporting mega-events, to look at the case of the governor of the Reserve Bank of New Zealand, whose contract extension was linked to performance – in this instance, targeted inflation rates not being exceeded.[14] Similarly, the contract and/or the payment of chairmen or -women for organising sporting mega-events could be linked to not exceeding event budgets.

Notes

1   Wolfgang Maennig is professor of economics at Hamburg University and an Olympic champion (rowing eights at the 1988 Summer Olympics).

2   Some argue that it may have even started earlier (see section headed 'Referenda and participation as formal prerequisites'); *New York Times* (US), 'Olympics: leaders of Salt Lake Olympic bid are indicted in bribery scandal', 21 July 2000, *www.nytimes.com/ 2000/07/21/sports/olympics-leaders-of-salt-lake-olympic-bid-are-indicted-in-bribery-scandal.html.*

3   ESPN (US), 'Sale, Pelletier share gold with Russian pair', 15 February 2002, *http://sports. espn.go.com/oly/winter02/figure/news?id=1333280.*

4   For an overview up to 2004, see Wolfgang Maennig, 'Corruption in international sports and sport management: forms, tendencies, extent and countermeasures', *European Sport Management Quarterly,* vol. 2 (2005). In recent years most cases of corruption in sports have been betting-related; see Christian Kalb, *Integrity in Sport: Understanding and Preventing Match-Fixing* (Lausanne: SportAccord, 2011), *www.sportaccord.com/multimedia/ docs/2012/04/SportAccordIntegrityReport_A4_V2UpdatedApril2012.pdf*; and David Forrest and Wolfgang Maennig, 'The threat to sports and sports governance from betting-related corruption: causes and solutions', in Paul Heywood (ed.), *Routledge Handbook of Political Corruption* (Abingdon: Routledge, 2015).

5   For more information on and a critique of the planning displacement, see Libby Porter, Margaret Jaconelli, Julian Cheyne, David Eby and Hendrik Wagenaar, 'Planning displacement: the real legacy of major sporting events', *Planning Theory and Practice,* vol. 10 (2009); for the other critical aspects in the case of Brazil 2014/2016, see Thêmis Aragão and Wolfgang Maennig, 'Mega sporting events, real estate, and urban social economics: the case of Brazil 2014/2016', in Paulo Esteves, Andrew Zimbalist and Luis Fernandes (eds), *BRICS and the Sports Mega Events: Experience and Perspectives* (Rio de Janeiro: BRICs Policy Center, forthcoming).

6   This is typically a period of six years, though the awarding of the 2022 World Cup to Qatar in 2010 was an exception.

7   *Boston Globe* (US), 'Olympic bid draws fire over funding omissions', 28 May 2015, *www. bostonglobe.com/metro/2015/05/28/walsh-says-public-money-can-used-for-olympic-infrastructure/aljtE75n1JDIVe2nCqsz2N/story.html*; *Frankfurter Allgemeine* (Germany), 'Keine öffentlichen Gelder für Olympia!', *www.faz.net/aktuell/sport/sportpolitik/keine-oeffentlichen-gelder-fuer-olympia-13331809.html.*

8   Andrew Zimbalist, *Circus Maximus: The Economic Gamble Behind Hosting the Olympics and the World Cup* (Washington, DC: Brookings Institution Press, 2015).

9   *Boston Globe* (US), 'Atlanta Games' venues left some lessons for Boston', 3 August 2014, *www.bostonglobe.com/metro/2014/08/02/atlanta-games-venues-from-left-legacy-some-lessons/Jj8zlJqrUcdTT6sEXUjseK/story.html.*

10 Free TV could nevertheless be a prerequisite.

11 United Nations Office on Drugs and Crime (UNODC), *The United Nations Convention Against Corruption: A Strategy for Safeguarding Against Corruption in Major Public Events* (Vienna: UNODC, 2013), p. 19, *www.unodc.org/documents/corruption/Publications/2013/13-84527_Ebook.pdf.*

12 Editor's note: Transparency International understands that, although the organisations do not publish salary bands and salaries of executive officials, these officials already receive sufficiently high if not exceedingly high salaries, and does not advocate raising them.

13 Edward Lazear, 'Why is there mandatory retirement?', *Journal of Political Economy*, vol. 87 (1979); Wolfgang Maennig, 'On the economics of doping and corruption in international sports', *Journal of Sports Economics*, vol. 3 (2002).

14 David Archer, 'Inflation targeting in New Zealand', paper presented to the International Monetary Fund, Washington, DC, 20 March 2000, sect. I, *www.imf.org/external/pubs/ft/seminar/2000/targets/archer.htm#iiia.*

3.8

Malpractice in the 2010 Delhi Commonwealth Games and the renovation of Shivaji Stadium

Ashutosh Kumar Mishra[1]

The 2010 Commonwealth Games, held in New Delhi, were marred by allegations of corruption and mismanagement, which tarnished the image of India by presenting it as a country blighted by high levels of fraud and malpractice.[2] From the very beginning the event was shrouded in controversies, which continually surfaced and have still not been fully resolved. Concerns were raised during the preparatory phase, with construction work falling behind schedule and volunteers quitting in large numbers because of dissatisfaction with their assignments and with the training programme. Gross violations of workers' rights were reported at construction sites, where workers were forced into *begar*.[3] The conclusion of the Games brought to the fore further issues, such as the reported flouting of contracting rules by officials of the organising committee and the awarding of work contracts to incompetent agencies at hugely inflated prices.[4]

At the start it was not clear whether the organising committee would be covered under the national Right to Information (RTI) Act, as it did not come under the purview of the definition of 'state'.[5] Such grey areas can create a sense of immunity from rules, procedures and accountability.

Concerns about the management of the project were raised when the British revenue and customs department (HMRC) raised objections over a substantial amount of money transferred to a UK company, AM Films.[6] The potential discrepancies surfaced in March 2010 when the organising committee reportedly asked HMRC for a VAT refund on its payments to AM Films, thus opening a Pandora's box.[7] It was reported that AM Films claimed that the payments were for car hire services, toilets, barriers and electricity, with the organising committee saying that they were for the purchase of video equipment, while HMRC held that no services had been procured in line with a proper tendering process.[8]

A judgment from the Delhi High Court in January 2010 brought the whole gamut of activities related to the Commonwealth Games within the ambit of the RTI, however. The High Court sided with the government's claim that the RTI laws were applicable to these activities on the grounds that nearly all the funding for the organising committee was provided by the government and that the committee was not an independent body.[9] This provided a fillip to various activists and members of the media in their efforts to expose potential malpractice.[10]

A special committee led by the former comptroller and auditor general of India, V.K. Shunglu (the 'Shunglu Committee'), was set up by the government on 25 October 2010 to probe the allegations of corruption and mismanagement in organising the Commonwealth Games. Given the colossal amount of public money that was involved, several other investigative agencies, such as the Central Bureau of Investigation (CBI), the Central Vigilance Commission (CVC), the Directorate General of Income Tax Investigation and the Enforcement Directorate, also scrutinised the financial irregularities.

The chairman of the organising committee, Suresh Kalmadi, and several others were subsequently arrested by the CBI on 25 April 2011, linked to the awarding of the timing/scoring/result system contract to a Swiss firm, Swiss Timing Omega, at an exorbitant cost of Rs. 141 crore (some US$23 million) and the rejection of Spanish firm MSL's much lower bid of Rs. 62 crore (around US$10 million), which resulted in a loss of over Rs. 80 crore (about US$13 million) to the exchequer.[11] They were charged with cheating, forgery and criminal conspiracy, criminal intimidation and destruction of evidence under the Prevention of Corruption Act.[12]

Several other serious allegations came to light, relating in particular to the Queen's Baton Relay, held in London and coordinated by the Organising Committee. This included the awarding of transportation work to AM Car and Van Hire and the aforementioned contracting of AM Films, which reportedly entailed irregular contracting processes and the charging of exorbitant rates.[13]

The example of the renovation of the Shivaji Stadium

The renovation of the Shivaji Stadium, located in New Delhi, is a classic case of the potential risks involved with large construction projects. Concerns of corruption have been exposed mainly through information procured by whistleblowers and RTI applications. The Shivaji Stadium was to be used solely as a practice stadium for women's hockey teams, rather than for any event during the Commonwealth Games. However, the renovation of the stadium proceeded so slowly that it could not be used even for practices during the Commonwealth Games. Although the tender for the renovation of the stadium stipulated that experience working with the Indian authorities was required, the New Delhi Municipal Council (NDMC) contracted M/s China Railway Shisiju Group Corporation (CRSGC), which did not have such experience.[14] The tender estimated that Rs. 808,518,605 (some US$11.5 million) was needed for the renovation, but CRSGC negotiated a sum of Rs. 1,602,716,430 (around US$23 million) for the contract.[15] The company then subcontracted the work in its entirety, contrary to the terms of its contract, to M/s Simplex Projects Ltd (SPL) and allegedly at half the cost of its original contract.[16]

Although there have not been conclusive findings to date that the work or procurement activities carried out in relation to the renovation involved corruption, there are incidents that raise serious concern. For instance, CRSGC, via SPL, allegedly purchased stadium chairs from abroad at six to seven times the price of chairs locally available in Delhi.[17] During the execution of the project the work was investigated by various government bodies, including the Shunglu Committee, the comptroller and auditor general, and the chief technical examiner of the CVC. The investigations found that CRSGC was not eligible to apply for the tender, that its subletting of the work to SPL was illegal and that the contract was awarded at an inflated cost.[18]

Based on the various irregularities, the NDMC revoked CRSGC's contract, reassigned the renovation to other agencies and debarred CRSGC.[19] Soon afterwards the Shunglu Committee submitted its report, and the government formed a committee consisting of a group of ministers to look into its findings and recommendations. As of July 2013, a case had been registered against the former NDMC chairman for alleged irregularities relating to the awarding of the contract to CRSGC.[20] Since then, however, no further known action has been taken on the Shunglu Committee's recommendations, and there is no evidence that any advances have been recovered from CRSGC.

After Transparency International India learnt from a whistleblower about various potential irregularities and malpractices that had occurred during the award and execution of the contract, and in an effort to find out what actions had been taken by the government on the recommendations of the Shunglu Committee, TI India filed an RTI application. After the initial application, and a subsequent appeal, government officials refused to share critical information, citing section 8(1)(i) of the Right to Information Act, which empowers the government to exempt certain information from disclosure; the authorities stated that the CBI was still investigating the matter, and questioned the need for an RTI request to be filed.

Of the Rs. 1,602,716,430 (about US$23 million) negotiated by CRSGC for its work on the renovations of Shivaji Stadium, it ultimately received Rs. 987,231,667 (some US$12.5 million) for the work.[21] Since the work is still ongoing at the time of writing and the final bills are yet to be paid to the agencies completing the project, there is no estimate of the actual expenditure incurred for the stadium's renovation.

It remains the case, at present, that the authorities are uncertain as to the expected date of completion and the total expenditure that is being incurred to upgrade this stadium.[22] The investigations are still ongoing, without any tangible outcome. The renovations were scheduled to be completed before the 2010 Commonwealth Games, but the fact that the work is still in progress even though the 2014 Commonwealth Games, in Glasgow, are already over points to the laxity that has seeped into the political system, allowing corruption to become endemic and deep-rooted.

Notes

1 Ashutosh Kumar Mishra is executive director of Transparency International India.
2 NDTV (India), 'Commonwealth Games scam may be to the tune of R8,000 crore: CVC', 20 October 2010, *www.ndtv.com/article/india/commonwealth-games-scam-may-be-to-the-tune-of-rs-8-000-crore-cvc-60984*.
3 '*Begar*' is a Hindi term for 'forced labour': *Economic and Political Weekly* (India), 'Violation of workers' rights at the Commonwealth Games construction site', 13 June 2009.
4 NDTV (India), 'CWG scam: Kalmadi's aide caught on camera', 28 April 2011, *www.ndtv.com/india-news/cwg-scam-kalmadis-aide-caught-on-camera-454204*; the organising committee was composed of an executive board and a 500-member general body, within which there were special subcommittees (for accreditation, transport, publicity, etc.) and functional area subgroups (sanitation, accommodation, catering, etc.). The 15-member executive board was led by a chair, vice chair, secretary general and treasurer: *http://d2010.thecgf.com/organisation_structure*.
5 Article 12 of the Indian constitution defines what is meant by the term 'state', and the Right to Information Act, 2005, is applicable to only those institutions that are covered under the definition of 'state'.
6 *The Hindu* (India), 'Shadow over Commonwealth Games', 1 August 2010, *www.thehindu.com/todays-paper/tp-national/tp-newdelhi/shadow-over-commonwealth-games/article545691.ece*.

7   *The Hindu* (India), 'Major scam hits Commonwealth Games', 31 July 2010, www.thehindu.
    com/news/national/major-scam-hits-commonwealth-games/article542593.ece.
8   *The Hindu* (1 August 2010).
9   *The Hindu* (India), 'CWG committee, IOA come under RTI Act: court', 7 January 2010,
    www.thehindu.com/sport/other-sports/cwg-committee-ioa-come-under-rti-act-court/
    article77008.ece.
10 The verdict was pronounced on 7 January 2010; see *http://lobis.nic.in/dhc/SRB/*
    judgement/20-01-2010/SRB07012010CW8762007.pdf.
11 NDTV (India), 'CWG case: Suresh Kalmadi, Lalit Bhanot and 9 others charged with
    corruption, conspiracy', 21 December 2012, *www.ndtv.com/article/india/cwg-case-*
    suresh-kalmadi-lalit-bhanot-and-9-others-charged-with-corruption-conspiracy-308113.
12 *Governance Now* (India), 'CWG scam: court frames charges against Kalmadi, 9 others',
    4 February 2013, *www.governancenow.com/news/regular-story/cwg-scam-court-*
    frames-charges-against-kalmadi-9-others.
13 *Economic Times* (India), 'CBI arrests Suresh Kalmadi in Commonwealth Games corruption
    investigation: report', 25 April 2011, *http://articles.economictimes.indiatimes.com/*
    2011-04-25/news/29471351_1_dig-s-k-palsania-suresh-kalmadi-cwg-scam.
14 The following bidders participated in the tender: M/s China Railway Shisiju Group
    Corporation; M/s Ahluwalia Corporation (India) Ltd; M/s JMC Projects Ltd; M/s Nagarjuna
    Const Co.; M/s YMC Buildmore; and M/s Unity India Projects Ltd. This information was
    provided by the Office of the Executive Engineer (Stadia Project), Civil Engineering
    Department, New Delhi Municipal Council on 5 August 2014, in response to an RTI
    application filed by TI India.
15 Information provided by the Office of the Executive Engineer (Stadia Project), Civil
    Engineering Department, New Delhi Municipal Council on 28 November 2014, in response
    to an RTI application filed by TI India; a report by the Office of the Chief Technical Examiner
    of the Central Vigilance Commission was also provided in response to the RTI request.
16 Information provided by the Office of the Executive Engineer (Stadia Project), Civil Engineering
    Department, New Delhi Municipal Council on 28 November 2014, in response to an RTI
    application filed by TI India. *Outlook* (India), 'Was Rs 185 Cr wasted on Shivaji Stadium
    renovation?', 10 April 2011, *www.outlookindia.com/news/article/was-rs-185-cr-wasted-on-*
    shivaji-stadium-renovation/718288.
17 This was among the irregularities reported by a whistleblower to TI India.
18 Information provided by the Office of the Executive Engineer (Stadia Project), Civil
    Engineering Department, New Delhi Municipal Council on 28 November 2014, in response
    to an RTI application filed by TI India.
19 M/s Johnson Lifts Pvt Limited and M/s Ingersoll Rand Climate Solution: ibid.
20 *Economic Times* (India), 'NDMC annuls Rs 160 crore contract with Chinese firm', 23 July
    2013, *http://articles.economictimes.indiatimes.com/2013-07-23/news/40749697_1_*
    commonwealth-games-chinese-firm-crore-contract.
21 This information was provided to TI India by the Office of the Executive Engineer (Stadia
    Project), Civil Engineering Department, New Delhi Municipal Council on 5 August 2014 and
    7 November 2014, in response to an RTI application filed by TI India.
22 Ibid.

3.9

Preventing corruption ahead of major sports events

Learning from the 2012 London Games

Kevin Carpenter[1]

Introduction

The hosting of major sporting tournaments is the most sought after of all types of major events by countries, with the pinnacle of all those to be awarded being the Summer Olympic and Paralympic Games. Once the Games have been awarded by the International Olympic Committee (IOC), the host country's thoughts must immediately turn to implementing the bid proposal by thoroughly planning the event. London was awarded the 2012 Olympic Games by the IOC on 6 July 2005.[2] One of the key risks the London organisers had to plan carefully for was the threat from corruption in its various guises.[3] This was reflected in preamble R of the Host City Contract: 'WHEREAS [London] and the [British Olympic Association] acknowledge and agree to carry out their activities pursuant to this Contract in full compliance with universal fundamental ethical principles, including those contained in the IOC Code of Ethics.'[4] Giving corruption the widest ambit possible, a number of areas of the delivery of the Olympic and Paralympic Games can be affected, including: financial management, public procurement, major infrastructure and construction, and security and private sector involvement.[5]

Establishing the organisational structure to deliver the London 2012 Games

The obligations under the Host City Contract, particularly preamble T and section 2,[6] led the UK government to enact special legislation to establish two new bodies to plan, organise and deliver the 2012 Games. First, the London Organising Committee of the Olympic Games (LOCOG) was incorporated, as a private company limited by guarantee.[7] Second, the London Olympic Games and Paralympic Games Act 2006 (the Olympic Act) established, and set the mandate of, the Olympic Delivery Authority (ODA).[8] The difference between the two bodies has been described as follows: 'The two organisations have complementary but distinct roles: the ODA is a publicly funded body charged with building the venues and infrastructure for the 2012 Games; [LOCOG] stages the events of the 2012 Games, and is almost entirely funded by privately raised revenues and sponsorship.'[9]

The ODA constituted a single body with overall responsibility for the construction of the venues and the infrastructure, as well as the transfer of assets after the Games and the transition to legacy use.[10] The ODA also shared responsibility with LOCOG for delivering the services required for the Games. As a public body, the ODA was accountable for its work to the government, specifically the Secretary of State for Culture, Media and Sport (who had to consult with the Mayor of London on key issues).[11]

Pursuant to the Olympic Act, two Standing Orders were also issued in relation to the ODA, the first of which set out important anti-corruption provisions for the board.

Paragraph 7

In accordance with the Management Statement the Board is also responsible for the following:

. . .

b. ensuring that the high standards of corporate governance and financial management and control are observed at all times.

. . .

Paragraph 9

Board members are required to:

a. comply at all times with the Code of Practice adopted by the ODA and with all relevant rules relating to the use of public funds and to conflicts of interest;
b. act in good faith in the best interests of the ODA;
c. not misuse information gained in their capacity as Board members for personal gain or for political profit, nor seek to use the opportunity of public service to promote their private interests or those of connected persons or organisations;
d. comply with the ODA's rules on the acceptance of gifts and hospitality and of business appointments (Management Statement para 5.16).[12]

There were also provisions in relation to conflicts of interest on the part of board members, and the declaration of those interests, in paragraphs 35 to 40.

Such provisions are particularly important when engaging private organisations for aspects of the delivery work. Indeed, there were accusations of 'cronyism' when the ODA originally awarded the contract to build the centrepiece Olympic Village, as it was to be financed by Lend Lease, an Australian company previously headed by the then chief executive of the ODA, David Higgins.[13] In 2008, however, during the global credit crunch, Lend Lease's private financing project collapsed, and the British government had to finance the scheme using public funds instead.[14]

In addition to the Olympic Act, the United Kingdom already had a robust anti-corruption legislative framework in place, which included the Fraud Act 2006, the Prevention of Corruption Act 1906 (and later the Bribery Act 2010) and the Public Interest Disclosure Act 1998 for whistleblowing.[15]

Financial management

Sound financial management and preventing mismanagement through corruption are paramount to the success of any major sporting event. The UK government recognised this for the ODA when it passed the two Standing Orders, which included rigorous financial control and oversight mechanisms and set out in detail the delegated authority and financial limits of spending and who was authorised to sign contracts entered into by the ODA at different values.[16]

Despite these strict regulations, a troubling incident of fraud still struck the ODA before the Games, when a man wrote to the authority pretending to be the finance director of Skanska, the construction firm that had been awarded the contract for landscaping the Olympic Park, with a change of account details ahead of a payment. The details he provided were actually for his own bank account. The money was paid to him, and his fraud was discovered by the Crown Prosecution Service only when he tried to disguise the money trail by sending £2 million to Nigeria before planning to buy a number of shops in Wolverhampton. He, and two accomplices, were jailed for between three and a half and four and a half years for defrauding the ODA and Skanska out of a total of around £2.4 million. The ODA managed to recover almost all the money, but a spokesman admitted that '[o]ur payments system was reviewed and strengthened immediately after the incident to further limit the risk of fraud'.[17] This was quite a faux pas by the ODA, given the value of the corrupt transaction, and it stands as a stark warning to the organisers of major events, who have to deal with a vast volume and array of contracts and financial arrangements.

Public procurement

Public procurement for major events, including those in sport, is a function that has traditionally been beset by corruption. As a result, there is a particular need for transparency, competition and objective criteria in decision-making.[18]

As a non-departmental public body, the ODA had to comply with the stringent procurement regulations already in place in the United Kingdom.[19] It went one step further, however, and developed and published its own procurement policy.[20] Two chapters of this publication covered specific aspects of corruption: chapter 4, 'Governance', and chapter 5, 'Management of risk and opportunity'. Chapter 4.1 highlighted how aware the ODA was of the need for the procurement process to be clean: 'The ODA recognises that the programme will be subject to intense scrutiny at all levels. It has therefore decided to adopt a "balanced procurement" approach to cascade its requirements down from the policy to the small sub-contractor on a site.'[21] The need to ensure that such an approach was imposed upon all designers, contractors and subcontractors was paramount and required back-to-back obligations in all contracts, as well as diligent contract monitoring, supervision and enforcement.[22] Chapter 4 specifically mentioned corruption in procurement under the heading of 'Probity and business ethics', saying that it would 'damage the integrity of the programme and/or project and the image of the Games'.

Further areas covered in the policy document that are important for the prevention of corrupt practices in procurement were transparency, sponsorship rights and fair competition. The need for the ODA to be transparent was enshrined in UK law through the Freedom of Information Act 2000 (FOIA 2000), which, as explained in chapter 4.11, 'establishes a general right of access to all types of "recorded" information held by public authorities'.[23] To comply with any requests under FOIA 2000, the ODA needed to have good and secure storage and access to the information obtained through the tendering and procurement process, while also being mindful of any commercially sensitive information that had been provided. As for sponsors, chapter 6.11 made it clear that private bodies that were also sponsors of LOCOG could tender for ODA contracts, but with the safeguards that they would be treated equally with other bidders, and that any sponsorship payments were strictly between themselves and LOCOG and would not be considered.

Security arrangements

The delivery of security-related infrastructure and services requires particular attention for major sports events because of its political sensitivity. For this reason, security costs often constitute a large proportion of the overall costs of a major event. Indeed, London 2012 had the largest security investment of any event in the history of the United Kingdom.[24] The private security company G4S was selected by the ODA at a cost of £284 million, to provide security guards for the Games.[25] The anti-corruption safeguards in the ODA's procurement policy in the award of this contract were satisfied by the fact that G4S had a robust and comprehensive business ethics policy in place, available for public inspection, and the fact that the company regularly reported on the measures it took at all levels of the organisation to ensure the company's integrity. In addition, G4S had in place a programme on anti-bribery risk assessments, anti-bribery control and anti-bribery audits, and also had a whistleblowing hotline.[26]

Even with these safeguards in place, the decision to award the contract to G4S caused huge embarrassment to the ODA when it became apparent just weeks before the Games were due to get under way that G4S would be able to provide only 7,000 guards, at most, of the 10,400 promised, as a result of catastrophic recruitment and training failures.[27] This led to the police and armed forces having to plug the shortfall, and G4S's chief executive, Nick Buckles, being brought before a Commons Home Affairs Committee hearing at short notice and describing the company's handling of its Olympics contract as a 'humiliating shambles'.[28] Buckles subsequently stepped down as chief executive[29] amid a collapse in profits by one-third after the company was forced to pay out £88 million over its London 2012 failures, after much painful negotiation with LOCOG.[30]

Lessons for the planning of future major sporting events

The increasing commercialisation of sport, particularly the Olympic Games, means that the opportunities and incentives for unscrupulous individuals to gain unlawful profits through corrupting major sporting events are continually growing. London 2012 was in a good starting position to fight corrupt practices because of the United Kingdom's legislative instruments already in place, but LOCOG, and particularly the ODA, enhanced this further through their processes in planning and delivering the Games, with the result that they were kept largely free from corruption and provided a good framework for other host countries in the future – the latter being part of the requirement in preamble P of the Host City Contract.[31] The sheer size and complexity of the event, and the commercial arrangements that had to be entered into, meant nevertheless that there was always a risk of some isolated instances of corruption in the lead-up to the Games. Such incidents did, unfortunately, occur, but LOCOG, the ODA and/or the UK government acted decisively to ensure that the impact of such events was lessened to the fullest extent. The combination of the largely successful organisation and the outstanding sporting achievements in London during that magical summer left the IOC and other Olympic stakeholders broadly in agreement that they were the best Games to date.

Notes

1   Kevin Carpenter is a principal and consultant for Captivate Legal and Sport Solutions.
2   *Guardian* (UK), 'London wins 2012 Olympics', 6 July 2005, *www.theguardian.com/uk/2005/ jul/06/olympics2012.olympicgames1.*
3   House of Commons Committee of Public Accounts, *Preparations for the London 2012 Olympic and Paralympic Games: Risk Assessment and Management* (London: The Stationery Office, 2007), *www.publications.parliament.uk/pa/cm200607/cmselect/ cmpubacc/377/377.pdf.*

4   International Olympic Committee, *Host City Contract: Games of the XXX Olympiad in 2012* (Lausanne: IOC, 2005), *www.gamesmonitor.org.uk/files/Host%20City%20Contract.pdf.*
5   United Nations Office on Drugs and Crime (UNODC), *United Nation Convention against Corruption: A Strategy for Safeguarding against Corruption in Major Public Events* (Vienna: UNODC, 2013), *www.unodc.org/documents/corruption/Publications/2013/13-84527_Ebook.pdf.*
6   IOC (2005).
7   See Finance Act 2006, section 65, *www.legislation.gov.uk/ukpga/2006/25/contents.*
8   See London Olympic Games and Paralympic Games Act 2006, sections 3–9 and Schedule 1, *www.legislation.gov.uk/ukpga/2006/12/contents.*
9   House of Commons, Culture, Media and Sport Committee, *London 2012 Olympic Games and Paralympic Games: Funding and Legacy*, vol. II (London: The Stationery Office, 2007), *www.publications.parliament.uk/pa/cm200607/cmselect/cmcumeds/69/69ii.pdf.*
10 Ibid.
11 Ibid.; London Olympic Games and Paralympic Games Act 2006, Schedule 1, Part 2.
12 Olympic Delivery Authority Standing Orders (1), revised 20 June 2013, *www.gov.uk/government/uploads/system/uploads/attachment_data/file/208226/Standing_Orders_1.pdf.*
13 Corruption UK, 'What is the real price of the London Olympics?', 4 April 2012, *www.corruptionuk.net/what-is-the-real-price-of-the-london-olympics.*
14 Ibid.
15 London Organising Committee of the Olympic Games and Paralympic Games, *LOCOG Sustainability Obligations Register, Version 4, LOCOG in Confidence* (London: The Stationery Office, 2012), *http://learninglegacy.independent.gov.uk/documents/pdfs/sustainability/cp-sustainability-obligations-register.pdf.*
16 Olympic Delivery Authority Standing Orders (1), paras. 32 and 33; Olympic Delivery Authority Standing Orders (2), para. 3(d) and appendix 1, revised 20 June 2013, *www.gov.uk/government/uploads/system/uploads/attachment_data/file/208227/Standing_Orders_2.pdf.*
17 BBC (UK), 'Two jailed over £2.3m Olympic authority fraud', 24 April 2012, *www.bbc.co.uk/news/uk-england-17829021.*
18 United Nations Convention against Corruption, article 9, 31 October 2003, *www.unodc.org/documents/treaties/UNCAC/Publications/Convention/08-50026_E.pdf.*
19 UNODC (2013), p. 35.
20 Olympic Delivery Authority, *Procurement Policy* (London: The Stationery Office, 2007), *http://webarchive.nationalarchives.gov.uk/20120403073945/http://www.london2012.com/documents/business/oda-procurement-policy.pdf.*
21 Ibid.
22 UNODC (2013), p. 37.
23 ODA (2007).
24 UNODC (2013), p. 46.
25 *Guardian* (UK), 'Olympic security chaos: depth of G4S security crisis revealed', 13 July 2012, *www.theguardian.com/sport/2012/jul/12/london-2012-g4s-security-crisis.*
26 UNODC (2013), p. 48.
27 *Guardian* (2012); *Financial Times* (UK), 'MPs lambast G4S Olympics shambles', 17 July 2012, *www.ft.com/cms/s/0/344a0e3c-d001-11e1-a3d2-00144feabdc0.html#axzz3F51aCS29.*
28 Ibid.
29 *Daily Telegraph* (UK), 'Timeline: how G4S's bungled Olympics security contract unfolded', 21 May 2013, *www.telegraph.co.uk/finance/newsbysector/supportservices/10070425/Timeline-how-G4Ss-bungled-Olympics-security-contract-unfolded.html.*
30 *Guardian* (UK), 'G4S profits tumble on Olympics failings', 13 March 2013, *www.theguardian.com/business/2013/mar/13/g4s-profits-tumble-olympics-failings.*
31 IOC (2005).

3.10

The 2014 Sochi Winter Olympics

Who stands to gain?

Oleg Golubchikov[1]

Introduction

The Sochi Winter Olympics and Winter Paralympics, which took place in February/March 2014, made the news worldwide as the most expensive events in history. While the initial bid's cost estimate for the Games was in the range of US$11 billion, the final bill skyrocketed to US$50 billion. Much of this cost has been borne by the federal budget, state-owned corporations and state-underwritten loans.[2]

It is easy to assume, as many did,[3] that the high cost was merely a testimony to mismanagement and corruption. This is to ignore the results of earnest probing into the causes and implications of expensive sporting mega-events, however, including how symptomatic they are of the wider tendencies of transnational sport to intersect with national economies and politics. Global sporting events, including the Olympic Games, are some of the most conspicuous mega-projects. What is the function of mega-projects, though? As Bent Flyvbjerg argues, mega-projects 'are designed to ambitiously change the structure of society, as opposed to smaller and more conventional projects that . . . fit into pre-existing structures and do not attempt to modify these'.[4] It can be further contended that, as nation states 'hollow out' (that is, experience a weakened capacity to project their economic powers over their own territories in the face of globalisation, welfare state retrenchment and the increasing self-reliance of subnational regions), mega-projects remain one of the few important means still available to national governments to pursue radical structural strategies with respect to national spatial development.

Similarly, the Sochi Olympic project reflects a strategy of the Putin government to modernise Russian geography. Indeed, as documented below, almost 80 per cent of the Sochi cost was unrelated to sport. This is well reflected in the official rhetoric: the Winter Olympic Games were seen as a lever for an overhaul of Sochi and making it a new 'growth pole' in the country.[5] This rationale goes beyond the direct calculus of the Games themselves, or even the expectation of a direct financial payback. This is not without controversies, however, including over issues such as the transparency of decision-making and the juxtaposition of the costs versus wider benefits of such geographically concentrated modernisation projects.

This chapter further outlines the context behind the Sochi project and its costs, and provides an assessment of the Olympic legacy in the aftermath of these Games.

Counting the cost of Sochi

The political dimension of the Sochi Games is well recognised; indeed, most commentators have argued that, much like, for example, the Beijing Olympics before them, the Sochi Games were an attempt to display Russia's re-emerging power to the rest of the world.[6] What is missing in this discourse, however, is the fact that the Sochi Games sought not only (and probably not so much) to put Russia on the map of world powers but to put Sochi on Russia's (and the world) map.[7] Here, the Sochi Games should be seen in the context of the Putin government's attempts to restructure Russia's regional geography, based on the premise of promoting a few select locations as 'strategic' (economically and geopolitically) and making them the key nodes of Russia's spatial modernisation.[8] Sochi has been 'appointed' as one such location; the city has long been favoured by President Putin as a sea resort, and it has an important geostrategic location at the Black Sea and the Caucasus. The Winter Olympics worked as the catalyst for the city's elevation within Russian geography.

This politics of growth poles is by no means idiosyncratic to Russia, nor was it born there;[9] but Russia, like other quasi-authoritarian emerging economies, does particularly rely on government spending and administrative leverages. The main sponsors of the Olympics have been large corporations, most of which are state-controlled (such as Gazprom and Rosneft), while key private investors took state-underwritten credits from state-owned banks (such as VEB and Sberbank).[10]

Sochi has become the first Olympic city for which the entire main sports infrastructure was constructed from scratch and the existing transport infrastructure and hospitality sector were thoroughly remade. Overall, more than 800 construction objects were built in Sochi. Some of these were, of course, sporting facilities, but most of the cost was associated with a generic upgrade of the urban and regional infrastructure, including power stations and supply, new water and sewerage systems, telecommunications, a massive transport network, and so forth.[11]

The resultant Sochi expenses are commonly reported as some US$50 billion – a considerable portion of Russia's GDP (Figure 3.7). This roughly corresponds to the official figures of Olympstroy, the state corporation managing and overseeing the preparations for Sochi.[12] In its 2013 (final) budget statement from June 2014, it reported total allocated funds of RUB 1,524.4 billion (US$49.4 billion) and funds actually spent by the end of 2013 as RUB 1,415.2 billion (US$45.9 billion).[13]

How much of this was directly related to sport? According to the Accounts Chamber of the Russian Federation,[14] the direct cost of the Games and the sporting facilities was RUB 324.9 billion (US$10.5 billion), including RUB 103.3 billion (US$3.3 billion) directly funded by the federal budget. This suggests that around 21 per cent of the total Sochi spending can be attributed to the sporting side.[15]

This peculiar cost structure was already part of Russia's original bid; the total budget was then envisaged at RUB 313.9 billion (or some US$11.3 billion at the exchange rate prevailing then), however.[16] These moneys were allocated for the Federal Target Programme (FTP) for the Development of Sochi as a Mountain Climate Resort, which framed the Olympic bid.[17] What is interesting is that the FTP was also allocated RUB 122.9 billion (US$4.4 billion) in case Russia's bid for the Winter Olympics was declined in 2007. Although that was much less than in the Olympic scenario, it still signifies the strategy of making Sochi a development hotspot.

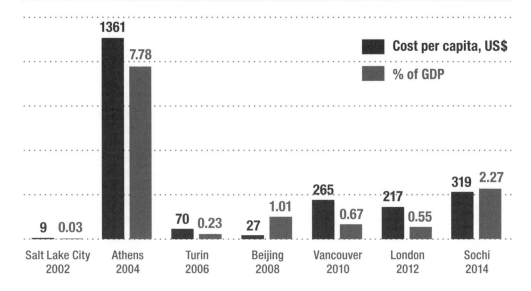

Figure 3.7 Costs of the Olympic Games per capita and as a percentage of GDP, 2002–2014

Source: Anti-Corruption Foundation, *Sochi 2014: Encyclopedia of Spending* (Moscow: Anti-Corruption Foundation, 2014), *http://sochi.fbk.info/en*.

Public participation and transparency investigations

The high bill for the Winter Olympics, and particularly its inflation since 2007, have attracted much criticism within and outside Russia.[18] State finances were greatly involved, and the main corporate investors and banks were also heavily exposed to the overspending.[19] The overspends are attributed to a number of factors – notably a lack of sufficient preparatory investigations at the bidding stage, and underestimations of the challenging engineering conditions in the swampy Imereti Valley, as well as other areas where the projects were built; other factors included the poor quality of the initial design specifications, additional emerging requirements of the International Olympic Committee (IOC) and inflation.[20] Embezzlement and kickbacks almost certainly played a role too – as proved by a number of official investigations.[21] The full extent of corruption is open to speculation, but such speculation often ignores the other factors leading to overspending.[22] Indeed, even private investors experienced considerable overspends; for example, Interros, the main investor and owner of the Rosa Khutor Alpine resort, saw a sixfold increase in its costs, from the planned US$350 million to US$2.07 billion.[23]

Nevertheless, there has been a perceived lack of follow-up investigations to existing corruption allegations. Despite the official rhetoric of transparency and participation, the Olympic monetary flows and, in particular, contract allocation procedures, were not exposed to public scrutiny in a systematic manner, while public participation commonly remained nominal.[24]

The most prominent and critical public investigation reviews have been those prepared by representatives of Russia's opposition, including with the participation of the opposition leaders Alexei Navalny[25] and the late Boris Nemtsov.[26] A report produced by Nemtsov in collaboration with Leonid Martynyuk, for example, accused the Putin government of a deliberate plot to make the most expensive games in a challenging location as an opportunity for malfeasance and the distribution of state resources to the benefit of 'Putin's cronies'. A report by Navalny's Anti-Corruption Foundation quoted personal ties between contractors and government officials as the most frequent point of concern over the Olympic projects. It needs to be borne in mind, however, that this reflects the objective realities of corporate capacity to undertake large-scale projects, given the oligarchic structure of Russia's economy.[27]

At the same time, there has surely been a lack of information about government-led investigations, even though it is known that a number of criminal investigations were launched following inspections by the Accounts Chamber of the Russian Federation, the country's principal financial watchdog.[28] Most of the Accounts Chamber's discoveries seem to have not led anywhere, however. For example, it was reported that in its 2012 annual report the Accounts Chamber accused Olympstroy's executives of creating the conditions for an unjustified increase in the estimated costs of the sports facilities, resulting in a cost increase of RUB 15.5 billion (around US$500 million).[29] Ever since the resignation of its long-serving head, Sergei Stepashin, in September 2013, however, little has emerged about further investigations. Moreover, the Account Chamber's full reports have not been made available to the public, on the pretext that to do so would disclose commercially sensitive information.[30]

Generally, the extant expectations of widespread corruption investigations once the Games were over have failed to materialise.[31] This may be attributable to the post-Olympic environment of public satisfaction with the successful execution of the Games in general and the outstanding performance of the Russian team in particular, as well as the ensuing geopolitical tensions over Ukraine, which overshadowed Sochi.

Usually, an important role in directing public attention is played by the mass media and investigative journalism. During the preparations for the Games, however, their interventions with respect to corruption were limited. The Western media gave prominence to a series of stories that exploited the stereotypes of the Western audiences but provided little evidence of investigative journalism. Some Russia-based journalists and organisations attempted more in-depth investigations, highlighting structural problems such as environmental concerns in the Sochi National Park, migrant labour exploitation and resettlement problems.[32] Even so, there were no sustained and unbiased follow-ups to the cases of alleged corruption.

Sochi in the aftermath of the Winter Olympic Games

The high Sochi spending aside, what is the economic impact of the Games on the host city? The Olympic legacy in the immediate aftermath of the Games appears to be rather mixed.

To start with, the city has been thoroughly retrofitted, while the continuous media and government focus on the Sochi Winter Olympics and other events in Sochi has made the city an easily recognisable 'brand'. Without doubt, the holding of the Winter Olympics in Sochi has changed not only the hitherto deteriorating resort city, but also the mental geography of Russia in the eyes of the Russian population itself. This is reflected in the rise of tourism to Sochi. After the years when Sochi was 'Russia's largest construction site', with all the associated hassles and troubles, since 2014 Sochi has begun to enjoy an increase in visitor numbers. The Winter Olympics appear to have made the largest contribution to this, but the trend has been maintained through the rest of 2014 and into 2015. The city's mayor is reported to expect 5.5 million tourists coming to Sochi in 2015, a rise from the 5.18 million arrivals in 2014,[33] and sharply up on the 3.7 million in 2006 before the Olympic project got under way.[34]

The rise in tourism is a welcome trend to city residents, who endured the years of construction disruption, often combined with a loss of tourism-related income and, sometimes, employment. In addition, hundreds of people were removed from their former sites when they were subject to compulsory purchase, and were compensated only for legally registered properties, not for any informal extensions, including those used as guest rooms.[35] Therefore, one year on from the Games, Sochi residents remained divided as to whether the Winter Olympics had benefited them or not.[36]

Tourists are attracted to Sochi for various reasons: the new or modernised skiing resorts; the Olympic Park; the sea resort facilities; and the post-Olympic sporting and business events and conferences that the government encourages to go to the city, such as the Formula One Grand Prix in 2014, some matches of the 2018 men's football World Cup and many others.[37] Tourism helps in returning capital invested in the hospitality business and bringing in jobs and tax revenues.[38] Nonetheless, tourism in Sochi cannot escape the wider geopolitical context, and Russia's economic troubles because of the fall in oil prices since 2014.[39] On the one hand, as the real incomes of the Russian population have dropped, many Russians can no longer spend money on tourism – disadvantaging Sochi. On the other hand, as the Russian rouble has lost its international value, many have switched their holiday plans to internal tourism, thus benefiting the city. As a further complication, the annexation of Crimea – another prime holiday destination for Russians – will probably represent a competitive challenge for Sochi's tourism.

Uncertainties remain over the economic future of some key sporting facilities in Sochi.[40] The Games themselves were held in two clusters, largely separated and distant from the main urban areas and the city centre. The coastal cluster contains the Olympic Park, where the main sports facilities and the Olympic Village are located. The mountain cluster contains the skiing facilities and alpine resort infrastructure. Although the cluster approach produced a concentration of all activities in these two areas, thus preventing traffic congestion, providing easier access and facilitating security measures, it also raised the issue of remoteness. For example, when no sporting or other events are taking places in the Olympic Park, the facilities appear to be rather empty. On this basis, many commentators have been quick to prophesy that the key stadiums are doomed to collect dust and fall into disrepair. Although a direct payback on the investment in these facilities is indeed questionable (also exposing the lack of planning for a post-Olympic legacy),[41] the future is by no means predetermined here. What is necessary is a sustained effort, smart management and coordinated actions on the part of the governments of different levels and other stakeholders to make sure that the sporting facilities do not become white elephants, but bring further social (if not financial) value.

Another point of public criticism has concerned the most expensive non-sporting investment in the Sochi project: a combined motorway and railroad link, comprising tunnels and bridges through the mountains and connecting the coastal and mountain clusters. Olympstroy reported that the project had cost RUB 317.9 billion (some US$10.3 billion),[42] or 21 per cent of Sochi's total allocated funds (effectively, this project alone cost more than the wide majority of the Olympic Games beforehand). It was built to serve as the main traffic artery during the Games, allowing a flow of up to 20,000 passengers per hour.[43] The utilisation of the roads has been low ever since, however, undermining the rationale for its expensive construction and maintenance.[44]

Ahead of the Sochi Games, much investment, especially private, went into the real-estate construction sector, and not just into hotels but housing as well. Sales of residential properties have not been as intensive as expected, however, especially in the wake of the economic slowdown – though this is, overall, a highly speculative market.[45] Of particular concern are reports of 'ghost settlements' emerging around housing originally built for residents relocated from expropriated plots. For example, in one settlement, only 17 of the total 79 detached homes are reported to have been occupied since they were built in 2011, some others being vandalised.[46]

On balance, it appears that the extent to which Sochi will actually become a magnet for tourism, further sporting events, conferences and other commercial and non-commercial activities – and, indeed, a growth pole of national (and international) significance – is not as yet certain but, rather, remains dependent on the sustained effort to further capitalise on the work already undertaken, including by government itself.

Conclusion

As already stated, Sochi needs to be seen in the context of the wider political project of Russian modernisation, the logic of which stretches beyond pure financial calculus. Although this approach has been conventionally criticised (as being wasteful, ad hoc and exposed to corruption risks),[47] one result is the re-emergence of spatial policy in Russia, which seeks to rebalance growth away from Moscow and to recalibrate the traditional sectoral approach of the federal government's modus operandi to the spatial approach of territorial development and urban policy. Following the disorganisation (and even degradation) of the national regional policy and spatial planning in Russia after the collapse of the planned economy of state socialism in the 1990s, various mega-events and mega-projects have recently become a 'hook' for the government to regain control over spatial and urban redevelopment policy. Sochi has become one of the most prominent cases in this new spatial policy in Russia.[48]

The urban conditions and infrastructure of Sochi prior to the Games were certainly poor, and the Winter Olympics have radically changed the city's fortune. Focusing on selected locations intensifies the spatial and social inequalities of a country that has already been unevenly developed and socially divided, however. The scale of the mega-projects also makes them less sensitive to public oversight, exposing the democratic deficit and corruption risks. This is a generic problem inherent to all mega-events, but it is more conspicuous in quasi-authoritarian emerging capitalist economies. It is yet a matter of political choices: political elites undertake such projects over and over again in hopes of certain gains, disregarding their opportunity costs. Ultimately, a key factor for politicians is the electorate's support. In this respect, it must be encouraging for the Putin government that, a year after the Winter Olympics, according to a survey by the Russian Public Opinion Research Center, 75 per cent of Russians said they would still support the holding of further sporting mega-events in the country.[49]

Notes

1   Oleg Golubchikov is senior lecturer in human geography at Cardiff University's School of Planning and Geography.
2   Anti-Corruption Foundation, *Sochi 2014: Encyclopedia of Spending* (Moscow: Anti-Corruption Foundation, 2014), *http://sochi.fbk.info/en*.
3   See, for example, *The Economist* (UK), 'Castles in the sand: the most expensive Olympic games in history offer rich pickings to a select few', 13 July 2013, *www.economist.com/news/europe/21581764-most-expensive-olympic-games-history-offer-rich-pickings-select-few-castles*; *The Economist* (UK), 'Sochi or bust: the conspicuous dazzle of the games masks a country, and a president, in deepening trouble', 1 February 2014, *www.economist.com/news/briefing/21595428-conspicuous-dazzle-games-masks-country-and-president-deepening-trouble-sochi*.
4   Bent Flyvbjerg, 'What you should know about megaprojects and why: an overview', *Project Management Journal*, vol. 45 (2014), p. 6.

5   See Martin Müller, 'After Sochi 2014: costs and impacts of Russia's Olympic Games', *Eurasian Geography and Economics*, vol. 55 (2014).

6   See, for example, Emil Persson and Bo Petersson, 'Political mythmaking and the 2014 Winter Olympics in Sochi: Olympism and the Russian great power myth', *East European Politics*, vol. 30 (2014).

7   Oleg Golubchikov and Irina Slepukhina, 'Russia: showcasing a "re-emerging" state?', in Jonathan Grix (ed.), *Leveraging Legacies from Sports Mega-Events: Concepts and Cases* (Basingstoke: Palgrave Macmillan, 2014).

8   Oleg Golubchikov, 'World-city-entrepreneurialism: globalist imaginaries, neoliberal geographies, and the production of New St Petersburg', *Environment and Planning A*, vol. 42 (2010).

9   See, for example, Neil Brenner, *New State Spaces: Urban Governance and the Rescaling of Statehood* (Oxford: Oxford University Press, 2004).

10 See, for example, Anti-Corruption Foundation (2014).

11 For an overview of Sochi projects and the Olympic legacy from the Games there, see International Olympic Committee, 'Sochi 2014: facts and figures', factsheet (Lausanne: IOC, 2015), *www.olympic.org/Documents/Games_Sochi_2014/Sochi_2014_Facts_and_Figures.pdf*.

12 The costs reported in US dollars depend on the exchange rates used for the Russian rouble, which have fluctuated much during the execution of the project (and even more so after the Games). It is not entirely correct to convert the costs into dollars at the date of their reporting, as investments are cumulative, so that each period needs to be converted separately. However, this makes it difficult to make conversions in practice. For the purpose of simplification, this chapter uses the average annual nominal exchange rates of 30.86 roubles per US$1 for the five-year period of 2009–2013, when the overwhelming majority of spending was made. The Central Bank of Russia reports daily rates and average nominal exchange rates; see *www.cbr.ru/currency_base/dynamics.aspx and www.cbr.ru/statistics/?Prtid=svs&ch=Par_57946*.

13 See the Olympstroy website for its financial reports: *www.sc-os.ru/ru/about/financial/index.php?id_101=3153*; *www.sc-os.ru/common/upload/otchet_2013/form_14.pdf*.

14 The Accounts Chamber of the Russian Federation, 'Analiz mer po ustraneniyu narusheniy pri podgotovke i provedenii XXII Olimpiyskikh zimnikh igr i XI Paralimpiyskikh zimnikh igr 2014 goda v Sochi', 10 April 2015, *http://audit.gov.ru/press_center/news/21280*.

15 Müller (2014) claims that more than half the non-sports-related costs were cost inflation on account of the Olympics that would not have occurred otherwise.

16 At the average nominal exchange rate of 27.68 in the first half of 2006 (according to the Central Bank of Russia). If rouble inflation is factored in, RUB 313.9 billion in December 2005 translates into RUB 618.5 billion in December 2013, meaning that the final overspend was much less than on dollar-based calculations. Price inflation was already assumed in the FTP, however.

17 Government of the Russian Federation, 'Decree from 08.06.2006 N357 on the Federal Target Programme "The Development of the City of Sochi as a Mountain Climate Resort (in 2006–2014)"'.

18 Large overspends are not unique in the worldwide context of mega-projects. As indicated by one of the most prominent commentators on the subject, Flyvbjerg (2014, p. 6), there is the 'iron law of megaprojects': 'over budget, over time, over and over again'. At one extreme, the budget for the 1976 Montreal Summer Olympics was overspent 14 times.

19 The Anti-Corruption Foundation (2014), on the basis of an analysis of corporate reports and federal budgets, has estimated the following breakdown of RUB 1.5 trillion of the total Sochi costs: direct public budget costs – RUB 855 billion; expenses of state corporations – RUB 343 billion; VEB loans to private companies – RUB 249 billion; equity of private companies – RUB 53 billion.

20 RBC (Russia), 'Stoimost' Olimpiady v Sochi perevalila za 1.5 trln rub.', 4 February 2013, *http://top.rbc.ru/economics/04/02/2013/843458.shtml*.

21   For example, for earlier corruption cases in Olympstroy, see Gazeta.ru, 'Sledovateli zayavili o korruptsii v "Olimpstroye" na 23 mln rubley posle otstavki Bolloeva', 31 January 2011, *www.gazeta.ru/news/business/2011/01/31/n_1682318.shtml*.

22   Famously, Jean Franco Kasper, then president of the International Ski Federation (FIS) and a member of the International Olympic Committee, was reported saying that one-third of the budget of the Games was stolen. He later underplayed the claim as rumours rather than his personal estimate, however. See *Vedomosti* (Russia), 'Chlen MOK: Tret' deneg na Olimpiadu v Schoi rastrachena iz-za "razgula korruptsii"', 10 January 2014, *www.vedomosti. ru/business/articles/2014/01/10/chlen-mok-tret-deneg-na-olimpiadu-v-sochi-rastracheno-iz-za*; and RT (Russia), 'Sochi Olympics venues, sports infrastructure most modern in the world: IOC official', 28 January 2014, *http://rt.com/news/sochi-modern-venues-ioc-273*.

23   This also exposed the state-owned bank VEB, which provided a loan of US$1.67 billion for this particular development; see *Forbes*, 'Milliarder na Olimpe: kak Potanin stal glavnym chastnym investorom Sochi-2014', 30 January 2014, *www.forbes.ru/milliardery/250267-milliarder-na-olimpe-kak-vladimir-potanin-stal-glavnym-chastnym-investorom-sochi*. It is also noteworthy that the Accounts Chamber of the Russian Federation complained in 2012 about VEB financing knowingly loss-making projects; see, for example, *Izvestia* (Russia), 'Olimpiyskiye kredity ushli v ofshor', 29 August 2012, *http://izvestia.ru/news/ 533192*.

24   Boris Nemtsov and Leonid Martynyuk, 'Zimnyaya Olimpiada v Subtropikakh' (Moscow, Nemtsov: 2013), *www.putin-itogi.ru/zimnyaya-olimpiada-v-subtropikax*; *Nezavisimaya Gazeta* (Russia), 'Korruptsiya ustanovila olimpiyskiy rekord', 7 June 2010, *www.ng.ru/ economics/2010-06-07/1_corrupciya.html*.

25   Anti-Corruption Foundation (2014).

26   Nemtsov and Martynyuk (2013).

27   On progress with transparency in Russia's state corporations, see Transparency International Russia, 'Monitoring the transparency and compliance of state-owned enterprise in Russia', *http://transparency.org.ru/en/news/russian-state-corporations-need-to-take-further-anti-corruption-measures*.

28   See, for example, *Izvestia* (Russia), 'Olimpiyskiye stroyki poluchili pervye ugolovnye dela', 9 August 2012, *http://izvestia.ru/news/532535*.

29   RT (Russia), 'Olympic overstate: Sochi embezzlement reaches $506mn', 6 March 2013, *http://rt.com/news/sochi-embezzlement-overstating-costs-901*.

30   See, for example, a response of the Accounts Chamber to a request of Russia's Republican Party following Nemtsov and Martynyuk's (2013) report: *http://svobodanaroda.org/news_ part/4144*.

31   *Vedomosti* (Russia), 'Olimpiyskiye geroi', 3 June 2014, *www.vedomosti.ru/newspaper/ articles/2014/06/03/olimpijskie-geroi*.

32   For example, Human Rights Watch produced an extensive report on migrant workers: Human Rights Watch (US), *Race to the Bottom: Exploitation of Migrant Workers Ahead of Russia's 2014 Winter Olympic Games in Sochi* (New York: Human Rights Watch, 2013), *www.hrw.org/sites/default/files/reports/russia0213_ForUpload.pdf*. For references to other concerns, see Human Rights Watch (US), 'Russia's Olympian abuses', 8 April 2013, *www.hrw.org/video-photos/interactive/2013/04/08/russias-olympian-abuses*.

33   *Vedomosti* (Russia), 'Trassa svernula v Sochi', 29 April 2015.

34   According to travel agencies, during Russia's traditional May holiday break, Sochi in 2015 replaced Paris as the most popular destination among Russians, seeing an 80 per cent increase in ticket sales for this period from a year earlier: RBC (Russia), 'Kuda edut na mayskiye prazdniki: Sochi, Simferopol i Tel-Aviv', 17 April 2015, *http://top.rbc.ru/business/1 7/04/2015/55310fc79a7947d461cb9607*.

35   Gazeta.ru, '"Vse eto delalos' ne dlya sochintsev"', 5 February 2015, *www.gazeta.ru/social/ 2015/02/04/6399989.shtml*.

36   Ibid.

37   See International Olympic Committee (2015).

38 Sochi has 55,000 hotel rooms, exceeding the 41,300 in Moscow: *Vedomosti* (Russia), 'Sostyazaniye za 1.5 trln', 27 December 2013.

39 *Washington Post* (US), 'Russian economic crisis helps save Putin's post-Olympic dream at Sochi', 18 January 2015, *www.washingtonpost.com/world/europe/russian-economic-crisis-helps-save-putins-post-olympic-dream-at-sochi/2015/01/17/d8c7bbd8-92b1-11e4-a66f-0ca5037a597d_story.html?Post+generic=%3Ftid%3Dsm_twitter_washingtonpost.*

40 For a review of the planned and current use of sporting facilities in Sochi, see Gazeta.ru, 'Olimpiada v Sochi: God Spustya', *www.gazeta.ru/sport/sochi2015*.

41 For further discussions on this, see, for example, Müller (2014).

42 Olympstroy (Russia), 'Otchet ob osuschestvlenii stroitel'stva olimpiyskikh obyektov i vypolnenii inykh meropriyatiy, svyezannykh so stroitelstvom olimpiyskikh obyektov za 2013 god', p. 16, *www.sc-os.ru/common/upload/otchet_2013/form_14.pdf*.

43 *Rossiyskaya Gazeta* (Russia), 'Igry vysshey proby', 12 April 2013.

44 Some estimates suggest that the costs that the government has to incur in order to subsidise, operate and maintain post-Olympic venues and tourist and transport infrastructures in Sochi may remain well above US$1 billion per year; see Müller (2014).

45 *Kommersant* (Russia), 'Igry, v kotorye igrayut v Sochi: kogda okupitsa olimpiyskoye nasledstvo', 8 September 2014, *www.kommersant.ru/doc/2554133*.

46 *Kavkazskiy Uzel* (Russia), 'V Sochi predstaviteli obschestvennosti napravili prezidentu akt obsledovaniya pustuyuschego poselka dlya olimpiyskikh pereselentsev', 3 April 2015, *www.kavkaz-uzel.ru/articles/259950*.

47 See, for example, Martin Müller, 'Higher, larger, costlier: Sochi and the 2014 Winter Olympics', *Russian Analytical Digest*, vol. 143 (2014); Robert Orttung and Sufian Zhemukhov, 'The 2014 Sochi Olympic mega-project and Russia's political economy', *East European Politics*, vol. 30 (2014).

48 See Golubchikov (2010); and Nadir Kinossian, 'Stuck in transition: Russian regional planning policy between spatial polarization and equalization', *Eurasian Geography and Economics*, vol. 54 (2013).

49 Russian Public Opinion Research Center, 'Olimpiada v Sochi: god spustya', 5 February 2015, *http://wciom.ru/index.php?id=236&uid=115138*.

3.11

The need for transparency and monitoring ahead of the 2018 World Cup in Russia

Anna Koval and Andrey Jvirblis[1]

In 2010 Russia was awarded the right to host the next Fédération Internationale de Football Association (FIFA) World Cup. After the Sochi 2014 Winter Olympics, the 2018 World Cup will become the second major international sports event held in the country in its recent history.

In contrast to the Sochi Olympics, the geography of the World Cup is much broader. The matches will be held in 12 stadiums in 11 Russian cities. The Russian government approved a total budget of 660 billion roubles (US$16 billion) for the event.[2] There will be 335 billion roubles (US$8 billion) allocated from the federal budget, 223 billion roubles (US$5.5 billion) will come from private investment and 102 billion roubles (US$2.5 billion) will be provided from the budgets of the 11 constituent regions that host the World Cup matches.[3] In particular, 174 billion roubles have been allocated for the construction of sport facilities, with 120 billion from the federal budget, 44 billion from the respective regional budgets and nine billion from private investors.[4]

Such a high amount of public spending requires increased transparency and accountability in order to prevent corruption and any abuse of public funds. Already, however, Transparency International Russia has concerns regarding the transparency of the organisations responsible for the World Cup and their activities.

Transparency in the preparations for the 2018 World Cup

A number of organisations have been created and entrusted with providing support to and monitoring the preparation process: the Bid Committee, named Russia 2018; the Local Organising Committee (LOC); Arena-2018, the organisation tasked with monitoring the stadiums' compliance with FIFA recommendations; and the Centre for Planning and Monitoring of the official 2018 World Cup preparation programme. According to the website of the Ministry of Justice, the Bid Committee and the Centre for Planning and Monitoring have not submitted any annual reports despite the legal requirement to do so before 15 April each year.[5] The LOC

	Federal	Regional	Local	Total
Ekaterinburg	4,232	21,790	739	**26,761**
Kaliningrad	6,722	1,403	17	**8,142**
Kazan	2,907	1,686	–	**4,593**
Moscow	94	64,280	–	**64,374**
Nizhniy Novgorod	12,583	6,755	8,742	**28,080**
Rostov-on-Don	26,969	10,895	11,474	**49,338**
St Petersburg	22,168	51,223	–	**73,391**
Samara	17,595	26,823	1,699	**46,117**
Saransk	6,724	9,452	–	**16,176**
Sochi	1,461	997	27	**2,485**
Volgograd	8,174	3,595	929	**12,698**
Total	**109,629**	**198,899**	**23,627**	**332,155**

Table 3.3 Public funds budgeted for the 2018 World Cup preparations (millions of roubles)

Source: Governmental decrees from each of the respective regions.

submitted its 2013 annual financial reports to the ministry on time, but its 2012 reports appeared online with a remarkable delay of about one year – in July 2014.[6] Only Arena-2018 has met all its legally required reporting obligations, with not just its 2013 report but also its 2014 report already available online.[7]

Another key organisation involved in the preparations for the 2018 World Cup is the state-owned Federal State Unitary Enterprise named Sport-Engineering (Sport-In), which answers to the Ministry of Sport. The company, first registered in 2006, was appointed in 2013 to manage the construction and subcontracting for the seven stadiums to be built for the FIFA World Cup.[8] The company also won the contracts to design five of the stadiums. Sport-In does not do the design work alone, but actively engages subcontractors, some of which are designing more than one stadium.[9] According to the official bidding information, in certain cases a contract was awarded to the only bidder.[10] This arrangement, as well as a number of other aspects concerning the selection of companies responsible for the stadiums, calls for the careful monitoring and evaluation of transparency and compliance with the requirements of Russian anti-corruption legislation.

The high level of expenditures allocated for the football World Cup preparations, together with the shortcomings in the transparency of the actors and activities involved, led Transparency International Russia to call on the Ministry of Sport to establish a comprehensive monitoring system for public spending on World Cup preparation activities. The system should make the details of public spending openly available and easy to access, so that any interested person or group can track how the funds are allocated and used. The portal should contain information on the awarding of contracts and other selection procedures and outcomes; a list of all the companies, contractors and consultants involved, including any

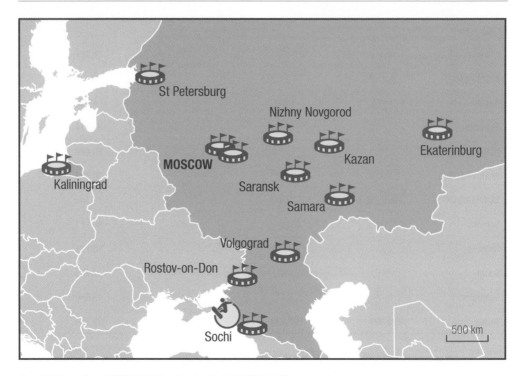

Sochi Olympics: US$12 billion budgeted, US$51 billion spent
2018 World Cup: US$16 billion budgeted, amount spent TBD

Figure 3.8 The geography and funding of mega-events in Russia

Sources: *Guardian* (UK), 'Sochi 2014: the costliest Olympics yet but where has all the money gone?', 9 October 2013; and *Vedomosti* (Russia), 'Оргкомитет ЧМ-2018:Объем финансирования ЧМ по футболу в России – 664,1 млрд рублей', 15 October 2015.

beneficial owners; and updates on the progress and implementation of stadium and facility construction. Finally, the portal should be updated on a regular basis, accumulating and featuring any relevant information made available elsewhere on public resources dedicated to the World Cup.

Looking back: the need for transparency in the preparations for the Sochi Olympics

Turning to the Sochi experience, no such comprehensive system was ever established for that event. Those wanting to track the flows of money had to consult a range of different sources and double-check any information they found. The most successful attempt to bring together and analyse the details behind the preparation for the Sochi games has come from civil society. The Anti-Corruption Foundation (ACF),[11] a Russian non-profit organisation, has issued a comprehensive report covering the main actors, sports venues and money flows, purely on the basis of open sources (federal laws, governmental decrees, public procurement contracts, annual reports of involved entities, among others). The ACF also launched an interactive website presenting the report's findings.[12]

The main problems with the preparations for the Sochi Olympic Games identified in the ACF report were overpricing (with Sochi venues costing much more than comparable venues elsewhere), offshore ownership stakeholders, the starting of construction without permission, environmental violations and, most frequently, personal ties between contractors and government officials.[13] According to the report, 'A significant part of the money was received by companies explicitly or implicitly related to several Russian officials.'[14] The result was delays in the completion of stadiums, as well as poor quality and/or inflated prices. Had civil society been better informed as to which actors were involved, how they were selected and how the contracts were awarded and implemented, some of these 'red flag' points could have been identified in time and avoided.

The current state of transparency and disclosure for the World Cup

At present only limited information is available on public spending for the 2018 World Cup preparations. It is possible to find data on how the public contracts have been awarded, as this information has to be made available by law on the official government portal on public procurement.[15] Little to nothing is known about what happens with the contracts then, however. We know only that there are more private subcontractors that take over the contracts, and there is no open official information on how the process actually carries on from there.

The main official source on the preparation process at present is the information published by the LOC. As stated in its *2012 Annual Report* on the FIFA website,[16] the LOC does not run a separate official website, but uses the FIFA website to cover relevant news and its own activities, both in Russian and in English. The LOC also has an official Russian-language Twitter account. Both sources focus on the news and very basic information on the stadiums and host cities.[17] They do not provide documents or procedural or financial information on how the main actors are selected, nor do they provide information on how funds are allocated or spent, or even links to other sources containing this type of data. The sole annual report on the LOC's activities that is available on the FIFA website covers 2012 only, and it is not available on the Russian-language version of the website.[18]

The other official source of information is the website of the Accounts Chamber of the Russian Federation, which audits the effectiveness of the use of public funds for the World Cup preparations. Only one report with information on public spending on the design and construction of new stadiums has been published, in May 2014.[19] The report highlights overpricing, delays in construction and payments, conflicts over land rights, and non-delivery by subcontractors, and addresses governance-related problems, such as timely issuance of governmental decrees and the development of project evaluation methodologies.[20] The auditors concluded that diligent monitoring of the spending process is required, due to the high amount of public expenditures.[21] A new audit was planned for December 2014,[22] but there is no information on its progress yet. Such reports are a valuable resource, but they are sporadic and disclose only the audit results, thereby falling well short of the standard that Transparency International Russia recommends be provided: the regular disclosure of comprehensive information.

There is also an unofficial website that, according to its description, was launched in 2011 by a group of football fans to 'cover the preparation process in a transparent way'.[23] The website features an array of news sources on the 2018 World Cup preparations. In a manner similar to the LOC page on the FIFA website, however, the information is news-oriented and misses the depth and the detail that would allow tracking and control of the money flows around the preparation activities. On the positive side, the website is updated regularly and covers a broad range of relevant news, so it can at least be used as a starting point for an activist's own investigation. The content sometimes lacks links to original sources, however, so the reliability of the information needs to be double-checked.

Applying the lessons learnt from Sochi

If information about activities and public expenditures for the World Cup preparations is not disclosed on time, the same issues faced in Sochi could resurface. Creating a portal to disclose information about the spending and the actors involved in the preparation process would be a crucial step to mitigate the various corruption risks – such as over-invoicing, bribery and conflicts of interest – that come from the high costs of the event and a lack of transparency and competitiveness. Making information publicly available and easy to access may help prevent many of the corruption-related problems that accompanied the Sochi Olympics. The Ministry of Sport should take responsibility for creating such a portal for the 2018 World Cup.

The government has shown that it has the capacity to create such systems, namely in the portals for the Federal Target Programmes and the Federal Investment Programmes.[24] Both are large-scale, costly programmes that are funded in part by the federal budget and cover structural reforms and capital investment, respectively. Both have portals hosted on the official website of the Ministry for Economic Development that provide information on the volume of funding for the programmes, progress in their implementation and the results achieved by the programmes, The disclosure of this information is required by federal law.[25] These portals could serve as a general model for creating a comprehensive resource on the 2018 event, but the World Cup portal should present the information in a more accessible and interactive way.

Public officials also appear to recognise the need for a comprehensive resource to track public spending on the 2018 World Cup. One Accounts Chamber auditor has admitted that the general public receives little information on the preparation process, from a variety of scattered sources, after which he suggested a comprehensive resource be created to address the problem.[26] At the moment, however, it is not clear if his recommendation will be acted upon.

Finally, it needs to be stated that it is not only the in-country actors that are responsible for transparency and disclosure regarding the 2018 World Cup. FIFA itself should also make greater efforts to promote transparency. FIFA should require all bidding and winning countries to publish their bid books, and should also require the host country's LOC, or the relevant government actors, to maintain a comprehensive resource about the preparation process, focusing on the use of public money. It should also insist that the organising committee publish annual reports in the official language(s) of the host country.

Notes

1   Anna Koval and Andrey Jvirblis are project manager and deputy director for Transparency International Russia, respectively.
2   The Programme of Preparation of 2018 World Cup in Russia, approved by Governmental Decree no. 518 of 20 June 2013, last updated 22 May 2015.
3   Ibid.; FIFA, 'Destination: host cities', *www.fifa.com/worldcup/destination/index.html*.
4   Ibid.
5   Article 32 of the federal law on non-profit organisations (these organisations are considered non-profit entities under Russian law). Any reports submitted are available here: *http://unro. minjust.ru/NKOReports.aspx*. A specific report may be found by the non-governmental organisation's (NGO) unique registration number.

6   Ibid.

7   Ibid.

8   Ministry of Sport, *Правительство Российской Федерации: Постановление от 20 июня 2013 г. no. 518* (Moscow: Ministry of Sport, 2013), *www.minsport.gov.ru/documents/518.pdf*.

9   The data have been collected from the official portal for public procurement: *http://zakupki.gov.ru/epz/main/public/home.html*. Part of it can also be found at the website of Sport-In, under the sections of the corresponding stadiums: *http://sportin.su/activity/championship-2018*.

10 The data have been collected from the official portal for public procurement: *http://zakupki.gov.ru/epz/main/public/home.html*. The site does not allow for direct links to the search results.

11 The Anti-Corruption Foundation is a Russian NGO based in Moscow. It was founded in 2011, is involved with the Progress Party and is highly critical of the current administration.

12 Anti-Corruption Foundation, *Sochi 2014: Encyclopedia of Spending* (Moscow: Anti-Corruption Foundation, 2014), *http://sochi.fbk.info/md/file/sochi_fbk_report_en_1.pdf*. The interactive website is available at *http://sochi.fbk.info/en*.

13 Ibid.

14 Ibid.

15 Официальный сайт Российской Федерации в сети Интернет, для размещения информации о размещении заказов на поставки товаров, выполнение работ, оказание услуг, *http://zakupki.gov.ru/epz/main/public/home.html*.

16 Local Organising Committee for the FIFA 2018 World Cup in Russia, *2012 Annual Report* (Moscow: Local Organising Committee, 2012), *http://resources.fifa.com/mm/document/tournament/loc/02/07/81/59/2012-annual-report_eng.pdf*.

17 Ibid.; Twitter, 'Футболисты и тренеры "Крылья Советов" посетили место строительства стадиона', 8 April 2015, *https://twitter.com/fifaworldcup_ru*.

18 Ibid.

19 Accounts Chamber of the Russian Federation, 'A summary report on the results of "Testing the effectiveness of budget spending for the design and construction of sports facilities being built for the World Cup 2018" (with Control Directorate of the President of the Russian Federation)', *Бюллетень Счетной палаты no. 5 (май) 2014* [*Bulletin of the Accounts Chamber no. 5 (May) 2014*], *www.ach.gov.ru/activities/bulleten/783/17773/?sphrase_id=645495* (available in Russian only).

20 Ibid.

21 Ibid.

22 Accounts Chamber of the Russian Federation Press Center, 'Счетная палата начнет проверку расходования государственных средств на ЧМ-2018 в конце года – аудитор Владимир Катренко', 27 October 2014, *www.ach.gov.ru/press_center/news/19423*.

23 See Россия 2018, *http://россия2018.рф* (available in Russian only).

24 Available at *http://fcp.economy.gov.ru/cgi-bin/cis/fcp.cgi/Fcp/Title/1/2015* and *http://faip.economy.gov.ru/cgi/uis/faip.cgi/G1*, respectively.

25 See Ministry of Economic Development of the Russian Federation website, *http://economy.gov.ru/wps/wcm/connect/economylib4/en/home/activity/sections/ftp*.

26 Accounts Chamber of the Russian Federation Press Center (27 October 2014).

3.12

Sporting mega-events, corruption and rights

The case of the 2022 Qatar World Cup

Sharan Burrow[1]

The concentration of wealth, corporate interests and unregulated international bodies in sport has grown to unprecedented levels. Sporting mega-events jostle for space each year, and with them comes a growing body of evidence around abuse of power, abuse of workers' rights and corruption. The investigations by the Swiss and US authorities into corruption allegations linked to the Fédération Internationale de Football Association (FIFA) have put the global spotlight on this issue as never before.

The international trade union movement, not least the International Trade Union Confederation (ITUC), began to take a close interest in sporting mega-events during the 1990s, when it documented the scandal of child labour being used in the production of footballs with 'FIFA Approved' emblems in Sialkot, Pakistan, to be sold during the 2002 FIFA World Cup.[2] The child labour was linked to violations of other international labour standards, with adult workers in Sialkot effectively being denied the right to organise unions and bargain for decent wages.[3]

In September 1996 FIFA eventually agreed that a 'Code of Labour Practice' would incorporate, in its commercial contracts, respect for a package of core labour rights based on International Labour Organization (ILO) conventions on freedom of association, collective bargaining, non-discrimination and protection from child labour and forced labour.[4] A cornerstone of the agreement was transparency: factory owners would need to declare their 'hidden' workforce – the large numbers of football stitchers, many of them women and children, working long hours at home to supply footballs to the factories in return for poverty-level wages.[5] FIFA subsequently transferred responsibility for the Code to the World Federation of the Sporting Goods Industry, an employer body.[6]

Some progress was made on tackling child labour, but, when measured against the objectives of ensuring respect for core ILO standards on freedom of association, collective bargaining, non-discrimination and protection from forced labour and child labour, the Code became yet another failed example of voluntary 'corporate social responsibility'. Moreover, although the Code was brought in specifically in connection with merchandise, the violation of labour rights is also a concern for sporting events, in particular relating to the construction and renovation of infrastructure for World Cups and other major events.[7]

Sialkot and the inadequate FIFA Code are just two examples of how today's 'supply chain' or 'value chain' business model, after three decades of globalisation, is still failing to ensure decent lives and decent jobs for millions of people. Lax or absent regulation in many countries in which production is based, combined with the multiple tiers of contractual relationships between producer factories, intermediaries and the global brand names, frequently leave workers without protection or rights.

The compromising of human rights for the 2022 World Cup

These fault lines are evident in the organisation and marketing of sporting mega-events. The relentless quest for profit, through merchandise deals and in building stadiums and other infrastructural elements for high-profile events, continues to outweigh public concern over the exploitation of the workers who deliver them.

One of the most disturbing features of the labour market today is the prevalence of modern slavery in global value chains. Here again, major sports events are part of the problem. Although workers facing 'slave-like conditions' in the building of World Cup infrastructure in Brazil were freed through government action,[8] the opposite is the case for the US$140 billion World Cup infrastructure programme in Qatar.[9] There, the government itself is responsible for modern slavery, through the 'kafala' system, used widely across the Middle East, which ties impoverished migrant workers to their employer.[10]

Under kafala, workers cannot change jobs without the permission of their employer. Their freedom of movement is heavily restricted, and they cannot leave Qatar without an exit visa signed by the employer. The ITUC has dealt with many cases of construction workers, company executives[11] and even professional football players[12] who have been stuck in Qatar for months – even years – because their employer refuses, or simply doesn't bother, to give them an exit visa. Qatar even refused to suspend kafala to allow grieving Nepalese workers to return home for the funerals of their loved ones after the massive earthquake in May 2015 that killed thousands in Nepal.[13]

As many as 1.75 million workers in the construction, domestic service and other sectors are trapped in this system of modern slavery.[14] Unregulated migration agencies promise young people from Nepal, India, the Philippines and elsewhere the chance to work in Qatar for a good wage in a decent job.[15] The practice of 'contract substitution', whereby workers are informed prior to departure that they will work in a particular job for a particular wage, only to find things very different when they arrive in Qatar, remains common.[16] This practice is made possible – in addition to kafala law and the absence of ILO-compliant labour laws – by the failure of Qatar and country-of-origin governments alike to ensure proper regulation of migration agencies.[17] Despite efforts by some government agencies in workers' countries of origin, as well as pre-departure outreach programmes by non-governmental organisations (NGOs) and trade unions, many migrant workers do not know about the kafala system.[18]

Once the workers have set foot in Qatar the reality hits, as they find themselves entrapped in a wage system that pays them according to their race or nationality rather than the nature of their job.[19] After work days of 12 hours or more, on construction sites in temperatures that regularly exceed 40° C, the workers return to sprawling labour camps on the outskirts of Doha, with unsanitary and filthy conditions.[20] Dissent is not tolerated, however: workers who join together to complain are detained and deported, while foreign journalists who look too deeply behind Qatar's public relations facade may receive the same treatment.[21]

Hundreds of thousands of workers have been and continue to be enlisted to build the infrastructure for the 2022 World Cup. Qatar asserts that the only infrastructure construction currently under way in the country that is relevant to the World Cup relates to the stadiums themselves, maintaining that the construction of roads, public transport infrastructure, accommodation and all the other facilities and services required to host the 2022 event are instead for more general purposes.[22] This is at odds with the announcements made during and immediately after the World Cup bidding process, in 2010, which placed the World Cup at the centre of Qatar's infrastructure-building programme.[23]

Over the past several years an annual average of around 200 migrant workers from each of India and Nepal have died as a result of the appalling working and living conditions[24] (figures for other countries of origin are often suppressed by the local embassies in Doha, pressured by the Qatari authorities). The cause of death is rarely established, as there are no post-mortems, and usually there is no compensation for the families left destitute by the loss of remitted income. The death rate of migrant workers from India actually increased from 2013 to 2014 by 16 per cent.[25]

The role of external influencers

The ITUC initiated new discussions with FIFA after their awarding of the 2022 World Cup hosting rights to Qatar, which was tainted by allegations of corruption. The ITUC and FIFA met at the latter's Zurich headquarters in 2011, with the ITUC insisting that the event should go ahead in Qatar only if the country changed its medieval labour laws. Despite some public statements,[26] FIFA has nevertheless failed to put the necessary pressure on Qatar, with serious consequences for the huge and growing migrant workforce as it races against time to deliver the vast World Cup infrastructure programme.

The ILO supervisory bodies have made strident criticism of Qatar's labour laws and called on the authorities to bring them into line with ILO standards.[27] These standards are widely adhered to around the world, yet Qatar and its fellow Gulf states Saudi Arabia and the United Arab Emirates refuse to respect them.[28] In March 2014 the ILO reported that the kafala system in Qatar constituted a violation of its Convention 29, the Forced Labour Convention,[29] which was adopted nearly a century ago but strengthened in 2014 because of the persistence of trafficking in forced labour worldwide. In the same month the ILO urged Qatar to address the absence of freedom of association for migrant workers – and, indeed, for the limited rights afforded even to Qatari workers.[30] Regrettably, Qatar has not acted on the ILO's calls for reform; rather, it has used its economic power to bully other governments in an attempt to stall plans for an ILO Commission of Inquiry into its system of forced labour, or even to allow an ILO mission of government, employer and worker representatives into the country.[31]

The ongoing tragedy for Qatar's migrant workforce is not a government responsibility alone. Multinational construction companies, which are generating huge profits from their joint ventures in Qatar, should also be held responsible. These companies are now under the spotlight. Litigation has been launched in France against construction giant Vinci,[32] and the main World Cup contractor, CH2M Hill, is under heavy public pressure.[33] Further legal action against other companies involved in World Cup construction is understood by the ITUC to be in progress. Global brands that sponsor FIFA are also feeling the pressure.[34] The international trade union movement is in talks with several of the major companies, demanding that they ensure that international labour standards be respected in every part of their Qatar operations.[35] Another important stakeholder is the Sports and Rights Alliance of NGOs,[36] which is pressing for reform of FIFA and has demonstrated its impact, with progress now being made at the International Olympic Committee (IOC) with its Agenda 2020.

The interdependence of transparency and labour rights: Qatar and beyond

Qatar today is a prime example of the link between corruption and the repression of workers' rights in global value chains, though it is far from alone in this respect. The absence of respect for international labour standards, and in particular the kafala system, leave workers exposed to corrupt practices in relation to their recruitment, including through the contract substitution described above, as well as their actual work in Qatar. Time and again the absence of transparency and the rule of law is a key factor in industrial tragedies, such as the Rana Plaza building collapse in Bangladesh in 2013, in which over 1,000 workers were killed. One of the key achievements of the union-endorsed Bangladesh Accord for Fire and Building Safety was to secure the disclosure of the supply chains of roughly 200 companies sourcing from the country, which has finally allowed them to be inspected by competent, honest inspectors.[37] The Bangladesh example shows how, on labour rights issues, constructive engagement by the private sector with trade unions increases protection and fairness for workers and contributes to ethical production, with consequent benefits for companies' reputations as well as returns to local communities. Such opportunities for engagement are why the ITUC places such a high value on cooperation between labour rights and anti-corruption groups, as demonstrated by the Sports and Rights Alliance.

International pressure on FIFA and Qatar, and on other sporting mega-event host countries, including from governments, international sporting bodies and corporate sponsors, must be stepped up. Many lives are at stake, and failure on the part of the international community on these issues would further entrench corruption and the exploitation of workers as accepted ways of doing business. The same challenge is faced by the IOC, to turn its Agenda 2020 into a real vehicle for change.

Notes

1   Sharan Burrow is the general secretary of the International Trade Union Confederation.
2   International Labour Office, *Action Against Child Labour* (Geneva: International Labour Office, 2000), p. 267; India Committee of the Netherlands, 'Child labour used to manufacture "World Cup" balls', 22 May 2002, *www.indianet.nl/a020522.html*; International Labor Rights Fund, *Child Labor in the Soccer Ball Industry: A Report on Continued Use of Child Labor in the Soccer Ball Industry in Pakistan* (Washington, DC: International Labor Rights Fund, 1999), *www.laborrights.org/sites/default/files/publications-and-resources/ILRF%20Soccer%20Balls%20in%20Pakistan%20report%20Feb99.pdf*.
3   See International Labor Rights Forum, *Missed the Goal for Workers: The Reality of Soccer Ball Stitchers in Pakistan, India, China and Thailand* (Washington, DC: International Labor Rights Forum, 2010), *www.cleanclothes.org/resources/recommended-reading/ilrf-soccerball-report.pdf*; and see also the letter sent to FIFA by the International Confederation of Free Trade Unions, the International Textile, Garment and Leather Workers' Federation and the Union Network International on 6 July 2000, which is available at *www.indianet.nl/ivvvbr.html*.
4   Fédération Internationale de Football Association, 'Labour codes for footballs', 3 September 1996, *http://m.fifa.com/newscentre/news/newsid=70068/index.html*.
5   'Code of labour practice for the production of goods licensed by the International Federation of Association Football (FIFA)', *www1.umn.edu/humanrts/links/fifa.html*.
6   Rhys Jenkins, Ruth Pearson and Gill Seyfang (eds), *Corporate Responsibility and Labour Rights: Codes of Conduct in the Global Economy* (London: Earthscan, 2002); Fédération Internationale de Football Association, 'Social responsibility', *http://quality.fifa.com/en/Footballs/Quality-Programme-for-Footballs/Social-responsibility*.

7   International Trade Union Confederation, *The Case against Qatar: Host of the FIFA 2022 World Cup* (Brussels: ITUC, 2014), p. 15, www.ituc-csi.org/IMG/pdf/the_case_against_qatar_en_web170314.pdf.

8   BBC (UK), 'Brazil World Cup workers "face slave-like conditions"', 26 September 2013, *www.bbc.co.uk/news/world-latin-america-24292174.*

9   ITUC (2014).

10 Ibid.

11 Human Rights Watch (US), 'Qatar: abolish exit visas for migrant workers', 30 May 2013, *www.hrw.org/news/2013/05/30/qatar-abolish-exit-visas-migrant-workers.*

12 Ibid.; Euronews (France), '"Desperate" French footballer trapped in Qatar', 14 November 2013, *www.euronews.com/2013/11/14/desperate-french-footballer-trapped-in-qatar.*

13 International Business Times (US), 'Nepali minister blasts Qatar, FIFA, over treatment of World Cup migrant workers', 24 May 2015, *www.ibtimes.com/nepali-minister-blasts-qatar-fifa-over-treatment-world-cup-migrant-workers-1936125.*

14 *Guardian* (UK), 'Revealed: Qatar's World Cup "slaves"', 25 September 2013, *www.the guardian.com/world/2013/sep/25/revealed-qatars-world-cup-slaves*; *Independent* (UK), 'FIFA's real crime with Qatar 2022 is ignoring the workers' plight', 3 March 2015, *www.independent.co.uk/sport/football/news-and-comment/sam-wallace-fifas-real-crime-with-qatar-2022-is-ignoring-the-workers-plight-10081450.html.*

15 Human Rights Watch (US), 'Qatar: migrant construction workers face abuse', 12 June 2012, *www.hrw.org/news/2012/06/12/qatar-migrant-construction-workers-face-abuse.*

16 International Labour Organization, 'Representation (Article 24): Qatar – Co29', 24 March 2014, *www.ilo.org/dyn/normlex/en/f?p=NORMLEXPUB:50012:0::NO::P50012_COMPLAINT_PROCEDURE_ID,P50012_LANG_CODE:3113101,en.*

17 United Nations, *Report of the Special Rapporteur on the Human Rights of Migrants, François Crépeau: Addendum: Mission to Qatar* (New York: United Nations, 23 April 2014), *www.ohchr.org/Documents/Issues/SRMigrants/A-HRC-26-35-Add1_en.pdf.*

18 Just Here (Qatar), 'Quota system for issuing work visas may stop soon', 2 December 2014, *www.justhere.qa/2014/12/quota-system-issuing-work-visas-may-stop-soon*; Business for Social Responsibility, *Migrant Workers and the FIFA World Cup 2022 in Qatar: Actions for Business* (New York: Business for Social Responsibility, 2012), *www.bsr.org/en/our-insights/report-view/migrant-workers-and-the-fifa-world-cup-2022-in-qatar-actions-for-business*; *The Peninsula* (Qatar), 'The rising cost of hiring maids', 2 November 2013, *http://thepeninsulaqatar.com/news/qatar/259293/the-rising-cost-of-hiring-maids.*

19 ITUC (2014).

20 Ibid.

21 National Public Radio (US), 'Talking to Qatar's World Cup workers gets BBC reporter arrested', 22 May 2015, *www.npr.org/2015/05/22/408680072/talking-to-qatar-s-world-cup-workers-gets-bbc-reporter-arrested.*

22 Qatar News Agency, 'Qatar's government communication office denies Washington Post article about worker conditions in Qatar', 2 June 2015, *www.qna.org.qa/en-us/News/15060218340056/Qatars-Government-Communication-Office-Denies-Washington-Post-Article-about-Worker-Conditions-in-Qatar.*

23 Hukoomi (Qatar), 'FIFA World Cup 2022', *http://portal.www.gov.qa/wps/portal/topics/Tourism,+Culture+and+Leisure/FIFA+World+Cup+2022*; Online Qatar, 'Qatar World Cup 2022', *www.onlineqatar.com/worldcup-2022*; Online Qatar, 'The 2022 World Cup countdown begins', *www.onlineqatar.com/worldcup-2022/world-cup-countdown.aspx.*

24 *Guardian* (UK), 'Qatar World Cup construction "will leave 4,000 migrant workers dead"', 26 September 2013, *www.theguardian.com/global-development/2013/sep/26/qatar-world-cup-migrant-workers-dead*; Human Rights Watch, *Building a Better World Cup: Protecting Migrant Workers in Qatar ahead of FIFA 2022* (New York: Human Rights Watch, 2012), *www.hrw.org/sites/default/files/reports/qatar0612webwcover_0.pdf*; International Trade Union Confederation, 'New evidence of abuses of workers' rights in Qatar prompts ITUC investigation', 16 May 2012, *www.ituc-csi.org/new-evidence-of-abuses-of-workers*;

Al Jazeera America, 'Qatar migrant workers die by hundreds', 18 February 2014, *http://america.aljazeera.com/articles/2014/2/17/hundreds-of-migrantworkersfacedeathin qatar.html.*

25 *Times of India*, '279 Indians died in Qatar in 2014', 31 January 2015, *http://time sofindia.indiatimes.com/nri/other-news/279-Indians-died-in-Qatar-in-2014/articleshow/ 46079097.cms.*

26 Fédération Internationale de Football Association, 'Meeting between FIFA and the ITUC', 21 November 2013, *www.fifa.com/worldcup/videos/y=2013/m=11/video=meeting-between-fifa-and-the-ituc-2227304.html*; ESPN (UK), 'Blatter: Qatar World Cup labour issues unacceptable', 20 November 2013, *http://en.espn.co.uk/football/sport/story/ 259317.html.*

27 International Labour Organization, 'Eighth supplementary report: report of the committee set up to examine the representation alleging non-observance by Qatar of the Forced Labour Convention 1930 (no. 29), made under Article 24 of the ILO Constitution by the International Trade Union Confederation and the Building and Woodworkers International', 24 March 2014, *www.ilo.org/wcmsp5/groups/public/---ed_norm/---relconf/documents/meeting document/wcms_239846.pdf.*

28 International Trade Union Confederation, 'ITUC Global Rights Index names world's ten worst countries for workers', 10 June 2015, *www.ituc-csi.org/ituc-global-rights-index-names*; Migration Policy Institute (US), 'Global civil society in Qatar and the Gulf Cooperation Council: emerging dilemmas and opportunities', 9 April 2014, *www.migrationpolicy.org/ article/global-civil-society-qatar-and-gulf-cooperation-council-emerging-dilemmas-and-opportunities.*

29 ILO (24 March 2014).

30 International Labour Organization, *371st Report of the Committee on Freedom of Association* (Geneva: ILO, 2014), *www.ilo.org/wcmsp5/groups/public/---ed_norm/---relconf/documents/ meetingdocument/wcms_239692.pdf.*

31 International Trade Union Confederation, 'Qatar buys time at the ILO', 30 March 2015, *www.ituc-csi.org/qatar-buys-time-at-the-ilo.*

32 *Guardian* (UK), 'France: Vinci Construction investigated over Qatar forced labour claims', 26 April 2015, *www.theguardian.com/world/2015/apr/26/france-vinci-construction-qatar-forced-labour-claims-2022-world-cup.*

33 *Independent* (3 March 2015).

34 *Guardian* (UK), 'Visa expresses "grave concern" to Fifa over migrant workers in Qatar', 20 May 2015, *www.theguardian.com/football/2015/may/20/visa-fifa-migrant-workers-qatar-world-cup.*

35 Building and Wood Worker's International, 'BWI meeting on working conditions of migrant workers in Qatar hosted by ILO sets path for joint strategy', 27 October 2014, *www.bwint. org/default.asp?index=5813&Language=EN.*

36 The Sports Rights Alliance is a coalition of leading human rights and sports groups, including Amnesty International, FIFPro – World Players' Union, Football Supporters Europe, Human Rights Watch, the International Trade Union Confederation, Supporters Direct Europe, Terre des Hommes and Transparency International Germany.

37 Accord on Fire and Building Safety in Bangladesh, *http://bangladeshaccord.org/progress.*

3.13

The Brazilian experience as 'role model'

Christopher Gaffney[1]

Brazil's World Cup experience has been instructive for future hosts, in that it has presented a number of problems related to the transparency of the bidding process, the size of the country and the ambitions of urban authorities, the emergence of strong opposition to infrastructure spending and privatisation, and critical governmental interventions that eventually allowed for the successful realisation of the event.

The major Brazilian sports confederations, the Confederação Brasileira de Futebol (CBF) and the Comitê Olímpico Brasileiro (COB), have tended to be dominated by a narrow range of vested interests for decades.[2] As these two organisations took the lead role in the bidding for the World Cup and Olympics, respectively, their institutional cultures have negatively impacted the transparency of the events themselves.[3] The lack of public consultation and open debate in the preparation of bid dossiers continues to be one of the major obstacles to ensuring that mega-events serve the broadest range of stakeholders.[4]

The case of Brazil is exemplary in that the bid dossier for the 2014 World Cup was never made public and the Rio 2016 bid book has become the de facto urban planning document for the city of Rio de Janeiro.[5] These are problematic developments because, in the former case, there is no public record of what the CBF and the Brazilian government proposed or promised to the Fédération Internationale de Football Association (FIFA); subsequent developments had major impacts on 12 Brazilian cities. In the latter case, the city of Rio de Janeiro is being transformed to match the proposed 'Olympic city', with dire consequences for tens of thousands of families, which have been forcibly removed from their homes.[6]

The logistical challenges of organising a World Cup in Brazil were exacerbated by the ambitions of the Brazilian executive branch to have as many host cities as possible; FIFA required between eight and ten host cities, but the Brazilians opted for 12. None of the 18 potential host cities circulated their proposals for public input prior to or during the bidding process. This meant not only an increase in costs and impacts, but that several cities without notable football traditions would acquire FIFA-standard stadiums, five-star hotels and world-class training facilities. Although the realisation of the World Cup in Manaus, Cuiabá, Brasília and Natal may have accelerated necessary upgrades to airports, these cities have not experienced an improvement in urban mobility or basic services, or an increase in tourism.[7] To the contrary, these cities have gone into debt since the World Cup to maintain 'white elephant' stadiums that will remain a burden on municipal budgets for the foreseeable future.[8]

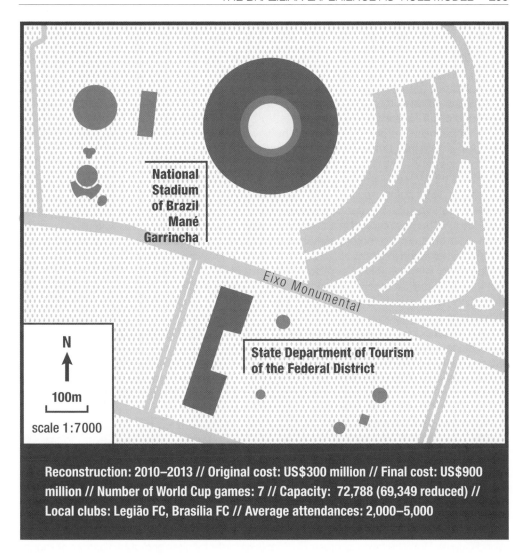

Figure 3.9 Estádio Nacional de Brasília Mané Garrincha: Brasilia's white elephant

Sources: Fédération Internationale de Football Association, Estádio Nacional de Brasília – Brasília, *http://pt.fifa.com/worldcup/destination/stadiums/stadium=5002284/index. html*; *Washington Post*, 'High costs, corruption claims mar Brazil World Cup', 12 May 2014.

In addition to the problem of 'white elephant' infrastructure, all the World Cup projects were exempted from normal contracting procedures so that the building process could be accelerated. The combined effects of the so-called Differential Public Procurement Regime (RDC in Portuguese) and an exemption to the Law of Fiscal Responsibility, which requires cities to have balanced budgets, have pushed all the World Cup host cities into debt, as municipal and state governments took advantage of the situation to build on a massive scale in an accelerated time frame.[9] The inclusion of infrastructure projects in World Cup development agendas typically falls under the category of 'legacy', but when these projects occur under emergency planning and execution regimes their transparency tends to decrease.[10]

Another problematic of the 2014 World Cup was the way in which municipal and state governments interpreted FIFA's host city demands. When FIFA declared, as early as 2007, that Brazil did not possess a single stadium capable of hosting a World Cup match, the Brazilians interpreted this to mean that they should build or renovate 12 stadiums that met or exceeded all FIFA's technical requirements.[11] As the FIFA documents had no provisions for social, economic or urban sustainability, however, the Brazilians constructed stadiums that are isolated from their urban contexts, very expensive to maintain and dependent on imported technologies, and that do not fit within the cultural paradigms of Brazilian 'fandom'. The majority of the World Cup stadiums were formerly public installations that were demolished and rebuilt with public money, and are now operated through so-called public–private partnerships (typically 30-year concessions won by the civil construction firms hired for the rebuilding).[12] This has resulted in a transfer of public space to private interests and an increase in the cost of attending football matches, and further exacerbated the crises of social and urban fragmentation in Brazil.[13]

Beginning with the FIFA Confederations Cup in 2013, it became apparent that Brazil had exposed itself to significant risk in the pursuit of mega-events. An a priori assumption of hosting mega-events is that they will serve to attract international media attention, and stimulate tourism, business and national pride. With the advent of massive protests against the exorbitant public spending on the World Cup, it became clear that Brazil was risking its international image and that the Workers' Party, the largest element in the governing coalition, was alienating its political base through its acquiescence to FIFA's stringent demands. The chronic lateness or incompleteness of stadium, airport, communications and transportation infrastructure, as well as the public displays of disaffection between the 2014 Local Organising Committee (LOC) and FIFA, further hurt Brazil's image abroad.[14]

The unprecedented scale and intensity of the protests during the 2013 Confederations Cup focused greater international attention on FIFA's business model than ever before. The federal government dealt with this crisis situation through heavy-handed policing and strategic negotiations with key social actors.[15] Despite the very real threats to a successful staging of the contest, including pitched battles between police and protesters at many venues, and repeated denunciations of human rights abuses, event organisers and international observers alike declared it a success.

Emboldened by the effectiveness of protests in bringing attention to the impact of the World Cup on Brazilian cities, protesters organised further strikes and public actions throughout 2013 and into 2014. One of the federal government's primary responses was to create a 10,000-strong military shock force that could be rapidly deployed to potential trouble spots during the World Cup.[16] This force, combined with an estimated BRL 1.9 billion (some US$780 million) in federal security spending and an additional 15,000 security officers, ensured that protesters threatening the staging of the World Cup would be contained.[17] For the final, there were no fewer than 25,000 police personnel in Rio de Janeiro, and 19 activists were arrested on the eve of the match.[18]

Another major risk to the realisation of the 2014 World Cup was the derelict state of Brazil's urban and inter-urban transportation. In order to guarantee uninterrupted urban traffic circulation and inter-city flights during the World Cup, each host city decreed a holiday on game days. This effectively cleaned the streets of their habitual users, diminishing the risk of traffic jams, overstretched metro services or crowded airports.[19] The suspension of urban normalcy across the Brazilian host cities was key to the operational success of the World Cup.

The response of the international sports organisations to the problems of hosting the 2014 World Cup and 2016 Olympics has been tepid. Partially as a result of the pursuit of FIFA-standard stadiums for the World Cup, Brazilian football tickets are now the most expensive in the world relative to the national minimum wage.[20] There has been no institutional reform of the cloistered and opaque CBF, and FIFA appears content to follow the Brazilian model of hosting in Russia and Qatar, where dissent and public protests are much less likely.

The preparations for the 2016 Summer Olympics are worryingly similar to those of the World Cup, although their effects are concentrated in Rio de Janeiro. The construction of three non-governmental regulatory agencies to deal with the financing and execution of Olympic-related projects has eroded democratic institutions and created significant vacuums of responsibility.[21] Large-scale infrastructure projects that are part of Olympic and Paralympic transportation planning have removed tens of thousands from their homes without due process or compensation.[22] These projects are accelerating and their impacts increasing as the Olympic deadline approaches.

The multiple levels of authority and bureaucracy have created a kind of shell game, in which no one agency or individual is responsible for the impact of a given project. The International Olympic Committee (IOC), for example, is focused only on the delivery of housing, transportation, brand protection and venues for its competition; it is not concerned with how these projects are developed, or their impacts on residents.[23] The Comitê Organizador dos Jogos Olímpicos e Paralímpicos Rio de Janeiro 2016 (Rio 2016) is preoccupied with Games operations, not infrastructure development.[24] Two governmental oversight organisations (the Autoridade Público Olímpico and Empresa Municipal Olímpica) are responsible for project delivery, but the city government has taken the lead on the transportation infrastructure that will link the nominal Olympic zones.[25] These multi-layered interventions are predicated on the content of and subsequent changes to the Rio 2016 bid book – a document that was prepared behind closed doors and chosen as the winning bid in the October 2009 IOC session in Copenhagen. All these projects benefit elite sectors of Rio's vast metropolitan area, while socialising the costs and localising the negative impacts in Rio's poorest communities.[26]

It may be that the experience of Brazil 2014 and Rio 2016 will mark both the interventionist apogee and the social nadir of the era of mega-event gigantism.[27] The massive public protests that rocked Brazil have sent a strong signal to the international community: sports mega-events are not worth it. While it is yet to be seen what the public reaction to Rio 2016 will be, the declining number of cities that are willing to host the Summer and Winter Olympics is perhaps a sign that the protesters' message has been heard. Unfortunately, the FIFA World Cup in Russia looks as if it will employ the same kinds of security measures, privatisations and suspensions of urban normalcy learnt from Brazil's 'successful' World Cup.[28]

At the heart of the mega-event problem is a lack of transparency in bidding and building, an absence of public participation and deliberation and an unequal sharing of the economic burden between hosts and rights holders. Because the IOC and FIFA are monopolistic rights holders that enforce strict financial, political, infrastructural, security, communication and other requirements for their events, but are unwilling to pay for any of these, the result is that citizens, cities and countries are forced to pay so that others can play.[29] Global and local resistances to these processes have been growing for some time.[30] The bidding process continues to be as opaque and non-participatory as ever. As the Brazilian experience has shown, this has dire consequences for cities, for economies and for the guarantee of human rights.

Notes

1   Christopher Gaffney is a senior research fellow in the Department of Geography, University of Zurich.
2   Amaury Ribeiro Jr, Leandro Cipoloni, Luiz Carlos Azenha and Tony Chastinet, *O Lado Sujo do Futebol: A Trama de Propinas, Negociatas e Traições que Abalou o Esporte Mais Popular do Mundo* (São Paulo: Planeta, 2014).
3   The CBF has been mired in corruption and malfeasance scandals for decades, controlling Brazilian football through nepotism and political favouritism: Terra (Brazil), 'Promotor confirma que MP entrará com Ação Civil Pública contra CBF', 3 February 2014, *http://esportes.terra. com.br/flamengo/,9c5a1bc3b59f3410VgnVCM20000099cceb0aRCRD.html*; Folha de S. Paulo (Brazil), 'Receita Federal Multa a CBF Em R$ 3 Milhões Por Sonegação de Imposto de Renda', 29 August 2010, *www1.folha.uol.com.br/esporte/790573-receita-federal-multa-a-cbf-em-r-3-milhoes-por-sonegacao-de-imposto-de-renda.shtml*. The same individual who has used intimidation tactics to maintain power while limiting the development of Brazilian Olympic sports has dominated the COB for two decades: Blog Do Juca Kfouri (Brazil), 'COB acusado de calote', 22 January 2013, *http://blogdojuca.uol.com.br/2013/01/cob-acusado-de-calote*; ESPN (Brazil), 'Exclusivo: Confederação brasileira de esportes no gelo é perseguida pelo COB por não apoiar Nuzman', 3 October 2012, *http://m.espn.com.br/ video/284999_exclusivo-confederacao-brasileira-de-esportes-no-gelo-e-perseguida-pelo-cob-por-nao-apoiar-nuzman*.
4   3 Wire Sports (US), 'The IOC's big bid problem', 5 May 2014, *www.3wiresports.com/ 2014/05/05/iocs-big-bid-problem*.
5   Christopher Gaffney, 'Mega-events and socio-spatial dynamics in Rio de Janeiro, 1919–2016', *Journal of Latin American Geography*, vol. 9 (2010).
6   Articulação Nacional das Comitês Populares da Copa e Olimpíadas, *Megaeventos e violações de direitos humanos no Brasil*, 2nd edn (Rio de Janeiro: ANCOP, 2014), *www.portalpopulardacopa.org.br/index.php?option=com_k2&view=item&id=198:dossi% C3%AA-nacional-de-viola%C3%A7%C3%B5es-de-direitos-humanos*.
7   Agência Brasil, 'Falta de planejamento pode comprometer mobilidade urbana da Copa do Mundo e Olimpíadas, diz especialista', 15 May 2011, *http://memoria.ebc.com.br/ agenciabrasil/noticia/2011-05-15/falta-de-planejamento-pode-comprometer-mobilidade-urbana-da-copa-do-mundo-e-olimpiadas-diz-especialis*; Instituto Humanitas Unisinos (Brazil), 'Estádio de Manaus poderá se pagar em 198 anos', 7 March 2012, *www.ihu. unisinos.br/noticias/507238-estadiodemanauspoderasepagarem198anos*; G1 Amazonas (Brazil), 'Artur e Omar descartam BRT e Monotrilho para Copa em Manaus', 30 October 2012. *http://g1.globo.com/am/amazonas/noticia/2012/10/artur-e-omar-descartam-brt-e-monotrilho-para-copa-em-manaus.html*.
8   BBC (UK), 'Copa: prejuízo de "elefantes brancos" já supera R$ 10 milhões', 19 February 2015, *www.bbc.co.uk/portuguese/noticias/2015/02/150212_elefantes_brancos_ copa_rm*.
9   Law no. 12.348, Lei que permite a alteração de limite de endividamento dos municípios envolvidos com a Copa 2014 e Olimpíadas 2016, *www2.camara.gov.br/legin/fed/lei/2010/ lei-12348-15-dezembro-2010-609683-norma-pl.html*; Law no. 12.462, Regime diferenciado de contratações públicas, *www2.camara.gov.br/legin/fed/lei/2011/lei-12462-4-agosto-2011-611147-norma-pl.html*.
10 Alberto de Oliveira, 'O emprego, a economia e a transparência nos grandes projetos urbanos', paper presented at the Congress of the Associação de Estudos Latino-Americanos (Rio de Janeiro, 11 June 2009), *http://pfdc.pgr.mpf.mp.br/atuacao-e-conteudos-de-apoio/publicacoes/direito-a-moradia-adequada/artigos/o-emprego-a-economia-alberto-de-oliveira*; Carta Maior (Brazil), 'Pouco transparente, Copa de 2014 já estoura prazos e orçamento', 25 March 2010, *www.cartamaior.com.br/templates/ materiaMostrar.cfm?materia_id=16485&editoria_id=4*.

11 Fédération Internationale de Football Association, *Brazil Bid Inspection Report for the 2014 FIFA World Cup* (Zurich: FIFA, 2007), *www.fifa.com/mm/document/affederation/mission/ 62/24/78/inspectionreport_e_24841.pdf*.

12 Christopher Gaffney, 'A World Cup for whom? The impact of the 2014 World Cup on Brazilian football stadiums and cultures', in Paulo Fontes and Bernardo Buarque de Hollanda (eds), *The Country of Football: Politics, Popular Culture and the Beautiful Game in Brazil* (London: Hurst, 2014), *www.academia.edu/8528132/A_World_Cup_for_Whom_The_ Impact_of_the_2014_World_Cup_on_Brazilian_Football_Stadiums_and_Cultures*.

13 Gilmar Mascarenhas and Christopher Gaffney, 'A Festa Acabou? Esta recomeçando? Os Novos Estádios de Futebol e a Disciplina Socioespacial', in Bernardo Buarque de Hollanda and Guilherme Burlamaqui (eds), *Desvendando o Jogo: Nova Luz Sobre o Futebol* (Rio de Janeiro: EDUFF, 2014).

14 *Guardian* (UK), 'Brazil's World Cup courts disaster as delays, protests and deaths mount', 16 February 2014.

15 France24 (France), 'Clashes mar Brazil Confederations Cup opener', 16 June 2013, *www. france24.com/en/20130616-brasilia-clashes-confederations-cup-opener-police-world-cup- protest*; BBC (UK), 'Brazil unrest: "million" join protests in 100 cities', 21 June 2013, *www. bbc.com/news/world-latin-america-22992410*; Amnesty International, *'They Use a Strategy of Fear': Protecting the Right to Protest in Brazil* (London: Amnesty International, 2014), *www.amnesty.org.uk/sites/default/files/brazil_world_cup_-_aibr_briefing_eng.pdf*; *Daily Mail* (UK), 'Protests rumble on at Confederations Cup as violent scenes tarnish Spain win over Italy in Brazil . . . and FIFA announce £45-a-bottle champagne as partner for World Cup', 28 June 2013, *www.dailymail.co.uk/sport/football/article-2350595/Confederations- Cup-2013-Brazil-protests-continue-FIFA-announce-Taittinger-champagne-partner. html#ixzz3QD8CMnMO*; Inter Press Service, 'Police brutality fuels protests in Brazil', 25 June 2013, *www.ipsnews.net/2013/06/police-brutality-fuels-protests-in-brazil*.

16 Consultor Jurídico (Brazil), 'Legado da Copa para a segurança pública é discutível', 24 June 2014, *www.conjur.com.br/2014-jun-24/josias-alves-legado-copa-seguranca-publica- discutivel*; Portal Brasil, 'Dez mil profissionais da Força Nacional atuarão na segurança das cidades-sede', 8 January 2014, *www.brasil.gov.br/defesa-e-seguranca/2014/01/ dez-mil-profissionais-da-forca-nacional-atuarao-na-seguranca-das-cidades-sede*.

17 Index on Censorship (UK), 'Brazil: bills rushed through congress in bid to suppress World Cup protests', 17 February 2014, *www.indexoncensorship.org/2014/02/brazil- bills-world-up-protest*; Portal Da Copa, 'Conheça detalhes dos investimentos em segurança previstos para a Copa', 19 November 2012, *www.copa2014.gov.br/pt-br/ noticia/diario-oficial-traz-resolucao-do-gecopa-que-inclui-atividades-de-seguranca- na-matriz-da-copa*.

18 BBC (UK), 'World Cup final security: Brazil plans huge security op', 12 July 2014, *www.bbc. com/news/world-latin-america-28274738*; Folha de S. Paulo (Brazil), 'Doze ativistas presos na véspera da final da Copa são liberados no Rio', 17 July 2014, *www1.folha.uol.com. br/poder/2014/07/1487192-doze-ativistas-presos-na-vespera-da-final-da-copa-sao- libertados-no-rio.shtml*.

19 *O Globo* Extra (Brazil), 'Paes decreta feriados e suspende obras durante a Copa', 12 March 2014.

20 *O Globo* Extra (Brazil), 'Ingressos para futebol no Brasil são os mais caros do mundo, aponta pesquisa', 24 March 2013.

21 Autoridade Publíco Olímpico (APO), *Matriz de Responsibilidades: 2016 Jogos Olímpicos e Paralimpicos de Rio de Janeiro* (Rio de Janeiro: APO, 2014), *www.apo.gov.br/downloads/ matriz/201401/livro_matriz_20140128.pdf*; Gazeta Esportiva (Brazil), 'APO divulga incompleta Matriz de Responsabilidades de Rio-2016', 29 January 2014; Arnaldo Cedraz de Oliveira, *O TCU e as Olimpíadas de 2016: Relatório de Situação* (Brasília: Tribunal de Contas da União, 2013); *Wall Street Journal* (US), 'Brazil Olympic Committee raises budget estimate for 2016 Games', 23 January 2014.

22 Comitê Popular da Copa e Olimpíadas do Rio de Janeiro, *Megaeventos e Violações dos Direitos Humanos no Rio de Janeiro* (Brasilia: Comitê Popular da Copa/Olimpíadas do Rio de Janeiro, 2012), *http://comitepopulario.files.wordpress.com/2012/04/dossic3aa-megaeventos-e-violac3a7c3b5es-dos-direitos-humanos-no-rio-de-janeiro.pdf*.

23 Terra (Colombia), 'El COI se impresiona con los avances de Río', 9 June 2012, *http://deportes.terra.com.co/mas-deportes/el-coi-se-impresiona-con-los-avances-de-rio, f7717eb12b670310VgnVCM20000099f154d0RCRD.html*.

24 Rio 2016, 'Frequently asked questions', *www.rio2016.org/en/transparency/frequently-asked-questions*.

25 *O Globo* (Brazil), 'Projeto de Paes muda lei ambiental para setor privado construir campo de golfe na Barra', 2 November 2012, *http://oglobo.globo.com/rio/projeto-de-paes-muda-lei-ambiental-para-setor-privado-construir-campo-de-golfe-na-barra-6618880*; *O Globo Extra* (Brazil), 'Rio dá a largada para transcarioca', 19 December 2009, *http://extra.globo.com/noticias/rio/rio-da-largada-para-transcarioca-387421.html*.

26 *Observatório das Metrópoles* (Brazil), 'Sobre o relatório do ONU – Copa 2014, Olimpíadas 2016 e megaprojetos: remoções em curso no Brasil', 4 May 2011; *O Globo*, 2 November 2012; À Beira do Urbanismo (Brazil), 'O Rio de Janeiro e as Olimpíadas 2016: "Nós Lucramos, Vocês Pagam a Conta – O Retorno"', 19 January 2008; *Folha de S. Paulo* (Brazil), 'TCU vê falta de planejamento da Rio-2016', 26 September 2013.

27 *O Globo* Esporte (Brazil), '"Gigantismo" ameaça o sucesso dos Jogos do Rio 2016 e futuras edições', 11 April 2013, *http://globoesporte.globo.com/olimpiadas/noticia/2013/04/gigantismo-ameaca-o-sucesso-dos-jogos-do-rio-2016-e-futuras-edicoes.html*; Al Jazeera (Qatar), 'Brazil: protests of discontent', 19 June 2013, *www.aljazeera.com/programmes/insidestoryamericas/2013/06/20136197823131177.html*; Amnesty International (UK), 'Right to protest under threat as Brazil pushes "terrorism" law ahead of World Cup', 12 May 2014, *www.amnesty.org.uk/press-releases/right-protest-under-threat-brazil-pushes-terrorism-law-ahead-world-cup*; *CourierMail* (Australia), 'Video shows Rio police officer firing live shots at World Cup protesters', 16 June 2014, *www.news.com.au/sport/football/video-shows-rio-police-officer-firing-live-shots-at-world-cup-protesters/story-fnkjl6g2-1226956079539*.

28 BBC (UK), 'Russia 2018: major challenges for next World Cup hosts', 22 July 2014, *www.bbc.com/news/world-europe-28409784*.

29 *Boston Globe* (US), 'IOC and FIFA: monopoly power makes pricey games', 6 June 2014, *www.bostonglobe.com/opinion/2014/06/07/ioc-and-fifa-monopoly-power-makes-pricey-games/hK7oGc2KZkJxZxx8fVXzRK/story.html*.

30 Kevin Gotham, 'Resisting urban spectacle: the 1984 Louisiana World Exposition and the contradictions of mega-events', *Urban Studies*, vol. 48 (2011); Mary Ann Glynn, 'Configuring the field of play: how hosting the Olympic Games impacts civic community', *Journal of Management Studies*, vol. 45 (2008); Malte Warburg Sørensen, 'Mega events in Rio de Janeiro: the case of Vila Autódromo – community planning as resistance to forced evictions', master's thesis, Roskilde University, 2013; Graeme Hayes and John Karamichas (eds), *Olympic Games, Mega-Events and Civil Societies* (Basingstoke: Palgrave Macmillan, 2011); Christopher Gaffney, 'Virando o Jogo: the challenges and possibilities for social mobilization in Brazilian football', *Journal of Sport and Social Issues*, vol. 37 (2013).

3.14

Rio 2016 and the birth of Brazilian transparency

Andy Spalding, Pat Barr, Albert Flores, Kat Gavin, Shaun Freiman, Tyler Klink, Carter Nichols, Ann Reid and Rina Van Orden[1]

Brazil's modern democracy is but three decades old. With the Brazilian people now taking to the streets in protest at public corruption, the government is enacting new laws and learning to effectively enforce them. The nation is thus feeling the growing pains of an emergent commitment to transparency.

In this, the window between Brazil's hosting of the 2014 Fédération Internationale de Football Association (FIFA) World Cup and the 2016 Summer Olympics, it is timely to ask what the spotlight of these two events has revealed about the nation's anti-corruption measures. How is the government responding to exposed corruption risk? Will the Olympics ultimately make good on their promise to be an agent of positive change? This chapter discusses issues related to Brazil's federal anti-corruption laws generally, its changing procurement laws and the Olympic contracts and governance organisations.

A rapidly evolving legal system

After the monarchy was overthrown in the late nineteenth century, Brazil went through four distinct government models before emerging as a democracy in 1985.[2] The cultural belief that corruption was inherent, acceptable and necessary – the 'jeitinho brasileiro' (loosely translated as the 'Brazilian way') – emerged from the wreckage of a century of unstable and/ or authoritarian rule.[3]

Many Brazilians believe that Brazil is changing culturally, however, and that the people will have a measure of success in rooting out corruption.[4] Young Brazilians especially are calling for reform both within the government and society. This movement is exemplified by recent protests against President Dilma Rousseff and the perceived corruption in her administration.[5]

Brazil's system of government is itself designed, at least in part, to curb corruption. Seemingly heeding Lord Acton's famous admonition that 'absolute power corrupts absolutely', the constitution grants an extraordinary amount of authority to the states and local governments to govern themselves.[6] The country's brand of federalism appears to be grounded in an institutional and cultural distrust for centralised power, probably borne of its recent history. To the extent that Brazil's federalism succeeds in preventing the concentration of power, it creates conditions that have historically tended to limit corruption.

In seeking to check corruption, however, Brazilian federalism also creates a distinct corruption risk. This risk is exemplified, perhaps ironically, in Brazil's recent landmark federal statute, referred to variously as the Anti-Corruption Law or the Clean Companies Act. The statute creates corporate liability for bribery, and contains various provisions that incentivise compliance and facilitate public enforcement.[7] Although the passage of the Clean Companies Act is a watershed moment for Brazil's anti-corruption movement, the law was enacted without an integrated national enforcement system. What exists now is a fragmented enforcement regime consisting of autonomous entities that compete both within and between the federal, state and municipal levels. It remains uncertain as to how the new statute will eventually be enforced, or by whom; it was hardly used at all to curb World Cup corruption. In response both to this uncertainty and to the continuing anti-corruption protests, the Rousseff administration has recently passed a decree that clarifies key areas of the statute.[8] Many believe that it will be years before scholars, lawyers and judges are able sort it all out, however. Only time will tell whether the government can effectively enforce this law to reduce corruption in connection with the Olympics.

Brazil's procurement regime is also now evolving, with implications for curbing Olympic corruption that remain unclear. The applicable law for public procurement purposes prior to the 2014 football World Cup was Federal Law no. 8,666/1993.[9] The main criticism of this law was that it required the government to go through two requests for proposals (RFPs), the first for the project design, called the 'technical project', the second for the actual construction. Typically, different companies would win each of the bids, leading to a misalignment of incentives. Procurement lawyers frequently lamented this messy state of affairs, from which litigators profit handsomely.[10]

The Olympics and World Cup gave Brazil a chance to experiment with a new bidding law. In 2011 the government enacted Federal Law no. 12,462, the Regime Diferenciado de Contratações Públicas, or RDC.[11] The RDC seeks to make bidding procedures more efficient by removing the requirement for a technical project RFP. Another provision included in the RDC makes the budget for government projects confidential. In theory, a 'blind' bidding process should produce more competitive offers for the government: bidders are forced to set prices without knowing their competitors' prices, potentially preventing bid inflation. Anonymity in bidding may also create corruption risk, however, as bidders cannot keep each other in check. Furthermore, two lawsuits have been filed that challenge the constitutionality of the blind bidding process.[12]

The RDC and the Clean Companies Act, as well as the enforcement mechanisms that give life to each of them, will of course remain long after the Olympic Games are gone. They are part of the legal infrastructure that will prove an important component of the Games' legacy. Brazil has also adopted a number of measures specifically for the Olympics, however, as discussed below.

Olympic anti-corruption measures

Brazil has implemented a number of anti-corruption laws and institutions specifically for the Olympics. The Autoridade Pública Olímpica (APO) is the primary Olympic authority in Rio de Janeiro, and it integrates the federal, state and municipal governments in the planning of the Games.[13] This is a unique body in Brazil – the first and only public body to bring all three levels of the government together – and it was one of the strongest points of Rio's bid.[14] The organisation allocates responsibilities and coordinates preparation for the Games among the many entities, public and private, that are overseeing the construction infrastructure, and revitalisation projects taking place around Rio. These entities include the Empresa Olímpica

Municipal (the municipal body in charge of many of the stadium and infrastructure projects and operating out of the Rio mayor's office)[15] and Rio 2016 (the private organisation responsible for the events and athletes during the Olympic Games),[16] as well as the participating offices of the federal and state governments.[17]

Given the large sums of money at play in preparation for the Olympics, and Brazil's rank as the 69th perceived least corrupt country in the world,[18] speculation involving construction-related corruption for the games is prevalent. This speculation is only compounded by the recent corruption scandals involving Petrobras and the construction industry.[19] The two overarching features providing public transparency and hedging against corruption for the games are the Responsibility Matrix (Matriz de Responsibilidades) provided by the APO and the auditing provided by the Tribunal de Contas do Município do Rio de Janeiro (TCMRJ).[20]

The Responsibility Matrix, as mentioned above, tracks all commitments of government agencies for projects directly related to the Rio 2016 Games, be they the responsibility of the federal government, the state government or the municipal government. Although a useful tool in tracking construction progress, the document has its limits: it is effectively available only in Portuguese, as the English version[21] is updated infrequently; it lists a budget and deadlines only for those projects with a 'maturation level' of 3, on a scale from 1 to 6; and it tracks projects only within its one-third of the budget.[22]

The TCMRJ is one of two municipal auditing oversight courts in Brazil. In this capacity, it monitors government procurement activities by analysing construction bidding documents, before the execution of the contract and during inspections, and it also examines the rendering of accounts.[23] It is the body responsible for ensuring that the people of Rio have fair government contracting and that these contracts are completed on time and on budget. One of the major issues that the TCMRJ faces leading up to 2016 is the sheer volume of contracts that it has to oversee. In one of the largest cities in the world, already overseeing all government expenditures, the body must now add to its administrative burden all municipal contracting arising from the Olympic Games.

These infrastructure projects create an additional corruption risk of a very different kind. As with the 2014 World Cup, the Olympics will almost inevitably elicit protests by Brazilian citizens living in the favelas, and other disaffected citizens who have grown tired of corruption. Corruption is particularly prevalent within the Pacifying Police Units, whose purpose is to bring security to favelas. These officers are reported to steal personal and residential property to sell and make a profit from, without any kind of accountability.[24]

An additional source of Olympic law relevant to corruption risk is the contractual obligations that the bid city undertakes with the International Olympic Committee (IOC). When a city is selected to host the Games, the promises made in the course of the bid become contractual obligations. The pressure to deliver on these obligations has the potential to encourage corner-cutting, and to open the way for corruption. Some of the promises made in Rio's Candidature File are the expansion of the capacity of Rio International Airport, a renovation of Rio's port and a guarantee that all three of Brazil's levels of government (federal, state and municipal) will cover any economic shortfall encountered by the Local Organising Committee (LOC).[25] The LOC has estimated that more than 30 million items are needed to meet the demands of the 2016 Olympic and Paralympic Games.[26]

Despite these myriad risks, the IOC does not appear to be helping much to reduce Olympic corruption in Rio. In contrast to the highly detailed sponsor- and trademark-related guarantees that the IOC typically demands from host cities, none of the host-city documents contains an anti-corruption guarantee. Similarly, our interviews with various individuals doing Olympics-related work revealed a widely held perception that the IOC simply is not concerned about host-city corruption. While insisting on protecting the commercial interests of its sponsors, the IOC does not seem to have a comparable insistence on protecting the host city's citizens from corruption.

Conclusion

This chapter has provided just a cursory discussion of Brazil's anti-corruption framework in advance of Rio 2016. Ultimately, it remains to be seen whether enforcement will prove more robust for the Olympics than it was for the World Cup. A full report, to be released in the spring of 2016, will discuss these and many other issues in substantial detail. The world deserves to know all that Brazil has done to curb public corruption, and all it still has to do.

Box 3.3 Projeto Jogos Limpos: the 'Clean Games' project in Brazil

Instituto Ethos[27]

When Brazil was chosen to host the FIFA 2014 World Cup and the 2016 Olympic and Paralympic Games, the Ethos Institute of Business and Social Responsibility launched the 'Clean Games: Inside and Outside Stadiums' project, with the goal of increasing transparency and preventing corruption in the preparation of the events.[28] Companies and public officials signed transparency and anti-corruption agreements, and the project also created tools for government and civil society to monitor public expenditure related to both events.

Following the approval of the federal Anti-Corruption Law[29] and the Access to Information Law in recent years,[30] both of which the project campaigned for, the Ethos Institute has seen greater transparency in the dealings between and among local governments and an increase in the willingness of companies to engage in collaboration towards integrity.

Engaging governments

The Ethos Institute has employed three strategies to pressure local governments to increase transparency in public expenditure. First, it set up a network of local branches in each of the 12 World Cup host cities. Second, it secured the commitment of mayoral candidates in these cities to increase transparency and engaged them to ensure that anti-corruption measures were on their agendas for the 2012 municipal elections (in which 89 per cent of the candidates committed themselves to 'transparency pacts').

The project also developed 'Transparency Indicators for Local and State Governments', which enabled media and civil society to monitor governments' expenditure effectively, and governments to improve transparency by using the indicators as a checklist. The success of these strategies is visible in the improved performance of cities and states according to the Transparency Indicators; in one year 11 of the 12 cities improved their performance, as well as 10 of the 11 states (the Federal District was counted only as a city). Moreover, the Ethos Institute was able to engage governments by holding high-level meetings in seven cities in three different states.

Engaging companies

There have been two main approaches for engaging and supporting companies. The first is the publication *Fighting Corruption in Sport Sponsorship and Hospitality: A Practical Guide for Companies* (and the discussions organised around it), developed in collaboration with the UN Global Compact to prevent corruption by providing a practical framework for managing sports sponsorship in a transparent and responsible manner.[31] The second approach consists of 'sectoral agreements': voluntary anti-corruption agreements signed by individual companies from given sectors. This collective action model was inspired by a similar initiative in Colombia, whereby companies commit to observe various transparency and anti-corruption principles.

Although there was considerable difficulty at first in persuading companies to commit to these agreements, two sectoral agreements have now been secured since the Anti-Corruption Law entered into force. The first, among companies from the health product sector and headed by the Ethos Institute with the support of the Brazilian Association of Importers and Distributors of Implants (Abraidi), was signed in mid-2015. The second, involving a number of sports sponsorship companies, has been led by Ethos in partnership with the Atletas pelo Brasil (Athletes for Brazil, composed of current and former athletes) non-governmental organisation. Several sponsors of FIFA and the Confederação Brasileira de Futebol are due to sign in a ceremony in August 2015.

Notes

1   The authors are a professor and eight students from the University of Richmond School of Law, Virginia, studying Brazil's anti-corruption reforms. Their complete report should be available in the spring of 2016.
2   From 1889 to 1930 the country was a 'democracy-in-kind', influenced by the coffee and rubber industries in an oligarchical form. Between 1930 and 1945 a military junta led to Getúlio Vargas being installed after a successful coup. After another coup in 1945 a weak democratic government ruled from Rio de Janerio, and later Brasilia, before falling to a third coup in 1964. From then a series of five generals controlled the country as dictators until democracy was again restored in 1985. A new constitution was drafted in 1988. See *New York Times* (US), 'A brief history of Brazil', *www.nytimes.com/fodors/top/features/travel/destinations/centralandsouthamerica/brazil/riodejanerio/fdrs_feat_129_9.html?pagewanted=1&n=Top/Features/Travel/Destinations/Central%20and%20South%20America/Brazil/Rio/%20de%20Janeiro*.
3   Fernando Prestes Motta and Rafael Alcadipani, 'Jeitinho brasileiro, controle social e competição', *Revista de Administração de Empresas*, vol. 39 (1999), *www.scielo.br/pdf/rae/v39n1/v39n1a02.pdf*.
4   This includes the Autoridade Pública Olímpica (APO), which in a presentation reiterated the fact that Brazil is an emerging young nation that is changing in order to adapt to Western norms. This includes the implementation of the Transparency Matrix, which the APO argued was a sign of Brazil's changing approach to corruption.
5   Beginning in the middle of March 2015, several nationwide protests have called for the president's impeachment.
6   For an English translation of the constitution of the Federative Republic of Brazil, see *www.stf.jus.br/repositorio/cms/portalstfinternacional/portalstfsobrecorte_en_us/anexo/constituicao_ingles_3ed2010.pdf*.
7   Brazilian Anti-Corruption Act, Lei no. 12.846 (Federal Law no. 12,846/2013), *www.planalto.gov.br/ccivil_03/_ato2011-2014/2013/lei/l12846.htm*.

8   Leonardo Ruiz Machado, 'President Dilma Rousseff regulates the Brazilian Anti-Corruption Act' (São Paulo: Machado, Meyer, Sendacz e Opice Advogados, 2015) (on file with lead author).
9   Lei no. 8.666 (Federal Law no. 8,666/1993), *www.planalto.gov.br/ccivil_03/leis/l8666cons. htm*.
10   Interview with lawyers at Machado Meyer, March 2015 (on file with lead author).
11   Lei no. 12.462 (Federal Law no. 12,462/2011), *www.planalto.gov.br/ccivil_03/_ato2011- 2014/2011/Lei/L12462.htm*.
12   For the lawsuit filed by various political parties, see *www.stf.jus.br/portal/processo/ verProcessoAndamento.asp?incidente=4131802* (in Portuguese). For a lawsuit filed by the Attorney General of the Republic, see *www.stf.jus.br/portal/processo/verProcesso Andamento.asp?incidente=4138546*. See also Daniel Teixeira, 'The differential public procurement regime ("RDC") for the 2014 Brazil FIFA World Cup and the 2016 Rio Olympics', paper presented at 6th International Public Procurement Conference, 15 August 2014.
13   Autoridade Pública Olímpica, 'About APO', *www.apo.gov.br/index.php/about-apo*.
14   Interview with the Autoridade Pública Olímpica, Rio de Janeiro, 13 March 2015 (notes on file with lead author).
15   See Cidade Olímpica, 'Empresa Olímpica Municipal', *www.cidadeolimpica.com.br/ empresaolimpica*.
16   See Rio 2016, *Candidature File for Rio de Janeiro to Host the 2016 Olympic and Paralympic Games* (Brasília: Ministério do Esporto, 2009), vol. I, p. 53, *www.rio2016.com/en/organising- committee/transparency/documents*.
17   Interview with the APO, 13 March 2015.
18   This ranking is according to the Corruption Perceptions Index: *www.transparency.org/ cpi2014/results*.
19   *Guardian* (UK), 'Petrobras scandal: Brazilian oil executives among 35 charged', 12 December 2014, *www.theguardian.com/world/2014/dec/12/petrobras-scandal- brazilian-oil-executives-among-35-charged*.
20   Brasil 2016, 'Matriz de Responsabilidades', *www.brasil2016.gov.br/en/paraolimpiadas/ governan%C3%A7a/matriz-de-responsabilidades*; and see the website of Tribunal de Contas do Município do Rio de Janeiro: *www.tcm.rj.gov.br*.
21   See *http://brasil2016.gov.br/en/noticias/olympic-public-authority-apo-publishes-update- responsibility-matrix*.
22   Brasil 2016, 'Matriz de Responsabilidades'.
23   Lei no. 289 (Federal Law no. 289/1981).
24   Rio Olympics Neighborhood Watch (Brazil), 'Pacifying Police Unit (UPP installations) part 3: 2012', *www.rioonwatch.org/?p=20694*. RioOnWatch is a programme managed by Catalytic Communities (CatComm), a non-profit organisation with a US 501(c)(3) charitable status based in Rio de Janeiro that advocates for the rights of favela communities impacted by the upcoming 2016 Summer Olympic Games in the city. The website RioOnWatch.org is the principle means whereby CatComm publishes reports and relevant news stories.
25   Rio 2016 (2009).
26   João Saravia, *Procurement for Rio 2016™ Olympic and Paralympic Games* (São Paulo: Rio 2016, 2012), *www.brazilcouncil.org/sites/default/files/OlympicCommittee_Procurement%20 Presentation2012.pdf*; Rio 2016, 'Rio 2016 launches procurement portal in order to meet Games demands', 8 August 2013, *www.rio2016.org/en/news/news/rio-2016-launches- procurement-portal-in-order-to-meet-games-demands*.
27   Instituto Ethos is based in São Paulo, and seeks to mobilise, encourage and help companies manage their business in a socially responsible manner.
28   See the Clean Games website: *www.jogoslimpos.org.br*.
29   Federal Law no. 12,846, Lei anticorrupção, entered into force on 1 August 2013.
30   Law no. 12.527, Lei de acesso à informação, entered into force on 18 November 2011; see *www.planalto.gov.br/ccivil_03/_ato2011-2014/2011/lei/l12527.htm*.

31   United Nations Global Compact, *Combatendo a Corrupção no Patrocínio Esportivo e nas Ações de Hospitalidade: Um Guia Prático para Empresas* [*Fighting Corruption in Sport Sponsorship and Hospitality: A Practical Guide for Companies*] (New York: UN Global Compact Office, 2014), *www.jogoslimpos.org.br/wp-content/uploads/2014/06/Guia_Combate_Corrupcao_no_Patrocionio.pdf.*

3.15

Sports mega-event legacies

From the beneficial to the destructive

Helen Lenskyj[1]

Sports mega-events, most notably the Olympic Games, have generated legacies that range from beneficial to destructive. Potentially positive outcomes include short-term boosts to tourism and local economies, and improved sporting facilities and infrastructure. Although negative financial, social and environmental impacts are widespread and thoroughly documented, they are overshadowed by the Olympic industry's 'feel-good' mythology and mainstream media's pro-Olympic bias. An understanding of exaggerated and misleading legacy promises related to recent Olympics will help to inform future 'resistance' efforts.

Olympic principles and promises

In common usage, a 'legacy' is a benefit handed down by one's predecessors. In the context of the Olympic industry,[2] the term includes the post-Olympic boost to civic pride and world-class city status, as well as improvements to infrastructure and sporting facilities. Since Olympic organisers' accounting methods usually exclude capital spending, however, it is misleading to present construction projects as a legacy.[3] New infrastructure and sporting facilities concentrated in one urban area, but heavily subsidised with public money from all citizens in the host state/province and country, do not constitute an Olympic windfall. They are, in effect, a cash purchase made on behalf of taxpayers by elected representatives, who are frequently pressured by the government in power to vote in a non-partisan manner on Olympic spending. Even at the bid stage, opposition or critique by local politicians is rare, although, in 2014, in what may prove to be an emerging trend, Munich, Oslo and St Moritz all withdrew their bids for the 2022 Winter Olympics following negative referendum results and concerns about mounting costs.[4] Similarly, in Boston, the US bid city for the 2024 Olympics, community opposition has forced organisers to agree to a referendum on the bid in 2016.[5]

The internal structure of the International Olympic Committee (IOC), bid committees and organising committees is characterised by a critical lack of accountability and transparency, while the myth that sport is, or should be, apolitical silences critics.[6] The popular call to 'keep politics out of the Olympics' belies the fact that they are by definition political: they involve politicians and significant amounts of public money. By officially recognising a country's Olympic committee and welcoming it to the Olympic fold, the IOC has long had significant political power on the world stage, in effect 'conferring political recognition although [it] had no formal diplomatic status'.[7]

The IOC, a self-appointed, self-perpetuating body, views its members as representatives *to*, not representatives *of*, their home countries.[8] It is difficult to imagine any other international body that could function in this way, although one researcher has suggested parallels with the Roman Catholic Church.[9] Given the pseudo-religious mythology surrounding *Olympism*, the Olympic *spirit* and the Olympic *Movement*, as well as the IOC's self-defined status as the 'supreme authority on world sport', the analogy is fitting.

Following the bribery and corruption scandals of 1998/1999, linked to the bid for the 2002 Winter Games in Salt Lake City, Utah, the IOC has claimed to have introduced significant reforms.[10] However, since that time there have been at least two examples in the public domain of questionable arrangements relating to the bid process, one involving two prime ministers, Tony Blair and Silvio Berlusconi,[11] and the other Vancouver bid committee chair John Furlong and Russian oligarch Yury Luzhkov.[12] Blair described a private visit in 2004 to his 'friend' Berlusconi, who subsequently assured him that the Italian IOC members would support London's 2012 bid. In Furlong's case, during the 2003 bid process for the 2010 Winter Olympics, he promised to give Luzhkov Vancouver's campaign strategy to aid Russia's 2014 bid, in exchange for Russian votes for Vancouver's 2010 bid. The fact that Blair and Furlong both disclosed details of these events in their published memoirs reflects a sense of entitlement and immunity that is common in Olympic decision-making circles. For its part, the IOC sided with Furlong's assertion that the deal was neither illegal nor unethical. After a superficial investigation, it claimed that those involved were not bound by the IOC's code of conduct – despite the fact that the code clearly governs bid committee members – and dismissed the matter.[13]

The single goal of a bid committee is to win the right to host the games, and generating support through promises in its bids of affordable housing, sporting facilities and infrastructure makes the bid more appealing to the taxpaying public. Regardless of social and environmental impact assessments, community consultations and government involvement, the organising committee is under no direct obligation to that public. In fact, in the case of Sydney 2000, the organising committee protected itself from Freedom of Information requests by using private subcontractors that were by definition non-government bodies.[14] Oversight of Olympic preparations lies in the hands of a coordination commission appointed by the IOC, whose chief concern is timely completion of Olympic-related construction. At the local level, public order bylaws, municipal development applications and social/environmental impact assessments are frequently fast-tracked, and, in these scenarios, the rights of homeless people and tenants are disregarded, low-income housing is gentrified and environmental damage is incurred.[15]

The IOC introduced the principle of environmentally sustainable development (ESD) as a requirement for Olympic host cities in 1991, but this policy is, at best, of the 'light green' or 'greenwashing' variety – appearing environmentally sustainable while not threatening corporate profit. In the case of the Sydney 2000 Summer Olympics, for example, two rare and protected woodlands were demolished to construct a cycling track, while, in preparations for the Vancouver 2010 Winter Games, an endangered ecosystem was destroyed to make way for Olympic highway construction.[16]

In 2014, when the official IOC strategic plan, Agenda 2020, was introduced, ESD requirements were diluted when the document encouraged the use of temporary or demountable facilities 'where no long-term legacy need exists or can be justified' – a move that, ironically, also eroded bid boosters' legacy promises. As the same document also requires 'state-of-the-art' facilities, it seems unlikely that a temporary building would suffice.[17] Furthermore, one of the criteria for evaluation bids refers to pre-existing facilities, which obviously cannot be considered 'state-of-the-art' if they are standing when the bid is prepared, seven years before the event. On a more positive note, Agenda 2020 managed to include some changes that made the bid process less expensive and cumbersome. However, in the face of diminished interest in hosting the 2022 Winter Olympics – with only two bid cities in the running by the end of 2014 – the motive for these changes may have been self-interest.

Legacies: unplanned and undelivered

Given the critical lack of transparency and accountability relating to Olympic bids, preparations and outcomes, it is not surprising that many planned or promised legacies fail to materialise. Vancouver's 2010 bid committee redefined 'legacy' by creating an organisation called 2010 Legacies Now in 2000, three years before the bid was submitted, with the goal of 'leveraging' the Olympics into 'local, tangible legacies' in hundreds of communities in the province.[18] In reality, as investigative journalist Bob Mackin reported in 2013, there were numerous broken promises. These related to the failure to develop affordable housing, the gentrification of the low-income Downtown Eastside, the use of public money to subsidise the high operating costs of the curling centre, speed skating oval, sliding centre and athletes' village, and the dramatic leap in the province's public debt between 2001 and 2011.[19]

Legacy rhetoric claims that hosting the Olympics will inspire young and old across the host country to become more physically active; that increased rates of sporting participation will flow from the new facilities and opportunities; that the television spectacle of sports played on the 'home field' will spark interest; and that the influence of Olympic 'role models' will promote young people's participation. London's 2012 bid promised 'to inspire a new sporting generation to play sport', but allocated only 1.5 per cent of its budget to a programme called Places People Play.[20] England received the full 1.5 per cent (£135 million, or some US$215 million), while Scotland, which had contributed £150 million (about US$239 million) to staging the games, received none, as did Wales and Northern Ireland.[21] An extensive 2008 Australian government survey covering the post-Olympic period from 2001 to 2008 found that the biggest increases were in non-organised, non-Olympic sports, as well as in aerobics and fitness, while participation in Olympic sports did not grow.[22] These and similar findings point to the difference between Olympic sports, many of which are elitist, expensive and unpopular, and non-Olympic sports, such as cricket, netball and the various codes of football, as well as aerobics and fitness activities, that attract mass participation. Hence, existing recreational interests and priorities will largely determine if an Olympic facility will become a valued legacy or a white elephant. Furthermore, some Olympic venues – ski jumps and sliding centres, for example – can be used safely only by high-performance athletes. Olympic stadiums, constructed with public money, are often turned over to professional sports teams, while maintenance fees for underused facilities continue to demand government subsidies.[23]

In 2008 the state government of New South Wales fast-tracked legislation to convert the central boulevard at the Sydney Olympic site into a car-racing circuit, destroying hundreds of trees in the process, and generating noise, crowds and the risk of toxic spills.[24] Following a similarly problematic conversion, Sochi hosted the Formula One Grand Prix a few months after the 2014 Winter Olympics.[25] In addition, on the issue of 'repurposing', in 2015 Sochi's regional government approved some US$46 million to have the stadium roof removed for the 2018 football World Cup.[26] Other Sochi 'repurposing' projects included converting the speed skating arena into an exhibition centre and tennis academy, dismantling the temporary freestyle skiing venue and using the curling centre as a concert venue – all projects that fail to meet the IOC's environmental principles and Sochi's legacy promises.[27]

Steps towards anti-corruption principles

Since the 1980s anti-Olympic and Olympic watchdog groups in bid and host cities have had some successes in raising public awareness of the financial, social and environmental costs of hosting the Games, as well as identifying the lack of accountability and transparency in relation to public spending for construction and the post-Olympic maintenance of often underused facilities. The biggest challenge facing Olympic resisters is the mythology that surrounds all things Olympic. With seemingly limitless funds for propaganda, the Olympic industry has successfully perpetuated the myths of the 'pure Olympic athlete' and 'pure Olympic sport' – both serving as a smokescreen for the 'underestimated costs and overestimated benefits' that characterise Olympic legacy rhetoric.[28] Thorough documentation of the factual evidence, obtained, for example, through freedom-of-information channels, is a key first step in challenging the hyperbole and holding elected representatives accountable.

Notes

1 Helen Lenskyj is professor emerita at the University of Toronto, Ontario Institute for Studies in Education.
2 The term 'Olympic industry' is used to emphasise the profit motive and the involvement of corporate sponsors, broadcast rights holders, developers, resort and hotel owners, and other business stakeholders. See, for example, Helen Lenskyj, *Inside the Olympic Industry: Power, Politics and Activism* (Albany, NY: SUNY Press, 2000).
3 The omission of capital spending was identified as early as September 2000, at the time of the Sydney Olympics: *Globe and Mail* ('Report on Business') (Canada), 'Summer Olympic red alert', September 2000.
4 *Guardian* (UK), 'Oslo withdrawal from Winter Olympics bidding is missed opportunity – IOC', 2 October 2014, *www.theguardian.com/sport/2014/oct/02/oslo-withdrawal-winter-olympics-2022-ioc*.
5 *Boston Globe* (US) 'With referendum, Boston residents to have say on 2024 Olympics', 24 March 2015, *www.bostonglobe.com/metro/2015/03/24/boston-calls-for-statewide-referendum-olympic-plans/KVjS0zU1jRjexUa3ElstfM/story.html*.
6 Helen Lenskyj, 'Olympic power, Olympic politics: behind the scenes', in A. Bairner and Gyozo Molnar (eds), *The Politics of the Olympics* (London: Routledge, 2010).
7 Richard Espy, *The Politics of the Olympic Games* (Berkeley, CA: University of California Press, 1979), p. 28.
8 See the IOC member list and description on the IOC website: *www.olympic.org/ioc-members-list*.
9 Saul Fridman, 'Conflict of interest, accountability and corporate governance: the case of the IOC and SOCOG', *University of New South Wales Law Journal*, vol. 22 (1999), *www.austlii.edu.au/au/journals/UNSWLJ/1999/28.html*.
10 *Guardian* (UK), 'Bribes scandal forces Olympics shake-up', 29 January 1999, *www.theguardian.com/sport/1999/jan/25/olympic-bribes-scandal-investigation*.
11 Tony Blair, *A Journey: My Political Life* (Toronto: Knopf, 2010), p. 546.
12 John Furlong, with Gary Mason, *Patriot Hearts: Inside the Olympics that Changed a Country* (Vancouver: Douglas & McIntyre, 2011), pp. 46–47; National Public Radio (US), 'IOC scrutinizes Vancouver Olympics bidding deal', 24 February 2011, *www.npr.org/2011/02/24/134015260/ioc-scrutinizes-vancouver-olympics-bidding-deal*.
13 ESPN (US), 'IOC clears John Furlong', 12 March 2011, *http://sports.espn.go.com/oly/news/story?id=6209719*.
14 See Helen Lenskyj, *The Best Olympics Ever? Social Impacts of Sydney 2000* (Albany, NY: SUNY Press, 2002), pp. 26–28.
15 Centre on Housing Rights and Evictions (COHRE), *Fair Play for Housing Rights: Mega-Events, Olympic Games and Housing Rights* (Geneva: COHRE, 2007).

16 Lenskyj (2002), p. 160; Helen Lenskyj, *Olympic Industry Resistance: Challenging Olympic Power and Propaganda* (Albany, NY: SUNY Press, 2008), p. 62.

17 International Olympic Committee, *Olympic Agenda 2020: 20+20 Recommendations* (Lausanne: IOC, 2014), *www.olympic.org/Documents/Olympic_Agenda_2020/Olympic_Agenda_2020-20-20_Recommendations-ENG.pdf.*

18 See the 2010 Legacies Now website: *http://2010andbeyond.ca.*

19 *The Tyee* (Canada), 'Ten legacies of the Vancouver Olympics', 2 July 2013, *http://thetyee.ca/News/2013/07/02/Vancouver-Olympics-Legacies.*

20 *Independent* (UK), 'The last word: London's legacy is a big fat myth', 26 June 2011, *www.independent.co.uk/sport/olympics/the-last-word-londons-legacy-is-a-big-fat-myth-2303005.html.*

21 Ibid.

22 Australian Sports Commission and Department of Health and Ageing, *Participation in Exercise, Physical Activity and Sport: Annual Report 2007–2008* (Canberra: Australian Sports Commission, 2008), p. 18.

23 See, for example, *The Tyee* (2 July 2013).

24 *Sydney Morning Herald* (Australia), 'Tree felling for V8 Supercars gets black flag', 31 July 2009.

25 *CNN News* (US), 'Sochi's formula for the future: "fantasy" becomes reality', 22 February 2014, *www.edition.cnn.com/2014/02/21/sport/sochi-formula-one-winter-olympics-ecclestone-tilke-f1/index.html.*

26 *Moscow Times* (Russia), 'Russia to spend $50 million taking roof off Sochi Olympic stadium', 20 January 2015, *www.themoscowtimes.com/article.php?id=514657.*

27 Architecture of the Games blog, 'Sochi 2014: one year on', 24 February 2015, *http://architectureofthegames.net/2014-sochi/sochi-2014-one-year-on/; Nemtsov* (Moscow), '**Зимняя Олимпиада в субтропиках: коррупция и произвол**', 7 June 2013, *www.nemtsov.ru/old.phtml?id=718790*. For a full discussion of the Sochi 2014 Winter Olympics, see Helen Lenskyj, *Sexual Diversity and the Sochi 2014 Olympics* (Basingstoke: Palgrave Macmillan, 2014).

28 David Whitson and John Horne, 'Underestimated costs and overestimated benefits? Comparing the outcomes of sports mega-events in Canada and Japan', in John Horne and Wolfram Manzenreiter (eds), *Sports Mega-Events: Social Scientific Analyses of a Global Phenomenon* (Oxford: Blackwell, 2006).

3.16

Urban speculation by Spanish football clubs

Nefer Ruiz Crespo[1]

Corruption and football have always gone hand in hand. The 'beautiful game' deals with huge amounts of money, and public institutions have all too often been accused of possible corrupt involvement.

The fact that a 2013 Europol report exposed a corruption network in professional football involving match-fixing in more than 15 countries and 425 individuals around the world,[2] but with no Spanish among them, might suggest that Spanish football is not implicated. The reality is quite different, however. Corruption in Spanish football tends to assume a different form, through urban-planning speculation, with clubs becoming involved in land 'rezoning',[3] and often, allegedly, collaborating with government institutions.

Urban-planning corruption in Spanish football derives from the rezoning of land that is a consequence of the real-estate boom in recent decades, combined with the growing political and social influence of football clubs. Social pressures generated by these football authorities first led the Spanish government, primarily the Treasury and the Ministry of Employment and Social Security,[4] to allow clubs to become burdened with progressively higher levels of indebtedness.[5] Debts became so high that it was clear the clubs could never realistically pay them back.[6]

A new Sports Act (Law 10/1990) was therefore enacted to redress the debt imbalance and improve the transparency of companies operating in professional sports in Spain.[7] The law obliged an indebted club to be legally categorised as a 'sociedad anónima deportiva' (SAD), a 'public limited sports company' – a special form of public limited company in Spain. This allowed the government to negotiate with these clubs on how to repay their debts in instalments, according to their economic circumstances.[8] In Spain there are only four football clubs that are not SADs: Real Madrid CF, FC Barcelona, Athletic Club Bilbao and Osasuna Athletic Club.

Conversion to SAD status also meant that clubs' social capital was put on sale through company shares. When this coincided with a national urban development model that encouraged speculation, the absence of anti-corruption oversight, coupled with an abuse of public power arising from massive political decentralisation, created the ideal conditions for criminal enterprise.[9]

Boom times to 2010

After 1990 the construction of most football fields in Spain has consisted of relocating the new stadium to the outskirts of the city on land of little value, which has then been rezoned by the municipalities, thus converting rural land into urban areas and giving rise to speculation and profiteering from the sale of the remaining land.[10] The clubs of the Spanish First and Second Divisions have collectively made more than €1 billion from rezoning to date.[11]

Illegal activities were carried out through agreements between the clubs' management and public agencies with zoning authority.[12] Rural land or spaces were rezoned for public facilities and services (parks, petrol stations, etc.) through clause modifications not requiring the revision of the General Urban Plan.[13] The intensity of the alterations carried out by these clause modifications was significant enough to merit a review by higher authorities but, because they were simply clause modifications, they were approved.[14] With this rezoning, deviating from the common interest and the spirit of the law, large sports facilities were built and, at the same time, commercial complexes were constructed around the facilities, on land that now had a much higher value than before the rezoning.[15] In this way, clubs received large revenues, which served to stabilise their finances, and, in turn, the local councils benefited from the rezoning and increased their assets.

Many SAD clubs and boards of directors have been investigated for rezoning corruption or illegal transfers[16] since the enactment of Law 10/1990.[17] These have largely been cases of mismanagement conducted by club leaders, most of them businessmen linked to building businesses (19 of La Liga's 42 teams in the First and Second Divisions have fallen into bankruptcy since the creation of SAD clubs).[18] These leaders, elevated to administrative roles in top clubs by purchasing blocks of shares, took advantage of their position and sought solutions to debt through speculation on urban land, often with the participation of public agencies.[19]

Examples of this practice include the city council of Murcia, which purchased one million square metres of rural land for €3 per square metre, reclassified it and then valued it at €600 per square metre, with an increase of 20,000 per cent for the construction of a new stadium: the New Condomina.[20] Similarly, Valencia Football Club announced plans to demolish the Mestalla stadium, sell the site and build a new field on newly reclassified land to the north of the city (the stadium is still standing but a court order has mandated its demolition soon).[21] Even the Royal Spanish Football Federation (RFEF) was implicated in a 1998 urban-planning scandal for an irregular transfer of 120,000 square metres of public land by the municipality of Las Rozas, just outside Madrid. In 2007 the Superior Court of Madrid confirmed the illegality of the transfer of public land, and ruled that the land be returned to Las Rozas.[22]

Investigations of the multiple and complex relationships between private football clubs and public money led in 2011 to the approval of a Regulation of Economical Control to promote accountability, increase transparency and protect creditors. In 2013 the regulation was completed with the 'rules of economic control a priori of 2013', ratified by the Sports Council of the Spanish government. Similarly, article 74.2 (d) of Law 10/1990, the Sports Act, gives professional leagues the administrative authority to discipline and sanction clubs in order to establish order and rationalise club finances.[23]

Urban-planning regulation needs to improve in Spain, as current standards are ineffective in controlling land speculation activity. One of the greatest problems in urban development control is the wide range of agents who have discretion over matters of urban planning, leading to confusion and legal uncertainty. If all the state and regional regulations were published together, the document would be over 5,000 pages long.[24] Implementing the legal framework contained in the Land Act of 2008 could be a good step towards reducing the number of competing authorities in this area, though it would probably fall short in this respect.[25]

Any urban-planning anti-corruption strategy requires several instruments to be effective: a clear and strong political will to raise collective awareness and provide the means to overcome it; strong sanctions for perpetrators; citizen involvement; and the assessment of both public

The city council of the City of Murcia purchased 1 million square metres of rural land for €3 per square metre, reclassified it, and then valued it at €600 per square metre for the construction of the New Condomina stadium.

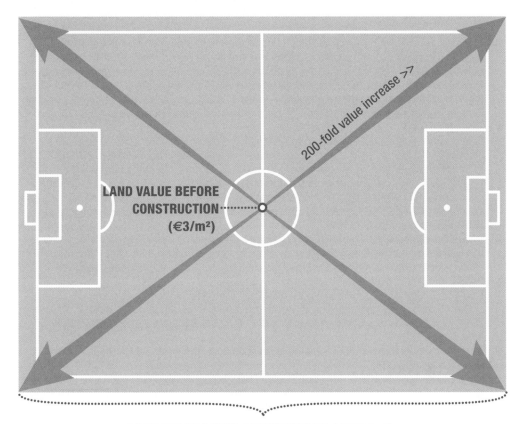

LAND VALUE AFTER CONSTRUCTION (€600/m²)

Figure 3.10 Land value before and after construction of the New Condomina stadium, Murcia

Source: *El Periódico Extremadura*, 'El presidente del Real Murcia protagoniza un sonoro pelotazo', 16 February 2004, *www.elperiodicoextremadura.com/noticias/deportes/presidente-real-murcia-protagoniza-sonoro-pelotazo_96698.html*.

and private institutions' vulnerability to corruption.[26] Rigorous administrative control is necessary in Spain, but is in short supply. Such oversight is at the discretion of the local councils themselves, with no real control exercised by the regional governments, even though this is stipulated by law. Greater legal/administrative control should begin with the creation of a state agency that monitors urban planning, as well as a reformulation of urban-planning laws in the country.[27]

Notes

1   Nefer Ruiz Crespo is a lawyer working at A25 Abogados y Economistas sl, and is a member of Transparency International Spain.

2 Europol, 'Results from the largest football match-fixing investigation in Europe', 6 February 2013, *www.europol.europa.eu/content/results-largest-football-match-fixing-investigation-europe.*

3 See Público (Spain), 'Bruselas confirma el expediente a Real Madrid y Barça por recibir ayudas públicas ilegales', 18 December 2013, *www.publico.es/deportes/490070/ bruselas-confirma-el-expediente-a-real-madrid-y-barca-por-recibir-ayudas-publicas-ilegales.*

4 The debt incurred with the social security corresponds to the proportion of the IRPF (personal income tax) of the player's salary that has to be paid by the club (third paragraph of the reference). See article V of the Finance Law, chapter II, Del régimen de la Hacienda Pública estatal, section 1a, Derechos de la Hacienda Pública estatal, at 'Ley 47/2003, de 26 de noviembre, General Presupuestaria' ['Law 47/2003, of 26 November, on the General Budget']: *www.seg-social.es/Internet_1/Normativa/index.htm?ssUserText=188871&dDocN ame=195014#5.*

5 *El Economista* (Spain), 'El fútbol profesional español debe 752 millones de euros sólo a Hacienda', 13 March 2015, *http://ecodiario.eleconomista.es/futbol/noticias/3816543/03/12/ El-futbol-profesional-espanol-debe-a-Hacienda-752-millones-de-euros.html#Kku8Wm V3SS234GfV;* El Confidencial (Spain), 'Montoro da vida a los clubes de fútbol al aplazarles deuda por 255 millones de euros', 29 September 2014, *www.elconfidencial.com/ economia/2014-09-29/montoro-da-vida-a-los-clubes-de-futbol-al-aplazarles-deuda-por-255-millones-de-euros_216617.*

6 See El Confidencial (Spain), 'Atlético y Deportivo lideran el ranking de la deuda con 120 y 90 millones de euros', 8 July 2013, *www.elconfidencial.com/deportes/futbol/2012/03/15/ atletico-y-deportivo-lideran-el-ranking-de-la-deuda-con-120-y-90-millones-de-euros-94365.*

7 Law 10/1990 of 15 October, on Sport; effective from 6 November 1990.

8 *El País* (Spain), 'La Liga intensifica la presión para aplazar la deuda de los clubes', 7 October 2014, *http://deportes.elpais.com/deportes/2014/10/06/actualidad/1412620473_204155. html.*

9 Juan-Cruz Alli Aranguren, 'Del inicio de la prueba de la corrupción urbanística', *Auditoría Pública*, no. 46 (2008).

10 For a detailed assessment, see Jordi Blasco Díez, 'La especulación inmobiliaria de los clubs de fútbol en España', *Revista Bibliográfica de Geografía y Ciencias Sociales*, vol. 13 (2008).

11 Ibid.

12 Ibid.

13 Ibid.

14 See, for example, 20 Minutos (Spain), 'El ladrillazo: los ayuntamientos con urnaismo polémico', 18 June 2008, *www.20minutos.es/noticia/165247/0/corruptelas/urbanisticas/ ediles.* See also Alli Aranguren (2008).

15 Manuel Villoria Mendieta, 'Corrupción en España', in Peter Eigen (ed.), *Las Redes de la Corrupción: La Sociedad civil contra los Abusos del Poder* (Barcelona: Planeta, 2003).

16 See, for example, IUSport.es, 'El Supremo reitera la ilegalidad de la Ciudad Deportiva de Las Rozas', 4 March 2010, *www.iusport.es/php2/index.php?option=com_content&task=vie w&id=1158&Itemid=27.*

17 The European Union has indicted seven Spanish football clubs for possible violations of EU free competition regulations regarding the acceptance of state aid. See El Diario (Spain), 'Los "señores" del fútbol español, de la A a la Z', 26 January 2015, *www.eldiario.es/ deportes/duenos-futbol-espanol_0_221528591.html.*

18 They include Alfonso García Gabarron (president of Union Deportiva Almería), Enrique Ortiz (president of Hercules Football Club), Agapito Iglesias (former president of the Real Zaragoza SAD) and Jesus Samper Vidal (Real Murcia Football Club). For a recent case and background, see *As* (Spain), 'Se abre una causa general de la FIFA contra el fútbol español', 27 January 2015, *http://futbol.as.com/futbol/2015/01/27/primera/1422317098_357755. html;* and *El País* (Spain), 'A diabolical business', 17 April 2013, *http://elpais.com/elpais/ 2013/04/17/inenglish/1366204502_127818.html.*

19 For a detailed assessment, see Jordi Blasco Díez, 'La especulación inmobiliaria de los clubs de fútbol en España', *Revista Bibliográfica de Geografía y Ciencias Sociales*, vol. 13 (2008).

20 *El Periódico Extremadura* (Spain), 'El presidente del Real Murcia protagoniza un sonoro pelotazo', 16 February 2004, *www.elperiodicoextremadura.com/noticias/deportes/ presidente-real-murcia-protagoniza-sonoro-pelotazo_96698.html*.

21 *El Mundo* (Spain), 'El Valencia será multado si la UE prueba que recibió ayudas ilegales', 18 September 2014, *www.elmundo.es/comunidad-valenciana/2014/09/18/541a888ce2704 ed6768b456c.html*; Valencia Plaza (Spain), 'Recados para Lim: La Generalitat reactiva el proyecto del nuevo campo de Mestalla', 4 June 2015, *www.valenciaplaza.com/ver/ 132642/-recados-para-lim--la-generalitat-reactiva-el-proyecto-del-nuevo-campo-de-mestalla.html*.

22 See *Marca* (Spain), 'Bruselas expedienta a Real Madrid y Barça por ayudas de Estado ilegales', 16 December 2013, *www.marca.com/2013/12/16/futbol/1adivision/1387212302. html?a=5c595d78d2f1353e1ba3e6dd975a8977&t=1423264575*; *La Vanguardia* (Spain), 'Bruselas expedient a Madrid, Barça y otros cinco clubes', *www.lavanguardia.com/ deportes/20131218/54398344430/bruselas-expedienta-a-madrid-barca-y-otros-cinco-clubes.html*; *El Mundo* (Spain), 'Bruselas expedienta a España por ayudas ilegales a a siete clubes de fútbol', 16 December 2013, *www.elmundo.es/deportes/2013/12/16/52af2b9f61f d3de1798b4599.html*; and IUSport.es, 'El Supremo reitera la ilegalidad de la Ciudad Deportiva de Las Rozas', 4 March 2010, *www.iusport.es/php2/index.php?option=com_ content& task=view&id=1158&Itemid=27*.

23 Noticias Jurídicas (Spain), 'Ley 10/1990, de 15 de octubre, del Deporte: titulo XI' ['Law 10/1990, of 15 October, on Sport: article XI'], *http://noticias.juridicas.com/base_datos/ Admin/l10-1990.t11.html#t11*.

24 Fundación Alternativas, *Urbanismo y Democracia: Alternativas para Eviter la Corrupción* (Madrid: Fundación Alternativas, 2007).

25 Ibid.

26 See Spanish-language edition (Buenos Aires: Editorial Sudamérica, 1994), pp. 10 et seq., of Robert Klitgaard, *Controlling Corruption* (Berkeley, CA: University of California Press, 1988).

27 Fundación Alternativas (2007).

PART 4

Match-fixing

4.1

Why sport is losing the war to match-fixers

Declan Hill[1]

The war against match-fixers is being lost. Part of the reason for the defeat is that the anti-match-fixing industry is drowning in nonsense – nonsense that is being propagated by a mixture of commercial agendas, professional conflicts of interest and ignorance. This chapter will do two things: first, it will show the *real* situation of current-day match-fixing; second, it will explain some of the key mistakes in contemporary research into match-fixing.

Methods

This chapter is based on a mixture of quantitative and qualitative research techniques. I conducted over 400 interviews with players, referees, coaches, team managers, league officials, policemen, prosecutors, bookmakers, gamblers and match-fixers who have direct experience in match-fixing. Along with the interviews, there has also been a text analysis of a 'confession databank', consisting of documents (over 450,000 words) gathered from 30 jurisdictions.

The research has also been shaped by behavioural observation, when I directly witnessed match-fixers attempting to corrupt matches at major international football tournaments. In addition, there is a quantitative analysis from the construction of several databases. The two key databases relate to fixed/non-fixed games and fixing/non-fixing players.[2]

Match-fixing explained

There has always been match-fixing in sport. If you had gone to the stadium of the ancient Olympics in Greece, you would have found a row of statues. These statues had been built with fines paid by athletes who had fixed a result or cheated thousands of years ago. Fixing has a long history and has touched many sports.

We of this generation are facing an almost entirely new form of match-fixing, however. It is as if someone had taken fixing and injected it with the steroid of globalisation. This new form of match-fixing is sweeping through sport. It has destroyed many Asian sports. It is now threatening tennis, cricket, football and a host of other sports based in Europe. This wave of corruption is also lapping at the doors of North American sport.

In the last five years over 1,000 sports events – from top-level soccer games to Olympic badminton matches to international cricket competitions – have been fixed. Hundreds of athletes, coaches, referees and gamblers have been arrested. It is a revolution in sport, which reaches from dingy bookmakers on the streets of Asia to some of the largest stadiums in the world.

The essential issue of this new wave of match-fixing is the globalisation of the sports gambling market. A generation ago it was not worth fixing many events in relatively minor sports leagues. Nowadays, though, three factors drive the profitability of modern-day fixing:[3]

1. the liquidity of the sports gambling market has grown and become unified;
2. it is now possible to bet money on more games in more leagues; and
3. international broadcasts are bringing sports to new audiences.

Contemporary match-fixing

In the early 1990s a group of match-fixers based in Malaysia/Singapore and Indonesia began to travel to international football tournaments to corrupt teams and games. In interviews with these fixers, corroborated by football officials, referees and players, their presence was confirmed at the women's World Cup, the Under-17 and the Under-20 World Cups, the Olympic football tournament and the men's World Cup itself between 1991 and 2014.[4]

By the early 2000s, these fixers were also working as brokers for corrupted players/ referees and team officials in dozens of countries in five different continents. Their essential modus operandi was that the players/referees/officials would do the actual fixing of the game. Then they would pass the information to the Asian-based fixers, who would fix the gambling market in a series of manoeuvres to conceal the fix from bookmakers.[5]

Despite the publication of an international best-selling book that revealed the existence of these gangs and a series of successful prosecutions led by German police investigators in Bochum (2011) and Finnish police in Rovaniemi (2011), the fixers continued almost unabated until 2013, when the Singapore authorities finally arrested key leaders of the group.[6] The fixing gangs continue to work in this region, however.[7] Worse for sport, the match-fixing has now spread to a variety of different criminal groups in Russia and China.[8]

The red flags of nonsense

Much of the research into this new form of fixing has been hampered by a series of commercial agendas, conflicts of interest and ignorance. In this section some of these problems are examined.

'Illegal betting'

A few members of the gambling industry have misdirected the debate by emphasising the issue of 'illegal betting' rather than match-fixing. One potential motive for this misdirection is that it helps bookmakers gain a commercial advantage over their rivals if they can declare them 'illegal'.

Despite contemporary match-fixing being driven by the globalisation of the sports gambling market, the discussion of 'illegal betting' is a side issue in the debate on fixing. Almost all bookmakers are legal, wherever their headquarters are located. What they are doing is providing a commercial service that some members of the public want. A senior Asian bookmaker from a company that his European rivals declare to be 'illegal' said in an interview, 'What is "illegal" gambling? What I do is legal on this side of the street. On the other side of the street, it is illegal.'

The real issue is match-fixing. Fixing defrauds bookmakers, whether they are regulated by governments, are private European companies or are located in an Asian tax-free zone.

'The police are not fighting match-fixing'

Sports authorities have an inherent conflict of interest in reporting corruption in their own industry. Their position is akin to that of the owner of a sausage factory who discovers a tainted product: he may try to stop the bad meat being sold, but he also does not want his customers to find out about it.[9]

Accordingly, many sports associations tend to emphasise two flawed concepts when speaking about match-fixing: first, that the police and the government authorities are not doing anything to help them; second, that fixing is largely the preserve of ethically challenged players or referees, who can be educated back to morality.

Even the normally sound researcher Kevin Carpenter may have been swayed by this myth in his 'key framing article' for Transparency International's Corruption in Sport Initiative when he argues that police generally do little work in stopping match-fixing because it is not a priority.[10] The facts are almost completely opposite to this view. Many people involved in official law enforcement actions against match-fixing speak of the difficulty of working with sports officials. This is an excerpt from a typical interview with a senior prosecutor involved in a European match-fixing investigation: 'We [the law enforcement agencies] received no help from the football association. In fact, quite the opposite; they closed ranks. They do not want to admit publicly that it [match-fixing] goes on.' In 2013 I did research on the question 'Who began the investigations of match-fixing?'. This work showed that fewer than 2 per cent of cases were initiated by sports associations; more than 40 per cent were begun by the police.[11]

In Europe alone there have been high-level judicial investigations into match-fixing in 27 countries since 2009. In 24 of them the prosecutors secured convictions of players/referees and team officials.[12] The trials have produced hundreds of thousands of legal documents on fixing. Almost everything evidence-based that is known about the fixers comes from these documents or researchers with first-hand experience of the fixers.[13]

The failure of education campaigns

In early 2015 the Cycling Independent Reform Commission (CIRC) released a report into the failure of anti-doping controls in professional cycling.[14] In the anti-doping world during the 1990s and early 2000s the blame was often pushed onto the athletes rather than officials, who administered a system that covertly encouraged doping. Millions of anti-doping dollars were put into projects to 'educate' athletes. In particular, there was an attempt to portray doping in cycling as an ethical failure on the part of a very few cyclists.

The findings of the CIRC report are very explicit, however. The decision to dope in the 1990s and early 2000s was mostly a result of rational choice. In that era, if a young cyclist wanted to win, he or she was, essentially, forced to dope. Many cyclists who had other ways of making a living left the sport rather than cheat. The athletes who had few other career options stayed in the sport – and, to win, many of them doped.

There are similarities in match-fixing. Currently, there are groups of relatively well-paid consultants and gambling companies giving lectures to relatively badly paid players about the 'ethics' of match-fixing.[15] The ongoing Italian investigations of Serie C and Pro-Lega show the relative failure of the 'education' of players. The police allege that a fixing ring existed in over 30 professional teams in southern Italy. The investigators claim the fixing was organised by the team owners. National police forces in other European countries allege that similar conditions exist in their countries.[16] Milan Sapina was one of the most successful modern-day fixers, with a network of corruption stretching across three continents until he was arrested by German police in 2011. He stated, when I interviewed him in 2007, that there was a similar pattern. Hill: 'Why is there fixing?' Sapina: 'Sometimes it is the clubs who are friends with each other. They may want to help each other. Sometimes it is the president who arranges with the other president. Or sometimes it is the boss of the club. The bosses then bet on the results. It happens a lot in lower divisions.'

These team owners are, in some cases, the same people who help organise anti-match-fixing sessions for their players. This dynamic, whereby the corruptors may be in the room, effectively turns some anti-match-fixing education campaigns into lessons in hypocrisy.

A number of players who were interviewed claim that a similar phenomenon exists in Asian leagues. This is one typical example:[17]

Our team was run by a group of top politicians and I am not saying they were fixing, but I am saying that there were very strong rumours and suspicions around them for several years. I can't accuse him. You have to get proof. These guys are untouchable. You are talking about corruption at the highest level of society. If there is corruption going on at the level that there is no hope, the game has absolutely no hope.

Conclusion

Match-fixing has taken on a new manifestation, linked to the globalised sports gambling market. It is threatening sports around the world. Much of the research on contemporary match-fixing has been misdirected, however; it is time for a return to evidence-based work. As the police investigations into the Fédération Internationale de Football Association (FIFA) in May 2015 have shown, there is a possible nexus between bad sports governance and match-fixing. An executive who commits commercial fraud cannot be expected to crack down on match corruption.

One potential example concerns the South African men's football World Cup in 2010, which was marred by fixers corrupting exhibition matches in the days before the start of the tournament (as well as approaching referees and, potentially, players at the tournament itself).[18] They were helped by at least one person inside the South African Football Association, but there has been no official investigation based in South Africa. In the 164-page indictment released by the US Department of Justice in May 2015 in connection with the FIFA investigations, however, it was alleged, in part, that the South Africans had paid bribes to secure the World Cup hosting rights.[19] If this is correct, it is a potential reason why there has been no South African investigation into the match-fixing.

There are similar cases in other football associations around the world. A recent confidential interview with a senior person involved with sports integrity revealed that, in his opinion, at least half a dozen of the presidents of national football associations have been involved in fixing matches. If this is correct, then the sport needs new solutions in the fight against match-fixing.

One practical solution is to create an independent, anti-corruption agency for sport. Ideally, it would be akin – or even linked – to the World Anti-Doping Agency. It would be financed by arm's-length sponsors and operate separately from sport governance control. It would give whistleblowers and people fighting against sports corruption a secure place to report corruption. If organised and staffed correctly, it would be free from the commercial agendas, professional conflicts of interests and ignorance that clog so much of today's struggle against match-fixing.

Notes

1 Declan Hill is an investigative journalist, academic and documentary-maker.
2 For a more detailed examination of the research methods, see Declan Hill, *The Insider's Guide to Match-Fixing in Football* (Toronto: Anne McDermid, 2013), pp. 14–27.
3 Ibid.
4 Declan Hill, *The Fix: Soccer and Organized Crime* (Toronto: McClelland & Stewart, 2008); Ralf Mutschke, interviewed in *Frankfurter Allgemeine* (Germany), 'Fifa-Sicherheitschef: "Kriminelle wollen WM-Spiele manipulieren"', 12 January 2014, *www.faz.net/aktuell/sport/ fussball-wm/fifa-sicherheitschef-kriminelle-wollen-wm-spiele-manipulieren-12747485.html*; Wilson Perumal, Alessandro Righi and Emanuele Piano, *Kelong Kings: Confession of the World's Most Prolific Match-Fixer* (New York: Invisible Dog Press, 2014).
5 Declan Hill, 'How gambling corruptors fix football matches', *European Sport Management Quarterly*, vol. 9 (2009); Tribunale Ordinario di Cremona, 'Ordinanza di Applicazione della Misura della Custodia Cautelare in Carcere', 9 December 2011, *www.invisible-dog.com/ DOC%20FIX/LAST_BET_ORDINANZA_DIC_2011.pdf*.
6 Hill (2008); Rovaniemen Toimipiste KRP, 'Report on the activities of Wilson Raj Perumal', August 2011; Tribunale Ordinario di Cremona (2011).
7 See, for example, AsiaOne (Singapore), 'SEA Games football hit by fix claims', 20 June 2015, *http://news.asiaone.com/news/sports/sea-games-football-hit-fix-claims*.
8 *Il Messaggero* (Italy), 'Calcioscommesse nella Lega Pro, 50 arresti e 70 indignati tra dirigente e giocatori', 20 May 2015, *http://sport.ilmessaggero.it/calcio/newscalcioscommesse_ arresti_lega_pro_serie_d_giocatori_dirigenti/1362124.shtml*.
9 Hill (2013), p. 248.
10 See Kevin Carpenter, 'Why are countries taking so long to act on match-fixing?', *www. transparency.org/files/content/feature/Feature_TakingLongMatchFixing_Carpenter_GCR Sport.pdf*. Carpenter's analysis is correct in a few jurisdictions, such as Canada, where the police and sports associations *both* claim that 'there is nothing they can do'.
11 Hill (2013), pp. 250–252.
12 In the other three countries – the Netherlands, Spain and Sweden – the investigations are still continuing (as of June 2015).
13 See, for example, Rovaniemen Toimipiste KRP (2011); Tribunale Ordinario di Cremona (2011); Preumal, Righi and Piano (2014); Hill (2008, 2013).
14 Cycling Independent Reform Commission, *Report to the President of the Union Cycliste Internationale* (Aigle, Switzerland: Union Cycliste Internationale, 2015), *https://docs.google. com/viewerng/viewer?url=http://www.cyclisme-dopage.com/actualite/2015-03-08-circ- report.pdf*.
15 Some of the consultants giving these educational sessions have received funding from organisations that suffer from credibility issues on integrity, such as the Fédération Internationale de Football Association and the Qataris.
16 See, for example, Fédération Internationale des Associations Footballeurs Professionnels (FIFPro), *FIFPro Black Book Eastern Europe: The Problems Professional Football Players Encounter* (Hoofddorp, Netherlands: FIFPro, 2012); Inside World Football, 'Greek corruption: Olympiacos owner charged in match-fixing ring round-up', 28 April 2015, *www.insideworld football.com/world-football/europe/16904-greek-corruption-olympiacos-owner-charged- in-match-fixing-ring-round-up*; B92 (Serbia), '"Clubs organize match fixing," says sports minister', 16 June 2015, *www.b92.net/eng/news/politics.php?yyyy=2015&mm=06&dd= 16&nav_id=94455*.
17 Hill (2013), p. 226.
18 *New York Times* (US), 'Fixed soccer matches cast shadow over the World Cup', 31 May 2014, *www.nytimes.com/2014/06/01/sports/soccer/fixed-matches- cast-shadow-over-world-cup.html?_r=0*.
19 United States District Court, Eastern District of New York, Indictment 15 CR 0252 (RJD) (RML), 20 May 2015, *www.justice.gov/opa/file/450211/download*.

4.2

The role of
the betting industry

Ben Van Rompuy[1]

Although match-fixing is not a new phenomenon, the rapid expansion of the global sports betting market and the involvement of transnational organised crime has substantially increased the threat of betting-related match-fixing. This is not only a critical issue for sport, but also for the betting industry – a point that is often overlooked. Apart from the direct losses that they may face in the event of match-fixing, betting operators are also adversely affected in the long term since consumers' confidence in the integrity of sports competitions is vital to their business. In light of this convergence of interests, this chapter explores the pivotal role that the betting industry, operating in a regulated environment, can play in the prevention and fight against betting-related match-fixing.

The Asian betting market

Sports betting has grown into a multi-billion-dollar industry. The gross gaming revenue (GGR) of the regulated sports betting market was estimated at US$58 billion in 2012 and is forecast to reach US$70 billion in 2016.[2] The volume of sports betting on the illegal markets is believed to dwarf the turnover on the regulated market. Some estimates put the total turnover of illegal sports betting at US$500 billion per annum,[3] but the lack of transparency evidently makes it hard to approximate the size of the illegal betting market reliably. Most of this activity emanates from south-east Asian countries, where the failure to provide an attractive, regulated betting market coupled with a culture of gambling has allowed enormous illegal betting networks to flourish. Unfortunately, most of these countries continue to demonstrate a lack of political will to take (more) aggressive action against this black economy.

There is a growing consensus that professional match-fixers predominantly use the illegal Asian betting markets to place their bets directly.[4] Regulated bookmakers generally restrict stakes, require registration and identification of the player and even withdraw betting markets in the case of irregular betting activity. In contrast, the Asian system of bookmaking – in which bets are collected from the street, in betting shops, online and through telephone betting, and are passed up through a hierarchical agent system – allows bets to be placed anonymously and without betting limits. To manage their risks, local illegal operators lay off their unbalanced bets along the chain to the next tier. Eventually many of the bets end up with the largest Asian bookmakers licensed in loosely regulated jurisdictions, such as the Philippines. By then the bets are hidden in larger parcels and almost impossible to trace back to their source.[5]

It would be too easy to put all the blame on the illegal Asian betting markets, however. As various documented cases exemplify, betting-related match-fixing can and does occur also in regulated betting markets. The point is rather that keeping sports betting activity within well-regulated, and therefore controlled, channels is the best way to identify and manage integrity risks. As the remainder of this chapter will demonstrate, in such a regulated environment the betting industry can be an important part of the solution.

Betting monitoring and fraud detection

Like any other type of corruption, betting-related match-fixing is a covert and consensual activity, which makes it extremely difficult to detect instances of fraud. Proactive intelligence-gathering and the sharing of information are therefore critical components of the fight against match-fixing. It is here that regulated betting operators can play a fundamental role.

Over the last decade a number of betting-monitoring systems have been put in place by betting industry bodies (such as the European Sports Security Association and the Global Lottery Monitoring System), sports organisations (for example, the FIFA Early Warning System), commercial monitoring companies (such as Sportradar) and gambling regulators. In parallel to these systems, each betting operator has its own surveillance system, to monitor the betting activity of its customers and to spot unusual movements across the betting market. This is an integral part of betting operators' internal risk management analysis, carried out to control financial risks and thus improve their profitability.

Many sports organisations, especially the better-resourced ones, have entered into voluntary memoranda of understanding (with betting operators or betting industry bodies) and/or commercial agreements (with monitoring companies) to keep themselves informed about irregular betting activities relating to their events. Even so, it is of vital importance that national gambling regulations oblige regulated betting operators to report information on suspicious betting activity to the authorities or the national platform, as envisaged by the Council of Europe Convention on the Manipulation of Sports Competitions.[6] While each of the betting monitoring systems mentioned above have their specific features and assets, typically only the betting operators have access to the records of individual transactions, including the amounts of the bet and the identity of the customer.

Good practice in the European Union highlights the fact that having a centralised platform that coordinates the gathering, analysis and exchange of information-sharing at the national and supranational levels is crucial in addressing the match-fixing threat to sport.[7] A good example is the Sports Betting Intelligence Unit (SBIU), which was created within the United Kingdom's Gambling Commission in 2010. The SBIU acts as the gateway for information on potentially corrupt betting activity related to British sports events. In the vast majority of cases this information is submitted by betting operators.[8] Once a piece of information has been received, such as a report on suspicious betting activity, the SBIU corroborates the report with other pieces of intelligence and decides on the most appropriate course of action, right through to when the case is closed. A detailed investigative decision-making framework documents how the SBIU determines whether to refer the case to a sports governing body or betting operator, proceed to criminal prosecution, issue a caution or take no further action.[9] The underlying presumption of this decision-making framework is that only the more serious cases are likely to be appropriate for criminal sanction. Given that criminal prosecution is a challenging task that requires satisfying a high burden of proof (beyond reasonable doubt), disciplinary action by the sports governing body can often be the most effective – and even, sometimes, the only possible – course of action. Of course, sports organisations are powerless against criminal gangs and individuals outside their sport. Yet one must not forget that while not every match-fixing case has a criminal component, it always has a disciplinary component: a fix can only occur with the involvement of at least one person covered by the regulations of the sports governing body. Preparing and progressing disciplinary proceedings for breaches of these regulations is a necessary component of an effective strategy to combat match-fixing.[10]

Obviously, the operation of national betting integrity platforms raises important questions about adequate resourcing, staffing and the granting of the necessary clearance to process and investigate betting data. Thought would have to be given to how the betting industry might assist in capacity-building at a national level, financially or otherwise. Moreover, it is important to develop guiding principles for what constitutes suspicious betting activity. The requirement for betting operators to report irregular betting patterns to the regulator or the national platform loses much of its relevance if it is left entirely to them to decide when and what to report. The setting of such integrity industry standards demands the involvement of all the relevant stakeholders who have built up experience in this regard. The Follow-up Committee to the Convention on the Manipulation of Sports Competitions would be well placed to foster the development and convergence of standards at the European level.

Betting bans for sportspeople

In most of the leading sports, sports organisations have made it a disciplinary offence for athletes, their support personnel and/or officials to (1) bet on sports events in which they are involved and (2) disclose inside information. Some sports organisations, such as the English Football Association, extend this prohibition to all betting on their sport. Betting bans for sportspeople can also be found in a number of national gambling regulatory frameworks.[11] Although such rules target only possible instances of individual fraud (such as a football player or referee conceiving and exploiting his or her own manipulation), which do not pose the threat that corruption involving criminal organisations does, they have an important educational and deterrence function. By precluding improper influence due to conflicts of interest, these prohibitions embed awareness and compliance in relation to betting-related match-fixing.

The enforcement rate of these betting bans is extremely low, however.[12] The main impediment to effective enforcement is that generally only betting operators, which have a duty to identify their customers, are able to detect non-compliance. In fact, the majority of sports betting operator's terms and conditions equally prohibit people who may influence the results of sports events from placing bets on those events. In the event of any breach of these terms and conditions, the operator may refuse payment of any winnings or cancel the bet (on the grounds of a breach of the contractual basis of the bet), but is not necessarily obliged to report this to the relevant sports organisation. Once again, cooperation between the different stakeholders and information-sharing are essential for the effective protection of integrity in sport and sports betting.

In Australia, for instance, sports organisations may request licensed betting operators to undertake integrity checks, such as an annual check that players and officials have not placed bets on their own sport.[13] In France, pursuant to information obligations imposed on licensed betting operators, the Online Gaming and Regulatory Authority (ARJEL) has access to all betting information related to players registered with these operators (that is, their identity, postal and IP addresses, and details of every gaming activity).[14] Sports federations may request ARJEL to cross-check this information with a data-filing system of all competition stakeholders subject to a betting ban (also specifying the scope of this ban).[15] If the analysis reveals that a person featuring on the 'ban list' has placed any bets, ARJEL informs the federation, which can then initiate disciplinary proceedings for breach of the betting ban.

In the United Kingdom, licensed operators that accept sports bets are required to 'provide the relevant sports governing body with sufficient information to conduct an effective investigation' if the licensee suspects that information in its possession may relate to a breach of a rule applied by a sports governing body.[16] The information provided by the operator can then be used to prepare and progress disciplinary proceedings.

Whatever mechanism is used, the enforcement of betting bans for sportspeople necessitates information-sharing between betting operators and sports organisations (with the regulator or national platform acting as a coordinator). Without such means of collaboration, the bans contained in disciplinary regulations or gambling regulations are of merely symbolic value.

Other conflict-of-interest provisions

The Convention on the Manipulation of Sports Competitions also places considerable emphasis on the need to subject regulated betting operators to strict requirements to prevent conflicts of interest. Among other things, it calls on the signatories to prohibit (1) persons involved in developing sports betting products from betting on these products and (2) the offering of bets on sports events when the operator has a controlling interest in the event or its participants.[17]

The identification and management of potential conflicts of interest on the betting industry's side remains largely unexplored. In Europe, for instance, only a minority of EU member states currently have such arrangements in place: the national gambling regulatory frameworks of only eight such countries impose a betting ban for the operators' owners and employees. While in some cases this betting ban applies solely to those directly involved in the development of the (sports) betting offering (in the Czech Republic, Italy and Sweden, for example), in other member states the ban extends to participation via third persons such as close relatives (such as France, Hungary and Spain).[18] Only six members prohibit regulated betting operators from accepting bets on sports events that they control by way of ownership or employment. In France, betting operators must even notify the regulator of sponsorship agreements with organisers of sports events or their participants. The regulator then scrutinises the agreement to see whether it might conceal an indirect form of control by one party over the other.[19]

Even when prohibitions and restrictions are in place, putting them into daily practice has proved to be a challenge. While most of the gambling regulators check compliance with the regulatory framework (including the conflict-of-interest provisions) in the context of the licensing process, limited staff and resources often impede sufficient or active post-licensing monitoring. Voluntary commitments contained in self-regulatory codes of conduct of betting industry bodies[20] are a useful complement, but not a substitute for implementing binding regulatory requirements. Of the many unknowns connected to the implementation of the recommendations of the Council of Europe's convention, the question of how to ensure compliance with these conflict-of-interest provisions deserves particularly careful attention.

Conclusion: friend or foe?

In recent years the betting industry has become a significant source of sponsorship funding for professional sport, and commercial partnership agreements continue to increase in number. When it comes to preserving the integrity of sport, however, the relationship between the sports world and the betting industry goes from hot to cold. Many international and national sports organisations still fail to understand that close cooperation between all stakeholders, including betting operators, is indispensable in order to combat match-fixing in an effective way. As highlighted in this chapter, regulated betting operators have a crucial role to play, especially in supporting preventative and investigative measures against betting-related match-fixing through the sharing of information.

Notes

1   Professor Ben Van Rompuy is a senior researcher at the TMC Asser Instituut in The Hague, where he heads the Asser International Sports Law Centre, and is a guest professor at the Vrije Universiteit Brussel (Free University of Brussels).
2   GGR is the difference between the wagered amounts and the winnings returned to players. Jason Foley-Train, *Sports Betting: Commercial and Integrity Issues* (Brussels: European Gaming and Betting Association, 2014).
3   Université Paris I Panthéon–Sorbonne, *Fighting Against the Manipulation of Sports Competitions* (Paris: Université Paris I Panthéon–Sorbonne, 2014).
4   See, for example, Interpol, *Match-Fixing in Football: Training Needs Assessment 2013* (Lyon: Interpol, 2013), p. 16; University Paris I Panthéon–Sorbonne and International Centre for Sport Security, *Protecting the Integrity of Sport Competition: The Last Bet for Modern Sport* (London: SportBusiness Communications, 2014), pp. 81–83; Sportradar, *World Match-Fixing: The Problem and the Solution* (St Gallen, Switzerland: Sportradar, 2014), p. 10.
5   David Forrest and Wolfgang Maennig, 'The threat to sports and sports governance from betting-related corruption: causes and solutions', in Paul M. Heywood (ed.) *Routledge Handbook of Political Corruption* (Abingdon: Routledge, 2015).
6   Council of Europe Convention on the Manipulation of Sports Competitions, 18 September 2014, *http://conventions.coe.int/Treaty/EN/Treaties/Html/215.htm*. In Europe, this is currently the case for fewer than half of the EU member states: Oxford Research, *Study on the Sharing of Information and Reporting of suspicious Sports Betting Activity in the EU 28* (Frederiksberg, Denmark: Oxford Research, 2014).
7   TMC Asser Instituut, *Study on Risk Assessment and Management and Prevention of Conflicts of Interest in the Prevention and Fight against Betting-Related Match Fixing in the EU 28* (The Hague: TMC Asser Instituut, 2014).
8   Gambling Commission, *Gambling Industry Statistics April 2009 to March 2014* (Birmingham: Gambling Commission, 2014).
9   Gambling Commission, *The Gambling Commission's Betting Industry Decision Making Framework* (Birmingham: Gambling Commission, 2013), *www.gamblingcommission.gov.uk/pdf/Betting%20integrity%20decision%20making%20framework.pdf*.
10   After all, empirical deterrence research persistently finds that the perceived likelihood of detection and punishment has the most powerful influence on compliance behaviour. For references, see Ben Van Rompuy, 'Effective sanctioning of match-fixing: the need for a two-track approach', *ICSS Journal*, vol. 1 (2013), *http://icss-journal.newsdeskmedia.com/images/Upload/Vol_1_no_3/ICSS_Journal_Vol1.3.pdf*.
11   Seven EU member states have introduced legislative provisions prohibiting people who may influence the outcome or course of sports events: Belgium, the Czech Republic, Estonia, France, Germany, Hungary and Spain.
12   TMC Asser Instituut (2014, *Study on Risk Assessment*).
13   TMC Asser Instituut, *Study on Sports Organisers' Rights in the EU* (The Hague: TMC Asser Instituut, 2014), pp.130–135.
14   Loi no. 2010-476 du 12 mai 2010 relative à l'ouverture à la concurrence et à la régulation du secteur des jeux d'argent et de hasard en ligne, articles 31 and 38; Décret no. 2010-509 du 18 mai 2010 relatif aux obligations imposées aux opérateurs agréés de jeux ou de paris en ligne en vue du contrôle des données par l'autorité de régulation des jeux en ligne.
15   French Sports Code (*Code du Sport*), articles L131-161, R131-37 to R131-45.

16   Gambling Commission, *Licence Conditions and Codes of Practice: February 2015* (Birmingham: Gambling Commission, 2015), *www.gamblingcommission.gov.uk/pdf/ Latest-LCCP-and-Extracts/Licence-conditions-and-codes-of-practice.pdf*, condition 15.1.2.
17   Council of Europe Convention on the Manipulation of Sports Competitions, 18 September 2014, article 10, *http://conventions.coe.int/Treaty/EN/Treaties/Html/215.htm*.
18   TMC Asser Instituut (2014, *Study on Risk Assessment*), pp. 34–35.
19   Ibid., pp. 32–33.
20   See, for example, European Sports Security Association, 'Code of conduct', *www.eu-ssa. org/code-of-conduct*; and European Lotteries, 'Code of conduct', *www.european-lotteries. org/el-code-conduct*.

4.3

Cricket in Bangladesh

Challenges of governance and match-fixing

Iftekhar Zaman, Rumana Sharmin and Mohammad Nure Alam[1]

The context

Cricket, the proverbial gentlemen's game,[2] has only recently become the most popular sport in Bangladesh. Although cricket was introduced in Bengal by the British East India Company in the eighteenth century, Bangladesh did not become an associate member of the International Cricket Council (ICC) until 1977, or a regular member until 1997, finally achieving the status of test-playing nation in June 2000. Bangladesh has increasingly become an important actor in global cricket,[3] and has captured the imagination of millions of Bangladeshis at home and abroad, men and women, and especially youth and children. Cricket is not simply a game in the country; it is a symbol of national unity.[4] Corresponding to this growth in domestic interest, however, and in keeping with global and regional trends, Bangladeshi cricket has also become a huge money-making mechanism,[5] making the game vulnerable to corruption and in need of strengthened, robust and effective governance structures.

As with other cricket-playing nations, competitive matches in Bangladesh were played until recently in the form of test matches and one-day tournaments between national teams. When the Bangladesh Premier League (BPL) was introduced in 2012 as a competition of franchises – clubs formed specifically for the league and essentially as business enterprises – profit-making became a key factor in cricket. The Bangladesh Cricket Board (BCB, described further below) demonstrated an enthusiasm for this short-term profitability, even at the possible expense of the longer-term development of the sport. This was evident when the BPL was given a better time slot in the 2013/2014 domestic cricket calendar at the expense of the Bangladesh Cricket League, a first-class (that is, higher-quality, and thus more important for national development) competition.[6] Profit-making became clubs' preoccupation, leading to irregularities in the form of match-fixing and spot-fixing,[7] linked with betting, in which players and officials became easy recruits. The governance deficit in the game has compounded the problem further.

The main theme of this study is that the two parallel sets of challenges – of the governance of the BCB, on the one hand, and of the wider problem of match-fixing, on the other – need to be addressed effectively, in the interests of cricket in Bangladesh and for it to realise its full potential. Much-needed improvements in the governance of the BCB will also enhance the capacity to prevent and control match-fixing.

Cricket governance

The Bangladesh Cricket Board, affiliated with the National Sports Council of Bangladesh (NSCB)[8] within the Ministry of Youth and Sports, is responsible for the operation and development of cricket in the country.[9] The Parliamentary Standing Committee of the Ministry of Youth and Sports, as the oversight body for the ministry, is also tasked with overseeing the work of the BCB.

The BCB generates income from TV rights, sponsorship,[10] donations, income-sharing with the ICC from global cricket, and tournament fees as an organiser of ICC events, among other sources.[11] It also receives government allocations (through the NSCB), and generates revenue from investments. The BCB is governed by its own constitution[12] and is composed of 27 board directors, a board president and 20 operational committees.[13]

The legal classification of the BCB's corporate structure is uncertain. It is neither a corporate body, such as the ICC, nor a statutory body, as is its counterpart in Pakistan, nor a 'registered society' (typical of charities), as is the case with India.[14] There is no formal mechanism within Bangladesh to hold the BCB accountable. It operates as an autonomous body, and is regarded as a subsidiary of the Ministry of Youth and Sports. In practice, however, the BCB operates on its own with hardly any relationship of accountability with the Ministry and the NSCB, while the Parliamentary Standing Committee rarely exercises or enforces its oversight functions.[15]

This is consistent with ICC guidelines for national cricket boards, so that government interference in cricket governance is minimal and the autonomy of the national cricket associations is maintained.[16] Former BCB officials have nevertheless claimed that the BCB is subject to government and political influence, especially in terms of its leadership and management, and in the election of its board president and members.[17] The BCB directors amended the BCB's constitution on 1 March 2012, following which an election was held for the first time within the BCB to choose board directors. The current president was also chosen, unanimously, in this election. Despite the introduction of elections, partisan and political interests still prevailed in the nomination process for the president's and directors' posts.[18]

Although the BCB constitution calls for representation from all over the country, most board members represent Dhaka-based clubs and have links to the ruling party. There are also allegations of board directors arbitrarily amending the constitution to suit the interests of the current leadership.[19] The president nominates five councillors of the General Council[20] and chooses the operational committee members, thus paving the way for BCB operations to be controlled by the president or his chosen few. The selection of certain match venues is also alleged to take place according to political interests.[21] In addition, there are allegations of conflicts of interest, including, for instance, a BCB director who worked as a coach for a franchise team in the BPL.[22] The BCB is also criticised for having no long-term plan for the development of cricket, and no specific programmes for behavioural change and ethics education.[23]

There is no specific law addressing corruption in sports in Bangladesh.[24] The Bangladesh Penal Code of 1860 and the Anti-Corruption Commission Act of 2004 include provisions against dishonest conduct and corruption in general, but there is no particular set of rules, regulations or protocols for the investigation of allegations of corruption in cricket. The ICC has its Anti-Corruption Code for Participants, to try to prevent corruption in global cricket, and has set up an Anti-Corruption Security Unit (ACSU), both of which have responsibility for ensuring discipline and integrity in international cricket. The BCB adopted its own such code on 1 October 2012, and revised it on 1 January 2013 to ensure consistency with the ICC Code. The BCB's Anti-Corruption Code allows a two-stage appeal process.[25] If there is a complaint against a player or player support personnel, under article 5.1.1 of the Code, the BCB will formulate a 'provisional' disciplinary panel (DP), headed by a chairman, who will establish an Anti-Corruption Tribunal of three individuals who are independent of the parties and have had no prior involvement with the case.[26] The tribunal will hear the case and make a judgement, and parties can lodge an appeal with the DP. Should the complaint still not be resolved, the second stage allows an appeal to the Court of Arbitration for Sport (CAS), based in Switzerland.[27]

Establishment of the Bangladesh Premier League

Against this governance backdrop came the tumultuous establishment of the BPL, which was done in an ad hoc manner without proper policies and rules for the tournament. The franchises determined the rates and payments of players' fees without following any well-defined criteria. The BCB and the franchises failed to secure permission for income-generating activities or foreign currency payments from the National Board of Revenue and Bangladesh Bank, the central bank, making franchises unable to pay some players' signing fees.[28] This oversight and the common use of cash payments to players create circumstances conducive to tax evasion.[29] There are also allegations of a lack of transparency in procurement activities.[30]

Match-fixing: money the spoiler

Sport has enormous influence in shaping social values and attitudes, because it provides role models, particularly for young people.[31] The popularity and influence of cricket, particularly among the youth, have been huge in Bangladesh, where 63 per cent of the population is under the age of 25.[32]

The increased flow of money has exposed cricket to higher risks of bribery and other illegal practices, including match-fixing and spot-fixing, and has raised concerns about an erosion of integrity in the game. The shorter version of cricket, especially the Twenty20 format of the BPL, is considered a quick profit-making venture for cricketers, teams, organisers and other stakeholders.[33] Fixers allegedly infiltrate in the guise of being involved in one or other aspects of the business venture, all the while building relationships with teams, players, umpires and sponsors. Some of these relationships transform into collusion and even coercion, especially in the case of young players, many of whom come from modest backgrounds and are more vulnerable to corruption.[34]

With regard to players, in a high-profile case of corruption, former national captain Mohammad Ashraful – who made history in 2001 by being the youngest cricketer to score a test century, at the age of 17 – accepted a substantial sum of money for spot-fixing in various matches and tournaments. Ashraful ultimately admitted to accepting an advance from a bookie of BDT 0.7 million (some US$10,000) for his complicity in spot-fixing in a test match in January 2010, though in the end he had failed to deliver as a result of being out early.[35] He admitted this was later transferred to another match in the 2012 Twenty20 World Cup in Sri Lanka[36] and also admitted to accepting US$10,000 in another deal for spot-fixing during the 2012 Sri Lanka Premier League.[37] In addition, he was reported to have taken part in spot-fixing during a match in the 2012 Twenty20 World Cup in exchange for BDT 2.5 million (around US$30,000).[38] The BCB Anti-Corruption Tribunal found Ashraful guilty of spot-fixing in the second edition of the BPL, fined him BDT 1 million (some US$13,000) and banned him from cricket for eight years; this was later reduced to five years upon appeal, with a possibility of a further reduction by two years contingent upon a certificate of 'good conduct' from the ICC.[39]

Umpires have also been involved in match-fixing. Take the case of Nadir Shah, for example, who was banned by the BCB in March 2013 for ten years for allegedly agreeing to give decisions favouring players in exchange for a fee in an undercover sting broadcast by India TV.[40] Bookies have also been found to be actively encouraging corrupt practices in the game. In February 2012 Sajid Khan, a Pakistani citizen, was apprehended while trying to enter the players' zone illegally, and was handed over to police, suspected of match-fixing in a BPL match between the Chittagong Kings and the Barisal Burners.[41] In the 2014 Twenty20 World Cup in Dhaka, Indian national Atanu Dutta[42] was reportedly arrested three times in April for alleged involvement in illegal betting related to the tournament.[43] Both were arrested and released on bail with no further action to date.[44]

The BPL itself has not proved immune to these threats of corruption. The ACSU brought charges against the Dhaka Gladiators after reportedly receiving a complaint from their head coach, Ian Pont.[45] Pont stated that he had been asked by team owner Shihab Chowdhury to lose a match in November 2013 against the Chittagong Kings by fixing certain elements.[46] The ACSU did not inform the BCB or the law enforcement authorities about the disclosure, despite the BCB having earlier entered into an agreement with the ACSU under which the latter was to assist the BCB in overseeing, managing, implementing and enforcing all aspects of the BCB Anti-Corruption Code.[47] The ACSU did not exercise its authority to call off the match, and allowed it to go ahead despite the credible risk of match-fixing.

On receiving notice from the ACSU, the BCB formed a tribunal, which charged nine cricketers and officials, including three foreign nationals.[48] It found Shihab Chowdhury guilty, barred him from cricket for ten years and fined him BDT 2 million (about US$25,000).[49] The fine was later withdrawn upon appeal. The tribunal acquitted six others accused for lack of evidence of involvement, while two confessed.[50] The BCB and ACSU later filed a joint appeal against the acquittal of Salim Chowdhury, another owner of the Dhaka Gladiators and father of Shihab Chowdhury; ultimately he also received a ten-year ban.

Looking ahead

The BCB has recently made efforts to strengthen its Anti-Corruption Unit (ACU), by taking actions such as sending an officer to South Africa for anti-corruption training. With the help of the ACSU, the BCB now also conducts anti-corruption orientation sessions before every international match or series.[51] While this is useful, more fundamental reforms are needed, especially in terms of a long-term anti-corruption strategy. The independence, professionalism and effectiveness of the ACU must be ensured by the provision of the necessary human and technical skills, giving it the capacity to prevent corruption as well as to control it, by means of prompt and efficient investigation and prosecution. The ACU should be endowed in particular with capacities to strictly monitor compliance with the BCB's Anti-Corruption Code. Legal provisions must be created to criminalise match-fixing, spot-fixing and other forms of cheating.

An independent, permanent Office of Ombudsman for Cricket should be set up by law, and endowed with the power to investigate and prosecute allegations of corruption and irregularities in the game. While administrative sanctions in the event of violation of the Code should continue to remain within the jurisdiction of the BCB, the ombudsman should be empowered to ensure the accountability of all stakeholders, including players, coaches, umpires, clubs, franchises and the BCB board and top management. The Office of Ombudsman should also receive and act upon complaints of irregularities, corruption and conflicts of interest in financial arrangements and related business aspects, including the allocation of media rights and sponsorships and other risk areas involving the integrity and reputation of the game. Given the full independence of the Office, the ombudsman ought to be able to ensure the desired autonomy of the sport.

In order to improve the governance of the BCB, it should be accountable to and subject to oversight from the Sports Ministry and the Parliamentary Standing Committee. Consistent with the government's National Integrity Strategy for fighting corruption,[52] the mandate of the BCB's ACU should be expanded to become an Integrity and Anti-Corruption Unit, with the objective of strengthening the preventive work, including greater integrity and ethics awareness and education.

It is imperative that all stakeholders involved in cricket matches and tournaments, especially the franchises, managers, coaches, captains, players and media houses, whether national or international, formally sign a commitment to uphold the ICC's Anti-Corruption Code, and thereby deter illicit conduct. All such individuals, including those involved with the BCB and their immediate families, agents and gate-keepers, should be subjected to the proactive disclosure of their income and wealth and to disciplinary action in cases when income and wealth are disproportionate to legitimate earnings. Specific programmes of information, education and communication need to be undertaken to change behaviour in young cricketers, strengthening both the demand and the supply sides of the governance and anti-corruption infrastructure of cricket.[53]

Notes

1 Iftekhar Zaman is executive director of Transparency International Bangladesh. The author was assisted by Rumana Sharmin and Mohammad Nure Alam. Data and information for this case study have been collected through primary and secondary sources. Interviews with former and current players, Bangladesh Cricket Board officials, sports journalists and experts have been conducted to collect primary data, and websites, media reports and relevant documents have been reviewed for secondary data.

2 Reference to the game of cricket can be traced to the thirteenth century. It gained popularity among English aristocrats in the seventeenth century; they insisted cricket would be played in 'a gentlemanly manner'. For example, if a batsman knew he should be out, he should walk, even if the umpire judged otherwise. See *Times of India*, 'Why is cricket called a gentleman's game?', 17 April 2011, *http://timesofindia.indiatimes.com/home/stoi/Why-is-cricket-called-a-gentlemans-game/articleshow/8003522.cms*; and Quora.com, 'Why is cricket called a gentleman's game?', 18 November 2012, *www.quora.com/Why-is-cricket-called-a-%E2%80%98gentleman%E2%80%99s-game%E2%80%99*.

3 A former president of the BCB became president of the ICC in June 2014: Cricbuzz.com, 'Mustafa Kamal becomes 11th ICC president', 26 June 2014, *www.cricbuzz.com/cricket-news/64129/mustafa-kamal-becomes-11th-icc-president*. A Bangladeshi also serves as chief executive of the Asian Cricket Council.

4 Saber Hossain Chowdhury, former BCB president, quoted by the BBC on 9 March 2011: *http://news.bbc.co.uk/sport2/hi/cricket/other_international/bangladesh/9420128.stm*.

5 The influence of money has become so pervasive that the 'gentlemanship' of the game is considered to have been compromised. As the legendary Indian cricketer Erapalli Prasanna said, 'Money is ruling the sport now and it is no more a gentleman's game': *http://sports.ndtv.com/cricket/news/208732-cricket-no-more-a-gentlemans-game-erapalli-prasanna*.

6 ESPN Cricinfo, 'Preference to BPL leads to clash in BCB', 6 August 2013, *www.espncricinfo.com/bangladesh/content/story/659477.html*.

7   'Match-fixing' takes place when the entire result of a match is determined in advance. 'Spot-fixing' takes place when specific incidents within the game are prearranged. Match-fixing is considered more difficult than spot-fixing because, as a minimum, it requires more players, including the captain, to build a nexus.

8   The NSCB is an autonomous government organisation under the Ministry of Youth and Sports, established by the National Sports Council Act 1974, which was later amended in 1991, 2003 and 2011. It is an apex organisation, mandated to develop and control sports. See *www.nsc.gov/bd*. As is the case with other federations, there is BCB representation on the NSCB (article 4(e), National Sports Council Act 1974, amended 19 February 1991): *www.nsc.gov.bd/rules/nscact.pdf*.

9   See the BCB's website, *www.tigercricket.com.bd/bcb/aboutbcb*.

10 The BCB controls cricket sponsorship business. India's business giant Sahara Group became the sponsor of the Bangladesh cricket team after offering US$9.4 million over four years in a tender process. Previously Grameenphone had paid the BCB US$1.22 million for a two-year deal, which expired in December 2011. See *http://uk.mobile.reuters.com/article/idUKL4E8GU6Y820120530?irpc=932*.

11 Data obtained from key informant interviews with BCB officials on 19 October 2014 (anonymity requested) and other secondary sources, including the BCB constitution.

12 See Bangladesh Cricket Board, 'Constitution: amended in 2012' (Dhaka: BCB, 2012), *www.tigercricket.com.bd/assets/pdf/BCB-Constitution-2012.pdf*.

13 The committees are: Cricket Operations, Media and Communications, Disciplinary, Game Development, Tournament, Age-Group Tournament, Grounds, Facilities Management, Umpires, Marketing and Commercial, Medical, Tender and Purchase, Finance, Audit, Women's Wing, Logistic and Protocol, Security, Cricket Committee of Dhaka Metropolis, High Performance (newly formed) and Technical (newly formed).

14 Bangladesh Cricket Board, 'Before the chairman, the disciplinary panel' (Dhaka: BCB, 2014), p. 41, *www.tigercricket.com.bd/assets/pdf/apeal/decision.pdf*.

15 Key informant interviews with BCB officials on 19 October and 22 November 2014, and former directors on 30 September and 19 October 2014 (anonymity requested).

16 Article 2.9, 'Independence of member boards', of the amended and restated memorandum and articles of association of the International Cricket Council.

17 Key informant interviews, former BCB directors, 30 September and 19 October 2014.

18 The current president is also a Member of Parliament from the ruling party. The same is true for previous presidents. See Bangladesh Cricket Board, 'List of presidents', *www.tigercricket.com.bd/bcb/former-president*.

19 Key informant interviews, former BCB directors, 30 September and 19 October 2014, and other secondary sources.

20 BCB (2012), 'Constitution', article 9.3 (9.3.8), p. 7.

21 For instance, Bogra was not selected under one administration for an event despite having a world-class venue (Bogra-Shahid Chandu Stadium), and similarly Sylhet was not selected under another despite its international-standard stadium, in both cases under the consideration that the respective venues were built during the time when political opponents were in power. Source: Key informant interviews, former BCB directors, 30 September and 19 October 2014.

22 The franchise system (leasing the rights of a team and its brand) was originally introduced in Bangladesh for a period of three years, and because of its success it has now become a permanent part of domestic cricket.

23 Key informant interviews with current national cricket team player on 23 October 2014, and former national cricket team captain and current BCB Operations Committee member on 28 October 2014 (anonymity requested).

24 Bangladesh Cricket Board, 'Before the Anti-Corruption Tribunal: Case no. 1/2013' (Dhaka: BCB, 2014), p. 16, *www.tigercricket.com.bd/assets/pdf/anticorr/detfinal.pdf*.

25 ESPN Cricinfo, 'ICC, BCB to appeal BPL anti-corruption tribunal's verdict', 18 July 2014, *www.espncricinfo.com/bangladesh/content/story/761553.html*.

26 According to clause 5.1.2 of the BCB's Anti-Corruption Code, 'One member of the anti-corruption tribunal, who shall be a retired justice of Supreme Court of Bangladesh/retired District Judge, shall sit as the convener of the tribunal. One member shall be drawn from the persons having expertise in cricket. The other one shall be appointed from socially well-recognised civilians.'

27 The CAS is an international quasi-judicial body established to settle disputes related to sport. Its headquarters are in Lausanne, and its courts are located in New York, Sydney and Lausanne.

28 For instance, because written permission was not received from the revenue board or central bank, contracting fees have still not been paid to a number of foreign players. As a guarantor, the ultimate responsibility for paying these fees goes to the BCB, which has been gradually paying them. The BCB never acquired any formal document from the franchises or players detailing these payments, however. The BCB board has continued to extend deadlines for the franchises to provide this information, which is still pending at present. Key informant interviews, BCB officials, 19 October and 22 November 2014; *Daily Star* (Bangladesh), 'BCB chasing its own tail', 2 November 2012, *http://archive.thedailystar.net/newDesign/print_news.php?nid=255855*.

29 Key informant interviews, BCB officials, 19 October and 22 November 2014.

30 Key informant interviews, BCB officials, 19 October and 22 November 2014; journalists on 28 September and 3 November 2014; former BCB Directors, 30 September and 19 October 2014.

31 Transparency International, ICC *Governance Review: Submission on behalf of Transparency International* (London: TI, 2011).

32 US Department of Commerce, 'Population trends: Bangladesh', PPT92-4 (Washington, DC: Department of Commerce, 1993), *www.census.gov/population/international/files/ppt/Bangladesh93.pdf*.

33 Key informant interviews with journalists on 28 September and 3 November 2014 (anonymity requested).

34 Key informant interviews, BCB officials, 19 October and 22 November 2014; former national cricket team captain and current BCB Operations Committee member, 28 October 2014; and current national cricket team player on 23 October 2014 (anonymity requested).

35 Bangladesh Cricket Board, 'Before the Anti-Corruption Tribunal: Case no. 1/2013: Determination' (Dhaka: BCB, 2014), *www.tigercricket.com.bd/assets/pdf/anticorr/detreason.pdf*; *Prothom Alo* (Bangladesh), 31 May 2013.

36 *Prothom Alo* (Bangladesh), 31 May 2013.

37 Ibid.

38 Ibid.

39 The tribunal took into consideration his confession of guilt, on the basis of articles 6.4, 6.3.3, 6.1.2.1, 6.1.2.2, 6.1.2.3, 6.1.2.7 and 6.1.2.8 of the Anti-Corruption Code: BCB (2014), 'Determination'; *Daily Star* (Bangladesh), 'Ashraful's ban now for 5 yrs', 30 September 2014, *www.thedailystar.net/ashrafuls-ban-now-for-5-yrs-43961*; BCB (2014), 'Before the chairman'.

40 ESPN Cricinfo, 'BCB allows Nadir Shah to officiate in match', 28 September 2014, *www.espncricinfo.com/bangladesh/content/story/785529.html*.

41 ESPN Cricinfo, 'Cloud over BPL after fixing arrest', 27 February 2012, *www.espncricinfo.com/bangladesh-premier-league-2012/content/story/555380.html*.

42 The 40-year-old had previously been arrested at Benapole Land Port, Bangladesh, on 3 April 2014, with the World Twenty20 under way. Three days later he was again arrested, in Dhaka, by the Rapid Action Battalion (RAB).

43 Bdnews24.com (Bangladesh), 'Indian bookie arrested for third time', 13 April 2014, *http://bdnews24.com/bangladesh/2014/04/13/indian-bookie-arrested-for-third-time*.

44 *New Age*, 'Arrested Indian "bookie" released on bail', 11 April 2014, *http://newagebd.net/1831/arrested-indian-bookie-released-on-bail/#sthash.i4bskmlr.LMM7KrPK.dpbs*.

45 Ian Leslie Pont is a former English cricketer, who mainly played for Essex. He served as head coach of the Dhaka Gladiators franchise during the second BPL edition and was the first individual to inform ACSU officials about the match-fixing conspiracy: *Daily Star* (Bangladesh), 'Reason judgement on BPL corruption', 11 June 2014, *www.thedailystar.net/ sports/reason-judgement-on-bpl-corruption-28052.*

46 Details of the match-fixing and spot-fixing were discussed during the night of 1 February 2013 and disclosure was made by Pont the following day to Peter O'Shea, the ACSU anti-corruption manager. It was also clear from the witnesses that, well before the match was played, details of how the Dhaka Gladiators would lose the match, who would be involved and how the acts of spot-fixing would take place were known to the ACSU. BCB (2014), 'Case no. 1/2013'.

47 Bangladesh Cricket Board, 'Before the Anti-Corruption Tribunal: Case no. 1/2013: Determination: Conclusions and Orders' (Dhaka: BCB, 2014), *www.tigercricket.com.bd/ assets/pdf/anticorr/detconclusion.pdf*; key informant interviews, journalists, 28 September and 3 November 2014.

48 Shihab Jishan Chowdury (owner of the Dhaka Gladiators), Salim Chowdury (owner of the Dhaka Gladiators), Gaurav Rawat (Dhaka Gladiators official), Mohammad Rafique (player), Mosharaff Hossain (Rubel) (player), Mahbubul Alam (Robin) (player), Darren Stevens (player), Kaushal Lokurachchi (player) and Mohammad Ashraful (player): BCB (2014), 'Case no. 1/2013'.

49 BCB (2014), 'Determination'.

50 *Daily Star* (11 June 2014).

51 Key informant interviews, BCB officials, 19 October 2014; other secondary sources.

52 The National Integrity Strategy is a comprehensive set of goals, strategies and action plans aimed at increasing the level of independence to perform, accountability, efficiency, transparency and effectiveness of state and non-state institutions in a sustained manner over a period of time: Chancery Law Chronicles (Bangladesh), 'Framework of National Integrity Strategy: an inclusive approach to fight corruption' (Dhaka: Government of Bangladesh, 2008), *www.clcbd.org/document/download/143.html.*

53 In a unique example of such an initiative, as a result of advocacy by TI Bangladesh, the country's national cricket team took a pledge to 'Say No to Corruption' on the eve of the International Anti-Corruption Day 2013, demonstrating their public commitment to abstain from corruption: Transparency International Bangladesh, 'Bangladesh national cricket team says no to corruption', 8 December 2013, *www.ti-bangladesh.org/beta3/index.php/en/ activities/4460-bangladesh-national-cricket-team-says-no-to-corruption*. The need to sustain and scale up such efforts and engage more stakeholders, including the BCB, cannot be underestimated.

4.4

The gap between sports institutions and the public will

Responses to match-fixing in Lithuania

Rugile Trumpyte[1]

Until recently it seemed as if there was no match-fixing in Lithuania, with no information on the subject available and no publicly known investigations. Suddenly in 2011, however, players from the Lithuanian Basketball League (Lietuvos krepšinio lyga – LKL) club Naglis were alleged to have bet on themselves to lose a game by 30 points.[2] Not only was this was the first ever known case of match-fixing in the country, but it occurred in Lithuania's most beloved sport, its 'second religion'. Despite this, no public debates about integrity in sport or the possible scale of the problem followed. The LKL and the Lithuanian Basketball Federation (Lietuvos krepšinio federacija – LKF) imposed monetary and disciplinary sanctions[3] – and that was pretty much the end of the story.

Lithuanians next heard about corruption in sport at the end of 2012, when the Swiss-based monitoring organisation Sportradar claimed that Lithuania was among the top ten European countries with the highest number of likely fixed football matches.[4] It were another red flag raised to the sport community, but, again, neither the LKF nor the Lithuanian Football Federation (Lietuvos futbolo federacija – LFF) seemed ready to publicly admit the existence of the problem, and the issue remained largely behind closed doors.

The sporting authorities might have been making little effort to advocate for honest sport, but the Lithuanian people clearly stated that both the LFF and the LKF had a responsibility for integrity in sports and should be the ones to address the issue. According to the research by Transparency International Lithuania in 2014, integrity and honesty in sports were important to 68 per cent of Lithuanian people, and most of them would be prepared to punish their beloved sports clubs in the event of match-fixing;[5] 57 per cent of those betting said they would stop doing so; 44 per cent of those watching games on television said they would not do that anymore; and half of all those buying tickets to watch sport matches live said they would abandon the habit.

How did Lithuanian sportsmen respond to this demand by sports fans for fair play? To find out, TI Lithuania conducted the first ever representative research into match-fixing in the professional basketball and football leagues, surveying 100 football players and 259

TI Lithuania research suggested that basketball may be as vulnerable to match-fixing as football – rarely raised when reporting match-fixing worldwide.

Figure 4.1 Match-fixing: football versus basketball

basketball players[6] about their experience and perceptions. The results suggested that basketball may be as vulnerable to match-fixing as football – a fact that is hardly raised when reporting match-fixing worldwide.

The findings clearly showed that Lithuanian sport faces big challenges, including that every fifth football player and every seventh basketball player is likely to have taken part in a fixed match, whether knowingly or otherwise.[7] According to the data collected, team-mates, former colleagues and club owners are the ones suggesting that players participate in match-fixing. Some 15 per cent of football players and 21 per cent of basketball players admitted to having been personally approached to agree to fix matches.

The research received a considerable amount of media attention, and provided a good catalyst for public debate. Even after all this, however, more than half the players interviewed said they still did not perceive the practice of match-fixing to be a problem.[8]

Root causes

Why do players get involved in such agreements? The results of the research showed that football and basketball players alike face a number of issues in their daily lives that, in the end, greatly influence their decision to engage in match-fixing. Primarily, players highlighted financial reasons: they were either looking for extra money (52 per cent) or found themselves in a poor personal financial situation (16 per cent), sometimes because of delays in the payment of their salaries (13 per cent).

Not all the players were aware of the rights and basic entitlements that they could demand from their clubs.[9] According to the research, 18 per cent of players have not even signed a contract with their clubs; 62 per cent stated that their wages were not paid on time at least once during the last year, most often with a delay of three to five months.[10] Those who did have contracts did not always understand the legal guarantees a contract brings, or what clauses the contracts should contain to protect them fully in the event of injury, for example. Injuries are one of the most pressing problems, as not all players receive their salaries when they are injured.

The results of the research inspired TI Lithuania to organise integrity seminars for professional players across the country. This provided a unique opportunity to talk face to face and develop a better understanding of the context they operate in. After discussing the risks of match-fixing, what it can mean for their professional career and how to avoid it, players consistently highlighted the fact that there are currently no effective measures to solve match-fixing and help athletes.

First and foremost, there is no legal protection for whistleblowers, and there are no safe reporting channels. Even if a player decides to report anything related to match-fixing, he or she is never sure what exactly will be done with the information and what the personal consequences could be. More broadly, TI analysis shows that Lithuania is among the weakest EU states in terms of protection for whistleblowers.[11] At the same time, there is no special provision for fraud in sport in Lithuania's criminal code, so law enforcement institutions have never been able to bring any investigation to a successful conclusion.

Findings

It is now known that match-fixing exists in Lithuania's sports. The necessary first step is to make a public admission of its existence and state clearly that it will not be tolerated. This would be a tremendously important move, as local sports fans already appear to be prepared to begin sanctioning their favourite sports teams and athletes if they are found out to have engaged in match-fixing.

Notes

1   Rugile Trumpyte is a project manager at Transparency International Lithuania.
2   Players from the club Naglis were alleged to have bet on their loss against the club Zalgiris by 30 points on 5 April 2011; see BasketNews.lt, 'Skandalas LKL: "Naglio" žaidėjai statė prieš savo komandą (papildyta – komentarai)', 6 April 2011, *www.basketnews.lt/news-38465-skandalas-lkl-naglio-zaidejai-state-pries-savo-komanda-papildyta-komentarai.html#.VOx3vizEpKo*.

3   Each player who participated in match-fixing was fined €869: BasketZone.lt, 'LKL skyrė baudas lažybose dalyvavusiems "Naglio" žaidėjams', *www.basketzone.lt/naujienos/7651-lkl-skyr-baudas-laybose-dalyvavusiems-qnaglioq-aidjams-.html*.

4   Albania Screen, '"Sportradar": Albanian football, the most corrupted in Europe', 30 November 2012, *http://news.albanianscreen.tv/pages/news_detail/51996/ENG*.

5   See Transparency International Lithuania, 'Lietuvos gyventojai apie nesąžiningus susitarimus sporte' (Vilnius: TI Lithuania, 2014), *http://transparency.lt/media/filer_public/2014/01/21/gyventojai_futbolas_krepsinis_2014.pdf*.

6   The survey of players was carried out in December 2013. The representative survey of Lithuanian citizens was also commissioned by TI Lithuania, and carried out in October/November 2013 by VISEO.

7   Transparency International Lithuania, 'Nesąžiningi susitarimai sporte' (Vilnius: TI Lithuania, 2014), *http://transparency.lt/media/filer_public/2014/01/22/sportininku_apklausos_rezultatai_2014_1.pdf*.

8   45.1 per cent of players said that match-fixing is a minor problem; 16.4 per cent said it is not a problem at all.

9   This became even more obvious when integrity seminars were organised for professional football and basketball players.

10 Ibid.

11 Transparency International, *Whistleblowing in Europe: Legal Protections for Whistleblowers in the EU* (Berlin: TI, 2013), *http://transparency.lt/media/filer_public/2013/11/05/praneseju_apsaugos__ataskaita_es.pdf*.

4.5

Australia's 'National Policy on Match-Fixing in Sport'

Jane Ellis[1]

Prior to 2011 Australia had been lulled into a false sense of security that it was immune from the more rapacious forms of corruption so prevalent in sport elsewhere. With online betting and organised crime ignoring borders, however, times have changed. Subsequent national inquiries made it increasingly clear that Australia needed to change as well.[2]

Actions taken

Australia is a federation, and the national government does not have the power to introduce national laws to address match-fixing in sport. Through its Council of Australian Governments framework, however, relevant ministers in the Commonwealth of Australia and all the state and territory governments negotiated, and reached an agreement to introduce reforms in each state and territory to expressly address sport, match-fixing and gambling.

The outcome of the negotiations was the 'National Policy on Match-Fixing in Sport', agreed in June 2011 and published in a report with the same title.[3] The National Policy is underpinned by the following principles:

- a nationally consistent approach to deterring and dealing with match-fixing in Australia;
- information sharing and highly efficient networks between governments, major sports, betting operators and law enforcers;
- a consistent national code of conduct principles for sport; and
- active participation in international efforts to combat corruption in sport, including an international code of conduct and an international body.

Relevant to match-fixing, the National Policy specifies the conduct that all governments agreed must be prohibited, the contravention of which attracts a maximum penalty of ten years' imprisonment:

- engaging in conduct that corrupts or would corrupt a betting outcome;
- facilitating conduct that corrupts or would corrupt a betting outcome;
- concealing such conduct, agreements or arrangements; and
- using corrupt information for betting purposes.

The governments also agreed to implement nationally consistent legislative arrangements, pursuant to which:

- a Sport Controlling Body for each sport or competition is identified, recognised in each jurisdiction and registered by an appropriate regulator;
- the Sport Controlling Body is to deal with those betting agencies that are licensed on behalf of their sport; and
- the Sport Controlling Body is to register all events subject to betting with the relevant regulator.

The governments also agreed that it was necessary to adopt a national approach to governing the implementation of the National Policy, to ensure cooperation and collaboration across all relevant agencies and governments, their gaming commissions, sporting organisations and betting agencies. The National Integrity of Sport Unit provides this oversight, monitoring and coordinating role.[4]

Laws prohibiting match-fixing include the following:

- Crimes Amendment (Cheating at Gambling) Act 2012 (New South Wales);
- Crimes Amendment (Integrity in Sports) Act 2013 (Victoria);
- Criminal Law Consolidation (Cheating at Gambling) Amendment Act 2013 (South Australia);
- Criminal Code (Cheating at Gambling) Amendment Act 2013 (Australian Capital Territory);
- Criminal Code (Cheating at Gambling) Amendment Act 2013 (Queensland); and
- Criminal Code Amendment (Cheating at Gambling) Act 2013 (Northern Territory).

The sporting sector is also implementing its own procedures to ensure that integrity in sport is not compromised. The Coalition of Major Professional and Participation Sports (COMPPS) shares information on sports gaming integrity education, sports gaming disciplinary and code of conduct processes, and integrity processes.[5]

More to be done

Most states and both territories have now introduced laws prohibiting match-fixing and other objectives of the National Policy. Some states, Victoria in particular, are vigorously enforcing this law. For example, in 2013 Victoria police arrested nine European soccer players and one coach who had allegedly been recruited by a match-fixing syndicate and were playing professionally in Australia.[6] In July 2014 Victoria police arrested six men for allegedly participating in a tennis match-fixing syndicate, involving players and linked to national and international matches.[7]

The action agreed and adopted by governments is commendable. Rigorous enforcement by all authorities is essential, however. Victoria is unlikely to be the only state in which match-fixing occurs. Concerns continue to be raised about the increasing risks of match-fixing across Australia,[8] particularly in football and cricket.[9] Enforcement alone is insufficient to address the problem of match-fixing, though. Many sporting codes continue to have poor governance structures that lack transparency and accountability. This means that there is a greater likelihood of any potential abuses not being identified and quickly and robustly addressed, or even potentially being suppressed by players, coaches and/or sports administrators.

Notes

1 Jane Ellis is a director of Transparency International Australia and principal of Assertia Pty Ltd.

2 The 2011 Australian Government Joint Select Committee conducted an inquiry into interactive and online gambling and gambling advertising, highlighting the dangers of Australian sport being corrupted; see *www.aph.gov.au/Parliamentary_Business/ Committees/Joint/Former_Committees/gamblingreform/completedinquires/2010-13/ interactiveonlinegamblingadvertising/index#*. An August 2011 report by the New South Wales Law Reform Commission, entitled *Cheating at Gambling*, made similar observations; see *www.lawreform.justice.nsw.gov.au/agdbasev7wr/lrc/documents/pdf/r130.pdf*. The Australian Crime Commission's report *Organised Crime and Drugs in Sport*, from February 2013, detailed how organised crime has become involved in sport, that clubs rarely questioned the source of money offered to them and that athletes who took illicit drugs were exposed to co-option into corrupt conduct by organised crime; see *www.crimecommission. gov.au/sites/default/files/organised-crime-and-drugs-in-sports-feb2013.pdf*.

3 See *www.health.gov.au/internet/main/publishing.nsf/Content/F6DB8637F05C9643CA257C 310021CCE9/$File/National%20Policy%20on%20Match-Fixing%20in%20Sport%20%28 FINAL%29.pdf*.

4 The National Integrity of Sport Unit, located in the Commonwealth Department of Health, provides national oversight, monitoring and coordination of governments' efforts to protect the integrity of sport in Australia from the threats of doping, match-fixing and other forms of corruption. It provides integrity tools for sporting organisations (including an anti-match-fixing policy template), conducts anti-match-fixing education programmes and provides guidance to sports betting agencies. Its profile continues to be developed. See *www.health. gov.au/internet/main/publishing.nsf/Content/national-integrity-of-sport-unit*.

5 COMPPS includes the Australian Football League, Australian Rugby Union, Cricket Australia, Football Federation Australia, National Rugby League, Netball Australia and Tennis Australia; see *www.compps.com.au/index.html*.

6 Football Federation Australia, 'Victoria police make arrests into alleged match-fixing', 15 September 2013, *www.footballaustralia.com.au/article/victoria-police-make-arrests-into-alleged-match-fixing/168hht90cmc0r137n9p4vcb5el*.

7 *The Age* (Australia), 'Gangland police arrest six men on tennis match fixing allegations', 18 July 2014, *www.theage.com.au/victoria/gangland-police-arrest-six-men-on-tennis-match-fixing-allegations-20140718-zucky.html*.

8 See, for example, *Sydney Morning Herald* (Australia), 'Match-fixing fears as Malaysian team joins Queensland football league', 16 February 2014, *www.smh.com.au/sport/soccer/ matchfixing-fears-as-malaysian-team-joins-queensland-football-league-20140215-32sdz. html*.

9 Australia and New Zealand were joint hosts of the International Cricket Council cricket World Cup in 2015.

4.6
Match-fixing
The role of prevention

Ulrike Spitz[1]

The need for prevention measures

The causes of and influences on match-fixing are complex.[2] Sporting events can be fixed to gain financial advantage or they can be fixed for sporting reasons – that is, to get the desired result. A pervasive culture of cash payments – from referees' travel expenses to players' goal bonuses to agents' transfer fees – reduces misgivings about illegal activity and increases the risk of individuals becoming involved. High wages, abundant free time and exposure to gambling also heighten the vulnerability of professional athletes, while the huge rise of online gambling, in real time and across borders, has led to a sharp increase in activity by organised crime, which sees match-fixing as a low-risk venture with high returns.

When sports organisations started to recognise the problem of match-fixing around 15 years ago, reactions varied. Some sports such as tennis or cricket put prevention programmes in place as early as 2000, but football did not start to tackle match-fixing seriously until 2009, when the big European football betting scandals were uncovered.[3] Previously the initial reaction to any allegations had been to call in the police, as the problem was seen to belong exclusively to criminal elements from outside the game. However, no match-fixing can take place without the involvement of individual players, referees or officials, and it therefore requires interrelated responses, from adequate legal frameworks and law enforcement procedures to public awareness and the engagement of sport supporters. It is also clear that sport organisations carry the primary responsibility for developing prevention programmes in order to protect their competitions and athletes.

For a long time, however, sport organisations refused to accept this responsibility. Although awareness of the problem has slowly but steadily grown in recent years, even now many organisations require a great deal of persuasion before they put effective prevention measures in place.

Establishing the proper environment for prevention

Many athletes and referees do not appreciate the step-by-step risks of becoming sucked into criminal behaviour, and as a result are easy prey. Raising awareness, education and training for all target groups, including athletes, coaches, referees and officials, are therefore key elements of prevention.

Knowing the problem and recognising the risks

First and foremost, awareness-raising in sport is needed. All people involved – athletes, coaches, referees, officials, parents – should know the danger, where it starts and how to detect it before any manipulation takes place. They should know the specific risks of a particular sport, and which behaviour fosters manipulation; they need to know that there is a link between some habits in sport and match-fixing – such as cash payments, gambling or the manipulation of competitions for sporting reasons. Only through being aware of these challenges is there any chance of successful prevention.

Rules

For prevention programmes to succeed, it is important to have fixed rules and regulations against match-fixing already in place inside the sport organisations, so that administrative sanctions can be applied separately from criminal prosecutions. It should be mandatory for violations to be punished internally, not only as violations of public laws, and this should be known within the sport. Penalties serve as a preventative deterrent, and athletes and other concerned individuals must be fully informed about these rules and regulations, as well as the consequences for violations.

There is at present no global model of comparable rules for all athletes and others in connection with match-fixing, as there is, for example, in the fight against doping.[4] In some countries and certain sports, participants are prohibited from betting on the results of the competitions they take part in, and their club's matches. In the case of the German Football League, the Bundesliga, this also extends to friends and relatives of the players.[5] A global

In some countries participants are prohibited from betting on their own team matches. A global standard could include an outright prohibition of athletes betting not only on their own competition/league but on their own sport on the whole.

Figure 4.2 All bets are off

standard could include just such an outright prohibition of athletes and other involved people betting not only on their own competition/league but on their own sport on the whole. Such a rule would be very clear, and it could help to diminish the danger of gambling addiction as well as reducing match-fixing risks.

Ombudsmen and whistleblowing

Whistleblowing is a well-known means for fighting corruption in politics and business, and increasingly in sport, and is important to the success of prevention programmes. Some countries and/or sports already have established whistleblowing systems to report hints of matches being fixed. For example, the Bundesliga established an ombudsman in 2011, to receive information (anonymously, if required), on the one hand, and to consult and assist every involved person, on the other hand.[6] Such an ombudsman must be independent and obliged to uphold secrecy. It is absolutely necessary that the main focus of attention must be on the protection of whistleblowers, and that any and all regulations to be introduced are working towards this end.

Tone from the top

One of the most important principles in the fight against all kinds of wrongdoing is that the need to behave well applies at all times; in the case of corruption and match-fixing, this means that fair play on the pitch is possible only in connection with fair play off the pitch. How, for example, would a young athlete realise the danger of gambling when the president of his club talks about gambling in an easy and casual way in public, as if there is no problem of addiction?[7] How would club officials be able to protect their athletes if they were incapable of paying them? The risks are high when professional athletes are badly paid, or sometimes not paid at all, potentially driving them to match-fixing just to be able to feed their family. Alternatively, how would young athletes get a sense of wrongdoing in daily situations if the officials they report to are making headlines for alleged corruption or other irregularities?

The success or failure of prevention programmes therefore depends on the behaviour of front-line management. To gain credibility, managers have to stick to the rules, to set a good example, to avoid ambiguity, to stand for ethical behaviour and to promote an awareness of the risks involved in sport. This means that the first line of management in federations, associations and clubs has to apply principles of transparency and integrity through systems of good governance if managers really are interested in combating match-fixing.

Content and methods of prevention

Background information

First it is necessary for all potentially involved people to receive background information on the most important issues concerning match-fixing. Basic knowledge for coaches or officials allows them, in turn, to provide advice or train athletes. It is also necessary for athletes themselves to have background information about betting in order to understand the dangers of match-fixing or gambling addiction, or to know how inside information can have a value for individuals seeking to profit from the betting markets. Often there is little awareness about this issue among sportspeople. Inside information can include:

- injury – new injuries to athletes or athletes failing fitness tests;
- team selection – line-ups before the match;

- transfers – players transferred in/out of the club;
- managerial changes – news of who the new manager may be;
- financial problems – clubs not paying players' wages or other bills;
- motivational issues – such as a club not worried about being knocked out of a cup because promotion is more important to it; and
- any personal situations – such as a fight between players in training.[8]

Athletes should also understand the dangers and consequences of gambling addiction. Coaches, athletes' parents and teachers at special sport boarding schools should know how to recognise any gambling problem at an early stage.

Box 4.1 Gambling risks within professional football

Current studies[9] together with some individual cases reveal the high risk of gambling addiction on the part of football players because of their particular environment. Players are young, often have a lot of slack time, as on bus trips to away games, and have little to do on these trips, leading to boredom. In combination with the competitive mentality of athletes, and the fact that they are used to taking risks, this time is often used for games, whether it is poker or card games or internet gambling on sport results. Rush betting can provide an obvious temptation. Additionally, an often large salary at a young age, in comparison to athletes' peers, can increase recklessness. Athletes who have lost high sums or suffer from gambling addiction then become easy prey for match-fixers, such as German footballer René Schnitzler, who developed a gambling addiction that led him to get involved in match-fixing – as told in the book about his story.[10]

Target groups

As athletes very often start their careers at a young age, prevention and education must also begin when they are young. Most of the current prevention programmes start with athletes from 15 or 16 years of age. Programmes should reach athletes taking part in minor competitions, because they are at a high risk. As they are often not well paid by their clubs, or not paid on time, and there is less public attention, they are easier prey for fixers. Education must not be limited to athletes, though: all people involved – coaches, officials, referees and parents – should be integrated into the prevention programmes, and they should know all the important issues and dangers.

Methods

The focus must be on awareness-raising, education and training. A number of countries and sports, such as Germany (football), Austria (football) and Lithuania (basketball), have already produced information brochures and flyers, while in Germany, Greece, Croatia and Austria e-learning programmes are being implemented for different target groups, as well as workshops and face-to-face training sessions (Germany, Austria, Italy). Working with case studies and situations encountered on a daily basis should hold out the greatest promise of success. Everyone involved should be made aware of how easily a harmless situation can turn into a critical one. Those taking part in the training sessions should be able to react in a proper way and know where to get help when confronted with critical situations in real life.

The methods should be communicative and participative, with all attendees actively taking part; only participation guarantees learning.

These meetings or workshops should take place regularly, at least once per year, not just a single time in a player's career. In the professional German football leagues, for example, prevention programmes are mandatory for youth centres. It is also important for coaches to be aware of the problem in everyday life, in training and on trips to away games. In the case of special boarding schools for athletes, the responsible persons should also be trained on the need for ongoing monitoring and oversight.

Conclusion

Prevention is the most important weapon in the fight against match-fixing. Together with the required rules and a disciplinary system, it is what the sport organisation can do to minimise the risk of result manipulation. When athletes, referees and officials resist, no sporting competition can be manipulated, not even by organised crime. It is not sufficient just to educate athletes, coaches and referees, however. It is also essential to establish a culture of transparency, honesty and integrity in all sectors of sport. Sport organisations have a responsibility to promote good governance, so it has to be introduced and implemented – and seen to be implemented. The principles of fair play and setting a positive example have to be applied in daily life, not just written down in a declaration.

Notes

1   Ulrike Spitz is a member of the Working Group on Sport of Transparency International Germany.
2   'Match-fixing' is a catch-all term covering both the manipulation of the results of sporting events and one-off incidents during a sporting event (or in direct connection with a sporting event) by one or more persons deliberately losing or acting in a specific way contrary to the laws of the game. The Council of Europe's Convention on the Manipulation of Sports Competitions defines 'manipulation of sports competitions' as 'an intentional arrangement, act or omission aimed at an improper alteration of the result or the course of a sports competition in order to remove all or part of the unpredictable nature of the aforementioned sports competition with a view to obtaining an undue advantage for oneself or for others': chapter 1, article 3, definition no. 4.
3   *Guardian* (UK), 'Europe hit by "biggest-ever" match-fixing scandal', 20 November 2009, *www.theguardian.com/sport/2009/nov/20/uefa-match-fixing-germany*.
4   World Anti-Doping Agency (Canada), 'The code', *www.wada-ama.org/en/what-we-do/the-code*.
5   See *www.dfb.de/fileadmin/_dfbdam/50986-08_Rechts-Verfahrensordnung.pdf* (§1, no. 2).
6   Gemeinsam-gegen-Spielmanipulation.de (Germany), 'Spiel Kein falsches Spiel', *http://gemeinsam-gegen-spielmanipulation.de/pdf/Broschuere_Spielmanipulation.pdf*.
7   Sport.de (Germany), 'Hoeneß feiert Gewinn durch Zockerei', 10 November 2013, *www.sport.de/medien/fussball/bundesliga-1/33883-19de9b-52f1-13/hoeness-feiert-gewinn-durch-zockerei.html*.
8   Transparency International, 'Tackling match fixing needs good governance' (Berlin: TI, 2012), *http://blog.transparency.org/2012/09/24/tackling-match-fixing-needs-good-governance*.
9   See, for example, Heather Wardle and Andrew Gibbons, 'Gambling among sports people', *www.thepca.co.uk/assets/files/pdfs/Embargoed%20gambling%20research%5B4%5D.pdf*; ESPN (UK), 'Sport's gambling problems revealed in new research', 3 December 2014, *www.espn.co.uk/football/sport/story/375657.html*.
10 See Wigbert Löer and Rainer Schäfer, *René Schnitzler: Zockerliga: Ein Fußballprofi packt aus* (Gütersloh: Gütersloher Verlagshaus, 2011).

4.7

New media approaches to tackling match-fixing in Finnish football

Annukka Timonen[1]

While the magnitude of the problem is not yet known, it is clear that Finland is very vulnerable to match-fixing. The fact that most matches are played in the summer, when other countries' leagues are off-season, draws the attention of match-fixers, while financial difficulties then allow them to influence football clubs and players more easily.[2]

There are also few deterrents to international fixers. The gathering of sufficient evidence to start investigations is a slow and difficult process, and there are no existing laws or institutions that address match-fixing specifically.[3] Instead, cases are either heard under the law of bribery in business (football cases to date) or treated as fraud (for which 20 people were convicted in a high-profile baseball match-fixing case).[4] To date only five football cases from the men's premier division (Veikkausliiga) and from the lower divisions have ended up before the Finnish courts[5] and none have progressed to the High Court of Finland.[6] The absence of a law against match-fixing means that such cases usually result in probation.[7]

This means that international fixers face few risks but can reap high rewards. The most high-profile example was Wilson Raj Perumal, who was sentenced to the maximum two years' imprisonment for match-fixing between 2008 and 2011, then expelled and denied re-entry into Finland on his release. This did not stop him from entering Finland four more times, however. In May 2014 he was finally arrested and sentenced to three months' conditional imprisonment on the grounds of illegal entry and forgery.[8]

Preventative technology

Finland has now woken up to the problem. In 2010 the Finnish professional football players' association (the Jalkapallon Pelaajayhdydtis – JPY) established a five-member working group to design a mobile application against match-fixing called the 'Players Red Button'. The final app became part of the 'Don't Fix It' campaign of the Fédération Internationale des Associations de Footballeurs Professionnels (FIFPro), which also features the Union of European Football Associations (UEFA), Birkbeck – University of London and the Finnish Ministry of Culture and Education as partners in the project.[9]

The app was launched in Finland in 2013 and was downloaded by 1,200 Finnish professional football players.[10] Its main purpose is to allow the players to report information about match-fixing cases anonymously and securely. The app is usually downloaded by players in their dressing rooms following JPY presentations against match-fixing. The players are given individual codes to access the app for security reasons.

The app then allows players to report contact from a match-fixer or their colleagues or even rumours of potential match-fixing. The information is sent directly to the security company chosen by the JPY.[11] The security company processes messages around the clock and, if necessary, forwards the data to the police.[12]

The JPY recognises that the software is just one more tool in the arsenal against match-fixing, and that it does not by itself solve the problem. It also reports that the app has been received in different ways. Younger players tend not to see the need for it, as they have not been exposed to match-fixing, and the idea seems strange; according to the JPY, they have often claimed that they would never need to use the app. Older players, on the other hand, with their greater experience, understand the significance of the app, and they have been encouraging the JPY to take the idea forward.

If the app is shown to be secure, the plan is to test in eight other EU countries: Italy, Romania, Hungary, Norway, England, Scotland, Greece and Slovenia.[13]

Notes

1 Annukka Timonen is chairperson of Transparency International Finland.
2 Johanna Peurala, 'Match-manipulation in football: the challenges faced in Finland', *International Sports Law Journal*, vol. 13 (2013).
3 Police University of Applied Science. 'Rikoslaki puree heikosti jalkapallotulosten' vääristelyyn' [The Penal Code and football's poor representation'], 13 March 2014, *www.polamk.fi/ polamk_tiedottaa/1/0/rikoslaki_puree_heikosti_jalkapallotulosten_vaaristelyyn_17088*.
4 Peurala (2013).
5 JPY (Finland), 'Alhaisilla palkoilla ja ottelumanipulaatioilla selvä yhteys' ['Low salary and match-fixing have clear link to each other'], 28 March 2014, *www.jpy.fi/?pageid=136& newsitemid=450*; Peurala (2013).
6 Police University of Applied Science, 'Rikoslaki puree heikosti jalkapallotulosten vääristelyyn', press release, *www.poliisi.fi/poliisi/bulletin.nsf/vwSearchView/919C6FE29379B977C2257C91 003C0E3E*.
7 Police University of Applied Science (2014).
8 *Helsingin Sanomat* (Finland), 'Pahamaineinen Perumal kävi Suomessa kahdesti viime syyskuussa' ['Perumal visited Finland twice last September'], 3 June 2014, *www.hs.fi/ urheilu/a1401769592143*.
9 *Helsingin Sanomat*. 'Suomen jalkapallo sai ilmiantopalvelun' ['Finland has match-fixing denunciation application'], 23 July 2013, *www.hs.fi/urheilu/a1374465967454*.
10 FIFPro (Netherlands), 'Finnish match-fixing app shows its value', 25 April 2014, *www.fifpro. org/en/news/finnish-match-fixing-app-shows-its-value*.
11 The name of the security company is confidential, for security reasons.
12 *Helsingin Sanomat* (2013).
13 FIFPRo (Netherlands), 'FIFPro and Finnish players union test match-fixing app', 16 July 2013, *www.fifpro.org/en/news/fifpro-and-finnish-players-union-test-match-fixing-app*.

4.8

Prevention and education in match-fixing

The European experience

Deborah Unger[1]

The sheer number of match-fixing scandals[2] in the past decade has shown that football matches can be, and are, fixed anywhere in the world, even top-flight fixtures and inter-national friendlies. A trillion-dollar global betting market,[3] much of it unregulated, makes fixing games a lucrative target for criminals and organised crime. In Europe a series of scandals, most notably the well-publicised story of how a German referee was co-opted by a Singaporean match-fixer in 2005[4] and a sensational trial in 2010 (also in Germany),[5] of four defendants in a case in which it was alleged more than 250 matches were fixed world-wide, focused the attention of football's administrators and politicians. The very integrity of sport was at stake.

The common reaction to match-fixing scandals in the past had always been to consider them one-off events, an aberration that could be stopped simply by sorting out a few 'bad apples'. Clubs and leagues focused on singling out the players or participants involved.[6] With evidence of systemic corruption and international criminal networks targeting Europe, however, it was clear that a different approach would be required.

In 2011 the European Commission allocated resources[7] to combat match-fixing as part of its sports initiative and the Fédération Internationale de Football Association (FIFA), world football's governing body, signed a ten-year €20 million deal[8] with Interpol to raise awareness of the risks. In 2012 the Fédération Internationale des Associations de Footballeurs Professionnels (FIFPro), the players' union, published shocking research into the causes of match-fixing in eastern Europe; the *Black Book*[9] showed how vulnerable players and match officials are in leagues in which clubs fail to pay wages and players are bullied. Two years later the Union of European Football Associations (UEFA), European football's governing body, FIFPro, the European Club Association and the European Professional Football Leagues (EPFL) announced[10] a new code of conduct, specifying that their members take anti-match-fixing measures. By the end of 2014 the Council of Europe had adopted the Convention on the Manipulation of Sports Competitions, open to ratification by all states even beyond the Council of Europe,[11] which established a framework for tackling match-fixing that included education as well as better law enforcement.[12]

Prevention and education

It is important that criminal investigations into match-fixing and prosecutions of those involved are actively pursued to deter criminals from further infiltrating European football, but prevention is also key because it is here that those inside football can make a difference: if you can stop the most vulnerable targets for match-fixers – players and match officials – from participating, matches cannot be fixed. How this is to be done was the target of five education projects, three aimed at football, funded by the European Commission under its 'European Partnerships in Sport' programme,[13] which ran from January 2013 to June 2014.

One of these projects, 'Staying on Side', brought together Transparency International chapters and football leagues in Germany, Greece, Italy, Lithuania, Portugal and the United Kingdom (plus basketball in Lithuania). The project partners were the EPFL and its German member, the German Football League (DFL). The development and outcomes of the project provided a useful lens with which to assess the overall challenges of implementing effective prevention and education programmes in a world struggling to come to grips with the issue of match-fixing, despite the fact the various sport governing bodies were in the process of making such training mandatory. Football leagues in Germany and Poland have already amended their statutes to mandate education programmes to prevent match-fixing and UEFA has introduced an Integrity Resolution that was adopted by its 54 member associations in March 2014, stipulating the need for preventative programmes.[14]

Building trust

Match-fixing in football is a sensitive subject. Clubs and football administrators do not like to talk about it because they fear the media will immediately cast doubt on the integrity of the games. This in turn can have disastrous financial cost, as was shown in Italy after the Calciopoli match-fixing scandal in 2006 that saw gate receipts go down.[15] One important aim of the project was therefore to find how the leagues can show leadership in managing the risk of match-fixing both internally and in their communication to the public.[16]

It was in 2010 that TI Germany started supporting the German Football League in its work to develop prevention programmes to educate players and clubs about the risks of match-fixing.[17] This formed the basis of the 'Staying on Side' project, and helped build the trust that allowed anti-corruption organisations to work with football leagues. It also provided the pedagogical underpinnings for the training approach. It looked at all the risk factors facing those vulnerable to match-fixing (psychological, financial and gambling issues), as well as the infrastructure needed to support them (a safe and secure whistleblower system, plus accessible education) in difficult situations, the goal being to show them how to resist match-fixing approaches.[18]

Everyone acknowledged the importance of communicating this message, but there was reluctance among the participants from the leagues to speak out about the specific actions the clubs and leagues were taking. When there were match-fixing incidents reported in participating leagues during the life of the programme, for example, there was little mention of the prevention and education programmes already in place. Even today this information is not forthcoming when club officials talk about match-fixing, and it is hard to find reference on the leagues' websites to what they are doing to combat match-fixing, with the possible exception of leagues in Austria and Germany.[19]

Scope

The project 'Staying on Side' had three main components: to gather information and evidence about match-fixing, to develop and test training and education programmes and materials, and to seek a more pro-active approach to addressing the problem within the football leagues. Of the six countries where the Transparency International chapter paired with a football league, three collaborations – those in Greece, Italy and Lithuania (in addition to Germany, where the project was already established and then further developed)[20] – led to trials of the educational materials with players and coaches.

In Greece, the project took place at a very challenging time as a high-profile corruption case was ongoing involving officials and players from the Super League – the partner of TI Greece for this project.[21] According to Nagia Mentzi, who supervised the project for TI Greece, it was a challenging but fruitful relationship that took significant effort on both sides and produced some impressive results: TI Greece developed educational materials and arranged workshops with more than 665 players from the Under 17 and Under 20 age groups to discuss honesty and integrity with young players and coaches in all 18 academies of the Super League clubs. It also gave a presentation at the Super League's 2014 annual conference, at which 30 athletes, coaches, referees and sports officials attended a session describing the project and the materials.

In Italy, TI educators visited clubs in Palermo and Brescia in addition to hosting media events in Milan and Rome, where the Serie B league representatives spoke about their commitment to long-term educational efforts to raise awareness of match-fixing. The sessions were attended by more than 100 people.[22] TI Italy also carried out research in collaboration with Catholic University of the Sacred Heart of Milan and the AIC Italian Professional Footballers Association. The research aimed to identify the main behavioural dynamics in Italian football that contributed to the phenomenon of match-fixing. More than 430 questionnaires were completed by players, coaches, and technical and management staff. One striking result was that 42 per cent said there was a medium risk they would be involved in match-fixing and 10 per cent of players thought there was even a high likelihood of involvement.[23]

In Portugal, the TI chapter was able to undertake research in collaboration with the referees' association. It surveyed 1,185 referees of amateur, professional and international competitions about the perception of the problem of match-fixing in Portugal. The respondents believed that as many as eight out of 100 referees participated in match-fixing, primarily because they suffer from economic problems. A second survey, of sports management students, found that more than half believed there was match-fixing in Portugal; a further survey of supporters found that two-thirds believed that match-fixing in Portugal was a result of clubs seeking to get results for sporting reasons, rather than organised crime getting involved for betting reasons (the belief of 18 per cent).[24]

In the United Kingdom, the chapter produced research on the various existing codes of conduct and education materials and subsequently developed a prevention resource manual entitled *Safeguarding the Beautiful Game: A Guide to Preventing Match-Fixing in Football at Club Level*. This guide was developed with input from a number of key stakeholders in the United Kingdom, including the Football Association, the Premier League, the Scottish Professional Football League and the Professional Footballers' Association. The guide is primarily aimed at club officials and coaches with professional football club youth academies having shown the most interest to date. The number of pre-existing initiatives relating to preventing match-fixing within football in the United Kingdom made it impossible to gain buy-in for the project to engage directly with players at football clubs.[25]

The experience in Lithuania, where the first task was to raise awareness of the issue and explain when and how match-fixing happens, is described in a separate chapter.[26]

Longer-term impact

Today no one questions the need for European football to be vigilant about the threat of match-fixing or that it is the responsibility of clubs and leagues to be proactive in preventing it by ensuring those involved in the sport are aware of the dangers and alert to approaches by match-fixers. The single most important longer-term impact of the project was the acknowledgement that football leagues need to adopt good whistleblower protection systems that are safe and secure. This is all the more important now that players and club officials are encouraged or even required to report any match-fixing approaches.[27] The first workshop that brought together all the participants for the 'Staying on Side' project focused on how the German Football League is doing this, via an independent and external ombuds-man, a lawyer and a former referee. These discussions were instrumental in the Scottish Football Association deciding to set up a secure hotline for players and club staff using Crimestoppers, a well-known and respected organisation, to run its reporting hotline.[28] Leagues in Greece and Italy are also discussing what model to use. The EPFL and Transparency International are working to produce guidelines for safe and secure whistleblower systems.

The project also produced a reference guide to the actions and materials produced over the 18-month period.[29] These materials have contributed to a growing library of education resources that clubs and leagues can adopt and use[30] as they mainstream education and prevention into training programmes for all players and officials.

The 'Staying on Side' collaborations underlined the difficulties that organisations face when they have to deal with corruption; they also showed, however, how much can be done in a short time frame. European football and other sports now have a legal framework to fight match-fixing, in the form of the Council of Europe convention cited above and a resolution from the sport's governing body, UEFA, to enforce prevention and education programmes across the continent. There is now a volume of materials and experiences produced in the context of pilot projects such as 'Staying on Side' to help institutionalise and optimise the prevention programmes that will reinforce the integrity of the game.

Notes

1   Deborah Unger is manager of the Rapid Response Unit at Transparency International and was part of the management group for the project 'Staying on Side'.
2   *Guardian* (UK), 'Europol's match-fixing bombshell leaves football authorities in the dark', 4 February 2013, *www.theguardian.com/football/blog/2013/feb/04/europol-match-fixing-football*.
3   Jason Foley-Train, European Gaming and Betting Association, *Sports Betting: Commercial and Integrity Issues* (Brussels: EGBA, 2014), *www.egba.eu/facts-and-figures/studies/6-sports-betting-report*.
4   *Guardian* (UK), 'Two years in jail for match-fixing German referee', 18 November 2005, *www.theguardian.com/football/2005/nov/18/newsstory.sport4*.
5   CNN (US), 'Soccer match-fixing trial begins in Germany', 6 October 2010, *http://edition.cnn.com/2010/WORLD/europe/10/06/germany.match.fixing.trial*.
6   *Daily Express* (UK), 'Cameroon FA brands seven bad apples amid match-fixing probe', 2 July 2014, *www.express.co.uk/sport/worldcup2014/486088/Cameroon-FA-brands-seven-bad-apples-amid-match-fixing-probe*.

7   See European Commission website: *http://ec.europa.eu/sport/policy/organisation_of_sport/match_fixing_en.htm*.

8   Interpol, 'FIFA makes historic contribution to INTERPOL in long-term fight against match-fixing', press release, 9 May 2011, *www.interpol.int/News-and-media/News/2011/PR035*.

9   FIFPro, *Black Book Eastern Europe: The Problems Professional Football Players Encounter* (Hoofddorp, Netherlands: FIFPro, 2012).

10 UEFA, 'European football adopts code of conduct on integrity', media release, 18 September 2014, *www.uefa.org/stakeholders/professional-football-strategy-council/news/newsid=2149775.html*.

11 Council of Europe, 'Council of Europe Convention on the Manipulation of Sports Competitions', *http://conventions.coe.int/Treaty/EN/Treaties/Html/215.htm*.

12 See Stanislas Frossard, Chapter 6.2 'Combatting the risk of corruption in sport: an integovernmental perspective', in this report.

13 European Commission, 'Preparatory actions: 2012', *http://ec.europa.eu/sport/policy/preparatory-actions/preparatory-actions-2012_en.htm*.

14 UEFA's 'European football united for the integrity of the game', 28 March 2013, point 5 (e), says: 'Establish and run comprehensive education programmes, especially for young players, to increase awareness of the risks of match-fixing and to ensure that all those involved in football are aware of, and respect, the relevant rules.'

15 Babatunde Buraimo, Giuseppe Migali and Rob Simmons, *An Analysis of Consumer Response to Italy's Calciopoli Scandal*, Economics Working Paper no. 2014/006 (Lancaster: Lancaster University Management School, 2014).

16 *Ibid.*

17 See Sylvia Schenk, Chapter 6.12 'What the anti-corruption movement can bring to sport: the experience of Transparency International Germany', in this report.

18 See Ulrike Spitz, Chapter 4.6 'Match-fixing: the role of prevention', in this report.

19 When Transparency International was founded in 1993, no one in business or politics wanted to use the word 'corruption'. It took ten years of hard lobbying to create the United Nations Convention against Corruption (2003).

20 See Ulrike Spitz, Chapter 4.6 'Match-fixing: the role of prevention', in this volume.

21 *Financial Times* (UK), 'Football fixing scandal rocks Greek elite', 24 June 2011, *www.ft.com/cms/s/0/70d92868-9e8b-11e0-9469-00144feabdc0.html#axzz3QsY28of8*.

22 Technical Implementation Report submitted by Transparency International to the European Commission in August 2014, p. 17.

23 Sport Economy (Italy), 'La Lega serie B con Transparency International per combattere il match fixing', *www.sporteconomy.it/La+Lega+serie+B+con+Transparency+International+per+combattere+il+match+fixing_49496_8_1.html*.

24 Technical Implementation Report, p. 5.

25 Football in the United Kingdom is administered by four bodies in England and Scotland at the higher level: the Football Association, the Premier League, the Football League and the Scottish Football Association. The Premier League is part of the European Professional Football Leagues and was the main partner in TI's 'Staying on Side' project. All these bodies have training programmes and materials for players, which left little room for Transparency International UK to contribute. The coaching manual was the agreed output after several months of talks.

26 See Rugile Trumpyte, Chapter 4.4 'The gap between sports institutions and the public will: responses to match-fixing in Lithuania', in this report.

27 UEFA (2013), point 5 (c), (d).

28 Crimestoppers and Scottish Football Association set up a hotline in January 2014: *https://crimestoppers-uk.org/in-your-area/scotland/crimestoppers-unites-with-scottish-football-to-keep-it-clean*.

29 Transparency International, *Staying on Side: How to Stop Match-Fixing* (Berlin: TI, 2014), *www.transparency.org/whatwedo/publication/staying_on_side_how_to_stop_match_fixing*.

30 Many organisations have produced match-fixing guides, including FIFA and SportAccord.

4.9

The Austrian approach

How to combat match-fixing and promote integrity in sport

Severin Moritzer[1]

Prior to 2012 the complex set of questions relating to how to deal with the controversial issues of match-fixing and betting fraud had never been tackled in a comprehensive manner in Austria. This changed substantially when the Austrian Ministry of Sport, the Austrian Football Association (AFA) and the Austrian Football League collectively founded the Association for Protecting the Integrity in Sport. Using the brand name 'Play Fair Code'[2] in its day-to-day activities, the association has subsequently been joined by a series of other major sports stakeholders, including the Austrian Federal Sports Organisation, the Austrian Olympic Committee, the Austrian Ski Federation, the Bookmakers' Federation, the Austrian Lotteries and the Austrian Ice Hockey League (Erste Bank Eishockey Liga), together with a range of Austrian betting providers.

The Play Fair Code is primarily funded by the Austrian Ministry of Sport, as well as through annual membership fees and sponsor contributions. The operating team consists of two full-time employees, headquartered in Vienna; the president is former international footballer Günter Kaltenbrunner. There is also ongoing close cooperation with the Austrian Ministry of the Interior, in particular the ministry's Integrity in Sports Unit.

The operating strategy of the Play Fair Code, which was laid down as soon as the organisation was founded and remains clearly defined, lies in prevention and monitoring, and has included the creation of an ombudsman facility to receive communications related to match-fixing in Austrian sport.

Prevention

From the very beginning the Play Fair Code applied a top-down education strategy, with professional athletes (including future professional athletes) constituting the first target group, followed by the interface between professional, semi-professional and amateur athletes, referees and sport representatives. As an estimated 80 per cent of match-fixing cases worldwide take place in football, the Play Fair Code initially focused its efforts on preventative activities in this sport.

Since 2012 all the players in Austria's top two professional leagues, the Austrian Football Association's national youth teams (both men's and women's football), players at its youth academies and the country's top match officials have been trained using a tool developed especially for professional footballers, professional youth team players, referees and linesmen.[3] All nine of the AFA's regional divisions have also received their own information and training, focusing specifically on match-fixing.

Since the beginning of 2013, by combining direct lectures, seminars and workshops focusing on integrity in sport and match-fixing at around 150 training courses, the Play Fair Code has been able to reach approximately 5,000 people within its core target audiences of players, association officials, sports organisation employees and media representatives, amounting to close to 100 per cent of the Austrian professional footballers and referees. A 12–18-month rotating refreshment of the training courses and seminars is also in place to ensure sustainability.

In line with the Code's top-down strategy, 2015's priority is the expansion of training activities into amateur sport, specifically the 48 football clubs of the third-highest Austrian division (regional league). The Erste Bank Eishockey Liga achieved full membership of the Play Fair Code in September 2014, resulting in a new training module being rolled out from spring 2015 for players at the top of the league.[4]

Experience to date has confirmed that the one-to-one athlete education approach is a sustainable and verifiable model of raising awareness and understanding.[5] It also provides a means to speak directly about the penalties for involvement in match-fixing, such as criminal law prosecution, consequences from the point of view of the AFA's regulations, labour law implications and, last but not least, the loss of social reputation.

Monitoring

A system of observation and analysis of matches and match results is now being employed in professional football at almost all levels, providing effective protection against match-fixing. The approximately 30,000 matches played in the top two divisions in each of UEFA's 54 member countries, all European club competitions, and matches between national teams are already subject to professional monitoring.

As a member of the Union of European Football Associations (UEFA), the Austrian Football Association is part of the UEFA monitoring system operated by Sportradar. This protective tool provides sports stakeholders with an effective means of monitoring matches and match results. The Play Fair Code uses the monitoring tool with a didactic approach in order to raise awareness from the athlete's perspective that behaviour on the pitch has a strong impact in terms of transparency and credibility, as athletes understand that their individual behaviour may be analysed from the perspective of potential match-fixing efforts.

The legal situation in Austria and the ombudsman

From a criminal law perspective, match-fixing is currently dealt with as the criminal offence of fraud. This was the basis for criminal convictions in the major football match-fixing scandal that took place in Austria's first division in 2013.[6]

As in the rest of Europe, there are ongoing discussions in Austria about whether the introduction of a specific sports integrity and anti-match-fixing section into the existing criminal law code might facilitate the fight against match fixing. For the moment, however, it would appear that no such addition is on the political and legislative agenda.

Besides the criminal law, there is a strong focus in Austria on the consequences of match-fixing in terms of the AFA's own regulations. As in other countries, there is a specific stipulation in the association's rules requiring players, referees and officials to report suspicions of match-fixing.[7] The report has to be filed with the competent Austrian regional football association.

This obligation to report is particularly emphasised within every training session of the Play Fair Code.

With the idea of creating incentives for informants, the Play Fair Code, in collaboration with the Ministry of Sport,[8] has set up an ombudsman's office through the law firm Niederhuber & Partner Rechtsanwälte GmbH (NHP) since 1 February 2014 as a confidential first point of contact for athletes and participants in sport in the event of issues related to match-fixing. The contacts have been extensively promoted in the Austrian world of sport, and they can be reached by e-mail or telephone around the clock. They are available to help and offer advice free of charge, to receive information and tips about match-fixing that is either being planned or has already taken place, and to investigate the concern.

The ombudsman's office is required to treat any information it receives from informants in total confidence, and it can be contacted anonymously. Working in close collaboration and harmony with the informant/person seeking advice – and, most importantly of all, only ever with their explicit agreement – the ombudsman will then contact the Play Fair Code, in order to find a tailored solution, together with the sports association involved. The ombudsman's activities are evaluated twice per year in order to strengthen the fields of operation and to improve the services offered.

National and international projects on sport integrity

As a national focal point on sports integrity, the work of the Play Fair Code extends beyond match-fixing, and even beyond Austria, to encompass wider activities related to strengthening integrity in sport in the country. As a result of an inter-ministerial working group initiated by the sports minister, Gerald Klug, that proposed texts for provisions relating to its super-structure ('General Commitment to Integrity in Sport') and substructure ('Inadmissible Influence'), the Play Fair Code was entrusted in March 2014 to develop unified conditions governing integrity in sport for all the Austrian professional sports associations. These texts are currently in the process of being integrated with the official statutes and regulations of the professional sports associations. In January 2015 the American Football Federation Austria became the first such association to incorporate these new conditions, and other professional sports associations are expected to follow on a step-by-step basis.

The Play Fair Code is also engaged in efforts to strengthen European cooperation in sport. The European Union's 'Workplan of the European Union for Sport 2014–2017', approved in May 2014, set out a series of concrete measures to be implemented by the Commission and the EU member states, including 'developing a European dimension to the integrity of sport, taking the combating of match-fixing into account in particular'.[9] The Play Fair Code is a member of the 'match-fixing' Expert Group established to exchange best-practice methods in combating match-fixing.

In addition, on 9 July 2014, the Council of Europe approved the Council of Europe Convention on the Manipulation of Sports Competitions within the framework of the Enlarged Partial Agreement on Sport (EPAS). Article 13 of the convention provides for the setting up of a national platform. In this context, the Play Fair Code is a designated part of the network of national regulatory authorities of the sports betting market.

Conclusion

Combating match-fixing demands far-reaching and ongoing efforts from sports associations, law enforcement agencies, betting operators, governmental institutions and other stake-holders. The Play Fair Code has dealt with these demands now for more than three years, gaining experience and developing know-how and good practices by acquiring and involving the relevant stakeholders and exchanging best-practice approaches on a national and international level. This centralised model is the Austrian approach for one of the biggest threats in sport today.

With the prospect of a national platform being established in the future in the context of the EPAS convention against match-fixing, it is satisfying that some milestones have already been achieved in Austria with the Play Fair Code.[10]

Notes

1 Severin Moritzer is chief executive officer for the Play Fair Code, based in Vienna, dealing with prevention, information, training, knowledge transfer and awareness-raising programmes.
2 See the Play Fair Code website: *www.playfaircode.at/startseite*.
3 An overview of the training tool and a full version of a videotaped training session are available on the Play Fair Code website: *www.playfaircode.at/downloads*.
4 The Austrian Ice Hockey League has also received funding from the European Union for a project named 'EU Rookie Cup' as part of the Erasmus+ promotional programme. In this project, the Play Fair Code is an expert partner of the Austrian Ice Hockey League on the issue of integrity in sport and match-fixing.
5 As an accompanying measure, the Play Fair Code offers various e-learning tools, such as those from UEFA, FIFA and the Deutsche Fußball Bund/Deutsche Fußball Liga, on its website based on a link service.
6 For the case of Dominique Taboga, see Reuters (UK), 'Former Austria forward Kuljic jailed over match-fixing', 3 October 2014, *http://uk.reuters.com/article/2014/10/03/uk-soccer-austria-matchfixing-idUKKCN0HS1S120141003*.
7 Article 115a of the Austrian Football Association's rules explicitly states that a failure in reporting perceptions with regard to match-fixing from players, referees or officials may result in sanctions, such as a warning, financial fines or bans.
8 The details can be found on the Play Fair Code website: *www.playfaircode.at/1/ombudsstelle*.
9 Council of the European Union, 'Resolution of the Council and of the representatives of the governments of the member states, meeting within the Council, of 21 May 2014 on the European Union Work Plan for Sport (2014–2017)', 2014/C 183/03 (Brussels: Council of the European Union, 2014), *http://eur-lex.europa.eu/legal-content/EN/TXT/?uri=CELEX:42014Y0614%2803%29*.
10 The Play Fair Code was awarded with the European Play Fair Diploma 2014 by the European Fair Play Movement; see the European Fair Play Movement website: *www.fairplayeur.com*.

PART 5

The US model
Collegiate sports and corruption

5.1

The roots of corruption in US collegiate sport

Donna Lopiano[1]

The United States has one of the few educational systems in the world that integrates high-level sport into secondary and post-secondary education as a financially well-supported extra-curricular programme in which teams from educational institutions compete against each other on a regular basis, including state championship competition at the secondary level and national championship competition at the post-secondary level. At the college and university level, there are over 2,000 higher education institutions in the United States with such sport programmes, called 'intercollegiate athletic programs'. While 'athletics' is a term used worldwide to describe track and field programmes, in the United States 'athletics' is synonymous with 'sport'.

Each of these institutional athletic programmes belongs to some type of regional or national governance association that offers a common set of athletic programme and academic eligibility rules and publishes or recognises sport-playing rules to guide competition between members. Each member institution also belongs to a smaller subset of members, called a 'league' or 'conference', that governs the majority of its regular season competitions against other conference members, usually within a limited geographic area. These conferences are also members of the national governance association and may conduct conference championships as qualifying events for national championships sponsored by the national governance organisation. The governance organisation may establish multiple competitive divisions, requiring member institutions to meet certain minimum and/or maximum limits with regard to the number of sports offered by the athletics programme, the number of contests in a playing season, the beginning and end dates for practice and competition seasons, the number of athletic scholarships that may be awarded in each sport, the number of coaches, and recruiting rules and calendars; these are among the most common forms of control. The association may also establish conditions under which member institutions may participate in pre- or post-season events sponsored by third parties.

Typically, these governance associations limit or prohibit the offering of financial aid to athletes, which are usually termed 'athletic grants-in-aid' or 'athletic scholarships', setting maximum limits to the value of an individual athletic scholarship and limiting the number of scholarships that can be granted in each sport and the number of years students are permitted to receive such grants. Academic eligibility rules usually include requirements for full-time enrolment, minimum grade point averages for initial and continuing eligibility and the requirements related to normal progress towards graduation.[2]

The excessive cost of Division I football and basketball programmes

The largest such association is the National Collegiate Athletic Association (NCAA), which consists of 1,281 institutions. Of these 1,281 institutions, 351 conduct highly commercialised men's football (American tackle football) and/or men's basketball programmes as members of the NCAA's most elite competitive division, Division I.[3] This chapter focuses on the financial and other excesses of this group of institutions in these two sports. It should be noted, however, that the practices described herein can occur at any level of competition and within any educational institution that chooses to place an emphasis on winning at all costs in any sport. Such 'costs' include the loss of academic integrity, sex discrimination and the academic and health exploitation of student-athletes, and these themes are addressed later in this chapter.

NCAA Division I consists of three subdivisions: the Football Bowl Subdivision (FBS; 128 members), the Football Championship Subdivision (FCS; 124 members) and non-football-playing institutions (99 members).[4] FBS members have the richest and most commercial athletic programmes, with annual athletics budgets ranging from US$10.7 million to US$138.2 million in 2012.[5] Notably, only 23 NCAA programmes, all FBS members, representing 2 per cent of all NCAA active members, actually generated more revenues than they spent.[6] The operating losses of the remaining FBS institutions ranged from a high of US$44 million to a low of US$476,000.[7] In 2012 20 per cent of these athletic programmes were supported by institutional allocations from general funds and/or student fees.[8]

The Football Championship Subdivision athletic programme annual budgets range from US$4.6 million to US$44.9 million.[9] No institution generates more revenues than it spends.[10] They are heavily subsidised by institutional allocations (71 per cent of their total operating budgets).[11] The median operating losses in 2012 of US$10.2 million represent a 73 per cent increase since 2004,[12] with losses ranging from a high of US$13.9 million to a low of US$330,000.[13]

The third Division I subdivision consists of athletic programmes that do not sponsor football. Their total operating budgets range from US$3.5 million to US$33.8 million. No institution generates more revenues than it spends. These athletic programmes are also heavily subsidised by institutional allocations (77 per cent of their total operating budgets).[14] The median operating losses in 2012 were US$9.8 million, ranging from a high of US$24.5 million to a low of US$2.8 million.[15]

All these Division I programmes spend disproportionate amounts of their men's sport operating budgets on two sports: football and basketball. In the FBS, 78 per cent of the men's sport budgets is spent on football and basketball, 66 per cent in the FCS and 42 per cent at the basketball-only institutions.[16] With regard to the basketball institutions, this means that the 16 basketball players in these programmes are receiving an incredible proportion of the men's total sport operating expenditures.[17] Athletic department budgets also significantly favour men's sports, with institutions spending two to three times more on men's than on women's. Further, in the past two decades many institutions have dropped sponsorship of many men's Olympic sports in order to fuel the seemingly insatiable 'arms race' among Division I football and men's basketball programmes.[18]

Notably, while FBS institutions are less dependent on institutional allocations, all Division I programmes are still dependent on institutional general-fund budgets or mandatory student fees for large annual subsidies. In the FBS, the median is US$12.2 million, which represents a 19 per cent increase over the previous year.[19] This subsidy is fairly close to the institutional subsidies, which cover median operating losses of US$10.2 million in the FCS and US$9.8 million in the basketball-only subdivision. Herein lies the first problem: athletics as an extracurricular programme whose costs are excessive compared to all other non-academic programmes at the institution. These subsidies have been relatively immune from the recent economic downturn affecting educational institutions worldwide. To the extent that the revenues generated are significant, they do not accrue to the larger institution. Rather, athletic programmes are allowed to use whatever they earn to compete in an 'arms race' that is unrestricted except for benefits that accrue to college athletes. Even if institutions believe that the branding and marketing benefits afforded by athletic programmes are beneficial, the enormous size of the institutional subsidies and their drain on limited resources that could be used for the primary academic purpose of the institution are difficult to rationalise.[20]

The institutionalisation of Division I self-interest within the NCAA

The second problem is the lack of a demonstrated ability to control the growth and excesses of these commercialised programmes at the NCAA or institutional level. This loss of control of Division I sport commercialism is primarily a result of changes in the NCAA governance structure. In 1997 the full NCAA membership gave legislative and financial control to the institutions with the most commercialised athletic programmes, thereby creating a plutocracy that does not exist in amateur or professional sports governance association anywhere else in the world.[21] Even professional sport league owners do not give majority voting power to a minority of the richest owners, enabling the rich to get richer and producing a downward decline in the parity that makes for healthy sports competition. In the United States, the blame for this increasingly unregulated and commercialised Division I sport is a direct result of two factors. First, college presidents say they are unable to control these programmes because of the political realities of alumni and trustee pressure to have winning teams and escalate coaches' salaries.[22] Further, unilateral 'disarmament' is virtually impossible, because it would put the individual institution at a competitive disadvantage vis-à-vis its regular opponents. Second, the NCAA membership's loss of control is directly attributable to threats by the most powerful and successful athletic programmes to leave the organisation (thereby removing the NCAA's primary funding source) if they weren't given legislative and financial control.[23] This control was not ceded just to Division I but specifically to the FBS, the most powerful institutions in Division I.[24] Moreover, in August 2014 the five largest and most powerful conferences or leagues[25] within the FBS, consisting of 65 institutions, were given further autonomy.[26]

This institutionalisation of Division I FBS self-interest, and now particularly the 65 institutions of the 'Big Five' conferences, is all about keeping as much national championship and other non-regular season and post-season championship revenues (the most valuable sport properties) as possible for these institutions themselves. Thus, it is important to understand the sources of this national championship revenue, how it is distributed and who determines the distribution. The NCAA makes most of its money by owning and selling marketing rights to its national championships, and most of the remainder from national championship gate receipts. The bulk of current NCAA revenue is derived from one property: the 68-team single-elimination Division I national basketball championship. This championship generates approximately US$770 million annually in NCAA media rights fees, and in 2013 represented 84 per cent of the NCAA's total revenues of US$913 million.[27]

A small percentage of this revenue is used to operate the NCAA's national office, including the operation of championship events. In the end, though, more than 90 cents of every dollar the NCAA generates are returned to member institutions, for specified purposes in support of student-athletes or based on Division I basketball championship participation, and, within this amount, approximately 90 per cent is returned to Division I institutions.[28] Thus, the NCAA has established a revenue distribution system that is dominated by the philosophy of returning the most money to the members responsible for earning that money rather than using it in a way that benefits the greatest number of student-athletes.

The threats by Division I schools in 1997 to leave the NCAA and the subsequent NCAA restructuring to give controlling power to the FBS were all about the FBS stopping the NCAA from establishing a national FBS football championship so it could own and keep these championship proceeds for itself. Notably, the NCAA does not sponsor an FBS football championship.[29] The College Football Playoff, a four-team play-off accepted by the public as the FBS national championship, begins in the autumn of 2014 and is the sequel to the Bowl Championship Series and its two-team play-off, which existed from 1998 to 2013. The value of the new four-team College Football Playoff is approximately US$470 million per year, and it is owned jointly by all FBS conferences plus Notre Dame, rather than the NCAA.[30] These College Football Playoff national championship proceeds are not shared equally among all FBS members. The 65 'Big Five' conference members take home 75 per cent of the proceeds, and the remaining 25 per cent is distributed to the 60 remaining institutions via other FBS conferences.[31] It is only a matter of time before the College Football Playoff is expanded to eight teams, or more, which would most likely increase its value to the US$1 billion per year level. The goal of the 65 'Big Five' conference institutions is clear: they want to win, and are prepared to spend whatever it takes to win, while maintaining a resource advantage over the other 94 per cent of NCAA member institutions.

Overt exploitation of higher education and college athletes

US institutions of higher education (and the athletic programmes they sponsor) are considered under US law to be not-for-profit educational programmes. As such, they receive significant tax concessions. They do not pay the taxes that businesses or professional sports franchises do. In addition, donors to athletic programmes are permitted to claim individual and business tax deductions for such donations to non-profit organisations. Division I athletic programmes further exploit these tax preferences when they tell their alumni that they can get a better season ticket seat location at football or basketball games on the basis of their total tax-deductible contributions to the athletics programme. This non-profit status also permits athletic programmes to classify athletes as students rather than employees. Further, this preferential tax status allows these institutions to provide football and basketball players with athletic scholarships covering tuition, required fees, room and board and other education-related expenses, and these athletes do not pay taxes on this income. The NCAA restricts the total amount the athlete can receive, however, and this amount is far lower than a professional athlete's salary, and lower than the actual cost of attending college. These NCAA scholarship rules permit the financial exploitation of college athlete talent.

Billion-dollar collegiate national championship sport properties, multi-million-dollar institutional athletic programmes, the full control of athlete talent expenses, a small minority of the most commercialised athletic programmes controlling NCAA rules and financial distributions, and weak presidential control at the institutional level constitute the sources of the myriad corrupt practices that taint the conduct of US intercollegiate athletics, a number of which are addressed in more detail in this chapter. The most prominent of these issues are briefly described here.

Academic exploitation

● Institutions waive normal admissions requirements for academically underprepared but highly talented athletes, thereby placing them in an academic environment in which they cannot reasonably be expected to compete.

● Athletic departments directly or indirectly control academic advising processes, placing athletes in the easiest academic majors and courses, creating a subset of students majoring in athletic eligibility rather than academic degrees with future career value.

● Athletic departments find friendly faculty and engage them as co-conspirators to offer one-on-one 'independent project' courses, for which athletes get academic credit and high grades for doing little or no work, or regular academic courses, in which athletes get grades they do not earn.

● Athletic departments administer their own academic support programmes and hire tutors for college athletes, looking the other way when tutors rather than athletes complete academic assignments.

● Those who report academic fraud have no 'whistleblower' protection. These individuals are most at risk of being chastised and retaliated against.

Restriction of college athletes' academic freedom

● Coaches require their athletes only to take courses that don't conflict with practice times, thereby limiting college athletes' academic choices.[32]

● NCAA rules penalise athletes who transfer to other institutions with the loss of a year of athletic eligibility.[33]

● Requirements to maintain a full-time student schedule of courses and to maintain academic progress over a five-year eligibility period severely limit students with lesser academic ability from trying new courses or majors for fear they may not meet academic eligibility standards for athletic competition and the retention of their athletic scholarships.

Race and gender inequities

● Students of colour are over-represented in the sports of football and basketball and under-represented in most other NCAA sports.[34]

● Female coaches and administrators and male and female coaches and administrators of colour are severely under-represented at all competitive levels of college sport, and even more so in the jobs with the most prestige and highest salaries.[35]

● Despite the United States having one of the strongest laws on gender equity in education in the world, female athletes are still under-represented as participants in intercollegiate sport, and schools spend less money recruiting them than they do for their male counterparts, and do not provide them with the same treatment.[36]

Financial improprieties

● There are over 100 head coaches in Division I institutions making US$1 million or more annually, and in 40 of the 50 states in the United States the highest-paid public employee is the head coach of a collegiate athletic team.[37] The only reason these salaries are possible is that there is no paid athletic talent.

● The athletic department builds facilities and restricts access to these facilities to college athletes only, frequently using tax-free public bonds to finance such projects.[38]

In 40 of the 50 states in the USA, the highest-paid public employee is the head coach of a collegiate athletic team.

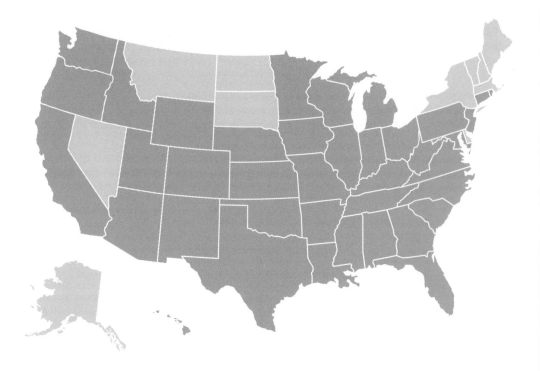

Figure 5.1 Highest-paid public employee = collegiate sports head coach

Source: Based on Deadspin (US), 'Is your state's highest-paid employee a coach? (Probably)', 9 May 2013, *http://deadspin.com/infographic-is-your-states-highest-paid-employee-a-co-489635228.*

- Many athletics facilities are extravagant. Here are some examples.
  - The University of Oregon Ducks' Football Performance Center, a 145,000-square-foot building that cost a reported US$68 million, contains amenities that include a lobby with 64 55-inch televisions that can combine to show one image, a weight-room floor made of Brazilian hardwood, custom 'foosball' tables on which one team is Oregon and the other team has 11 players each representing the rest of the Pac-12 (league opponents), a barber shop and a coaches' locker room with TVs embedded in the mirror.[39] Athletics already has an indoor practice field, an athletic medical centre and a brand new basketball arena and academic study centre for athletes. The new University of Oregon football programme complex contains, among other things, movie theatres, an Oregon football museum, a players' lounge and deck, a dining hall and private classrooms for top players.[40]
  - Athletics-only practice facilities at West Virginia University are utilised solely by the men's and women's athletic teams.[41] In addition to top-tier practice areas, strength and conditioning space, sports medicine needs, team meeting rooms and video and facility equipment, there are first-class locker-room facilities, players' lounges and study areas.[42]

o The Texas A&M University football programme has a 5,000-square-foot players' lounge and academic centre conveniently located one floor above the football locker room, training room and meeting rooms, and across the hall from the new, state-of-the-art, athletics-only academic centre. The players' lounge has oversized leather lounge chairs that recline to a fully prone position so that players can watch the huge widescreen high-definition television – which is equipped with a DVD player. The lounge also contains table tennis, foosball, pool and gaming tables, and several arcade-style gaming stations feature the latest PlayStation 2, XBox and other video games. Mounted in corners of the room are several flat-screen TVs. Immediately to the left of the lounge's entrance is a marble-top bar that contains soft drink and confectionery machines for the players' use.[43]

- Academic support facilities for athletes are often of higher quality than those available to the student body. Weight-training facilities are often larger and include higher-quality equipment than those available to the student body. Gymnasia or fields that are used only for basketball or athletics team practices are left unused for the majority of the day.
- Many FBS teams travel by chartered aeroplane – a financial extravagance.

Academic eligibility and related academic issues

- The NCAA invented its own graduation rate definition, which is less rigorous and not comparable to the federal definition of graduation rate.[44] Thus, the performance of college athletes cannot be easily compared to other students not participating in athletics.
- The initial eligibility requirements for incoming freshman athletes are low and excessively dependent on high-school grade point averages, which are commonly viewed as inflated.
- The continuing academic eligibility requirements are minimal, enabling some athletes to spend only two or three semesters in college doing little academic work before leaving to play professional sports.
- Many sports permit a large number of regular season contests, resulting in an excessive number of classes being missed.
- FBS national conferences have been formed to ensure large television audience reach. As a result, cross-country or long-distance team travel is commonplace, again meaning that too many classes are missed.

Athletes treated as employees

- Most institutions award athletics scholarships for one year at a time, allowing coaches to pressure athletes to leave if they find better-talented alternatives (the equivalent of termination of employment).
- In season, coaches require athletes in football and basketball to put in 40–50 hours per week in athletics-related activities, leaving little time for academic responsibilities.
- Coaches establish team rules that allow them to control almost everything an athlete does, with penalties for violations of team rules including loss of athletic scholarship support (again, the equivalent of termination of employment).
- Due-process protection of athletes is extremely limited. Athletic department employees are often involved in institutional appeals processes when athletics financial aid is terminated and then challenged by students.[45]
- Because athletes are not employees, they are not permitted under US law to unionise and work together to address grievances.[46]

- The NCAA does not have a code of ethics for coaches that protects athletes from verbal, mental or physical abuse or defines improper behaviour with regard to coach–athlete relationships.
- Even though US education law prohibits sexual abuse and harassment in educational settings, 20 per cent of higher education institutions allow athletic departments to investigate and adjudicate athlete or coach transgressions.[47]

Absence of athlete health protection

- The NCAA provides catastrophic insurance, but neither the NCAA nor its member institutions provide athletes with basic injury insurance. Although NCAA rules prohibit students from participating in athletics without athletic injury insurance, most institutions require athletes and their parents to purchase these policies. Most institutions carry secondary coverage policies.
- The NCAA is facing a series of lawsuits related to concussions in contact sports such as football. Plaintiffs allege that the institutions allowed athletes to return too soon and without physician clearance or that the NCAA had knowledge of the effect of concussions but failed to adopt policies to protect athletes, with those athlete now suffering early-onset dementia or similar disabilities.[48] In the United States, professional football players are limited to no more than two contact practices each week during the season (the result of players' union agreements). There are no similar restrictions for collegiate football, however. It was only recently that the NCAA adopted a concussion treatment policy.

Is reform possible?

Given the current structure of the NCAA – one of control by the Division I FBS – it appears highly unlikely that commercialised athletic programmes will act to restrain themselves from continuing to act against the best interests of college athletes and their host higher education institutions. It has been suggested by many that only action by the United States Congress will produce the necessary reforms. Several proposals have been advanced: (1) the establishment of a federally chartered non-profit organisation that would replace the NCAA with an independent board of expert directors and strict reform instructions; (2) a federal regulatory commission; or (3) establishing US Higher Education Act reform conditions that, if not met, would result in ineligibility for federal funding or a loss of tax privileges.[49] It appears to be time for the US Congress to act.

Notes

1   Donna Lopiano is president and founder of Sports Management Resources, based in Shelton, Connecticut, which brings the knowledge of educational sports experts to help athletics directors solve the integrity, equity, growth and development challenges of their respective athletics programmes.

2   For further information on the general structure and function of interscholastic and intercollegiate sport in the United States, see Mary Hums and Joanne MacLean, *Governance and Policy in Sport Organizations* (Scottsdale, AZ: Holcomb Hathaway, 2004). For further information on the most commercialised and problematic US college sport programmes, see Ronald Smith, *Pay for Play: A History of Big-Time College Athletic Reform* (Urbana, IL: University of Illinois Press, 2011); Wilford Bailey and Taylor Littleton, *Athletics and Academe: An Anatomy of Abuses and a Prescription for Reform* (New York: American

Council on Education, 1991); and James Duderstadt, *Intercollegiate Athletics and the American University: A University President's Perspective* (Ann Arbor, MI: University of Michigan Press, 2003).

3   National Collegiate Athletic Association, 'NCAA members by division' (report run 10 April 2015), *http://web1.ncaa.org/onlineDir/exec2/divisionListing*.

4   Ibid.

5   National Collegiate Athletic Association, *Revenues and Expenses 2013: NCAA Division I Intercollegiate Athletics Program Report* (Indianapolis: NCAA, 2013), p. 44, *www.ncaapublications.com/p-4306-revenues-and-expenses-2004-2012-ncaa-division-i-intercollegiate-athletics-programs-report.aspx* (based on 121 members reporting). It should be noted that, while NCAA data are based on audited financial statements provided by institutions, they cover operating expenses only, thereby excluding millions of dollars of capital costs per school each year. A study commissioned by the NCAA has estimated that the average FBS athletic programme had annual capital costs of over US$20 million: see Robert Litan, Jonathan Orszag and Peter Orszag, *The Empirical Effects of Intercollegiate Athletics: An Interim Report* (Indianapolis: NCAA, 2003), *www.ncaa.org/sites/default/files/empirical_effects_of_collegiate_athletics_interim_report.pdf*. These losses must be financed by university or state funds, further diminishing already thin educational and fiscal resources.

6   Ibid., p. 8.

7   Ibid., p. 46.

8   Ibid., p. 8.

9   Ibid., p. 72.

10 Ibid., p. 14.

11 Ibid., p. 8.

12 Ibid., p. 19.

13 Ibid., p. 70.

14 Ibid., p. 8.

15 Ibid., p. 96.

16 Ibid., pp. 32, 36 (FBS), pp. 58, 62 (FCS), pp. 84, 88 (non-football). This is not to suggest that the players are receiving the funds. In fact, player benefits are strictly limited by the NCAA to the value of an athletic scholarship, while no such restrictions apply to coaches' salaries, which may be in the multiple millions of dollars.

17 National Collegiate Athletic Association, *Student-Athlete Participation: 1981/82–2013/14* (Indianapolis: NCAA, 2014), p. 76. The average number of athletes on a Division I men's basketball team is 15.7.

18 Ibid. Institutions usually do not try to eliminate female sports programmes, because of a fear of lawsuits. Females are significantly under-represented at most institutions, in violation of US education law.

19 Ibid., p. 12.

20 Drake Group, 'Student fee and institutional subsidy allocations to fund intercollegiate athletics', position statement, 2 March 2015, *https://drakegroupblog.files.wordpress.com/2015/04/position-statement-student-fees-final-3-2-15.pdf*.

21 Donna Lopiano, 'Fixing enforcement and due process will not fix what is wrong with the NCAA', *Roger Williams University Law Review*, vol. 20 (2015).

22 Knight Commission on Intercollegiate Athletics, *Quantitative and Qualitative Research with Football Bowl Subdivision University Presidents on the Costs and Financing of Intercollegiate Athletics: Report of Findings and Implications* (Baltimore, MD: Art & Science Group, 2009), *www.knightcommissionmedia.org/images/President_Survey_FINAL.pdf*; Amy Perko and Rick Hesel, 'A sustainable model? University presidents assess the costs and financing of intercollegiate athletics', *Journal of Intercollegiate Sport*, vol. 3 (2010).

23 Lopiano (2015).

24 Ibid.

25 These conferences are the Atlantic Coast Conference (ACC), the Big 12, the Big Ten, the Southeastern Conference (SEC) and Pac-12.

26 ESPN (US), 'NCAA board votes to allow autonomy', 8 August 2014, *http://espn.go.com/college-sports/story/_/id/11321551/ncaa-board-votes-allow-autonomy-five-power-conferences*.

27 *Indianapolis Star* (US), 'NCAA approaching $1 billion per year amid challenges by players', 27 March 2014, *www.indystar.com/story/news/2014/03/27/ncaa-approaching-billion-per-year-amid-challenges-players/6973767*. Note that the data are based on NCAA tax forms, NCAA bond prospectuses, NCAA financial statements and interviews, and are consistent with 2013 NCAA financial statements: see *www.ncaa.org/sites/default/files/NCAA_FS_2012-13_V1%20DOC1006715.pdf*; see also US News, 'The case for paying college athletes', 6 January 2014, *www.usnews.com/opinion/articles/2014/01/06/ncaa-college-athletes-should-be-paid*.

28 National Collegiate Athletic Association, '2014 finances', *www.ncaa.org/about/resources/finances*.

29 Lopiano (2015).

30 *USA Today*, 'Power Five's college football playoff revenues will double what BCS paid', 16 July 2014, *www.usatoday.com/story/sports/ncaaf/2014/07/16/college-football-playoff-financial-revenues-money-distribution-bill-hancock/12734897*.

31 *Chronicle of Higher Education* (US), 'The "Big Five" power grab: the real threat to college sports', 19 June 2014, *http://chronicle.com/article/The-Big-Five-Power-Grab-/147265*.

32 Robert A. McCormick and Amy Christian McCormick, 'The myth of the student-athlete: the college athlete as employee', *Washington Law Review*, vol. 81 (2006), p. 71.

33 National Collegiate Athletic Association, *2014–15 NCAA Division I Manual* (Indianapolis: NCAA, 2014), *www.ncaapublications.com/productdownloads/D115.pdf*; see article 14.5.1, p. 168.

34 National Collegiate Athletic Association, 'Race and gender demographic search', *http://web1.ncaa.org/rgdSearch/exec/main*.

35 Ibid.

36 Amy Wilson, *The Status of Women in Intercollegiate Athletics as Title IX Turns 40* (Indianapolis: NCAA, 2012), *www.ncaapublications.com/p-4289-the-status-of-women-in-intercollegiate-athletics-as-title-ix-turns-40-june-2012.aspx*. Even if one argues that schools are spending most money in the sports that generate the most revenues, with male and female athletes in non-revenue sports suffering equally, there can be no economic justification for violating federal laws prohibiting discrimination. If economic justifications were permitted, wealthy individuals and institutions would be allowed to violate discrimination laws.

37 Deadspin (US), 'Infographic: is your state's highest paid employee a coach? (Probably)', 9 May 2013, *http://deadspin.com/infographic-is-your-states-highest-paid-employee-a-co-489635228*.

38 Drake Group, 'Establishment of a presidential commission on intercollegiate athletics reform', position statement, 31 March 2015, *https://drakegroupblog.files.wordpress.com/2015/03/final-presidential-commission-position-paper.pdf*.

39 Business Insider (US), 'Oregon's new $68-million football facility is like nothing we've ever seen in college sports', 31 July 2013, *www.businessinsider.com/new-oregon-football-building-photos-2013-7#*; *Register-Guard* (US), *www.registerguard.com/rg/news/local/30050174-75/football-autzen-oregon-center-building.html.csp*.

40 Inside Higher Ed (US), 'Money still talks', 23 July 2012, *www.insidehighered.com/news/2012/07/23/criticism-athletics-spending-wake-penn-state-unlikely-slow-growth*.

41 Mountaineer Athletic Club (US), 'Current projects', *www.mountaineerathleticclub.com/page.cfm?storyid=103*.

42 Ibid.

43 Texas A&M University, 'Athletics', *www.aggieathletics.com/ViewArticle.dbml?DB_OEM_ID=27300&ATCLID=205237707*.

44 The Federal Graduation Rate (FGR) for all students includes all entering full-time students but excludes transfers in or out. The NCAA's Graduation Success Rate (GSR) adjusts

institutional rates for transfers, however, even though there is currently no method of verifying that athletes who transfer out actually graduate. The FGR is also inflated compared to the GSR because it includes entering full-time students who drop down to part-time status and take longer to graduate, whereas athletes are required to be full-time students making normal progress towards a degree. The GSR also includes 11,000 Ivy League and military academy students who (1) do not receive athletic-related aid, (2) are not admitted as athletes and (3) are considered properly as regular students in the FGR. In other words, the GSR is 'spin' and 'padded'.

45 Drake Group, 'Fixing the dysfunctional NCAA enforcement system', position statement, 7 April 2015, *https://drakegroupblog.files.wordpress.com/2015/04/tdg-position-fair-ncaa-enforcement.pdf*.

46 Currently under appeal is a Region 13 National Labor Relations Board decision that ruled that Northwestern University football players were employees and would be permitted to unionise: see *www.nlrb.gov/news-outreach/news-story/nlrb-director-region-13-issues-decision-northwestern-university-athletes* for the full text of the decision.

47 US Senate Subcommittee on Financial Contracting and Oversight, 'Survey of campus sexual violence policies and procedures', *www.mccaskill.senate.gov/pdf/McCaskill SurveyCampusSexualAssaults.pdf*.

48 In July 2014 the NCAA negotiated a US$75 million settlement to resolve the initial group of these lawsuits, which is currently being challenged. The settlement proposes a 50-year medical monitoring programme, estimated to cost US$55 million, and US$5 million for concussion research, with up to US$15 million designated for attorney's fees. The settlement proposes that plaintiffs as a class give up their rights to seek personal injury damages. In August 2014 formal objection to the settlement was filed, and the objection is still under consideration at the time of this writing. See *USA Today*, 'Opposition to NCAA concussion settlement filed in federal court', 23 August 2014, *www.usatoday.com/story/sports/college/2014/08/23/objection-to-ncaa-concussion-settlement-filed-anthony-nichols/14490501*.

49 Drake Group (31 March 2015).

5.2

Academic fraud and commercialised collegiate athletics

Lessons from the North Carolina case

Jay M. Smith[1]

The recent revelation of the scale of the academic/athletic fraud scandal at the University of North Carolina – Chapel Hill (UNC) has exposed a systemic weakness in the US higher education structure: the financial lure of sporting success can easily lead to the widespread and systematic compromising of academic standards.

UNC is a highly regarded institution ranked among the so-called 'public ivies' that provide affordable educations comparable in quality to those offered at Harvard, Yale and Princeton. It has top-flight graduate programmes and a diverse undergraduate population of approximately 18,000. It boasts illustrious alumni – including one US president and multiple Pulitzer Prize winners – from many fields. Since 1987, UNC students have won more Rhodes scholarships than students at any other public research university.[2]

UNC also enjoys a sporting identity known the world over. The alma mater of Michael Jordan and soccer superstar Mia Hamm, the winner of 40 national championships in six different sports, one of the world's leading merchandisers of sports apparel, and a partner (with Duke University) in what many regard as the best rivalry in all of US sports, UNC is a colossus of collegiate athletics. By the importance it confers on sports, and through its cultivation of an institutional 'brand' partly defined by its sporting success, UNC exemplifies the peculiarly American melding of higher education and commercialised sports. Unlike university systems in any other country, American institutions of higher learning sponsor sports programmes in which recruited 'student-athletes' participate (UNC has approximately 800 athletes in 28 sports) and which fans and alumni of the institution support through cash donations, the purchase of game tickets, and consistently high television ratings. American universities have created an enormously profitable entertainment enterprise – college sports programmes, especially in basketball and football, take in approximately $11 billion annually – and they have become psychologically and even financially dependent on the goodwill created by their teams' successes on the field.[3]

The institution's recent experience therefore stands as a cautionary tale. Between the early 1990s and 2011, UNC was host to the largest and longest-running academic scandal in the history of intercollegiate athletics, the full dimensions of which university leaders assiduously tried to cover up for years.[4] The course fraud scheme, which Drake Group[5] president Gerald Gurney has called 'the largest and most egregious case of academic fraud by far' in the history of the National Collegiate Athletic Association (NCAA), sends one unmistakable message about college athletics in the United States: university structures will inevitably be pressured to accommodate the needs of their respective athletic departments.[6] Too often, the will to accommodate those needs opens the road to corruption.

The fundamentals of the long-running UNC course fraud scheme are well known. In the former Department of African and Afro-American Studies (AFRI/AFAM), the chair and his administrative assistant arranged for the creation of 'Potemkin courses'[7] that enrolled athletes in disproportionate numbers, required no attendance and little real work (the worst of the courses were called 'paper classes') and invariably awarded students marks that boosted their grade point average (GPA)[8] – and provided other academic benefits – as needed.[9] The scheme unfolded over two decades; there were more than 3,000 student enrolments in the sham courses, almost half of which involved athletes, even though athletes account for no more than about 4 per cent of undergraduate enrolments at UNC. The department chair, Julius Nyang'oro, and his administrative assistant, Debby Crowder, were the central figures in facilitating the fraud.[10]

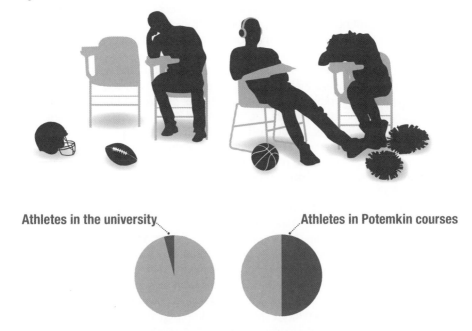

Athletes in the university   **Athletes in Potemkin courses**

From the early 1990s to 2011, the University of North Carolina – Chapel Hill Department of African and Afro-American Studies enrolled more than 3,000 students in 'Potemkin courses' that required no attendance and little real work and awarded marks that boosted their grade point average and provided other academic benefits. Almost half these students were athletes.

Figure 5.2 'Potemkin' courses for athletes

Adapted from: University of North Carolina – Chapel Hill, 'Investigation of irregular classes in the Department of African and Afro-American Studies at the University of North Carolina at Chapel Hill', 16 October 2014, *http://tinyurl.com/p7eqxrb*.

The pretext that college athletes in the highly commercialised sports of American football and basketball are actually 'students first' forces the NCAA and its member institutions to develop elaborate disguises for the priorities they pursue. Keeping athletes academically eligible to play, constantly available to their teams and to their coaches, is in fact the chief function of academic support centres in athletic departments. Because the athletes' 'amateur' (meaning unpaid) status depends legally and morally on their presumed identities as 'students first', however, the eligibility manoeuvres that determine course schedules, choice of major field and academic workloads must be dressed up so that casual observers will assume that athletes are following authentic and typical educational pursuits.[11] This is a massive operation that requires the complicity and active planning of many. UNC provides an ideal case study in the forms of hypocrisy that big-time athletic programmes require of the universities that host them. Its example should be studied intently by institutions of higher learning the world over, to help them avoid succumbing to similar pressures.

For three years and more, UNC's leaders tried to foist on an inquisitive public a tightly focused narrative of corruption. They insisted that the problems with phoney courses (revealed by a local newspaper in 2011) were all the fault of two 'rogue' individuals centred in a single academic department.[12] Thanks to the recent investigation headed by Kenneth Wainstein,[13] the world has now seen that academic fraud was in fact pervasive in Chapel Hill.[14] Evidence from the Wainstein report, together with an insiders' account of the UNC scandal recently published by Mary Willingham and me, shows that the UNC experience was symptomatic of a dysfunctional academic culture in the commercialised athletic programmes of American universities.[15]

Evidence now made public establishes beyond doubt that the academic corner-cutting and administrative chicanery that were part and parcel of UNC's athletic eligibility system required the willing participation of a great number of people on the athletic and academic sides of campus. Those willing to facilitate fraud, or to turn a blind eye to its un-folding, included many members of the faculty in addition to Nyang'oro. Whether through apathy and indifference, their own enthusiasm for sports or fear of administrative reprisal on a campus where most faculty do not enjoy the protections of tenure, faculty members and other staff in departments across campus proved 'useful' to the academic counsellors for athletes during the scandal years. In the Wainstein documents, regular academic advisers are shown facilitating the 'adding' of sham independent study courses for irregular credit hours. The athletics compliance director – the person whose job it was to ensure that the UNC athletic department violated no NCAA standards – is shown joking about the 'notorious' paper classes and the uses to which they were being put by academic counsellors. Tutors are caught revising athletes' 'paper class' papers for them. A head coach asks the academic counsellor for his team to place one of his players in an 'ace in the hole' independent study course. A powerful dean is revealed to have had suspicions about AFRI/AFAM independent study courses – which were offered by the hundreds each year – while doing nothing to investigate the department's curriculum or its course scheduling practices. A professor in the geography department is shown acquiescing in a request to offer an 'independent study' to five women's basketball players during a summer session – the request coming not from the students but from their academic counsellor in athletics.[16]

This particular academic counsellor was one of the most prominent and notorious participants in the UNC course fraud scheme because in the years between 2011 and 2014 she also happened to serve as the elected chair of the university's faculty. Jan Boxill joined the philosophy department as a lecturer in 1988, when she also began her service as academic counsellor for the women's basketball team. A former player and coach, and an announcer for the Lady Tar Heels basketball broadcasts, Boxill was fiercely dedicated to the athletic programme and to the athletes she advised. Just how far she took her dedication to athletics became clear with the release of the Wainstein report, which included damning e-mail exchanges between Boxill and Crowder. In one particularly egregious case, from 2008, Boxill is shown haggling over the grade that one of her own women's basketball advisees was set to receive. The e-mail exchange indicates clearly that Boxill understood that Crowder – and not a faculty member – would be assigning the grade, and that the grade would be given in exchange for a 'recycled' paper that had been written (or plagiarised) in an earlier school year.[17] On learning that the paper's deficiencies had even caught the attention of Crowder, and that the administrative assistant was not especially inclined to be generous in this case, Boxill responded that 'a "D" will be fine, that's all she needs'. And that's what she got. Both Boxill and Crowder were willing to overlook the faked writing assignment in order to push this student over the graduation finish line with an independent study that had involved little or no actual 'study'.

Boxill, whose term as chair of the faculty coincided with a period when faculty and non-faculty critics of the university were pushing hard for a real investigation of the athletic programme, worked to stave off any probing of the academic support centre for athletes. In a prime position to cover up her own complicity in a corrupt system, she did what she could to direct critical attention elsewhere.[18] She even endorsed an external report that erroneously laid much of the blame for years of unchecked curricular fraud on a faculty committee.[19] As faculty leader, Boxill played a confidence game that required real chutzpah – a game that might well have worked, had it not been for the commissioning of the Wainstein report.

Anger over the revelations of Boxill's complicity in the athletic scandal helps to explain why she has been removed from her teaching position.[20] Meanwhile, Nyang'oro and Crowder have gone into retirement and the 'paper classes' have been terminated. UNC would have the world believe that the removal of a few scapegoats and the ending of the most offensive curricular abuses from the scandal era have thwarted threats to academic integrity and have placed the university back on a healthy path. In fact, however, the evidence shows that the tentacles of corruption spread far, and that the corruption came in many flavours – some more subtle than others. Only when the disease is treated, and the symptoms recognised as the tell-tale signs of illness that they are – an illness created and driven by the imperative to maintain athletes' eligibility to play – will UNC and other participants in commercialised college athletics be able to restore themselves to health.

The financial pressures intrinsic to the commercial enterprise of collegiate sport inevitably create breaches in the wall defending academic integrity. At UNC, the scheduling of bogus AFRI/AFAM paper classes was the most egregious tactic used to propel the athletic eligibility system, but there were many other long-standing tricks, and many compromised individuals in addition to the two shamed AFRI/AFAM staff. For many years athletes were funnelled to notorious slide courses in geography, French, philosophy, drama, Portuguese, exercise and sport science, education and library science – places that hosted either 'friendly faculty' known for their athlete favouritism, or courses whose real purpose was to boost enrolments by keeping all students happy. Academic counsellors in the athletic programme found all these courses and directed all their needy students into each one.[21] The admission to universities of athletes unprepared or unwilling to tackle genuine college-grade work, a problem exacerbated by the NCAA's lowering of admission standards in 2003,[22] only reinforced athletic department reliance on such courses and such faculty. At UNC, the broad temptation to sympathise with and 'help out' athletes with weak GPAs and impossible practice schedules led to the hardening of suspect curricular patterns.[23]

The Wainstein report shows that, at UNC, academic counsellors knew exactly where to look and whom to approach when athletes had special needs: GPA boosts, grade changes, late course additions or schedules that imposed little to no burden. Moreover, AFRI/AFAM was only one of several units on campus where athletes could get the special treatment they 'needed'.[24] UNC's failure to acknowledge this widespread and deeply ingrained tendency to cut corners – the institution's failure to acknowledge its flourishing culture of 'look the other way' compromise – may prevent it from ever contemplating the sorts of reforms needed to avoid repeat embarrassments in the future.

American universities have been indelibly compromised by their willingness to subordinate academic integrity and educational outcomes to the eligibility imperatives of commercialised sport. Sports, it goes without saying, are worthwhile endeavours in themselves. Extra-curricular activities are nourishing and can enrich the educational experiences of college students everywhere. Participation in activities whose primary purpose is entertainment, such as musical or dramatic performance, is not inherently problematic; but the drive to compete for national championships – a drive fuelled by the massive and continuing infusion of money into athletic departments and the unchecked popular craving for televised sport entertainment – means that coaches and the many people who enable them will almost inevitably facilitate corruption within the academy in the absence of effective anti-corruption systems. Eligibility will always mean more to the stewards of the athletic machine than the educational experiences of the students in their charge. Consequently, faculty will be placed time and again in the uncomfortable position of having to sacrifice their integrity or inflict academic hardship on athletes who have previously been led to believe they would be 'taken care of'. Too often, faculty will choose the path of least resistance, and educational integrity will go by the wayside.

Only a bracing 'coming to consciousness' among faculty and college administrators across the United States, and a vigorous new commitment to transparency in all matters athletic, can offer any hope of ending the hypocritical charade that US universities are currently enacting. American universities might wish to learn from the examples set by other academic communities the world over. Only in the Unites States do for-profit sporting enterprises operate alongside and mingle with the academic infrastructure of universities, and there are many good reasons why this practice is unique. In Europe, Asia and elsewhere, universities remain faithful to their missions and are reflexively regarded as places of learning, research and discovery. Their refusal to become entangled in commercialised sports and the corruption that comes in their wake helps to explain why their reputations as centres of learning remain fully intact – and it points to the tragic bargain with commercialism that has led American institutions of higher education to actively subvert their own values and standards in the name of wins, championships and revenue. To avoid the temptation to make such compromises in their own missions and values, universities across the globe should heed the cautionary tale of UNC and definitively reject the American model for integrating academics and athletics.

Notes

1 Jay M. Smith is a professor in the department of history, University of North Carolina – Chapel Hill.
2 See 'Carolina's Rhodes Scholars', *https://alumni.unc.edu/news/rhodes-scholars-from-unc/*.
3 On revenues, see Al Jazeera America, 'Experts weigh in: should college athletes get paid?', 27 March 2014, *http://america.aljazeera.com/watch/shows/inside-story/articles/2014/3/27/should-college-athletesgetpaidtoplay.html*.
4 *News & Observer* (US), 'UNC scandal ranks among the worst, experts say,' *www.news observer.com/news/local/education/unc-scandal/article10107554.html*.
5 The Drake Group, established in 1999, is a network of academics in the United States with the shared belief that college athletics has become too dominant a presence on US university campuses.

6   CBS Sports (US), 'UNC's unprecedented academic fraud case will test the NCAA', 24 October 2014, *www.cbssports.com/collegefootball/writer/jon-solomon/24765822/ uncs-unprecedented-academic-fraud-case-will-test-ncaa*.
7   The term 'Potemkin courses' is an allusion to 'Potemkin villages', the fake settlements built by Grigory Potemkin along the banks of the river Dnieper in eighteenth-century Russia purely to impress Empress Catherine II. 'Potemkin' is now used as an adjective to describe anything built solely to deceive people that a situation is better than it really is.
8   In the United States, grades from all current classes are averaged to generate a grade point average, which is an important factor for university applicants in the country.
9   UNC's former Department of African and Afro-American Studies now carries the name African, African-American, and Diaspora Studies.
10   For an overview of the UNC course fraud scandal, see *News & Observer* (US), 'Fake-class scheme aided UNC players' eligibility, Wainstein report says,' 22 October 2014, *www. newsobserver.com/news/local/education/unc-scandal/article10104428.html*.
11   For an incisive discussion of the eligibility pressures that bear down on academic counsellors in athletic departments, see Inside Higher Ed (US), 'Academic fraud in collegiate athletics', 2 October 2007, *www.insidehighered.com/news/2007/10/02/fraud#sthash.K81KvTEj. dpbs*.
12   See, for example, the UNC-sponsored report by Governor Jim Martin in December, 2012 (James G. Martin, University of North Carolina at Chapel Hill Academic Anomalies Review: Report of Findings, 19 December 2012, *http://3qh929iorux3fdpl532k03kg.wpengine. netdna-cdn.com/wp-content/uploads/2013/01/UNC-Governor-Martin-Final-Report-and-Addendum.pdf*) as described by the UNC alumni magazine at *https://alumni.unc.edu/news/ martin-says-fraud-isolated-to-african-studies-department*.
13   Kenneth Wainstein, a highly regarded lawyer who served as homeland security advisor to President George W. Bush, was appointed to lead the independent inquiry into the academic irregularities at UNC – Chapel Hill in early 2014.
14   University of North Carolina – Chapel Hill, 'Investigation of irregular classes in the Department of African and Afro-American Studies at the University of North Carolina at Chapel Hill', 16 October 2014, *http://carolinacommitment.unc.edu/reports-resources/ investigation-of-irregular-classes-in-the-department-of-african-and-afro-american-studies-at-the-university-of-north-carolina-at-chapel-hill-2*; see also both the 'Wainstein final report: exhibits' at *https://docs.google.com/file/d/0B9a7FfkXuvZUOGR6ZU5WX3d5TkE/edit* and the 900-page 'Final report supplements' that were issued on the day of the report: *http://3qh929iorux3fdpl532k03kg.wpengine.netdna-cdn.com/wp-content/uploads/ 2014/10/UNC-FINAL-REPORT-SUPPLEMENTS.pdf*.
15   For discussion of the problems afflicting other universities, see Jay M. Smith and Mary Willingham, *Cheated: The UNC Scandal, the Education of Athletes, and the Future of Big-Time College Sports* (Lincoln, NE: Potomac Books, 2015), pp. 207–234.
16   On the adviser, see 'Final report supplements', p. 610; on the compliance officer, see ibid., p. 248; on the coach, see ibid., p. 24; on the dean, see 'Investigation of irregular classes', p. 25; on the tutors, see, for example, 'Wainstein final report: exhibits', p. 16; on the geography professor, see 'Final report supplements', p. 271.
17   'Investigation of irregular classes', p. 44.
18   On Boxill's role in the UNC cover-up, see Smith and Willingham (2015), pp. 96–105.
19   For the reception of the infamous 'Martin report' in UNC's Faculty Council, and Boxill's management of that reception, see Smith and Willingham (2015), pp. 141–143.
20   *News & Observer* (US), 'Jan Boxill, implicated in UNC scandal, resigns', 5 March 2015, *www.newsobserver.com/news/local/education/unc-scandal/article12601562.html*.
21   See Smith and Willingham (2015), pp. 171–174, 186–190.
22   Inside Higher Ed (US), 'NCAA reform gone wrong', 14 February 2013, *www.insidehighered. com/views/2013/02/14/ncaa-academic-reform-has-hurt-higher-eds-integrity-essay*.
23   Alabama law professor Gene Marsh, who once chaired the NCAA's Division I Committee on Infractions, has noted that the presence in the student body of people 'who really don't

belong' because of their academic deficiencies has the inevitable effect of inducing corruption. The imperative to keep players eligible 'means you're going to get more people getting cute, more professors who lose their will and their ethics'. See Inside Higher Ed (US), 'Bad apples or more?', 7 February 2011. On the changed admissions standards introduced in 2003, and their unintended consequences, see Inside Higher Ed (14 February 2013).

24 See the Wainstein 'Final report supplements', *http://3qh929iorux3fdpl532k03kg.wpengine. netdna-cdn.com/wp-content/uploads/2014/10/UNC-FINAL-REPORT-SUPPLEMENTS.pdf*.

5.3

The evolution of professional college sport in the United States

Allen Sack[1]

The United States is the only country in the world in which colleges and universities stage mass athletic spectacles for commercial gain. In 2013 athletic programmes in higher education accounted for an estimated US$6.1 billion in revenue from activities such as ticket sales, television and radio receipts, alumni contributions, guarantees, royalties and association distributions.[2] Given that the athletes in this industry receive only room, board, tuition and fees as compensation, it is not surprising that the issue of providing college athletes with a greater share of the revenues has generated heated debate. This chapter examines the evolution of professional college sport in the United States, and makes recommendations for how to defend academic integrity in higher education from the corrosive aspects of the college sport industry.

Historical context

At its first business meeting, in 1906, the National Collegiate Athletic Association (NCAA) took a position on amateurism that was unequivocal and perfectly consistent with the model inherited from elite British universities and public schools.[3] According to article VI of the bylaws, each institution was required to enforce amateur principles. The 'offering of inducements to players to enter colleges or universities because of their athletic abilities, or maintaining players while students on account of their athletic abilities' were treated as blatant violations of amateurism. Need-based aid not related to sports did not violate amateurism. Athletic scholarships did.[4]

As the twentieth century progressed, rampant commercialism in college sports and the NCAA's lack of enforcement power made violations of amateur rules a national scandal.[5] As the financial stakes increased, so too did the pressure to recruit and subsidise the best players. In an effort to regulate behaviour it could not totally prevent, the NCAA compromised its amateur code in 1956 by allowing subsidies in the form of athletic scholarships. An official interpretation in the 1957 NCAA constitution limited these subsidies to room, board, tuition, fees, books and US$15 a month for laundry.[6]

According to Walter Byers, the NCAA executive director during this period, the new scholarships, which were awarded for up to four years, could not be withdrawn if the recipient chose not to play. He did not want players to be mistaken for employees. When a college player was killed in an aeroplane crash while on an American football trip in the early 1960s, however, his family was awarded workers' compensation benefits, on the grounds that the payments he received each school quarter and his rent money during the playing season were conditioned on his playing football. This ruling was taken very seriously by the NCAA.[7]

Byers was concerned that some colleges were offering one-year grants that could be cancelled if athletes voluntarily withdrew from sports, arguing that these grants 'came perilously close to employment contracts'.[8] Everett Barnes, the NCAA secretary/treasurer, contacted Warren Ashmead, an attorney, to get his opinion, which he shared with Byers. Ashmead's opinion was that, 'if scholarships are not contingent on athletic activity, the athlete would not come under workman's compensation as there would be no penalty to students when and if they cease athletic endeavors'.[9]

The issue seemed settled, until coaches, athletic directors and others began to complain in the late 1960s that athletes were accepting scholarships but deciding not to play. In other words, by granting 'no cut' four-year scholarships, the NCAA was protecting itself from workers' compensation lawsuits, but leaving the membership vulnerable to athletes who correctly concluded that they were not employees under contract and could therefore walk away from sporting activities if they so desired. To address this problem, the NCAA passed rules in 1967 to allow the immediate cancellation of the scholarship of an athlete who voluntarily withdrew from sport or who violated team rules.[10]

The 1967 decision allowed universities to cancel the scholarship of players who decided to quit or who violated team rules, but it did not allow coaches to get rid of 'dead wood' whose lack of skills put their teams at a competitive disadvantage. The NCAA dealt with this problem in 1973 by introducing one-year-renewable scholarships – a strategy that Byers had rejected earlier. This rule, which went unchanged until 2012, allowed the cancellation of an athlete's scholarship at the end of one year for virtually any reason, including injury, contribution to team success, the need to make room for a more talented recruit or failure to fit into a coach's style of play. The contractual nature of this relationship is unmistakable.[11] Athletic performance in one year now became a condition for retaining the grant in a subsequent year.

Not long after the 1973 decision a number of players claimed that they were employees at the time they sustained serious injuries while playing college football. In one case, an athlete relied on what is often called an 'economic realities test' to support his claim to be an employee.[12] According to this test, as used in the state of Michigan, four factors must be present in a contract for hire: the proposed employer's right to control the activities of the proposed employee; the proposed employer's right to discipline or fire the proposed employee; the payment of wages or other benefits for daily living expenses; and whether the task performed was an integral part of the employer's business. The athlete lost his case in this instance, because the judge ruled that college football is not a university business.

Over the next four decades one-year-renewable scholarships provided the burgeoning multi-billion-dollar college sports business with a reliable and disciplined source of cheap labour. Athletes who have not met a coach's performance expectations can be encouraged to transfer, or simply stripped of financial aid. Although several workers' compensation cases have been taken to court over the past couple of decades, NCAA attorneys and NCAA member institutions have been able to persuade judges that college athletes are merely students engaged in an amateur extracurricular activity.[13]

The twenty-first century: the NCAA under attack

Although the NCAA's amateur rhetoric dominated legal thinking throughout the twentieth century, the unbridled commercialisation of big-time college sport in the United States during the opening years of the new century has left the NCAA more exposed to legal attacks than ever.[14] Among the plaintiffs who have sued the NCAA during this period is Ed O'Bannon, a former NCAA basketball player, who challenged the NCAA rule that bars college athletes from receiving a share of the revenue the NCAA and its member institutions earn from the sale of licences to use players' names, images and likenesses. The players contend that these rules are an unreasonable restraint of trade and thus violate the Sherman Antitrust Act, which aims to prohibit anti-competitive practices.

In 2014 the federal judge in the O'Bannon case ruled that the NCAA's limits on what major college football and men's basketball players can receive for playing sports unreasonably restrain trade, in violation of the antitrust laws.[15] The ruling enables football players in the top Division I Football Bowl Subdivision (FBS) and male basketball players in Division I to receive a stipend of US$5,000 a year, taken from the revenue the NCAA generates from the licensing of players' names, images and likenesses. These stipends will remain in trust while athletes are at school. The players will also receive the full cost of attendance, which generally exceeds the current scholarship of room, board, tuition and fees by several thousand dollars, depending on the location of the college or university attended.[16]

According to the judge in the O'Bannon case, the historical record reveals that the NCAA has revised its rules governing athlete compensation numerous times over the years: 'Rather than evincing the association's adherence to a set of core principles, this history documents how malleable the NCAA's definition of amateurism has been since its founding.'[17] This characterisation of the current use and misuse of the term 'amateur' by the NCAA adds considerable support to the central thesis of this chapter, namely that the definition of amateurism used by the founding fathers of the NCAA has been transformed on a number of occasions to suit the NCAA's political agenda. A counterfeit version has replaced the real thing.

The NCAA appealed this case,[18] and other antitrust cases against the NCAA are still in the pipeline. But the most significant challenge to the NCAA's argument that big-time college athletes are amateurs and not professional employees is currently taking place in the state of Illinois, where the National Labor Relations Board (NLRB) has recently ruled that the Northwestern University football team has the right to unionise.[19] Under the common law definition of employment, an employee is a person who performs services for another under a contract for hire, subject to the other's control or right of control and in return for payment.[20] College athletes would appear to fit the common law definition, and the NLRB in Illinois recently used this common law definition to argue its case.

It is significant to note that the NCAA, under pressure from the US Department of Justice, has recently changed its rules to give colleges and universities the option to return to the multi-year scholarships that were in effect before 1973, and that Northwestern is one of the schools that has done so.[21] The NLRB argues, however, that a football player's scholarship can be cancelled immediately if the athlete voluntarily withdraws from sport or abuses team rules. Training for football at Northwestern University continues on a year-round basis. According to the NLRB decision, Northwestern players must devote 40–50 hours per week during the football season to their football duties. Athletes have to schedule classes to meet the demands of sport, and sometimes switch to easier majors to have more time for football. Failure to follow these rules puts an athlete's scholarship at risk.[22] Northwestern has appealed the NLRB decision to the full NLRB. Just as in the O'Bannon case, this is still a work in progress. Nonetheless, it is fair to say that the very thought that plaintiffs might ultimately win these cases has created the greatest crisis in the history of college sport in the United States.

Discussion and recommendations for reform

Throughout the early twentieth century the NCAA was unwavering in its commitment to the core amateur principle that college athletes should receive no financial inducements for participating in collegiate sports. During this same period college sport in many colleges and universities became a very popular form of mass commercial entertainment. As the decades passed, and college sport became a multi-billion-dollar industry, it made no business sense to trust the industry's fortunes to amateur college athletes pursuing sports in their spare time. The NCAA solution was to create a scholarship system that had all the trappings of employment but capped compensation at room, board, tuition and fees.

It was only a matter of time before the fundamental contradiction in this model would lead players to challenge the NCAA in court. If coaches can make millions of dollars a year from these mass athletic spectacles, how is it legal or fair to exclude athletes from this market? Perhaps anticipating a loss in the O'Bannon case, the NCAA's five richest and most powerful conferences have already formed an autonomous unit within the NCAA that can share some of the US$1.5 billion it generates every year with football and men's basketball players. The problem with this strategy is that schools that are already struggling to compete in football with the 'Big Five' conferences will find it impossible to do so without budget cuts that could lead to the elimination of non-revenue-producing sports on many campuses.[23]

While the strategy of the 'Big Five' may lead to reforms that produce financial benefits for a limited number of big-time college athletes, it does nothing whatsoever to address the complex problems facing sport in higher education in the United States today. To quote Congressman Jim Moran, who recently sponsored a bill to establish a Presidential Commission on Intercollegiate Athletics Reform: 'We need to give our colleges and universities the tools they need to sustain healthy intercollegiate athletic programs that benefit the schools and protect our student-athletes.'[24] Moran was not referring only to the athletes in the sports that produce the most revenue, but to all NCAA athletes.

The near-total emphasis on college sport as commercial entertainment creates excessive institutional expenditures on certain sports and has resulted in burdensome mandatory student fees as a funding source for athletic programmes. Money that should support academic programmes and educational opportunities for students is often siphoned into palatial stadiums, training facilities and coaches' salaries.[25] Elite athletes are often relegated to the periphery of student life. Again to quote Congressman Moran, 'Recent scandals involving . . . a number of the nation's most prestigious institutions reveal the absence of policy and practice that would ensure a level of academic integrity, athletic welfare and financial soundness appropriate for non-profit institutions of higher education.'[26]

What may be needed is for Congress to consider replacing the NCAA with a federally chartered corporation that would have a laser focus on education. Professionalism and commercialism cannot be eliminated, but athletes should not be university employees like players in the National Football League. This federally chartered organisation would funnel benefits back to the athletes, but they would be educational and healthcare benefits, not cash payments. This new organisation, which could be called the Collegiate Athletic Association of the United States (CAAUS), would promulgate and enforce rules and regulations in order to achieve reforms such as the following.

- Ownership of the national Bowl Championship Series (BCS) should be given to CAAUS, with the proceeds being used to subsidise member institution programmes that contribute directly to the health, educational success and welfare of college athletes.
- Ensure that athletes are treated as students rather than employees or just athletes by mandating scholarship awards that extend through graduation and prohibiting cancellation for reasons of athletic performance or injury. Cancellation should be permitted only for voluntary withdrawal or serious violations of team rules.
- Require that all full scholarships awarded to Division I athletes cover the full cost of attendance as defined by the federal government, not merely the cost of education – the present NCAA limit.
- A committee composed of members of each faculty senate should closely review the disciplinary rules and regulations created by coaches and athletic directors to ensure they are consistent with academic best practices.
- Require CAAUS and its members each to retain 5 per cent of their gross annual media rights fees in an academic trust fund, to be utilised to disburse education grants to college athletes who have not completed their undergraduate degrees or wish to continue their education.
- Provide strong CAAUS due-process protection for college athletes, institutions and employees in danger of losing participation privileges or incurring financial penalties for alleged rule violations.
- Give CAAUS a limited antitrust exemption to control the cost of athletic programmes by capping sport programme operating expenditures and salary and wage budgets and preventing excessive expenditures.
- Allow freshman eligibility for only those athletes whose high-school grade point average or standardised test scores are within one standard deviation of the mean academic profile of their entering class, thus giving 'special admit' students time to adjust to a more competitive academic environment than they may be used to.
- Provide extensive academic remediation for athletes who are ineligible to play as freshmen and limit their practice time to ten hours a week. Remediation should begin in the summer, before these athletes enter college.
- Require that all academic and counselling support services for college athletes be under the direct supervision and budgetary control of the institution's academic authority, administered externally to the athletic department, and be consistent with counselling and support services for all students.
- Require institutions to provide 'whistleblower protections' for those who disclose unethical conduct or institutional rules violations related to the conduct of athletics programmes.
- Limit athletic playing and practice seasons so as to minimise interference with athletes' opportunities for acquiring a high-quality education in a manner consistent with that afforded to the general student body.
- Institutions should work with faculty senates to ensure that athletic contests are scheduled such that they minimise conflict with class attendance, and no athlete should be prohibited from taking a class that may occasionally conflict with a practice, or team, meeting.

These are just a few suggestions, to demonstrate the priorities of this new organisation. The CAAUS would allow universities to continue to provide a point of emotional attachment for fans, alumni and students. In fact, it could increase fan interest in athletic programmes that are not part of the major conferences. This model contains some of the best aspects of college sports in the United States, where competitive sport has always been a part of campus life.

Notes

1   Allen Sack is professor in the College of Business at the University of New Haven, Connecticut, and was a member of the University of Notre Dame's 1966 National Championship football team. He is immediate past president of the Drake Group, an organisation committed to defending academic integrity in college sports.

2   See the National Collegiate Athletic Association's revenue page: *www.ncaa.org/about/ resources/finances/revenue*.

3   Howard Savage, *Games and Sports in British Schools and Universities* (New York: Carnegie Foundation for the Advancement of Teaching, 1927), p. 78.

4   NCAA, formerly the Intercollegiate Athletic Association of the United States (IAAUS), *Proceedings of the First Annual Meeting* (New York: IAAUS, 1906), p. 33.

5   Jack Falla, *NCAA: The Voice of College Sports* (Mission, KS: NCAA, 1981), pp. 9–17.

6   'Constitution of the National Collegiate Athletic Association, including official interpretations: article III', in *NCAA 1956–57 Yearbook* (Kansas City, MO: NCAA, 1956), p. 4.

7   In a letter from Robert F. Ray, NCAA president, and Everett D. Barnes, secretary/treasurer, to faculty representative and athletic directors of member institutions, a request was made for institutions to protect themselves from further workmen's compensation claims by student athletes by changing the wording of grants-in-aids to ensure that there did not appear to be an employment relationship: see Unorganized Walter Byers Papers, Workman Compensation Folder, 21 December 1964, NCAA headquarters, Overland Park, Kansas. See also Allen Sack and Ellen Staurowsky, *College Athletes for Hire: The Evolution and Legacy of the NCAA's Amateur Myth* (Westport, CT: Praeger, 1999), pp. 81–82

8   Walter Byers, *Unsportsmanlike Conduct: Exploiting College Athletes* (Ann Arbor, MI: University of Michigan Press, 1995), p. 75.

9   Everett D. Barnes, letter to Walter Byers, 6 July 1964, Walter Byers Papers, Long Planning Folder, NCAA headquarters, Overland Park, Kansas.

10 M.R. Clausen, the person who proposed this amendment, argued that it would allow an athlete who had voluntarily left sport to be referred for disciplinary action, which could lead to the withdrawal of financial aid; see NCAA, *Proceedings of the 61st Annual Convention* (Kansas City, MO: NCAA, 1967), p. 122.

11 Robert A. McCormick and Amy Christian McCormick, 'The myth of the student athlete: the college athlete as employee', *Washington Law Review*, vol. 8 (2006).

12 *Coleman* v. *Western Michigan University*, 336 N. W. 2n 224 (1983).

13 See *Rensing* v. *Indiana State University*, 444 N.E. 2d. 1173 (1983). Kent Waldrep was rendered a quadriplegic in a Southeast Conference football game in 1974. Waldrep lost his final appeal in his legal quest for workman's compensation benefits in 2000. It may be prophetic that the judges concluded their opinion by noting that 'college athletics has changed dramatically over the years', and they could not say what their ruling would be 'if an analogous case were to arise today'. See *Waldrep* v. *Texas Employers Insurance Association*, 21 S.W.3d 692 (Tex. App. 2000).

14 Mary Grace Miller, 'NCAA and the student-athlete: reform is on the horizon', *University of Richmond Law Review*, vol. 46 (2012).

15 *New York Times* (US), 'N.C.A.A. must allow colleges to pay athletes, judge rules', 8 August 2014, *www.nytimes.com/2014/08/09/sports/federal-judge-rules-against-ncaa-in-obannon-case.html*.

16 *New York Times* (US), 'What the O'Bannon ruling means for colleges and players', 8 August 2014, *www.nytimes.com/2014/08/09/sports/what-the-obannon-ruling-means-for-colleges-and-players.html*.

17 *Edward O'Bannon* et al., *Plaintiffs* v. *National Collegiate Athletic Association; Electronic Arts Inc.; and Collegiate Licensing Company, Defendants*, no. C 09-3329 CW (N. D. Cal. 2014), *www.nacua.org/documents/Wilken-NCAA-Order_8-11-14.pdf*, p. 80.

18 *New York Times* (US), 'After ruling in O'Bannon case, determining the future of amateur athletics', 21 October 2014, *www.nytimes.com/2014/10/22/sports/after-obannon-ruling-figuring-out-whats-next.html.*

19 ESPN (US), 'Northwestern players get union vote', 27 March 2014, *http://espn.go.com/college-football/story/_/id/10677763/northwestern-wildcats-football-players-win-bid-unionize.*

20 Charles Muhl, 'What is an employee? The answer depends on the federal law', *Monthly Labor Review* (January 2002), p. 3.

21 Thomas Bright, 'NCAA institutes multi-year scholarships', *DePaul Journal of Sports Law and Contemporary Problems*, vol. 8 (2011).

22 NLRB, Illinois, 'United States Government before the Labor Relations Board, Region 13', Northwestern, Employee, and College Athletes Players Association (CAPA), Petitioner, case 13-RC-121359, *www.cnn.com/2014/images/03/26/Decision_and_Direction_of_Election.pdf.*

23 *Chronicle of Higher Education* (US), 'The "Big Five" power grab: the real threat to college sports', 19 June 2014, *http://chronicle.com/article/The-Big-Five-Power-Grab-/147265.*

24 *Fairfax News* (US), 'Rep. Moran introduces bill to reform NCAA', 1 December 2014. For a discussion of the bill, see *News & Observer* (US), 'US legislation would create presidential commission for college sports', 4 December 2014, *www.newsobserver.com/2014/12/04/4376880_federal-legislation-would-create.html?rh=1.*

25 David Ridpath, Brian Porto, Gerald Gurney, Donna Lopiano, Allen Sack, Mary Willingham and Andrew Zimbalist, 'The Drake Group position statement: student fee allocations to fund intercollegiate athletics', 2 March 2015.

26 See *www.arlnow.com/2014/12/02/moran-introduces-bill-to-reform-broken-college-sports-system.*

5.4

Inequality, discrimination and sexual violence in US collegiate sports

Erin Buzuvis and Kristine Newhall[1]

College athletics is a popular cultural institution, attracting thousands of participants and millions of fans each year. Yet, examining US college athletics reveals a pattern of inequality, discrimination and abuse, which operates to foreclose women's access and suppress women's interest in athletic participation and leadership. This chapter examines three gender-related issues of integrity in college athletics: gender discrimination in athletic participation and opportunity; barriers to leadership for women coaches and administrators; and the relationship between athletics and sexual violence at college and universities.

Discrimination in athletic participation and opportunity

Colleges and universities provide the majority of athletic opportunities to men,[2] even though women make up a majority of college students.[3] This imbalance exists despite the fact that Title IX, a federal statute passed in 1972, prohibits discrimination on the basis of sex in educational programmes that receive federal financial assistance.[4] Title IX is credited with increasing the number and quality of opportunities for female athletes, yet many schools still struggle with compliance. Under the law, colleges and universities must provide equitable athletic opportunities to men and women using one of three possible compliance tests.[5] Some institutions seek to avoid the expense of compliance with any of these tests – which generally require[6] adding new opportunities for women – by manipulating their rosters to give the appearance of providing a proportionate distribution of athletic opportunities. For example, litigation exposed one university's practice of 'triple-counting' female runners as members of cross-country, winter track and spring track teams, even though, for many of the runners, the track teams operated as an 'adjunct' to the cross-country team: merely a source of off-season training rather than as a source of athletic opportunity in their own right.[7] Colleges and universities have over-counted women's athletic opportunities, as well as under-counting those for men,[8] to create the appearance of proportionality and thus avoid the legal obligation to create new athletic opportunities for women that would exist under either of the two alternative measures of compliance.

Title IX also requires that athletics departments provide equal treatment to men's and women's programmes in the aggregate, as measured by factors such as the quality of facilities, equipment and uniforms; the schedule of games and practices; the quality of coaching and of the academic and medical services received; and publicity and promotion.[9] Relatedly, the law requires athletics departments to distribute scholarship dollars proportionately to the percentage of athletes of each sex.[10] The fact that men's athletic programmes generally receive more resources than women's,[11] as well as the fact that female college athletes receive a smaller share of scholarship dollars,[12] suggests that there is likely widespread non-compliance with these requirements as well.[13] Although the revenue-generating potential of men's football and basketball may explain why schools are willing to provide greater support to men's programmes, Title IX does not permit athletics departments to provide inferior treatment to women's teams on the basis of consumer preferences for men's sports.[14]

Barriers to leadership for women coaches and administrators

Women constitute a minority (23 per cent) of head coaches at the college level, and are similarly under-represented at the highest levels of administration. Notably, women are even minorities among coaches of women's teams (43 per cent), and are hardly represented at all (3 per cent) among coaches of men's teams.[15] Additionally, while African-American female athletes and coaches are not under-represented relative to the population data, their participation is overwhelmingly confined to basketball and running sports, suggesting that race and gender combine to erect barriers to entry into other sports.[16]

Several cases have revealed how retaliation, hostile environments and double standards operate to exclude women from the ranks of coaches and administrators.[17] For example, litigation exposed several instances in which athletics administrators at California State University, Fresno, retaliated against female coaches and administrators for advocating for gender equity on behalf of themselves and their players.[18] The lawsuits also revealed the athletics department's homophobic atmosphere, tolerance for sexual harassment and tendency to single out female coaches for discipline. The plaintiffs in these cases prevailed in multi-million-dollar settlements and jury awards.[19] While these cases and others show that it is possible to use Title IX and other anti-discrimination laws to successfully challenge these practices, the high social and financial costs of challenging inequality, as well as the difficulty proving discriminatory motivation, deter many potential plaintiffs from pursuing legal recourse. The fact that coaches of women's teams earn less than those of men's teams has also proved impervious to legal recourse, even though it suggests the possibility of pay discrimination against female coaches, who are virtually excluded from the opportunities in higher-paying jobs coaching men.[20]

Student-athletes and sexual violence

Sexual assault and violence is an epidemic across American college campuses.[21] Although there is no definitive data[22] that athletes – at any level – are more prone to violence than their non-athlete peers, the culture of college athletics has created a unique environment in which there has been significant mishandling of sexual violence accusations against student athletes. This is the result of both a culture of entitlement for student athletes and a win-at-all-costs mentality within athletics departments and schools.[23]

Historically, student athletes have received various privileges and perks, often in violation of National Collegiate Athletic Association (NCAA) rules and Title IX, including preferential housing, gifts and money from alumni, and unique academic considerations including special classes, scheduling and assignments.[24] Although some of these have been eliminated, the sentiment remains that athletes, and by extension athletics departments, occupy a high position in the campus hierarchy. One result of this has been that student-athletes who are accused of sexual assault and violence are often shielded from formal investigations, or even basic questioning, after an incident. In 2010, at the University of Notre Dame, the campus police were not allowed access to a football player who had been accused of rape because he was in athletics department facilities.[25]

One explanation for the practices that privilege student-athletes is the increasing pressure on athletics departments to be successful on the playing field in order to increase athletics department revenue via sponsorships, television rights, alumni donations and, potentially, increased student enrolment. The win-at-all-costs mentality that results has shielded accused student-athletes whom coaches, administrators and even fans believe are essential for achieving or maintaining winning traditions and providing entertainment. Thus they are willing to bend, stretch or ignore the rules governing the handling of reported sexual assaults when the accused are student-athletes. Evidence of this can be seen at the above-mentioned University of Notre Dame, as well as at Florida State University and the University of Missouri.[26]

The visibility of big-time college athletics programmes and their star athletes has played a significant role in the recent awareness about campus sexual assault in the United States, however, as seen in the public attention to several high-profile legal cases.[27] In 2011 the Office for Civil Rights (OCR), a sub-agency of the US Department of Education, responsible for the oversight of Title IX, issued a 'Dear Colleague' letter that explicitly states the responsibilities of schools under Title IX to investigate claims of sexual violence. This letter of clarification was motivated in part by cases involving student-athletes, including a 2001 university-sanctioned party at the University of Colorado for football players and recruits at which two female students reported being raped.[28] The 'Dear Colleague' letter states that all schools must institute proper procedures for investigating accusations, and notes that they 'must apply to all students, including athletes'. Schools are required to do their own independent investigations, and 'complaints must not be addressed solely by athletics department procedures'.[29] The Colorado case ended with a large settlement for the victims and changes to the university's policies and procedures regarding the investigation of incidents.

Nonetheless, athletics departments continue to protect athletes accused of sexual violence, often in violation of the OCR's mandate that schools 'take immediate and effective steps to end sexual harassment and sexual violence'.[30] These illegal practices include dismissing student-athletes from the team but allowing them to remain on campus, facilitating transfers to new schools by exempting them from their athletic commitment, handling accusations solely within athletic departments, not reporting incidents to the proper university officials and delaying investigation until an athlete's season is over. These are all ongoing practices, as evidenced in cases in the past ten years including at Florida State University, the University of Oregon, the University of Missouri, the University of Tulsa and the University of Notre Dame.[31]

Conclusion

There are a number of remedies that can mitigate the problems within college athletics related to discrimination, inequality and sexual violence. Some of these remedies require government intervention. For example, the Department of Education could engage in more aggressive Title IX enforcement to ensure that institutions are held accountable for non-compliance even when victims of discrimination are deterred from filing lawsuits by the associated financial, emotional, social and professional costs. Congress could put pressure on the NCAA, via an exemption from antitrust law, for example, to reform itself in such a way that reduces the commercialised nature of college athletics, thus reducing economic pressure on athletics departments to engage in the corrupt practices discussed above.

Colleges and universities could do a better job of policing themselves, such as by agreeing to condition NCAA membership status on Title IX compliance. As a step in this direction, the NCAA could restore the self-study process it once required of its Division I members, which conditioned membership on the institution's ability to evaluate and demonstrate its commitment to gender equity across a variety of measures. The NCAA could also implement policies that promote transparency in the handling of cases of athletes accused of assault, including penalising institutions that are found to have sheltered athletes from discipline or that have accepted the transfer of student-athletes found responsible for sexual violence.[32]

Colleges and universities could also improve the education and training they provide to staff on how to attain and sustain equitable participation opportunities, combat the implicit bias that serves as a barrier to women's athletic leadership, and effectively carry out their duties to report and address accusations of sexual violence.

Finally, the public in general, including fans, alumni, students and parents, have a role to play. By choosing carefully which college athletics programmes to attend and support, they can increase the pressure on universities to denounce and desist the inequitable allocation of resources, biased hiring practices and tolerance of sexual violence. Withholding support from athletics programmes that engage in these practices will ensure that they lack the resources to continue to engage in them.

Notes

1 Erin Buzuvis is a professor of law at Western New England University, Springfield, Massachusetts, and Kristine Newhall is a lecturer in sport management at the University of Massachusetts, Amherst. Together they founded and contribute to the Title IX Blog.

2 See National Collegiate Athletic Association, *Student-Athlete Participation 1981/82– 2013/14: NCAA Sports Sponsorship and Participation Rates Report* (Indianapolis: NCAA, 2015), pp. 75–76 (reporting a total of 207,814 opportunities in women's sports and 271,055 in men's).

3 National Center for Education Statistics, 'Digest of education statistics', table 303.10, *http://nces.ed.gov/programs/digest/d13/tables/dt13_303.10.asp.*

4 Code of Laws (US), Title 20, chapter 38, § 1681: 'Sex', *www.law.cornell.edu/uscode/text/ 20/1681.*

5 First, they may comply by showing that the distribution of athletic opportunities is proportionate to the percentage of each sex in the student body. Alternatively, they may comply by showing a 'history and continuing practice' of expanding athletic opportunities for women as 'the underrepresented sex'. Another possibility is that they may demonstrate that they offer enough athletic opportunities to fully satisfy the interests and abilities of the under-represented sex. Department of Health, Education and Welfare, 'Policy interpretation: Title IX and intercollegiate athletics', *Federal Register*, vol. 44 (11 December 1979), pp. 71413, 71418.

6 As an alternative to adding opportunities for women, it is possible for institutions to comply with the proportionality prong by contracting opportunities for men, as this practice is not prohibited by Title IX or any law. Nevertheless, notwithstanding the fact that the Department of Education calls cutting men's teams a 'disfavored' compliance, institutions regularly blame Title IX for such decisions rather than acknowledge the fact that the law preserves institutions' own autonomy to decide whether to comply by adding teams for women instead of cutting teams for men.

7 *Biediger* v. *Quinnipiac University*, 728 F. Supp. 2d62, 101–108 (D. Conn. 2010).

8   *New York Times* (US), 'College teams, relying on deception, undermine gender equity', 25 April 2011, *www.nytimes.com/2011/04/26/sports/26titleix.html?_r=0.*

9   US Code of Federal Regulations, 34 C.F.R. 106.41(c).

10   US Code of Federal Regulations, 34 C.F.R. 106.37(c).

11   National Collegiate Athletic Association, *Gender-Equity 2004–2010: NCAA Gender-Equity Report* (Indianapolis: NCAA, 2012).

12   Ibid.

13   Erin Buzuvis and Kristine Newhall, 'Equality beyond the three-part test: exploring and explaining the invisibility of Title IX's equal treatment requirement', *Marquette Sports Law Review*, vol. 22 (2012).

14   Erin Buzuvis, 'Athlete compensation for women too? Title IX implications of Northwestern and O'Bannon', *Journal of College and University Law*, vol. 41 (2015).

15   Vivian Acosta and Linda Carpenter, 'Women in college sport: a longitudinal, national study – thirty-seven year update, 1977–2014', *http://acostacarpenter.org//2014%20Status%20 of%20Women%20in%20Intercollegiate%20Sport%20-37%20Year%20Update%20-%20 1977-2014%20.pdf.*

16   Richard Lapchick, 'The 2012 racial and gender report card: college sport', *www.tidesport. org/RGRC/2012/2012_College_RGRC.pdf.*

17   Erin Buzuvis, 'Sidelined: examining barriers to women's leadership in college athletics through the lens of Title IX retaliation cases', *Duke Journal of Gender Law and Policy*, vol. 17 (2010).

18   Ibid.

19   Ibid.

20   NCAA (2012).

21   *Mother Jones* (US), 'This new study shows sexual assault on college campuses has reached "epidemic" levels', 20 May 2015, *www.motherjones.com/mixed-media/2015/05/ campus-sexual-assault-study*; Kate Carey, Sarah Durney, Robyn Shepardson and Michael Carey, 'Incapacitated and forcible rape of college women: prevalence across the first year', *Journal of Adolescent Health*, vol. 56 (2015), pp. 678–680.

22   Findings from several studies suggest that college athletes *may* commit sexual assault at rates higher than their non-athlete undergraduate peers and/or that male athletes in certain sports (that is, football and wrestling) may demonstrate higher levels of sexual aggression. These findings have not been replicated, however, as researchers face significant constraints in the collection of data (such as privacy rights and under-reporting).

23   *New York Times* (US), 'Errors in inquiry on rape allegations against FSU's Jameis Winston', 16 April 2014, *www.nytimes.com/interactive/2014/04/16/sports/errors-in-inquiry-on-rape- allegations-against-fsu-jameis-winston.html*; *Huffington Post* (US), 'University of Missouri mishandled sexual assault case, review finds', 11 April 2014, *www.huffingtonpost.com/ 2014/04/11/missouri-sexual-assault-review-university_n_5134699.html*; The Big Lead (US), 'Missouri failed to conduct Title IX investigation on sexual assault allegation against football player', 21 August 2014, *http://thebiglead.com/2014/08/21/missouri-failed-to-conduct- title-ix-investigation-on-sexual-assault-allegation-against-football-player.*

24   *Huffington Post* (US), 'These college athletes say they deserve special treatment', 2 September 2014, *www.huffingtonpost.com/2014/09/02/college-athletes-deserve- special-treatment_n_5749758.html.*

25   Kirby Dick, *The Hunting Ground* (California: RADiUS-TWC, 2015).

26   Ibid., note 23.

27   ESPNW (US), 'Athletic departments handing sexual assault cases: never a good idea', 21 August 2014, *http://espn.go.com/espnw/news-commentary/article/11386174/why- athletic-departments-clueless-handling-sexual-assaults*; ESPN (US), 'Outside the lines: Missouri, Tulsa, southern Idaho face allegations they did not investigate Title IX cases', 25 August 2014, *http://espn.go.com/espn/otl/story/_/id/11381416.*

28   ESPN (US), 'Timeline: Colorado recruiting scandal', 27 May 2004, *http://sports.espn. go.com/ncf/news/story?id=1803891.*

29   US Department of Education, 'Dear Colleague letter: Office of the Assistant Secretary',
     4 April 2011, *www2.ed.gov/about/offices/list/ocr/letters/colleague-201104.html*.
30   Ibid.
31   *Huffington Post* (11 April 2014); The Big Lead (2014); *New York Times* (2014); *Huffington
     Post* (US), 'Notre Dame, stung by "The Hunting Ground," is under US investigation for
     sexual harassment cases', 17 April 2015, *www.huffingtonpost.com/2015/04/17/notre-
     dame-sexual-harassment-hunting-ground_n_7082702.html*; *USA Today*, 'Ex-NFL player's
     son, Patrick Swilling Jr., implicated in sexual assault lawsuit', 18 August 2014, *www.
     usatoday.com/story/sports/ncaab/2014/08/18/patrick-swilling-tulsa-sexual-assault-lawsuit-
     title-ix/14104075*; *The Oregonian* (US), 'University of Oregon and Dana Altman sued over
     alleged sexual assault', 8 January 2015, *www.oregonlive.com/ducks/index.ssf/2015/01/
     university_of_oregon_and_dana.html*.
32   The Southeastern Conference, one of the most powerful intercollegiate athletics conferences
     in the United States, recently instituted a policy preventing the acceptance of transfer
     student-athletes who had been found guilty of 'serious misconduct', including sexual
     assault and domestic violence, at their previous institutions. It remains unknown whether
     other conferences or the NCAA will adopt similar policies. *Sports Illustrated* (US), 'SEC bars
     transfer athletes dismissed for "serious misconduct"', 29 May 2014, *www.si.com/college-
     football/2015/05/29/sec-transfer-rule-serious-misconduct-domestic-violence*.

PART 6

The role of participants

Within and beyond the sports family

6.1

The International Olympic Committee's actions to protect the integrity of sport

Pâquerette Girard Zappelli[1]

> *We need to change because sport today is too important in society to ignore the rest of society. We are not living on an island, we are living in the middle of a modern, diverse, digital society . . . This society will not wait for sport to change. If we want our values of Olympism – the values of excellence, respect, friendship, dialogue, diversity, non-discrimination, tolerance, fair play, solidarity, development and peace – to remain relevant in society, the time for change is now.*
> *International Olympic Committee president Thomas Bach*

As leader of the Olympic Movement, the International Olympic Committee (IOC) encourages all other sports organisations to follow its lead in regard to strengthening integrity in sport.

Shaken by the corruption scandal related to the awarding of the Salt Lake City Winter Olympic Games in 2002, the IOC reacted strongly by adopting a large number of regulations and processes aimed at severely limiting the risk of recurrence. In addition to ensuring good governance, the IOC also has a duty to safeguard clean athletes and competitions. Corrupt competition makes sport a meaningless spectacle, and nobody is interested in watching or taking part in a competition whose outcome is tainted or – worse – already determined before it begins. Furthermore, failing to protect the integrity of sport means the IOC cannot promote positive values through sport.

As a result, the IOC applies a zero-tolerance policy when it comes to manipulation at the Olympic Games. The two biggest threats to the integrity of sport are doping and the manipulation of competitions, also known as match-fixing. The IOC has put a number of measures in place to protect the Olympic Games, many of which have been offered for wider use among the Olympic movement stakeholders.

Following are some of the key actions taken by the IOC since 1999 to protect the integrity of sport.

1999: actions taken in the aftermath of the Salt Lake City scandal

The Salt Lake City scandal – in which IOC members were accused of taking bribes from the Salt Lake Organizing Committee (SLOC) during the bidding process – was one of the most serious situations the IOC has ever been confronted with.[2] The IOC's reaction was swift and strong. All of the following occurred within six months of the allegations coming to light:

● an Ad-Hoc Committee investigated the various events;
● six IOC members were expelled; seven others were sanctioned;
● the IOC set up a permanent and independent Ethics Commission involving a majority of independent, high-ranking international personalities including a former UN secretary-general, judges from the supreme court and International Court of Justice, as well as a former head of the Swiss Confederation;[3] and
● the IOC Code of Ethics was developed and approved.

At the same time the IOC Session, which is the annual assembly of the full IOC membership, approved a number of new reforms, including a limit to the IOC president's term and a ban on IOC members not serving on the Evaluation Commission from visiting candidate cities.[4]

In the following years the Ethics Commission created the position of permanent secretary and approved a large number of implementing provisions, such as its independent status, rules of procedure, directions for the election of the IOC president, regulations concerning conflict of interest, and rules of conduct for the bidding process for hosting the Olympic Games.

These regulations have since been updated regularly and are explained to the IOC membership at every IOC Session.

2003–2005: the bidding process for the Olympic Games in 2012

For the first time, a full set of Rules of Conduct was approved and implemented, thereby providing bid cities with a clear framework for their international promotion and relations with IOC members. While this process was ongoing it was revealed that an IOC member and various consultants had breached the Code of Ethics in regard to bids.[5] The respective IOC member was expelled and the consultants were declared personae non gratae.

These decisions show the IOC's firm stance in regard to any form of corruption. This zero-tolerance policy underpinned a number of other decisions to sanction any IOC member proved to have breached the IOC Code of Ethics.[6]

2009: the XIII Olympic Congress in Copenhagen

The 2009 Congress provided a rare opportunity for the entire Olympic family (i.e. IOC members, representatives of national Olympic committees (NOCs), international federations (IFs), the organising committees of the Olympic Games (OCOGs), athletes, coaches, media, sponsors and other stakeholders) to meet and discuss issues of importance to the Movement. In the field of ethics, this Congress allowed all the Olympic Movement stakeholders, including all the NOCs, IFs and recognised sports organisations, to approve and take on board the following:

● the Basic Principle of Good Governance for the Sports Organisations;[7]
● recommendation 41, which states that the 'legitimacy and autonomy of the Olympic Movement depend on upholding the highest standards of ethical behaviour and good governance'; and
● recommendation 42, which states that all members of the Olympic movement should 'adopt and implement a code of ethics based on the principles and rules of the IOC Code of Ethics'.[8]

2014: Olympic Agenda 2020

Following his election in September 2013, IOC president Thomas Bach launched an open, inclusive and wide-ranging debate called Olympic Agenda 2020. Discussions centred on recommendations for a strategic roadmap for the future of the Olympic movement and involved all Olympic Movement stakeholders, external stakeholders and the public. Following this consultation, 40 recommendations were formulated and unanimously approved by the IOC Session in December 2014.[9] The protection of clean athletes forms an essential part of Olympic Agenda 2020. The six recommendations relating to increased transparency and strengthened ethics measures will have been implemented by the time of the IOC Session in Kuala Lumpur in July–August 2015.

Introducing the Olympic Agenda 2020 recommendations to the IOC Session in December ahead of the vote, President Bach summed up the new philosophy and reasoning behind the reforms through the words of Nelson Mandela, that 'sport has the power to change the world', and that 'you can inspire others to change, only if you are ready to change yourself'.[10] This begins with people getting the Olympic message of dialogue, of respect for rules, of tolerance, solidarity and peace.

Olympic Agenda 2020 addresses the issue of credibility for competitions as well as for organisations. It will encourage potential candidate cities to present a holistic concept of respect for the environment, feasibility and of development, to leave a lasting legacy, respecting that there is no one-size-fits-all solution for the sustainability of the Olympic Games, while 'at the same time safeguarding the unity of the Olympic Movement by ensuring the respect of the host for our values and the respect for the athletes who are at the heart of the Olympic Games'.[11]

Olympic Agenda 2020 also commits the IOC to strengthen good governance, transparency and ethics. This includes that members of the Ethics Commission will be elected by the IOC Session rather than the IOC executive board. The Ethics Commission will draft new rules in line with the Olympic Agenda 2020.The IOC will also create the position of a compliance officer.

Financial statements will be prepared and audited by the benchmark International Financial Reporting Standards (IFRS), even if from the legal perspective much less transparent standards would be sufficient. The IOC will provide an annual activity and financial report, including the allowance policy for IOC members, which will give evidence for the fact that the IOC members are genuine volunteers.

With regard to the credibility of sports competitions and of athletes, President Bach stated that 'we have first and foremost to protect the clean athletes . . . from doping, match-fixing, manipulation and corruption. We have to change our way of thinking. We have to consider every single cent in the fight against these evils not as an expense but as an investment in the future of Olympic Sport.'[12] This will include supporting innovative anti-doping research, which leads to a better and less onerous protection of the clean athlete, and creating robust education, awareness and prevention programmes against match-fixing, manipulation and corruption.

2006–2015: protection of clean athletes against competition manipulation

The manipulation of sports competitions, in particular when linked to betting activities, has become an area of great concern in recent years. Like doping, such corruption threatens the very integrity of sport. Recommendation 16 of Olympic Agenda 2020 aims to protect Olympic events from any kind of manipulation through robust education and awareness programmes.

This threat has been on the IOC's radar for many years already. Since 2006 the IOC has implemented wide-ranging measures to deal with the threat. These include rules prohibiting Olympic Games participants from betting on Olympic events; the monitoring of betting patterns related to Olympic events; educational programmes for athletes; cooperation with Interpol to raise awareness at all levels; and a whistleblower system.[13]

A major step forward was taken in 2014 with the launch of the IOC's Integrity Betting Intelligence System (IBIS),[14] a centralised mechanism for the exchange of information and intelligence. IBIS enables the sport movement to allocate and analyse information and intelligence about potential manipulation of competitions efficiently at one source and to communicate with entities on the sports betting side and/or governmental agencies. It covers all Olympic sports (except football, which is dealt with by the Union of European Football Associations (UEFA) and the Fédération Internationale de Football Association (FIFA)), and, after the Olympic Games in Rio 2016, will come into force at other multi-sports events.

To maximise the impact of its actions, the IOC works in close partnership not only with Olympic Movement stakeholders, but with key international players such as the United Nations, the European Union, the Council of Europe, Interpol, the United Nations Office on Drugs and Crime and UNESCO, to name just a few.

Strengthening good governance and protecting clean athletes is a top priority for the IOC. Through Olympic Agenda 2020 and other measures taken since 1999, the IOC remains fully committed to protecting them from doping, match-fixing, manipulation and corruption.

Notes

1   Pâquerette Girard Zappelli is chief ethics and compliance officer of the International Olympic Committee.
2   See Bill Mallon, 'The Olympic bribery scandal', *Journal of Olympic History*, vol. 8 (2000).
3   For a summary of the mandate of the Ethics Commission, see *www.olympic.org/ethics-commission*.
4   For further details, please refer to the full report by the IOC 2000 Commission to the 110th IOC Session: *www.olympic.org/Documents/Reports/EN/en_report_588.pdf*.
5   See 'Decision no. 5/04 dated 25.10.04 Mr Ivan Slavkov – decision by the 117th IOC Session, Singapore, 07.07.05, to expel Mr Ivan Slavkov from the IOC', *www.olympic.org/Documents/Reports/EN/en_report_912.pdf*.
6   For more information, please consult our website, where all the texts and decisions have been published: *www.olympic.org/ethics-commission*.
7   For an overview of the Basic Principle of Good Governance for the Sports Organisations, see *www.olympic.org/ethics-commission?tab=good-governance*.
8   Read the full set of the Olympic Congress 2009 recommendations: 'The Olympic Movement in society', *www.olympic.org/Documents/Congress_2009/Recommendations-eng.pdf*.
9   Read the full document: International Olympic Committee, *Olympic Agenda 2020: 20+20 Recommendations* (Lausanne: IOC, 2014), *www.olympic.org/documents/olympic_agenda_2020/olympic_agenda_2020-20-20_recommendations-eng.pdf*.
10 Thomas Bach, 'Speech on the occasion of the opening ceremony, 127th IOC Session, Monaco, 7 December 2014', *www.olympic.org/Documents/IOC_Executive_Boards_and_Sessions/IOC_Sessions/127_Session_Monaco_2014/127th_IOC_Session_Speech_Opening_Ceremony_President_Bach-English.pdf*.
11 Ibid.
12 Ibid.
13 See the Integrity and Compliance Hotline: *www.olympic.org/integrityhotline*.
14 For more information, see 'IOC Integrity Betting Intelligence System (IBIS)', factsheet (Lausanne: IOC, 2015), *www.olympic.org/Documents/Reference_documents_Factsheets/Integrity_Betting_Intelligence_System_IBIS.pdf*.

6.2

Combating the risk of corruption in sport

An intergovernmental perspective

Stanislas Frossard[1]

Introduction

Promotion of the Council of Europe's values – human rights, democracy and the rule of law – cannot be reserved for specialists, whether diplomats, officials or judges. These values must be experienced on a daily basis. They are not just matters for the organs of state but need to be adopted by civil society, promoted through education and fully integrated into our culture. It is in this spirit that the European Cultural Convention has, since 1955, taken the work of the Council of Europe into sectors such as education, culture, youth and sport.

The sport movement, in particular, is a part of civil society, which concerns a high proportion of the population as either participants or spectators. It is also an economic sector that is not negligible: economic activities related to sport represent 2 per cent of the European Union's total GDP, and sports activities generate the equivalent of 7.3 million jobs, equivalent to 3.5 per cent of the working population.[2] Sport can contribute to education by developing knowledge, skills and attitudes such as commitment within an organised group, respect for opponents and rules, team spirit, and so on. Sport can promote these values within society, and also contributes to public health and social inclusion.

The fight against corruption in sport is central to the role of the Council of Europe, which entails the promotion of the rule of law and democracy. Protecting sport from corruption not only makes sport more efficient and its organisations more reliable partners, but also sends out an important message about the fight against corruption in society. The governments that allocate, directly or indirectly, large sums of money to sports organisations and events are accountable to their taxpayers for the good use made of those funds. Preserving sport's autonomy and ensuring that the funds have been used for the purposes for which they were allocated is a challenge to governments. Quite clearly, both autonomy and transparency are important, and governments must verify that the public money allocated to sport is spent in accordance with the applicable rules and with the commitments made, but without unduly or arbitrarily interfering with the decisions of sports organisations.

Over the past ten years the fight against corruption in sport has forced its way onto the political agenda. In view of the European involvement in the international sport movement, European states' role as hosts of events or as countries where sports organisations are headquartered, and public authorities' financial participation in sport, the Council of Europe has played a part in this movement, promoting the good governance of sport, combating the manipulation of sports competitions (e.g. match-fixing) and, more recently, combating corruption in the governance of sports organisations or events. This subject, long a 'hot potato' tackled only indirectly by public authorities, is now therefore on the political agenda of intergovernmental cooperation. States, while reaffirming their attachment to the principle of autonomy for the sport movement, wish to back sports organisations' initiatives with a view to better governance and to shoulder their share of the responsibility as partners of the sport movement and as guarantors of the punishment of criminal offences.

Moving towards better governance in sport

The Council of Europe broached the issue of good governance in sport at its 10th Conference of Ministers responsible for Sport (Budapest, 2004). In the wake of the conference the Committee of Ministers adopted recommendation REC(2005)8 to member states on the principles of good governance in sport. This recommendation specifies effective policies and measures of good governance in sport, which comprise, as a minimum:

- democratic structures for non-governmental sports organisations based on clear and regular electoral procedures open to the whole membership;
- organisation and management of a professional standard, with an appropriate code of ethics and procedures for dealing with conflicts of interest;
- accountability and transparency in decision-making and financial operations, including the open publication of yearly financial accounts duly audited; and
- fairness in dealing with membership, including gender equality and solidarity.

The issue has subsequently assumed growing importance in many sports organisations and international organisations.

The promotion of good governance in sport is a long, drawn-out process, entailing cultural and structural changes. Sometimes, however, 'good governance' is a concept used as a positive alternative to the word 'corruption', a euphemism or a means of avoiding the term. The 11th Conference of Ministers responsible for Sport (Athens, 2008) went further, however, concluding its discussions on sports ethics by identifying 'corruption in sport' as one of the new challenges to sports ethics, and asking the Enlarged Partial Agreement on Sport (EPAS) to deal with the subject.

Action against match-fixing: a promising step against corruption in sport

Narrowing down the scope of its work, EPAS decided to concentrate on the manipulation of sports competitions, postponing to a later date the more general issue of the fight against corruption in the governance of sport. This process culminated in the adoption of a recommendation of the Committee of Ministers to member states on the manipulation of sports results, adopted in 2011, followed by the new Convention on the Manipulation of Sports Competitions (CETS no. 215), which was opened for signature on 18 September 2014 in Magglingen/Macolin (Switzerland). The adoption of this new treaty has placed the Council of Europe in a prominent position in the fight against the manipulation of sports competitions. The Convention is the only rule of international law on the subject. As of May 2015 the Convention had been signed by 18 states and ratified by Norway, and it will come into force after the fifth ratification.

The manipulation of sports competitions has proved to be a complex issue. Not only is the integrity of sport at stake, but the fight against organised crime and corruption as well. A closer analysis of manipulation cases has shown that corruption is not the only method used by those who falsify competitions. There have been cases of manipulation involving violence, intimidation, threats, poisoning, and so on. Others may be based on a friendly agreement, without any pecuniary arrangement or promise or without any coercion, while the manipulation may nevertheless lead to a fraudulent gain. Combating manipulation requires the cooperation and expertise of the authorities in fields including sport, gambling, anti-corruption measures, criminal law, cybercrime, personal data protection and money-laundering. In this context, the Council of Europe has obtained the support of numerous networks of governmental experts and managed to unite the sporting movement and betting operators.

There are various reasons why European states have been able to take such an initiative. The development of the betting market, which really took off in the early years of the new millennium, has sometimes taken place in a legal vacuum, but the legal framework has been speedily brought up to date: the states of Europe have equipped themselves with means of regulating the market, granting licences to operators who offer bets on their territory or defending their national lottery's monopoly position. The attention given to regulating betting services, for many reasons (combating of addiction, consumer protection, integrity of sport, taxation, combating of money-laundering), has made clearer the risks associated with this market. Europe also has the privilege of having at its disposal research and international cooperation institutions that have been able to study the problem and put forward international solutions. The increased attention has led to a huge increase in the number of cases: in 2009 EPAS examined 70 cases of manipulation reported by the press since 2000. There have been revelations of new cases every week since 2012. According to Interpol, the criminal justice systems in 80 countries are investigating or holding trials in cases of manipulation of competitions.

This is not a specifically European problem, however, and the challenge today is to expand intergovernmental action to other continents, *inter alia*, by welcoming all the states interested in signing the Convention, whether they are European or not. Some promising signals have been sent by various states that are not members of the Council of Europe (Australia, Belarus, Canada, Israel, Japan, Morocco and New Zealand) but took part in the negotiations.

The Community institutions have also been active on the issue, for the manipulation of sports competitions is on the agenda of the Commission, Council and Parliament, which are looking at the combating of corruption, the fight against organised crime, the regulation of the gambling market and sports ethics. The Commission took part in the negotiations on the Council of Europe Convention alongside the EU member states, and on 2 March 2015 it proposed to the Council of the EU that the European Union sign the Convention.

Combating the corruption that affects the governance of sports organisations

Notwithstanding the thorough work done to promote good governance in sport and some promising developments in the fight against match-fixing, allegations and cases of corruption in sport have continued to hit the headlines and be the subject of questions in parliament. Corruption relating to the governance of sport, tendering processes or the preparation of major sports events has drawn the attention of governments and national parliaments in such countries as Switzerland and the United Kingdom.[3]

Thus a subject that has long been a 'hot potato', dealt with only indirectly by governments, is now on the political agenda of intergovernmental cooperation. States, while reaffirming their attachment to the principle of the autonomy of the sport movement, wish to back sports organisations in their initiatives with a view to improved governance and to shoulder their share of the responsibility as partners of the sport movement and as guarantors of the punishment of criminal offences. The risk of corruption in the governance of sport was the main theme of the 13th Conference of Ministers responsible for Sport, held in Macolin/ Magglingen on 18 September 2014. It discussed numerous examples of corruption in sport, the challenges presented to public authorities by this scourge and the initiatives that might be coordinated.

Conclusion

For the past 15 years or so, states and sports organisations have shown a greater capacity for dialogue and cooperation. The introduction of coordinated arrangements to combat doping and the manipulation of sports competitions is evidence of this. So far as the risk of corruption is concerned, the current tendency is towards recognition that there is a common interest, towards awareness among the various players of their own limitations and towards complementary means of action available to each. Effective cooperation and creation of the requisite trust are realistic longer-term objectives. It is possible that the development of cooperation on less sensitive issues (combating the manipulation of competitions and the trafficking of doping substances) will open the way for closer cooperation on punishing corruption.

Another line of action would be to increase collaboration with the anti-corruption and law enforcement authorities, not only at governmental authority level but also in the context of cooperation between the sport movement and the public authorities. In this context, the reports written on the implementation of anti-corruption rules, including those produced by the Council of Europe's Group of States against Corruption (GRECO),[4] might be helpful in the preparation of standards and policies. These reports could, *inter alia*, look at the state of cooperation between the sport movement and the public authorities in the effort to prevent and combat corruption in sport and to preserve sport's values, image and benefits to society.

Greater coordination is necessary in respect of international sports organisations. Countries applying to host international sports events and those where international sports organisations have their headquarters should play a leading role. As most international sports organisations are located in Council of Europe member states, over 70 per cent of the posts of president and secretary general at international sports federations are held by Europeans,[5] and many international sports events take place in European states, these countries, which have made firm commitments on the combating of corruption, have a particular responsibility to bear.

Finally, it is not only international sports organisations and states that are concerned. National sports organisations must also set an example, and, within their continental and international structures, could demand greater accountability. Athletes could be more involved in decision-making. There should also be a role for other players, such as sponsors, who should also contribute to the promotion of ethics in sport through their businesses' social responsibility programmes. Civil society holds sports organisations and governments to account. The media, too, are in a position to raise awareness of corruption in sport and to show what is being done to curb it. By taking action in this way, the sector could rediscover its reputation for fair play.

Notes

1   Stanislas Frossard is the executive secretary of the Enlarged Partial Agreement on Sport of the Council of Europe. The opinions expressed in this chapter are the responsibility of the author and do not necessarily reflect the official policy of the Council of Europe.

2   European Commission, 'Sport as a growth engine for EU Economy', Memo 14–432
     (Brussels: European Commission, 2014).
3   The Parliamentary Assembly of the Council of Europe adopted a resolution in 2012
     concerning the good governance and ethics of sport, backed up by a report that highlighted
     recent scandals and decisions taken in relation to the governance of international football.
     In April 2015 it adopted another resolution on football governance, based on a report
     analysing, in particular, Union of European Football Associations (UEFA) and Fédération
     Internationale de Football Association (FIFA) rules of governance, and condemning the
     procedure that led to the award of the 2022 World Cup to Qatar. Other international
     organisations have also tackled in a more head-on fashion the subject of corruption in
     sport. The declaration adopted by the United Nations Educational, Scientific and Cultural
     Organization's (UNESCO's) fifth World Conference of Sport Ministers (MINEPS V, Berlin)
     places corrupt practices in sport on the same footing as doping and the manipulation of
     sports competitions.
4   These reports are available on GRECO's webpage: *www.coe.int/greco*.
5   Arnout Geeraert, Jens Alm and Michael Groll, 'Good governance in international non-
     governmental sport organisations: an empirical study on accountability, participation and
     executive body members in sport governing bodies', in Jens Alm (ed.), *Action for Good
     Governance in International Sports Organisations: Final Report* (Copenhagen: Danish
     Institute for Sports Studies, 2013), *www.playthegame.org/fileadmin/documents/Good_
     governance_reports/AGGIS_Final_report.pdf*.

6.3

UNESCO

Building on global consensus to fight corruption in sport

Nada Al-Nashif[1]

The educational and ethical dimensions of sport, and its multidisciplinary nature, form the core of the United Nations Educational, Scientific and Cultural Organization's (UNESCO's) mandate as the UN custodian of sport policy development. When sport emerged as an international policy issue in the 1970s, through 'ping-pong diplomacy'[2] and the boycott of the white-only South African Springboks rugby team, UNESCO responded by convening in 1976 the International Conference of Ministers and Senior Officials Responsible for Physical Education and Sport (MINEPS). MINEPS I played an important role in the development of the International Charter of Physical Education and Sport, adopted in 1978 by UNESCO's General Conference. The Charter establishes the practice of physical education and sport as a fundamental right for all, and thereby places emphasis on equality and grassroots sport. The longest article of the Charter is devoted to 'the protection of ethical and moral values of physical education and sport', with respect to violence, doping and 'commercial excesses'.[3]

The term 'corruption' does not feature in the 1978 Charter, however. More than 20 years after its adoption the third session of MINEPS (MINEPS III), held in 1999, recognised 'the risks threatening competition sport, such as excessive commercialisation and advertising, doping, violence and chauvinism, distorted, corrupted and discredited sport'.[4] Building on the Council of Europe's Anti-Doping Convention, MINEPS IV, held in 2004, prepared the grounds for the adoption by the General Conference of UNESCO's International Convention against Doping in Sport[5] in 2005. Ratified by 180 member states, it constitutes today, in combination with the World Anti-Doping Code, the only binding, international legal framework on sport integrity and governance.

MINEPS V, held in Berlin in 2013, covered all the main national and international sport policy issues with a focus on emerging challenges of sport integrity. The Declaration of Berlin contains a detailed set of recommendations concerning the manipulation of sport competitions, as well as the conditions for hosting major sports events. Two of the central assertions of the Declaration are that, 'due to the involvement of transnational organised crime, doping in sport, the manipulation of sport competitions and corruption are not only a threat to sport itself but to society at large' and that 'various national and international authorities and stakeholders need to concert their efforts in order to combat threats to the integrity of sport through doping, corruption and the manipulation of sport competitions, and that sport ministers play a leadership role in federating these efforts'.[6] Ministers also recommended a revision of the International Charter of Physical Education and Sport – a fundamental benchmark for the universal principles underpinning sport policies and programmes.[7]

The new article 10 on the 'Protection and promotion of the integrity and ethical values of physical education, physical activity and sport' reaffirms that 'phenomena such as violence, doping, political exploitation, corruption and manipulation of sports competitions endanger the credibility and integrity of physical education, physical activity and sport and undermine their educational, developmental, and health promoting functions'. Furthermore, it highlights that 'to reduce the risk of corruption and overspending related to major sport events, event owners, public authorities and other stakeholders must take measures to maximise transparency, objectivity and fairness in the bidding, planning and hosting of these events'. This article also includes provisions concerning national and international cooperation against the manipulation of sport competitions, the respect of international labour conventions and basic human rights, the implementation of principles of good governance, the rigorous enforcement of the principles of accountability and transparency, and the provision by all stakeholders of prevention programmes, as well as an invitation to the media to fulfil their role as critical and independent observers of events, organisations and stakeholders.

Above all, the Charter underlines the critical linkages of sport integrity principles with the ethical values and benefits of physical education, physical activity and sport, including equal access, non-discrimination, safety, sustainability and lifelong learning. This basic agreement on the reasons, purpose and main modalities of protecting and developing sport is powerful – both as a baseline for designing and measuring policy implementation and as a lever for future multi-stakeholder cooperation. MINEPS VI, to be held in the spring of 2017, will focus on the follow-up to the Declaration of Berlin and the revised International Charter of Physical Education and Sport – an agenda marking a move towards measurable action. For this endeavour to succeed, the sharing of 'good practice' will be important. However, these practices must be qualified, codified and disseminated.

It is therefore critical that we leverage the existing policy consensus to build a globally recognised, coherent framework of indicators, benchmarks and self-assessment tools. These would allow public sport authorities around the world to objectively determine policy gaps and needs, solutions and progress to be targeted in the field of sport integrity. Such a framework would cover four main areas: awareness-raising and prevention education; legislation; multi-stakeholder cooperation and governance; and effective exchange of information among athletes, sports organisations, public authorities and other sports-related rights holders. Our experience with the follow-up to MINEPS V shows that sport authorities welcome such harmonisation – a common set of monitoring tools would reduce transaction costs and strengthen their capacity to implement core policies. Nonetheless, the development, harmonisation and deployment of sport policy monitoring tools require political will and dedicated resources at international and national levels. In this context, the revised International Charter of Physical Education and Sport, as the common denominator of sports stakeholders, can serve as an anchor for gathering, standardising and disseminating more effectively practical experience and scientific evidence that is relevant for the governments of *all* UNESCO member states, and not only for individual countries or regions.

Through its standard-setting instruments and in close cooperation with other intergovernmental organisations in this domain, UNESCO offers a unique platform to harness a universal protection of the integrity of sport. This platform is a precious asset for the collective effort that is now required to strengthen the power of sport for all members of society, across the diverse interpretations and reflections of our multiple stakeholders. This is the common endeavour we must unite to uphold and defend.

Notes

1   Nada Al-Nashif is assistant director-general for social and human sciences, United Nations Educational, Scientific and Cultural Organization.
2   The term 'ping-pong diplomacy' refers to the organising of table tennis matches between the United States and the People's Republic of China in the early 1970s as a means to relax tensions at a time when the two countries did not have diplomatic relations.
3   See *www.unesco.org/education/nfsunesco/pdf/SPORT_E.PDF*, article 7.
4   UNESCO, *Third International Conference of Ministers and Senior Officials Responsible for Physical Education and Sport (MINEPS III), Punta del Este, Uruguay, 30 November–3 December 1999: Final Report* (Paris: UNESCO, 1999), p. 12.
5   UNESCO, *Fourth International Conference of Ministers and Senior Officials Responsible for Physical Education and Sport (MINEPS IV), Athens, Greece (6–8 December 2004): Final Report* (Paris: UNESCO, 2005), point 4, p. 1.
6   The Declaration of Berlin was adopted by the 121 member states of UNESCO that participated in MINEPS V, based on a draft elaborated by some 100 expert organisations, including Transparency International: *www.unesco.org/new/en/social-and-human-sciences/themes/physical-education-and-sport/mineps-2013/declaration*.
7   This revision was carried out in 2014–2015 in a collective process involving all 195 UNESCO member states, as well as international experts and practitioners representing sports organisations, academia and non-governmental organisations. The final draft of the revised Charter is presented in the annex of Document 196EX/9: *www.unesco.org/new/index.php?id=121368* ('Main series'). The executive board recommended that the General Conference adopt this final draft, *excluding* article 10.8 on the 'autonomy of sport', at its 38th session in November 2015 (see decision 196EX/9).

6.4

The role of Switzerland as host

Moves to hold sports organisations more accountable, and wider implications

Lucien W. Valloni and Eric P. Neuenschwander[1]

Background

Switzerland is an attractive base for international sports organisations,[2] on account of its geographic location, highly qualified workforce, political stability, neutrality, security, quality of life and, most importantly, its very liberal legal code and attractive tax regime.[3] It is no coincidence that these important bodies organising worldwide sports have all chosen the legal form of a Swiss association, granting maximum flexibility and autonomy to the organisation.[4]

Although the importance of Swiss law for international sporting associations is considerable, the importance of these organisations for Switzerland is also not to be underestimated. A recent survey by the International Academy of Sports Science and Technology (AISTS) showed that the 45 main international sporting associations headquartered in Switzerland contributed an average of CHF 1.07 billion (some US$1.16 billion) annually to the Swiss economy between 2008 and 2013.[5]

These numbers show that sport and sporting associations have experienced significant professionalisation and commercialisation in recent years. In line with this growth, numerous measures are either in the process of being implemented or at the planning stage to combat the increased scope for corruption and betting manipulation in sport at the national and international levels. It is therefore incumbent on Switzerland, as a hub of international sporting associations, to rise to the challenge with a range of measures of its own. This chapter highlights the most important changes under way in Switzerland regarding the investigation and prosecution of corruption in sport.

The current situation

Although Switzerland is perceived to be one of the countries least affected by corruption,[6] regular amendments to the criminal law on corruption are necessary as it applies to international sports organisations.[7] The seven-member Swiss Federal Council – which serves as the Swiss head of state – approves such amendments.

Bribery under Swiss criminal law

Article 332 of the Swiss Criminal Code punishes the active and passive bribery of Swiss or foreign public officials. These rules are special torts, which means that bribery is punishable under criminal law only if the individual bribed is a public official. A public official must be either a member of an authority or a court, an official, an officially appointed expert, a translator, an interpreter, a referee or a member of the army.[8] Sports organisations as legal entities under Swiss private law and their officials cannot be categorised as public officials in the meaning of the Swiss Criminal Code.[9] Therefore, according to the law at the time of writing, there is no criminal liability for the bribery of officials of international sports organisations.

Bribery under Swiss competition law

In addition to the criminalisation of the bribery of officials there also exists a legal basis against private bribery in Switzerland. Under the law at present, private corruption is a criminal offence only if it leads to a distortion of competition within the meaning of the Federal Act against Unfair Competition (UWG). Article 4(a) of the act covers both active (granting of an advantage) and passive (acceptance of an advantage) corruption, but it is pursued only if an individual who is affected files a complaint.[10] An affected person can be a worker, a partner, an agent or an assistant of any other third person.[11] Private bribery is always based on a triangular relationship, whereas the bribed individual (the agent) stands in a fiduciary relationship with the primarily damaged individual (the principal).[12]

The applicability of the Federal Act against Unfair Competition presupposes a competitive relationship between the participating parties in such an act, however.[13] Therefore, it was unclear whether the act was applicable in the field of sport or not. In a ruling given in 2004, the Federal Council expressed the opinion that article 4(a) of the act did apply to non-governmental organisations (NGOs) – and therefore sports organisations – if they are in a competitive relationship.[14] In our opinion, there can be no doubt that organisations such as the Fédération Internationale de Football Association (FIFA) and the International Olympic Committee (IOC) are in a competitive relationship. The Federal Council also said, however, that it doubted whether it would be 'business conduct' within the meaning of the UWG if members of an association received financial benefits in preferring the bid of a city that was aiming to host a major sporting event.[15] Otherwise, if an attempt was being made, with bribery payments to or from private companies, to influence a competitive relationship, such as the conclusion of sponsorship agreements, then such an act could already qualify as bribery under the current Federal Act against Unfair Competition.[16]

Box 6.1 Match-fixing and the law in Switzerland

One might have expected match-fixing to qualify as a crime under applicable laws in Switzerland. In 2012, however, the Federal Criminal Court held that football players allegedly involved in match-fixing could not be subject to criminal sanctions.[17]

The court came to its conclusion on the grounds that, under the Swiss Criminal Code (article 146), for the crime of fraud to have been committed it was necessary for a human being to have been misled, not an electronic betting system.[18] In the case before the court, however, three football players had been accused of manipulating, or trying to manipulate, football games and generate winnings on electronic betting platforms. As no specific individuals had been misled or manipulated, the court was of the opinion that it had no choice other than to discharge the accused players.[19]

There are other ways to approach this matter, however, as the example of the Swiss Association of Football Players shows; the association, as part of its 'Show Respect – Don't Fix It!' campaign, has implemented a match-fixing hotline, through which players and coaches can confidentially and anonymously report notices of alleged match-fixing.[20] State rules protecting whistleblowers are still absent in Switzerland, however, even though they are crucial to combating any kind of corruption.

Legal changes under way

Swiss Criminal Code

Improvement is in sight. There have been moves in the Swiss Parliament to change the law so that private bribery becomes an ex officio crime (meaning that such crime has to be prosecuted by the state prosecutor without any intervention of any third party) in the future and punishable under the Swiss Criminal Code.[21] Following the same recommendation from a Groupe d'États contre la Corruption (GRECO) report,[22] the Federal Council therefore commissioned the Swiss Federal Department of Justice and Police to consider making private bribery an ex officio crime and transferring it from the UWG to the Swiss Criminal Code. Unlike the Act, the Criminal Code does not have a requirement that a competitive relationship has to be proved.

The Commission for Legal Affairs of the Council of States adopted the outline proposal against private bribery unanimously on 25 April 2015. Contrary to the proposal of the Federal Council, however, the majority of the Commission did not want ex officio prosecution in less serious cases. The majority of the Council of States followed the recommendation of the Commission and wanted to ensure that no criminal proceedings should be carried out in minor cases. One member of the Council of States, Pirmin Bischof of the Christian Democratic People's Party of Switzerland (Kanton Solothurn), claimed that if, for example, the employee of a baker accepts a bribe to buy a particular furnace for the bakery, his supervisor should decide on the conduct of criminal proceedings. This led to the decision by the Commission that private bribery should be prosecuted only on request, if by doing so no public interests were injured or endangered.[23] In the overall vote, held on 3 June 2015, the Council of States approved the new law by 23 votes to four, with 16 abstentions. At the time of writing, the law still has to be approved by the House of Representatives.[24]

New money-laundering rules

One of the major changes in Swiss law regarding the fight against corruption in sport associations has concerned the amendments to the money-laundering rules. In recent years the Organisation for Economic Co-operation and Development (OECD), through its Financial Action Task Force (FATF) on money-laundering (also known as the Groupe d'Action Financière, or GAFI), has urged its member countries – including Switzerland – to tighten their money-laundering regulations.[25] On 12 December 2014 the Act on the Implementation of the Revised Recommendations of FATF was adopted by the Swiss Parliament.[26] In these amended recommendations the FATF has extended the definition of a politically exposed person (PEP) to include senior politicians and officials of international sports organisations based in Switzerland.[27]

The most important amendments, which now also affect officials of sports organisations, are that cash transactions may not exceed CHF 100,000 (some US$108,000) and that serious tax offences are considered as a predicate offence to money-laundering.[28] This means that a seller has to identify and register any person who wants to pay more than CHF 100,000 in cash, or the money has to be transferred.

Conclusion

As the most important hub for the world's most important sports organisations, it is crucial that Switzerland leads by example in the fight against corruption in sport. It would seem that the country's legislature is now starting to see this; this may be why Switzerland is the first signatory of the Convention on the Manipulation of Sports Competitions.[29]

Protecting the integrity and credibility of sport requires enhanced governmental regulation. The indictment by US authorities and arrest of 14 current and former FIFA officials in Zurich on 27 May 2015[30] clearly shows that sports organisations' corporate governance rules are insufficient. The fight against corruption in sport is primarily the task of the private sports organisations, but states' legal systems and their governments must provide these organisations with the necessary legal framework. In the past, sports organisations in Switzerland always asserted their autonomy, and until now the state has granted this autonomy. With autonomy comes responsibility, however, and whether this responsibility has been lived up to or not in the past remains an open question. Given that an organisation of the stature of FIFA was apparently unable to do so, it seems the only logical consequence that the state should now try to intervene in a regulatory way.

Corruption in sport must be combated by all stakeholders joining forces, working together with the state authorities. Legal reforms are a first and important step in the right direction. It is clear that, in Switzerland at least, the force of criminal authority is required, to make use of compulsory measures, as the civil law is inadequate to deal with illegal activities carried out by the most powerful organisations, such as FIFA and the IOC.

Notes

1   Dr Lucien W. Valloni, attorney at law, is a partner at Froriep, and Eric P. Neuenschwander is a trainee lawyer at Froriep. Froriep is one of the leading law firms in Switzerland, with around 90 lawyers and offices in Zurich, Geneva, Lausanne and Zug, as well as foreign offices in London and Madrid, serving clients seeking Swiss law advice.

2   These include the International Olympic Committee (IOC), the Fédération Internationale de Football Association (FIFA), the Union of European Football Associations (UEFA), the Union Cycliste Internationale and the International Federation of Gymnastics.

3   Swissinfo.ch, 'Swiss set to get tough over sports corruption', 2 October 2014, *www.swissinfo. ch/eng/new-rules_swiss-set-to-get-tough-over-sports-corruption/40801520*.

4   Pursuant to article 60 et seq. of the Swiss Civil Code: Lucien Valloni and Thilo Pachmann, *Sports Law in Switzerland*, 2nd edn (Alphen aan den Rijn, Netherlands: Wolters Kluwer, 2014), §1 no. 1.

5   Amandine Bousigue and Claude Stricker, *The Economic Impact of International Sports Organisations in Switzerland 2008–2013* (Lausanne: International Academy of Sports Science and Technology, 2015), *www.aists.org/sites/default/files/publication-pdf/aists_ economic_impact_study-english-web.pdf*. All but one organisation participated in the study.

6   See Transparency International, 'Corruption by country/territory: Switzerland', *www.transparency.org/country#CHE*.

7   See the press release of the Federal Council from 30 April 2014 about the amendments to the Swiss Criminal Code (criminal law on corruption).

8   See articles 322ter and 322[quater] of the Swiss Criminal Code.
9   Kommission für Wissenschaft, Bildung und Kultur des Ständerates, 'Korruptionsbekämpfung und Wettkampfmanipulation im Sport: Bericht in Erfüllung des Postulats 11.3754' (Berne: Kommission für Wissenschaft, Bildung und Kultur des Ständerates, 28 June 2011), p. 35, *www.baspo.admin.ch/internet/baspo/de/home/aktuell/bundesrat_genehmigt_ korruptionsbericht.parsys.83108.downloadList.8434.DownloadFile.tmp/28529.pdf*.
10 Marco Balmelli and Damian Heller, 'Gutachten Sportbetrug und Good Governance' (Basel: Basel Institute on Governance, 5 December 2012), p. 25, no. 81.
11 Ibid.
12 Deborah Hauser, 'Korruption im Sport', in *Jusletter* (Switzerland), 13 May 2012, no. 9.
13 'Message of the Federal Council concerning the approval and implementation of the Criminal Law Convention and the Additional Protocol of the Council of Europe on Corruption (amendment of the Swiss Criminal Code and the Federal Law against Unfair Competition)', BBl 2004 6983.
14 Ibid., p. 7007.
15 Ibid., pp. 7009 f.
16 Ibid., p. 7010.
17 The judgement is available at *http://bstger.weblaw.ch/cache/pub/cache.faces?file=20121113_ SK_2012_21.htm&query=Sport&ul=de*.
18 Sportslawcircle.ch, 'Match fixing no crime', 16 November 2012, *http://sportslawcircle.com/ sports-law/blog/match-fixing-no-crime*.
19 Ibid.
20 Swiss Association of Football Players, 'Show Respect – Don't Fix It! Hotline Regeln', *www.safp.ch/show-respect-dont-fix-it-hotline-regeln*.
21 Federal Assembly of Switzerland, 'Parlamentarische Initiative 10.516, Fifa: Bestechung von Privatpersonen als Offizialdelikt', *www.parlament.ch/d/suche/seiten/geschaefte.aspx? gesch_id=20100516*.
22 Groupe d'États contre la Corruption, 'Council of Europe Group of States against Corruption calls for rules on political funding and increased effectiveness of certain anti-corruption provisions in Switzerland', press release, 2 December 2011, *www.coe.int/t/dghl/monitoring/ greco/news/News(20111202)Eval3_Switzerland_en.asp*.
23 See the media release of the Commission for Legal Affairs of the Council of States of the Federal Assembly of Switzerland, 'Einschränkung der Verfolgung von Amtes wegen', 24 April 2015, *www.parlament.ch/d/mm/2015/Seiten/mm-rk-s-2015-04-24.aspx*.
24 Current status, 26 June 2015. See *www.parlament.ch/d/suche/seiten/legislaturrueckblick. aspx?rb_id=20140035*.
25 Swissinfo.ch, 'Switzerland tightens its money-laundering rules', 13 December 2014, *www.swissinfo.ch/eng/business/coming-clean_switzerland-tightens-its-money-laundering- rules/41168000*.
26 The Federal Council decided on 29 April 2015 to set the federal law into force in two steps. First, the autumn 2015 peer review of the Global Forum on transparency and exchange of information for tax purposes requires the enactment of the provisions on transparency of legal entities and bearer shares as soon as possible, which is why these provisions are set in force on 1 July 2015. The remaining legislative amendments then require either the drafting of implementing regulations at ordinance level or certain implementation work by the affected norm addressees. With enactment planned for 1 January 2016, the necessary time should be given in particular to financial intermediaries and self-regulatory organisations according to the Money Laundering Act in order to arrange implementation. See *www.sif. admin.ch/sif/de/home/themen/bekaempfung-der-finanzkriminalitaet.html*.
27 'Message of the Federal Council concerning the implementation of the recommendations of the Financial Action Task Force, revised in 2012, SR 13.106', BBl 2014 585, p. 620.
28 Swissinfo.ch (13 December 2014).
29 See Council of Europe, 'Convention on the Manipulation of Sports Competitions', *http://conventions.coe.int/Treaty/EN/Treaties/Html/215.htm*. This treaty, pledging better

prevention and prosecution of match-fixing and corruption in sports, was discussed and signed by 30 European sports ministers in Magglingen/Macolin, Switzerland, in 2014, and according to the Swiss Federal Office of Sport (Bundesamt für Sport: BASPO) the Swiss sports minister, Ueli Maurer, led the meeting: *www.baspo.admin.ch/internet/baspo/de/home/aktuell/sportminister_unterzeichnen_konvention_gegen_wettkampfmanipulation.html.*

30 This is the scandal surrounding FIFA regarding the arrests in Zurich on 27 May 2015, as well as the start of criminal proceedings in the United States against several FIFA officials: see, for example, Schweizer Radio und Fernsehen, 'Zum Nachlesen: Protokoll der Ereignisse um den Fifa-Skandal', 27 May 2015, *www.srf.ch/news/international/zum-nachlesen-protokoll-der-ereignisse-um-den-fifa-skandal.*

6.5

Promoting integrity in sport

A sponsor's perspective

Jaimie Fuller[1]

Brands pay millions to sponsor sport. In return, they are able to call themselves the 'Official Timekeeper of the UCI', the 'Worldwide TOP Partner of the Olympic Movement' or the 'Official Partner of the FIFA World Cup'.

These significant naming rights sponsorships – especially among the top sporting properties and their major sponsors – bring benefits beyond the bottom-line return on investment. Increasingly, corporations' mission statements proclaim that the purpose of their 'brand' is not simply about being a household name, having their logo recognised and making profits; it is also about how they are perceived, what their values are and a broader obligation to support societal values.

Governments and fans

Experience suggests that the key to whether sponsors take a lead in strengthening integrity in sport is dependent on two other key stakeholders: governments and fans.

Some sports governing bodies may object to intervention from governments in internal affairs from time to time, especially around governance issues.[2] Nevertheless, governments have a major role in sport in support of civil society, in building social inclusion and in terms of probity. Sport (and how it is perceived) is important in shaping overall societal values, and, because of this, governments cannot and should not ignore its impact on communities. At best, governments need to take a leading role in making change happen, and advocating and pursuing improved governance practices; at the least, they need to encourage and facilitate it, in particular among their local sporting organisations.

The fans are likewise critical actors in ensuring integrity in sport, with their willingness to lobby and express their opinions to sponsors constituting an important force for achieving change. Fans are more vocal and easier to organise, and technology allows them to make their views known instantly around the world. Brands are more likely to react to 'fan power', even if slowly. The challenge in encouraging fans to push for change in a mass movement is to ensure they set their natural love of their sport aside from the need for reform of the administration of that sport.

History lessons

The IOC reforms

The reforms that the International Olympic Committee (IOC) were forced to undertake in the late 1990s, to strengthen the integrity of the Olympic Movement, are a good example of something that would not have happened without the active intervention of government.[3] The original transgression that led to the IOC's moment of reckoning – known as the 'Salt Lake City scandal' – involved university scholarships being awarded to children of IOC members.[4] The ensuing revelations, which included both the winning Nagano 1998 Winter Olympic and Sydney 2000 Summer Olympic bids, showed the use of a host of favours to garner votes, including cosmetic surgery, medical care, employment, expensive gifts and cash bribes.[5]

While the major sponsors of the IOC, which included large American companies such as Coca-Cola, McDonald's, UPS and Home Depot, were instrumental in placing pressure on the IOC, what really sparked the reaction of the sponsors was the attention of both the FBI and the US legislature. The FBI looked at the potential application of the Foreign Corrupt Practices Act,[6] and Congressman Henry Waxman introduced legislation that required US companies sponsoring the IOC to comply with an inquiry headed up by another Congressman, George Mitchell. Waxman said in 1999:

> The bill I have introduced today would prohibit American corporations from providing any financial support to the IOC until the IOC adopts the Mitchell commission reforms. [. . .] I regret that this legislation has to be introduced. I had hoped that the IOC would adopt the necessary reforms on its own accord. It is apparent, however, that the IOC is reluctant to take strong and immediate action. Perhaps, the only thing that will get the IOC's attention is if American corporate money is cut off.[7]

The IOC simply couldn't function without the financial input of US sponsors and broadcast rights, and the American sponsors and broadcasters were forced to demand action. IOC sponsors made it clear that they did not want to be 'stampeded' by public opinion, and that a lack of attention to reform could potentially be 'fatal'.[8]

Nike

Nike, a sponsor of many major sports events, teams and players, such as Manchester United, Cristiano Ronaldo, Rory McIlroy and Serena Williams, first came under public pressure to introduce reforms at the turn of the century, around the same time as the IOC reforms were taking place.[9] This related in particular to its supply chain and a code of conduct on workers' rights in its overseas factories.[10] The campaign largely began with organised labour groups in the United States, but was sustained, and achieved success, because of its overwhelming support from the communities in which Nike had its major markets.[11]

According to the editor of *Ethical Consumer*, Rob Harrison, Nike was targeted because it was big, successful and initially denied any responsibility for what went on half a world away.[12] Fifteen years later, the 'sweatshop' issues for Nike and other sportswear manufacturers may not have completely disappeared but, as a minimum, most of the companies point to systems being in place for identifying problems and processes for dealing with them.[13]

This serves as a valuable example of how consumers can successfully demand and encourage large, successful corporations to reform. Nike's response to public pressure permeated not only supply chain issues associated with its workforce, but also environmental issues such as the use of water, the creation and reuse of waste and the toxicity of materials and processes used in manufacturing.[14]

A current challenge

The Fédération Internationale de Football Association (FIFA) has been scandal-plagued for years.[15] The flawed governance of the organisation was brought sharply into focus for the wider football community in 2010, when the Executive Committee awarded the 2018 and 2022 World Cup tournaments to Russia and Qatar, respectively. Among other things, such quixotic decisions showed the FIFA Executive Committee's disregard for independent expert advice on issues such as technical capacity, financial cost–benefit analysis and security concerns when assessing the merits of the nine bidders for the two tournaments.[16]

Since then, FIFA has bumbled along from one off-field issue to another, without much real impact on its financial bottom line. While the organisation's reputation (and that of its president, Sepp Blatter) has taken a battering, Blatter was re-elected comfortably for a fifth term in May 2015.[17] FIFA and its sponsors have so far benefited from the fans' love of the sport outweighing concerns about how the sport is managed.

Some experts argue[18] that, when an event is as big and as popular as the FIFA World Cup, the appetite to push for change by sponsors is relatively small, as there are other sponsors ready to take their place for a chance to be the focus of world attention for four weeks every four years. In other words, FIFA, coupled with football, is simply too big to fail. Encouragingly, there have been a number of 'non-renewals' of sponsorship of FIFA, namely by Emirates, Sony, Johnson & Johnson, Continental Tyres and Castrol.[19] Less encouragingly, though, the readiness of companies such as Gazprom to fill the breach suggests that there remain brands that are not concerned with the reputational risk of association with FIFA.[20]

After the events of late May 2015 involving FIFA, however, the propensity of the competitor brands to 'leap into the breach' and put themselves forward as new sponsors is probably rather subdued. It is difficult to imagine Mastercard stepping into such a toxic environment when phrases such as 'money-laundering', 'racketeering', 'bribery' and 'corruption' are being used so freely by the FBI and the US Department of Justice.

This is why recent attempts by a coalition of advocacy groups and commercial interests[21] to put pressure on FIFA to reform has focused on eight of FIFA's major sponsors,[22] and the gap between their stated values of business ethics and human rights and their significant financial support for the scandal-plagued FIFA. The long-term aim of #NewFIFANow is to establish a FIFA Reform Commission, led by an eminent person, to overhaul FIFA's statutes, committee and electoral system in order to bring greater democracy, transparency and accountability to the organisation. The short-term aim is focused specifically on highlighting the inconsistencies between the sponsors' public commitments to the Universal Declaration of Human Rights and their failure to speak out against the use of the 'kafala' system in Qatar, which is the host of the 2022 FIFA World Cup.

Sponsors as change agents

Seventeen years on from the IOC reforms, the world is a different place. There is an expectation that the sport, event or individual sportsperson that a corporation sponsors should align with the values of the brand. Depending on the circumstances, sponsors have options that range from quiet behind-the-scenes pressure on the properties or individuals they sponsor to public statements of their own policies and expectations, and active advocacy of change through taking a leadership role in making it happen.

In our 'global village', as fans become more informed and engaged in what happens off the field, brands and sponsors must anticipate, and be responsive to, their customers and community values and expectations. The promotion by sponsors of integrity in sport is a challenge that will only grow as fans become more knowledgeable, more demanding, more organised and more vocal.

A failure to respond to fans' and community concerns will not only compromise the authenticity of an individual sponsor's values but, as the examples of the IOC sponsors and Nike demonstrate, will ultimately mean that they are on the wrong side of history as well. The challenge, therefore, is for corporations that sponsor sport not just to espouse societal values, but to live them.

Notes

1 Jaimie Fuller is chairman of SKINS, the ultra-performance sportswear manufacturer, based in Steinhausen, Switzerland, and an active member of the #NewFIFANow coalition.
2 FIFA has frequently and regularly complained about governments that seek to 'intervene' in the affairs of football; examples include the governmental dissolution of local football boards that had lost the confidence of the government and the football community in countries as diverse as Nigeria, Iraq, Greece, Kuwait and Peru, among others.
3 BBC (UK), 'Congress grills Olympic chief', 16 December 1999, *http://news.bbc.co.uk/2/hi/sport/566228.stm*; BBC (UK), 'Cleaning up the Olympics', 10 December 1999, *http://news.bbc.co.uk/2/hi/sport/558815.stm*.
4 *New York Times* (US), 'Olympics: leaders of Salt Lake Olympic bid are indicted in bribery scandal', 21 July 2000, *www.nytimes.com/2000/07/21/sports/olympics-leaders-of-salt-lake-olympic-bid-are-indicted-in-bribery-scandal.html*.
5 Ibid.
6 Bill Mallon, 'The Olympic bribery scandal', *Journal of Olympic History*, vol. 8 (2000).
7 Sunlight Foundation (US), 'The International Olympic Committee Reform Act: a speech in Congress by Rep. Henry Waxman (D–CA)', 12 April 1999, *https://scout.sunlightfoundation.com/item/speech/CREC-1999-04-12-pt1-PgE607-2.chunk0/rep-henry-waxman-the-international-olympic-committee-reform-act*.
8 Stephen Wenn, Robert Barney and Scott Martyn, *Tarnished Rings: The International Olympic Committee and the Salt Lake City Bid Scandal* (Syracuse, NY: Syracuse University Press, 2011).
9 *Guardian* (UK), 'Under pressure: campaigns that persuaded companies to change the world', 9 February 2015, *www.theguardian.com/sustainable-business/2015/feb/09/corporate-ngo-campaign-environment-climate-change*.
10 Nike, 'Code of conduct', *www.nikeresponsibility.com/report/uploads/files/Nike_Code_of_Conduct.pdf*.
11 *Guardian* (UK), 'How activism forced Nike to change its ethical game', 6 July 2012, *www.theguardian.com/environment/green-living-blog/2012/jul/06/activism-nike*.
12 Ibid.
13 Ibid.
14 Nike, 'Sustainable business reporting and governance', *http://about.nike.com/pages/sustainability*.
15 Andrew Jennings' book *Foul! The Secret World of FIFA: Bribes, Vote Rigging and Ticket Scandals* (London: HarperCollins, 2006) was the first to highlight FIFA's way of doing business, specifically highlighting its TV marketing rights, in what has become known as the 'ISL scandal'. Others include Alan Tomlinson's *FIFA (Fédération Internationale de Football Association): The Men, the Myths and the Money* (London: Routledge, 2014), Andrew Jennings' *Omertà: Sepp Blatter's FIFA Organised Crime Family* (London: Transparency Books, 2014) and Heidi Blake and Jonathan Calvert's *The Ugly Game: The Qatari Plot to Buy the World Cup* (London: Simon & Schuster, 2015).

16   *Daily Mirror* (UK), 'Qatar hero? Why Michel Platini might not be the man to save FIFA',
     29 May 2015, *www.mirror.co.uk/sport/football/news/qatar-hero-michel-platini-might-5783843.*

17   Four days after his re-election, Blatter announced his intention to call a fresh presidential
     election some time later in the year, while at the same time a start was made on proposals
     to 'reform' the organisation.

18   Sports marketing consultant Hermut Zastrow, in an interview with Reuters (UK), 'After
     scandal, will FIFA follow the IOC's lead?', 1 June 2011, *www.reuters.com/article/*
     2011/06/01/us-soccer-fifa-ioc-idUSTRE7505J020110601.

19   *Daily Telegraph* (UK), 'Fifa loses three key sponsors as Castrol, Continental and Johnson
     & Johnson sever ties with world governing body', 22 January 2015, *www.telegraph.co.uk/*
     sport/football/world-cup/11364195/Fifa-loses-three-key-sponsors-as-Castrol-Continental-
     and-Johnson-and-Johnson-sever-ties-with-world-governing-body.html.

20   Gazprom, 'Gazprom becomes official partner of FIFA and 2018 FIFA World Cup',
     14 September 2013, *www.gazprom.com/press/news/2013/september/article171325.*

21   The organisations/groups collaborating to put pressure on FIFA because of the kafala
     system are #NewFIFANow, the International Trade Union Congress, Playfair Qatar and the
     SKINS group of companies, which is also an 'official non-sponsor' of FIFA.

22   These are, namely, Adidas, Budweiser, Coca-Cola, Gazprom, Hyundai, Kia, McDonald's
     and Visa.

6.6

A player's perspective on the need for reform to enhance transparency and integrity in sports

Louis Saha[1]

As demonstrated by the arrests of Fédération Internationale de Football Association (FIFA) executives in late May 2015 and the subsequent resignation of FIFA's president, Sepp Blatter, a lack of transparency can mean nasty surprises, with all sorts of skeletons coming out of the closet. This can potentially involve offshore dealings, bribery, electoral fraud and agents and managers taking cuts from transfers. All too commonly, however, it is not until a major incident happens that people start talking about transparency and why the sports industry urgently needs to address the lack thereof.

The scope of the problem of corruption in sports

The scandal over the awarding of the 2022 men's World Cup to Qatar and FIFA's refusal to publish the full report prepared by Michael Garcia,[2] who was commissioned to look into the bidding and awarding of the 2018 and 2022 World Cups, raised even more concerns that corruption was taking place within the organisation, yet the most severe allegations of corruption died off fairly quickly in the minds of many in the global football community.

Unethical agents and intermediaries are also a concern when discussing corruption and sport. These powerful individuals often benefit from payoffs that come about as a result of doing business in a 'hidden' and complex environment. This also creates a barrier to entry, as many find the functioning of these environments difficult to grasp. During transfer and contract negotiations, for example, players are not invited to participate in the discussions, and, as a result, they remain unaware of what the deal actually involves. Agents, club directors, lawyers, club chairmen, unions and federations are the ones aware of the details. Ill-intentioned or not, they are following the 'procedures' that they must, in order to keep their jobs.

At the end of the day, football is a business, with fans as the main stakeholders. With a general trend towards companies and organisations becoming socially responsible and transparent, FIFA's activities have run contrary to what is expected from ordinary businesses.

More is expected from the organisation that is in place to uphold and protect the reputation of the 'beautiful game', which has billions of followers worldwide. Football's age-old heritage and tradition are something to be proud of. In addition, there are many amazing football-related projects around the globe, many of which help underprivileged children and families, which makes it disappointing that these initiatives are drowned out by the news of corruption and scandal in football governance and management.

The lack of transparency can mean unpleasant surprises for investors, sponsors, players and fans. It is crucial to bring the focus back to entertainment and positive sporting values. As a result of not prioritising the sport, however, decision-makers have lost the power to implement and enforce much-needed changes, and the industry will now have to look elsewhere to restore its well-deserved reputation. Unfortunately, as things have gone from bad to worse, to the point that people are focusing on money and arrests rather than actually enjoying the game, this is a call for the industry to change from its core.

Transparency as a solution

Transparency shows everyone that the 'restaurant' is clean. An open kitchen means a clean kitchen, a good kitchen. Surely that's what we're aiming for? As with any other business, stakeholders and investors should expect and demand transparency.

It is important to determine what we actually want to achieve through increased transparency, and who is responsible for demanding this, be it FIFA, players, club owners, agents, fans or civil society as a whole. It is critical for all these participants to be involved in an ongoing conversation, and not only when it is 'appropriate' to do so after major scandals. In a post-Blatter era it will be essential that FIFA implements both appropriate stakeholder engagement and audit systems, to ensure that cultural change within the organisation is driven by those involved in the game who so desperately want greater transparency, and that it responds to any suspicions of corruption promptly and diligently.

Promisingly, there are FIFA executives, such as England's David Gill, who are indeed calling for increased transparency.[3] Encouraging transparency through detailed internal and independent audit and accounting procedures, reported in full and publicly, would allow for a better understanding of what's going on and would also create opportunities for more people to succeed in a fair and proper way. It would also prevent well-connected individuals from being prioritised ahead of others through corruption, nepotism and undue influence.

Taking the lead in engendering change

Like a bad illness, I'm fed up hearing about researchers nearly finding a cure. I want to hear about results. It's as though we've become numb, thinking that there's no point trying to change something we can't. Many believe that, if you want to continue in the game, the only option is to ignore it all, thinking that, although there is clear evidence of what is going on, nothing can be done to bring about effective change.

Footballers, and all sportspeople, should be the best possible role models, and take a greater stand in the fight against corruption by advocating the principles of fair play not only to those on the pitch but also to those who hold the balance of power off it.

Understandably, it can be difficult to do so within an industry that is based on confusion, lies and often illogical decisions. For me, a good step towards increased transparency would be to open up the voting system for the FIFA president to allow other key industry personnel, such as representatives from players' unions, to participate in the voting process.

Although we have seen some positive steps being taken towards opening up the industry, such as Blatter's stepping down, much more needs to be done.

Reform of the processes and procedures will take time. In the meantime we can make a real difference by providing new tools and technology that will make the vetting and negotiating process much cleaner, easier to understand and completely transparent: a new way to bring about the much-needed restoration of trust. My new company, Axis Stars, aims to address many of these concerns, by bringing a once elusive clarity to the murky world of contract negotiations. By providing an online platform for professional athletes, we aim to make all business transactions transparent to all the relevant parties, so that sponsors, agents and players all receive a fair deal. As sports professionals, we hope that this much-desired increase in transparency will transform the situation for fans and governing officials alike.

Armed with the power of communicating with the masses through social networks and communities, we can now all help to make a difference by putting pressure on those at the top. Hopefully, this will help foster a clear and open business environment, in which the focus will be on the game, the players and the best interests of the fans.

Axis Stars has recruited established sportsmen such as Didier Drogba, Mo Farah, Boris Diaw and Gary Neville to break down the barriers regarding the lack of transparency in sport. It has established lists of companies that have been vetted and are trusted to provide advice and services, with the aim of establishing a culture of fair play, on and off the pitch, for sports stars. Cultural change takes time, but Axis Stars is committed to ensuring that the athletes of tomorrow can do business in a protected environment, and that the only stories on them will be about success on the field, not a fall from grace off it.

Notes

1   Louis Saha is a former professional and international footballer who played for the French national team as well as Manchester United, Everton and Fulham football clubs in the United Kingdom. He is the founder of Axis Stars, a social network that provides support to professional athletes and helps them manage their contracts, agent relations and post-football career planning.

2   When FIFA published a summary of the Garcia report, there was international outcry that the full 430-page document was not going to be made available. Garcia said of FIFA that its 'investigation and adjudication process operates in most parts unseen and unheard. That's a kind of system which might be appropriate for an intelligence agency but not for an ethics compliance process in an international sports institution that serves the public and is the subject of intense public scrutiny.' See Fox (US), 'Chief ethics investigator Michael Garcia criticizes FIFA's culture of secrecy', 13 October 2014, *www.foxsports.com/soccer/story/chief-ethics-investigator-michael-garcia-criticizes-fifa-s-culture-of-secrecy-101314*.

3   *Guardian* (UK), 'Manchester United director David Gill set to become Fifa vice-president', 22 March 2015, *www.theguardian.com/football/2015/mar/22/david-gill-manchester-united-fifa-vice-president*.

6.7

Organised athletes

A critical voice in sports governance

Brendan Schwab[1]

Football is at its most important juncture since the very establishment of the Fédération Internationale de Football Association (FIFA) over a century ago; and, with football at a historic juncture, so too is all of sport. Never before have so many of the game's fans and stakeholders acknowledged the need for fundamental change in the governance of the world's most popular and important sport.

In a surprise announcement on 2 June 2015 that he would 'lay down' his mandate at a to-be-convened extraordinary congress, FIFA president Sepp Blatter said: 'While I have a mandate from the membership of FIFA, I do not feel that I have a mandate from the entire world of football – the fans, the players, the clubs, the people who live, breathe and love football. . .' A brief statement, but one that says much about the governance issues that have plagued FIFA – and, indeed, many international sporting federations – for a number of years.

Simply put, sport's major international bodies lack the accountability needed to ensure the good governance that is essential if sport is to uphold the social, cultural and economic significance that many attach to it.

The accountability deficit and the rights of athletes

Since professional and commercial interests first entered sport in the nineteenth century, those vested with the privilege of governing sport have championed its special characteristics and even suggested that its governance should sit outside the high standards that the law applies across society. Central to this has been an intense and sustained focus on limiting the incomes and career opportunities of professional athletes, whose human and legal rights have been subjected to vague notions such as the autonomy or specificity of sport.[2]

English football adopted a transfer system as early as 1891 and a maximum wage of £4 per week ten years later. It was not until 1963 that football's governors were brought to account, by professional footballer George Eastham and future English Lord Justice Richard Wilberforce, who asserted that the law was competent to examine football's transfer system despite claims that its abolition would result in the death of professional football itself. Wilberforce considered the system

> *an employers' system, set up in an industry where the employers have succeeded in establishing a monolithic front all over the world, and where it is clear that for the*

purpose of negotiation the employers are vastly more strongly organized than the employees. No doubt the employers all over the world consider the system a good system, but this does not prevent the court from considering whether it goes further than is reasonably necessary to protect their legitimate interests.[3]

Jean Marc Bosman won a similar legal victory 30 years later with the clear statement that professional footballers, like all workers within the European Union, have the right to move freely within the Union and that the special interests demanded by sport do not sit above, nor justify a departure from, the rule of law.[4]

The positive growth and reforms to football that followed both legal cases attest to the benefits that flow to sport when it, like the rest of society, is made subject to the rule of law. The political and diplomatic skills of sport's administrators have succeeded in convincing many that not only does sport require special protection, it should also be autonomous from democratically elected governments and political institutions.

Article 165 of the Treaty on the Functioning of the European Union, which entered into force on 1 December 2009, calls on the European Union to 'take account of the specific nature of sport and the structures of sport'.[5] In October 2014 the United Nations General Assembly passed a resolution ostensibly about the role of sport in advancing education, health, development and peace. The resolution, passed at a time of great consternation in the governance of sport globally, '[s]upports the independence and autonomy of sport'.[6] In a similar vein, the FIFA statutes provide for the suspension of member football associations when that autonomy has been breached by possible 'influence from third parties'.[7] All three instruments present a threat to the rights of athletes and, in turn, the good governance of sport.

The ineffectiveness of the World Anti-Doping Agency has been condemned by athlete unions,[8] and critical legal proceedings involving German speed skater Claudia Pechstein rightly question the independence of the Court of Arbitration for Sport and the absence of any free choice on the part of athletes to submit their very costly and often career-defining disputes to it.[9]

What needs to change

Fortunately, change is afoot.

One example is that Paraguay's lawmakers are moving to remove the diplomatic immunity of the Confederación Sudamericana de Fútbol (CONMEBOL), which has been on the country's statute books since 1997. With several CONMEBOL officials among those arrested as part of the May 2015 crackdown on FIFA, the counterproductive impact of the special privileges afforded international sporting bodies is finally being understood.

Such change is a small step towards the broad societal acknowledgement that is required: that, as sports are structured as cartels, they warrant not privilege and protection but enhanced scrutiny and accountability. Whether the requisite change to sport's governance occurs in a lasting manner will largely depend on what happens at FIFA.

The Fédération Internationale des Associations Footballeurs Professionnels (FIFPro), the world footballers' association, is determined to ensure that the change is both fundamental and lasting. Honorary president Gordon Taylor OBE spoke unequivocally when addressing the FIFPro Europe General Assembly in Bulgaria in June 2015, saying that 'there has never been a better or more opportune time' for change, and that the player unions 'cannot and must not leave a vacuum in FIFA to be filled with the same toxic problems as before'.[10] The failure of FIFA's own efforts to reform its governance in the wake of the decision of the FIFA

Executive Committee to award the 2018 and 2022 men's football World Cups to Russia and Qatar, respectively, needs to be borne in mind. The recommendations of the Independent Governance Committee (IGC), chaired by Professor Mark Pieth of the Basel Institute on Governance and made up of critical stakeholders, including the players through then FIFPro president Leonardo Grosso, were largely ignored, resulting in the failure of the reform effort.

Some key lessons from the IGC report of 22 April 2014 are particularly relevant.[11] These include the roles played by the six FIFA confederations in defeating principal reforms, the uncertainty that continues to surround the awarding of the hosting rights for the 2018 and 2022 World Cups and how the reform process is to be driven if it is to succeed.

Key athlete-driven organisations, such as FIFPro and UNI World Athletes, insist that fundamental reform is required at the global and continental levels as well as in many countries. Knowledge and principle must drive the reform agenda. The conduct, governance and structure of FIFA, all confederations and complicit national football associations must be fully examined to properly inform the change process. Other key stakeholders, such as players, leagues, clubs, fans, corporate partners, governance and human rights lobbies and governments, must unite around the key planks of reform; otherwise they will face defeat through fragmentation against the football establishment, which will aim to secure its hegemony.

The key governance principles that must be embraced are well known, and include:

- a fundamental dedication to advancing the essence of sport, and a commitment to avoid compromising it for commercial or political purposes;
- subrogation to, and respect for, the rule of law;
- an independent governing board with the requisite skills and diversity to provide the necessary leadership and quality of decision-making – appropriate electoral rules, including term limits, should be clearly provided for;
- accountability of the governing board to the game's key stakeholders, which must include the right to elect and remove members of the board;
- the separation of powers between the regulatory, executive and dispute resolution functions;
- standards of transparency and disclosure in keeping with public companies, particularly regarding the finances of sporting organisations, the making of critical decisions, such as the right to host mega-events, and the conduct of elections – these should all be subject to independent audits and public disclosure;
- an obligation to uphold international and national law and standards regarding human rights and the environment in relation to the conduct of sport, including major events; and
- the recognition and involvement of the athletes, especially through independent athlete associations and collective bargaining agreements negotiated at arm's length and in good faith.

History and the prevailing culture at FIFA both suggest that such change cannot be achieved from within. The IGC report acknowledges this problem, and concludes by stating:

In order to promote genuine cultural change, the IGC believes that some outside independent body should continue to work with FIFA to ensure that the road to reform is completely finished. This outside body can be small but must be adequately resourced to do the work.[12]

Recent revelations demonstrate that a much more substantial external effort is required. In particular, this effort cannot succeed without organised athletes acting through independent trade unions. As Taylor said in Bulgaria:

> *Our record is one of transparency not opaqueness, accountability not of obfuscation. We adhere to rules or change them openly through negotiations or by the law of the land. We believe in monitoring, appraising and assessing the projects we set out to deliver from start to finish.*

Above all else, he emphasised: 'A game for players about players has NOT been run by players and we are now seeing the results.'[13]

Notes

1   Brendan Schwab is vice president of the Fédération Internationale des Associations Footballeurs Professionnels and the newly appointed head of UNI World Athletes, a global collective of 85,000 athletes through major player associations including FIFPro, the Federation of International Cricketers' Associations, the International Rugby Players' Association, EU Athletes, the US National Basketball Players Association, the US National Football League Players Association, the National Hockey League Players Association (United States and Canada), the Japanese Baseball Players Association and the Australian Athletes' Alliance. He is the former general secretary of the Australian Athletes' Alliance and chief executive of Professional Footballers Australia.

2   See, for example, Braham Dabscheck, 'Sport, human rights and industrial relations', *Australian Journal of Human Rights*, vol. 6 (2000).

3   Ibid.

4   *Wall Street Journal* (US), 'Bosman still struggling with ruling that rewards soccer's free agents', 2 July 2014, *www.wsj.com/articles/the-jean-marc-bosman-ruling-benefited-soccers-free-agents-but-the-man-himself-is-still-struggling-1404327335*.

5   See article 165 of the Treaty of Lisbon, at *www.lisbon-treaty.org/wcm/the-lisbon-treaty/treaty-on-the-functioning-of-the-european-union-and-comments/part-3-union-policies-and-internal-actions/title-xii-education-vocational-training-youth-and-sport/453-article-165.html*.

6   International Olympic Committee, 'Historic milestone: United Nations recognises autonomy of sport', 3 November 2014, *www.olympic.org/news/historic-milestone-united-nations-recognises-autonomy-of-sport/240276*.

7   FIFA statute article 13.1(i): *www.fifa.com/mm/Document/AFFederation/Generic/02/58/14/48/2015FIFAStatutesEN_Neutral.pdf*.

8   *Sydney Morning Herald* (Australia), 'Why Australian sports must cut ties with WADA', 15 June 2014, *www.smh.com.au/sport/why-australian-sports-must-cut-ties-with-wada-20140615-zs8k1.html#ixzz34ION5nPL*.

9   Asser International Sports Law, 'The Pechstein ruling of the Oberlandesgericht München: time for a new reform of CAS?', 19 January 2015, *www.asser.nl/SportsLaw/Blog/post/the-pechstein-ruling-of-the-oberlandesgericht-munchen-time-for-a-new-reform-of-cas*.

10 Professional Footballers' Association (UK), 'Taylor addresses FIFPro European congress', 11 June 2015, *www.thepfa.com/news/2015/6/11/taylor-addresses-fifpro-european-congress*.

11 Independent Governance Committee, *FIFA Governance Reform Project: Final Report by the Independent Governance Committee to the Executive Committee of FIFA* (Basel: Basel Institute on Governance, 2014).

12 Ibid. p. 15.

13 Professional Footballers' Association (11 June 2015).

6.8

The role of supporters in effective governance

Ben Shave and Antonia Hagemann[1]

Introduction

When it comes to examining sports governance, one is inevitably compelled to reflect upon larger themes of identity, ownership and the varied nature of the relationships between sports, sports organisations and their numerous stakeholders. In order to achieve effective, transparent and robust governance of international sports organisations, governing bodies, competitions and clubs, the significance of the role of supporters cannot be underestimated.

Supporters are the lifeblood of sport – economically, culturally and socially. More than any other category of stakeholder, they make lifelong commitments, and invest in sport (economically and emotionally, as well as in terms of their time) on a similar basis. Supporters have an interest in sport that is qualitatively and quantitatively different from that of any other group.[2]

The involvement of supporters in sport's decision-making processes is facing considerable pressure, however. In some countries, the tradition of member ownership – most sports clubs began as associations of people wanting to organise collective leisure and social activities – has been replaced or threatened by more overtly commercial or corporate models of governance and structure.

> ### Box 6.2 The changing face of club ownership
>
> In some countries, such as Germany and Sweden, the member-run model remains.[3] In other countries, such as Spain, clubs were structured as members' associations until the early 1990s. In 1992 all professional football clubs – with the exceptions of Athletic Club, FC Barcelona, Osasuna CF and Real Madrid – whose finances showed a negative balance had to transform from members' associations into Sports Public Limited Companies (SADs). This changed the structure of Spanish football and the status of supporters dramatically. Some supporters did acquire shares in their clubs, thus becoming owners, in response to calls from the clubs' directors about managing the debt problem. However, their stake became progressively less significant after several capital increase ventures. Today, most clubs are owned primarily by wealthy individuals, who have

established numerous corporations to further limit their potential liability, which has led to the minority shareholders feeling at risk from management abuse – something which has indeed come to pass on many occasions.[4] In the ten years following the introduction of a Bankruptcy Law for sports clubs in 2003, 22 Spanish clubs entered administration,[5] and current debt levels throughout the professional game are significantly higher than in 1992.[6]

Despite a significant increase in football's revenues in recent decades, the financial stability of clubs has been undermined across Europe. The key reason for this is simple: clubs have a pronounced tendency to spend more than they earn.[7] Prior to the introduction of the Club Licensing and Financial Fair Play regulations by the Union of European Football Associations (UEFA) (which are applicable to clubs applying for licenses to compete in the Champions and Europa League), the net debt of Europe's top divisions was an estimated €6.9 billion (US$7.8 billion), and '36% [of clubs surveyed by UEFA] reported negative equity (more liabilities than assets) in their balance sheets'.[8] The relationship between these stark figures and ownership structures could not be clearer: in the same financial year, owner and benefactor capital injections were an estimated €3.4 billion (US$3.8 billion).[9]

This chapter sets out the case for supporter involvement in sports governance, at international, national and club level. It also outlines Supporters Direct (SD) Europe's perspective on three key issues relevant to the battle against corruption in sport, and provides an outlook for the future.

The need for supporter involvement in the governance of international sports organisations

In many countries, professional sport is experiencing the adverse effects of unsustainable financial models, weak governance and a lack of democratic accountability – all of which are key contributing factors to the emergence of corruption.[10] As well as the resulting instability, this also damages the social impact that sport can have. This assertion has been recognised by almost all major stakeholders in sport.[11]

It is also increasingly recognised that good governance is fundamental to bolstering financial sustainability and delivering social benefits, and is a condition for the self-regulation of sport organisations[12] – something they hold in great value. In the context of sport, good governance can also help promote a range of positive values and aims: democratic participation, citizenship, transparency, financial sustainability, community development, education and training – which can all play an active role in combating corruption.

The involvement of supporters in decision-making across Europe and further afield has demonstrated that clubs can be successful while also following good governance guidelines. The most notable recent example came in the 2012/2013 UEFA Champions League final, which was contested by FC Bayern and Borussia Dortmund – two clubs where the annual members' meeting is the highest decision-making body, and principles of transparency and financial sustainability are upheld. For the benefits of this to be fully harnessed, however, and for anti-corruption efforts to achieve maximum effectiveness, overarching governance structures in sport (to provide a framework under which sustainable supporter-run clubs can compete meaningfully alongside other ownership models) are required.[13]

The prevalence of commercially minded structures means that clubs are organised so as to prioritise shareholder interests above all others. Growth in broadcast revenues, commercial sponsorship and advertising has exacerbated this trend, as decisions are made in order to

Supporters, the financial and cultural mainstays of sport, are almost universally absent from the executive bodies of national and international governing bodies and leagues.

Figure 6.1 Support versus influence

maximise these new streams to the exclusion of supporter interests and concerns, such as those listed above.[14] It has also compromised the ability (and, in some cases, the desire) of governing bodies to impose robust, independent regulation.

Supporters, the financial and cultural mainstays of sport, are almost universally absent from the executive bodies of national and international governing bodies and leagues. SD Europe believes that the involvement of supporters in governance at club, national and international governing body levels can provide a greater level of scrutiny, independence, accountability and transparency, and that it will lead to better and more balanced decision-making, in the best long-term interests of sport, in the clubs and institutions that play such an important role in the life of communities; whether that be through delivering social value (clubs) or providing a framework through which that social value is delivered (institutions).[15]

Case study: match-fixing

Match-fixing ultimately leads to a decrease in the attractiveness of sport and has a negative impact on sponsors, the media and the public. Sport's intrinsic appeal is based on trust, fair competition and uncertainty of outcome. If these are no longer guaranteed then the status quo will not last.

For supporters, there is a clear interest in joining efforts to combat match-fixing, whether this takes the form of participation in EU expert groups examining the issue (as SD Europe will do under the new EU Work Plan for Sport) or organising campaigns to highlight the issue. There is also added value to be gleaned: the fight against match-fixing does not begin with sanctions or prosecutions, but rather with the dissemination of information and education about the negative impact it has on sport as a whole. This applies to supporters as much as it does to other stakeholders, and the backing of supporters for initiatives undertaken by public institutions, governing bodies, competition organisers or other stakeholders will lend such initiatives considerable weight. Only through such a coordinated approach can the fight against match-fixing be won.

In addition, SD Europe believes that better governance of clubs, competitions and governing bodies (including supporter ownership and involvement) will reduce the risk of match-fixing. Basic good governance principles, such as democratic representation and transparency, create an environment in which match-fixing is less likely, and sport's social value can be realised. If we accept that supporters have an interest in sport that is qualitatively and quantitatively different from that of any other group, SD Europe believes that clubs where supporters are part of the ownership and decision-making structures are less likely to see match-fixing incidents occur. Prevention, education and enforcement are crucial, but would be underpinned in the long term by more sustainable, transparent club structures across sport as a whole. Research undertaken by FIFPro Division Europe clearly shows that when clubs are operating unsustainable and non-transparent structures, instances of match-fixing are significantly more likely to occur.[16]

Case study: sports agents

The regulations for agents (also known as intermediaries) of the Fédération Internationale de Football Association (FIFA) have been the fundamental basis of the regulatory framework for transfers since first being implemented in 1991. FIFA has acknowledged that the regulations are not operating effectively in practice, however, and are not being observed in the majority of transfers.

The main problems in the operation and regulation of this aspect of the transfer market are as follows.

- There are a significant number of unlicensed (and therefore unregulated) agents operating in the global market.
- There is very little transparency regarding the role, involvement and payment of agents in football, despite FIFA statistics indicating that payments to agents acting on international player transfers for clubs rose to US$236 million in 2014.[17]
- Transactions are often complex and cross-border, making meaningful enforcement action difficult and rare.
- The often unregulated and clandestine nature of agent involvement, coupled with the significant sums of money involved, creates potential risks of misconduct/market abuse as well as financial crime, corruption and money-laundering.
- There are also ethical risks, including misrepresentation, conflicts of interest and the exploitation of young players.[18]

These risks are significant, and endanger football's integrity. FIFA has indicated that it intends to abandon the existing licensing regime and has proposed new draft regulations. These would leave the control of the activities of agents to clubs and players. This is potentially a backward step, as parties will often not be in a position to effectively control the behaviour of intermediaries.

In order for long-term improvements to be made, the overall regulatory framework will need to be significantly adjusted in order to deal with the new challenges outlined above. Principles of transparency (in relation to market information, decision-making and outcomes) and accountability will provide a system of 'checks and balances', therefore lowering the risk of misconduct.[19] SD Europe believes that these principles can be promoted through the democratic representation of supporters in the decision-making processes of clubs and governing bodies, which will ultimately lead to better governance and a more transparent trading environment. In the long term, better governance and improved transparency will promote greater levels of sustainability – something that will increase the possibility and viability of supporter-owned clubs, many of which are currently competing on an unlevel playing field, against clubs with less rigorous standards of governance, transparency and sustainability.

Conclusion

Clearly, the quality of the people involved in administering any structure is at least as important as the structure itself in terms of preventing corruption. A privately owned sports club is not inherently more susceptible to corruption than a community-owned one. It is the belief of SD Europe, however, that the structured involvement of supporters in the ownership, governance and decision-making processes of sports organisations, clubs and sport as a whole brings an important added value, at the core of which is a long-term interest in sport's sustainability. In terms of anti-corruption efforts, supporters are also natural allies, on account of the ruinous effect of such practices in the long term.

A core part of SD Europe's mission is to broaden the network of organisations in Europe that are seeking to develop supporter ownership and involvement. SD Europe's work to date has shown how much value can be generated, and how many benefits to the governance of sport can be delivered, by democratic supporter involvement. Thanks to the work of supporters' groups across Europe since 2000, we estimate that approximately 100 football clubs have been preserved for their communities to enjoy, while national organisations have been established across the continent – providing partners in dialogue for public authorities, governing bodies, leagues and clubs. Many challenges remain, but a coordinated approach involving all stakeholders is the only way forward.

Notes

1   Ben Shave is development manager at Supporters Direct Europe and Antonia Hagemann is head of Supporters Direct Europe. SD Europe assists supporters' organisations in achieving formal structured involvement in their clubs and associations and developing supporter ownership of sports clubs. SD Europe also advises clubs on their ownership and governance structure and works with associations, leagues, the Union of European Football Associations (UEFA) and EU institutions. Established in 2007 with funding from UEFA, SD Europe has helped meet these objectives by advising supporters across Europe, increasing the resources at their disposal to improve both the governance of sport and the social function it serves. SD Europe's position paper *The Heart of the Game: Why Supporters Are Vital to Improving Governance in Football* (London: SD Europe, 2012) was launched at the European Parliament in Brussels, and outlines the organisation's positions on key policy issues. To read more, see *www.supporters-direct.org/homepage/what-we-do/europe-2/sd-europe-paper.*
2   Supporters Direct Europe (2012), p. 6.
3   See Supporters Direct Europe, 'The "German model" explained: governance, regulation and financial performance', *www.supporters-direct.org/news-article/the-german-model-explained-governance-regulation-and-financial-performance.*
4   Supporters Direct Europe, *What is the Feasibility of a Supporters Direct Europe?* (London: Supporters Direct Europe, 2009), pp. 108–109.
5   Supporters Direct Europe (2012), p. 16.
6   La Nueva España, 'Situación Económica del Fútbol Español a 30/06/13: 1. Deuda Total', *www.lne.es/blogs/el-blog-de-roberto-bayon/situacion-economica-del-futbol-espanol-a-30-06-2013-1-deuda-total.html.*
7   Supporters Direct Europe (2012), p. 16.

8 Union of European Football Associations, *The European Club Footballing Landscape: Club Licensing Benchmarking Report Financial Year 2010* (Nyon, Switzerland: UEFA, 2012), p. 88.

9 Ibid., p. 88.

10 See *www.transparency.org/topic/detail/sport*.

11 Communication from the Commission to the European Parliament, the Council, the European Economic and Social Committee and the Committee of the Regions: developing the European dimension in sport, *http://eur-lex.europa.eu/legal-content/EN/TXT/PDF/?uri=CELEX:52011DC0012&from=EN*; and Supporters Direct Europe, *Improving Football Governance through Supporter Involvement and Community Ownership: Project Final Report* (London: Supporters Direct Europe, 2013), p. 3.

12 EU Expert Group '"Good Governance" deliverable 2: principles of good governance in sport', *http://ec.europa.eu/sport/library/policy_documents/xg-gg-201307-dlvrbl2-sept2013.pdf*.

13 Supporters Direct Europe (2012), p. 9.

14 Ibid., p. 10.

15 This view has been endorsed by bodies such as UEFA, through their support of SD Europe's work since 2007; and the European Union, which financed the 'Improving football governance through supporter involvement and community ownership' preparatory action. See *www.supporters-direct.org/homepage/what-we-do/europe-2/official-support*.

16 FIFPro, *FIFPro Black Book Eastern Europe: The Problems Professional Football Players Encounter* (Hoofddorp, Netherlands: FIFPro, 2012), pp. 5–7.

17 *Guardian* (UK), 'Agents made £155m on international transfers in 2014, FIFA reveals', 28 January 2015.

18 Supporters Direct Europe (2012), p. 32.

19 Ibid.

6.9

Learning from others

The Kick It Out campaign

Richard Bates[1]

English football has evolved in many ways over the last two decades. The Premier League is a huge commercial enterprise that generates billions of pounds each year on a global scale, and managers, coaches and players are afforded the best facilities and most up-to-date technology with which to do their jobs. The upper echelons of the English game are now full of impressive all-seater stadiums, and millions of fans around the world tune in to watch their favourite teams every weekend.

The issue of discrimination in the game has changed dramatically during this time too, with new challenges constantly arising. Throughout the 1970s and 1980s the most overt forms of discrimination, abuse and prejudice were on display for all to see, yet little was done to confront this. Lord Herman Ouseley, chairman of Kick It Out, first sought to change this when working for the Greater London Council in 1984, but professional clubs were not receptive then, with some even denying that problems existed.

When Lord Ouseley became the chairman of the Commission for Racial Equality (CRE) in 1993, he saw another opportunity to try to galvanise the football authorities and professional clubs into recognising the problems that continued to tarnish the game's reputation. Lord Ouseley and colleagues at the CRE swiftly gained the backing of over 50 per cent of professional clubs, and had secured all but two clubs within a year. There was now an acknowledgement of the seriousness of the issue.

There had been certain difficulties with the football authorities, but Gordon Taylor of the Professional Footballers' Association (PFA), David Dein of the Premier League, David Davies of the national Football Association (FA) and Richard Faulkner of the Football Trust were all enthusiastic about the campaign, originally called 'Let's Kick Racism Out of Football', and its intentions. This high-level leadership support was crucial in getting their own organisations to understand the problem that many maintained wasn't there.

From the outset players had said 'I hope you know what you're taking on' to Lord Ouseley, because they could see the knockbacks he was taking. Having such a figurehead, who was willing to put his head above the parapet and use his position to challenge those with the power to change things, was instrumental in putting equality high up on football's agenda. He understood the struggle and the sacrifices so many had undertaken in trying to achieve similar feats across society.

The use of striking branding also played an important part of the 'Let's Kick Racism Out of Football' campaign, becoming part of the structure of the English game. T-shirts were being donned by high-profile players across the Premier League, magazines were sent out to schools, grassroots clubs and community groups, and campaign videos containing players such as Eric Cantona and Les Ferdinand were developed. The campaign was deliberately kept at the forefront of people's minds.

Fans played a huge part from the start. Many supporters' groups had been active over the years prior to 'Let's Kick Racism Out of Football' by initiating campaigns themselves to address the issue of racism in the game. Making these connections was very important, and there was an early realisation of how vital the role of fans would be in trying to stop others from behaving in a discriminatory manner. These fans in particular, including groups such as Foxes Against Racism of Leicester City FC and Leeds Fans United Against Racism and Fascism of Leeds United FC, were seeing the abuse first-hand and had a powerful message to convey.

With the backing of the PFA, the Premier League, the FA and the Football Foundation, 'Let's Kick Racism Out of Football' evolved into Kick It Out in 1997 as it widened its remit to tackle all forms of discrimination. This was a major development for the campaign, reflecting how well integrated within football it had become. It proved the power of partnerships – a key element of Kick It Out's success to this day, giving the organisation greater leverage with which to push for more inclusive practices.

A gradual approach has been taken over the years to edging equality and diversity into the day-to-day operations of professional clubs and the agencies tackling their policies. Kick It Out introduced its own Equality Standard in 2003, which expects clubs to achieve graded levels by demonstrating their commitment towards making football accessible, and opening up opportunities to everybody, ensuring clubs become more representative of the communities they serve.

Hosting specific awareness-raising periods, such as the 'Weeks of Action', launched by Kick It Out in 2001, has proved to be a very effective way of engaging clubs in equality activity. This has been replicated by a number of initiatives and campaigns, including the Football Against Racism in Europe network – a body that Kick It Out works with closely on overseas matters. Kick It Out will always seek to maintain its independence while working closely with all of football's stakeholders, providing a consistent public voice on the issues that matter and giving support to those who are discriminated against and denied the chance to fully participate in a game that purports to be open to all.

Note

1   Richard Bates is media and communications manager at Kick It Out, which is based in London. His main role is to generate awareness of the campaign's projects at all levels – local, regional, national and international.

6.10

Big business blurs sports journalism's critical eye

Peter English[1]

The increased commercialisation of the media is having a visible effect on sports journalism and has the potential to diminish its ability to monitor and scrutinise. With its focus on athletes and results, sports journalism has not always been the natural domain of detached watch-dogs and investigative journalists. Its function extends beyond reporting scores and press conferences, however, with the requirement to analyse and interpret the work, decisions and actions of players, officials and administrators.

There is no suggestion that the contemporary commercial environment is leading to the *corruption* of sports journalists or their journalism. The combination of corporate influences, reduced staffing and increased workloads has caused sports journalism to be practised differently in comparison with more traditional approaches, however. As a result, there are pressing issues in relation to objectivity, ethics, the merging of business and editorial links, and the number of in-depth investigations. These conclusions are made from a study that combined in-depth interviews with 36 sports journalists from six broadsheet/quality publications from Australia, India and the United Kingdom, with a content analysis of 4,541 articles from the sports sections of these outlets.[2]

Concerns outlined by the journalists, particularly in the United Kingdom and Australia, focused on the increase of commercial aspects in their coverage, as well as fewer financial and human resources to undertake investigations, or detailed analysis of issues that were previously covered.[3] It is important to recognise that these factors are not exclusive to the sports section, but their impact can be especially significant in sport – for journalists, supporters and those controlling the games.

Falling staff numbers are a major reason for the decline in sports scrutiny. The current economic climate, with dramatic reductions in print circulation and media advertising in Western markets, means that fewer sports journalists are doing more of the work. This can lead to a reliance on press releases and sports-administration-driven 'news' items. It also leads to there being fewer critical eyes to peer away from their computer screens or social media accounts. Therefore, most sports journalists are unable to consider issues that are not occurring right in front of them. This allows the big players, whether sports companies, agents or athletes, to operate without being monitored closely by those capable of exposing any mistakes or misdeeds.

Declining revenues in many Western media companies are having a greater influence in another way, with limited resources meaning that staged events by sports organisations are cheap and easy for the media to cover. While traditional print-based media are operating on smaller budgets, many professional sports organisations are thriving due to broadcast deals and sponsorships, providing greater control over access to sources, content and, in some cases, matches.

Athletes still provide the bulk of quotes and material for news reports, features or profiles. Sports organisations regulate day-to-day news-gathering through press conferences or media events, however, and by limiting access to athletes (often in conjunction with their agents). These organisations control the message of the players through briefings and media training. As a result, contemporary journalists can find themselves tied to sports bodies or administrators, afraid to criticise for fear of being cut off from their official source, and comfortable running the ruling company's line. This clearly impacts on the objectivity of the reporters, as well as limiting the investigation of any wrongdoing by the sporting bodies.

A further complication for sports journalists is that gaining exclusive access to athletes (news is about new or unique information, after all) can now be a complex process involving journalistic and business forces. In some countries, such as Australia and the United Kingdom, a one-on-one interview can come with the baggage of a corporate promotion as part of the story. In these instances, the interview will not occur without the promise of a sponsor or advertising mention. At *The Daily Telegraph*, one reporter said they were 'not embarrassed to use any means' when it came to utilising business and sponsors to secure interviews with elite sportspeople.[4] While commercial promotions may not be 'immoral or harmful' in journalism, they go against the tradition of newspapers being 'promoters of public interests' and representatives of the people.[5] Journalists are still in a position to ask hard questions in these interviews, but they say they are also aware of repercussions in terms of restricted or no access in the future, and story opportunities being offered to rival publications. On account of financial factors, however, these organisations have adapted to the commercial environment, arguing that accepting this deal was the only way a journalist might attend such an event or interview.

The compromise of the public interest extends to advertising or funding deals to allow journalists to travel to events.[6] For example, a sports journalist from Australia's *The Sydney Morning Herald* went to Europe to report on cycling races while being partially funded by Orica-GreenEdge cycling and EuroSport television.[7] In the United Kingdom, a senior writer from *The Guardian* was sent to interview an Olympic athlete with all flights and accommodation paid for – provided there was a photograph with sponsors' logos.[8] These examples are particularly relevant given that both of the organisations previously operated under regulations that prevented travel being paid from outside sources.[9] A senior manager at *The Guardian* noted how the rules that existed in print were 'starting to dissolve on the web, particularly in areas like sport'. As he said:

> Let's face it, we're not covering revolutions and uprisings and corporate scandals, by and large, although there's a certain extent of it. A lot of newspapers come to the conclusion – and we're no different – that sport is one of the areas that could and should be monetised. And that will allow you that level of whiter-than-white representation around your news coverage, domestic and foreign, which you need and cannot be influenced by any sort of commercial factors if you are going to be a serious paper.[10]

This approach resulted in a 'more relaxed' relationship with sponsors in sports coverage. It must be noted that both organisations made attempts to retain their journalistic integrity in these situations. At *The Sydney Morning Herald*, a disclosure agreement was signed with the sponsors that the news organisation did not have to be supportive of the companies in print.

The Guardian refused to give the commercial organisation copy approval.[11] Despite the potential for being compromised, there remained a desire to retain editorial freedom.

These types of commercial tie-ins expand the list of potential media restrictions on sports journalists. Of the 36 sports journalists interviewed in this study, almost one-third were required by their organisational guidelines or individual roles and routines to mention commercial aspects in their published articles; 50 per cent did this 'occasionally'.[12] Five of the 12 UK sports journalists interviewed said they were required to mention these factors, while seven of the 12 Australian respondents said they did it occasionally. There was less pressure in India to promote corporate aspects, although some journalists at *The Times of India* noted that it was important not to upset their advertisers.

The presence of commercial inclusions in stories is a key indicator of the success of corporate influence. One study shows that more than one-quarter of the articles in an analysis of 4,103 newspaper and online sports stories contained business, sponsor or product placement mentions.[13] Examples included using a stadium title bought by a financial institution instead of the traditional name;[14] a cycling team name;[15] including newspaper advertisers in a story (for example, betting agencies);[16] and a tagline in an interview.[17] Commercial mentions were included in approximately one-third of stories in the Australian and UK publications, but fewer than one-quarter in India. It was clear that commercial influences had an impact on the content in these sports sections, and highlighted the increased commercialisation of sports journalism. When corporate organisations have a presence on the sports page, and wield financial power over news organisations with shrinking margins, the upshot can be a reduction in the critical analysis of those businesses.

Interestingly, the trend towards economic factors influencing sports journalism began before the global financial crisis. A global study published in 2005 describes the sports media as 'the world's best advertising agency', and goes on to say that commercial pressure has made it 'almost impossible to work' within journalism's 'classic ideals'.[18] Now the question is asked whether sports journalism is 'news' or 'publicity'.[19]

The commercial creep onto the sports pages raises ethical concerns and questions over objectivity. In strict interpretations of each nation's ethical codes, issues surrounding corporate mentions contravene the conditions.[20] For example, in Australia, journalists do not allow 'advertising or other commercial considerations to undermine accuracy, fairness or independence'.[21] While it can be difficult to determine when fairness or independence is compromised, it is evident that by accepting commercial mentions – and at times even embracing them – news organisations have stepped away from the pure truth-telling of journalism. This shift towards a more corporate orientation has therefore created a haze over objective reporting. As one sports journalist from *The Guardian* said:

> *You've got to have complete editorial freedom and write about the stories you want to. If you've got a big sponsor and you've done something wrong, you've got to write about it. That's your role as a newspaper, you can't brush something under the carpet just because they give you someone [to interview] every now and then.*[22]

Of course, news organisations are predominantly for-profit organisations, and work within these ideals. The landscape has changed significantly across many media markets, however. In Australia, for example, it was mentioned by the interview respondents that editorial sports staff could meet with advertisers to determine possible stories on which they might work together.[23] Even in recent history this would not have occurred, in an effort to keep the two departments separate. The sports journalists said that this did not mean that advertisers had a right to demand copy or approve it, but that there was cooperation between two former foes. The blurring of business boundaries inside and outside the sports departments has resulted in the diminishing of journalistic independence.

The range of factors discussed above suggests that the traditional print-oriented news organisations are increasingly unable to focus on in-depth investigative reporting because of workloads, financial factors and commercial influences. It appears that, in most cases, the days when a reporter could spend an extended period focusing on one issue are over. In subsequent interviews with sports journalists in Australia and India, I have found that most believe that in-depth investigations are important for sports journalism, and they want to undertake them, but staff levels, time constraints and heavy workloads mean they are virtually impossible, and the focus has to remain on day-to-day news events and matches.

Overall, these issues affecting sports journalism have reduced its potency for investigation and critical analysis. In order to remedy this situation, and ensure greater scrutiny of the major forces in sport, news organisations would need to reduce their involvement with internal and external commercial interests. It would mean a return to a time when advertising and editorial were separate, and journalists were not measured by the number of stories they wrote in a day, or the online 'hits' they received. In reality, though, commercial influences have now become a key ingredient at many news organisations, and removing them from circulation appears to be an impossible ideal.

Notes

1 Peter English is a journalist and lecturer in journalism in the School of Communication, Faculty of Arts and Business, University of the Sunshine Coast, Queensland, Australia.
2 Peter English, 'Sports coverage in print and web newspapers: how online journalism has changed sports journalism', PhD thesis (Sippy Downs: University of the Sunshine Coast, 2014), *http://research.usc.edu.au/vital/access/manager/Repository;jsessionid=2557 EC901B8B33E0BAE1D730BA91C7C7/usc:13122?exact=sm_creator%3A%22English% 2C+P+A%22*.
3 Ibid.
4 Ibid.
5 Robert Picard, 'Commercialisation and newspaper quality', *Newspaper Research Journal*, vol. 25 (2004).
6 English (2014).
7 Ibid., p.186.
8 Ibid., p.187.
9 In interviews with the author, the sports journalists were asked how economic factors had changed over the previous five years. This covered the period back to 2007, and the start of the Global Financial Crisis.
10 Interview with the author, 10 April 2014.
11 English (2014), p. 186.
12 Ibid.
13 Peter English, 'Sports journalism's relationship with sport's corporate sector: a comparison between Australia, India and the United Kingdom', *Australian Journalism Review*, vol. 35 (2013).
14 Ibid., p. 51.
15 Ibid.
16 Ibid.
17 Ibid.
18 *Mandag Morgen* (*Monday Morning*) (Denmark), 'The world's best advertising agency: the sports press', 31 October 2005, *www.playthegame.org/upload//Sport_Press_Survey_ English.pdf*.
19 Ibid.

20 See Media, Entertainment and Arts Alliance (Australia), 'Media Alliance code of ethics', *www.alliance.org.au/code-of-ethics.html*; National Union of Journalists (UK), 'NUJ code of conduct', *www.nuj.org.uk/about/nuj-code*; and Press Council of India, 'Norms of journalistic conduct', *www.unesco.org/new/fileadmin/MULTIMEDIA/HQ/CI/3.%20Press%20Council%20 of%20India%20Norms%20of%20Journalistic%20Conduct.pdf*.
21 'Media Alliance code of ethics'.
22 Interview with author, 3 May 2014.
23 English (2014), p.184.

6.11

New ball game

Covering sports, with teams as competitors

John Affleck[1]

In the spring of 2014, as the Baltimore Ravens began the long build-up to that year's National Football League (NFL) season, the team's public relations staff let local media know about an important event: star quarterback Joe Flacco was going to hold a news conference to discuss the upcoming season. It seemed at the time like a particularly important moment, because, in 2013, the Ravens had failed to make the American football play-offs for the first time since Flacco had arrived in Baltimore five years previously. The news conference would establish a new tone for the club.

Then, however, as Ron Fritz of *The Baltimore Sun* tells it, the story changed[2] – not because of something that happened to Flacco, but because the team published a story under the news section of its website ahead of the session with reporters. It was an exclusive interview with the quarterback, giving an upbeat assessment of the Ravens and a new offensive scheme.[3] In essence, the team had scooped the media ahead of its own news conference. When Fritz – head of sports for *The Baltimore Sun* – complained to team officials that that wasn't playing fair, violating the traditional 'We ask the questions, you give the answers' formula of journalism, the response from the Ravens, he said, was that they were trying to drive traffic to their website just like any for-profit entity, including the news media.

Now move ahead to 8 September 2014. The Ravens and the NFL were overwhelmed with negative publicity that day when a security video obtained by the website TMZ Sports was released that showed running back Ray Rice knocking out his then fiancé and now wife, Janay, with one punch in the lift of an Atlantic City casino.[4] The video caused an uproar, transcending the sports pages and sparking a national discussion in the United States about domestic violence.[5] Coverage on ESPN, the broadcast giant of American sports media, was virtually constant, and the Ravens dropped Rice. The approach to the scandal on Baltimore's team website was muted, however. Videos, since removed, were posted of coach John Harbaugh facing the media, a news conference that was broadcast live nationally by ESPN, among others, and of several sombre players expressing their shock and personal support for Rice. By the time the team competed in the NFL play-offs in January 2015, all that remained of those moments on BaltimoreRavens.com was an interview transcript file.[6]

A review of the website's archive shows that the Rice firing – the top story in all US sports coverage that day – was handled in text with a short statement:

The Ravens terminated the contract of running back Ray Rice on Monday afternoon. NFL Commissioner Roger Goodell also announced that based on new video evidence that became available today, he has indefinitely suspended Rice. Rice was previously serving a two-game suspension. Ravens Head Coach John Harbaugh is scheduled to speak with the media today at 7:15 p.m.[7]

Put these two moments back to back, and they frame a rising concern among American sports journalists: teams covering themselves through their own websites, and pitching that material as virtually indistinguishable from the mainstream media's work. In one case the Baltimore team undercut local media to put out what amounted to a good-news story, while in the other it handled a major scandal with little more than a media advisory in text.

'It's just a whole new ball game,' Fritz says – and, to journalists, a disturbing one.

Why it matters

The reality is that teams in the United States' four major professional sports leagues (American football, baseball, ice hockey and men's basketball), along with top college athletic programmes, have an increasingly robust web presence. Although news companies worry about the financial consequences when fans turn primarily to team sites for information – the general wisdom being that, the fewer the clicks, the harder it is to attract advertisers – reporters and editors insist that their dissatisfaction runs deeper than money.

Teams and leagues are bound to produce content with an edge of favouritism, even if only in the editorial choices they make, editors argue. Readers need to know that, they say. 'You can't be part of the story and report the story – another tenet we all know as journalists', says Gerry Ahern, vice president of content for *USA Today*, Sports. 'The notion that teams or schools or leagues can cover themselves and do so in an unbiased fashion is – you know, the Ray Rice situation was empirical evidence that that's just not gonna happen.'[8]

The product on many team websites, journalists say, is content that reads more like spin than news. 'It's the difference between reading propaganda and information,' says Vicki Michaelis, the John Huland Carmical distinguished professor in sports journalism at the University of Georgia.[9] Readers may scoff and believe that, since the subject is sports, it means that this issue doesn't matter, Michaelis says, but even a quick run-through of major scandals in America's massive sports industry reveals that its 'Keep it inside the team' culture can cause problems to fester. Now, with the teams and institutions covering themselves, a cloistered group becomes even more closed, and journalists' work is that much tougher. The issue has become of enough concern that the Associated Press Sports Editors, the major body of sports editors in the United States, is devoting a general session to the topic at its annual convention in June.[10] 'Shouldn't we be learning the unfiltered truth?' Michaelis asks.[11]

Of course, the Ravens' digital wing doesn't see itself as corrupting American journalism, just fighting for clicks. Local television and newspapers 'are competitors in so much as we are all vying for the same fan eyeballs and, in some cases, the same advertisers. And those advertising dollars are limited. We must have compelling content to keep readers coming back to then secure advertisers,' says Michelle Andres, vice president of digital media and broadcasting for the Ravens.[12] 'The purpose of our site is to serve our fans first and foremost with the best, most compelling, timely coverage – news and otherwise – we can produce or get access to,' she says, adding that the site's focus exclusively on the Ravens is a selling point. 'Are there things we will cover differently because we are the team? Of course. But, we work hard to write legitimate, fair, honest, compelling, timely content, just like any other news outlet.'

Impact of team reporters

The idea of having reporters from the team work right alongside mainstream journalists is aggravating to the independent media. Why? To illustrate, put yourself in the position of a reporter writing the story for a National Basketball Association (NBA) game, which ends late and pushes print deadlines. Josh Robbins, president of the Professional Basketball Writers Association, describes the scenario:

> One of the things our members are finding is that a team will hire its own reporter, and that reporter will attend a post-game press conference, and, even if the team loses a game by a wide margin, the question that that reporter might throw to the coach is 'Well, how happy are you with how your players battled?'[13]

Such easy questions – 'softballs', in American parlance – mean that independent reporters don't get good information about what's wrong with the team, and then neither does the public.

To understand further why this causes such outrage among reporters, imagine the same scenario moved into a political setting. Would it be acceptable if, after a major piece of legislation had failed, a state governor held a ten-minute news conference for the mainstream media at which an operative from a website owned by the governor's political party asked two of the questions? That, journalists argue, is what sports teams are doing all the time. 'The team,' Robbins says, 'is stacking the deck. And it's a tremendous problem.'

When the Atlanta Falcons reported to training camp last summer – an annual ritual of American football that occurs roughly six weeks before the regular season – D. Orlando Ledbetter, president of the Pro Football Writers of America in 2014, and his colleagues counted 13 media people from the team.[14] 'Website folks, camera people, tweet people and writers from the website,' Ledbetter recalls. 'And from mainstream media there was three of us: *The Atlanta Journal-Constitution* [Ledbetter himself], AP [Associated Press] and ESPN. com [. . .] So they were going to great lengths to cover themselves in a flowery way, all positives, happy-go-lucky stuff – "Jim Bob arrived at camp today". Nothing newsy.'

When there is transactional news – such as a signing or trade – the team's media operation routinely publishes and tweets first with its own angle and then calls the mainstream press, he says. As with the NBA, team website employees join in NFL news conferences, Ledbetter says. And his working life can be made that much more difficult during the open locker room periods throughout the practice week leading up to games, when players are to be made available to reporters, because the team's public relations people will often move into a spot to listen in on interviews.

Put another way, an employee (the player) will be talking to a reporter with a representative of his employer standing close by. 'There's a chilling effect of having those [PR] people around,' Ledbetter says. 'There's an attempt to control the message that's getting out.' This means that journalists have to do more work outside team headquarters, or even the playing arena, which reporters say are diminishing as places to get worthwhile material. Agents have become more important sources for news on signings, hirings and firings, but, inevitably, they have their own agenda. 'It should trouble everyone who works within the sports journalism industry,' says Robbins, who writes for the *Orlando Sentinel*, talking about the overall effects of team self-coverage. 'And it should trouble everyone who consumes pro[fessional] basketball journalism as well, because it is colouring everything that is done, and it's colouring everything that independent journalists are attempting to do.'[15]

Switching sides

Despite their complaints, however, journalists do not necessarily begrudge those who take jobs with teams and leagues. They understand that people have to make personal and financial decisions, and that frequently these people have a background in daily journalism. Andres notes that one writer for the Ravens is a former *Baltimore Sun* columnist – just one of many examples throughout American sports. Some journalists also draw a distinction of sorts between league sites, which they say tend to be somewhat more objective, because they represent all the teams, and locally based team sites, which target home-town fans. Major League Baseball, for instance, has regional editing desks to which copy is sent.

There is strong evidence, however, that writing for a team or a league can come with special pitfalls not found in mainstream media. The website Deadspin – a popular US blog that describes itself as 'sports news without access, favor or discretion' – reported in October 2014 that Chris Bianchi, a reporter employed by the website of Major League Soccer (MLS) to cover the Colorado Rapids, was fired after he had answered a fan's question on Twitter by saying that the Rapids' top executives were more to blame for a bad Colorado season than the coaching staff.[16] The Deadspin piece included a testy exchange between team president Tim Hinchey and Bianchi, the clear implication being that, angry about Bianchi's tweet, Hinchey pushed to get him fired. Bianchi and an MLS spokesman both declined to comment further on the Deadspin article, which included claims in the comments section that other reporters had faced similar treatment while covering the league.

Media failures and possible solutions

When it comes to responding to teams covering themselves, sometimes the independent media don't do themselves any favours. Take the case of Josh Shaw, a starting football player for the University of Southern California (USC), an institute that, like scores of others in the United States, has a large, well-funded and popular sports programme. In late August 2014 the school put out a story on its sports blog to the effect that Shaw had injured both ankles leaping off a balcony to save his seven-year-old nephew from drowning in the pool at an apartment complex.[17] Fox Sports and the Associated Press each picked up on the tale with stories that did not question the account, or even attribute the source to a team website in the first few paragraphs.[18] Within hours USC began to get calls questioning the story, and it quickly became apparent that Shaw was lying; he had been hurt in a fall, but not a heroic one. The mainstream media, operating in an environment of constant competition, had already repeated the false tale, however.

To Ahern, of *USA Today*, there is a cautionary lesson in such cases: the media need to treat the material released by team websites with the same scepticism that they would bring to a government news release or a police report. Failing to confirm or refute independently such stories only damages the mainstream media's credibility. 'I think this is a hugely important point in today's 24/7 news cycle, where everybody's running and gunning to get that quick post-up,' Ahern says. 'I think that speed-to-market notion puts us in some potential jeopardy, because sometimes people that are in that rush to match entity X are skipping steps, and that's pretty scary to an editor or anybody who really takes pride in protecting our business and our brands and our profession.'[19] For editors, putting more emphasis on credibility, as well as stressing to readers that their organisation will report all the news about the local team, whether it's good or bad, may well be a way to compete in the face of what is likely to be an increasing flow of team-generated content.

Ahern is also part of an effort to get major American colleges to offer more access to their athletic teams – or, at least, not less access. He is a representative from the Associated Press Sports Editors (the nationwide body of sports editors) on a committee that also includes representatives of the National Collegiate Athletic Association (which governs US college sports) and the group that represents the sports information officers at American universities. These low-key conference calls and meetings are aimed at rolling back measures that the press sees as particularly draconian, and that, Ahern says, have worked to defuse some situations that otherwise could have evolved into public spats and hardened positions.

The media stance going into those college-level talks, and with regard to professional leagues, is basically this. Many colleges and universities in the United States are public institutions, and even the private ones receive federal funding. The professional leagues and teams, meanwhile, benefit from stadiums built with public money, from police and emergency services to get fans in and out of the ballpark safely and from the enormous goodwill of those supporters. As a result, teams need to play fair with the media in terms of access and website competition, because the press represents the public. And the public deserves the straight story about the teams they love and pay for.

Final thoughts

Naturally, the media understand that their calls to the better nature of wealthy and powerful organisations such as professional teams, leagues and major universities will, in many cases, go unheeded.

For reporters trying to do their jobs effectively and stay relevant in the current sports media landscape, then, here are three simple practices based on research for this story, my 22 years with the Associated Press and my work as a journalism professor at Pennsylvania State University. They are aimed at helping reporters break news on the beat.

- Be the tough one. Source development is always a challenge on any beat, and, with players often available only at certain designated times, the chance to break the ice and foster a relationship can be increasingly difficult. My personal observation is that many reporters take the route of being overly complimentary to coaches, players and other team officials, in the hope that one day they will be given a scoop as a reward. As this contribution has demonstrated, however, teams have their own media strategy: go right to the public and ignore the media. Smart reporters should therefore abandon the 'nice guy' approach and ask hard-nosed questions, even if they irritate the sources, for three reasons. First, it is journalists' role to be independent and sceptical. Second, tough questions elicit the most newsworthy responses. Third, in any sports organisation there are disgruntled people, particularly in an unsuccessful sports organisation; being a fair, engaged, independent journalist signals to sources who don't think they've received a fair deal that there is someone they can talk to.
- Work outside the lines I. As Ledbetter notes, access to players and coaches inside team headquarters is limited and monitored closely. This means that reporters must work outside the building, setting up interviews off-premises when possible and catching stars – who rarely grant such individual access – at moments when they are in public, such as charity events (US players often have foundations) or when they are appearing on behalf of a corporate sponsor.
- Work outside the lines II. The most important thing that sports writers can keep in mind is that the results of competition are, ultimately, not the most important journalistic aspect of sports. Reporting on the way sports are run, the Rice case being one small example,[20]

is critical to the press fulfilling its watchdog role in society. In the United States, where many colleges with large sports programmes are public institutions whose records are open to scrutiny, it is crucial that independent media covering a team have someone on staff who can lead efforts to obtain records.[21] Help is also available through the journalists' group Investigative Reporters and Editors (IRE), which has focused on sports on several occasions over the years. A recent IRE podcast outlined successes in the use of records to blow the lid off a scandal at the US Air Force Academy, examine the driving records of football players at Ohio State University and review the work of team physicians.[22] Finally, the enormous financial resources devoted to sports (an estimated US$67.7 billion in revenue in North America alone by 2017)[23] demands that journalists and journalism organisations cover sports for what it is, at least to a large extent – and that is a business beat. College journalism departments can help train the next generation of reporters in this area.[24]

Given the media landscape, it is inevitable that sports coverage will continue to evolve in the coming years, but, by taking a tough, sceptical approach to the beat, developing sources other than in team or corporate headquarters, making better use of open records and developing expertise in business reporting, journalists will do a better job for the public.

Notes

1   John Affleck is Knight Chair in Sports Journalism and Society at the John Curley Center for Sports Journalism, Pennsylvania State University.
2   Author interview with Ron Fritz, *The Baltimore Sun*.
3   BaltimoreRavens.com, 'Joe Flacco offers opinion of Gary Kubiak's offense', 29 May 2014, *www.baltimoreravens.com/news/article-1/Joe-Flacco-Offers-Opinion-Of-Gary-Kubiaks-Offense/134b3f78-3c8f-4663-ae53-d57a9280a738.*
4   SB Nation (US), 'A complete timeline of the Ray Rice assault case', 28 November 2015, *www.sbnation.com/nfl/2014/5/23/5744964/ray-rice-arrest-assault-statement-apology-ravens.*
5   See, for example, CBS News (US), 'Ray Rice scandal: how people are reacting', 8 September 2014, *www.cbsnews.com/news/reaction-to-ray-rice-suspension-spans-a-range-of-anger.*
6   Original files seen by author in October 2014. BaltimoreRavens.com, 'Ravens Monday transcripts', 8 September 2014, *www.baltimoreravens.com/news/article-1/Ravens-Monday-Transcripts/186b86cc-ccbd-417d-a6e8-18997834cbf4.*
7   BaltimoreRavens.com, 'Ravens terminate Ray Rice's contract', 8 September 2014, *www.baltimoreravens.com/news/article-1/Ravens-Terminate-Ray-Rices-Contract/17178ebd-005f-4176-b1cb-d6acd8980be4.*
8   Author interview with Gerry Ahern, *USA Today*, Sports.
9   Author interview with Vicki Michaelis, University of Georgia.
10 Associated Press Sports Editors conference, 24–27 June 2015, San Diego; see *http://apsportseditors.org/conference-2015.*
11 Author interview with Michaelis.
12 Author interview, via e-mail, with Michelle Andres, vice president of digital media and broadcasting for the Baltimore Ravens.
13 Author interview with Josh Robbins, president of the Professional Basketball Writers Association.
14 Author interview with D. Orlando Ledbetter, president of the Pro Football Writers of America.
15 Author interview with Robbins.
16 Deadspin (US), 'Former MLS reporter: team pushed to get me fired', 20 October 2014, *http://screamer.deadspin.com/former-colorado-rapids-reporter-team-pushed-to-get-me-1647752540.*

17 USCTrojans.com (US), 'Shaw suffers injury while rescuing nephew', 25 August 2014, originally at *www.usctrojans.com/blog/2014/08/shaw-injured.html* (since removed). See also *Washington Post* (US), 'The bizarre case of Josh Shaw's sprained ankles, a drowning nephew and a baffled USC football team', 27 August 2014, *www.washingtonpost. com/news/morning-mix/wp/2014/08/27/the-bizarre-case-of-josh-shaws-sprained-ankles-a-drowning-nephew-and-a-baffled-usc-football-team*.

18 Fox Sports (US), 'USC starting CB Josh Shaw injures both ankles saving nephew from pool', 25 August 2014, originally at *www.foxsports.com/college-football/story/usc-trojans-josh-shaw-suffers-injury-saving-nephew-082514* (since removed); *Daily News* (US), 'USC CB Josh Shaw leaps from balcony to save 7-year-old nephew from drowning, sprains both ankles', 25 August 2014, *www.nydailynews.com/sports/more-sports/usc-cb-josh-shaw-jumps-balcony-save-drowning-nephew-sprains-ankles-article-1.1916583*; *Huffington Post* (US), 'Josh Shaw jump saves nephew', *www.huffingtonpost.com/2014/08/25/josh-shaw-jumps-saves-nephew_n_5713047.html*.

19 Author interview with Ahern.

20 ESPN (US), 'Rice case: purposeful misdirection by team, scant investigation by NFL', 19 September 2014, *http://espn.go.com/espn/otl/story/_/id/11551518/how-ray-rice-scandal-unfolded-baltimore-ravens-roger-goodell-nfl*.

21 Reporters Committee for Freedom of the Press; see website: *www.ifoia.org/#!*.

22 Investigative Reporters and Editors (US), sports podcast, 'Policing the players', 3 October 2014, *www.ire.org/blog/ire-radio/2014/10/03/ire-radio-podcast-policing-players*.

23 Bloomberg (US), 'Sports revenue to reach $67.7 billion by 2017, PwC report says', 13 November 2013, *www.bloomberg.com/news/2013-11-13/sports-revenue-to-reach-67-7-billion-by-2017-pwc-report-says.html*.

24 It is worth noting that Pennsylvania State University has offered an introduction to the sports industry for years within the College of Communications and offered a course specifically about writing on sports business in the spring of 2015.

6.12

What the anti-corruption movement can bring to sport

The experience of Transparency International Germany

Sylvia Schenk[1]

When Transparency International Germany established its Working Group on Sport[2] in 2006, it was pioneering work at the time. 'Sport and corruption? We have more important issues than that!' was the view of the international anti-corruption movement, on the one hand; 'There is no corruption in sport!' insisted the sport movement, on the other. Experience in national and international sport organisations, and reading between the lines, told TI Germany otherwise, however. Accordingly, although the prevailing view was displayed by a high-ranking German football official when informed about this new work (he responded by saying: 'German football clubs will not be able to buy any South American player without paying some money behind the scenes. You may call that a bribe – but there is nothing we can do about it!'), TI Germany thought that something could indeed be done. It took time, and trial and error, but that thinking has subsequently been shown to be right.

TI Germany's primary asset from the very beginning was its roots in the sport movement. It knew what it was talking about, and, even if sportspeople still believed that sport was inherently fair and ethical, they understood that TI Germany was speaking from experience. Gradually they started to listen.

The 2005 Hoyzer match-fixing scandal, involving a referee from the second division of the German Bundesliga,[3] did not serve as a wake-up call. Neither did the subsequent distribution of 2006 football World Cup tickets by World Cup sponsor Energie Baden-Württemberg (EnBW) to governors and a state secretary 'who were . . . mandated with matters that had direct influence on the economic performance of EnBW'.[4] In May 2008, when Declan Hill published his book on international match-fixing, *The Fix: Soccer and Organized Crime*, the reaction in Germany – as in many other countries – was that its claims were largely exaggerated.[5]

Match-fixing as an entry point

In the meantime, TI Germany was developing its strategy in order to fight against corruption in sport. It seemed most promising to start with match-fixing: it was a single issue, easy to explain and understand, and it was becoming an increasingly prominent issue, especially at the international level.

TI Germany pointed to the obvious and important fact that no manipulation of a sporting competition can take place on the pitch without the involvement of sportspeople – above all, players and referees. It was not just about (organised) crime attacking sport from the outside; sport itself was part of the problem. Therefore, prevention, to be arranged by the sport organisations, had to be part of the solution. With this in mind, TI Germany was well prepared in 2009 when police in Bochum uncovered a criminal network that might have fixed as many as 300 matches in Europe.[6] Following this news the German Bundestag, in December that year, organised a hearing on match-fixing and this specific case, inviting the Deutsche Fußball-Bund (DFB), the Deutsche Fußball Liga (DFL), the Early Warning System[7] and TI Germany. As a result of the hearing, TI Germany contacted the DFL with a proposal for a joint match-fixing prevention programme. TI Germany provided detailed inputs on the basis of its experience with compliance programmes and corruption prevention in the business sector, stressing the importance of awareness-raising, education and whistleblowing, and a pilot project was launched in September 2010.[8]

In May 2011, following assistance by TI Germany with the tender and the selection process, the DFL established an ombudsman for sport;[9] subsequently, in the summer and autumn of that year, it organised three pilot workshops on the prevention of match-fixing, with managers, coaches and players taking part.[10] With the support of the DFL, TI Germany was invited to present its ideas at the General Assembly of the European Professional Football Leagues (EPFL) in October 2011. On the basis of this experience and its partnership-building, TI Germany then initiated an EU-funded match-fixing prevention project in 2012, at the International Secretariat of Transparency International, co-funded by DFL and the EPFL and extending across six European professional leagues.[11]

For Transparency International Germany, the public recognition by the DFL was just as important as this developing work on match-fixing itself: that TI Germany had become a player in the nation's sporting life and the 'go-to' institution for the media on any wrongdoing or specific problems occurring in sport helped with the improvement of its impact. Members of the TI Germany working group gave interviews, made presentations and sat on panels,[12] addressing not only match-fixing but, increasingly, integrity and fair play in sport, the role of sponsors, sustainability in sport and anti-corruption activities.

Expanding to good governance in sport

Beyond addressing match-fixing, TI Germany's aim was to increase transparency and accountability in sport organisations by introducing and strengthening good governance. The approach was twofold. First, to build up know-how, TI Germany became a partner in the EU-funded project entitled 'Good Governance in Grassroots Sport', led by the International Sport and Culture Association (ISCA).[13] The project concluded in April 2013 with the publication of a handbook, *Guidelines for Good Governance in Grassroots Sport*.[14]

Second, TI Germany, in autumn 2010, used the German bid for the Olympic and Paralympic Winter Games of 2018 to be acknowledged by the German Olympic Sports Confederation (DOSB) as a partner, asking for anti-corruption measures to be included as part of the bidding strategy. The request was both too early and too late, however: too early, as the DOSB was not yet ready to take up such ideas from an external stakeholder; and too late, as the bid was already far advanced. TI Germany was even informed that the request from an organisation with an English name to translate the bid book into German in order to let the population know about the details was perceived as strange.

Several months after the failed bid, another bid discussion in Germany, for 2022, began. TI Germany jumped in immediately. In January 2013 it submitted its 'Principles for a Transparent Olympic Bid'[15] to the DOSB and to the media. On this occasion the timing was right. In summer 2013 a working group on good governance in sport was established by the DOSB,[16] with TI Germany as a member giving advice. Within two months an ethics code and guidelines on gifts, invitations and conflicts of interest had been drafted and approved by the bidding committee, which included the DOSB, the city of Munich and the smaller cities involved in the bid.[17] When the bid was rejected by a public poll in November 2013, the DOSB continued its work on good governance, with TI Germany remaining a part of it, advising the DOSB and other national sport federations on how to implement the principles of good governance – transparency, accountability, integrity and democracy – in their day-to-day work and in shaping their internal compliance systems.[18]

Thinking globally

It is not sufficient to limit one's efforts to the national level, however; sport is a global business. The ongoing crisis of sporting mega-events – controversy surrounding the Winter Olympics in Sochi 2014 and the FIFA World Cups in Brazil 2014, Russia 2018 and Qatar 2022 – opens up an opportunity for reform. To join forces in order to increase civil society pressure on national and international sport organisations, in the summer of 2014 TI Germany and Football Supporters Europe initiated a meeting of leading non-governmental organisations, comprising Amnesty International, the International Federation of Terre des Hommes, Human Rights Watch and the International Trade Union Confederation, as well as Supporters Direct and FIFPro, the professional football players' association, from the world of sport. In December 2014 the group sent a letter to the president of the International Olympic Committee, Dr Thomas Bach, asking for 'future Olympic and Paralympic Games as well as Youth Olympic Games and other [sporting mega-events]' to

> be organised in a way that respects human rights, labour rights, the environment and anti-corruption requirements during the entire life cycle of the event – that is, from the early bidding stage on national level to the closing ceremony and final reporting.[19]

Thus extending its field of activity, after eight years struggling to establish 'sport and corruption' in the anti-corruption and the sports movements, TI Germany can conclude that it was – and is – hard work, but worthwhile. Sport is an important part of the lives of so many, especially young people, whether actively participating or as spectators. Sending a strong anti-corruption message within and through sport may prove a cornerstone in the fight for a world free of corruption.

Notes

1 Sylvia Schenk is chair of the Working Group on Sport of Transparency International Germany.
2 The Working Group on Sport includes several people with experience in sport, such as an athlete who competed up to the level of Olympic participation and an official who worked in national and international sport organisations.
3 *Guardian* (UK), 'Two years in jail for match-fixing German referee', 18 November 2005, *www.theguardian.com/football/2005/nov/18/newsstory.sport4*.
4 See section C of Lentze Stopper (Germany), 'Guideline compliance', *www.ufasports-hospitality.com/fileadmin/user_upload/documents/Guideline_Compliance_-_Lentze_Stopper_Rechtsanwaelte.pdf*.

5   Spielverlagerung.de (Germany), 'Interview mit Declan Hill: "Hoyzer ist ein Held!"', 4 February 2013, *http://spielverlagerung.de/2013/02/04/interview-mit-declan-hill.*

6   See Wikipedia, '2009 European football betting scandal', *http://en.wikipedia.org/wiki/ 2009_European_football_betting_scandal*; and *Daily Telegraph* (UK), 'How German police fell on European football's biggest match-fixing scandal by accident', 5 February 2013, *www.telegraph.co.uk/sport/football/news/9851507/How-German-police-fell-on-European- footballs-biggest-match-fixing-scandal-by-accident.html.*

7   The Fédération Internationale de Football Association (FIFA) founded the Early Warning System as a subsidiary (EWS GmbH) in 2007; based in FIFA's Zurich offices, it has its own dedicated personnel. See *www.fifa-ews.com/en.*

8   Soccer by the Numbers (UK), 'Fixing matches: mapping corruption', 6 September 2010, *www.soccerbythenumbers.com/2010/09/fixing-matches-mapping-corruption.html.*

9   European Professional Football Leagues (Switzerland), 'German Bundesliga and DFB "Together against match fixing"', *www.epfl-europeanleagues.com/bundesliga_DFB. htm*; Gemeinsam-gegen-Spielmanipulation.de (Germany), 'Spiel Kein falsches Spiel', *http://gemeinsam-gegen-spielmanipulation.de/index.php/startseite.*

10 Transparency International Germany, 'Gemeinsam gegen Spielmanipulation', *www.transparency.de/Gemeinsam-gegen-Spielmanipulat.2261.0.html.*

11 See Deborah Unger, Chapter 4.8 'Prevention and education in match-fixing: the European experience', in this report. See also European Professional Football Leagues (Switzerland), 'EPFL, DFL and Transparency International join forces', 27 March 2013, *www.epfl- europeanleagues.com/pilot_project.htm.*

12 See, for example, *www.nh24.de/index.php/panorama/22-allgemein/36194-fussball-liga- sagt-spielmanipulationen-den-kampf-an*; *www.faz.net/aktuell/sport/fussball/sylvia-schenk- im-gespraech-blatter-mangelt-es-an-glaubwuerdigkeit-1578488.html*; *www.faz.net/aktuell/ sport/fussball/faz-net-fruehkritik-anne-will-die-welt-ist-so-verkommen-12054208.html*; *www.welt.de/print/die_welt/wirtschaft/article13842991/Angst-vor-leeren-VIP-Logen.html*; and *www.wuv.de/marketing/compliance_expertin_sylvia_schenk_die_verflechtungen_ im_sport_sind_zu_eng.*

13 See Mogens Kirkeby, Chapter 1.13 'Challenges and approaches to ensuring good governance in grassroots sport', in this report. See also the 'Good Governance in Grassroots Sport' website: *www.goodgovsport.eu/home.*

14 International Sport and Culture Association, *Guidelines for Good Governance in Grassroots Sport* (Copenhagen: ISCA, 2013), *www.isca-web.org/files/GGGS_WEB/Files/Guidelines_ for_Good_Governance_in_Grassroots_Sport.pdf.*

15 Transparency International Germany, 'Grundsätze einer transparenten Olympiabewerbung', 15 January 2013, *www.transparency.de/fileadmin/pdfs/Themen/Sport/Positionspapier_ Grundsaetze_einer_transparenten_Olympiabewerbung_13-03-05.pdf.*

16 Deutsche Olympische Sportbund, 'EU unterstützt Umsetzung von Good Governance', 8 December 2014, *www.dosb.de/de/organisation/internationales/detail/news/eu_ unterstuetzt_umsetzung_von_good_governance.*

17 Deutsche Olympische Sportbund, 'Ethik-Code für die Bewerbung', 23 October 2013, *www.dosb.de/fileadmin/Bilder_allgemein/Veranstaltungen/Muenchen2022/Ethik-Code_ und_Richtlinien_Bewerbungs-GmbH_231013.pdf.*

18 Deutsche Olympische Sportbund, 'Bob- und Schlittensport: BSD [Bob- und Schlittenverband für Deutschland] beschließt Compliance-Richtlinien', 5 November 2014, *www.dosb.de/de/ leistungssport/spitzensport-news/detail/news/bob_und_schlittensport_bsd_beschliesst_ compliance_richtlinien*; Deutsche Olympische Sportbund, 'Der Deutscher Turner-Bund beschließt einen Ethik-Code', 26 November 2014, *www.dosb.de/de/leistungssport/ spitzensport-news/detail/news/der_deutsche_turner_bund_beschliesst_einen_ethik_code.*

19 See Transparency International Germany, press release, 'Zivilgesellschaftliches Bündnis fordert vom IOC eine Vorreiterrolle für saubere internationale Sportveranstaltungen', 5 December 2014; *www.transparency.de/14-12-05_IOC-Vorreiterrolle-Sp.2578.0.html? &contUid=5939*; and *Guardian* (UK), 'IOC urged to make human rights key part of major sporting events', 5 December 2014, *www.theguardian.com/sport/2014/dec/05/ioc- human-rights-major-sporting-events.*

Index